T0385031

Skoda Octavia
Owner's Workshop Manual

Chris Randall & Pete Trott

Models covered

(5549 - 7AY2 - 288)

Hatchback & Estate with 1.9 litre (1896cc) & 2.0 litre (1968cc) PD and common rail turbo-diesel engines

Does NOT cover models with petrol engines, 1.6 litre diesel engine, 4x4 models, Scout or Tour
Does NOT cover new Octavia 'third generation' range introduced March 2013

© Haynes Group Limited 2019

A book in the **Haynes Owners Workshop Manual Series**

All rights reserved. No part of this book may be reproduced or transmitted in any form or by any means, electronic or mechanical, including photocopying, recording or by any information storage or retrieval system, without permission in writing from the copyright holder.

ISBN **978 1 78521 430 1**

British Library Cataloguing in Publication Data
A catalogue record for this book is available from the British Library.

Haynes Group Limited
Haynes North America, Inc

www.haynes.com

Disclaimer

There are risks associated with automotive repairs. The ability to make repairs depends on the individual's skill, experience and proper tools. Individuals should act with due care and acknowledge and assume the risk of performing automotive repairs.

The purpose of this manual is to provide comprehensive, useful and accessible automotive repair information, to help you get the best value from your vehicle. However, this manual is not a substitute for a professional certified technician or mechanic.

This repair manual is produced by a third party and is not associated with an individual vehicle manufacturer. If there is any doubt or discrepancy between this manual and the owner's manual or the factory service manual, please refer to the factory service manual or seek assistance from a professional certified technician or mechanic.

Even though we have prepared this manual with extreme care and every attempt is made to ensure that the information in this manual is correct, neither the publisher nor the author can accept responsibility for loss, damage or injury caused by any errors in, or omissions from, the information given.

Contents

LIVING WITH YOUR SKODA OCTAVIA

Illegal Copying

It is the policy of the Publisher to actively protect its Copyrights and Trade Marks. Legal action will be taken against anyone who unlawfully copies the cover or contents of this Manual. This includes all forms of unauthorised copying including digital, mechanical, and electronic in any form. Authorisation from the Publisher will only be provided expressly and in writing. Illegal copying will also be reported to the appropriate statutory authorities.

Contents

REPAIRS AND OVERHAUL

Engine and Associated Systems

Transmission

Brakes and Suspension

Body Equipment

REFERENCE

Index

The Skoda Octavia models covered by this manual were first introduced to the UK in 2004. Hatchback and Estate models are available, equipped with a variety of engine sizes. This manual covers the 4-cylinder turbocharged diesel engine models of 1.9 or 2.0 litre capacity, with SOHC 8v or DOHC 16v cylinder heads. Until 2008, all diesel engines were equipped with unit injectors, utilising a rocker shaft and arm assembly with a second set of camshaft lobes to compress each unit injector in turn to provide higher injection pressures, and increased accuracy of injection timing. From 2009, a 2.0 litre DOHC 16v engine was available with conventional common rail fuel injection.

Fully-independent front and rear suspension is fitted, with the components attached to a subframe assembly.

A five- or six-speed manual gearbox is fitted as standard to all models, with a six-speed DSG (Direct Shift Gearbox) automatic transmission available as an option on most 2.0 litre models.

A wide range of standard and optional equipment is available within the model range to suit most tastes, including an anti-lock braking system and air conditioning.

For the home mechanic, the Octavia is quite straightforward to maintain, and most of the items requiring frequent attention are easily accessible.

Your Skoda Octavia Manual

The aim of this manual is to help you get the best value from your vehicle. It can do so in several ways. It can help you decide what work must be done (even should you choose to get it done by a garage). It will also provide information on routine maintenance and servicing, and give a logical course of action and diagnosis when random faults occur. However, it is hoped that you will use the manual by tackling the work yourself, with the potential to save a lot of money by avoiding the costs a garage must charge to cover its labour and overheads.

The manual has drawings and descriptions to show the function of the various components so that their layout can be understood. Tasks are described and photographed in a clear step-by-step sequence. The illustrations are numbered by the Section number and paragraph number to which they relate – if there is more than one illustration per paragraph, the sequence is denoted alphabetically.

References to the 'left' or 'right' of the vehicle are in the sense of a person in the driver's seat, facing forwards.

Acknowledgements

Thanks are due to Draper Tools, who provided some of the workshop tools, and to all those people at Sparkford who helped in the production of this manual.

This manual is not a direct reproduction of the vehicle manufacturer's data, and its publication should not be taken as implying any technical approval by the vehicle manufacturers or importers.

We take great pride in the accuracy of information given in this manual, but vehicle manufacturers make alterations and design changes during the production run of a particular vehicle of which they do not inform us. No liability can be accepted by the authors or publishers for loss, damage or injury caused by any errors in, or omissions from, the information given.

Project vehicles

The main vehicle used in the preparation of this manual, and which appears in many of the photographic sequences, was a 2008 Skoda Octavia 1.9 PD diesel Hatchback. An Estate model was also used.

Working on your car can be dangerous. This page shows just some of the potential risks and hazards, with the aim of creating a safety-conscious attitude.

General hazards

Scalding

• Don't remove the radiator or expansion tank cap while the engine is hot.
• Engine oil, transmission fluid or power steering fluid may also be dangerously hot if the engine has recently been running.

Burning

• Beware of burns from the exhaust system and from any part of the engine. Brake discs and drums can also be extremely hot immediately after use.

Crushing

• When working under or near a raised vehicle, always supplement the jack with axle stands, or use drive-on ramps.
Never venture under a car which is only supported by a jack.
• Take care if loosening or tightening high-torque nuts when the vehicle is on stands. Initial loosening and final tightening should be done with the wheels on the ground.

Fire

• Fuel is highly flammable; fuel vapour is explosive.
• Don't let fuel spill onto a hot engine.
• Do not smoke or allow naked lights (including pilot lights) anywhere near a vehicle being worked on. Also beware of creating sparks (electrically or by use of tools).
• Fuel vapour is heavier than air, so don't work on the fuel system with the vehicle over an inspection pit.
• Another cause of fire is an electrical overload or short-circuit. Take care when repairing or modifying the vehicle wiring.
• Keep a fire extinguisher handy, of a type suitable for use on fuel and electrical fires.

Electric shock

• Ignition HT and Xenon headlight voltages can be dangerous, especially to people with heart problems or a pacemaker. Don't work on or near these systems with the engine running or the ignition switched on.

• Mains voltage is also dangerous. Make sure that any mains-operated equipment is correctly earthed. Mains power points should be protected by a residual current device (RCD) circuit breaker.

Fume or gas intoxication

• Exhaust fumes are poisonous; they can contain carbon monoxide, which is rapidly fatal if inhaled. Never run the engine in a confined space such as a garage with the doors shut.
• Fuel vapour is also poisonous, as are the vapours from some cleaning solvents and paint thinners.

Poisonous or irritant substances

• Avoid skin contact with battery acid and with any fuel, fluid or lubricant, especially antifreeze, brake hydraulic fluid and Diesel fuel. Don't syphon them by mouth. If such a substance is swallowed or gets into the eyes, seek medical advice.
• Prolonged contact with used engine oil can cause skin cancer. Wear gloves or use a barrier cream if necessary. Change out of oil-soaked clothes and do not keep oily rags in your pocket.
• Air conditioning refrigerant forms a poisonous gas if exposed to a naked flame (including a cigarette). It can also cause skin burns on contact.

Asbestos

• Asbestos dust can cause cancer if inhaled or swallowed. Asbestos may be found in gaskets and in brake and clutch linings. When dealing with such components it is safest to assume that they contain asbestos.

Special hazards

Hydrofluoric acid

• This extremely corrosive acid is formed when certain types of synthetic rubber, found in some O-rings, oil seals, fuel hoses etc, are exposed to temperatures above 4000C. The rubber changes into a charred or sticky substance containing the acid. *Once formed, the acid remains dangerous for years. If it gets onto the skin, it may be necessary to amputate the limb concerned.*
• When dealing with a vehicle which has suffered a fire, or with components salvaged from such a vehicle, wear protective gloves and discard them after use.

The battery

• Batteries contain sulphuric acid, which attacks clothing, eyes and skin. Take care when topping-up or carrying the battery.
• The hydrogen gas given off by the battery is highly explosive. Never cause a spark or allow a naked light nearby. Be careful when connecting and disconnecting battery chargers or jump leads.

Air bags

• Air bags can cause injury if they go off accidentally. Take care when removing the steering wheel and trim panels. Special storage instructions may apply.

Diesel injection equipment

• Diesel injection pumps supply fuel at very high pressure. Take care when working on the fuel injectors and fuel pipes.

⚠ *Warning: Never expose the hands, face or any other part of the body to injector spray; the fuel can penetrate the skin with potentially fatal results.*

Remember...

DO

• Do use eye protection when using power tools, and when working under the vehicle.
• Do wear gloves or use barrier cream to protect your hands when necessary.
• Do get someone to check periodically that all is well when working alone on the vehicle.
• Do keep loose clothing and long hair well out of the way of moving mechanical parts.
• Do remove rings, wristwatch etc, before working on the vehicle – especially the electrical system.
• Do ensure that any lifting or jacking equipment has a safe working load rating adequate for the job.

DON'T

• Don't attempt to lift a heavy component which may be beyond your capability – get assistance.
• Don't rush to finish a job, or take unverified short cuts.
• Don't use ill-fitting tools which may slip and cause injury.
• Don't leave tools or parts lying around where someone can trip over them. Mop up oil and fuel spills at once.
• Don't allow children or pets to play in or near a vehicle being worked on.

The following pages are intended to help in dealing with common roadside emergencies and breakdowns. You will find more detailed fault finding information at the back of the manual, and repair information in the main chapters.

If your car won't start and the starter motor doesn't turn

- ☐ If it's a model with automatic transmission, make sure the selector is in P or N.
- ☐ Open the bonnet and make sure that the battery terminals are clean and tight.
- ☐ Switch on the headlights and try to start the engine. If the headlights go very dim when you're trying to start, the battery is probably flat. Get out of trouble by jump starting using a friend's car.

If your car won't start even though the starter motor turns as normal

- ☐ Is there fuel in the tank?
- ☐ Is there moisture on electrical components under the bonnet? Switch off the ignition, then wipe off any obvious dampness with a dry cloth. Spray a water-repellent aerosol product (WD-40 or equivalent) on ignition and fuel system electrical connectors like those shown in the photos.

A Check the condition and security of the battery connections.

B Check the fuel injection system airflow meter wiring is secure.

Check that electrical connections are secure (with the ignition switched off) and spray them with a water-dispersant spray like WD-40 if you suspect a problem due to damp.

C Check the fuses in the panel under the bonnet.

D Check the starter motor wiring.

Jump starting

When jump-starting a car using a booster battery, observe the following precautions:

✔ Before connecting the booster battery, make sure that the ignition is switched off.

Caution: Remove the key in case the central locking engages when the jump leads are connected

✔ Ensure that all electrical equipment (lights, heater, wipers, etc) is switched off.

✔ Take note of any special precautions printed on the battery case.

✔ Make sure that the booster battery is the same voltage as the discharged one in the vehicle.

✔ If the battery is being jump-started from the battery in another vehicle, the two vehicles MUST NOT TOUCH each other.

✔ Make sure that the transmission is in neutral (or PARK, in the case of automatic transmission).

HAYNES HiNT *Jump starting will get you out of trouble, but you must correct whatever made the battery go flat in the first place. There are three possibilities:*

1 *The battery has been drained by repeated attempts to start, or by leaving the lights on.*

2 *The charging system is not working properly (alternator drivebelt slack or broken, alternator wiring fault or alternator itself faulty).*

3 *The battery itself is at fault (electrolyte low, or battery worn out).*

1 Connect one end of the red jump lead to the positive (+) terminal of the flat battery

2 Connect the other end of the red lead to the positive (+) terminal of the booster battery.

3 Connect one end of the black jump lead to the negative (-) terminal of the booster battery

4 Connect the other end of the black jump lead to a bolt or bracket on the engine block, well away from the battery, on the vehicle to be started.

5 Make sure that the jump leads will not come into contact with the fan, drive-belts or other moving parts of the engine.

6 Start the engine using the booster battery and run it at idle speed. Switch on the lights, rear window demister and heater blower motor, then disconnect the jump leads in the reverse order of connection. Turn off the lights etc.

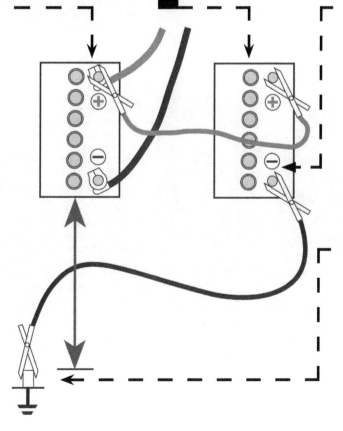

Wheel changing

Some of the details shown here will vary according to model. For instance, some models may have steel wheels with plastic covers rather than the alloy wheels shown, and others will have a sealant and pump kit rather than a spare wheel; follow the procedure with the kit.

 Warning: Do not change a wheel in a situation where you risk being hit by other traffic. On busy roads, try to stop in a lay-by or a gateway. Be wary of passing traffic while changing the wheel – it is easy to become distracted by the job in hand.

Preparation

- ☐ When a puncture occurs, stop as soon as it is safe to do so.
- ☐ Park on firm level ground, if possible, and well out of the way of other traffic.
- ☐ Use hazard warning lights if necessary.
- ☐ If you have one, use a warning triangle to alert other drivers of your presence.
- ☐ Apply the handbrake and engage first or reverse gear (or Park on models with automatic transmission).
- ☐ Chock the wheel diagonally opposite the one being removed – a couple of large stones will do for this.
- ☐ If the ground is soft, use a flat piece of wood to spread the load under the jack.

Changing the wheel

1 The spare is stored beneath the luggage compartment floor covering. The jack and tool kit are located in a tray within the spare wheel. Lift out the tray, undo the plastic nut and lift the spare wheel from the well in the floor.

2 Where fitted, use the tool provided to remove the covers from the bolts.

3 Loosen each wheel bolt by half a turn. Use the special adapter where a locking wheel bolt is fitted.

4 Locate the jack head below the reinforced jacking point nearest the wheel to be changed. The jacking point is indicated by a triangle pressed into the sill, visible when the door is opened. Once the vehicle is raised and the wheel has been removed, the wheel should be placed beneath the sill as a precaution against the jack failing.

5 Fit the spare wheel, then tighten the bolts moderately with the wheel brace. Lower the vehicle to the ground then finally tighten the wheel bolts in a diagonal sequence. Refit the wheel cover/bolt caps as applicable. Note that the wheel bolts should be tightened to the specified torque at the earliest opportunity.

Finally . . .

- ☐ Remove the wheel chocks.
- ☐ Stow the jack and tools in the correct locations in the car.
- ☐ Check the tyre pressure on the wheel just fitted. If it is low, or if you don't have a pressure gauge with you, drive slowly to the nearest garage and inflate the tyre to the right pressure.
- ☐ Have the damaged tyre or wheel repaired at the earliest opportunity.

Note: *If a temporary 'space-saver' spare wheel has been fitted, special conditions apply to its use. This type of spare wheel is only intended for use in an emergency, and should not remain fitted any longer than it takes to get the punctured wheel repaired. While the temporary wheel is in use, do not exceed 50 mph, and avoid harsh acceleration, braking or cornering. Note that, besides being narrower than a normal roadwheel, the temporary spare wheel is of smaller diameter; therefore, since ground clearance will be slightly reduced with the temporary spare in use, take care when travelling over rough ground.*

Identifying leaks

Puddles on the garage floor or drive, or obvious wetness under the bonnet or underneath the car, suggest a leak that needs investigating. It can sometimes be difficult to decide where the leak is coming from, especially if an engine undershield is fitted. Leaking oil or fluid can also be blown rearwards by the passage of air under the car, giving a false impression of where the problem lies.

 Warning: Most automotive oils and fluids are poisonous. Wash them off skin, and change out of contaminated clothing, without delay.

 The smell of a fluid leaking from the car may provide a clue to what's leaking. Some fluids are distinctively coloured. It may help to remove the engine undershield, clean the car carefully and to park it over some clean paper overnight as an aid to locating the source of the leak.
Remember that some leaks may only occur while the engine is running.

Sump oil

Engine oil may leak from the drain plug...

Oil from filter

...or from the base of the oil filter.

Gearbox oil

Gearbox oil can leak from the seals at the inboard ends of the driveshafts.

Antifreeze

Leaking antifreeze often leaves a crystalline deposit like this.

Brake fluid

A leak occurring at a wheel is almost certainly brake fluid.

Power steering fluid

Power steering fluid may leak from the pipe connectors on the steering rack.

Towing

When all else fails, you may find yourself having to get a tow home – or of course you may be helping somebody else. Long-distance recovery should only be done by a garage or breakdown service. For shorter distances, DIY towing using another car is easy enough, but observe the following points:

☐ Use a proper tow-rope or solid towing bar – they are not expensive. The vehicle being towed must display an ON TOW sign in its rear window.

☐ Always turn the ignition key to the 'on' position when the vehicle is being towed, so that the steering lock is released, and the direction indicator and brake lights work.

☐ A rear towing eye is provided below the right-hand side of the bumper. The front towing eye is provided behind the cover on the right-hand side of the front bumper – pull the cover from the bumper and screw in the towing hook supplied with the vehicle.

☐ Before being towed, release the handbrake and select neutral on the transmission. On models with automatic transmission, do not exceed 30 mph or tow for more than 30 miles. If in doubt, do not tow, or transmission damage may result.

☐ The driver of the car being towed must keep the tow-rope taut at all times to avoid snatching.

☐ Note that greater-than-usual pedal pressure will be required to operate the brakes, since the vacuum servo unit is only operational with the engine running.

☐ Greater-than-usual steering effort will also be required.

☐ Make sure that both drivers know the route before setting off.

☐ Only drive at moderate speeds and keep the distance towed to a minimum. Drive smoothly and allow plenty of time for slowing down at junctions.

Introduction

There are some very simple checks which need only take a few minutes to carry out, but which could save you a lot of inconvenience and expense.

These *Weekly checks* require no great skill or special tools, and the small amount of time they take to perform could prove to be very well spent, for example:

☐ Keeping an eye on tyre condition and pressures, will not only help to stop them wearing out prematurely, but could also save your life.

☐ Many breakdowns are caused by electrical problems. Battery-related faults are particularly common, and a quick check on a regular basis will often prevent the majority of these.

☐ If your car develops a brake fluid leak, the first time you might know about it is when your brakes don't work properly. Checking the level regularly will give advance warning of this kind of problem.

☐ If the oil or coolant levels run low, the cost of repairing any engine damage will be far greater than fixing the leak, for example.

Underbonnet check points

◀ **1.9 litre PD engine shown, other models similar**

A *Engine oil level dipstick*

B *Engine oil filler cap*

C *Coolant expansion tank*

D *Brake (and clutch) fluid reservoir*

E *Screenwash fluid reservoir*

F *Battery*

Engine oil level

Before you start

✔ Make sure that the car is on level ground.
✔ Check the oil level before the car is driven, or at least 5 minutes after the engine has been switched off.

 HAYNES HiNT *If the oil is checked immediately after driving the vehicle, some of the oil will remain in the upper engine components, resulting in an inaccurate reading on the dipstick.*

The correct oil

Modern engines place great demands on their oil. It is very important that the correct oil for your car is used (see *Lubricants and fluids*).

Car care

● If you have to add oil frequently, you should check whether you have any oil leaks. Place some clean paper under the car overnight, and check for stains in the morning. If there are no leaks, then the engine may be burning oil.
● Always maintain the level between the upper and lower dipstick marks (see photo 3). If the level is too low, severe engine damage may occur. Oil seal failure may result if the engine is overfilled by adding too much oil.

1 The dipstick is located on the front of the engine (see *Underbonnet check points* for exact location). Withdraw the dipstick.

3 Note the oil level on the end of the dipstick, which should be between the upper and lower mark. Approximately 1.0 litre of oil will raise the level from the lower mark to the upper mark.

2 Using a clean rag or paper towel, wipe all oil from the dipstick. Insert the clean dipstick into the tube as far as it will go, then withdraw it again.

4 Oil is added through the filler cap on top of the engine. Turn the cap through a quarter-turn anti-clockwise and withdraw it. Top-up the level. A funnel may help to reduce spillage. Add the oil slowly, checking the level on the dipstick often. Do not overfill.

Coolant level

 Warning: Do not attempt to remove the expansion tank pressure cap when the engine is hot, as there is a very great risk of scalding. Do not leave open containers of coolant about, as it is poisonous.

Note: *Skoda recommend that demineralised / distilled water should be used with antifreeze in the preparation of coolant.*

Car care

● With a sealed-type cooling system, adding coolant should not be necessary on a regular basis. If frequent topping-up is required, it is likely there is a leak. Check the radiator, all hoses and joint faces for signs of staining or wetness, and rectify as necessary.
● It is important that antifreeze is used in the cooling system all year round, not just during the winter months. Don't top up with water alone, as the antifreeze will become diluted.

1 The coolant level varies with the temperature of the engine. When the engine is cold, the coolant level should be between the MIN and MAX marks.

2 If topping-up is necessary, wait until the engine is cold. Slowly unbolt the cap to release any pressure present in the cooling system, and remove the cap.

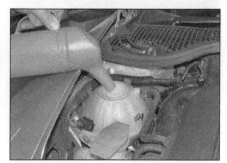

3 Add a mixture of water and antifreeze to the expansion tank until the coolant level is on the MAX mark.

Brake (and clutch) fluid level

 Warning:
• *Brake fluid can harm your eyes and damage painted surfaces, so use extreme caution when handling and pouring it.*
• *Do not use fluid that has been standing open for some time, as it absorbs moisture from the air, which can cause a dangerous loss of braking effectiveness.*

 HAYNES HiNT
• *Make sure that your car is on level ground.*
• *The fluid level in the reservoir will drop slightly as the brake pads wear down, but the fluid level must never be allowed to drop below the MIN mark.*

Safety first!
● If the reservoir requires repeated topping-up this is an indication of a fluid leak somewhere in the system, which should be investigated immediately.
● If a leak is suspected, the car should not be driven until the braking system has been checked. Never take any risks where brakes are concerned

1 The MIN mark is indicated on the reservoir. The fluid level must be kept above this mark at all times.

2 If topping-up is necessary, first wipe clean the area around the filler cap to prevent dirt entering the hydraulic system. Unscrew the reservoir cap.

3 Carefully add fluid, taking care not to spill it onto the surrounding components. Use only the specified fluid; mixing different types can cause damage to the system. On completion, securely refit the cap and wipe away any spilt fluid.

Battery

Caution: Before carrying out any work on the vehicle battery, read the precautions given in 'Safety first!' at the start of this manual.
✔ Make sure that the battery tray is in good condition, and that the clamp is tight. Corrosion on the tray, retaining clamp and the battery itself can be removed with a solution of water and baking soda. Thoroughly rinse

all cleaned areas with water. Any metal parts damaged by corrosion should be covered with a zinc-based primer, then painted.
✔ Periodically (approximately every three months), check the charge condition of the battery as described in Chapter 5.
✔ If the battery is flat, and you need to jump start your vehicle, see *Roadside Repairs*.

 HAYNES HiNT *Battery corrosion can be kept to a minimum by applying a layer of petroleum jelly to the clamps and terminals after they are reconnected.*

1 Check the tightness of battery clamps to ensure good electrical connections. You should not be able to move them. Also check each cable for cracks and frayed conductors.

2 If corrosion (white, fluffy deposits) is evident, remove the cables from the battery terminals, clean them with a small wire brush, then refit them. Automotive stores sell a tool for cleaning the battery post . . .

3 . . . as well as the battery cable clamps.

Electrical systems

✔ Check all external lights and the horn. Refer to the appropriate Sections of Chapter 12 for details if any of the circuits are found to be inoperative.

✔ Visually check all accessible wiring connectors, harnesses and retaining clips for security, and for signs of chafing or damage.

 HAYNES HiNT *If you need to check your brake lights and indicators unaided, back up to a wall or garage door and operate the lights. The reflected light should show if they are working properly.*

1 If a single indicator light, brake light or headlight has failed, it is likely that a bulb has blown and will need to be renewed. Refer to Chapter 12 for details. If both brake lights have failed, it is possible that the brake light switch operated by the brake pedal has failed. Refer to Chapter 9 for details.

2 If more than one indicator light or headlight has failed, it is likely that either a fuse has blown or that there is a fault in the circuit (see Chapter 12). The main fusebox is located beneath a cover on the driver's end of the facia panel; further fuses are located in the engine compartment.

3 To renew a blown fuse, pull it from its location in the fusebox. Fit a new fuse of the same rating, available from car accessory shops.

Screen washer fluid level

● Screenwash additives not only keep the windscreen clean during bad weather, they also prevent the washer system freezing in cold weather – which is when you are likely to need it most. Don't top-up using plain water, as the screenwash will become diluted, and will freeze in cold weather.

Caution: On no account use coolant antifreeze in the washer system – this could discolour or damage paintwork.

1 The reservoir for the windscreen and headlight washer systems is on the right-hand side of the engine compartment.

2 A screenwash additive should be added in the quantities recommended on the bottle.

Wiper blades

1 Check the condition of the wiper blades. If they are cracked or show any signs of deterioration, or if the glass swept area is smeared, renew them. For maximum clarity of vision, wiper blades should be renewed annually, as a matter of course.

2 To remove a windscreen wiper blade, place the wipers in the 'service position' as described in Chapter 12. Fold the wiper arm out from the windscreen and position the blade at right angles to the arm. Slide the blade from the locating pin on the arm

Tyre condition and pressure

It is very important that tyres are in good condition, and at the correct pressure - having a tyre failure at any speed is highly dangerous. Tyre wear is influenced by driving style - harsh braking and acceleration, or fast cornering, will all produce more rapid tyre wear. As a general rule, the front tyres wear out faster than the rears. Interchanging the tyres from front to rear ("rotating" the tyres) may result in more even wear. However, if this is completely effective, you may have the expense of replacing all four tyres at once! Remove any nails or stones embedded in the tread before they penetrate the tyre to cause deflation. If removal of a nail does reveal that the tyre has been punctured, refit the nail so that its point of penetration is marked. Then immediately change the wheel, and have the tyre repaired by a tyre dealer.

Regularly check the tyres for damage in the form of cuts or bulges, especially in the sidewalls. Periodically remove the wheels, and clean any dirt or mud from the inside and outside surfaces. Examine the wheel rims for signs of rusting, corrosion or other damage. Light alloy wheels are easily damaged by "kerbing" whilst parking; steel wheels may also become dented or buckled. A new wheel is very often the only way to overcome severe damage.

New tyres should be balanced when they are fitted, but it may become necessary to re-balance them as they wear, or if the balance weights fitted to the wheel rim should fall off. Unbalanced tyres will wear more quickly, as will the steering and suspension components. Wheel imbalance is normally signified by vibration, particularly at a certain speed (typically around 50 mph). If this vibration is felt only through the steering, then it is likely that just the front wheels need balancing. If, however, the vibration is felt through the whole car, the rear wheels could be out of balance. Wheel balancing should be carried out by a tyre dealer or garage.

1 Tread Depth - visual check
The original tyres have tread wear safety bands (B), which will appear when the tread depth reaches approximately 1.6 mm. The band positions are indicated by a triangular mark on the tyre sidewall (A).

2 Tread Depth - manual check
Alternatively, tread wear can be monitored with a simple, inexpensive device known as a tread depth indicator gauge.

3 Tyre Pressure Check
Check the tyre pressures regularly with the tyres cold. Do not adjust the tyre pressures immediately after the vehicle has been used, or an inaccurate setting will result.

Tyre tread wear patterns

Shoulder Wear

Underinflation (wear on both sides)
Under-inflation will cause overheating of the tyre, because the tyre will flex too much, and the tread will not sit correctly on the road surface. This will cause a loss of grip and excessive wear, not to mention the danger of sudden tyre failure due to heat build-up.
Check and adjust pressures
Incorrect wheel camber (wear on one side)
Repair or renew suspension parts
Hard cornering
Reduce speed!

Centre Wear

Overinflation
Over-inflation will cause rapid wear of the centre part of the tyre tread, coupled with reduced grip, harsher ride, and the danger of shock damage occurring in the tyre casing.
Check and adjust pressures

If you sometimes have to inflate your car's tyres to the higher pressures specified for maximum load or sustained high speed, don't forget to reduce the pressures to normal afterwards.

Uneven Wear

Front tyres may wear unevenly as a result of wheel misalignment. Most tyre dealers and garages can check and adjust the wheel alignment (or "tracking") for a modest charge.
Incorrect camber or castor
Repair or renew suspension parts
Malfunctioning suspension
Repair or renew suspension parts
Unbalanced wheel
Balance tyres
Incorrect toe setting
Adjust front wheel alignment
Note: *The feathered edge of the tread which typifies toe wear is best checked by feel.*

Lubricants and fluids

Note: *Using lubricants and fluids which do not meet the Skoda standard may invalidate the warranty.*

Engine

Models fitted with a particulate filter . . . .   LongLife oil
VW 507 00 only

Models without a particulate filter:
    Standard (distance/time) service interval . . . .   Multigrade oil
VW 505 01 or better

    LongLife (variable) service interval . . . .   LongLife oil*
VW 506 01 or better

Cooling system

Models up to 2007 model year . . . .   VW G12 Plus antifreeze
Models from 2008 model year . . . .   VW G12 Plus Plus antifreeze
Models from 2011 model year . . . .   VW G13 antifreeze

Transmission

Manual gearbox . . . .   Refer to dealer
Automatic gearbox G05 218 2A2

Braking and clutch systems . . . .   Hydraulic fluid to DOT 4

* A maximum of 0.5 litres of standard VW oil may be used for topping-up when LongLife oil is unobtainable.

Tyre pressures

Note: *The recommended tyre pressures for each vehicle are given on a sticker attached to the inside of the fuel filler flap. The pressures given are for the original equipment tyres – the recommended pressures may vary if any other make or type of tyre is fitted; check with the tyre manufacturer or supplier for latest recommendations.*

Chapter 1
Routine maintenance and servicing

Contents

Degrees of difficulty

Easy, suitable for novice with little experience | Fairly easy, suitable for beginner with some experience | Fairly difficult, suitable for competent DIY mechanic | Difficult, suitable for experienced DIY mechanic | Very difficult, suitable for expert DIY or professional

1 Servicing specifications

Lubricants and fluids. . . . . Refer to the end of *Weekly checks*

Capacities – all approximate

Engine oil (including filter):
  1.9 litre engines:
    Without particulate filter . . . . 3.8 litres
    With particulate filter. . . . . 4.3 litres
  2.0 litre engines . . . . 4.3 litres
Cooling system:
  1.9 litre engines . . . . 8.4 litres
  2.0 litre engines . . . . 8.4 litres
Transmission:
  Manual transmission:
    5-speed (0A4). . . . . 2.0 litres (initial/dry fill) 1.8 litres (oil change)
    6-speed (02Q) . . . . 2.3 litres (initial/dry fill) 2.15 litres (oil change)
  Automatic (DSG) transmission fluid:
    Initial filling . . . . 7.2 litres
    Fluid change . . . . 5.2 litres
Fuel tank :
  All models. . . . . 55 litres
Washer reservoirs:
  Without headlight washers. . . . . 3.0 litres
  With headlight washers . . . . 5.5 litres

Engine codes*

PD unit injector engines:
  1.9 litre . . . . BJB, BKC, BLS and BXE
  2.0 litre . . . . BKD, BMM and BMN
Common rail engines . . . . CBBB, CBDB, CLCA, CLCB, CFHF, CFHC and CEGA
* See '*Vehicle identification*' at the end of this manual for the location of engine code markings.

Cooling system

Antifreeze mixture: *
  40% antifreeze . . . . Protection down to -25°C
  50% antifreeze . . . . Protection down to -35°C
*Refer to *Lubricants and fluids*

Remote control battery

Type CR2032

Brakes

Brake pad minimum thickness (excluding backing plate) . . . . 2.0 mm

Torque wrench settings

	Nm	lbf ft
Engine sump drain plug	30	22
Engine oil filter cap.	25	18
Manual transmission level/drain plug:		
6-speed:		
Hexagon socket head plug.	30	22
Multi-point socket head plug	45	33
Roadwheel bolts.	120	89

2 Maintenance schedule

1 The maintenance intervals in this manual are provided with the assumption that you, not the dealer, will be carrying out the work. These are the minimum intervals recommended by us for vehicles driven daily. If you wish to keep your vehicle in peak condition at all times, you may wish to perform some of these procedures more often. We encourage frequent maintenance, since it enhances the efficiency, performance and resale value of your vehicle.

2 When the vehicle is new, it should be serviced by a dealer service department (or other workshop recognised by the vehicle manufacturer as providing the same standard of service) in order to preserve the warranty. The vehicle manufacturer may reject warranty claims if you are unable to prove that servicing has been carried out as and when specified, using only original equipment parts or parts certified to be of equivalent quality.

3 This manual is not a direct reproduction of the vehicle manufacturer's data, and its publication should not be taken as implying any technical approval by the vehicle manufacturers or importers.

4 All models are equipped with a service interval display indicator in the instrument panel. With the standard non-variable display, the service intervals are in accordance with specific distances and time periods. With the LongLife display, the service interval is variable according to the number of starts, length of journeys, vehicle speeds, brake pad wear, bonnet opening frequency, fuel consumption, oil level and oil temperature, however the vehicle must be serviced at least every two years. At approximately 15 days before a service is due, 'Service in --- miles' or 'Service in --- days' or a spanner symbol will appear for approximately 10 seconds at the bottom of the odometer or in the display in the centre of the instrument cluster. Once the service interval has been reached, the display will flash 'Service'. Note that if the variable (LongLife) service interval is being used, the engine must only be filled with the recommended LongLife engine oil (see *Lubricants and fluids*).

5 After completing a service, Skoda technicians use a special instrument to reset the service display to the next service interval, and a print-out is put in the vehicle service record. The display can be reset by the owner as described in Section 8, but note that the procedure will automatically reset the display to the 10 000 miles 'distance' interval. To have the display reset to the 'variable' (LongLife) interval, it is necessary to take the vehicle to a Skoda dealer or suitably-equipped specialist who will use a special instrument to encode the on-board computer.

Every 250 miles or weekly

☐ Refer to *Weekly checks*

SERVICE on display or every 12 months, whichever comes first

☐ Renew the engine oil and filter (Section 6)
Note: *Frequent oil and filter changes are good for the engine. We recommend changing the oil at least once a year.*
☐ Check the front and rear brake pad thickness (Section 7)
☐ Reset the service interval display (Section 8)
☐ Check the condition of the exhaust system and its mountings (Section 9)
☐ Check all underbonnet components and hoses for fluid and oil leaks (Section 10)
☐ Check the condition of the auxiliary drivebelt (Section 11)
☐ Check the antifreeze concentration (Section 12)
☐ Check the brake hydraulic circuit for leaks and damage (Section 13)
☐ Check the headlight beam adjustment (Section 14)
☐ Renew the pollen filter element (Section 15)
☐ Check the manual transmission oil level (Section 16)
☐ Check the underbody protection for damage (Section 17)
☐ Check the condition of the driveshaft gaiters (Section 18)
☐ Check the steering and suspension components for condition and security (Section 19)
☐ Check the battery condition, security and electrolyte level (Section 20)
☐ Lubricate all hinges and locks (Section 21)
☐ Check the condition of the airbag unit(s) (Section 22)
☐ Check the operation of the windscreen/tailgate/headlight washer system(s) (as applicable) (Section 23)
☐ Check the engine management self-diagnosis memory for faults (Section 24)
☐ Check plenum chamber drainage for dirt and debris and clean if necessary (Section 25)
☐ Replace the fuel filter (only when using fuel not conforming to DIN EN 590) (Section 30)
☐ Check the operation of the sunroof and lubricate the guide rails (Section 26)
☐ Carry out a road test and check exhaust emissions (Section 27)

Every 38 000 miles or 4 years, whichever comes first

Note: *Most dealers perform these tasks with the nearest SERVICE*
☐ Renew the automatic (DSG) transmission fluid and filter (Section 28)

Every 56 000 miles

☐ Renew the air filter element (Section 29)
☐ Replace the fuel filter (for vehicles using fuel conforming to DIN EN 590) (Section 30)

Every 75 000 miles or 4 years, whichever comes first

☐ Renew the timing belt and tensioning roller (PD unit injector engines up to 2006 model year) (Section 31)
Note: *Skoda recommend this interval for timing belt renewal. However, if the vehicle is used mainly for short journeys or a lot of stop-start driving it is recommended that the interval is shortened. Bearing in mind that severe engine damage will result if the belt breaks in use, we recommend you err on the side of caution.*
Note: *Although Skoda recommend that the tensioner roller is only replaced at every other belt change on this engine, it is increasingly considered best practice to always change the idlers, tensioner and coolant pump whenever the timing belt is replaced. Note also that most manufacturers will not guarantee a belt unless the tensioners and rollers have been replaced at the same time.*

After 93 000 miles then every 18 000 miles

☐ Check the particulate filter ash deposit mass (Section 32)
Note: *Carry out this check on all engines with diesel particulate filter (except engine codes CLCB, CFHC, CFHF)*

Every 95 000 miles or 4 years, whichever comes first

☐ Renew the timing belt and tensioner roller (PD unit injector engines from 2007 model year) (Section 33)

Note: *Skoda recommend this interval for timing belt renewal. However, if the vehicle is used mainly for short journeys or a lot of stop-start driving it is recommended that the renewal interval is shortened. Bearing in mind that severe engine damage will result if the belt breaks in use, we recommend you err on the side of caution.*

Note: *Although Skoda recommend that the tensioner roller is only replaced at every other belt change on this engine, it is increasingly considered best practice to always change the idlers, tensioner and coolant pump whenever the timing belt is replaced. Note also that most manufacturers will not guarantee a belt unless the tensioners and rollers have been replaced at the same time.*

After 112 000 miles then every 18 000 miles

☐ Check the particulate filter ash deposit mass (Section 32)

Note: *For engine codes CLCB, CFHC, CFHF.*

Every 112 000 miles or 5 years, whichever comes first

☐ Renew the timing belt and tensioning roller (first generation common rail injection engines with engine codes CEGA, CBBB and CBDB (Section 34).

Note: *Skoda recommend this interval for timing belt renewal. However, if the vehicle is used mainly for short journeys or a lot of stop-start driving it is recommended that the interval is shortened. Bearing in mind that severe engine damage will result if the belt breaks in use, we recommend you err on the side of caution.*

Note: *Although Skoda recommend that the tensioner roller is only replaced at every other belt change on this engine, it is increasingly considered best practice to always change the idlers, tensioner and coolant pump whenever the timing belt is replaced. Note also that most manufacturers will not guarantee a belt unless the tensioners and rollers have been replaced at the same time.*

Every 130 000 miles or 5 years whichever comes first

☐ Renew the timing belt and tensioning roller (second generation common rail injection engines with engine codes CLCA, CLCB, CFHC and CFHF (Section 35).

Note: *Skoda recommend this interval for timing belt renewal. However, if the vehicle is used mainly for short journeys or a lot of stop-start driving it is recommended that the interval is shortened. Bearing in mind that severe engine damage will result if the belt breaks in use, we recommend you err on the side of caution.*

Note: *It is increasingly considered best practice to always change the idlers, tensioner and coolant pump whenever the timing belt is replaced. Note also that most manufacturers will not guarantee a belt unless the tensioners and rollers have been replaced at the same time.*

Every 2 years

☐ Renew the brake and clutch fluid (Section 36)
☐ Renew the coolant* (Section 37)
☐ Renew the remote control battery (Section 38)

* Note: *This work is not included in the Skoda schedule and should not be required if the recommended coolant antifreeze/inhibitor is used.*

After 4 years and then annually

☐ Check tyre repair sealant " use by " date on vehicles equipped with a breakdown kit (Section 39)

3 Maintenance –
component location

Underbonnet view of a 1.9 litre PD engine – other models are similar

1   Engine oil filler cap
2   Fuel filter
3   Engine oil level dipstick
4   Air filter
5   Brake/clutch fluid
    reservoir
6   Battery
7   Oil filter
8   Coolant reservoir
9   Alternator
10 Air intake ducting
11 Fusebox
12 Common (fuel) rail

Front underbody view

1   Exhaust front downpipe
2   Brake caliper
3   Lower arm
4   Engine oil drain plug
5   Intercooler hoses
6   Anti-roll bar
7   Steering track rod
8   Driveshaft
9   Subframe
10 Air conditioning
    compressor

Rear underbody view

1 Track control rod
2 Trailing arm
3 Fuel tank
4 Rear silencer
5 Subframe
6 Anti-roll bar
7 Lower suspension arm

4 Introduction

1 This Chapter is designed to help the home mechanic maintain his/her vehicle for safety, economy, long life and peak performance.
2 The Chapter contains a master maintenance schedule, followed by Sections dealing specifically with each task in the schedule. Visual checks, adjustments, component renewal and other helpful items are included. Refer to the accompanying illustrations of the engine compartment and the underside of the vehicle for the locations of the various components.
3 Servicing your vehicle will provide a planned maintenance programme, which should result in a long and reliable service life. This is a comprehensive plan, so maintaining some items but not others will not produce the same results.
4 As you service your vehicle, you will discover that many of the procedures can – and should – be grouped together, because of the particular procedure being performed, or because of the proximity of two otherwise unrelated components to one another. For example, if the vehicle is raised for any reason, the exhaust can be inspected at the same time as the suspension and steering components.
5 The first step in this maintenance

programme is to prepare yourself before the actual work begins. Read through all the Sections relevant to the work to be carried out, then make a list and gather all the parts and tools required. If a problem is encountered, seek advice from a parts specialist, or a dealer service department.

5 Regular maintenance

1 If, from the time the vehicle is new, the routine maintenance schedule is followed closely, and frequent checks are made of fluid levels and high-wear items, as suggested throughout this manual, the engine will be kept in relatively good running condition, and the need for additional work will be minimised.
2 It is possible that there will be times when the engine is running poorly due to the lack of regular maintenance. This is even more likely if a used vehicle, which has not received regular and frequent maintenance checks, is purchased. In such cases, additional work may need to be carried out, outside of the regular maintenance intervals.
3 If engine wear is suspected, a compression test (refer to the relevant Part of Chapters 2A and 2B) will provide valuable information regarding the overall performance of the main internal components. Such a test can be used as a basis to decide on the extent of the work to be carried out. If, for example, a

compression test indicates serious internal engine wear, conventional maintenance as described in this Chapter will not greatly improve the performance of the engine, and may prove a waste of time and money, unless extensive overhaul work is carried out first.
4 The following series of operations are those most often required to improve the performance of a generally poor-running engine:

Primary operations

a) Clean, inspect and test the battery (See 'Weekly checks').
b) Check all the engine-related fluids (See 'Weekly checks').
c) Check the condition and tension of the auxiliary drivebelt (Section 11).
d) Check the condition of the air filter, and renew if necessary (Section 29).
e) Check the condition of all hoses, and check for fluid leaks (Section 10).

5 If the above operations do not prove fully effective, carry out the following secondary operations:

Secondary operations

6 All items listed under *Primary operations*, plus the following:
a) Check the charging system (see Chapter 5 Section 4).
b) Check the preheating system (see Chapter 5 Section 11).
c) Renew the fuel filter (Section 30) and check the fuel system (see Chapter 4A).

6 Engine oil and filter renewal

Note: *There are several designs of oil filter used on these engines, always ensure the replacement matches the one removed. In addition to the large O-ring fitted to the cap, there may be one or more smaller O-rings, included with the new filter, for fitting to the filter or cap. Ensure all O-rings are correctly located and lubricated before fitting the filter and observe any markings with regard to the filters correct orientation. Bearing in mind these points, the following procedure for changing the oil filter is essentially the same for all versions.*

1 Frequent oil and filter changes are the most important preventative maintenance procedures which can be undertaken by the DIY owner. As engine oil ages, it becomes diluted and contaminated, which leads to premature engine wear.

2 Before starting this procedure, gather all the necessary tools and materials. Also make sure that you have plenty of clean rags and newspapers handy, to mop-up any spills. Ideally, the engine oil should be warm, as it will drain better, and more built-up sludge will be removed with it. Take care, however, not to touch the exhaust or any other hot parts of the engine when working under the vehicle. To avoid any possibility of scalding, and to protect yourself from possible skin irritants and other harmful contaminants in used engine oils, it is advisable to wear gloves when carrying out this work. Access to the underside of the vehicle will be greatly improved if it can be raised on a lift, driven onto ramps, or jacked up and supported on axle stands (see *Jacking and vehicle support*). Whichever method is chosen, make sure that the vehicle remains level. Undo the retaining fasteners and remove the engine undershield, then remove the engine top cover. The cover simply pulls up from its rubber mountings **(see illustration)**.

3 Slacken the oil filter housing cap (located to the front of the cylinder head) to allow the oil within to drain into the sump. Although there is a special Skoda tool to undo the cap, a 32 mm socket or a strap wrench is a suitable alternative **(see illustration)**. Place absorbent cloths around the filter housing to catch any spilt oil. On common rail injection engines, undo the Torx bolt and move the EGR cooler 'change-over' vacuum-solenoid valve above the filter to one side, to give access to the filter cap **(see illustration)**.

4 Working underneath the vehicle, slacken the sump drain plug about half a turn. Position the draining container under the drain plug, then remove the plug completely **(see illustration)**. Recover the sealing ring from the drain plug. Note that on some engines the sealing ring is integral with the drain plug. On these engines the drain plug must be renewed.

6.2 Pull up the front edge of the engine cover first

6.3b On common rail engines, undo the bolt (arrowed) and move the vacuum-solenoid valve to one side

6.3a Use a 32 mm socket to unbolt the filter cap

6.4 Unbolt the engine oil sump drain plug (arrowed)

5 Allow some time for the old oil to drain, noting that it may be necessary to reposition the container as the oil flow slows to a trickle.

6 After all the oil has drained, wipe off the drain plug with a clean rag, and fit a new sealing washer. Clean the area around the drain plug opening, and refit the plug. Tighten the plug to the specified torque.

7 Completely unscrew the oil filter housing cap, and lift it from the housing. Pull the old filter element from the cap/housing.

8 Remove and discard the O-ring seal(s), then using a clean rag, wipe all oil and sludge from the inside of the filter housing and cap.

9 Fit the new O-ring(s) and lubricate with a little clean engine oil and fit the new filter element to the housing/cap. Note that on 1.9 litre engines, the filter element is marked TOP on one end **(see illustrations)**.

10 Screw the cap (initially by hand) into

the housing, and tighten it to the specified torque.

11 On common rail engines refit the vacuum valve bracket above the filter.

12 Remove the old oil from under the car, dispose of the used engine oil safely, with reference to General repair procedures in the Reference section of this manual.

13 Remove the dipstick, then undo the oil filler cap from the cylinder head cover. Fill the engine, using the correct grade and type of oil (see *Lubricants and fluids*). An oil can spout or funnel may help to reduce spillage. Pour in half the specified quantity of oil first, then wait a few minutes for the oil to run to the sump (see *Weekly checks*). Continue adding oil a small quantity at a time until the level is between the minimum and maximum mark on the dipstick. Refit the filler cap.

14 Start the engine and run it for a few minutes;

6.9a Renew the filter cap O-ring seal

6.9b Fit the new filter element to the cap

7.1 The outer brake pads can be observed through the holes in the wheels

check for leaks around the oil filter cap and the sump drain plug. Note that the oil pressure warning lamp will illuminate for a short period when the ignition is turned on and then go out. The oil will only take a few seconds to circulate through the engine oil galleries and new oil filter (where fitted) when the engine starts. If the oil pressure warning lamp illuminates continuously or flashes with the engine running, switch off immediately and investigate the cause.

⚠️ *Warning: Do not increase the engine speed above idling while the oil pressure light is illuminated, as considerable damage can be caused to the turbocharger.*

Note: *On vehicles fitted with an information display system, the oil pressure warning lamp does not come on with the ignition, if it illuminates red with an accompanying message, switch off the engine immediately and investigate the cause.*

15 Switch off the engine and wait a few minutes for the oil to settle in the sump, now with the new oil circulated and the filter completely full, recheck the level on the dipstick, and add more oil up to the maximum on the dipstick.

16 If no leaks are present, refit the undershield and engine top cover.

17 Lower the vehicle to the ground.

7.3 The thickness (a) of the brake pads friction material must not be less than the specified amount

7 Brake pad check

1 On some models, the outer brake pads can be checked without removing the wheels, by observing the brake pads through the holes in the wheels **(see illustration)**. If necessary, remove the wheel trim. The thickness of the pad (excluding backing plate) must not be less than the dimension given in the Specifications.

2 If the outer pads are worn near their limits, it is worthwhile checking the inner pads as well. Apply the handbrake then jack up vehicle and support it on axle stands (see *Jacking and vehicle support*). Remove the roadwheels.

3 Use a steel rule to check the thickness of the brake pads friction material (excluding the backing plate), and compare with the minimum thickness given in the Specifications **(see illustration)**.

4 For a comprehensive check, the brake pads should be removed and cleaned. The operation of the caliper can then also be checked, and the condition of the brake disc itself can be fully examined on both sides. Refer to Chapter 9.

5 If any pads are worn to the specified minimum thickness or less, all four pads at the front or rear, as applicable, must be renewed as a set.

6 On completion of the check, refit the roadwheels and lower the vehicle to the ground.

8 Resetting the service interval display

1 After all necessary maintenance work has been completed, the service interval display must be reset. Skoda technicians use a special dedicated instrument to do this, and a print-out is then put in the vehicle service record. It is possible for the owner to reset the display as described in the following paragraphs, but note that the procedure will automatically reset the display to a 10,000 mile interval. To continue with the 'variable' intervals which take into consideration the number of starts, length of journeys, vehicle

8.2 Service indicator reset button (arrowed)

speeds, brake pad wear, bonnet opening frequency, fuel consumption, oil level and oil temperature, the display must be reset by an Skoda dealership (or suitably equipped garage) using diagnostic equipment.

Vehicles without Information Display

2 To reset the standard display manually, switch off the ignition, then press and hold down the reset button of the trip counter located beside the speedometer**(see illustration)**.

3 Switch on the ignition, then release the reset button and turn it to the right.

4 The service interval display is now reset, and will return to the normal mode after a short delay. Switch off the ignition.

Vehicles with Information Display

5 On vehicles equipped with an information display system the service interval is reset using the buttons on either the wiper control stalk or multi function steering wheel **(see illustration)**.

6 Switch on the ignition, then press button **X** for at least one second to bring up the "Main Menu" in the display. **Note:** *If the "Main Menu" will not display it may be necessary to scroll through other warning messages using button Y first.*

7 Using button **Y** to make and confirm selections in the Main Menu, select "Setup" then "Service Intervals" and finally " Reset". On pressing button **Y** to confirm, the service interval will be reset to a standard 10,000 mile interval.

8 Switch off the ignition.

8.5 Use controls to reset service interval display

9 Exhaust system check

1 With the engine cold (at least an hour after the vehicle has been driven), check the complete exhaust system from the engine to the end of the tailpipe. The exhaust system is most easily checked with the vehicle raised on a hoist, or suitably supported on axle stands, so that the exhaust components are readily visible and accessible (see *Jacking and vehicle support*).

2 Check the exhaust pipes and connections for evidence of leaks, severe corrosion and damage. Make sure that all brackets and mountings are in good condition, and that all relevant nuts and bolts are tight **(see illustration)**. Leakage at any of the joints or in other parts of the system will usually show up as a black sooty stain in the vicinity of the leak.

3 Rattles and other noises can often be traced to the exhaust system, especially the brackets and mountings. Try to move the pipes and silencers. If the components are able to come into contact with the body or suspension parts, secure the system with new mountings. Otherwise separate the joints (if possible) and twist the pipes as necessary to provide additional clearance.

10 Hose and fluid leak check

Note: *Also refer to Section 13.*

1 Visually inspect the engine joint faces, gaskets and seals for any signs of water or oil leaks. Pay particular attention to the areas around the camshaft cover, cylinder head, oil filter and sump joint faces. Bear in mind that, over a period of time, some very slight seepage from these areas is to be expected – what you are really looking for is any indication of a serious leak. Should a leak be found, renew the offending gasket or oil seal by referring to the appropriate Chapters in this manual.

2 Also check the security and condition of all the engine-related pipes and hoses. Ensure that all cable-ties or securing clips are in place and in good condition. Clips which are broken or missing can lead to chafing of the hoses, pipes or wiring, which could cause more serious problems in the future.

3 Carefully check the radiator hoses and heater hoses along their entire length. Renew any hose which is cracked, swollen or deteriorated. Cracks will show up better if the hose is squeezed. Pay close attention to the hose clips that secure the hoses to the cooling system components. Hose clips can pinch and puncture hoses, resulting in cooling system leaks.

4 Inspect all the cooling system components (hoses, joint faces, etc) for leaks **(see Haynes Hint)**. Where any problems of this nature are

9.2 Check the condition of the rubber exhaust mountings

found on system components, renew the component or gasket with reference to the relevant section of Chapter 3.

 A leak in the cooling system will usually show up as white- or antifreeze coloured deposits in the area adjoining the leak.

5 Where applicable, inspect the automatic transmission fluid cooler hoses for leaks or deterioration.

6 With the vehicle raised, inspect the fuel tank and filler neck for punctures, cracks and other damage. The connection between the filler neck and tank is especially critical. Sometimes a rubber filler neck or connecting hose will leak due to loose retaining clamps or deteriorated rubber.

7 Carefully check all rubber hoses and metal fuel lines leading away from the fuel tank. Check for loose connections, deteriorated hoses, crimped lines, and other damage. Pay particular attention to the vent pipes and hoses, which often loop up around the filler neck and can become blocked or crimped. Follow the lines to the front of the vehicle, carefully inspecting them all the way. Renew damaged sections as necessary.

8 From within the engine compartment, check the security of all fuel hose attachments and pipe unions, and inspect the fuel hoses and vacuum hoses for kinks, chafing and deterioration.

11 Auxiliary drivebelt check and renewal

Check

1 The auxiliary drivebelt drives the alternator, and where applicable, the air conditioning compressor.

2 For access to the drivebelt, apply the handbrake, then jack up the front of the vehicle and support it on axle stands (see *Jacking and vehicle support*). Remove the engine undershield, and remove the engine top cover as well.

11.3 Use a mirror to check the condition of the auxiliary drivebelt

3 Examine the auxiliary drivebelt along its entire length for damage and wear in the form of cuts and abrasions, fraying and cracking. The use of a mirror and possibly an inspection lamp will help, and the engine may be turned with a spanner on the crankshaft pulley in order to observe all areas of the belt **(see illustration)**.

4 On most engines, the drivebelt tension is adjusted automatically by a spring-tensioned idler.

5 If a drivebelt requires renewal, proceed as follows:

Removal

Note: *When the belt is removed, check all pulleys are free from damage and secure. Check the operation of the freewheel alternator pulley (where fitted) with reference to Chapter 5 Section 7.*

6 To remove the drivebelt first apply the handbrake, slacken the right-hand front roadwheel bolts, then jack up the front of the vehicle and support it on axle stands (see *Jacking and vehicle support*). Remove the roadwheel, then remove the undershield from under the engine compartment.

7 Undo the fasteners and remove the lower part of the lower front right-hand wheel arch liner. **Note:** *If the belt is being removed as part of another procedure and the intention is to re-use the belt mark it's direction of rotation with pen or chalk.*

PD unit injector engines

8 Unbolt the fuel filter and move it to one side with the hoses still attached **(see illustration)**.

11.8 The fuel filter is secured by 2 bolts, and 1 nut (arrowed)

11.9 Rotate the tensioner and lock it in place with a suitable drill bit (arrowed)

11.11 Insert a 4.0 mm drill bit (arrowed) to lock the tensioner in place

11.13 Undo the tensioner adjusting bolt (arrowed)

If improved access is required, disconnect the hoses and completely remove the filter. Plug the openings to prevent contamination.

9 Use an open-ended spanner to rotate the tensioner, and relieve the tension on the belt. Once the tensioner and bracket holes are aligned, use a suitable drill bit to lock the tensioner in place (see illustration). Remove the belt from the pulleys.

Common rail injection engines with automatic tensioner and a/c

10 Using a spanner on the centre bolt, rotate the tensioner pulley clockwise.
11 As the holes in the tensioner hub and bracket align, insert a 4.0 mm drill bit/rod to lock them in place (see illustration).
12 Remove the drivebelt.

Common rail injection engines with manual tensioner and a/c

13 Undo the tensioner adjusting bolt on the underside of the tensioner assembly to slacken the belt, and remove the tensioner pulley (see illustration). Discard the bolt – a new one must be fitted. Remove the drivebelt.

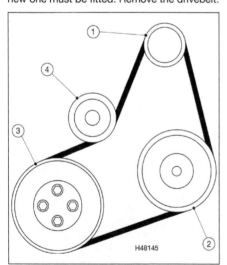

11.15 Auxiliary drivebelt routing – all models with air conditioning

1 Alternator pulley
2 Air conditioning compressor pulley
3 Crankshaft pulley
4 Tensioner pulley

Common rail injection engines without a/c

14 Models without air conditioning are fitted with a 'stretch' drivebelt which cannot be re-used and is removed by using a sharp knife to cut through the drivebelt.

Refitting

15 Locate the drivebelt on the alternator, crankshaft, air conditioning compressor (where applicable), making sure that each rib is correctly located in a groove (see illustration).

PD unit injector engines

16 Locate the drivebelt on the tensioner pulley, then release the tensioner to tension the drivebelt.

Common rail injection engines with automatic tensioner and a/c

17 Locate the drivebelt on the tensioner pulley, then release the tensioner to tension the drivebelt.

Common rail injection engines with manual tensioner and a/c

18 Coat the guide surfaces of the tensioner roller with high-temperature anti-seize grease, then locate the roller in position against the belt, and insert the new adjusting bolt.
19 The adjusting bolt must be tightened in 5 stages:
a) Hand-tighten the bolt.
b) Tighten the bolt with a spanner/socket until the bolt reaches its stop.
c) Slacken the bolt ¼ of a turn.

11.20 The end of the bolt must protrude approximately 2.5 mm above the pulley

d) Tighten the bolt to 30 Nm (22 lbf ft).
e) Tighten the bolt a further ¼ of a turn.
20 Check that the end of the bolt protrudes approximately 2.5 mm above the circumference of the tensioner pulley (see illustration).

Common rail injection engines without a/c

21 Models without air conditioning are fitted with a 'stretch' drivebelt. New drivebelts are supplied in a kit with a tool to slip the belt over the crankshaft pulley, and illustrated instructions. Follow the instructions supplied in the kit and fit the new belt.

All engines

22 The remainder of refitting is a reversal of removal.

12 Antifreeze concentration check

1 The cooling system should be filled with the recommended antifreeze and corrosion protection fluid, which is designed to last the life of the vehicle. Vehicles up to 2007 model year are filled with G12 Plus, vehicles from 2008 model year are filled with G12 Plus Plus and vehicles from 2011 with G13. Do not mix these antifreezes with any other type. If it is mixed with other types, it loses its 'filled for life' quality. The exceptions are that models filled with G12 Plus can be topped-up with G12 Plus Plus and G13. Models filled with G12 Plus Plus can be topped-up with G13 and vice-versa, but not G12 Plus. Over a period of time, the concentration of fluid may be reduced due to topping-up (this can be avoided by topping-up with the correct antifreeze mixture – see Specifications) or fluid loss. If loss of coolant has been evident, it is important to make the necessary repair before adding fresh fluid.
2 With the engine cold, carefully remove the cap from the expansion tank. If the engine is not completely cold, place a cloth rag over the cap before removing it, and remove it slowly to allow any pressure to escape.
3 Antifreeze checkers (hydrometers) are available from car accessory shops. Draw

some coolant from the expansion tank into the hydrometer and follow the manufacturer's instructions.

4 If the concentration is incorrect, it will be necessary to either withdraw some coolant and add antifreeze, or alternatively drain the old coolant and add fresh coolant of the correct concentration (see Section 37).

Note: *Skoda recommend that demineralised / distilled water should be used with antifreeze in the preparation of coolant, as normal tap water can vary in mineral and chemical content.*

13 Brake hydraulic circuit check

1 Check the entire brake hydraulic circuit for leaks and damage. Start by checking the master cylinder in the engine compartment. At the same time, check the vacuum servo unit and ABS unit for signs of fluid leakage.
2 Raise the front and rear of the vehicle and support it securely on axle stands (see *Jacking and vehicle support*). Check the rigid hydraulic brake lines for corrosion and damage.
3 At the front of the vehicle, check that the flexible hydraulic hoses to the calipers are not twisted or chafing on any of the surrounding suspension components. Turn the steering on full lock to make this check. Also check that the hoses are not brittle or cracked.
4 Lower the vehicle to the ground after making the checks.

14 Headlight beam adjustment

Halogen headlamps

1 Accurate adjustment of the headlight beam is only possible using optical beam setting equipment, and this work should therefore be carried out by a Skoda dealer or suitably-equipped workshop.
2 For reference, the headlights can be adjusted using the adjuster bolts, accessible at the top of each light unit **(see illustration)**.
3 Some models are equipped with an electrically-operated headlight beam adjustment system which is controlled through the switch in the facia. On these models, ensure that the switch is set to the basic 0 position before adjusting the headlight aim.

Gas discharge headlights

4 The headlamp range is controlled dynamically by an electronic control module which monitors the ride height of the vehicle by sensors fitted to the front and rear suspension. Beam adjustment can only be carried out using specialist test equipment and should therefore be entrusted to a suitably equipped workshop.

14.2 Headlight beam adjustment bolts (arrowed)

15.2a Slide the cover (arrowed) to the left...

15 Pollen filter element renewal

1 Undo the fasteners and remove the shield under the passenger side of the heater unit **(see illustration)**.
2 Slide the pollen filter cover to the left, and lower the filter from place **(see illustrations)**. Note how the filter is fitted.
3 Insert the new filter into the heater housing, and slide the cover to the right to secure it in place.
4 Refit the shield and tighten the fasteners securely.

16 Manual transmission oil level check

Note: *This operation is not included in the Skoda service schedule – the transmission is effectively sealed for life. However, if there is any evidence of leakage from the transmission, we would recommend that the level is checked. Where the vehicle is used in arduous conditions such as mainly for short journeys, taxi work, or towing, we recommend the oil is changed every 20 000 miles or 2 years.*

1 Apply the handbrake, then jack up the front and rear of the vehicle and support it on axle stands (see *Jacking and vehicle support*). To ensure an accurate check, make sure that the vehicle is level. Undo the fasteners and remove the engine/transmission undershield.

15.1 Undo the fasteners (arrowed) and remove the shield

15.2b... and lower the filter from place

5-speed transmissions (OA4)

2 The plug on the front face of this transmission cannot be used to check the oil level. The angle of the transmission in this installation means that the correct oil level is above the position of the plug.
3 The only method of establishing the correct oil level is to drain and refill the transmission with the specified quantity of oil as described in Chapter 7A Section 6

6-speed transmissions (O2Q)

4 On some versions of this transmission the oil level can only be checked by draining and refilling with the specified quantity, as described in Chapter 7A Section 6 as there is no filler/level plug.
5 Where fitted the oil filler/level plug is located on the front side of the manual transmission. The plug may be either an Allen key type, or a multisplined type **(see illustration)**. Remove

16.5 Oil level plug

18.1 Check the condition of the driveshaft gaiters

the oil level plug. The fluid must be level with the bottom of the hole. A certain amount of oil will have gathered behind the filler/level plug, and will trickle out when it is removed, this does not necessarily indicate that the level is correct. To ensure that a true level is established, wait until the initial trickle has stopped, then add oil as necessary until a trickle of new oil can be seen emerging. The level will be correct when the flow ceases.
6 When the oil level is correct, refit the filler/level plug and tighten it to the specified torque. Note that two versions of the oil filler plug are fitted and they have different torque settings.
7 Wipe off any spilt oil then refit the engine undershield and tighten the retaining screws securely. Lower the car to the ground.

17 Underbody protection check

1 Raise and support the vehicle on axle stands (see *Jacking and vehicle support*).
2 Using an inspection lamp, examine the entire underside of the vehicle, paying particular attention to the wheel arches. Look for any damage to the flexible underbody coating, which may crack or flake off with age, leading to corrosion.
3 Also check that the wheel arch liners are securely attached with any clips provided – if they come loose, dirt may get in behind the liners and defeat their purpose.
4 If there is any damage to the underseal, or any corrosion, it should be repaired before the damage gets too serious.

19.3 Check for wear in the hub bearings by grasping the wheel and trying to rock it

18 Driveshaft gaiter check

1 With the vehicle raised and securely supported on stands, slowly rotate the roadwheel. Inspect the condition of the outer constant velocity (CV) joint rubber gaiters, squeezing the gaiters to open out the folds. Check for signs of cracking, splits or deterioration of the rubber, which may allow the grease to escape, and lead to water and grit entry into the joint. Also check the security and condition of the retaining clips. Repeat these checks on the inner joints **(see illustration)**. If any damage or deterioration is found, the gaiters should be renewed (see Chapter 8 Section 3).
2 At the same time, check the general condition of the CV joints themselves by first holding the driveshaft and attempting to rotate the wheel. Repeat this check by holding the inner joint and attempting to rotate the driveshaft. Any appreciable movement indicates wear in the joints, wear in the driveshaft splines, or a loose driveshaft retaining nut.

19 Steering and suspension check

1 Raise the front and rear of the vehicle, and securely support it on axle stands (see *Jacking and vehicle support*).
2 Visually inspect the track rod end balljoint dust cover, the lower front suspension balljoint dust cover, and the steering rack-and-pinion gaiters for splits, chafing or deterioration. Any wear of these components will cause loss of lubricant, together with dirt and water entry, resulting in rapid deterioration of the balljoints or steering gear.
3 Grasp the roadwheel at the 12 o'clock and 6 o'clock positions, and try to rock it **(see illustration)**. Very slight free play may be felt, but if the movement is appreciable, further investigation is necessary to determine the source. Continue rocking the wheel while an assistant depresses the footbrake. If the movement is now eliminated or significantly reduced, it is likely that the hub bearings are at fault. If the free play is still evident with the footbrake depressed, then there is wear in the suspension joints or mountings.
4 Now grasp the wheel at the 9 o'clock and 3 o'clock positions, and try to rock it as before. Any movement felt now may again be caused by wear in the hub bearings or the steering track rod balljoints. If the inner or outer balljoint is worn, the visual movement will be obvious.
5 Using a large screwdriver or flat bar, check for wear in the suspension mounting bushes by levering between the relevant suspension component and its attachment point. Some

movement is to be expected as the mountings are made of rubber, but excessive wear should be obvious. Also check the condition of any visible rubber bushes, looking for splits, cracks or contamination of the rubber.
6 With the car standing on its wheels, have an assistant turn the steering wheel back-and-forth about an eighth of a turn each way. There should be very little, if any, lost movement between the steering wheel and roadwheels. If this is not the case, closely observe the joints and mountings previously described, but in addition, check the steering column universal joints for wear, and the rack-and-pinion steering gear itself.
7 Check for any signs of fluid leakage around the front suspension struts and rear shock absorber. Should any serious fluid leakage be noticed, it indicates that the suspension strut or shock absorber is defective, and should be renewed.
Note: *Suspension struts/shock absorbers should always be renewed in pairs on the same axle to ensure correct vehicle handling.*
8 The efficiency of the suspension strut/shock absorber may be checked by bouncing the vehicle at each corner. Generally speaking, the body will return to its normal position and stop after being depressed. If it rises and returns on a rebound, the suspension strut/shock absorber is probably suspect. Examine also the suspension strut/shock absorber upper and lower mountings for any signs of wear.

20 Battery check

1 The battery is located on the left-hand side of the engine compartment. Release the catch and remove the cover from the top of the battery (where fitted)**(see illustration)**.
2 Check that both battery terminals are securely attached and are free from corrosion.
3 Check the battery casing for signs of damage or cracking and check the battery retaining clamp bolt is securely tightened. If the battery casing is damaged in any way the battery must be renewed (see Chapter 5 Section 3).
4 On completion of the check, refit the cover.

20.1 Release the clip (arrowed) and lift up the battery cover

21 Hinge and lock lubrication

1 Lubricate the hinges of the bonnet, doors and tailgate with a light general-purpose oil. Similarly, lubricate all latches, locks and lock strikers. At the same time, check the security and operation of all the locks, adjusting them if necessary (see Chapter 11).
2 Lightly lubricate the bonnet release mechanism and cable with a suitable grease.

22 Airbag unit check

1 Inspect the exterior condition of the airbag(s) for signs of damage or deterioration. If an airbag shows signs of damage, it must be renewed (see Chapter 12 Section 24).
2 Note that it is not permissible to attach any stickers to the surface of the airbag, as this may affect the deployment of the unit.

23 Windscreen/tailgate/ headlight washer system check

1 Check that each of the washer jet nozzles are clear and that each nozzle provides a strong jet of washer fluid.
2 The windscreen washer nozzles should be aimed slightly above the centre of the screen and can be adjusted up and down using a small screwdriver (see illustration).
3 The aim of the headlight jets is set in the factory and there is no provision for adjustment.
4 Especially during the winter months, make sure that the washer fluid concentration is sufficient.

24 Engine management self-diagnosis memory fault check

1 This work should be carried out by a Skoda dealer or diagnostic specialist using special equipment. Note however that simple and relatively inexpensive diagnostic tools are now widely available, allowing access to at least the mandatory OBD (on board diagnostics) emissions related fault codes. The diagnostic socket is located beneath the right-hand side of the facia (see illustration).

25 Plenum chamber check

1 The plenum chamber is the area at the base of the windscreen, containing the wiper motor linkage and other components. The outer ends of the chamber have water drainage channels and these can become blocked with dirt and debris such as leaves, leading to possible water ingress and electrical problems. Inspect the chamber through it's cover and if necessary remove the cover (see Chapter 12 Section 13) and clear the channels.

26 Sunroof check and lubrication

1 Check the operation of the sunroof, and leave it in the fully-open position.
2 Wipe clean the guide rails on each side of the sunroof opening, then apply lubricant to them. Skoda recommend lubricant spray G 052 778 A2.

27 Road test and exhaust emissions check

Instruments and electrical equipment

1 Check the operation of all instruments and electrical equipment.
2 Make sure that all instruments read correctly, and switch on all electrical equipment in turn, to check that it functions properly.

Steering and suspension

3 Check for any abnormalities in the steering, suspension, handling or road feel.
4 Drive the vehicle, and check that there are no unusual vibrations or noises which may indicate wear in the driveshafts, wheel bearings, etc.
5 Check that the steering feels positive, with no excessive sloppiness, or roughness, and check for any suspension noises when cornering and driving over bumps.

Drivetrain

6 Check the performance of the engine, clutch (where applicable), gearbox/transmission and driveshafts.
7 Listen for any unusual noises from the engine, clutch and gearbox/transmission.
8 Make sure that the engine runs smoothly when idling, and that there is no hesitation when accelerating.
9 Check that, where applicable, the clutch action is smooth and progressive, that the drive is taken up smoothly, and that the pedal travel is not excessive. Also listen for any noises when the clutch pedal is depressed.
10 On manual gearbox models, check that all gears can be engaged smoothly without noise, and that the gear lever action is smooth and not abnormally vague or notchy.
11 On automatic transmission models, make sure that all gearchanges occur smoothly, without snatching, and without an increase in engine speed between changes. Check that all the gear positions can be selected with the

23.2 Use a small screwdriver to adjust the washer jet aim

vehicle at rest. If any problems are found, they should be referred to a Skoda dealer.
12 Listen for a metallic clicking sound from the front of the vehicle, as the vehicle is driven slowly in a circle with the steering on full-lock. Carry out this check in both directions. If a clicking noise is heard, this indicates wear in a driveshaft joint, in which case renew the joint if necessary.

Braking system

13 Make sure that the vehicle does not pull to one side when braking, and that the wheels do not lock when braking hard.
14 Check that there is no vibration through the steering when braking.
15 Check that the handbrake operates correctly without excessive movement of the lever, and that it holds the vehicle stationary on a slope.
16 Test the operation of the brake servo unit as follows. With the engine off, depress the footbrake four or five times to exhaust the vacuum. Hold the brake pedal depressed, then start the engine. As the engine starts, there should be a noticeable 'give' in the brake pedal as vacuum builds-up. Allow the engine to run for at least two minutes, and then switch it off. If the brake pedal is depressed now, it should be possible to detect a hiss from the servo as the pedal is depressed. After about four or five applications, no further hissing should be heard, and the pedal should feel considerably harder.
17 Under controlled emergency braking, the pulsing of the ABS unit must be felt at the footbrake pedal.

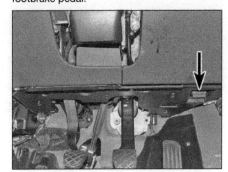
24.1 EOBD diagnostic plug (arrowed)

29.1 Undo the air filter cover bolts (arrowed)

29.2 Lift out the air filter element

Exhaust emissions check

18 Although not part of the manufacturer's maintenance schedule, this check will normally be carried out on a regular basis according to the country the vehicle is operated in. Currently in the UK, exhaust emissions testing is included as part of the annual MOT test after the vehicle is 3 years old.

28 Automatic (DSG) transmission fluid and filter renewal

1 Refer to Chapter 7B Section 6 for details of renewing the DSG transmission fluid and filter.

29 Air filter element renewal

1 Undo the bolts and lift away the upper part of the air cleaner housing**(see illustration)**.
2 Remove the air filter element, noting which way round it is fitted**(see illustration)**.
3 Wipe clean the main body, if necessary use a vacuum cleaner to remove any debris, then fit the new air filter, making sure it is the correct way round.
4 The remainder of refitting is a reversal of removal.

30 Fuel filter renewal

Note: *Various versions of fuel filter are fitted to these engines depending on model year and territory. The following procedures depict a common example. On some versions it may be necessary to change the central pillar seal in the lower filter housing or align the filter element with the upper housing before fitting, but the basic procedure is the same.*

1 The fuel filter is located on the right-hand side of the engine. To ease access, pull the engine cover upwards to release the rubber mountings. Place cloth rags around the area beneath the filter unit.
2 Position a container underneath the filter unit and pad the surrounding area with rags to absorb any fuel that may be spilt.
3 At the top of the filter unit, undo the Torx bolts around the circumference and remove the upper part, leaving the fuel hoses attached to it. If necessary, use a flat-bladed screwdriver in the slot provided to prise the upper part from the lower part**(see illustrations)**.
Caution: Be prepared for an amount of fuel loss. Do not allow diesel fuel to contact any of the coolant hoses.
4 Lift the filter element from the housing, and remove the O-ring seal **(see illustration)**.
5 Use a pipette/ syringe to remove the dirty fuel and water residue from inside the fuel filter lower housing and then use rags to remove any residue from its internal surfaces **(see illustration)**. Ensure that the fuel filter lower housing is completely clean.
6 Fit a new fuel filter into the housing, then moisten the new O-ring seal with clean fuel and fit it to the upper part of the filter housing **(see illustrations)**.
7 Fill the filter housing with clean diesel to aid restarting.
8 Refit the upper part to the lower part of the filter housing, ensuring its correctly

30.3a Undo the Torx bolts (arrowed)...

30.3b ... then prise the upper part of the filter up using the slot provided

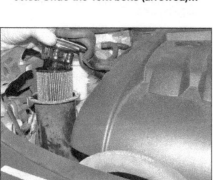

30.4 Lift the filter element from the lower housing

30.5 Use a pipette to draw out the old fuel

seated and pushed fully home, then refit the bolts and tighten them evenly in a diagonal sequence **(see illustration)**.

Note: *Do not use the bolts to pull the upper part into place as there is a risk of damage to the bolts and/or housing.*

9 Start and run the engine at idle, then check around the fuel filter for fuel leaks. Note that it may take a few seconds of cranking before the engine starts. If the engine does not start the system must be bled using a vacuum tool or hand primer **(see illustration)**. Identify the fuel return hose from the injectors and disconnect it from the filter. Connect the vacuum pump or primer and draw fuel to the filter. Reconnect the fuel hose to the filter and start the vehicle.

Note: *Skoda recommend that the common rail engine fuel systems are bled using diagnostic equipment to run the in-tank pump for three minutes to purge the system. This should not be required, provided the fuel filter lower housing is filled with clean diesel prior to fitting the upper part of the housing.*

10 Raise the engine speed to about 2000 rpm several times, then allow the engine to idle again.

11 Remove the collecting container and rags, then refit the engine top cover.

31 Timing belt and tensioning roller renewal (PD unit injector engines up to 2006)

1 Refer to Chapter 2A Section 7 and Chapter 2A Section 8 for details of renewing the timing belt and tensioning roller. Note that Skoda recommend that the tensioning roller is renewed every second timing belt change.

32 Particulate filter ash deposit mass check

1 Eventually the amount of ash deposited in the particulate filter by the filtration process will cause a blockage and engine running problems. Skoda state that the maximum amount of ash is 60g. At this point, the particulate filter must be renewed. Unfortunately, the mass of the ash can only be established using dedicated Skoda diagnostic equipment connected to the vehicle through the diagnostic plug under the driver's side of the facia **(see illustration 21.1)**. Consequently, we recommend this task is entrusted to a Skoda dealer or suitably-equipped specialist.

Note: *Access to diagnostic equipment will be required when fitting a new particulate filter to adapt the filter to the engine management system and reset the stored ash level to zero.*

33 Timing belt and tensioning roller renewal (PD unit injector engines after 2007)

1 Refer to Chapter 2A Section 7 and Chapter

30.6a Renew the O-ring seal…

2A Section 8 for details of renewing the timing belt and tensioning roller. Note that Skoda recommend that the tensioning roller is renewed every second timing belt change.

34 Timing belt and tensioning roller renewal (1st generation common rail injection engines)

1 Refer to Chapter 2B Section 7 and Chapter 2B Section 8 for details of renewing the timing belt and tensioning roller. Note that Skoda recommend that the tensioning roller is renewed every second timing belt change.

35 Timing belt and tensioning roller renewal (2nd generation common rail injection engines)

1 Refer to Chapter 2B Section 7 and Chapter 2B Section 8 for details of renewing the timing belt and tensioning roller.

36 Brake and clutch fluid renewal

⚠ *Warning: Brake hydraulic fluid can harm your eyes and damage painted surfaces, so use extreme caution when handling and pouring it. Do not use fluid that has been standing open*

30.8 Lower the upper part, complete with filter element, into the housing

30.6b.. and fit the new element to the upper housing

for some time, as it absorbs moisture from the air. Excess moisture can cause a dangerous loss of braking effectiveness.

1 The procedure is similar to that for the bleeding of the hydraulic system as described in Chapter 9 Section 2, except that the brake fluid reservoir should be emptied by siphoning, using a clean poultry baster or similar before starting, and allowance should be made for the old fluid to be expelled when bleeding a section of the circuit. Since the clutch hydraulic system on manual gearbox models also uses fluid from the brake system reservoir, it should also be bled at the same time by referring to Chapter 6, Section 2.

2 Working as described in Chapter 9 Section 2, open the first bleed screw in the sequence, and pump the brake pedal gently until nearly all the old fluid has been emptied from the master cylinder reservoir.

3 Top-up to the MAX level with new fluid, and continue pumping until only the new fluid remains in the reservoir, and new fluid can be seen emerging from the bleed screw. Tighten the bolt, and top the reservoir level up to the MAX level line.

4 Work through all the remaining bleed screws in the sequence until new fluid can be seen at all of them. Be careful to keep the master cylinder reservoir topped-up to above the MIN level at all times, or air may enter the system and greatly increase the length of the task.

5 When the operation is complete, check that all bleed screws are securely tightened, and that their dust caps are refitted. Wash off all

30.9 Bleeding the fuel system with a vacuum pump

37.4 Disconnect the hoses from the circulation pump (arrowed) – common rail injection engines only

traces of spilt fluid, and recheck the master cylinder reservoir fluid level.

6 On models with a manual transmission unit, once the brake fluid has been changed the clutch fluid should also be renewed. Referring to Chapter 6 Section 2, bleed the clutch until new fluid is seen to be emerging from the slave cylinder bleed screw, keeping the master cylinder fluid level above the MIN level line at all times to prevent air entering the system. Once the new fluid emerges, securely tighten the bleed screw then disconnect and remove the bleeding equipment. Securely refit the dust cap then wash off all traces of spilt fluid.

7 On all models, ensure the master cylinder fluid level is correct (see *Weekly checks*) and thoroughly check the operation of the brakes and (where necessary) clutch before taking the car on the road.

37 Coolant renewal

⚠ *Warning: Wait until the engine is cold before starting this procedure. Do not allow antifreeze to come in contact with your skin, or with the painted surfaces of the vehicle. Rinse off spills immediately with plenty of water. Never leave antifreeze lying around in an open container, or in a puddle in the driveway or on the garage floor. Children and pets are attracted by its sweet smell, but antifreeze can be fatal if ingested.*

37.18 A vacuum coolant refill tool

Note: *The cooling system should be filled with the recommended antifreeze and corrosion protection fluid, which is designed to last the life of the vehicle. Vehicles up to 2007 model year are filled with G12 Plus, vehicles from 2008 model year are filled with G12 Plus Plus and vehicles from 2011 with G13. Do not mix these antifreezes with any other type. If it is mixed with other types, it loses its 'filled for life' quality and may result in engine damage. The exceptions are that models filled with G12 Plus can be topped-up with G12 Plus Plus and G13. Models filled with G12 Plus Plus can be topped-up with G13 and vice-versa, but not G12 Plus.*

Note: *This work is not included in the Skoda schedule and should not be required if the recommended VW G12 Plus, G12 Plus Plus or G13 LongLife coolant antifreeze/inhibitor is used. However, if standard antifreeze/inhibitor is used, the work should be carried out at the recommended interval.*

Cooling system draining

1 With the engine completely cold, cover the expansion tank cap with a wad of rag, and slowly turn the cap anti-clockwise to relieve the pressure in the cooling system (a hissing sound will normally be heard). Wait until any pressure remaining in the system is released, then continue to turn the cap until it can be removed.
2 Firmly apply the handbrake, then jack up the front of the vehicle and support it on axle stands (see Jacking and support 13 Section 5). Release the fasteners and remove the engine undershield to gain access to the base of the radiator.
3 Some models are equipped with a drain plug in the radiator bottom hose, whilst on others, it's necessary to disconnect the bottom hose from the radiator. Position a suitable container beneath the radiator bottom hose, then prise out the retaining clip a little, and pull the bottom hose from the radiator, or undo the drain tap as applicable. Allow the coolant to drain into the container.
4 On common rail injection engines, release the clamps and disconnect the hoses from the coolant circulation pump located at the front side of the cylinder block, under the oil cooler **(see illustration)**.
5 On all engines, remove the lower (horizontal) or rear (vertical) coolant hose from the oil cooler on the oil filter housing and allow the coolant to drain. Note that on later common rail engines there is only one hose to the oil filter housing to remove.
6 If the coolant has been drained for a reason other than renewal, then provided it is clean, it can be re-used, but this is not recommended.
7 Once all the coolant has drained, refit the hoses ensuring that all retaining clips/clamps are properly located, or tighten the drain tap as applicable.
8 Refit the engine undershield and lower the vehicle onto its wheels.

Cooling system flushing

9 If coolant renewal has been neglected, or

if the antifreeze mixture has become diluted, then in time, the cooling system may gradually lose efficiency, as the coolant passages become restricted due to rust, scale deposits, and other sediment. Flushing the system clean can restore the cooling system efficiency.
10 The radiator should be flushed independently of the engine, to avoid unnecessary contamination.

Radiator flushing

11 To flush the radiator, disconnect the top and bottom hoses and any other relevant hoses from the radiator, with reference to Chapter 3 Section 2.
12 Insert a garden hose into the radiator top inlet. Direct a flow of clean water through the radiator, and continue flushing until clean water emerges from the radiator bottom outlet.
13 If after a reasonable period, the water still does not run clear, the radiator can be flushed with a good proprietary cooling system cleaning agent. It is important that their manufacturer's instructions are followed carefully. If the contamination is particularly bad, insert the hose in the radiator bottom outlet, and reverse-flush the radiator.

Engine flushing

14 To flush the engine, remove the thermostat housing as described in Chapter 3 Section 4.
15 With the top hose disconnected from the radiator, insert a garden hose into the radiator top hose. Direct a clean flow of water through the engine, and continue flushing until clean water emerges from the cylinder block.
16 On completion of flushing, refit the thermostat housing and reconnect the hoses with reference to Chapter 3 Sections 2 and 4.

Cooling system filling

17 Before attempting to fill the cooling system, make sure that all hoses and clips are in good condition, and that the clips/connections are secure. Note that an antifreeze mixture must be used all year round, to prevent corrosion of the engine components (see following sub-Section).
Note: *Skoda recommend that demineralised / distilled water should be used with antifreeze in the preparation of coolant, as normal tap water can vary in mineral and chemical content.*
18 If the coolant is being renewed, prepare the required quantity of coolant (to the correct concentration) with reference to Section 1.
Note: *For the second generation common rail engines, the recommended refill method is to use a vacuum type coolant filling tool **(see illustration)**. The tool vacuums the cooling system and then the vacuum is used to draw the coolant into the system. This method ensures there are no airlocks in the cooling system. It is possible to fill the cooling system manually, by adding coolant slowly through the coolant reservoir.*
19 Remove the expansion tank filler cap, and fill the system by slowly pouring the coolant into the expansion tank to prevent airlocks from forming.
20 Once the level in the expansion tank starts

38.2a Use a small screwdriver or a feeler gauge to separate the battery compartment from the key

38.2b With the key separated, the two halves of the battery compartment can be prised apart

38.3 Remote control sections separated to show battery

to rise, squeeze the radiator top and bottom hoses to help expel any trapped air in the system. Once all the air is expelled, top-up the coolant level to the MAX mark.
21 Start the engine and run it at a fast idle for up to two minutes, during this time top up and maintain the coolant level in the expansion tank at the maximum mark, then fit the coolant expansion tank cap and continue to run the engine until the cooling fan cuts in. Wait for the fan to stop then switch off the engine and allow the engine to cool.
22 When the engine has cooled, check the coolant level with reference to *Weekly checks*. Top-up the level if necessary and refit the expansion tank cap.

Antifreeze mixture

Note: *If the coolant visible in the expansion tank is brown in colour, then the cooling system may have been topped-up with coolant containing the wrong type of antifreeze. If you are unsure of the type of antifreeze used, or if you suspect that mixing may have occurred, the best course of action is to drain, flush and refill the cooling system.*
Note: *Skoda recommend that demineralised / distilled water should be used with antifreeze in the preparation of coolant, as normal tap water can vary in mineral and chemical content.*

23 If the recommended Skoda coolant is not being used, the antifreeze should always be renewed at the specified intervals. This is necessary not only to maintain the antifreeze properties, but also to prevent corrosion which would otherwise occur as the corrosion inhibitors become progressively less effective.
24 The quantity of antifreeze and levels of protection are indicated in the Specifications.
25 Before adding antifreeze, the cooling system should be completely drained, preferably flushed, and all hoses checked for condition and security.
26 After filling with antifreeze, a label should be attached to the expansion tank, stating the type and concentration of antifreeze used, and the date installed. Any subsequent topping-up should be made with the same type and concentration of antifreeze.
Caution: Do not use engine antifreeze in the windscreen/tailgate/headlight washer system, as it will cause damage to the vehicle paintwork.

38 Remote control battery renewal

1 Fold open the key.

2 Using a thin screwdriver or feeler gauge, carefully separate the front part of the key from the transmitter housing **(see illustrations)**.
3 Remove the cover of the transmitter housing, and remove the battery noting its orientation **(see illustration)**.
4 Fit the new battery with the positive (+) side facing downwards, as indicated on the transmitter cover housing.
5 The remainder of refitting is a reversal of removal.
6 If the vehicle does not lock or unlock after renewing the battery, you may need to synchronise the remote control.
7 Press any button on the remote control and unlock the driver's door with the key within 1 minute. The remote control should then function as normal.

39 Tyre repair sealant

1 On vehicles equipped with a tyre repair kit, the "use by" date should be checked after four years and then annually. Any sealant that is more than four years old should be replaced.

Notes

Chapter 2 Part A
PD unit injector engine in-car repair procedures

Contents

Degrees of difficulty

Easy, suitable for novice with little experience | Fairly easy, suitable for beginner with some experience | Fairly difficult, suitable for competent DIY mechanic | Difficult, suitable for experienced DIY mechanic | Very difficult, suitable for expert DIY or professional

Specifications

General

Manufacturer's engine codes: *
  1.9 litre (1896 cc), 8-valve, SOHC ... BJB, BKC, BLS and BXE
  2.0 litre (1968 cc):
    8-valve, SOHC ... BMM
    16-valve, DOHC ... BKD and BMN

Maximum outputs: **Power** / **Torque**
  1.9 litre ... 77 kW at 4000 rpm / 250 Nm at 1900 rpm
  2.0 litre:
    Engine codes BKD and BMM ... 103 kW at 4000 rpm / 320 Nm at 1750 to 2500 rpm
    Engine code BMN ... 125 kW at 4200 rpm / 350 Nm at 1800 rpm

Bore:
  1.9 litre ... 79.5 mm
  2.0 litre ... 81.0 mm
Stroke ... 95.5 mm
Compression ratio:
  1.9 litre ... 19.0 : 1
  2.0 litre ... 18.5 : 1
Compression pressures:
  Minimum compression pressure ... Approximately 19.0 bar
  Maximum difference between cylinders ... Approximately 5.0 bar
Firing order ... 1 – 3 – 4 – 2
No 1 cylinder location ... Timing belt end

*See 'Vehicle identification' at the end of this manual for the location of engine code markings.

Camshaft

Camshaft endfloat (maximum) ... 0.15 mm

Lubrication system

Oil pump type ... Gear type, chain-driven from crankshaft
Oil pressure (oil temperature 80°C, at idle) ... 0.8 bar (minimum)
Oil pressure (oil temperature 80°C, at 2000 rpm) ... 2.0 bar (minimum)
Oil pressure (oil temperature 80°C, at high rpm) ... 7.0 bar (maximum)

Torque wrench settings

	Nm	lbf ft
Ancillary (alternator, etc) bracket mounting bolts.................	45	33
Air conditioning compressor	25	18
Alternator and tensioner.....................................	23	17
Auxiliary drivebelt tensioner securing bolt	23	17
Big-end bearing cap bolts: *		
Stage 1..	30	22
Stage 2..	Angle-tighten a further 90°	
Camshaft bearing cap bolts (SOHC engines): *		
Stage 1..	8	6
Stage 2..	Angle-tighten a further 90°	
Camshaft bearing frame bolts (DOHC engines)*	20	15
Camshaft cover nuts/bolts...................................	10	7
Camshaft sprocket hub centre bolt	100	74
Camshaft sprocket-to-hub bolts: *		
SOHC engine		
Stage 1	20	15
Stage 2	Angle-tighten a further 45°	
DOHC engine	25	18
Coolant pump bolts	15	11
Crankshaft oil seal housing bolts.............................	15	11
Crankshaft pulley-to-sprocket bolts: *		
Stage 1..	10	7
Stage 2..	Angle-tighten a further 90°	
Crankshaft sprocket bolt: *		
Stage 1..	120	89
Stage 2..	Angle-tighten a further 90°	
Cylinder head bolts: *		
Stage 1..	35	26
Stage 2..	60	44
Stage 3..	Angle-tighten a further 90°	
Stage 4..	Angle-tighten a further 90°	
Engine mountings: *		
RH engine mounting:		
Mounting bracket to engine:		
Stage 1	40	30
Stage 2	Angle-tighten a further 180°	
Mounting to body:		
Stage 1	40	30
Stage 2	Angle-tighten a further 90°	
Mounting to bracket:		
Stage 1	60	44
Stage 2	Angle-tighten a further 90°	
Mounting movement limiter		
Stage 1	20	15
Stage 2	Angle-tighten a further 90°	
LH engine mounting:		
Mounting to body:		
Stage 1	40	30
Stage 2	Angle-tighten a further 90°	
Mounting to bracket on transmission:		
Stage 1	60	44
Stage 2	Angle-tighten a further 90°	
Rear mounting link:		
To transmission:		
Stage 1:		
8.8 strength class bolt............................	40	30
10.9 strength class bolt...........................	50	37
Stage 2	Angle-tighten a further 90°	
To subframe:		
Stage 1	100	74
Stage 2	Angle-tighten a further 90°	
Flywheel/driveplate: *		
Stage 1..	60	44
Stage 2..	Angle-tighten a further 90°	
Main bearing cap bolts: *		
Stage 1..	65	48
Stage 2..	Angle-tighten a further 90°	

Torque wrench settings (continued)

	Nm	lbf ft
Oil cooler bolt	25	18
Oil drain plug	30	22
Oil filter cover	25	18
Oil filter housing-to-cylinder block bolts: *		
Stage 1	15	11
Stage 2	Angle-tighten a further 90°	
Oil level/temperature sensor-to-sump bolts	10	7
Oil pick-up pipe securing bolts	15	11
Oil pressure relief valve plug	27	20
Oil pressure warning light switch	20	15
Oil pump chain tensioner bolt	16	12
Oil pump sprocket securing bolt: *		
Stage 1	20	15
Stage 2	Angle-tighten a further 90°	
Oil pump-to-crankcase securing bolts	15	11
Piston oil spray jet bolt	27	20
Rocker arm shafts: *		
Stage 1	20	15
Stage 2	Angle-tighten a further 90°	
Sump:		
Sump-to-cylinder block bolts	15	11
Sump-to-transmission bolts	45	33
Tandem pump	20	15
Thermostat housing	15	11
Timing belt idler roller (next to coolant pump sprocket) nut*	20	15
Timing belt idler roller bolt (DOHC engine upper idler):*		
Bolt (with internal thread for large engine mounting bracket):		
Stage 1	90	66
Stage 2	Angle-tighten a further 90°	
Bolt (small engine mount bracket):		
Stage 1	40	30
Stage 2	Angle-tighten a further 90°	
Timing belt outer cover bolts	10	7
Timing belt rear cover-to-cylinder head bolt	10	7
Timing belt tensioner mounting stud*	15	11
Timing belt tensioner roller securing nut: *		
Stage 1	20	15
Stage 2	Angle-tighten a further 45°	

* Do not re-use fasteners

1 General Information

How to use this Chapter

1 This Part of Chapter 2 describes those repair procedures that can reasonably be carried out on the engine while it remains in the vehicle. If the engine has been removed from the vehicle and is being dismantled as described in Part C, any preliminary dismantling procedures can be ignored.

2 Note that while it may be possible physically to overhaul certain items while the engine is in the vehicle, such tasks are not usually carried out as separate operations, and usually require the execution of several additional procedures (not to mention the cleaning of components and of oilways); for this reason, all such tasks are classed as major overhaul procedures, and are described in Part C of this Chapter.

Engine description

3 Throughout this Chapter, engines are referred to by type, and are identified and referred to by the manufacturer's code letters. A listing of all engines covered, together with their code letters, is given in the Specifications at the start of this Chapter.

4 The engines are water-cooled, single (1896 cc) or double (1968 cc) overhead camshaft(s), in-line four-cylinder units, with cast-iron cylinder blocks and aluminium-alloy cylinder heads. All are mounted transversely at the front of the vehicle, with the transmission bolted to the left-hand end of the engine.

5 The crankshaft is of five-bearing type, and thrustwashers are fitted to the centre main bearing to control crankshaft endfloat.

6 Drive for the single (1896 cc) or double (1968 cc) camshafts is by a toothed timing belt from the crankshaft. Each camshaft is mounted at the top of the cylinder head, and is secured by bearing caps (1896 cc) or a bearing frame/ladder (1968 cc).

7 The valves are closed by coil springs, and run in guides pressed into the cylinder head. On 1896cc engines, the camshaft actuates the valves directly, through hydraulic tappets; on 1968 cc engines, the valves are operated by roller rocker arms incorporating hydraulic tappets.

8 The gear-type oil pump is driven by a chain from a sprocket on the crankshaft. Oil is drawn from the sump through a strainer, and then forced through an externally-mounted, renewable filter. From there, it is distributed to the cylinder head, where it lubricates the camshaft journals and hydraulic tappets, and also to the crankcase, where it lubricates the main bearings, connecting rod big-ends, gudgeon pins and cylinder bores. A coolant-fed oil cooler is fitted to the oil filter housing on all engines. Oil jets are fitted to the base of each cylinder – these spray oil onto the underside of the pistons, to improve cooling.

9 All engines are fitted with a combined brake servo vacuum pump and fuel lift pump (tandem pump), driven by the camshaft on the transmission end of the cylinder head.

2.3 Disconnect the injector solenoids wiring plug (arrowed)

10 On all engines, engine coolant is circulated by a pump, driven by the timing belt. For details of the cooling system, refer to Chapter 3.

Operations with engine in car

11 The following operations can be performed without removing the engine:
a) Compression pressure – testing.
b) Camshaft cover – removal and refitting.
c) Crankshaft pulley – removal and refitting.
d) Timing belt covers – removal and refitting.
e) Timing belt – removal, refitting and adjustment.
f) Timing belt tensioner and sprockets – removal and refitting.
g) Camshaft oil seals – renewal.
h) Camshaft(s) and hydraulic tappets – removal, inspection and refitting.
i) Cylinder head – removal and refitting.
j) Cylinder head and pistons – decarbonising.
k) Sump – removal and refitting.
l) Oil pump – removal, overhaul and refitting.
m) Crankshaft oil seals – renewal.
n) Engine/transmission mountings – inspection and renewal.
o) Flywheel/driveplate – removal, inspection and refitting.

Note: It is possible to remove the pistons and connecting rods (after removing the cylinder head and sump) without removing the engine. However, this is not recommended. Work of this nature is more easily and thoroughly completed with the engine on the bench, as described in Chapter 2C.

2 Compression and leakdown tests – description and interpretation

Compression test

Note: A compression tester suitable for use with diesel engines will be required for this test.

1 When engine performance is down, a compression test can provide diagnostic clues as to the engine's condition. If the test is performed regularly, it can give warning of trouble before any other symptoms become apparent.

2 The engine must be fully warmed-up to normal operating temperature, the battery must be fully-charged, and you will require the aid of an assistant.

3 Disconnect the injector solenoids by disconnecting the connector at the end of the cylinder head **(see illustration)**. **Note:** As a result of the wiring being disconnected, faults will be stored in the ECU memory. These must be erased after the compression test.

4 Remove the glow plugs as described in Chapter 5 Section 11, then fit a compression tester to the No 1 cylinder glow plug hole. The type of tester which screws into the plug thread is preferred.

5 Have your assistant crank the engine for several seconds on the starter motor. After one or two revolutions, the compression pressure should build-up to a maximum figure and then stabilise. Record the highest reading obtained.

6 Repeat the test on the remaining cylinders, recording the pressure in each.

7 The cause of poor compression is less easy to establish on a diesel engine than on a petrol engine. The effect of introducing oil into the cylinders (wet testing) is not conclusive, because there is a risk that the oil will sit in the recess on the piston crown, instead of passing to the rings. However, the following can be used as a rough guide to diagnosis.

8 All cylinders should produce very similar pressures. Any difference greater than that specified indicates the existence of a fault. Note that the compression should build-up quickly in a healthy engine. Low compression on the first stroke, followed by gradually increasing pressure on successive strokes, indicates worn piston rings. A low compression reading on the first stroke, which does not build-up during successive strokes, indicates leaking valves or a blown head gasket (a cracked head could also be the cause).

9 A low reading from two adjacent cylinders is almost certainly due to the head gasket having blown between them and the presence of coolant in the engine oil will confirm this.

10 On completion, remove the compression tester, and refit the glow plugs, with reference to Chapter 5 Section 11.

11 Reconnect the wiring to the injector solenoids. Finally, have a Skoda dealer erase the fault codes from the ECU memory.

Leakdown test

12 A leakdown test measures the rate at which compressed air fed into the cylinder is lost. It is an alternative to a compression test, and in many ways it is better, since the escaping air provides easy identification of where pressure loss is occurring (piston rings, valves or head gasket).

13 The equipment required for leakdown testing is unlikely to be available to the home mechanic. If poor compression is suspected, have the test performed by a suitably-equipped garage.

3 Engine assembly and valve timing marks – general information and usage

General information

1 TDC is the highest point in the cylinder that each piston reaches as it travels up-and-down when the crankshaft turns. Each piston reaches TDC at the end of the compression stroke and again at the end of the exhaust stroke, but TDC generally refers to piston position on the compression stroke. No 1 piston is at the timing belt end of the engine.

2 Positioning No 1 piston at TDC is an essential part of many procedures, such as timing belt removal and camshaft removal.

3 The design of the engines covered in this Chapter is such that piston-to-valve contact may occur if the camshaft or crankshaft is turned with the timing belt removed. For this reason, it is important to ensure that the camshaft and crankshaft do not move in relation to each other once the timing belt has been removed from the engine.

Setting TDC on No 1 cylinder

Note: Skoda special tool T10050 (early) or T10100 (late) is required to lock the crankshaft sprocket in the TDC position. The early type tool locates directly onto the sprocket teeth, but the contour of the teeth on the later type means that the tool must be pushed onto the sprocket teeth from the right-hand end of the engine.

4 Remove the auxiliary drivebelt(s) as described in Chapter 1 Section 11.

5 Remove the crankshaft pulley/vibration damper as described in Section 5.

6 Remove the timing belt covers as described in Section 6.

7 Remove the glow plugs, as described in Chapter 5 Section 11, to allow the engine to turn more easily. Note that on DOHC engines the glow plugs are accessed by removing the camshaft cover, so this may not be considered an option.

8 Using a spanner or socket on the crankshaft sprocket bolt, turn the crankshaft in the normal direction of rotation (clockwise) until the alignment mark on the face of the sprocket is almost vertical for tool T10050, or at 2 o'clock for tool T10100 **(see illustrations)**.

9 On SOHC engines (codes BJB, BKC, BLS, BMM and BXE), the arrow (marked 4Z) on the rear section of the upper timing belt upper cover aligns between the two lugs on the rear of the camshaft hub sender wheel.

10 On DOHC engines (codes BKD and BMN), the pointer on the rear section of the timing belt inner cover aligns with the camshaft hub sender wheel, and the marks on the camshaft toothed segments and sprockets must be vertical.

11 While in this position it should be possible to insert the Skoda tool to lock the

3.8a TDC setting tools

3.8b Position the crankshaft so that the mark on the sprocket (arrowed) is almost vertical...

3.8c... or at the 2 o'clock position (arrowed) depending on the sprocket type

3.8d Then insert the locking tool...

3.8e... and align the marks (arrowed) on the tool and sprocket – round sprocket...

3.8f... and oval sprocket (arrowed)

3.11a Insert a 6 mm drill bit/rod (arrowed) through the camshaft hub into the cylinder head to lock the camshaft – SOHC engines...

3.11b... and DOHC engines (arrowed)

crankshaft, and a 6 mm diameter rod to lock the camshaft(s) **(see illustrations)**. **Note:** *The mark on the crankshaft sprocket and the mark on the Skoda tool must align, whilst at the same time the shaft of tool must engage in the drilling in the crankshaft oil seal housing.*
12 The engine is now set to TDC on No 1 cylinder.

4   Camshaft cover –
    removal and refitting

Removal

1 Remove the dipstick and prise off and remove the engine top cover, then disconnect the breather hose from the camshaft cover **(see illustrations)**.

2 Unscrew the camshaft cover retaining bolts and lift the cover away. If it sticks, do not attempt to lever it off – instead free it

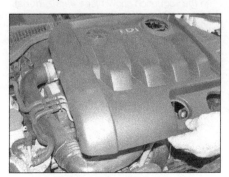

4.1a Pull the engine cover upwards to release it

by working around the cover and tapping it lightly with a soft-faced mallet. Note on DOHC engines, it will be necessary to unbolt the air

4.1b Disconnect the breather hose (arrowed)

4.2 Undo the bolts (arrowed) securing the pipes from the front of the cylinder head

4.3 Ensure the retaining bolts are pushed fully through the gasket before refitting the camshaft cover

4.5a Apply sealant to the points (arrowed) on the cylinder head

4.5b Camshaft cover tightening sequence (DOHC engines)

4.5c Camshaft cover tightening sequence (SOHC engines)

ducting from the rear of the cylinder head, and unbolt the fuel lines from the front of the cylinder head to provide additional clearance **(see illustration)**.

3 Recover the camshaft cover gasket **(see illustration)**. Inspect the gasket carefully, and renew it if damage or deterioration is evident – note that the retaining bolts must be pushed fully through the gasket before refitting the cover.

4 Clean the mating surfaces of the cylinder head and camshaft cover thoroughly, removing all traces of oil and old gasket – take care to avoid damaging the surfaces as you do this.

5.5 Crankshaft pulley retaining bolts (arrowed)

Refitting

5 Refit the camshaft cover by following the removal procedure in reverse, noting the following points:

a) *On SOHC engines (codes BJB, BKC, BLS, BMM and BXE), apply suitable sealant to the points where the camshaft bearing cap contacts the cylinder head* **(see illustration)**.

b) *Tighten the camshaft cover retaining nuts/ bolts progressively to the specified torque in the sequence shown* **(see illustrations)**.

5.7 Note the hole in the pulley which locates over the peg on the sprocket (arrowed)

5 Crankshaft pulley – removal and refitting

Removal

1 Switch off the ignition and all electrical consumers, and remove the ignition key.

2 For improved access, raise the front right-hand side of the vehicle, and support securely on axle stands (see *Jacking and vehicle support*). Remove the roadwheel.

3 Remove the securing screws and withdraw the engine undershield(s) and/or wheel arch liner panels. On turbo models, unscrew the nut at the rear, and the washer-type fasteners further forward, then release the air hose clip and manipulate out the plastic air duct for the intercooler.

4 Where applicable, prise the cover from the centre of the pulley to expose the securing bolts.

5 Slacken the bolts securing the crankshaft pulley to the sprocket **(see illustration)**. If necessary, the pulley can be prevented from turning by counterholding with a spanner or socket on the crankshaft sprocket bolt.

6 Remove the auxiliary drivebelt, as described in Chapter 1 Section 11.

6.1 Prise up the clips (arrowed) and remove the air pipe

6.2a Prise open the metal clips (arrowed) – SOHC engines...

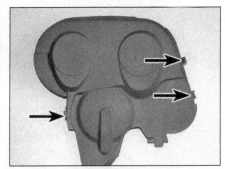

6.2b... and DOHC engines (arrowed)

7 Unscrew the bolts securing the pulley to the sprocket, and remove the pulley **(see illustration)**.

Refitting

8 Refit the pulley over the locating peg on the crankshaft sprocket, then refit the pulley securing bolts.

9 Prevent the crankshaft from turning as during removal, then tighten the pulley securing bolts to the specified torque.

10 Refit and tension the auxiliary drivebelt as described in Chapter 1 Section 11

11 Refit the engine undershield(s), wheel arch liners and the intercooler air duct, as applicable.

12 Refit the roadwheel and lower the vehicle to the ground.

6 Timing belt covers – removal and refitting

Upper outer cover

1 Where applicable, release the retaining clips and remove the air intake hose from across the top of the timing belt cover **(see illustration)**.

2 On SOHC engines, release the clip and remove the charge air pipe between the intercooler and the inlet manifold. Release the uppermost part of the timing belt outer cover by prising open the metal spring clips, then withdraw the cover away from the engine. On DOHC engines there are three clips, two at the front and a single one at the rear of the cover **(see illustrations)**.

3 Refitting is a reversal of removal, noting that the lower edge of the upper cover engages with the centre cover.

Centre outer cover

4 Remove the auxiliary drivebelt as described in Chapter 1 Section 11.

5 Remove the crankshaft pulley as described in Section 5. It is assumed that, if the centre cover is being removed, the lower cover will be also – if not, simply remove the components described in Section 5 for access to the crankshaft pulley, and leave the pulley in position.

6 With the upper cover removed (paragraphs 1 and 2), unscrew and remove the retaining bolts from the centre cover. Withdraw the centre cover from the engine, noting how it fits over the lower cover **(see illustration)**.

7 Refitting is a reversal of the removal procedure.

Lower outer cover

8 Remove the upper and centre covers as described previously.

9 If not already done, remove the crankshaft pulley as described in Section 5.

10 Unscrew the remaining bolt(s) securing the lower cover, and lift it out **(see illustration)**.

11 Refitting is a reversal of removal; locate the centre cover in place before fitting the top two bolts.

Rear cover

12 Remove the upper, centre and lower covers as described previously.

13 Remove the timing belt, tensioner and sprockets as described in Sections 7 and 8.

14 Slacken and withdraw the retaining bolts and lift the timing belt inner cover from the studs on the end of the engine, and remove it from the engine compartment.

15 Refitting is a reversal of removal.

7 Timing belt – removal, inspection and refitting

Note: *It is considered best practise to always*

replace the tensioner, idler and coolant pump whenever the timing belt is replaced. Any mounting studs should also be replaced at the same time. Most of the components (apart from the coolant pump) will be supplied with a timing belt kit. Note also that most manufactures will not guarantee a belt against premature failure if the idler(s) and tensioner are not replaced with the belt.

Removal

1 The primary function of the toothed timing belt is to drive the camshaft, but it also drives the coolant pump. Should the belt slip or break in service, the valve timing will be disturbed and piston-to-valve contact may occur, resulting in serious engine damage. For this reason, it is important that the timing belt is tensioned correctly, and inspected regularly for signs of wear or deterioration.

2 Switch off the ignition and all electrical consumers, and remove the ignition key.

3 Apply the handbrake, then jack up the front of the vehicle and support securely on axle stands (see *Jacking and vehicle support*).

4 Remove the securing screws and withdraw the engine undershield(s), and the front section of the right-hand wheel arch liner. Also, remove the engine top cover.

5 Remove the auxiliary drivebelt as described in Chapter 1 Section 11, then unbolt and remove the drivebelt tensioner **(see illustration)**.

6 Remove the crankshaft pulley/vibration damper as described in Section 5.

6.6 Centre cover retaining bolts (arrowed)

6.10 Lower cover bolts (arrowed)

7.5 Unbolt the drivebelt tensioner (DOHC engine)

7 Remove the timing belt covers as described in Section 6.

8 Remove the fuel filter from its bracket and place to one side. On 06/2006-on DOHC engines, disconnect the fuel supply and return lines.

9 Where necessary, remove the intercooler charge air pipe.

10 Unbolt the filler neck from the screen washer reservoir.

11 Where applicable, unbolt the fuel filter bracket from the engine mounting.

12 Unbolt the coolant expansion tank and position it to one side. Note that there is no need to disconnect the hoses.

13 Set the engine to TDC on No 1 cylinder as described in Section 3.

14 Support the engine and remove the right-hand engine mounting as described in Section 18.

7.17 Prevent the sprocket from rotating with a suitable tool, and slacken the retaining bolts

7.23 Position the sprocket so that the securing bolts are in the centre part of the elongated holes

15 Unbolt and remove the right-hand engine mounting bracket from the engine. It may be necessary to raise and lower the engine slightly to access the mounting bracket bolts.

16 If the original timing belt is to be refitted, mark the running direction of the belt, to ensure correct refitting.

Caution: If the belt appears to be in good condition and can be re-used, it is essential that it is refitted the same way around, otherwise accelerated wear will result, leading to premature failure.

17 Loosen the bolts securing the sprocket(s) to the camshaft(s) while holding the sprockets with a suitable tool **(see illustration)**.

18 Loosen the timing belt tensioner securing nut, then use circlip pliers or an Allen key (as applicable) to turn the tensioner anti-clockwise until a suitable pin or drill bit can be inserted through the locking holes. Now, turn the tensioner clockwise to the stop and tighten the securing nut **(see illustration)**.

19 Slide the belt from the sprockets, taking care not to twist or kink the belt excessively if it is to be re-used.

Inspection

20 Examine the belt for evidence of contamination by coolant or lubricant. If this is the case, find the source of the contamination before progressing any further. Check the belt for signs of wear or damage, particularly around the leading edges of the belt teeth. Renew the belt if its condition is in doubt; the cost of belt renewal is negligible compared

7.18 Tensioner securing nut, Allen key and locking pin (arrowed)

7.26 Align the pointer with the gap in the tensioner backplate (arrowed)

with potential cost of the engine repairs, should the belt fail in service. The belt must be renewed if it has covered the mileage given in Chapter 1, however, if it has covered less, it is prudent to renew it regardless of condition, as a precautionary measure.

21 If the timing belt is not going to be refitted for some time, it is a wise precaution to hang a warning label on the steering wheel, to remind yourself (and others) not to attempt to start the engine.

Refitting

22 Ensure that the crankshaft and camshaft are still set to TDC on No 1 cylinder, as described in Section 3.

23 Position the camshaft sprocket(s) so that the securing bolts are in the centre part of the elongated holes **(see illustration)**.

24 Loop the timing belt loosely under the crankshaft sprocket.

Note: *Observe any direction of rotation markings on the belt.*

25 Engage the timing belt teeth with the camshaft sprocket(s), then manoeuvre it into position around the tensioning roller, crankshaft sprocket, and finally around the coolant pump sprocket. Make sure that the belt teeth seat correctly on the sprockets. Note that slight adjustment to the position of the camshaft sprocket may be necessary to achieve this. Avoid bending the belt back on itself or twisting it excessively as you do this. Ensure that any slack in the belt is in the section of belt that passes over the tensioner roller.

26 Loosen the timing belt tensioner securing nut, and turn the tensioner anti-clockwise with the circlip pliers or an Allen key (as applicable) until the locking pin can be removed. Now, turn the tensioner clockwise until the pointer is in the middle of the gap in the tensioner backplate. With the tensioner held in this position, tighten the securing nut to the specified torque and angle **(see illustration)**.

Note: *The tensioner pointer may move to the right as the nut is tightened, up to 5 mm from the centre of the notch is permissible.*

27 Using a suitable tool, counter hold the camshaft sprocket(s) and tighten the camshaft sprocket bolts to the specified torque, remove the sprocket locking pin(s) and the crankshaft locking tool.

28 Using a spanner or wrench and socket on the crankshaft pulley centre bolt, rotate the crankshaft through two complete revolutions. As the engine approaches TDC be prepared to install the camshaft locking tool(s), installing the rear camshaft locking tool first on DOHC engines, once installed check that the crankshaft locking tool can be installed (see Section 3) and that the tensioner pointer is still aligned with the notch in the backplate or no more than 5 mm to the right.

29 On DOHC engines if the front camshaft locking tool cannot be installed with the rear camshaft and crankshaft locked, slacken the front camshaft sprocket bolts and move

8.3 Ensure that the lug on the tensioner backplate engages with the cut-out in the rear timing belt cover

the sprocket hub slightly until the tool can be fitted. Counterhold the sprocket and tighten the camshaft sprocket bolts to the specified torque, remove the camshaft and crankshaft locking tools and turn the crankshaft two revolutions clockwise, as the engine approaches TDC be prepared to install the camshaft locking tool(s), once installed check that the crankshaft locking tool can be installed and that the tensioner pointer is still aligned with the notch in the backplate or no more than 5 mm to the right.

30 If the crankshaft sprocket locking tool cannot be inserted, slacken the camshaft sprocket retaining bolts and turn the crankshaft counter clockwise slightly and then clockwise or just clockwise as required for the crankshaft sprocket tool to locate, (the crankshaft must always be rotated clockwise prior to fitting the locking tool to ensure correct belt tensioning) then counter hold the sprockets and tighten the camshaft sprocket bolts to the specified torque, remove the camshaft and crankshaft locking tools and turn the crankshaft two revolutions clockwise, as the engine approaches TDC be prepared to install the camshaft locking tool(s), once installed check that the crankshaft locking tool can be installed and that the tensioner pointer is still aligned with the notch in the backplate or no more than 5 mm to the right.

31 The timing belt is correctly installed when the engine is set to TDC (with camshaft and crankshaft locking tools installed) and the tensioner pointer is showing the correct tension.

32 Remove the crankshaft and camshaft locking tools.

33 Refit the engine mounting bracket, the bolts should be tightened to a torque in sequence, starting with the rear upper bolt, then the lower bolt and finally the front bolt and then angle tightened in the same order.

34 Refit and align the engine mounting.

35 Refit the coolant expansion tank.

36 Where applicable, refit the fuel filter bracket to the engine mounting.

37 Refit the screen washer reservoir filler neck.

38 Refit the fuel filter to its bracket, and where necessary reconnect the fuel lines and intercooler charge air pipe.

39 Refit the timing belt covers as described in Section 6.

40 Refit the crankshaft pulley/vibration damper as described in Section 5.

41 Refit the auxiliary drivebelt and tensioner with reference to Chapter 1 Section 11.

42 Refit the engine undershield(s), right-hand wheel arch liner and engine top cover, and lower the vehicle to the ground.

8 Timing belt tensioner and sprockets – removal and refitting

Timing belt tensioner

Removal

1 Remove the timing belt as described in Section 7.

2 Unscrew the timing belt tensioner nut, and remove the tensioner from the engine.

Note: *With the tensioner removed check that the mounting stud is securely fitted and is in good condition, where a new stud is being fitted, clean the mounting hole and check the condition of the threads. Ensure the new stud is correctly seated and secure.*

Refitting

3 When refitting the tensioner to the engine, ensure that the lug on the tensioner backplate engages with the corresponding cut-out in the rear timing belt cover, then refit the tensioner nut **(see illustration)**.

4 Refit and tension the timing belt as described in Section 7, making sure that the tensioner backplate is correctly engaged with the hole in the cylinder head.

Idler pulleys

Removal

5 Remove the timing belt as described in Section 7.

6 Unscrew the relevant idler pulley securing bolt/nut, then withdraw the pulley.

Refitting

7 Refit the pulley and tighten the securing bolt or nut to the specified torque. Note that a new nut/bolt may be required (see Specifications).

8 Refit and tension the timing belt as described in Section 7.

Crankshaft sprocket

Note: *A new crankshaft sprocket securing bolt must be used on refitting.*

Removal

9 Remove the timing belt as described in Section 7.

10 The sprocket securing bolt must now be slackened, and the crankshaft must be prevented from turning as the sprocket bolt is unscrewed. To hold the sprocket, make up a suitable tool, and screw it to the sprocket using two bolts screwed into two of the crankshaft pulley bolt holes.

8.14 Fit a new crankshaft sprocket bolt

11 Hold the sprocket using the tool, then slacken the sprocket securing bolt. Take care, as the bolt is very tight. Do not allow the crankshaft to turn as the bolt is slackened.

12 Unscrew the bolt, and slide the sprocket from the end of the crankshaft, noting which way round the sprocket's raised boss is fitted.

Refitting

13 The contact areas between the sprocket and crankshaft must be oil free, clean and dry before positioning the sprocket on the end of the crankshaft, with the raised boss fitted as noted on removal.

14 Fit a new sprocket securing bolt (do not lubricate the threads or head of the bolt), then counterhold the sprocket using the method employed on removal, and tighten the bolt to the specified torque in the two stages given in the Specifications **(see illustration)**.

15 Refit the timing belt as described in Section 7.

Camshaft sprocket

Removal

16 Remove the timing belt as described in Section 7.

17 Unscrew and remove the three retaining bolts and remove the camshaft sprocket from the camshaft hub.

Refitting

18 Refit the sprocket ensuring that it is fitted the correct way round, as noted before removal, then insert the sprocket bolts, and tighten by hand only at this stage.

19 If the crankshaft has been turned, turn the crankshaft clockwise 90° back to TDC.

20 Refit and tension the timing belt as described in Section 7.

Camshaft hub

21 Skoda technicians use special tool T10051 to counterhold the hub, however it is possible to fabricate a suitable alternative – see below.

Removal

22 Remove the camshaft sprocket as described previously in this Section.

23 Engage special tool T10051 with the three locating holes in the face of the hub to prevent the hub from turning. If this tool is

8.23 Use a fabricated tool to counterhold the camshaft hub

8.24 Attach a three-legged puller to the hub, and evenly tighten the puller until the hub is free of the camshaft taper

8.25 The integral key in the hub taper must align with the keyway in the camshaft taper (arrowed)

not available, fabricate a suitable alternative. Whilst holding the tool, undo the central hub retaining bolt about two turns **(see illustration)**.

24 Leaving the central hub retaining bolt in place, attach tool T10052 (or a similar three-legged puller) to the hub, and evenly tighten the puller until the hub is free of the camshaft taper **(see illustration)**.

Refitting

25 Ensure that the camshaft taper and the hub centre is clean and dry, locate the hub on the taper, noting that the built-in key in the hub taper must align with the keyway in the camshaft taper **(see illustration)**.

26 Hold the hub in this position with tool T10051 (or similar home-made tool), and

tighten the central bolt to the specified torque.

27 Refit the camshaft sprocket as described previously in this Section.

Coolant pump sprocket

28 The coolant pump sprocket is integral with the coolant pump. Refer to Chapter 3 Section 7 for details of coolant pump removal.

9 Pump injector rocker shaft assembly – removal and refitting

Removal

1 Remove the camshaft cover as described in Section 4. In order to ensure that the rocker

arms are refitted to their original locations, use a marker pen or paint and number the arms 1 to 4, with No 1 nearest the timing belt end of the engine. If the arms are not fitted to their original locations the injector basic clearance setting procedure must be carried out as described in Chapter 4A Section 5.

2 Slacken the locknut of the adjustment screw on the end of the rocker arm above the respective injector, and undo the adjustment screw until the rocker arm lies against the plunger pin of the injector. Starting at the outside and working in, gradually and evenly slacken and remove the rocker shaft retaining bolts. Lift off the rocker shaft. Discard the rocker shaft bolts, new ones must be fitted **(see illustrations)**.

Refitting

3 Thoroughly check the rocker shaft, rocker arms and camshaft bearing cap seating surface for any signs of excessive wear or damage.

4 Smear some grease (Skoda No G000 100) onto the contact face of each rocker arm adjustment screw, and refit the rocker shaft assembly, tightening the new retaining bolts as follows. Starting from the inside out, hand-tighten the bolts. Again, from the inside out, tighten the bolts to the Stage one torque setting. Finally, from the inside out, tighten the bolts to the Stage two angle tightening setting.

5 Attach a DTI (Dial Test Indicator) gauge to the cylinder head upper surface, and position the DTI probe against the top of the adjustment screw **(see illustration)**. Turn the crankshaft until the rocker arm roller is on the highest point of its corresponding camshaft lobe, and the adjustment screw is at its lowest. Once this position has been established, remove the DTI gauge, screw the adjustment screw in until firm resistance is felt, and the injector spring cannot be compressed further. Turn the adjustment screw **anti-clockwise** 180°, and tighten the locknut securely. Repeat this procedure for any other injectors that have been refitted.

6 Refit the camshaft cover and upper timing belt cover, as described in Sections 4 and 6.

7 Start the engine and check that it runs correctly.

9.2a Slacken the rocker shaft adjustment bolts

9.2b Start with the outer bolts first, carefully and evenly slacken the rocker shaft retaining bolts (SOHC engine)

9.2c Rocker shaft retaining bolts – 3 of 4 shown (DOHC engine)

9.5 Attach a DTI gauge to the cylinder head upper surface and position the DTI probe against the top of the adjustment bolt

10.4 Tandem fuel/vacuum pump (DOHC engine)

10.6 Check the camshaft bearing caps (arrowed) for markings

10.11 Remove the camshaft oil seal

10 Camshaft and hydraulic tappets – removal, inspection and refitting

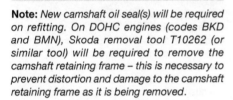

Note: New camshaft oil seal(s) will be required on refitting. On DOHC engines (codes BKD and BMN), Skoda removal tool T10262 (or similar tool) will be required to remove the camshaft retaining frame – this is necessary to prevent distortion and damage to the camshaft retaining frame as it is being removed.

Removal

1 Turn the crankshaft to position No 1 piston at TDC on the firing stroke, and lock the camshaft and the fuel injection sprocket in position, as described in Section 3.
2 Remove the timing belt as described in Section 7.
3 Remove the camshaft sprocket(s) and hubs as described in Section 8.
4 Remove the tandem fuel/brake vacuum pump as described in Chapter 4A Section 10 **(see illustration)**.
5 Remove the injector rocker arms and shaft as described in Section 9.

SOHC engines

6 Check the camshaft bearing caps for identification markings **(see illustration)**. The bearing caps are normally stamped with their respective cylinder numbers. If no marks are present, make suitable marks using a scriber or punch. The caps should be numbered from 1 to 5, with No 1 at the timing belt end of the

engine. Note on which side of the bearing caps the marks are made to ensure that they are refitted the correct way round.
7 The camshaft rotates in shell bearings. As the camshaft bearing caps are removed, recover the shell bearing halves from the camshaft. Number the back of the bearings with a felt pen to ensure that, if re-used, the bearings are fitted to their original locations.
Note: *Fitted into the cylinder head, under each camshaft bearing cap, is a washer for each cylinder head bolt.*
8 Unscrew the securing nuts, and remove Nos 1, 3 and 5 bearing caps.
9 Working progressively, in a diagonal sequence, slacken the nuts securing Nos 2 and 4 bearing caps. Note that as the nuts are slackened, the valve springs will push the camshaft up.
10 Once the nuts securing Nos 2 and 4 bearing caps have been fully slackened, lift off the bearing caps.
11 Carefully lift the camshaft from the cylinder head, keeping it level and supported at both ends as it is removed so that the journals and lobes are not damaged. Remove the oil seal from the end of the camshaft and discard it – a new one will be required for refitting **(see illustration)**.
12 Lift the hydraulic tappets from their bores in the cylinder head, and store them with the valve contact surfaces facing downwards, to prevent the oil from draining out. It is recommended that the tappets are kept immersed in oil for the period they are removed from the cylinder head. Make a

note of the position of each tappet, as they must be refitted in their original locations on reassembly – accelerated wear leading to early failure will result if the tappets are interchanged.
13 Recover the lower shell bearing halves from the cylinder head; number the back of the shells with a felt pen to ensure that, if re-used, the bearings are fitted to their original locations.

DOHC engines

14 Unscrew the upper bolt securing the EGR cooler bracket.
15 Disconnect the wiring from the unit injectors and glow plugs. To disconnect the wiring connector from the left-hand end of the cylinder head, use a screwdriver to pull out the plastic red lock, then unscrew the collar and pull the connector from the pins. To remove the wiring conduit, first undo the screws retaining it to the cylinder head, then release the multipin plug by raising the clip and unscrewing the outer threaded collar, ideally using the special Skoda tool T10310 which engages the three slots **(see illustrations)**.
16 Progressively unscrew the camshaft retaining frame bolts starting from the outside to inside.
17 The Skoda tool is now used to remove the retaining bearing frame. First, fully unscrew the ejector bolts, then fit the tool to the frame and tighten the bolts. Screw in the ejector bolts until they contact the cylinder head bolt(s), then progressively tighten them so that the bearing frame is released from the cylinder head.

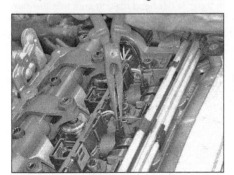

10.15a Disconnect the wiring from the unit injectors

10.15b Wiring loom connector, showing the 3 pins in the outer collar

10.15c Retaining clip on the inside of the wiring loom connector

10.24 Check the camshaft endfloat using a DTI gauge

18 Carefully lift the camshafts from the cylinder head, keeping them identified for location. Remove the oil seals from the ends of the camshafts and discard them – new ones will be required for refitting.

19 To remove the exhaust roller rocker fingers and hydraulic tappets, carry out the following:
a) Drain the coolant as described in Chapter 1 Section 37.
b) Remove the connecting pipe between the EGR valve and bypass flap.
c) Remove the thermostat housing as described in Chapter 3 Section 4.
d) Unscrew the plug from the end of the exhaust roller rocker shaft. **Note:** If the plug is very tight, the shaft may be deformed while unscrewing it, making the oil supply hole alignment incorrect. If this happens, renew the shaft.
e) Undo the screw securing the roller rocker shaft to the cylinder head.

20 To remove either exhaust or inlet roller rocker fingers and hydraulic tappets, use Skoda slide hammer/puller tool T10055 to pull the shaft from the cylinder head while removing the roller rockers. Store the rockers in a container with numbered compartments to ensure they are refitted to their correct locations. It is recommended that the tappets are kept immersed in oil for the period they are removed from the cylinder head.

10.42 Camshaft bearing frame bolt tightening sequence

Inspection – all engines

21 With the camshaft(s) removed, examine the bearing caps/frame and the bearing locations in the cylinder head for signs of obvious wear or pitting. If evident, a new cylinder head will probably be required. Also check that the oil supply holes in the cylinder head are free from obstructions.

22 Visually inspect the camshaft for evidence of wear on the surfaces of the lobes and journals. Normally their surfaces should be smooth and have a dull shine; look for scoring, erosion or pitting and areas that appear highly polished, indicating excessive wear. Accelerated wear will occur once the hardened exterior of the camshaft has been damaged, so always renew worn items. Note if these symptoms are visible on the tips of the camshaft lobes and check the corresponding tappet, as it will probably be worn as well.

23 If the machined surfaces of the camshaft appear discoloured or blued, it is likely that it has been overheated at some point, probably due to inadequate lubrication. This may have distorted the shaft, so have the run-out checked by an automotive engine reconditioning specialist.

24 To measure the camshaft endfloat, temporarily refit the camshaft to the cylinder head, then fit Nos 1 and 5 bearing caps and tighten the retaining nuts to the specified torque setting. Anchor a DTI gauge to the timing belt end of the cylinder head **(see illustration)**. Push the camshaft to one end of the cylinder head as far as it will travel, then rest the DTI gauge probe on the end face of the camshaft, and zero the gauge. Push the camshaft as far as it will go to the other end of the cylinder head, and record the gauge reading. Verify the reading by pushing the camshaft back to its original position and checking that the gauge indicates zero again. Note that the hydraulic tappets must not be fitted whilst this measurement is being taken.

25 Check that the camshaft endfloat measurement is within the limit listed in the Specifications. If the measurement is outside the specified limit, wear is unlikely to be confined to any one component, so renewal of the camshaft, cylinder head and bearing caps must be considered.

26 The camshaft bearing running clearance should now be measured. This will be difficult to achieve without a range of micrometers or internal/external expanding calipers, but involves measuring the outside diameters of the camshaft bearing surfaces and the internal diameters formed by the bearing caps/frame (and shell bearings where applicable) and the bearing locations in the cylinder head. The difference between these two measurements is the running clearance.

27 If you do not have access to suitable measuring tools, entrust the task to an automotive engine reconditioning specialist.

28 Inspect the hydraulic tappets for obvious signs of wear or damage, and renew if necessary. Check that the oil holes in the tappets are free from obstructions.

Refitting

SOHC engines

29 Smear some clean engine oil onto the sides of the hydraulic tappets, and offer them into position in their original bores in the cylinder head. Push them down until they contact the valves, then lubricate the camshaft lobe contact surfaces.

30 Lubricate the camshaft and cylinder head bearing journals and shell bearings with clean engine oil.

31 Carefully lower the camshaft into position in the cylinder head making sure that the cam lobes for No 1 cylinder are pointing upwards.

32 Refit a new camshaft oil seal on the end of the camshaft. Make sure that the closed end of the seal faces the camshaft sprocket end of the camshaft, and take care not to damage the seal lip. Locate the seal against the seat in the cylinder head.

33 Oil the upper surfaces of the camshaft bearing journals and shell bearings, then fit Nos 2 and 4 bearing caps. Ensure that they are fitted the right way round and in the correct locations, then progressively tighten the retaining nuts in a diagonal sequence to the specified torque. Note that as the nuts are tightened, the camshaft will be forced down against the pressure of the valve springs.

34 Fit bearing caps 1, 3 and 5 over the camshaft and progressively tighten the nuts to the specified torque. Note that it may be necessary to locate No 5 bearing cap by tapping lightly on the end of the camshaft.

35 Refit the injector rocker arms as described in Section 9.

DOHC engines

36 Oil the roller rocker fingers and hydraulic tappets together with the shafts, then insert each shaft into the cylinder head while at the same time fitting the roller rockers in their correct order. The inlet shaft must be inserted until flush with the cylinder head. The exhaust shaft must be correctly aligned with the retaining bolt hole. Insert and tighten the bolt securely.

37 Reverse the procedures listed in paragraph 19.

38 Lubricate the camshaft and cylinder head bearing journals with clean engine oil.

39 Carefully lower the camshafts into position in the cylinder head making sure that the cam lobes for No 1 cylinder are pointing upwards.

40 Fit new camshaft oil seals on the end of the camshafts. Make sure that the closed end of the seal faces the camshaft sprocket end of the camshaft, and take care not to damage the seal lip. Locate the seal against the seat in the cylinder head.

41 Oil the upper surfaces of the camshaft bearing frame journals, then apply sealant to the mating surfaces of the bearing frame and cylinder head.

42 Refit the bearing frame together with the rocker arms and shaft, using the Skoda tool, ensuring the frame is the correct way round. Progressively tighten the retaining bolts to the specified torque in the order shown**(see illustration)**, then remove the tool. Note that as the bolts are tightened, the camshafts will be forced down against the pressure of the valve springs.

43 Tighten the rocker arm shaft bolts to the specified angle. Refit the wiring conduit and secure the connectors.

All engines

44 Renew the camshaft oil seal(s) as applicable, and as described in this section.

45 Refit the tandem fuel/brake vacuum pump as described in Chapter 4A Section 10.

46 Refit the camshaft sprocket(s) and hubs as described in Section 8.

47 Refit the timing belt as described in Section 7.

11 Hydraulic tappets – testing

⚠ *Warning: After fitting hydraulic tappets, wait a minimum of 30 minutes (or preferably, leave overnight) before starting the engine, to allow the tappets time to settle, otherwise the valve heads will strike the pistons.*

1 The hydraulic tappets are self-adjusting, and require no attention whilst in service.

2 If the hydraulic tappets become excessively noisy, their operation can be checked as described below.

3 Start the engine, and run it until it reaches normal operating temperature, increase the engine speed to approximately 2500 rpm for 2 minutes.

4 If any hydraulic tappets are heard to be noisy, carry out the following checks.

5 Remove the camshaft cover as described in Section 4.

6 Using a socket or spanner on the crankshaft sprocket bolt, turn the crankshaft until the tip of the camshaft lobe above the tappet to be checked is pointing vertically upwards.

7 Using feeler blades, check the clearance between the top of the tappet, and the cam lobe. If the play is in excess of 0.1 mm, renew the relevant tappet. If the play is less than 0.1 mm, or there is no play, proceed as follows.

8 Press down on the tappet using a wooden or plastic instrument **(see illustration)**. If free play in excess of 1.0 mm is present before the tappet contacts the valve stem, renew the relevant tappet.

9 On completion, refit the camshaft cover as described in Section 4.

12 Camshaft oil seals – renewal

Right-hand oil seal(s)

1 Remove the timing belt as described in Section 7.

2 Remove the camshaft sprocket and hub, as described in Section 8.

3 Drill two small holes into the existing oil seal, diagonally opposite each other. Take great care to avoid drilling through into the seal housing or camshaft sealing surface. Thread two self-tapping screws into the holes, and using a pair of pliers, pull on the heads of the screws to extract the oil seal.

4 Clean out the seal housing and the sealing surface of the camshaft by wiping it with a lint-free cloth. Remove any swarf or burrs that may cause the seal to leak.

5 Do not lubricate the lip and outer edge of the new oil seal, push it over the camshaft until it is positioned in place above its housing. To prevent damage to the sealing lips, wrap some adhesive tape around the end of the camshaft.

6 Using a hammer and a socket of suitable diameter, drive the seal squarely into its housing. **Note:** *Select a socket that bears only on the hard outer surface of the seal, not the inner lip which can easily be damaged.*

7 Refit the camshaft sprocket and its hub, as described in Section 8.

8 Refit and tension the timing belt as described in Section 7.

Left-hand oil seal

9 The left-hand camshaft oil seal is formed by the brake vacuum pump seal. Refer to Chapter 9 Section 22 for details of brake vacuum pump removal and refitting.

13 Cylinder head – removal, inspection and refitting

Note: *The cylinder head must be removed with the engine cold. New cylinder head bolts and a new cylinder head gasket will be required on refitting, and suitable studs will be required to guide the cylinder head into position – see text.*

Removal

1 Switch off the ignition and all electrical consumers, and remove the ignition key. For improved access on DOHC engines, remove the battery as described in Chapter 5 Section 3.

2 Drain the cooling system and engine oil as described in Chapter 1 Section 6 and Chapter 1 Section 37.

11.8 Press down on the tappet using a wooden or plastic tool

3 Remove the cover from the plenum chamber (see Chapter 12 Section 13) located just in front of the windscreen. Also, undo the bolts at each end and remove the plenum chamber partition from the rear of the engine compartment.

4 Remove the air filter complete with the air mass meter and air ducts. Also, where applicable, unbolt and remove the duct from the turbocharger.

5 Disconnect the fuel supply and return lines, and also the coolant hoses from the cylinder head. In the interests of safety, it is recommended that the fuel is siphoned from the tandem pump on the left-hand end of the cylinder head. If necessary, the pump may be unbolted and removed **(see illustration)**.

6 Remove the fuel filter from its mounting bracket and position to one side.

7 Remove the front exhaust pipe as described in Chapter 4B Section 6.

8 Remove the turbocharger support and oil return line from the turbocharger. Also, remove the oil supply pipe and place to one side.

9 Remove the camshaft cover as described in Section 4.

10 Remove the timing belt as described in Section 7. Where the right-hand engine mounting has been removed, ensure the engine is supported adequately on a trolley jack and block of wood.

11 Remove the camshaft sprocket and timing belt tensioner as described in Section 8.

12 Where applicable, unscrew the bolt(s) securing the rear timing belt cover to the cylinder head **(see illustrations)**.

13.5 Undo the tandem pump retaining bolts (arrowed)

13.12a Undo the bolt from the inner cover (arrowed)...

13.12b... and the one (arrowed) on the side of the cover

13.13 Undo the bolt and remove the camshaft position sensor

13.14 EGR connecting pipe at the flap housing (arrowed)

13.15 Disconnect the central connector for the injectors

13.16a Disconnect the coolant hose from the end of the cylinder head

13.16b Disconnect the vacuum pipes (arrowed)

13 Remove the camshaft position sensor from the right-hand end of the cylinder head **(see illustration)**. Note that on DOHC engines, the idler roller must be loosened to release the sensor wiring.

14 Remove the exhaust gas recirculation connecting pipe **(see illustration)**.

15 Note the locations of all the electrical wiring, then disconnect them methodically **(see illustration)**.

16 Disconnect all vacuum and coolant hoses **(see illustrations)**.

17 On DOHC engines, unbolt and remove the injector rocker arm shaft as follows. Slacken the locknut of the adjustment screw on the end of the rocker arm above each of the injectors, and undo the adjustment screw until the rocker arm lies against the plunger pin of the injector. Starting at the outside and working in, gradually and evenly slacken and remove the rocker shaft retaining bolts. Lift

off the rocker shaft – this will allow access to the rear cylinder head bolts. Now unscrew the row of inner bolts securing the camshaft retaining frame – the bolts screw into the tops of the front cylinder head bolts, and are located behind the exhaust camshaft **(see illustration)**. As the bolts are removed, recover the large washers.

18 Using a multisplined tool, undo the cylinder head bolts, working from the outside-in, evenly and gradually **(see illustration)**. Check that nothing remains connected, and lift the cylinder head from the engine block. Seek assistance if possible, as it is a heavy assembly, especially as it is being removed complete with the manifolds.

19 Remove the gasket from the top of the block, noting the locating dowels. If the dowels are a loose fit, remove them and store them with the head for safe-keeping. Do not discard the gasket yet – it will be needed

for identification purposes. If desired, the manifolds can be removed from the cylinder head with reference to Chapter 4A Section 6 and Chapter 4B Section 4.

Inspection

20 Dismantling and inspection of the cylinder head is covered in Chapter 2C Section 6.

Cylinder head gasket selection

Note: *A dial test indicator (DTI) will be required for this operation.*

21 Examine the old cylinder head gasket for manufacturer's identification markings **(see illustration)**. These will be in the form of holes or notches, and a part number on the edge of the gasket. Unless new pistons have been fitted, the new cylinder head gasket must be of the same type as the old one.

22 If new piston assemblies have been fitted as part of an engine overhaul, or if a new

13.17 The camshaft retaining frame inner row bolts are tightened into the tops of the front cylinder headbolts

13.18 Cylinder head bolt slackening sequence

13.21 The thickness of the cylinder head gasket can be identified by notches or holes

short engine is to be fitted, the projection of the piston crowns above the cylinder head mating face of the cylinder block at TDC must be measured. This measurement is used to determine the thickness of the new cylinder head gasket required.

23 Anchor a dial test indicator (DTI) to the top face (cylinder head gasket mating face) of the cylinder block, and zero the gauge on the gasket mating face.

24 Rest the gauge probe on No 1 piston crown, and turn the crankshaft slowly by hand until the piston reaches TDC. Measure and record the maximum piston projection at TDC **(see illustration)**.

25 Repeat the measurement for the remaining pistons, and record the results.

26 If the measurements differ from piston-to-piston, take the highest figure, and use this to determine the thickness of the head gasket required as follows.

Gasket identification

Piston projection	Number of holes/notches
0.91 to 1.00 mm	1
1.01 to 1.10 mm	2
1.11 to 1.20 mm	3

27 Purchase a new gasket according to the results of the measurements.

Refitting

Note: *If a Skoda exchange cylinder head, complete with camshaft(s), is to be fitted, the manufacturers recommend the following:*

a) *Lubricate the contact surfaces between the tappets and the cam lobes before fitting the camshaft cover.*

b) *Do not remove the plastic protectors from the open valves until immediately before fitting the cylinder head.*

c) *Additionally, if a new cylinder head is fitted, Skoda recommend that the coolant is renewed.*

28 The mating faces of the cylinder head and block must be perfectly clean before refitting the head. Use a scraper to remove all traces of gasket and carbon, also clean the tops of the pistons. Take particular care with the aluminium surfaces, as the soft metal is easily damaged.

29 Make sure that debris is not allowed to enter the oil and water passages – this is particularly important for the oil circuit, as

13.24 Measure the piston projection at TDC using a DTI gauge

carbon could block the oil supply to the camshaft and crankshaft bearings. Using adhesive tape and paper, seal the water, oil and bolt holes in the cylinder block.

30 To prevent carbon entering the gap between the pistons and bores, smear a little grease in the gap. After cleaning a piston, rotate the crankshaft to that the piston moves down the bore, then wipe out the grease and carbon with a cloth rag. Clean the other piston crowns in the same way.

31 Check the head and block for nicks, deep scratches and other damage. If slight, they may be removed carefully with a file. More serious damage may be repaired by machining, but this is a specialist job.

32 If warpage of the cylinder head is suspected, use a straight-edge to check it for distortion, as described in Chapter 2C Section 6.

33 Ensure that the cylinder head bolt holes in the crankcase are clean and free of oil. Syringe or soak up any oil left in the bolt holes. This is most important in order that the correct bolt tightening torque can be applied, and to prevent the possibility of the block being cracked by hydraulic pressure when the bolts are tightened.

34 Turn the crankshaft anti-clockwise until all the pistons are at an equal height, approximately half-way down their bores from the TDC position (see Section 3). This will eliminate any risk of piston-to-valve contact as the cylinder head is refitted.

35 Where applicable, refit the manifolds with reference to Chapter 4A Section 6 and Chapter 4B Section 4.

13.36 Two of the old head bolts (arrowed) can be used as cylinder head alignment guides

36 To guide the cylinder head into position, screw two long studs (or old cylinder head bolts with the heads cut off, and slots cut in the ends to enable the bolts to be unscrewed) into the cylinder block **(see illustration)**.

37 Ensure that the cylinder head locating dowels are in place in the cylinder block, then fit the new cylinder head gasket over the dowels, ensuring that the part number is uppermost. Where applicable, the OBEN/TOP marking should also be uppermost. Note that Skoda recommend that the gasket is only removed from its packaging immediately prior to fitting.

38 Lower the cylinder head into position on the gasket, ensuring that it engages correctly over the guide studs and dowels.

39 Fit the new cylinder head bolts to the eight remaining bolt locations, and screw them in as far as possible by hand.

40 Unscrew the two guide studs from the exhaust side of the cylinder block, then screw in the two remaining new cylinder head bolts as far as possible by hand.

41 Working progressively, in sequence, tighten all the cylinder head bolts to the specified Stage 1 torque **(see illustrations)**.

42 Again working progressively, in sequence, tighten all the cylinder head bolts to the specified Stage 2 torque.

43 Tighten all the cylinder head bolts, in sequence, through the specified Stage 3 angle**(see illustration)**.

44 Finally, tighten all the cylinder head bolts, in sequence, through the specified Stage 4 angle.

13.41a Cylinder head bolt tightening sequence

13.41b Use a torque wrench to tighten the cylinder head bolts

13.43 Angle-tighten the cylinder head bolts

14.9 Apply sealant as shown by the black line

45 After finally tightening the cylinder head bolts, turn the camshaft so that the cam lobes for No 1 cylinder are pointing upwards.

46 Where applicable, reconnect the lifting tackle to the engine lifting brackets on the cylinder head, then adjust the lifting tackle to support the engine. Once the engine is adequately supported using the cylinder head brackets, disconnect the lifting tackle from the bracket bolted to the cylinder block, and unbolt the improvised engine lifting bracket from the cylinder block. Alternatively, remove the trolley jack and block of wood from under the sump.

47 The remainder of the refitting procedure is a reversal of the removal procedure, bearing in mind the following points.

a) *Refit the injector rocker shaft with reference to Section 9.*

b) *Refit the camshaft cover with reference to Section 4.*

c) *On turbo models, use new sealing rings when reconnecting the turbocharger oil return pipe to the cylinder block.*

d) *Reconnect the exhaust front section to the exhaust manifold or turbocharger, as applicable, with reference to Chapter 4B Section 6.*

e) *Refit the timing belt tensioner with reference to Section 8.*

f) *Refit the camshaft sprocket as described in Section 8, and refit the timing belt as described in Section 7.*

g) *Refill the cooling system and engine oil as described in Chapter 1 Section 6 and Chapter 1 Section 37.*

14 Sump – removal and refitting

Removal

1 Apply the handbrake, then jack up the front of the vehicle and support securely on axle stands (see *Jacking and vehicle support*).

2 Remove the securing bolts and withdraw the engine undershield(s).

3 Drain the engine oil as described in Chapter 1 Section 6.

4 Where fitted, disconnect the wiring connector from the oil level/temperature sender in the sump.

5 Unbolt and remove the bolts securing the sump to the cylinder block, and the bolts securing the sump to the transmission casing, then withdraw the sump. If necessary, release the sump by tapping with a soft-faced hammer.

6 If desired, unbolt the oil baffle plate from the cylinder block.

Refitting

7 Begin refitting by thoroughly cleaning the mating faces of the sump and cylinder block. Ensure that all traces of old sealant are removed.

8 Where applicable, refit the oil baffle plate, and tighten the securing bolts.

9 Ensure that the cylinder block mating face of the sump is free from all traces of old sealant, oil and grease, and then apply a 2.0 to 3.0 mm thick bead of silicone sealant (Skoda D 176 600 A1 or equivalent) to the sump**(see illustration)**. Note that the sealant should be run around the inside of the bolt holes in the sump. The sump must be fitted within 5 minutes of applying the sealant.

10 Offer the sump up to the cylinder block, then refit the sump-to-cylinder block bolts, and lightly tighten them by hand, working progressively in a diagonal sequence.If the sump is being refitted with the engine and transmission separated, use a straight edge to make sure that the sump is flush with the flywheel end of the cylinder block.

11 Refit the sump-to-transmission casing bolts, and tighten them lightly, using a socket.

12 Again working in a diagonal sequence, lightly tighten the sump-to-cylinder block bolts, using a socket.

13 Tighten the sump-to-transmission casing bolts to the specified torque.

14 Working in a diagonal sequence, progressively tighten the sump-to-cylinder block bolts to the specified torque.

15 Refit the wiring connector to the oil level/temperature sender (where fitted), then refit the engine undershield(s), and lower the vehicle to the ground.

16 Allow at least 30 minutes from the time of refitting the sump for the sealant to dry, then refill the engine with oil, with reference to Chapter 1 Section 6

15 Oil pump and drive chain – removal, inspection and refitting

Oil pump

Removal

1 Remove the sump as described in Section 14, and unbolt the baffle from the cylinder block.

2 Undo the securing bolt and remove the chain sprocket from the pump shaft.

3 Undo the two retaining bolts and release the oil pump from the dowels in the crankcase. Withdraw the oil pump and oil pick-up pipe from the engine.

4 If desired, unscrew the flange bolts and remove the pick-up pipe from the oil pump. Recover the O-ring seal. Unscrew the bolts and remove the cover from the oil pump.

Inspection

5 Clean the pump thoroughly, and inspect the gear teeth/rotors for signs of damage or wear. If evident, renew the oil pump.

Refitting

6 Prime the pump with oil by pouring oil into the pick-up pipe aperture while turning the driveshaft.

7 Refit the cover to the oil pump and tighten the bolts securely. Where applicable, refit the pick-up pipe to the pump using a new O-ring seal, and tighten the securing bolts.

8 The remainder of a refitting is a reversal of removal, tightening the oil pump retaining bolts to the specified torque. Note that the sprocket will only fit in one position.

Drive chain and sprockets

Note: *Skoda sealant D 176 404 A2 or equivalent will be required to seal the crankshaft oil seal housing on refitting, and it is advisable to fit a new crankshaft oil seal.*

Removal

9 Proceed as described in paragraphs 1 and 2.

10 To remove the chain, remove the timing belt as described in Section 7, then unbolt the crankshaft oil seal housing from the cylinder block. Unbolt the chain tensioner from the cylinder block, then unhook the chain from the sprocket on the end of the crankshaft.

11 The oil pump drive sprocket is a pressure fit on the crankshaft, and cannot easily be removed. Consult a Skoda dealer for advice if the sprocket is worn or damaged.

Inspection

12 Examine the chain for wear and damage. Wear is usually indicated by excessive lateral play between the links, and excessive noise in operation. It is wise to renew the chain in any case if the engine is to be overhauled. Note that the rollers on a very badly worn chain may be slightly grooved. If there is any doubt as to the condition of the chain, renew it.

13 Examine the teeth on the sprockets for wear. Each tooth forms an inverted V. If worn, the side of each tooth under tension will be slightly concave in shape when compared with the other side of the tooth (ie, the teeth will have a hooked appearance). If the teeth appear worn, the sprocket should be renewed.

Refitting

14 Refitting is a reversal of removal. It may be necessary to use a screwdriver to press the chain tensioner against its spring to provide sufficient slack in the chain to engage the sprocket with the oil pump.

16 Flywheel/driveplate –
removal, inspection and refitting

Removal

1 On manual gearbox models, remove the gearbox (see Chapter 7A Section 3) and clutch (see Chapter 6 Section 6).

2 On automatic transmission models, remove the automatic transmission as described in Chapter 7B Section 2.

3 These models are fitted with a dual-mass flywheel. Begin by making alignment marks between the flywheel and the crankshaft.

4 Rotate the outside of the dual-mass flywheel so that the bolts align with the holes **(see illustration)**.

5 Unbolt the bolts and remove the flywheel. Use a locking tool to counterhold the flywheel **(see illustration)**. Discard the bolts, new ones must be fitted. **Note:** *In order not to damage the flywheel, do not allow the bolt heads to make contact with the flywheel during the unbolting procedure.*

Inspection

6 Check the flywheel for wear and damage. Examine the starter ring gear for excessive wear to the teeth. If the driveplate or its ring gear are damaged, the complete driveplate must be renewed. The flywheel ring gear, however, may be renewed separately from the flywheel, but the work should be entrusted to a Skoda dealer. If the clutch friction face is discoloured or scored excessively, it may be possible to regrind it, but this work should also be entrusted to a Skoda dealer.

7 With the flywheel removed, check the spigot

16.4 Rotate the outside of the dual-mass flywheel to align the bolts with the holes

needle bearing (where fitted) in the end of the crankshaft for wear by turning it with a finger. If there is any evidence of excessive wear or if the bearing has been running dry, it must be renewed. To do this, use a bearing removal puller which engages the rear end of the bearing. Drive the new bearing into position until its outer end is 1.5 mm below the end of the crankshaft.

8 The following are guidelines only, but should indicate whether professional inspection is necessary. The dual-mass flywheel should be checked as follows:

9 There should be no cracks in the drive surface of the flywheel. If cracks are evident, the flywheel may need renewing.

Warpage

10 Place a straight-edge across the face of the drive surface, and check by trying to insert a feeler gauge between the straight-edge and the drive surface **(see illustration)**. The flywheel will normally warp like a bowl – ie, higher on the outer edge. If the warpage is more than 0.40 mm, the flywheel may need renewing.

Free rotational movement

11 This is the distance the drive surface of the flywheel can be turned independently of the flywheel primary element, using finger effort alone. Move the drive surface in one direction and make a mark where the locating pin aligns with the flywheel edge. Move the drive surface in the other direction (finger pressure only) and make another mark **(see illustration)**. The total of free movement should not exceed 10.0 mm. If it's more, the flywheel may need renewing.

16.5 Use a locking tool (arrowed) to prevent the flywheel from rotating

Total rotational movement

12 This is the total distance the drive surface can be turned independently of the flywheel primary element. Insert two bolts into the clutch pressure plate/damper unit mounting holes, and with the crankshaft/flywheel held stationary, use a lever/pry bar between the bolts and use some effort to move the drive surface fully in one direction – make a mark where the locating pin aligns with the flywheel edge. Now force the drive surface fully in the opposite direction, and make another mark. The total rotational movement should not exceed 44.0 mm. If it does, have the flywheel professionally inspected.

Lateral movement

13 The lateral movement (up and down) of the drive surface in relation to the primary element of the flywheel, should not exceed 2.0 mm. If it does, the flywheel may need renewing. This can be checked by pressing the drive surface down on one side into the flywheel (flywheel horizontal) and making an alignment mark between the drive surface and the inner edge of the primary element. Now press down on the opposite side of the drive surface, and make another mark above the original one. The difference between the two marks is the lateral movement **(see illustration)**.

Refitting

14 Refitting is a reversal of removal. Use new bolts when refitting the flywheel, and coat the threads of the bolts with locking fluid before inserting them. Tighten them to the specified torque.

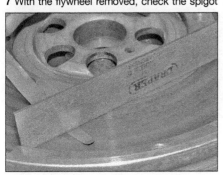

16.10 Flywheel warpage check – see text

16.11 Flywheel free rotational movement check alignment marks – see text

16.13 Flywheel lateral movement check marks – see text

17.2 Pull the screw and seal from place using pliers

17.3 Prise the oil seal from the crankshaft oil seal housing

17.9 Slide the oil seal housing over the end of the crankshaft

17 Crankshaft oil seals – renewal

Note: *The oil seals are a PTFE (Teflon) type and are fitted dry, without using any grease or oil. These have a wider sealing lip and have been introduced instead of the coil spring type oil seal.*

Note: *If the oil seal housing is removed, suitable sealant (Skoda D 176 404 A2, or equivalent) will be required to seal the housing on refitting.*

Timing belt end oil seal

1 Remove the timing belt as described in Section 7, and the crankshaft sprocket with reference to Section 8.

2 To remove the seal without removing the housing, drill two small holes diagonally opposite each other, insert self-tapping screws, and pull on the heads of the screws with pliers **(see illustration)**.

3 Alternatively, to remove the oil seal complete with its housing, proceed as follows.

a) *Remove the sump as described in Section 14. This is necessary to ensure a satisfactory seal between the sump and oil seal housing on refitting.*

b) *Unbolt and remove the oil seal housing.*

c) *Working on the bench, lever the oil seal from the housing using a suitable screwdriver. Take care not to damage the seal seating in the housing* **(see illustration)**.

4 Thoroughly clean the oil seal seating in the housing.

5 Wind a length of tape around the end of the crankshaft to protect the oil seal lips as the seal (and housing, where applicable) is fitted.

6 Fit a new oil seal to the housing, pressing or driving it into position using a socket or tube of suitable diameter. Ensure that the socket or tube bears only on the hard outer ring of the seal, and take care not to damage the seal lips. Press or drive the seal into position until it is seated on the shoulder in the housing. Make sure that the closed end of the seal is facing outwards.

7 If the oil seal housing has been removed, proceed as follows, otherwise proceed to paragraph 11.

8 Clean all traces of old sealant from the crankshaft oil seal housing and the cylinder block, then coat the cylinder block mating faces of the oil seal housing with a 2.0 to 3.0 mm thick bead of sealant (Skoda D 176 404 A2, or equivalent). Note that the seal housing must be refitted within 5 minutes of applying the sealant.

Caution: DO NOT put excessive amounts of sealant onto the housing as it may get into the sump and block the oil pick-up pipe.

9 Refit the oil seal housing, and tighten the bolts progressively to the specified torque **(see illustration)**.

10 Refit the sump as described in Section 14.

11 Refit the crankshaft sprocket with reference to Section 8, and the timing belt as described in Section 7.

Flywheel/driveplate end oil seal

Note: *For engines that have a sealing flange with integral timing sender wheel, refer to Chapter 2B Section 15. The seal housing and crank sender wheel must be correctly positioned, and this requires a special tool.*

12 Remove the flywheel/driveplate as described in Section 16.

13 Remove the sump as described in Section 14. This is necessary to ensure a satisfactory seal between the sump and oil seal housing on refitting.

14 Unbolt and remove the oil seal housing, complete with the oil seal.

15 The new oil seal will be supplied ready-fitted to a new oil seal housing.

16 Thoroughly clean the oil seal housing mating face on the cylinder block.

17 New oil seal/housing assemblies are supplied with a fitting tool to prevent damage to the oil seal as it is being fitted. Locate the tool over the end of the crankshaft **(see illustration)**.

Caution: DO NOT put excessive amounts of sealant onto the housing as it may get into the sump and block the oil pick-up pipe.

18 Carefully fit the oil seal/housing assembly over the end of the crankshaft, then refit the securing bolts and tighten the bolts progressively, in a diagonal sequence, to the specified torque **(see illustrations)**.

19 Remove the oil seal protector tool from the end of the crankshaft.

20 Refit the sump as described in Section 14.

21 Refit the flywheel/driveplate as described in Section 16

17.17 Locate the oil seal fitting tool over the end of the crankshaft

17.18a Fit the oil seal housing assembly over the end of the crankshaft...

17.18b... then tighten the securing bolts

18 Engine/transmission mountings – inspection and renewal

Where engine mountings are being removed as part of a procedure and the intention is to refit them, make alignment marks between the mounting, vehicle body and engine / transmission bracket, with paint or marker pen, to aid positioning on re-assembly.

Inspection

1 If improved access is required, jack up the front of the vehicle, and support it securely on axle stands (see *Jacking and vehicle support*). Remove the engine top cover which also incorporates the air filter, then remove the engine undershield(s).
2 Check the mounting rubbers to see if they are cracked, hardened or separated from the metal at any point; renew the mounting if any such damage or deterioration is evident.
3 Check that all the mountings are securely tightened; use a torque wrench to check if possible.
4 Using a large screwdriver or a crowbar, check for wear in the mounting by carefully levering against it to check for free play. Where this is not possible, enlist the aid of an assistant to move the engine/transmission back-and-forth, or from side-to-side, whilst you observe the mounting. While some free play is to be expected, even from new components, excessive wear should be obvious. If excessive free play is found, check first that the fasteners are correctly secured, then renew any worn components as described in the following paragraphs.

Renewal

Note: *New mounting securing bolts will be required on refitting.*

Right-hand mounting

5 Attach a hoist and lifting tackle to the engine lifting brackets on the cylinder head, and raise the hoist to just take the weight of the engine. Alternatively the engine can be supported on a trolley jack under the engine. Use a block of wood between the sump and the head of the jack, to prevent any damage to the sump.
6 For improved access, unbolt the coolant reservoir and move it to one side, leaving the coolant hoses connected.
7 Where applicable, move any wiring harnesses, pipes or hoses to one side to enable removal of the engine mounting.
8 Unbolt the bolts securing the mounting to the engine, then unbolt the bolts securing it to the body. Also, unbolt the movement limiter. Withdraw the mounting from the engine compartment.
9 Refitting is a reversal of removal, bearing in mind the following points.
a) *Use new securing bolts.*
b) *There must be at least 10 mm between the engine mounting bracket and the right-hand side chassis member*

c) *The side of the mounting support arm must be parallel to the side of the engine mounting bracket.*
d) *Tighten all fixings to the specified torque.*

Left-hand mounting

10 Remove the engine top cover.
11 Attach a hoist and lifting tackle to the engine lifting brackets on the cylinder head, and raise the hoist to just take the weight of the engine and transmission. Alternatively the engine can be supported on a trolley jack under the transmission. Use a block of wood between the transmission and the head of the jack, to prevent any damage to the transmission.
12 Remove the battery, as described in Chapter 5 Section 3, then disconnect the main starter motor feed cable from the positive battery terminal box.
13 Release any relevant wiring or hoses from the clips on the battery tray, then unbolt the 3 securing bolts and remove the battery tray.
14 Unbolt the bolts securing the mounting to the transmission, and the remaining bolts securing the mounting to the body, then lift the mounting from the engine compartment.
15 Refitting is a reversal of removal, bearing in mind the following points:
a) *Use new mounting bolts.*
b) *The edges of the mounting support arm must be parallel to the edge of the mounting.*
c) *Tighten all fixings to the specified torque.*

Rear mounting (torque arm)

16 Apply the handbrake, then jack up the front of the vehicle and support securely on axle stands (see *Jacking and vehicle support*). Remove the engine undershield(s) for access to the rear mounting (torque arm).
17 Support the rear of the transmission beneath the final drive housing. To do this, use a trolley jack and block of wood, or alternatively wedge a block of wood between the transmission and the subframe.
18 Working under the vehicle, unbolt and remove the bolt securing the mounting to the subframe.
19 Unbolt the two bolts securing the mounting to the transmission, then withdraw the mounting from under the vehicle **(see illustration)**.

18.19 Rear mounting-to-transmission bolts (arrowed)

20 Refitting is a reversal of removal, using new mounting securing bolts.
Note: *There are two different strengths specified for the bolts into the transmission with differing torque settings, check the bolt strength marking on head of the bolts and replace with bolts of the same specification.*

19 Engine oil cooler / oil filter housing – removal and refitting

Oil cooler

Note: *New sealing rings will be required on refitting.*

Removal

1 Raise the front of the vehicle and support it securely on axle stands (see *Jacking and vehicle support*) and remove the engine compartment undershield.
2 The oil cooler is mounted under the oil filter housing on the front of the cylinder block.
3 Position a container beneath the oil filter to catch escaping oil and coolant.
4 Clamp the oil cooler coolant hoses to minimise coolant spillage, then remove the clips, and disconnect the hoses from the oil cooler. Be prepared for coolant spillage.
5 Unscrew the oil cooler securing bolt from the bottom of the oil filter housing, then slide off the oil cooler. Recover the O-rings from the top and bottom of the oil cooler.

Refitting

6 Refitting is a reversal of removal, bearing in mind the following points:
a) *Use new oil cooler O-rings (Make sure the upper sealing ring / gasket is located correctly and does not obscure any oil passages).*
b) *Tighten the oil cooler securing bolt to the specified torque.*
c) *On completion, check and if necessary top-up the oil and coolant levels.*

Oil filter housing

7 For guidance on the removal and refitting of the oil filter housing refer to Chapter 2B Section 17 (engine code CEGA).

20 Oil pressure warning light switch – removal and refitting

Removal

1 The oil pressure warning light switch is fitted to the oil filter housing. Remove the engine top cover to gain access to the switch.
2 Disconnect the wiring connector and wipe clean the area around the switch.
3 Unscrew the switch from the filter housing and remove it, along with its sealing washer. If the switch is to be left removed from the engine for any length of time, plug the oil filter housing aperture.

21.4 Undo the 3 bolts (arrowed) and lower the sensor from the sump

Refitting

4 Examine the sealing washer for signs of damage or deterioration and if necessary renew.

5 Refit the switch, complete with washer, and tighten it to the specified torque.

6 Securely reconnect the wiring connector then check and, if necessary, top-up the engine oil as described in *Weekly checks*. On completion, refit the engine top cover(s).

21 Oil level/temperature sensor – removal and refitting

Removal

1 Where fitted, the engine oil level/temperature sensor is located in the base of the oil sump. Apply the handbrake, then jack up the front of the vehicle and support it on axle stands (see *Jacking and vehicle support*). Undo the fasteners, and remove the engine undershield.

2 Position a container beneath the sump, then unscrew the drain plug (refer to Chapter 1 Section 6) and drain the engine oil. Clean the plug and fit a new sealing washer (or replace plug with integral washer) refit and tighten, after the oil has drained.

3 Disconnect the oil level/temperature sensor wiring plug.

4 Undo the securing bolts, and lower the sensor from the sump. Discard the O-ring seal, a new one must be fitted**(see illustration)**.

Refitting

5 Clean the mating surfaces of the sensor and the sump. Smear the new O-ring seal with clean engine oil, and position it on the sensor.

6 Fit the sensor to the sump, insert the securing bolts and tighten them to the specified torque.

7 Reconnect the sensor wiring plug

8 Refit the engine undershield, lower the vehicle to the ground.

9 Refill the engine with new oil as described in Chapter 1 Section 6. Start the engine and check for leaks.

Chapter 2 Part B
Common rail injection engine in-car repair procedures

Contents

Degrees of difficulty

Easy, suitable for novice with little experience	Fairly easy, suitable for beginner with some experience	Fairly difficult, suitable for competent DIY mechanic	Difficult, suitable for experienced DIY mechanic	Very difficult, suitable for expert DIY or professional

Specifications

General

Manufacturer's engine codes: *
2.0 litre (1968 cc), 16-valve, DOHC . . . . CBBB, CBDB and CEGA (1st Generation)
CLCA, CLCB, CFHC and CFHF (2nd Generation)

Maximum outputs:

	Power	Torque
Engine code CLCA.	81 kw at 4200rpm	250 Nm at 1500 to 2500 rpm
Engine code CFHF.	81 kW at 4200 rpm	280 Nm at 1750 to 2750 rpm
Engine codes CLCB and CFHC.	103 kW at 4200 rpm	320 Nm at 1750 to 2500 rpm
Engine code CEGA.	125 kW at 4200 rpm	350 Nm at 1750 to 2500 rpm

Bore . . . . 81.0 mm
Stroke . . . . 95.5 mm
Compression ratio 16.5: 1
Compression pressures:
    Minimum compression pressure . . . . Approximately 19.0 bar
    Maximum difference between cylinders. . . . . Approximately 5.0 bar
Firing order . . . . 1 – 3 – 4 – 2
No 1 cylinder location. . . . . Timing belt end
*See 'Vehicle identification' at the end of this manual for the location of engine code markings.

Camshaft

Camshaft endfloat (maximum) 0.17mm

Lubrication system

Oil pump type. . . . . Gear type, chain or belt driven from crankshaft

Engine code	CEGA	CLCA, CLCB, CFHC, CFHF
Oil pressure (coolant temperature 80°C, at idle)	0.8 bar (minimum)	0.8 bar (minimum)
Oil pressure (coolant temperature 80°C, at 2000 rpm).	2.0 bar (minimum)	1.4 bar (minimum)
Oil pressure (coolant temperature 80°C,at high rpm).	7.0 bar (maximum)	5.2 bar (maximum)

Torque wrench settings

	Nm	lbf ft
Ancillary (alternator, etc) bracket mounting bolts: *		
Stage 1	Finger-tighten	
Stage 2	40	30
Stage 3 (2 centre bolts)	Angle-tighten a further 90°	
Stage 4 (2 lower bolts)	Angle-tighten a further 45°	
Stage 5 (2 upper bolts)	Angle-tighten a further 90°	
Auxiliary drivebelt tensioner securing bolt: *		
Stage 1	20	15
Stage 2	Angle-tighten a further 180°	
Balancer shaft drivegear bolts: *		
Stage 1	20	15
Stage 2	Angle-tighten a further 90°	
Balancer shaft housing to cylinder block: *		
M7:		
Stage 1	13	10
Stage 2	Angle-tighten a further 90°	
M8:		
Stage 1	20	15
Stage 2	Angle-tighten a further 90°	
Balancer shaft idler gear: *		
Stage 1	90	66
Stage 2	Angle-tighten a further 90°	
Big-end bearing cap bolts: *		
Stage 1	30	22
Stage 2	Angle-tighten a further 90°	
Camshaft bearing frame bolts/nut	10	7
Camshaft cover bolts	10	7
Camshaft sprocket hub centre bolt	100	74
Camshaft sprocket-to-hub bolts: *		
Stage 1	20	15
Stage 2	Angle-tighten a further 45°	
Common rail mounting bolts	22	16
Coolant pump bolts	15	11
Crankshaft oil seal housing/flange bolts*	15	11
Crankshaft pulley-to-sprocket bolts: *		
Stage 1	10	7
Stage 2	Angle-tighten a further 90°	
Crankshaft sprocket bolt: *		
Stage 1	180	133
Stage 2	Angle-tighten a further 90°	
Stage 3	Angle-tighten a further 45°	
Cylinder head bolts: *		
Stage 1	30	22
Stage 2	50	37
Stage 3	Angle-tighten a further 90°	
Stage 4	Angle-tighten a further 90°	
Engine mountings: *		
RH engine mounting:		
Mounting bracket to engine:		
Stage 1	7	5
Stage 2	40	30
Stage 3	Angle-tighten a further 180°	
Mounting to body:		
Stage 1	40	30
Stage 2	Angle-tighten a further 90°	
Mounting to bracket:		
Stage 1	60	44
Stage 2	Angle-tighten a further 90°	
LH engine/transmission mounting:		
Mounting to body:		
Stage 1	40	30
Stage 2	Angle-tighten a further 90°	
Mounting to bracket on transmission:		
Stage 1	60	44
Stage 2	Angle-tighten a further 90°	

Torque wrench settings (continued)	Nm	lbf ft
Engine mountings (continued): *		
Rear mounting link:		
To transmission:		
Stage 1:		
8.8 strength class bolt............................	40	30
10.9 strength class bolt...........................	50	37
Stage 2	Angle-tighten a further 90°	
To subframe:		
Stage 1	100	74
Stage 2	Angle-tighten a further 90°	
Flywheel/driveplate: *		
Stage 1	60	44
Stage 2	Angle-tighten a further 90°	
Fuel injector:		
Clamp nuts (CEGA)................................	10	7
Cover bolts (CEGA)	5	4
Clamp bolt (CLCA, CLCB, CFHC and CFHF): *		
Stage 1	8	6
Stage 2	Angle-tighten a further 270°	
Fuel pump hub nut...................................	95	70
Fuel pump sprocket bolts: *	20	15
Intermediate gear bolt: *		
Stage 1	90	66
Stage 2	Angle-tighten a further 90°	
Main bearing cap bolts: *		
Stage 1	65	48
Stage 2	Angle-tighten a further 90°	
Oil cooler bolt (CEGA)	25	18
Oil cooler to filter housing bolts (CLCA, CLCB, CFHC and CFHF):		
Stage 1	Hand-tighten	
Stage 2	5	4
Stage 3	11	8
Oil drain plug*.....................................	30	22
Oil filter cover	25	18
Oil filter housing-to-cylinder block bolts: *		
Stage 1:		
CEGA	15	11
CLCA, CLCB, CFHC and CFHF	14	10
Stage 2	Angle-tighten a further 90°	
Oil level/temperature sensor-to-sump bolts.....................	10	7
Oil pick-up pipe securing bolts (CEGA)	15	11
Oil pick-up pipe securing bolts (CLCA, CLCB, CFHC and CFHF).....	10	7
Oil pressure warning light switch (CEGA)......................	22	16
Oil pressure warning light switch (CLCA, CLCB, CFHC and CFHF) ...	20	15
Oil pump chain tensioner (CEGA)...........................	16	12
Oil pump cover bolts (CEGA)	10	7
Oil pump securing bolts	15	11
Oil pump sprocket bolt (CEGA)	25	18
Piston oil spray jet bolt (CEGA)	27	20
Piston oil spray jet bolt (CLCA, CLCB, CFHC and CFHF)	24	18
Sump:		
Sump-to-cylinder block bolts:		
Stage 1	5	4
Stage 2	15	11
Sump-to-transmission bolts............................	40	30
Thermostat housing	15	11
Timing belt idler pulleys:		
Lower idler roller nut.................................	20	15
Upper idler roller (small) bolt...........................	20	15
Upper idler roller (large) bolt: *		
Stage 1	50	37
Stage 2	Angle-tighten a further 90°	
Timing belt outer cover bolts	10	7
Timing belt tensioner roller securing nut: *		
Stage 1	20	15
Stage 2	Angle-tighten a further 45°	
Turbocharger oil supply pipe connection to oil filter housing (CEGA) ..	22	16

* Do not re-use fasteners

1 General Information

How to use this Chapter

1 This Part of Chapter 2 describes those repair procedures that can reasonably be carried out on the engine while it remains in the vehicle. If the engine has been removed from the vehicle and is being dismantled as described in Part C, any preliminary dismantling procedures can be ignored.

2 Note that while it may be possible physically to overhaul certain items while the engine is in the vehicle, such tasks are not usually carried out as separate operations, and usually require the execution of several additional procedures (not to mention the cleaning of components and of oilways); for this reason, all such tasks are classed as major overhaul procedures, and are described in Part C of this Chapter.

Engine description

3 Throughout this Chapter, engines are referred to by type, and are identified and referred to by the manufacturer's code letters. A listing of all engines covered, together with their code letters, is given in the Specifications at the start of this Chapter.

4 The engines are water-cooled, double overhead camshafts (DOHC), in-line four-cylinder units, with cast-iron cylinder blocks and aluminium-silicon alloy cylinder heads. All are mounted transversely at the front of the vehicle, with the transmission bolted to the left-hand end of the engine.

5 The crankshaft is of five-bearing type, and thrustwashers are fitted to the centre main bearing to control crankshaft endfloat.

6 Drive for the exhaust camshaft is by a toothed timing belt from the crankshaft, with the inlet camshaft driven by interlocking gears at the left-hand end of both camshafts. The gears incorporate a toothed backlash compensator element. Each camshaft is mounted at the top of the cylinder head, and is secured by a bearing frame/ladder.

7 The valves are closed by coil springs, and run in guides pressed into the cylinder head. The valves are operated by roller rocker arms incorporating hydraulic tappets.

8 On some models a twin, counter-rotating balancer shaft assembly is fitted to the base of the cylinder block. The rearmost balancer shaft is driven by a gear on the crankshaft, via an intermediate gear bolted to the balancer shaft housing. The two balancer shafts are geared together with the front balancer shaft driving the oil pump through a hexagonal drive.

9 On models with no balancer shaft assembly the gear-type oil pump is driven by a belt or chain from a sprocket on the crankshaft.

10 On all models the oil pump draws oil from the sump through a strainer, and then forces it through an externally-mounted, renewable filter. From there, it is distributed to the cylinder head, where it lubricates the camshaft journals and hydraulic tappets, and also to the crankcase, where it lubricates the main bearings, connecting rod big-ends, gudgeon pins and cylinder bores. A coolant-fed oil cooler is fitted to the oil filter housing on all engines. Oil jets are fitted to the base of each cylinder – these spray oil onto the underside of the pistons, to improve cooling.

11 All engines are fitted with a brake servo vacuum pump driven by the camshaft on the transmission end of the cylinder head.

12 On all engines, engine coolant is circulated by a pump, driven by the timing belt. For details of the cooling system, refer to Chapter 3.

Operations with engine in car

13 The following operations can be performed without removing the engine:
a) *Compression pressure – testing.*
b) *Camshaft cover – removal and refitting.*
c) *Crankshaft pulley – removal and refitting.*
d) *Timing belt covers – removal and refitting.*
e) *Timing belt – removal, refitting and adjustment.*
f) *Timing belt tensioner and sprockets – removal and refitting.*
g) *Camshaft oil seals – renewal.*
h) *Camshafts and hydraulic tappets – removal, inspection and refitting.*
i) *Cylinder head – removal and refitting.*
j) *Cylinder head and pistons – decarbonising.*
k) *Sump – removal and refitting.*
l) *Oil pump – removal, overhaul and refitting.*
m) *Crankshaft oil seals – renewal.*
n) *Engine/transmission mountings – inspection and renewal.*
o) *Flywheel – removal, inspection and refitting.*

Note: *It is possible to remove the pistons and connecting rods (after removing the cylinder head and sump) without removing the engine. However, this is not recommended. Work of this nature is more easily and thoroughly completed with the engine on the bench, as described in Chapter 2C.*

2 Compression and leakdown tests – description and interpretation

Compression test

Note: *A compression tester suitable for use with diesel engines will be required for this test.*

1 When engine performance is down, a compression test can provide diagnostic clues as to the engine's condition. If the test is performed regularly, it can give warning of trouble before any other symptoms become apparent.

2 The engine must be fully warmed-up to normal operating temperature, the battery must be fully-charged, and you will require the aid of an assistant.

3 Remove the glow plugs as described in Chapter 5 Section 11, then fit a compression tester to the No 1 cylinder glow plug hole. The type of tester which bolts into the plug thread is preferred. **Note:** *Part of the glow plug removal procedure is to disconnect the fuel injector wiring plugs. As a result of the plugs being disconnected and the engine cranked, faults will be stored in the ECM memory. These must be erased after the compression test.*

4 Have your assistant crank the engine for several seconds on the starter motor. After one or two revolutions, the compression pressure should build-up to a maximum figure and then stabilise. Record the highest reading obtained.

5 Repeat the test on the remaining cylinders, recording the pressure in each.

6 The cause of poor compression is less easy to establish on a diesel engine than on a petrol engine. The effect of introducing oil into the cylinders (wet testing) is not conclusive, because there is a risk that the oil will sit in the recess on the piston crown, instead of passing to the rings. However, the following can be used as a rough guide to diagnosis.

7 All cylinders should produce very similar pressures. Any difference greater than that specified indicates the existence of a fault. Note that the compression should build-up quickly in a healthy engine. Low compression on the first stroke, followed by gradually increasing pressure on successive strokes, indicates worn piston rings. A low compression reading on the first stroke, which does not build-up during successive strokes, indicates leaking valves or a blown head gasket (a cracked head could also be the cause).

8 A low reading from two adjacent cylinders is almost certainly due to the head gasket having blown between them and the presence of coolant in the engine oil will confirm this.

9 On completion, remove the compression tester, and refit the glow plugs, with reference to Chapter 5 Section 11.

10 Reconnect the wiring to the injector solenoids. Finally, have a Skoda dealer or suitably-equipped specialist erase the fault codes from the ECM memory.

Leakdown test

11 A leakdown test measures the rate at which compressed air fed into the cylinder is lost. It is an alternative to a compression test, and in many ways it is better, since the escaping air provides easy identification of where pressure loss is occurring (piston rings, valves or head gasket).

12 The equipment required for leakdown testing is unlikely to be available to the home mechanic. If poor compression is suspected, have the test performed by a suitably-equipped garage.

3 Engine assembly and valve timing marks – general information and usage

General information

1 TDC is the highest point in the cylinder that each piston reaches as it travels up-and-down when the crankshaft turns. Each piston reaches TDC at the end of the compression stroke and again at the end of the exhaust stroke, but TDC generally refers to piston position on the compression stroke. No 1 piston is at the timing belt end of the engine.

2 Positioning No 1 piston at TDC is an essential part of many procedures, such as timing belt removal and camshaft removal.

3 The design of the engines covered in this Chapter is such that piston-to-valve contact may occur if the camshaft or crankshaft is turned with the timing belt removed. For this reason, it is important to ensure that the camshaft and crankshaft do not move in relation to each other once the timing belt has been removed from the engine.

Setting TDC on No 1 cylinder

Note: *Skoda special tool T10050 is required to lock the crankshaft sprocket in the TDC position. Alternatively obtain a tool from automotive tool specialists.*

4 Raise the front of the vehicle and support it securely on axle stands (see *Jacking and vehicle support*). Undo the retaining fasteners and remove the engine undershield. Remove the front right-hand roadwheel, then release the fasteners and remove the lower section of the wheel arch liner.

5 Remove the auxiliary drivebelt as described in Chapter 1 Section 11.

6 Remove the crankshaft pulley/vibration damper as described in Section 5.

7 Remove the timing belt outer covers as described in Section 6.

8 Using a spanner or socket on the crankshaft sprocket bolt, turn the crankshaft in the normal direction of rotation (clockwise) until the alignment mark on the face of the sprocket is almost vertical, and the hole in the camshaft sprocket hub aligns with the hole in the cylinder head **(see illustration)**.

4.4 Disconnect the vacuum hoses from the camshaft cover (arrowed)

3.8 The alignment mark (arrowed) on the crankshaft sprocket should be almost vertical

3.9b... so the marks on the tool and sprocket align (arrowed)

9 While in this position it should be possible to insert the Skoda tool T10050 to lock the crankshaft, and a 6 mm diameter rod/drill bit to lock the camshafts **(see illustrations)**. **Note:** *The mark on the crankshaft sprocket and the mark on the Skoda tool must align, whilst at the same time the shaft of tool must engage in the drilling in the crankshaft oil seal housing.*

10 The engine is now set to TDC on No 1 cylinder.

4 Camshaft cover – removal and refitting

Removal

1 Remove the fuel injectors and common rail as described in Chapter 4A Section 5 and Chapter 4A Section 7.

4.5 Squeeze together the sides of the collar (arrowed) and disconnect the breather hose

3.9a Fit the tool to the hole in the oil seal housing (arrowed)...

3.9c Insert a 6 mm drill bit/rod to lock the camshaft hub (arrowed)

2 Remove the timing belt upper cover as described in Section 6.

3 Disconnect the wiring connector from the vacuum unit on top of the turbocharger.

4 Note their fitted positions, then disconnect the vacuum hoses from the camshaft cover, and release them and the wiring loom from the retaining clips at the left-hand end of the cover **(see illustration)**.

5 Squeeze together the sides of the collar, and disconnect the breather hose from the camshaft cover **(see illustration)**.

6 Release the wiring from the clips at the rear of the cover, then unbolt the camshaft cover retaining bolts and lift the cover away **(see illustration)**. Note that on some models the camshaft cover is fastened to the rear timing belt cover; carefully release the clips as the camshaft cover is removed.

7 Recover the camshaft cover gasket. Inspect the gasket carefully, and renew it if

4.6 Undo the bolts and lift away the camshaft cover

4.7a Renew the cover seal if necessary

4.7b The bolts and seals must be pushed fully through the cover before fitting the gasket

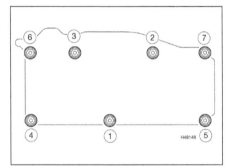

4.9 Cylinder head cover bolt tightening sequence

5.5 Undo the pulley bolts, counterholding it with a socket on the centre sprocket bolt

6.2 Disconnect the wiring plug and undo the retaining bolt (arrowed)

6.4a Note their positions, then disconnect the hoses from the fuel filter

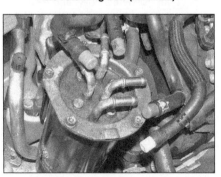

6.4b Plug the openings to prevent contamination

6.5 Undo the nut/bolts (arrowed) and remove the fuel filter

damage or deterioration is evident – note that the retaining bolts and seals must be pushed fully through the cover (see illustrations).

8 Clean the mating surfaces of the cylinder head and camshaft cover thoroughly, removing all traces of oil – take care to avoid damaging the surfaces as you do this.

Refitting

9 Refit the camshaft cover by following the removal procedure in reverse, tightening the cover retaining bolts to the specified torque in the sequence shown (see illustration).

5 Crankshaft pulley – removal and refitting

Removal

1 Switch off the ignition and all electrical consumers and remove the ignition key.
2 Raise the front right-hand side of the vehicle, and support securely on axle stands (see Jacking and vehicle support). Remove the roadwheel.
3 For improved access undo the retaining fasteners and remove the engine undershield.
4 Remove the securing fasteners and withdraw the lower section of the front wheel arch liner.
5 Slacken the bolts securing the crankshaft pulley to the sprocket (see illustration). If necessary, the pulley can be prevented from turning by counterholding with a spanner or socket on the crankshaft sprocket bolt.
6 Remove the auxiliary drivebelt, as described in Chapter 1 Section 11.
7 Unbolt the bolts securing the pulley to the sprocket, and remove the pulley. Discard the bolts – new ones must be fitted.

Refitting

8 Refit the pulley over the locating peg on the crankshaft sprocket, then fit the new pulley securing bolts.
9 Refit and tension the auxiliary drivebelt as described in Chapter 1 Section 11.
10 Prevent the crankshaft from turning as during removal, then fit the pulley securing bolts, and tighten to the specified torque.
11 Refit the wheel arch liner.
12 Refit undershield.
13 Refit the roadwheel and lower the vehicle to the ground.

6 Timing belt covers – removal and refitting

Upper outer cover

1 Pull the engine top cover upwards to release the mountings.
2 Disconnect the wiring plug, undo the retaining bolt, and release the exhaust gas pressure differential sensor and bracket by pushing it forwards(see illustration). Position the bracket clear of the timing cover, taking care with the sensor a it is easily damaged.
3 Remove the bolt securing the screen wash reservoir filler tube.
4 Disconnect the wiring plug, unclip the fuel hoses, then release the clamps and disconnect the hoses from the filter(see illustrations). Note the fitted locations of the hoses to aid refitting. Plug the openings to prevent contamination.
5 Undo the bolts/nut and remove the fuel filter

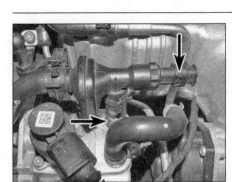

6.6 Disconnect the fuel supply hose and temperature sensor (arrowed)

6.7 Supplementary fuel pump retaining bolts (arrowed)

6.8a Disconnect the temperature sensor wiring plug (arrowed)

6.8b Release the clips (arrowed)...

6.8c... and manoeuvre the timing belt upper cover from place

6.12 Centre timing belt cover bolts

assembly **(see illustration)**. Release the hose clamp as the filter assembly is withdrawn.

6 Disconnect the fuel temperature sensor wiring plug, then release the clamp and disconnect the fuel supply pipe from the high-pressure fuel pump **(see illustration)**. Plug the openings to prevent contamination, and place a rag above the alternator to prevent fuel ingress.

7 Slide up the hose retaining clips, undo the 2 retaining bolts, disconnect the wiring plug and remove the supplementary fuel pump **(see illustration)**.

8 Disconnect the radiator outlet temperature sensor wiring plug, then release the 3 clips and remove the timing belt upper cover **(see illustrations)**.

9 Refitting is a reversal of removal, noting that the lower edge of the upper cover engages with the centre cover.

Centre outer cover (engine code CEGA)

10 Remove the crankshaft pulley as described in Section 5. It is assumed that, if the centre cover is being removed, the lower cover will be also – if not, simply remove the components described in Section 5 for access to the crankshaft pulley, and leave the pulley in position.

11 Undo the retaining nuts/bolts and move the coolant pipe that lies across the centre cover away, towards the inner wing.

12 With the upper cover removed (paragraphs 1 to 7), unbolt and remove the 3 retaining bolts from the centre cover. Withdraw the

centre cover from the engine, noting how it fits over the lower cover **(see illustration)**. Note: *If the auxiliary belt tensioner is in the 'locked' position as described in the belt removal procedure, the locking drill bit/rod must be removed for access to the cover retaining bolt.*

13 Refitting is a reversal of the removal procedure, using a little thread-locking compound on the retaining bolts.

Lower outer cover (engine code CEGA)

14 Remove the upper and centre covers as described previously.

15 If not already done, remove the crankshaft pulley as described in Section 5.

16 Undo the remaining bolts securing the lower cover, and remove it **(see illustration)**.

17 Refitting is a reversal of removal; locate the centre cover in place before fitting the top two bolts.

6.16 Lower cover retaining bolts (arrowed)

Lower cover (engine codes CFHC, CFHF, CLCA and CLCB)

18 Remove the upper cover as described previously.

19 If not already done, remove the crankshaft pulley as described in Section 5.

20 Unscrew the 5 bolts securing the lower cover and remove it **(see illustration)**.

21 Refitting is the reversal of removal, applying a small amount of suitable locking compound to the bolt threads; noting that the upper edge of the lower cover engages with the upper cover.

Rear cover

22 Remove the timing belt, tensioner and sprockets as described in Sections 7 and 8.

23 Slacken and withdraw the retaining bolts and lift the timing belt inner cover from the studs on the end of the engine, note that it

6.20 Remove lower cover

7.0 Two types of tensioner type (A) and (B)

may be required to remove the coolant pump (Chapter 3 Section 7) before the cover can be removed.

24 Refitting is a reversal of removal.

7 Timing belt –
removal, inspection and refitting

Note: *It is considered best practise to always replace the tensioner, idler and coolant pump*

7.4 Slacken the sprocket-to-hub bolts (arrowed)

7.6 Insert an Allen key, slacken the nut, and rotate the hub anti-clockwise until a 2 mm rod/drill bit (arrowed) can be inserted to lock the hub to the pulley

whenever the timing belt is replaced. Any mounting studs should also be replaced at the same time. Most of the components (apart from the coolant pump) will be supplied with a timing belt kit. Note also that most manufactures will not guarantee a belt against premature failure if the idler(s) and tensioner are not replaced with the belt

Note: *There are two types of tensioner fitted to this engine and they are not interchangeable* **(see illustration)**. *Check to see which type is fitted before removing the timing belt. Type A tensioner requires a locking pin for installation and it tensions the belt by rotating clockwise. Type B tensioner does not require a locking pin for installation and it tensions the belt by rotating anti-clockwise. See text.*

Removal

1 The primary function of the toothed timing belt is to drive the camshaft, but it also drives the coolant pump and high-pressure fuel pump. Should the belt slip or break in service, the valve timing will be disturbed and piston-to-valve contact may occur, resulting in serious engine damage. For this reason, it is important that the timing belt is tensioned correctly, and inspected regularly for signs of wear or deterioration.

2 Switch off the ignition and all electrical consumers, and remove the ignition key.

3 Set the engine to TDC on No 1 cylinder as described in Section 3.

4 Slacken the 3 bolts securing the sprocket to the camshaft hub by 90° **(see illustration)**.

7.5 Slacken the high-pressure fuel pump sprocket bolts (arrowed)

7.15 Rotate the high-pressure fuel pump clockwise until a 6 mm drill bit/rod can be inserted into the housing and hub (arrowed)

5 Slacken the 3 bolts securing the sprocket to the high-pressure fuel pump by 90°**(see illustration)**.

Type A tensioner

6 Insert a suitable Allen key into the tensioner hub, then slacken the retaining nut and rotate the tensioner hub anti-clockwise until it can be locked in place using a 2.0 mm pin/drill bit **(see illustration)**.

7 Now rotate the tensioner hub clockwise to the stop, and hand-tighten the retaining nut.

Type B tensioner

8 Insert a suitable Allen key into the tensioner hub, then slacken the retaining nut and rotate the tensioner hub clockwise, until the tension on the belt is released. When in this position hand-tighten the retaining nut.

All engines

9 If the original timing belt is to be refitted, mark the running direction of the belt, to ensure correct refitting.

Caution: Caution: If the belt appears to be in good condition and can be re-used, it is essential that it is refitted the same way around, otherwise accelerated wear will result, leading to premature failure.

10 Slide the belt from the sprockets, taking care not to twist or kink the belt excessively if it is to be re-used.

Inspection

11 Examine the belt for evidence of contamination by coolant or lubricant. If this is the case, find the source of the contamination before progressing any further. Check the belt for signs of wear or damage, particularly around the leading edges of the belt teeth. Renew the belt if its condition is in doubt; the cost of belt renewal is negligible compared with potential cost of the engine repairs, should the belt fail in service. The belt must be renewed if it has covered the mileage given in Chapter 1, however, if it has covered less, it is prudent to renew it regardless of condition, as a precautionary measure.

12 If the timing belt is not going to be refitted for some time, it is a wise precaution to hang a warning label on the steering wheel, to remind yourself (and others) not to attempt to start the engine.

Refitting

13 Ensure that the crankshaft and camshaft are still set to TDC on No 1 cylinder, as described in Section 3.

14 The camshaft sprocket and high pressure fuel pump sprocket bolts should be renewed one at a time and tightened only by hand sufficient to hold the sprockets against their respective hubs, whilst still allowing the sprockets to turn to the limits of their elongated slots.

15 Using a screwdriver on the bolts heads, rotate the high-pressure fuel pump clockwise until a 6.0 mm locking pin/drill bit can be inserted into the housing adjacent to the sprocket, locking the pump in place **(see illustration)**.

7.16a Rotate the sprockets fully clockwise until the fuel pump sprocket...

7.16b ... and camshaft sprocket bolts are at the end of the elongated slots

7.19 Timing belt routing

16 Rotate the camshaft sprocket and high-pressure fuel pump sprocket fully clockwise so that the securing bolts are at the end of the elongated slots **(see illustrations)**.
17 Loop the timing belt loosely under the crankshaft sprocket.
Note: *Observe any direction of rotation markings on the belt.*
18 Fit the belt around the tensioner pulley, engage the timing belt teeth with the camshaft sprockets, then manoeuvre it into position around the coolant pump sprocket and the fuel pump sprocket. Make sure that the belt teeth seat correctly on the sprockets. Note that slight adjustment to the position of the camshaft sprocket may be necessary to achieve this. Avoid bending the belt back on itself or twisting it excessively as you do this.
19 Finally, fit the belt around the idler roller **(see illustration)**. Ensure that any slack in the belt is in the section of belt that passes over the tensioner roller.

Type A tensioner

20 Loosen the timing belt tensioner securing nut, and pull out the tensioner locking pin. Turn the tensioner clockwise with an Allen key until the pointer is just past the middle of the gap in the tensioner backplate**(see illustration)**. With the tensioner held in this position, tighten the securing nut to the specified torque and angle.

Type B tensioner

21 Loosen the timing belt tensioner securing nut and turn the tensioner anti-clockwise

with an Allen key until the pointer is just past the middle of the gap in the tensioner base plate. At this point markings on the tensioner hub and pulley should also be in alignment **(see illustration)**. With the tensioner held in this position, tighten the securing nut to the specified torque and angle.

All engines

22 Counterhold the camshaft sprocket with a home-made tool to prevent any rotation, then tighten the camshaft sprocket and fuel pump sprocket bolts to 20 Nm (15 lbf ft). Remove the sprockets locking tools and the crankshaft locking tool.
23 Using a spanner or wrench and socket on the crankshaft pulley centre bolt, rotate the crankshaft clockwise through two complete revolutions. Reset the engine to TDC on No 1 cylinder, with reference to Section 3 and refit the crankshaft locking tool.
24 Check that the tensioner roller indicator arm is centred, or within a maximum of 5 mm to the right of the notch in the backplate **(see illustration)**. If not, hold the tensioner hub stationary with an Allen key, slacken the retaining nut and position the arm in the centre of the notch. Tighten the retaining nut to the specified torque and angle. Remove the Allen key.
25 Check that the camshaft sprocket locking pin can still be inserted. **Note:** *It's very difficult to align the locking point of the fuel pump hub again. However, a misalignment of holes will not affect engine performance.*

26 If the camshaft sprocket locking pin cannot be inserted, pull the crankshaft locking tool away from the engine, and rotate the crankshaft anti-clockwise slightly past TDC. Now slowly rotate the crankshaft clockwise until the camshaft sprocket locking tool can be inserted.
27 If the locating pin of the crankshaft locking tool is to the left of the corresponding hole, slacken the camshaft sprocket bolts, slowly rotate the crankshaft clockwise until the locking tool can be fully inserted. Tighten the camshaft sprocket bolts to 20 Nm (15 lbf ft).
28 If the locating pin of the crankshaft locking tool is to the right of the corresponding hole, slacken the camshaft sprocket bolts, rotate the crankshaft anti-clockwise slightly until the pin is to the left of the hole, then slowly rotate it clockwise until the lock tool can be fully inserted. Tighten the camshaft sprocket bolts to 20 Nm (15 lbf ft). **Note:** *The crankshaft must always be rotated clockwise prior to fitting the locking tool to ensure correct belt tensioning.*
29 Remove the crankshaft and camshaft locking tools, then rotate the crankshaft 2 complete revolutions clockwise and check the locking tools can be reinserted. If necessary, repeat the adjustment procedure.
30 When both crankshaft and camshaft locking tools can be inserted, with the engine at TDC on No 1 cylinder, the timing is correct, remove the locking tools, counterhold the camshaft sprocket and tighten the camshaft sprocket bolts to the specified torque and angle.

7.20 Rotate the tensioner clockwise until the pointer (arrowed) is just past the gap in the backplate

7.21 Turn type B tensioner anti-clockwise and secure with retaining nut (1)

7.24 The pointer should be centred in, or within 5 mm to the right of, the gap in the backplate

8.4 Coolant pipe upper mounting bolt and lower mounting nut (arrowed)

31 Carry out a final check by rotating the crankshaft two further turns clockwise and setting the engine to TDC on No 1 cylinder (Section 3). Check the crankshaft locking tool alignment markings and ensure that the crankshaft and camshaft locking tools are correctly inserted; check the correct belt tension is indicated by the belt tensioner pointer. Remove the locking tools and carry out the remainder of refitting, which is the reversal of removal.

8 Timing belt tensioner and sprockets – removal and refitting

Timing belt tensioner

Removal

1 In order to remove the timing belt tensioner, the engine mounting bracket must first be removed. Either support the engine from above using a crossbeam or an engine hoist, or support if from underneath with a trolley jack and block of wood.
2 Remove the timing belt as described in Section 7.
3 Make marks with paint or a pen between the engine mount and body and between the engine mount and mounting bracket to aid alignment when refitting, then undo the bolts and remove the right-hand engine mounting.
4 Undo the bolt securing the coolant pipe to the mounting bracket **(see illustration)**.

8.8 Ensure the lug on the backplate engages with the cut-out in the timing belt cover (arrowed)

8.6 Engine mounting bracket bolts (arrowed)

5 Working in the wheel arch area, undo the nut securing the lower end of the coolant pipe.
6 Undo the 3 retaining bolts and remove the engine mounting bracket **(see illustration**.
7 Unbolt the timing belt tensioner nut, and remove the tensioner from the engine. **Note:** *With the tensioner removed check that the mounting stud is securely fitted and is in good condition, where a new stud is being fitted, clean the mounting hole and check the condition of the threads. Ensure the new stud is correctly seated and secure.*

Refitting

8 When refitting the tensioner to the engine, ensure that the lug on the tensioner backplate engages with the corresponding cut-out in the rear timing belt cover, then refit the tensioner nut **(see illustration)**.
9 The remainder of refitting is a reversal of removal.
10 When refitting the engine mounting bracket, the bolts should be tightened in the stages specified and in the sequence 1-2-3 for each stage **(see illustration)**.

Idler pulleys

Removal

11 Remove the timing belt as described in Section 7.
12 Unbolt the relevant idler pulley/roller securing bolt/nut, then withdraw the pulley.

Refitting

13 Refit the pulley and tighten the securing bolt or nut to the specified torque, noting that

8.10 Engine mounting bracket bolts and tightening sequence.

the large roller/pulley retaining bolt must be renewed.
14 Refit and tension the timing belt as described in Section 7.

Crankshaft sprocket

Note: *A new crankshaft sprocket securing bolt must be used on refitting.*

Removal

15 Remove the timing belt as described in Section 7.
16 The sprocket securing bolt must now be slackened, and the crankshaft must be prevented from turning as the sprocket bolt is unbolted. To hold the sprocket, make up a suitable tool, and bolt it to the sprocket using a two bolts bolted into two of the crankshaft pulley bolt holes.
17 Hold the sprocket using the tool, then slacken the sprocket securing bolt. Take care, as the bolt is very tight. Do not allow the crankshaft to turn as the bolt is slackened.
18 Unbolt the bolt, and slide the sprocket from the end of the crankshaft, noting which way round the sprocket's raised boss is fitted.

Refitting

19 Ensure that the mating faces of the sprocket and crankshaft are clean and free of oil and grease, then position the sprocket on the end of the crankshaft.
20 Fit a new sprocket securing bolt (do not lubricate the threads or head of the bolt) then counterhold the sprocket using the method employed on removal, and tighten the bolt to the specified torque in the stages given in the specifications.
21 Refit the timing belt as described in Section 7.

Camshaft sprocket

Removal

22 Remove the timing belt as described in Section 7, then rotate the crankshaft 90° anti-clockwise to prevent any accidental piston-to-valve contact.
23 Unbolt and remove the three retaining bolts and remove the camshaft sprocket from the camshaft hub.

Refitting

24 Refit the sprocket ensuring that it is fitted the correct way round, then insert the new sprocket bolts, and tighten by hand only at this stage.
25 If the crankshaft has been turned, turn the crankshaft clockwise 90° back to TDC.
26 Refit and tension the timing belt as described in Section 7.

Camshaft hub

Note: *Skoda technicians use special tool T10051 to counterhold the hub, however it is possible to fabricate a suitable alternative.*

Removal

27 Remove the camshaft sprocket as described previously in this Section.
28 Engage special tool T10051 with the three

8.28 Fabricate a home-made tool to counterhold the hub. Undo the bolt...

8.29... and slide the hub from the camshaft

8.30 Ensure the integral key aligns with the keyway in the camshaft (arrowed)

locating holes in the face of the hub to prevent the hub from turning. If this tool is not available, fabricate a suitable alternative. Whilst holding the tool, undo the central hub retaining bolt about two turns **(see illustration)**.
29 Slide the hub from the camshaft. If necessary, attach Skoda tool T10052 (or a similar three-legged puller) to the hub, and evenly tighten the puller until the hub is free of the camshaft taper **(see illustration)**.

Refitting

30 Ensure that the camshaft taper and the hub centre are clean and dry, locate the hub on the taper, noting that the built-in key in the hub taper must align with the keyway in the camshaft taper **(see illustration)**.
31 Hold the hub in this position with tool T10051 (or similar home-made tool), and tighten the central bolt to the specified torque.
32 Refit the camshaft sprocket as described previously in this Section.

Coolant pump sprocket

33 The coolant pump sprocket is integral with the coolant pump. Refer to Chapter 3 Section 7 for details of coolant pump removal.

Fuel pump sprocket

34 The fuel pump sprocket removal is included in timing belt removal (Section 7).

9 Camshaft and hydraulic tappets – removal, inspection and refitting

Note: A new camshaft oil seal(s) will be required on refitting. Skoda removal tool T40094 (or similar tool) will be required to refit the camshafts – this is necessary to prevent damage to the retaining frame and cylinder head as the camshafts are refitted.
Note: For information on testing the hydraulic tappets, refer to Chapter 2A Section 11.

Removal

1 Remove the camshaft hub as described in Section 8.
2 Remove the camshaft cover as described in Section 4.
3 Remove the brake vacuum pump as described in Chapter 9 Section 22.

4 Progressively unbolt the camshaft retaining frame bolts in the reverse of the sequence shown in illustration 9.20, and carefully remove the retaining frame.
5 Carefully lift the camshafts from the cylinder head, keeping them identified for location. Remove the oil seal from the end of the camshaft and discard it – a new one will be required for refitting.
6 Lift the rocker arms and hydraulic tappets from place. Store the rockers and tappets in a container with numbered compartments to ensure they are refitted to their correct locations. It is recommended that the tappets are kept immersed in oil for the period they are removed from the cylinder head.

Inspection

7 With the camshafts removed, examine the retaining frame and the bearing locations in the cylinder head for signs of obvious wear or pitting. If evident, a new cylinder head will probably be required. Also check that the oil supply holes in the cylinder head are free from obstructions.
8 Visually inspect the camshafts for evidence of wear on the surfaces of the lobes and journals. Normally their surfaces should be smooth and have a dull shine; look for scoring, erosion or pitting and areas that appear highly polished, indicating excessive

wear. Accelerated wear will occur once the hardened exterior of the camshaft has been damaged, so always renew worn items. If these symptoms are visible on the tips of the camshaft lobes, check the corresponding rocker arm, as it will probably be worn as well.
9 If the machined surfaces of the camshaft appear discoloured or blued, it is likely that it has been overheated at some point, probably due to inadequate lubrication. This may have distorted the shaft, so have the camshaft runout and endfloat checked by an automotive engine reconditioning specialist.
10 Inspect the hydraulic tappets for obvious signs of wear or damage, and renew if necessary. Check that the oil holes in the tappets are free from obstructions.

Refitting

11 Oil the rocker arms and hydraulic tappets, then refit them to their original positions.

⚠ *Warning: After fitting hydraulic tappets, wait a minimum of 30 minutes (or preferably, leave overnight) before starting the engine, to allow the tappets time to settle, otherwise the valve heads will strike the pistons.*

12 To set up the tool, remove the supports number 3, 4 and 5, then install the supports number 1, 2, 9 and 10 as shown**(see illustrations)**.

9.12a The different elements of tool No T40094

9.12b Position supports No 1, 2, 9 and 10 as shown

9.13 Position the inlet camshaft on the tool with the bolt indent (arrowed) facing outwards, then slide tool No 8 in to the slot in the end of the camshaft and use a 0.50 mm feeler gauge to remove any free play

9.14 Fit tool No 11 into the slot (arrowed) in the end of the exhaust camshaft

9.15 Tighten the thumbwheel to align the gear teeth. Ensure the clamping jaw with the arrow is seated on the wider gear

9.18 Secure the camshafts in place in the frame using tool No T40095 (arrowed)

13 Position the inlet camshaft as shown with the cylinder head bolt indent facing outwards, then slide the support number 8 into the slot in the end of the camshaft and remove any free play with a 0.50 mm feeler gauge (see illustration).
14 Position the exhaust camshaft on supports numbers 9 and 10, and fit the tool No 11 into the slot in the end of the camshaft (see illustration).
15 Fit the clamping tool No T40096 to the gear on the exhaust camshaft, tightening the knurled thumb wheel until the faces of the gear teeth are in alignment. If necessary, use a 13 mm spanner (see illustration).

16 Slide the exhaust camshaft towards the inlet camshaft until the gear teeth engage.
17 Ensure the gasket faces of the retaining frame are clean, then apply a smear of clean engine oil to the bearing surfaces and lower the frame into position over the camshafts. Ensure the bearing surfaces locate correctly on the camshafts.
18 Fit the clamping tool No T40095 over the camshafts and frame, and tighten the thumbwheels to hold the camshafts in position in the frame (see illustration).
19 Ensure the sealing surfaces of the cylinder head are clean, then apply a 2.0 mm wide bead of sealant (Skoda D 176 501 A2 or equivalent) as shown. Take care not to apply too much sealant, ensuring the oil holes supply holes are not blocked (see illustration).
20 Slide out tool Nos 8 and 11, then lift the camshafts, retaining frame and clamping tool from the tool No 40094. Place the camshafts, frame and tool in place on the cylinder head. Progressively and carefully, hand-tighten the frame retaining bolts in the sequence shown, until the retaining frame makes contact with the cylinder head over the complete surface,

9.19 Apply a 2.0 mm thick bead of sealant to the area shown by the thick, black line. Take care not to block the oil holes (arrowed)

then tighten the bolts to the specified torque, again in the correct sequence**(see illustration)**.
21 Remove the gear aligning tool (T40096) and the clamping tool (T40095).
22 Renew the camshaft oil seal (Section 10), then drive in a new sealing cap.
23 The remainder of refitting is a reversal of removal.

10 Camshaft oil seals – renewal

Right-hand oil seal

1 Remove the camshaft sprocket and hub, as described in Section 8.
2 Take note of the fitted depth of the oil seal prior to it's removal.
3 Drill two small holes into the existing oil seal, diagonally opposite each other. Take great care to avoid drilling through into the seal housing or camshaft sealing surface. Thread two self-tapping screws into the holes, and using a pair of pliers, pull on the heads of the screws to extract the oil seal**(see illustration)**.
4 Clean out the seal housing and the sealing surface of the camshaft by wiping it with a lint-free cloth. Remove any swarf or burrs that may cause the seal to leak.
5 Do not lubricate the lip and outer edge of the new oil seal, push it over the camshaft until it is positioned in place above its housing. To prevent damage to the sealing lips, wrap some adhesive tape around the end of the camshaft.
6 Using a hammer and a socket of suitable diameter, drive the seal squarely into its housing.
Note: *Select a socket that bears only on the hard outer surface of the seal, not the inner lip which can easily be damaged*.
7 Refit the camshaft sprocket and its hub, as described in Section 8.

Left-hand oil seal

8 The left-hand camshaft oil seal is formed by the brake vacuum pump seal. Refer to Chapter 9 Section 22 for details of brake vacuum pump removal and refitting.

11 Cylinder head – removal, inspection and refitting

Note: *The cylinder head must be removed with the engine cold. New cylinder head bolts and a new cylinder head gasket will be required on refitting, and suitable studs will be required to guide the cylinder head into position – see text.*

Removal

All Engines

1 Remove the battery as described in Chapter 5 Section 3.

9.20 Camshaft retaining frame bolt tightening sequence

2 Drain the cooling system and engine oil as described in Chapter 1 Section 37 and Chapter 1 Section 6.
3 Pull the plastic cover on the top of the engine upwards from its mountings.
4 Remove the air filter housing as described in Chapter 4A Section 3.
5 Undo the 3 bolts and remove the battery tray **(see illustration)**.
6 Unbolt and remove the heatshield from above the right-hand driveshaft.
7 Remove the radiator cooling fan(s) and shroud as described in Chapter 3 Section 5.
8 Remove the camshaft cover as described in Section 4.
9 Remove the camshaft sprocket and hub as described in Section 8.

Engine code CEGA

10 Undo the bolts and remove the charge air hose/pipe from the intercooler to the turbocharger. Release the wiring looms from the clips as necessary to enable the pipe to be manoeuvred from place.
11 Disconnect the wiring plugs from the EGR valve and throttle body/inlet manifold flap.
12 Disconnect the charge air pressure sensor wiring plug, then undo the 2 retaining bolts, release the clamps, and remove the charge air pipe and hose from the front of the engine **(see illustrations)**.
13 Undo the bolt securing the oil level dipstick guide tube to the throttle body/inlet manifold flap **(see illustration)**.

10.3 Screw in a self-tapping screw, then pull the screw and seal from place

11.5 Battery tray bolts (arrowed)

11.12a Disconnect the pressure sensor wiring plug (arrowed)...

11.12b... then remove the charge air pipe and hose (arrowed)

11.13 Oil level dipstick guide tube bolt (arrowed)

11.14 EGR pipe-to-valve bolts (arrowed)

11.15 Charge air pipe retaining bolt (arrowed). Note the position of the vacuum hoses

11.16 With some lubrication, the hose connection pulls up from the vacuum pump

11.20 EGR pipe-to-cooler bolts (arrowed)

11.22 Remove the EGR pipe between the manifold and cooler

14 Undo the 2 bolts securing the connecting pipe to the EGR valve (see illustration).
15 Undo the front retaining bolt, twist the charge air pipe clockwise and disconnect it from the turbocharger. Note their fitted positions, and unclip the vacuum hoses from the charge air pipe (see illustration).
16 Apply a little lubrication spray to the rubber sleeve, pull up the pipe from the vacuum pump, then undo the 4 retaining bolts and remove the vacuum pump from the left-hand end of the cylinder head (see illustration). Renew the pump-to-cylinder head seal.
17 Disconnect the coolant temperature sensor wiring plug at the left-hand end of the cylinder head, and release the wiring loom from any retaining clips.

18 Disconnect the gearchange cables from the levers on the transmission as described in Chapter 7A Section 3 or Chapter 7B Section 4.
19 Undo the bolts/nut, securing the gearchange bracket to the top of the transmission. Move the bracket and cables to one side.
20 Undo the bolts securing the EGR pipe to the cooler at the left-hand end of the engine, and the nut securing the bracket to the cylinder head, then remove the pipe (see illustration). Recover the gasket at each end.
21 Slacken the Allen bolt and release the clamp securing the diesel particulate filter/catalytic converter to the turbocharger, then undo the bolts/nuts securing the brackets to the cylinder block/head and secure the filter/converter to one side.

22 Undo the nuts and multispline bolts securing the EGR pipe to the right-hand end of the exhaust manifold and EGR cooler (see illustration). Remove the pipe and recover the gaskets.
23 Trace the exhaust manifold gas temperature sensor wiring back, releasing it from any retaining clips, disconnect its wiring plug at the bulkhead, and slide it from the retaining bracket. Unclip the wiring loom from the top of the turbocharger heat shield.
24 Undo the bolt securing the support bracket/oil return pipe to the underside of the turbocharger, then undo the bolt securing the top of the support bracket to the underside of the turbocharger. Now pull and twist the support bracket to disconnect it from the oil return pipe at the top. Remove the pipe/bracket (see illustrations). Note the O-ring and copper sealing washer on the lower banjo bolt, and the two O-rings fitted to the base of the oil return pipe still fitted to the turbocharger.
25 Note their fitted locations, then release the clamps and disconnect the various coolant hoses from the cylinder head.
26 Undo the bolt securing the turbocharger oil supply pipe bracket at the left-hand end of the cylinder head, the nut securing the bracket on the rear of the head, then undo the union bolts and remove the pipe. Renew any seals.
27 Undo the bolt securing the timing belt guard adjacent to the timing belt tensioner, and the bolt securing the camshaft position sensor, then remove the tensioner retaining nut (see illustration).

11.24a Undo the banjo bolt (arrowed) at the base of the turbocharger support bracket/oil return pipe and the bolt at the top (arrowed)

11.24b Note the 2 O-ring seals (arrowed) at the base of the oil return pipe

11.27 Undo the bolt (arrowed) securing the timing belt guard

11.28 Undo the boost pressure solenoid valve nuts (arrowed)

11.36a EGR exhaust manifold to cooler pipe

28 Disconnect the turbocharger boost regulator position sensor wiring plug, and the inlet manifold changeover valve wiring plug. Note their fitted positions and disconnect the vacuum hoses from the EGR cooler (where the plastic pipe joins the metal pipe at the back of the cylinder head) and the turbocharger boost regulator actuator. Undo the nuts securing the boost pressure solenoid valve to the bulkhead. Release the loom wiring plug, lay the wiring loom and vacuum hoses over the front of the engine, clear of the cylinder head (see illustration). Make a final check to ensure all relevant wiring and vacuum hoses have been disconnected. Note the loom/hose routing to aid refitting.

Engine codes CFHC, CFHF, CLCA and CLCB

29 Remove the bolt securing the dipstick guide tube to the throttle flap housing.
30 Disconnect the wiring plug from the throttle flap housing.
31 Apply a little lubrication spray to the rubber sleeve, pull up the pipe from the vacuum pump.
32 Unclip any wiring and hoses from the charge air pipe between the turbocharger and the intercooler on the left side of the engine, unscrew the fixing bolts, release the clamp/clip at the ends and remove the charge air pipe.
33 At the front of the engine, release the clips at each end and remove the radiator lower coolant hose. Unscrew the fixings for the charge air pipe between the intercooler and inlet manifold, disconnect the wiring for the pressure/temperature sender, release the clamps at each end and remove the charge air pipe.
34 Undo the screws and remove the resonator assembly from the turbocharger outlet.
35 Release the clips and remove the coolant hoses from the housing at the left-hand side of the cylinder head; disconnect the coolant temperature sender wiring plug.
36 Undo the nuts/bolts securing the EGR pipes from the EGR valve/cooler assembly to the cylinder head and to the exhaust manifold (see illustrations).
37 From the underside, undo the 4 nuts and remove the diesel particulate filter/ catalytic converter support bracket.

11.36b EGR pipe to cylinder head bolts (arrowed)

11.36c EGR pipe to cooler bolts (arrowed)

38 Remove the bolt from the bracket at the right rear of the cylinder head, supporting the diesel particulate filter/ catalytic converter. Slacken and remove the clamp between the turbocharger and the diesel particulate filter/ catalytic converter; release and secure the diesel particulate filter/ catalytic converter away from the cylinder head.
39 Disconnect the wiring from the oil pressure switch at the rear of the engine.
40 At rear of engine, disconnect the rigid vacuum pipe for EGR by-pass, remove the bolt from support bracket and remove the pipe.
41 Undo the bolt securing the timing belt guard adjacent to the timing belt tensioner, and remove the timing belt tensioner retaining nut
42 Disconnect the camshaft position sensor wiring plug and release the wiring from any clips.
43 Disconnect the turbocharger boost regulator position sensor wiring plug (see illustration).
44 Take note of their fitted positions, then release and disconnect any relevant wiring plugs from their retainers on the bulkhead. Make a final check to ensure all relevant wiring and vacuum hoses have been disconnected.
45 Undo the oil feed pipe at the top of the turbocharger, counterhold the union whilst undoing the pipe nut to ensure that the connection to the turbocharger is not loosened. Once undone the pipe should be gently bent away from the turbocharger enough to enable the turbocharger to be removed with the cylinder head.
46 Undo the bolt securing the support

bracket/oil return pipe to the underside of the turbocharger, the oil return pipe will release from the support bracket as the cylinder head is lifted.

All Engines

47 Using an M12 multisplined tool (12-pointed star), undo the cylinder head bolts, working from the outside-in, evenly and gradually (see illustration). Remove the bolts and recover the washers. Check that nothing remains connected, and starting at the gearbox side, lift the cylinder head from the engine block, sliding the belt tensioner from the mounting stud as the cylinder head is removed. Seek assistance if possible, as it is a heavy assembly, especially as it is being removed complete with the manifolds. When putting the head down support it on blocks of wood or similar to avoid damage to the oil return pipe and the glow

11.43 Disconnect the wiring plug

11.47 Undo the cylinder head bolts using an M12 multisplined (12-pointed star) tool

11.50 The holes (arrowed) identify the thickness of the cylinder head gasket

11.53 Measure the piston protrusion using a DTI gauge

plugs, which protrude below the level of the cylinder head face.

48 Remove the gasket from the top of the block, noting the locating dowels. If the dowels are a loose fit, remove them and store them with the head for safe-keeping. Do not discard the gasket yet – it will be needed for identification purposes. If desired, the manifolds can be removed from the cylinder head with reference to Chapter 4A Section 6 and Chapter 4B Section 4.

Inspection

49 Dismantling and inspection of the cylinder head is covered in Chapter 2C Section 6.

Cylinder head gasket selection

Note: *A dial test indicator (DTI) will be required for this operation.*

50 Examine the old cylinder head gasket for manufacturer's identification markings **(see illustration)**. These will be in the form of holes, and a part number on the edge of the gasket. Unless new pistons have been fitted, the new cylinder head gasket must be of the same type as the old one.

51 If new piston assemblies have been fitted as part of an engine overhaul, or if a new short engine is to be fitted, the projection of the piston crowns above the cylinder head mating face of the cylinder block at TDC must be measured. This measurement is used to determine the thickness of the new cylinder head gasket required.

52 Anchor a dial test indicator (DTI) to the top face (cylinder head gasket mating face) of

the cylinder block, and zero the gauge on the gasket mating face.

53 Rest the gauge probe on No 1 piston crown, and turn the crankshaft slowly by hand until the piston reaches TDC. Measure and record the maximum piston projection at TDC **(see illustration)**.

54 Repeat the measurement for the remaining pistons, and record the results.

55 If the measurements differ from piston-to-piston, take the highest figure, and use this to determine the thickness of the head gasket required as follows.

Gasket identification

Piston projection	Number of holes
0.91 to 1.00 mm	1
1.01 to 1.10 mm	2
1.11 to 1.20 mm	3

56 Purchase a new gasket according to the results of the measurements.

Refitting

57 The mating faces of the cylinder head and block must be perfectly clean before refitting the head. Use a scraper to remove all traces of gasket and carbon, also clean the tops of the pistons. Take particular care with the aluminium surfaces, as the soft metal is easily damaged.

58 Make sure that debris is not allowed to enter the oil and water passages – this is particularly important for the oil circuit, as carbon could block the oil supply to the camshaft and crankshaft bearings. Using adhesive tape and paper, seal the water, oil and bolt holes in the cylinder block.

59 To prevent carbon entering the gap between the pistons and bores, smear a little grease in the gap. After cleaning a piston, rotate the crankshaft to that the piston moves down the bore, then wipe out the grease and carbon with a cloth rag. Clean the other piston crowns in the same way.

60 Check the head and block for nicks, deep scratches and other damage. If slight, they may be removed carefully with a file. More serious damage may be repaired by machining, but this is a specialist job.

61 If warpage of the cylinder head is suspected, use a straight-edge to check it for distortion, as described in Chapter 2C Section 6.

62 Ensure that the cylinder head bolt holes in the crankcase are clean and free of oil. Syringe or soak up any oil left in the bolt holes. This is most important in order that the correct bolt tightening torque can be applied, and to prevent the possibility of the block being cracked by hydraulic pressure when the bolts are tightened.

63 Turn the crankshaft anti-clockwise all the pistons at an equal height, approximately half-way down their bores from the TDC position (see Section 3). This will eliminate any risk of piston-to-valve contact as the cylinder head is refitted.

64 Where applicable, refit the manifolds with reference to Chapter 4A Section 6 and Chapter 4B Section 4.

65 Ensure that the cylinder head locating dowels are in place in the cylinder block, then fit the new cylinder head gasket over the dowels, ensuring that the part number is uppermost **(see illustration)**. Note that Skoda recommend that the gasket is only removed from its packaging immediately prior to fitting.

66 Lower the cylinder head into position on the gasket, ensuring that it engages correctly over the dowels. Refit the timing belt tensioner as the cylinder head is refitted.

67 Fit the washers in place then fit the new cylinder head bolts to the locations, and bolt them in as far as possible by hand. Do not oil the bolt threads.

68 Working progressively, in sequence, tighten all the cylinder head bolts to the specified Stage 1 torque **(see illustrations)**.

69 Again working progressively, in sequence,

11.65 Ensure the dowels are in place, then fit the new gasket with the part number uppermost (arrowed)

11.68a Cylinder head bolt tightening sequence

11.68b Tighten the cylinder head bolts to the Stage 1 torque

11.70 Use an angle-tightening gauge

12.4 Raise the clip (arrowed) and disconnect the air duct from the intercooler

tighten all the cylinder head bolts to the specified Stage 2 torque.

70 Tighten all the cylinder head bolts, in sequence, through the specified Stage 3 angle **(see illustration)**.

71 The remainder of the refitting procedure is a reversal of the removal procedure, noting the following points:

a) *Tighten all fasteners to their specified torque where given.*
b) *Renew all seals and gaskets.*
c) *Refill the cooling system as described in Chapter 1 Section 37.*
d) *Ensure all wiring is correctly routed.*

12 Sump –
removal and refitting

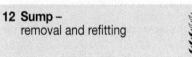

Removal

1 Apply the handbrake, then jack up the front of the vehicle and support securely on axle stands (see *Jacking and vehicle support*).

2 Remove the securing bolts and withdraw the engine undershield(s).

3 Drain the engine oil as described in Chapter 1 Section 6.

4 Release the clamp, raise the retaining clip and remove the air duct from the intercooler outlet **(see illustration)**.

5 Undo the retaining bolts, release the clamp and remove the charge air pipe from the front of the cylinder block **(see illustrations 11.11a and 11.11b)**. Disconnect the charge air pressure sensor wiring plug as the pipe is withdrawn.

6 Undo the retaining bolt and move the electric coolant circulation pump to one side **(see illustration)**.

7 Undo the bolt securing the turbo-to-intercooler air pipe to the sump.

8 Disconnect the wiring connector from the oil level/temperature sender in the sump **(see illustration)**.

9 Remove the sump insulation cover (where fitted); pull the sump insulation cover downwards at the rear to release the retaining clips, then prise down the centre pin and pull the clip on the front side of the cover downwards **(see illustration)**.

12.6 Electric coolant circulation pump retaining bolt (arrowed)

10 Unbolt and remove the bolts securing the sump to the cylinder block, and the bolts securing the sump to the transmission casing, then withdraw the sump. If necessary, release the sump by tapping with a soft-faced hammer.

Refitting

11 Begin refitting by thoroughly cleaning the mating faces of the sump and cylinder block. Ensure that all traces of old sealant are removed.

12 Ensure that the cylinder block mating face of the sump is free from all traces of old sealant, oil and grease, and then apply a 2.0 to 3.0 mm thick bead of silicone sealant (Skoda D 176 600 A1 or equivalent) to the sump **(see illustration)**. Note that the sealant should be run around the inside of the bolt holes in the sump. The sump must be fitted within 5 minutes of applying the sealant.

13 Offer the sump up to the cylinder block,

12.9 At the front, prise down the centre pin and pull the clip downwards

12.8 Oil level/temperature sensor location

then refit the sump-to-cylinder block bolts, and lightly tighten them by hand, working progressively in a diagonal sequence. If the sump is being refitted with the engine and transmission separated, use a straight edge to make sure that the sump is flush with the flywheel end of the cylinder block.

12.12 Apply a bead of sealant around the inside of the bolt holes

13.2a Remove the circlip...

13.3 Oil pump pick-up pipe bolts (arrowed)

14 Refit the sump-to-transmission casing bolts, and tighten them lightly, using a socket.
15 Again working in a diagonal sequence, lightly tighten the sump-to-cylinder block bolts to the first stage torque, using a socket.
16 Tighten the sump-to-transmission casing bolts to the specified torque.

13.4 Oil pump mounting bolts (arrowed)

13.12a Rotate the balance shaft until the groove (arrowed) on the end of the rear shaft is vertical...

13.2b... and pull out the oil pump shaft using an M3 bolt

17 Working in a diagonal sequence, progressively tighten the sump-to-cylinder block bolts to the specified second stage torque.
18 The remainder of refitting is a reversal of removal, noting to allow at least 30 minutes from the time of refitting the sump for the sealant to dry, then refill the engine with oil, with reference to Chapter 1 Section 6

13 Oil Pump –
removal, inspection and refitting

Oil pump and balancer shaft assembly

Removal

1 Remove the sump as described in Section 12.

13.9 Renew the pick-up pipe O-ring seal

13.12b... and tool No T10255...

Oil pump

2 Remove the retaining circlip, then pull the oil pump shaft out using an M3 bolt (see illustrations).
3 Undo the retaining bolts and detach the pick-up pipe from the pump(see illustration).
4 Undo the bolts and detach the oil pump from the balancer shaft assembly (see illustration).

Balancer shaft assembly

5 Lock the camshafts and crankshaft at TDC on No 1 cylinder as described in Section 3.
6 Working gradually and evenly, undo the retaining bolts and detach the balancer shaft assembly from the base of the cylinder block.

Inspection

7 Consult a Skoda dealer or parts specialist on the availability of parts for the oil pump or balancer shaft assembly.

Refitting

Oil Pump

8 Refit the pump to the balancer shaft assembly and tighten the retaining bolts to the specified torque.
9 Refit the oil pick-up pipe using a new O-ring, then tighten the retaining bolts to the specified torque(see illustration).
10 Push the driveshaft into place, and secure it with the circlip.
11 The remainder of refitting is a reversal of removal.

Balancer shaft assembly

Note: If the original balancer shaft assembly is being refitted, it's essential that neither the drivegear on the crankshaft or the crankshaft itself has been renewed, or the idler gear bolt has been slackened. If they have, proceed under the heading for the installation of a new balancer shaft assembly.

Refitting the original assembly

12 Rotate the balancer shaft until Skoda tool No T10255 can be fitted into the groove on the left-hand end of the rear shaft (see illustrations).
13 Ensure the engine is still locked at TDC for No 1 cylinder as described in Section 3, then position the balancer shaft assembly over the locating dowels on the base of the cylinder

13.12c... can be fitted

block. The idler gear must engage with the drivegear of the crankshaft, and there must be noticeable backlash.

14 Fit the new balancer shaft assembly retaining bolts, and working from the centre outwards, tighten them to the specified torque. Remove the Skoda tool.

15 The remainder of refitting is a reversal of removal.

Fitting a new balancer shaft assembly

16 New balancer shaft assemblies are supplied with an idler gear with a special coating. Once fitted, the coating wears down to give the correct backlash between the gears.

17 Ensure the engine is still locked at TDC for No 1 cylinder as described in Section 3.

18 Slacken the idler gear retaining bolt 90°.

19 Position the balancer shaft assembly over the locating dowels on the base of the cylinder block, ensuring the white mark on the idler gear is centrally aligned with the crankshaft drivegear. Idler gears not marked with a white mark can be installed in any position.

20 Fit the new balancer shaft assembly retaining bolts, and working from the centre outwards, tighten them to the specified torque.

21 Rotate the balancer shaft until Skoda tool No T10255 can be fitted into the groove on the left-hand end of the rear shaft (see illustrations 13.12a, 13.12b and 13.12c).

22 Fit the balancer shaft drivegear onto the shaft so the holes in the gear align with the holes in the shaft. Tighten the retaining bolts to the specified torque.

23 Have an assistant push the idler gear between the two gears to remove any backlash. At the same time, rotate the balancer shaft anti-clockwise slightly, and tighten the idler gear retaining bolt to the specified torque. Remove the balancer shaft locking tool.

24 The remainder of refitting is a reversal of removal.

Oil pump – chain driven (engine code CEGA)

Oil pump removal

25 Remove the sump as described in Section 12, and unbolt the baffle from the cylinder block.

26 Undo the securing bolt and remove the chain sprocket from the pump shaft.

27 Undo the two retaining bolts and release the oil pump from the dowels in the crankcase. Withdraw the oil pump and oil pick-up pipe from the engine.

28 If desired, unscrew the flange bolts and remove the pick-up pipe from the oil pump. Recover the O-ring seal. Unscrew the bolts and remove the cover from the oil pump.

Oil pump inspection

29 Clean the pump thoroughly, and inspect the gear teeth/rotors for signs of damage or wear. If evident, renew the oil pump.

13.39 Remove the oil pick -up pipe

Oil pump refitting

30 Refit the cover to the oil pump and tighten the bolts securely. Where applicable, refit the pick-up pipe to the pump using a new O-ring seal, and tighten the securing bolts.

31 Prime the pump with oil by pouring oil into the pick-up pipe aperture while turning the driveshaft sprocket.

32 The remainder of refitting is a reversal of removal, making sure that the pump locating dowels are in position before fitting the pump; installing and tightening the oil pump retaining bolts and sprocket bolt to the specified torque. Note that the sprocket will only fit in one position.

Drive chain and sprockets removal

Note: *Skoda sealant D 176 404 A2 or equivalent will be required to seal the crankshaft oil seal housing on refitting, and it is advisable to fit a new crankshaft oil seal.*

33 Proceed as described in paragraphs 25 and 26.

34 To remove the chain, remove the timing belt as described in Section 7, then unbolt the crankshaft oil seal housing from the cylinder block with reference to Section 15. Unbolt the chain tensioner from the cylinder block, then unhook the chain from the sprocket on the end of the crankshaft. Mark the chains direction of rotation if it is to be re-used.

Note: *The oil pump drive sprocket is a pressure fit on the crankshaft, and cannot easily be removed. Consult a Skoda dealer for advice if the sprocket is worn or damaged.*

Drive chain and sprockets inspection

35 Examine the chain for wear and damage. Wear is usually indicated by excessive lateral play between the links, and excessive noise in operation. It is wise to renew the chain in any case if the engine is to be overhauled. Note that the rollers on a very badly worn chain may be slightly grooved. If there is any doubt as to the condition of the chain, renew it.

36 Examine the teeth on the sprockets for wear. Each tooth forms an inverted V. If worn, the side of each tooth under tension will be slightly concave in shape when compared

13.40 Remove oil pump mounting bolt (also securing oil baffle plate)

with the other side of the tooth (ie, the teeth will have a hooked appearance). If the teeth appear worn, the sprocket should be renewed.

Drive chain and sprockets refitting

37 Refitting is a reversal of removal. It may be necessary to use a screwdriver to press the chain tensioner against its spring to provide sufficient slack in the chain to engage the sprocket with the oil pump.

Oil pump – belt driven (engine codes CFHC, CFHF, CLCA and CLCB)

Oil pump removal

38 Remove the sump as described in Section 12.

39 Unscrew the flange bolts and remove the oil pick-up pipe/filter from the oil pump (see illustration). Recover the O-ring seal and discard, as a new one will be required for refitting.

40 Unscrew and remove the oil pump mounting bolts and release and remove the baffle plate (see illustration). Release the oil pump from the dowels in the crankcase, unhook the oil pump drive sprocket from the belt and withdraw the oil pump from the engine.

Oil pump inspection

41 Turn the pump sprocket by hand and check for smooth operation and inspect for signs of damage or wear. If the pump is rough or tight to turn or if there is any evidence of wear or damage then renew the oil pump. Integral with the pump are an oil pressure control valve and an oil pressure safety release valve, replacment of these components can only be achieved by replacing the complete pump as at the time of writing no parts were available.

Oil pump refitting

42 Prime the pump with oil by pouring oil into the pick-up pipe aperture while turning the drive sprocket.

43 Engage the oil pump sprocket with the drive belt, and then locate the oil pump on the dowels, position the baffle plate, then refit and tighten the mounting bolts to the specified torque (see illustration).

13.43 Oil pump mounting bolt locations

44 Refit the pick-up pipe to the oil pump, using a new O-ring seal, and tighten the securing bolts **(see illustration)**.
45 Refit the sump as described in Section 12.

Drivebelt removal

46 Remove the sump Section 12 and oil pump as described in this section.
47 Remove the timing belt (Section 7) and the crankshaft oil seal housing with reference to Section 15
48 Unhook the oil pump drivebelt from the sprocket and remove it.Take note of the belts direction of rotation if the intention is to re-use it. **Note:** *The oil pump drive belt sprocket is a pressure fit on the crankshaft, and cannot easily be removed. Consult a Skoda dealer for advice if the sprocket is worn or damaged.*

Drivebelt inspection

49 The drivebelt can be seen after removing the sump and oil pump, it should be examined and replaced if showing signs of damage or wear.
50 If the belt has been removed completely then it would be considered best practice to replace it.

Drivebelt refitting

51 Fit the new drivebelt over the crankshaft sprocket.
52 Refit the oil pump as described earlier in this section.
53 Refit the crankshaft oil seal housing Section 15
54 Refit the crankshaft sprocket with reference to Section 8, and the timing belt as described in Section 7
55 Refit the sump as described in Section 12.

13.44 Fit new O-ring seal to oil pick-up pipe

14 Flywheel/driveplate –
removal, inspection and refitting

Removal

1 On manual gearbox models, remove the gearbox (see Chapter 7A Section 3) and clutch (see Chapter 6 Section 6).
2 On automatic transmission models, remove the automatic transmission as described in Chapter 7B Section 2.
3 These models are fitted with a dual-mass flywheel. The flywheel can only be fitted in one position due to the offset of the flywheel mounting holes in the end of the crankshaft.
4 Rotate the outside of the dual-mass flywheel so that the bolts align with the holes (if necessary).
5 Unbolt the bolts and remove the flywheel. Use a locking tool to counterhold the flywheel **(see illustration)**. Discard the bolts, new ones must be fitted.
Note: *In order not to damage the flywheel, do not allow the bolt heads to make contact with the flywheel during the unbolting procedure.*

Inspection

6 Check the flywheel for wear and damage. Examine the starter ring gear for excessive wear to the teeth. If the driveplate or its ring gear are damaged, the complete driveplate must be renewed. The flywheel ring gear, however, may be renewed separately from the flywheel, but the work should be entrusted

to a Skoda dealer. If the clutch friction face is discoloured or scored excessively, it may be possible to regrind it, but this work should also be entrusted to a Skoda dealer.
7 The following are guidelines only, but should indicate whether professional inspection is necessary. The dual-mass flywheel should be checked as follows:
8 There should be no cracks in the drive surface of the flywheel. If cracks are evident, the flywheel may need renewing.

Warpage

9 Place a straight-edge across the face of the drive surface, and check by trying to insert a feeler gauge between the straight-edge and the drive surface **(see illustration)**. The flywheel will normally warp like a bowl – ie, higher on the outer edge. If the warpage is more than 0.40 mm, the flywheel may need renewing.

Free rotational movement

10 This is the distance the drive surface of the flywheel can be turned independently of the flywheel primary element, using finger effort alone. Move the drive surface in one direction and make a mark where the locating pin aligns with the flywheel edge. Move the drive surface in the other direction (finger pressure only) and make another mark **(see illustration)**. The total of free movement should not exceed 20.0 mm. If it's more, the flywheel may need renewing.

Total rotational movement

11 This is the total distance the drive surface can be turned independently of the flywheel primary element. Insert two bolts into the clutch pressure plate/damper unit mounting holes, and with the crankshaft/flywheel held stationary, use a lever/pry bar between the bolts and use some effort to move the drive surface fully in one direction – make a mark where the locating pin aligns with the flywheel edge. Now force the drive surface fully in the opposite direction, and make another mark. The total rotational movement should not exceed 44.0 mm. If it does, have the flywheel professionally inspected.

Lateral movement

12 The lateral movement (up and down) of the drive surface in relation to the primary

14.5 Use a locking tool to counterhold the flywheel

14.9 Flywheel warpage check – see text

14.10 Flywheel free rotational movement check alignment marks – see text

element of the flywheel, should not exceed 2.0 mm. If it does, the flywheel may need renewing. This can be checked by pressing the drive surface down on one side into the flywheel (flywheel horizontal) and making an alignment mark between the drive surface and the inner edge of the primary element. Now press down on the opposite side of the drive surface, and make another mark above the original one. The difference between the two marks is the lateral movement **(see illustration)**.

Refitting

13 Refitting is a reversal of removal. Use new bolts when refitting the flywheel or driveplate, and coat the threads of the bolts with locking fluid before inserting them. Tighten them to the specified torque.

15 Crankshaft oil seals –
renewal

Note: *The oil seals are a PTFE (Teflon) type and are fitted dry, without using any grease or oil. These have a wider sealing lip and have been introduced instead of the coil spring type oil seal.*

Timing belt end oil seal

1 Remove the timing belt as described in Section 7, and the crankshaft sprocket with reference to Section 8.
2 To remove the seal without removing the housing, drill two small holes diagonally opposite each other, insert self-tapping screws, and pull on the heads of the screws with pliers**(see illustration)**. Prior to removing the seal, measure it's fitted depth in the housing so that the new seal can be fitted in the same position.
3 Alternatively, to remove the oil seal complete with its housing, proceed as follows.
a) *Remove the sump as described in Section 12. This is necessary to ensure a satisfactory seal between the sump and oil seal housing on refitting.*
b) *Unbolt and remove the oil seal housing.*
c) *Working on the bench, lever the oil seal from the housing using a suitable screwdriver. Take care not to damage*

14.12 Flywheel lateral movement check marks – see text

the seal seating in the housing **(see illustration)**.
4 During oil seal installation Skoda use a guide sleeve over the end of the crankshaft (tool T10053/1), if this tool is not available, wind a length of tape around the end of the crankshaft to protect the oil seal lips as the seal (and housing, where applicable)is fitted.
5 Thoroughly clean the oil seal seating in the housing.
6 Fit a new oil seal to the housing, pressing or driving it into position using a socket or tube of suitable diameter. Ensure that the socket or tube bears only on the hard outer ring of the seal, and take care not to damage the seal lips. Press or drive the seal into position until it is seated on the shoulder in the housing. Make sure that the closed end of the seal is facing outwards.
7 If the oil seal housing has been removed, proceed as follows, otherwise proceed to paragraph 11.
8 Clean all traces of old sealant from the crankshaft oil seal housing and the cylinder block, then coat the cylinder block mating faces of the oil seal housing with a 2.0 to 3.0 mm thick bead of silicone sealant (Skoda D 176 404 A2, or equivalent). Note that the seal housing must be refitted within 5 minutes of applying the sealant.
Caution: DO NOT put excessive amounts of sealant onto the housing as it may get into the sump and block the oil pick-up pipe.
9 Refit the oil seal housing, and tighten the bolts progressively to the specified torque **(see illustration)**.

15.9 Slide the oil seal housing over the end of the crankshaft

15.2 Pull the screw and seal from place using pliers

10 Refit the sump as described in Section 12.
11 Refit the crankshaft sprocket with reference to Section 8, and the timing belt as described in Section 7.

Flywheel end oil seal

Note: *In these engines, the seal, sealing flange and sender wheel are a complete unit. Special tools are required to refit the sealing flange, and press the sender wheel onto the end of the crankshaft. It is not possible to accurately fit these parts without the tools, which may be available from Skoda (part No T10134) and are available from aftermarket automotive tool specialists.*
12 Remove the flywheel as described in Section 14, then prise the intermediate plate from the locating dowels on the cylinder block.
13 Remove the sump as described in Section 12.
14 Set the engine to TDC on number 1 cylinder as described in Section 3.
15 Remove the engine speed sensor with reference to Chapter 4A Section 4.
16 Undo the bolts securing the sealing flange to the cylinder block **(see illustration)**.
17 Insert three 6 x 35 mm bolts into the threaded holes in the sealing flange. Tighten the bolts gradually and evenly, and press the sealing flange and sender wheel from the crankshaft/cylinder block **(see illustration)**. The seal, sender wheel and sealing flange are supplied as a complete unit.
18 Ensure the mating face of the cylinder block is clean and free from debris. The new sealing flange/seal/sender wheel assembly

15.3 Prise the oil seal from the crankshaft oil seal housing

15.16 Sealing flange bolts (arrowed)

15.17 Bolt in 6 x 35 mm bolts (arrowed) and draw the sealing flange and sender wheel from place

15.19a Rotate the nut until its level with the end of the clamping surface (arrowed)...

15.19b ... then clamp it in a vice

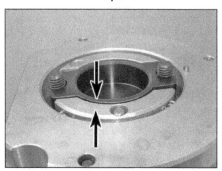

15.20 Rotate the nut until the inner part of the tool is flush with the housing (arrowed)

15.21a Remove the securing clip...

15.21b ... the hole in the sender wheel should align with the marking on the flange (arrowed)

is supplied with a sealing lip support ring, which serves as a fitting sleeve, and must not be removed prior to installation. Equally, the

sender wheel must not be separated from the assembly.

19 If using the Skoda tool, proceed as

15.22a Press the assembly downwards on a clean, flat surface...

15.22b... so the upper edge of the sender wheel is level with the edge of the flange (arrowed)

15.23 Fit the flange to the tool, ensuring the pin locates in the hole (arrowed)

15.24 With the pin engaged in the hole, tighten the 3 knurled bolts to secure the flange to the tool

follows. If using an aftermarket tool specialist's product, follow the instructions supplied with the tool. Rotate the large spindle nut until it's level with the end of the clamping surface of the spindle, then clamp the spindle in a vice **(see illustrations)**.

20 Press the tool housing downwards until it rests on the nut and washer. Rotate the nut until the inner part of the tool is at the same height as the housing**(see illustration)**.

21 Remove the seal securing clip. The hole on the sender wheel must align with the marking on the sealing flange**(see illustrations)**.

22 Place the flange outer side down on a clean, flat surface, then press the seal guide fitting sleeve (supplied ready fitted), housing, and sender wheel downwards until all the components are flat on the surface. In this position the upper edge of the sender wheel should be level with the edge of the sealing flange **(see illustrations)**.

23 Place the sealing flange on the assembly tool, so the pin locates in the hole in the sender wheel **(see illustration)**.

24 Push the sealing flange and guide fitting sleeve against the tool whilst tightening the 3 knurled bolts. Ensure the pin is still located in the sender wheel **(see illustration)**.

25 Ensure the end of the crankshaft is clean, and is locked at TDC on No 1 cylinder as described in Section 3.

26 Unbolt the large nut to the end of the spindle threads, then press the spindle inwards as far as possible**(see illustration)**.

27 Align the flat side of the assembly with the sump flange, then secure the tool to the

15.26 Unscrew the nut to the end of the thread, and push the spindle in as far as possible

15.27 Hand-tighten the Allen bolts to secure the tool to the crankshaft (arrowed)

15.28 Use 2 M7 x 35 mm bolts (arrowed) to guide the sealing flange

15.29 Push the black knob (arrowed) into the hole in the crankshaft

15.30 After tightening the spindle nut there should be an air gap between the sealing flange and the cylinder block (arrowed)

15.32 Measure the fitted depth of the sender wheel in relation to the end of the crankshaft

crankshaft using the integral Allen bolts (see illustration). Only finger-tighten the bolts.
28 Insert two M7 x 35 mm bolts to guide the sealing flange to the cylinder block (see illustration).
29 Using hand-pressure alone, push the tool assembly onto the crankshaft until the seal guide fitting sleeve contacts the crankshaft flange, then push the guide pin (black knob) into the hole in the crankshaft. This is to ensure the sender wheel reaches its correct installation position (see illustration).
30 Rotate the large nut until it makes contact with the tool housing, then tighten it to 35 Nm (26 lbf ft). After tightening this nut, a small air gap must still be present between the sealing flange and cylinder block (see illustration).
31 Unbolt the large nut, the two M7 x 35 mm bolts, the three knurled bolts and the Allen bolts securing the tool to the crankshaft. Remove the tool, and pull the seal guide fitting sleeve from place (if it didn't come out with the tool).
32 Use a vernier caliper or feeler gauge to measure the fitted depth of the sender wheel in relation to the crankshaft flange(see illustration). The correct depth is 0.5 mm.
33 If the gap is correct, fit the sealing flange bolts and tighten them to the specified torque.
34 If the gap is too small, re-attach the tool to the sealing flange and crankshaft, then refit the two M7 x 35 mm guide bolts to the flange. Tighten the large spindle nut to 40 Nm (30 lbf ft), remove the tool and measure the air gap. If the gap is still too small, re-attach the tool

and tighten the spindle nut to 45 Nm (33 lbf ft). Measure the gap again. When the gap is correct, refit the flange retaining bolts, and tighten them to the specified torque.
35 The remainder of refitting is a reversal of removal.

16 Engine/transmission mountings – inspection and renewal

Where engine mountings are being removed as part of a procedure and the intention is to refit them, make alignment marks around mounting bolts and between the mounting, vehicle body and engine / transmission bracket, with paint or marker pen, to aid positioning on re-assembly.

Inspection

1 If improved access is required, jack up the front of the vehicle, and support it securely on axle stands (see *Jacking and vehicle support*). Remove the engine top cover and the air filter, then remove the engine undershield(s).
2 Check the mounting rubbers to see if they are cracked, hardened or separated from the metal at any point; renew the mounting if any such damage or deterioration is evident.
3 Check that all the mountings are securely tightened; use a torque wrench to check if possible.
4 Using a large screwdriver or a crowbar, check for wear in the mounting by carefully

levering against it to check for free play. Where this is not possible, enlist the aid of an assistant to move the engine/transmission back-and-forth, or from side-to-side, whilst you observe the mounting. While some free play is to be expected, even from new components, excessive wear should be obvious. If excessive free play is found, check first that the fasteners are correctly secured, then renew any worn components as described in the following paragraphs.

Renewal

Note: *New mounting securing bolts will be required on refitting.*

Right-hand mounting

5 Attach a hoist and lifting tackle to the engine lifting brackets on the cylinder head, and raise the hoist to just take the weight of the engine. Alternatively the engine can be supported on a trolley jack under the engine. Use a block of wood between the sump and the head of the jack, to prevent any damage to the sump.
6 For improved access, unbolt the coolant reservoir and move it to one side, leaving the coolant hoses connected.
7 Where applicable, move any wiring harnesses, pipes or hoses to one side to enable removal of the engine mounting.
8 Unbolt the bolts securing the mounting to the engine bracket, then unbolt the bolts securing it to the body. Also, unbolt the movement limiter. Withdraw the mounting from the engine compartment.

16.9 There must be at least 10 mm between the bracket and the chassis member (arrowed)

9 Refitting is a reversal of removal, bearing in mind the following points.
a) *Use new securing bolts.*
b) *There must be at least 10 mm between the engine mounting bracket and the right-hand side chassis member* **(see illustration)**.
c) *The side of the mounting support arm must be parallel to the side of the engine mounting bracket.*
d) *Tighten all fixings to the specified torque.*

Left-hand mounting

10 Remove the engine top cover.
11 Attach a hoist and lifting tackle to the engine lifting brackets on the cylinder head, and raise the hoist to just take the weight of the engine and transmission. Alternatively the engine can be supported on a trolley jack under the transmission. Use a block of wood between the transmission and the head of the jack, to prevent any damage to the transmission.
12 Remove the battery and battery tray, as described in Chapter 5 Section 3.
13 Unbolt the bolts securing the mounting to the transmission, and the remaining bolts securing the mounting from the engine compartment.
14 Refitting is a reversal of removal, bearing in mind the following points:
a) *Use new mounting bolts.*
b) *The edges of the mounting support arm must be parallel to the edge of the mounting.*
c) *Tighten all fixings to the specified torque.*

16.18 Rear mounting arm-to-transmission bolts (arrowed)

Rear mounting (torque arm)

15 Apply the handbrake, then jack up the front of the vehicle and support securely on axle stands (see *Jacking and vehicle support*). Remove the engine undershield(s) for access to the rear mounting (torque arm).
16 Support the rear of the transmission beneath the final drive housing. To do this, use a trolley jack and block of wood, or alternatively wedge a block of wood between the transmission and the subframe.
17 Working under the vehicle, unbolt and remove the bolt securing the mounting to the subframe.
18 Unbolt the two bolts securing the mounting to the transmission, then withdraw the mounting from under the vehicle **(see illustration)**.
19 Refitting is a reversal of removal, but use new mounting securing bolts, and tighten all fixings to the specified torque.
Note: *There are two different strengths specified for the bolts into the transmission with differing torque settings, check the bolt strength marking on head of the bolts and replace with bolts of the same specification.*

17 Engine oil cooler / oil filter housing – removal and refitting

Oil cooler (engine code CEGA)

Removal

1 Raise the front of the vehicle and support it securely on axle stands (see *Jacking and vehicle support*), then remove the engine compartment undershield.
2 The oil cooler is mounted under the oil filter housing on the front of the cylinder block.
3 Position a container beneath the oil filter housing to catch escaping oil and coolant.
4 Clamp the oil cooler coolant hoses to minimise coolant spillage, then remove the clips, and disconnect the hoses from the oil cooler; be prepared for coolant spillage.
5 Undo the clamp and pull out the clip to release the right-hand charge air hose, remove the hose from the vehicle. Remove the two bolts securing the front charge air pipe to the engine, release the coolant hose clipped to it, disconnect the charge pressure sender wiring plug, release the upper clamp and move the charge air pipe to access the coolant recirculation pump mounting bracket.
6 Remove the bolt securing the coolant recirculation pump bracket to the block, and move the pump aside.
7 Unscrew the oil cooler securing bolt, using a 32m socket from the underside of the oil filter housing, then slide off the oil cooler. Recover the O-rings (taking note of their fitted positions) from the top and bottom of the oil cooler.

Refitting

8 Refitting is a reversal of removal, bearing in mind the following points:
a) *Use new oil cooler O-rings.(Make sure the upper sealing ring / gasket is located correctly and does not obscure any oil passages).*
b) *Tighten the oil cooler securing bolt to the specified torque.*
c) *On completion, check and if necessary top-up the oil and coolant levels.*

Oil filter housing (engine code CEGA)

Removal

9 Raise the front of the vehicle and support it securely on axle stands (see *Jacking and vehicle support*) and remove the engine compartment undershield.
10 Remove the air filter housing as described in Chapter 4A Section 3
11 Place the lock carrier assembly in the service position as described in Chapter 11 Section 10
12 Position a container beneath the oil filter housing to catch escaping oil and coolant.
13 Release the wiring and hoses secured to the bracket on the oil filter housing, undo the bolt securing the bracket to the filter housing and remove the bracket.
14 Release the clip and remove the charge air hose from the right side of the intercooler, undo the clamp and remove the charge air hose from the lower end of the charge air pipe. Disconnect the wiring from the charge air pressure sender and release the coolant hose clipped to the charge air pipe. Undo the charge air pipe mounting bolts and the upper hose clamp,release the charge air pipe and remove it.
15 Remove the bolt from the coolant circulation pump bracket and position the pump aside.
16 Pull out the engine oil dipstick, remove the bolts securing the dipstick guide tube, pull the guide tube out of the engine block and position it clear of the oil filter housing assembly.
17 Clamp both coolant hoses near to their connection to the oil cooler, release the hose clips and remove the hoses from their stubs on the oil cooler.
18 Release the wiring connector from the oil pressure switch, unscrew and remove the oil pressure switch. Counter-hold the union adapter and unscrew the union nut for the turbocharger oil feed pipe from the oil filter housing.
19 Unbolt the 4 bolts securing the oil filter housing to the block and remove the housing **(see illustration)**.

Refitting

20 Refitting is the reversal of removal, bearing in mind the following points.
a) *Replace all gaskets, O rings and seals.*
b) *Use new bolts to secure the oil filter*

housing, tightening in a diagonal sequence, to the specified torque.

c) *On completion, check engine oil and coolant levels and top-up if required.*

Oil cooler (engine codes CFHC, CFHF, CLCA and CLCB)

Note: *Access to the oil cooler will be greatly improved by placing the lock carrier assembly in the service position, as described in Chapter 11 Section 10*

Removal

21 Drain the cooling system with reference to Chapter 1 Section 37

22 Remove the air filter housing as described in Chapter 4A Section 3

23 Remove the oil filter element with reference to Chapter 1 Section 6

24 Position a container beneath the oil filter housing to catch escaping oil and coolant.

25 Remove the bolts securing the oil cooler to the oil filter housing, remove the oil cooler and recover the gasket **(see illustration)**.

Refitting

26 Refitting is the reversal of removal, bearing in mind the following points.

a) *Use a new gasket between the oil cooler and filter housing.*

b) *Ensure that the oil cooler is positioned on the dowel pins and mounted squarely on the gasket. Tighten the bolts in the specified torque stages using a diagonal sequence.*

c) *Fit a new filter element with new sealing ring with reference to Chapter 1 Section 6*

d) *Refill the cooling system with reference to Chapter 1 Section 37*

e) *Check and top-up the engine oil level (the level will drop especially if a new filter and/or cooler has been fitted).*

Oil filter housing (engine codes CFHC, CFHF, CLCA and CLCB)

Removal

27 Drain the cooling system with reference to Chapter 1 Section 37.

28 Remove the radiator fans and fan shroud as described in Chapter 3 Section 5

29 Remove the air filter housing as described in Chapter 4A Section 3

30 Position a container beneath the oil filter housing to catch escaping oil and coolant.

31 Remove the oil filter element with reference to Chapter 1 Section 6

32 Release the clip and remove the charge air hose from the right side of the intercooler, undo the clamp and remove the charge air hose from the lower end of the charge air pipe.

33 Disconnect the wiring from the charge air pressure/temperature sender and release the coolant hose clipped to the charge air pipe. Undo the charge air pipe mounting bolts and the upper hose clamp,release the charge air pipe and remove it.

34 Pull out the engine oil dipstick, prise out the clip securing the dipstick guide tube to the

17.19 Filter housing bolts (arrowed)

oil filter housing and remove the bolt attaching the guide tube to the throttle flap housing. Pull the dipstick guide tube out of the block and position it clear of the filter housing.

35 Release the hose clamp and remove the coolant hose from it's connection to the oil filter housing.

36 Slacken and remove the 4 bolts securing the oil filter housing to the cylinder block and remove the housing.

Refitting

37 Refitting is the reversal of removal, bearing in mind the following points.

a) *Replace all gaskets, O rings and seals.*

b) *Use new bolts to secure oil filter housing, tightening in a diagonal sequence to the specified torque.*

c) *Refill the cooling system with reference to Chapter 1 Section 37*

d) *Check and top-up the engine oil level.*

18 Oil pressure warning light switch – removal and refitting

Engine code – CEGA

Removal

1 The oil pressure warning light switch is fitted to the oil filter housing **(see illustration)**. Remove the engine top cover and air filter housing assembly (Chapter 4A Section 3) to gain access to the switch.

2 Disconnect the wiring connector and wipe clean the area around the switch.

3 Unbolt the switch from the filter housing and remove it, along with its sealing washer. If the switch is to be left removed from the engine for any length of time, plug the oil filter housing aperture.

Refitting

4 Skoda recommend that a new sealing washer is always fitted.

5 Refit the switch, complete with washer, and tighten it to the specified torque.

6 Securely reconnect the wiring connector then check and, if necessary, top-up the engine oil as described in *Weekly checks*. Refit the air filter housing assembly and the engine top cover.

17.25 Oil cooler bolts (arrowed)

Engine codes – CFHC, CFHF, CLCA and CLCB

Removal

7 The oil pressure warning light switch is fitted to the left-hand rear of the cylinder head. Remove the engine cover to gain access to the switch.

8 Squeeze and pull the connections at each end of the crankcase ventilation hose to release them and remove the hose.

9 Unfasten any vacuum pipes from the intake air ducting, release the retaining clips at each end and remove the air intake ducting from between the air mass meter and the turbocharger.

10 Disconnect the wiring connector from the oil pressure switch.

11 Remove the bolt securing the vacuum pipe to the engine lifting eye bracket, unbolt and remove the lifting eye bracket.

12 Unscrew the oil pressure switch and remove it, along with its sealing washer (where fitted). If the switch is to be left removed from the engine for any length of time, plug the oil filter housing aperture.

Refitting

13 Fit the switch, with new sealing washer (where fitted) and tighten it to the specified torque.

14 Refit the engine lifting eye bracket and fasten the vacuum pipe to it. Reconnect the oil pressure switch wiring plug.

15 Refit the intake air ducting, fastening any vacuum pipes to it that were removed during dismantling. Refit the crankcase ventilation hose by pushing together the connections.

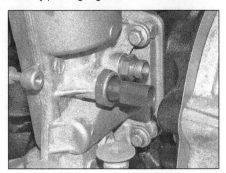

18.1 Oil pressure warning light switch

16 Check and top-up the engine oil, if required, as described in *Weekly checks*, then refit the engine top cover.

19 Oil level/temperature sensor – removal and refitting

Removal

1 Where fitted, the engine oil level/ temperature sensor is located in the base of the oil sump. Apply the handbrake, then jack up the front of the vehicle and support it on axle stands (see *Jacking and vehicle support*).

Undo the fasteners, and remove the engine undershield.
2 Position a container beneath the sump, then unscrew the drain plug (refer to Chapter 1 Section 6) and drain the engine oil. Clean the plug, fit a new sealing washer (or replace plug with integral washer) refit and tighten it to the specified torque.
3 Disconnect the oil level/temperature sensor wiring plug.
4 Release the retaining clips and remove the insulation cover from the sump.
5 Undo the securing bolts, and lower the sensor from the sump. Discard the O-ring seal, a new one must be fitted (see Chapter 2A Section 21).

Refitting

6 Clean the mating surfaces of the sensor and the sump. Smear the new O-ring seal with clean engine oil, and position it on the sensor.
7 Fit the sensor to the sump, insert the securing bolts and tighten them to the specified torque.
8 Refit the insulation cover.
9 Reconnect the sensor wiring plug
10 Refit the engine undershield, lower the vehicle to the ground.
11 Refill the engine with new oil as described in Chapter 1 Section 6.Start the engine and check for leaks.

Chapter 2 Part C
Engine removal and overhaul procedures

Contents

Degrees of difficulty

| Easy, suitable for novice with little experience | | Fairly easy, suitable for beginner with some experience | | Fairly difficult, suitable for competent DIY mechanic | | Difficult, suitable for experienced DIY mechanic | | Very difficult, suitable for expert DIY or professional | |

Specifications

Engine codes*

PD unit injector engines:
1.9 litre (1896 cc), 8-valve, SOHC	BJB, BKC, BLS and BXE
2.0 litre (1968 cc):	
8-valve, SOHC	BMM
16-valve, DOHC	BKD and BMN
Common rail injection engines:	
2.0 litre (1968 cc), 16-valve, DOHC	CBBB, CBDB and CEGA (1st Generation)
	CLCA, CLCB, CFHC and CFHF (2nd Generation)

*See 'Vehicle identification' at the end of this manual for the location of engine code markings.

Cylinder head

Cylinder head gasket surface, maximum distortion................	0.1 mm
Minimum cylinder head height................................	Head resurfacing not possible
Cylinder head gasket selection:	
Piston projection 0.91 to 1.00 mm...........................	1 hole/notch*
Piston projection 1.01 to 1.10 mm...........................	2 holes/notches*
Piston projection 1.11 to 1.20 mm...........................	3 holes/notches*

*Disregard single and double oval holes.

Valves

	Inlet	Exhaust
Valve stem diameter:		
PD unit injector engine:		
1.9 litre	6.980 mm	6.965mm
2.0 litre	5.980 mm	5.965mm
Common rail injection engine................................	5.975 mm	5.965mm
Maximum valve head deflection (end of stem flush with top of guide) .	1.3 mm	

Pistons and piston rings

Piston diameter:	
1.9 litre	79.470 mm nominal
2.0 litre	80.960 mm nominal
Ring-to-groove clearance:	
Compression rings	0.25 mm maximum
Oil control ring	0.15 mm maximum
Piston ring end gap clearance (ring 15 mm from bottom of bore):	
New:	
Compression rings	0.20 to 0.40 mm
Oil scraper ring	0.25 to 0.50 mm
Wear limit	1.0 mm

Cylinder block

Bore diameter:
1.9 litre . . . . 79.51 mm nominal
2.0 litre . . . . 81.01 mm nominal

Crankshaft

Spigot needle bearing depth . . . . 1.5 mm
Endfloat:
New . . . . 0.07 to 0.17 mm
Wear limit . . . . 0.37 mm
Main bearing journal diameter . . . . 54.00 mm nominal
Big-end bearing journal diameter . . . . 50.90 mm nominal

Torque wrench settings

Refer to Chapters 2A or 2B

---

1 General Information

1 Included in this Part of Chapter 2 are details of removing the engine from the car and general overhaul procedures for the cylinder head, cylinder block and all other engine internal components.
2 The information given ranges from advice concerning preparation for an overhaul and the purchase of parts, to detailed step-by-step procedures covering removal, inspection, renovation and refitting of engine internal components.
3 After Section 5, all instructions are based on the assumption that the engine has been removed from the car. For information concerning in-car engine repair, as well as the removal and refitting of those external components necessary for full overhaul, refer to the relevant in-car repair procedure section (Chapters 2A or 2B) and to Section 5 of this Chapter. Ignore any preliminary dismantling operations described in the relevant in-car repair sections that are no longer relevant once the engine has been removed from the car.
4 Apart from torque wrench settings, which are given at the beginning of the relevant in-car repair procedure in Chapters 2A or 2B, all specifications relating to engine overhaul are at the beginning of this Part of Chapter 2.

2 Engine overhaul –
general information

1 It is not always easy to determine when, or if, an engine should be completely overhauled, as a number of factors must be considered.
2 High mileage is not necessarily an indication that an overhaul is needed, while low mileage does not preclude the need for an overhaul. Frequency of servicing is probably the most important consideration. An engine which has had regular and frequent oil and filter changes, as well as other required maintenance, should

give many thousands of miles of reliable service. Conversely, a neglected engine may require an overhaul very early in its life.
3 Excessive oil consumption is an indication that piston rings, valve seals and/or valve guides are in need of attention. Make sure that oil leaks are not responsible before deciding that the rings and/or guides are worn. Perform a compression test, as described in the relevant Part A or B of this Chapter, to determine the likely cause of the problem.
4 Check the oil pressure with a gauge fitted in place of the oil pressure switch, and compare it with that specified (see Chapter 2A Specifications or Chapter 2B Specifications). If it is extremely low, the main and big-end bearings, and/or the oil pump, are probably worn out.
5 Loss of power, rough running, knocking or metallic engine noises, excessive valve gear noise, and high fuel consumption may also point to the need for an overhaul, especially if they are all present at the same time. If a complete service does not remedy the situation, major mechanical work is the only solution.
6 An engine overhaul involves restoring all internal parts to the specification of a new engine. During an overhaul, the pistons and the piston rings are renewed. New main and big-end bearings are generally fitted; if necessary, the crankshaft may be renewed, to restore the journals. The valves are also serviced as well, since they are usually in less-than-perfect condition at this point. While the engine is being overhauled, other components, such as the starter and alternator, can be overhauled as well. The end result should be an as-new engine that will give many trouble-free miles.
7 Critical cooling system components such as the hoses, thermostat and coolant pump should be renewed when an engine is overhauled. The radiator should be checked carefully, to ensure that it is not clogged or leaking. Also, it is a good idea to renew the oil pump whenever the engine is overhauled.
8 Before beginning the engine overhaul, read through the entire procedure, to familiarise

yourself with the scope and requirements of the job. Overhauling an engine is not difficult if you carefully follow all of the instructions, have the necessary tools and equipment, and pay close attention to all specifications. It can, however, be time-consuming. Plan on the car being off the road for a minimum of two weeks, especially if parts must be taken to an engineering works for repair or reconditioning. Check on the availability of parts and make sure that any necessary special tools and equipment are obtained in advance. Most work can be done with typical hand tools, although a number of precision measuring tools are required for inspecting parts to determine if they must be renewed. Often the engineering works will handle the inspection of parts and offer advice concerning reconditioning and renewal.
9 Always wait until the engine has been completely dismantled, and until all components (especially the cylinder block and the crankshaft) have been inspected before deciding what service and repair operations must be performed by an engineering works. The condition of these components will be the major factor to consider when determining whether to overhaul the original engine, or to buy a reconditioned unit. Do not, therefore, purchase parts or have overhaul work done on other components until they have been thoroughly inspected. As a general rule, time is the primary cost of an overhaul, so it does not pay to fit worn or sub-standard parts.
10 As a final note, to ensure maximum life and minimum trouble from a reconditioned engine, everything must be assembled with care, in a spotlessly-clean environment.

3 Engine removal –
preparation and precautions

1 If you have decided that the engine must be removed for overhaul or major repair work, several preliminary steps should be taken.
2 Locating a suitable place to work is extremely important. Adequate work space,

along with storage space for the vehicle, will be needed. If a workshop or garage is not available, at the very least a solid, level, clean work surface is required.

3 If possible, clear some shelving close to the work area and use it to store the engine components and ancillaries as they are removed and dismantled. In this manner, the components stand a better chance of staying clean and undamaged during the overhaul. Laying out components in groups, together with their fixings, bolts, screws, etc, will save time and avoid confusion when the engine is refitted.

4 Clean the engine compartment and engine before beginning the removal procedure; this will help visibility and help to keep tools clean.

5 The help of an assistant is essential; there are certain instances when one person cannot safely perform all of the operations required to remove the engine from the vehicle. Safety is of primary importance, considering the potential hazards involved in this kind of operation. A second person should always be in attendance to offer help in an emergency. If this is the first time you have removed an engine, advice and aid from someone more experienced would also be beneficial.

6 Plan the operation ahead of time. Before starting work, obtain (or arrange for the hire of) all of the tools and equipment you will need. Access to the following items will allow the task of removing and refitting the engine to be completed safely and with relative ease: a heavy-duty trolley jack – rated in excess of the weight of the engine, complete sets of spanners and sockets as described in the back of this manual, wooden blocks, and plenty of rags and cleaning solvent for mopping-up spilled oil, coolant and fuel. A selection of different sized plastic storage bins will also prove useful for keeping dismantled components grouped together. If any of the equipment must be hired, make sure that you arrange for it in advance, and perform all of the operations possible without it beforehand; this may save you time and money.

7 Plan on the vehicle being out of use for quite a while, especially if you intend to carry out an engine overhaul. Read through the whole of this Section and work out a strategy based on your own experience and the tools, time and workspace available to you. Some of the overhaul processes may have to be carried out by a Skoda dealer or an engineering works – these establishments often have busy schedules, so it would be prudent to consult them before removing or dismantling the engine, to get an idea of the amount of time required to carry out the work.

8 When removing the engine from the vehicle, be methodical about the disconnection of external components. Labelling cables and hoses as they are removed will greatly assist the refitting process.

9 Always be extremely careful when lifting the engine from the engine bay. Serious injury can result from careless actions. If help is required, it is better to wait until it is available rather than risk personal injury and/or damage to components by continuing alone. By planning ahead and taking your time, a job of this nature, although major, can be accomplished successfully and without incident.

10 Note that the engine should ideally be removed with the vehicle standing on all four roadwheels, but access to the exhaust system downpipe and lower bolts will be improved if the vehicle can be temporarily raised onto axle stands.

4 Engine – removal and refitting

Removal

1 On common rail injection models with air conditioning, have the refrigerant discharged by a suitably-equipped specialist.

2 Select a solid, level surface to park the vehicle on. Give yourself enough space to move around it easily.

3 Remove the battery and battery tray as described in Chapter 5 Section 3.

4 Apply the handbrake, then jack up the front of the vehicle and support it on axle stands (see *Jacking and vehicle support*). Remove both front roadwheels.

5 Remove the retaining bolts, and remove engine compartment undershield.

6 Remove the cover from the top of the engine.

4.12 Disconnect the pressure sensor wiring plug and undo the bracket retaining bolt (arrowed)

7 Move the lock carrier to the 'Service position' as described in Chapter 11 Section 10. If improved access is required, remove the lock carrier assembly as described in Chapter 11 Section 10.

8 Remove the air cleaner assembly as described in Chapter 4A Section 3.

PD unit injector engines

9 Note their fitted positions, and disconnect the coolant, fuel supply and return hoses at the right-hand end of the cylinder head. Plug the openings to prevent contamination.

10 Remove the auxiliary drivebelt as described in Chapter 1 Section 11.

11 On models with air conditioning, unbolt the compressor and secure it to the lock carrier without disconnecting, or kinking, the refrigerant pipes.

Common rail injection engines

12 Disconnect the wiring plug, undo the retaining bolt, and remove the exhaust gas pressure sensor bracket by pushing it forwards (see illustration).

13 Disconnect the wiring plug, unclip the fuel hoses from the clips, then release the clamps and disconnect the hoses from the filter (see illustrations).

14 Disconnect the fuel temperature sensor wiring plug, release the clamp and disconnect the fuel supply hose from the high-pressure pump (see illustration).

15 Undo the 2 retaining bolts and remove the supplementary fuel pump (see illustration).

16 Undo the retaining bolts and disconnect

4.13a Disconnect the wiring plug and unclip the hoses (arrowed)

4.13b Note their positions and disconnect the hoses from the filter

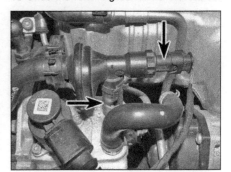
4.14 Disconnect the fuel temperature sensor and the supply hose (arrowed)

4.15 Undo the supplementary fuel pump retaining bolts (arrowed) at the right-hand end of the cylinder head

4.17 The coolant circulation pump bracket retaining bolt (arrowed – shown with the charge air pipe removed)

4.18 Charge pressure regulating valve (arrowed)

the refrigerant pipes from the air conditioning compressor. Plug the pipe openings to prevent contamination.

17 Undo the bolt securing the electric coolant circulation pump to the front of the cylinder block **(see illustration)**.

18 Detach the charge pressure regulating valve from the plenum chamber bulkhead and lay it on the engine, together with the vacuum hoses **(see illustration)**.

All engines

19 Remove the engine control module as described in Chapter 4A Section 4.

20 Open the wiring guide catches of the left-hand chassis member, then disconnect the engine wiring harness connector beneath the left-hand headlight, and lift the wiring harness from the guide **(see illustration)**. Lay the harness to one side.

21 Disconnect the wiring plug adjacent to the left-hand end of the radiator, and undo the bolt securing the earth strap to the chassis member **(see illustration)**.

22 Disconnect the alternator positive lead from the central electrics box, and the wiring from the starter motor**(see illustration)**.

23 On models with the DSG automatic gearbox, disconnect the selector cable from the transmission as described in Chapter 7B Section 4, then disconnect the Mechatronic connector from the gearbox by rotating the catch and pulling the connector from place**(see illustration)**.

24 On models with the manual gearbox, disconnect the gearchange cables from the transmission as described in Chapter 7A Section 2, then disconnect the hydraulic hose from the clutch slave cylinder as described in Chapter 6 Section 5 (plug the openings to

prevent contamination), and the wiring plug from the reversing light switch.

25 Slacken the clamp and detach the air pipe from the throttle body **(see illustration)**.

26 Disconnect the hose from the vacuum pump at the left-hand end of the cylinder head.

27 Remove both driveshafts as described in Chapter 8 Section 2.

28 Remove the front subframe with reference to Chapter 10 Section 21. Note that there is no need to detach the steering gear or anti-roll bar from the subframe.

29 Remove the particulate filter/catalytic converter (as applicable) as described in Chapter 4B Section 5.

30 Remove any remaining charge air pipes.

31 Disconnect the heater pipes at the quick-release couplings on the plenum chamber bulkhead**(see illustration)**.

4.20 Disconnect the wiring plug beneath the left-hand headlight (arrowed – headlight removed for clarity)

4.21 Disconnect the wiring plug and the earth strap (arrowed)

4.22 Alternator positive lead (arrowed) at the central electrics box

4.23 Disconnect the Mechatronic connector (arrowed) from the DSG transmission

4.25 Remove the air pipe (arrowed) – common rail engine shown

4.31 Prise out the clips, and disconnect the heater hoses at the bulkhead

32 Note their fitted positions and disconnect any remaining coolant/vacuum hoses from the engine/transmission assembly.

33 Attach a suitable hoist to the engine, and lift the engine and transmission slightly. Make sure that the engine is adequately supported. Alternatively, support the engine/transmission from underneath with trolley jacks, etc. Take the weight of the engine/transmission.

34 Unbolt the rear engine support/torque arm from the transmission**(see illustration)**. Note that the black steel bracket should not be separated from the aluminium arm.

35 Unbolt the right- and left-hand engine mountings with reference to Chapter 2A Section 18 or 2B Section 16.

36 Make a final check to ensure that all relevant wiring, hoses and pipes have been disconnected, then carefully lower the engine and transmission from the engine compartment, and withdraw forwards from the front of the car.

Separation

37 Remove the starter motor (Chapter 5 Section 9).

38 Where applicable, undo the bolt securing the small engine-to-transmission plate to the transmission adjacent to the right-hand driveshaft flange **(see illustration)**.

39 Ensure that both engine and transmission are adequately supported, then unbolt the remaining engine-to-transmission bolts, noting the location of each bolt, and the locations of any brackets secured by the bolts.

40 Carefully withdraw the transmission from the engine, ensuring that the weight of the transmission is not allowed to hang on the input shaft while it is engaged with the clutch friction disc. Recover the engine-to-transmission plate.

Reconnection and refitting

41 Reconnection and refitting are a reversal of removal, bearing in mind the following points:
a) Smear the splines of the transmission input shaft with a little high melting-point grease: Skoda G 052 133 A2 – auto models, or Skoda G 000 100 – manual models.
b) Ensure that any brackets noted before removal are in place on the engine-to-transmission bolts.
c) Tighten all fixings to the specified torque, where given.
d) Where applicable, have the air conditioning system recharged with refrigerant by a suitably-qualified professional.
e) Ensure that all wiring, hoses and pipes are correctly reconnected and routed as noted before removal.
f) Ensure that the fuel lines are correctly reconnected.
g) On completion, refill the cooling system as described in Chapter 1 Section 37

4.34 Rear engine support retaining bolts (arrowed)

5 Engine overhaul – preliminary information

1 It is much easier to dismantle and work on the engine if it is mounted on a portable engine stand. These stands can often be hired from a tool hire shop. Before the engine is mounted on a stand, the flywheel should be removed, so that the stand bolts can be tightened into the end of the cylinder block/crankcase. **Note:** *Do not measure cylinder bore dimensions with the engine mounted on this type of stand.*

2 If a stand is not available, it is possible to dismantle the engine with it blocked up on a sturdy workbench, or on the floor. Be very careful not to tip or drop the engine when working without a stand.

3 If you intend to obtain a reconditioned engine, all ancillaries must be removed first, to be transferred to the new engine (just as they will if you are doing a complete engine overhaul yourself). These components include the following:
a) Alternator (including mounting brackets) and starter motor (Chapter 5 Section 5 and Chapter 5 Section 9).
b) The glow plug/preheating system components (Chapter 5 Section 11).
c) All fuel system components, including all sensors and actuators (Chapter 4A).
d) The tandem/vacuum pump (Chapters 4A Section 10 and Chapter 9 Section 22).
e) All electrical switches, actuators and sensors, and the engine wiring harness (Chapter 12).
f) Inlet and exhaust manifolds, and turbocharger (Chapter 4A Section 6, Chapter 4A Section 11 and Chapter 4B Section 4).
g) The engine oil level dipstick and its tube.
h) Flywheel (Chapters 2A Section 16 and Chapter 2B Section 14).
i) Clutch components (Chapter 6 Section 6).
Note: When removing the external components from the engine, pay close attention to details that may be helpful or important during refitting. Note the fitted position of gaskets, seals, spacers, pins, washers, bolts, and other small components.

4.38 Remove the bolt (arrowed) securing the engine-to-transmission plate

4 If you are obtaining a short engine (the engine cylinder block/crankcase, crankshaft, pistons and connecting rods, all fully assembled), then the cylinder head, sump, oil pump, timing belt (together with its tensioner and covers), auxiliary belt (together with its tensioner), coolant pump, thermostat housing, coolant outlet elbows, oil filter housing and where applicable oil cooler will also have to be removed.

5 If you are planning a full overhaul, the engine can be dismantled in the order given below:
a) Inlet and exhaust manifolds (see Chapter 4A Section 6 and Chapter 4B Section 4).
b) Timing belt, sprockets and tensioner (see Chapter 2A Section 7 and 2A Section 8 or Chapter 2B Section 7 and 2B Section 8).
c) Cylinder head (see Chapter 2A Section 13 or Chapter 2B Section 11).
d) Flywheel (see Chapter 2A Section 16 or Chapter 2B Section 14).
e) Sump (see Chapter 2A Section 14 or Chapter 2B Section 12).
f) Oil pump and balancer shaft assembly (see Chapter 2A Section 15 or Chapter 2B Section 13).
g) Piston/connecting rod assemblies (see Section 7).
h) Crankshaft (see Section 8).

6 Cylinder head – dismantling, cleaning, inspection and reassembly

Note: *New and reconditioned cylinder heads are available from Skoda, and from engine specialists. Specialist tools are required for the dismantling and inspection procedures, and new components may not be readily available. It may, therefore, be more practical for the home mechanic to buy a reconditioned head, rather than to dismantle, inspect and recondition the original head.*

Dismantling

1 Remove the cylinder head from the engine block as described in Part A or B of this Chapter. Also remove the camshafts, rockers and hydraulic tappets as described in Part A or B of this Chapter.

6.4 Keep groups of components together in labelled bags or boxes

6.5 Compress the valve springs with a compressor tool

6.6a Remove the upper spring seat...

6.6b ...and valve spring

2 Remove the injectors (if not already done so) and glow plugs (see Chapters 4A Section 5 and Chapter 5 Section 11).

3 Where applicable, remove the rear coolant outlet elbow together with its gasket/O-ring.

4 It is important that groups of components are kept together when they are removed and, if still serviceable, refitted in the same groups. If they are refitted randomly, accelerated wear leading to early failure will occur. Stowing groups of components in plastic bags or storage bins will help to keep everything in the right order – label them according to their fitted location, eg, No 1 exhaust, No 2 inlet, etc **(see illustration)**. Note that No 1 cylinder is nearest the timing belt end of the engine.

5 Turn the cylinder head over, and rest it on one side. Using a valve spring compressor, compress each valve spring in turn, extracting the split collets when the upper valve spring seat has been pushed far enough down the valve stem to free them. If the spring seat sticks, tap the upper jaw of the compressor with a hammer to free it **(see illustration)**.

6 Release the valve spring compressor, and remove the upper spring seat and single valve spring or double valve springs (depending on model) **(see illustrations)**.

7 Use a pair of pliers or a special removal tool to extract the valve stem oil seal, then remove the lower spring seat from the valve guide. Withdraw the valve itself from the head gasket side of the cylinder head. Repeat this process for the remaining valves **(see illustrations)**.

Cleaning

8 Using a suitable degreasing agent, remove all traces of oil deposits from the cylinder head, paying particular attention to the journal bearings, hydraulic tappet bores, valve

guides and oilways. Scrape off any traces of old gasket from the mating surfaces, taking care not to score or gouge them. If using emery paper, do not use a grade of less than 100. Turn the head over and using a blunt blade, scrape any carbon deposits from the combustion chambers and ports. Finally, wash the entire head casting with a suitable solvent to remove the remaining debris.

9 Clean the valve heads and stems using a fine wire brush. If the valve is heavily coked, scrape off the majority of the deposits with a blunt blade first, then use the wire brush.

10 Thoroughly clean the remainder of the components using solvent and allow them to dry completely. Discard the oil seals, as new ones must be fitted when the cylinder head is reassembled.

Inspection

Cylinder head

11 Examine the head casting closely to identify any damage or cracks that may have developed. Pay particular attention to the areas around the valve seats and spark plug holes. If cracking is discovered in this area, Skoda state that the cylinder head may be re-used, provided the cracks are no larger than 0.5 mm wide. More serious damage will mean the renewal of the cylinder head.

12 Moderately pitted and scorched valve seats can be repaired by grinding in the valves in during reassembly, as described later in this Section. The valve seats must not be recut.

13 Measure any distortion of the gasket surfaces using a straight-edge and a set of feeler blades. Take one measurement longitudinally on both the inlet and exhaust manifold mating surfaces. Take several measurements across the head gasket surface, to assess the level of distortion in all planes **(see illustration)**. Compare the measurements with the figures in the Specifications. If the distortion exceeds the specification, the cylinder head may need to be renewed – no machining is recommended. Consult an engine reconditioning specialist.

Valves and associated components

Note: *On all engines, the valve heads cannot be recut, although they may be ground in.*

14 Examine each valve closely for signs of

6.7a Use a removal tool...

6.7b ...to pull the valve stem oil seal from place

6.7c Remove the valves from the gasket side of the cylinder head

6.13 Measure the gasket surface distortion with a straight-edge and feeler gauges

6.17 Measure the maximum deflection of the valve in its guide using a DTI gauge

6.19 Measure the free length of each valve spring

wear. Inspect the valve stems for wear ridges, scoring or variations in diameter; measure their diameters at several points along their lengths with a micrometer.

15 The valve heads should not be cracked, badly pitted or charred. Note that light pitting of the valve head can be rectified by grinding in the valves during reassembly, as described later in this Section.

16 Check that the valve stem end face is free from excessive pitting or indentation; this would be caused by defective hydraulic tappets.

17 Insert each valve into its respective guide in the cylinder head and set up a DTI gauge against the edge of the valve head. With the valve end face flush with the top of the valve guide, measure the maximum side-to-side deflection of the valve in its guide (see illustration).

18 If the measurement exceeds that given in the Specifications, the valve and valve guide should be renewed as a pair. Note that the valve guides are an interference fit in the cylinder head and their removal requires access to a hydraulic press. For this reason, it would be wise to entrust the job to an engine reconditioning specialist.

19 Using vernier calipers, measure the free length of each of the valve springs. As a manufacturer's figure is not quoted, the only way to check the length of the springs is by comparison with a new component. Note that valve springs are usually renewed during a major engine overhaul (see illustration).

20 Stand each spring on its end on a flat surface, against an engineer's square (see illustration). Check the squareness of the spring visually, and renew it if it appears distorted.

Reassembly

21 To achieve a gas-tight seal between the valves and their seats, it will be necessary to grind in (or lap in) the valves. To complete this process you will need a quantity of fine/coarse grinding paste and a grinding tool – this can either be of the rubber sucker type, or the automatic type which is driven by a rotary power tool.

22 Smear a small quantity of fine grinding paste on the sealing face of the valve head.

6.20 Check the squareness of the valve springs

Turn the cylinder head over so that the combustion chambers are facing upwards and insert the valve into the correct guide. Attach the grinding tool to the valve head and using a backward/forward rotary action, grind the valve head into its seat. Periodically lift the valve and rotate it to redistribute the grinding paste (see illustration).

23 Continue this process until the contact between valve and seat produces an unbroken, matt grey ring of uniform width, on both faces. Repeat the operation on the remaining valves.

24 If the valves and seats are so badly pitted that coarse grinding paste must be used, bear in mind that there is a maximum protrusion of the end of the valve stem from the valve guide. Refer to a Skoda dealer or engine reconditioning specialist. If this dimension is outside the limit due to excessive grinding-in, the hydraulic tappets may not operate correctly.

25 Assuming the repair is feasible, work as

6.27a Lubricate the valve stem with clean engine oil

6.22 Grind in the valves with a reciprocating rotary motion

described previously but use coarse grinding paste initially, to achieve a dull finish on the valve face and seat. Wash off the coarse paste with solvent and repeat the process using fine grinding paste to obtain the correct finish.

26 When all the valves have been ground in, remove all traces of grinding paste from the cylinder head and valves with solvent, and allow them to dry completely.

27 Working on one valve at a time, lubricate the valve stem with clean engine oil, and insert it into the guide. Fit one of the protective plastic sleeves supplied with the new valve stem oil seals over the valve end face – this will protect the oil seal whilst it is being fitted (see illustrations).

28 Fit the lower spring seat (where one is fitted) over the valve guide.

29 Dip a new valve stem seal in clean engine oil, and carefully push it over the valve and onto the top of the valve guide – take care

6.27b Fit a protective sleeve over the valve stem before fitting the oil seal

6.29a Fit a new stem seal over the valve

6.29b Use a special installer or long reach socket to fit the valve stem oil seals

6.30 Fit the valve spring(s)

6.31a Fit the upper seat over the top of the valve spring

6.31b Use grease to hold the two halves of the spring collets in the groove

not to damage the stem seal as it passes over the valve end face. Use a suitable long reach socket or special installer to press it firmly into position **(see illustrations)**. Remove the protective sleeve.

30 Locate the valve spring(s) over the valve stem **(see illustration)**.

31 Fit the upper seat over the top of the springs, then using a valve spring compressor, compress the springs until the upper seat is pushed beyond the collet grooves in the valve stem. Refit the split collet, using a dab of grease to hold the two halves in the grooves **(see illustrations)**. Gradually release the spring compressor, checking that the collet remains correctly seated as the spring extends. When correctly seated, the upper seat should force the two halves of the collet together, and hold them securely in the grooves in the end of the valve.

32 Repeat this process for the remaining

sets of valve components. To settle the components after installation, strike the end of each valve stem with a mallet, using a block of wood to protect the stem from damage. Check before progressing any further that the spilt collets remain firmly held in the end of the valve stem by the upper spring seat.

33 The remainder of refitting is a reversal of removal.

7 Piston/connecting rod assemblies – removal and inspection

Removal

1 Refer to Part A or B of this Chapter (as applicable) and remove the cylinder head, flywheel, sump and oil pump/balancer shaft assembly.

2 Inspect the tops of the cylinder bores for ridges at the point where the pistons reach top dead centre. These must be removed otherwise the pistons may be damaged when they are pushed out of their bores. Use a scraper or ridge reamer to remove the ridges.

3 Rotate the crankshaft until piston No 1 is at bottom dead centre; piston No 4 will also be at bottom dead centre. Unless they are already identified, mark the big-end bearing caps and connecting rods with their respective piston numbers, using a centre-punch or a scribe **(see illustration)**. Note the orientation of the bearing caps in relation to the connecting rod; it may be difficult to see the manufacturer's markings at this stage, so scribe alignment arrows on them both to ensure correct reassembly.

4 Unbolt the bearing cap bolts/nuts, half a turn at a time, until they can be removed and the cap withdrawn **(see illustrations)**. Recover the bottom shell bearing, and tape it to the cap for safe-keeping. Note that if the shell bearings are to be re-used, they must be refitted to the same connecting rod.

5 Drive the piston out of the top of the bore using a piece of wooden dowel or a hammer handle. As the piston and connecting rod emerge, recover the top shell bearing and tape it to the connecting rod for safe-keeping. On engines fitted with piston cooling jets at the bottom of the cylinders, take care not to allow the connecting rod to damage the jet as the piston is being removed.

6 Remove No 4 piston and connecting rod in the same manner, then turn the crankshaft through half a turn and remove No 2 and 3

7.3 Mark the big-end caps and connecting rods with their cylinder numbers

7.4a Unbolt the big-end cap bolts...

7.4b ...and remove the cap

7.7a Remove the piston cooling jet retaining bolts...

7.7b ...and withdraw the jets from their mounting holes

7.7c Piston cooling jet and retaining bolt

7.8a Insert a small screwdriver into the slot and prise out the circlips

7.8b Push out the gudgeon pin to separate the piston and connecting rod

7.9 Piston rings can be removed using an old feeler gauge

pistons and connecting rods. Remember to maintain the components in their cylinder groups whilst they are in a dismantled state.

7 If applicable, remove the retaining bolts and withdraw the piston cooling jets from the bottom of the cylinder **(see illustrations)**.

Inspection

8 Check the orientation of the piston to the connecting rod (see paragraph 19), then insert a small flat-bladed screwdriver into the removal slot and prise the gudgeon pin circlips from each piston. Push out the gudgeon pin, and separate the piston and connecting rod **(see illustrations)**. Discard the circlips as new items must be fitted on reassembly. If the pin proves difficult to remove, heat the piston to 60°C with hot water – the resulting expansion will then allow the two components to be separated.

9 Before an inspection of the pistons can be carried out, the existing piston rings must be removed, using a removal/installation tool, or an old feeler blade if such a tool is not available. Always remove the upper piston rings first, expanding them to clear the piston crown. The rings are very brittle and will snap if they are stretched too much – sharp edges are produced when this happens, so protect your eyes and hands. Discard the rings on removal, as new items must be fitted when the engine is reassembled **(see illustration)**.

10 Use a section of old piston ring to scrape the carbon deposits out of the ring grooves, taking care not to score or gouge the edges of the groove.

11 Carefully scrape away all traces of carbon from the tops of the pistons**(see illustration)**. A hand-held wire brush (or a piece of fine emery cloth) can be used, once the majority of the deposits have been scraped away. Be careful not to remove any metal from the piston, as it is relatively soft. **Note:** *Make sure each piston is kept identified for position during cleaning*.

12 Once the deposits have been removed, clean the pistons and connecting rods with paraffin or a suitable solvent, and dry thoroughly. Make sure that the oil return holes in the ring grooves are clear.

13 Examine the pistons for signs of excessive wear or damage. Some normal wear will be apparent, in the form of a vertical 'grain' on the piston thrust surfaces and a slight looseness of the top compression ring in its groove. Abnormal wear should be carefully

7.11 The piston crown

examined, to assess whether the component is still serviceable and what the cause of the wear might be.

14 Scuffing or scoring of the piston skirt may indicate that the engine has been overheating, through inadequate cooling or lubrication. Scorch marks on the skirt indicate that gas blow-by has occurred, perhaps caused by worn bores or piston rings. Burnt areas on the piston crown are usually an indication of pre-ignition, pinking or detonation. In extreme cases, the piston crown may be melted by operating under these conditions. Corrosion pit marks in the piston crown indicate that coolant has seeped into the combustion chamber. The faults causing these symptoms must be corrected before the engine is brought back into service, or the same damage will recur.

15 Check the pistons, connecting rods, gudgeon pins and bearing caps for cracks. Lay the connecting rods on a flat surface, and look along the length to see if it appears bent or twisted. If you have doubts about their condition, get them measured at an engineering workshop. Inspect the small-end bush bearing in the connecting rod for signs of wear or cracking.

16 Have the diameter of the pistons checked by an engine reconditioning specialist at the same time as the cylinder block is inspected.

17 Locate a new piston ring in the appropriate groove and measure the ring-to-groove clearance using a feeler blade **(see illustration)**. Note that the rings are of different widths, so use the correct ring for

7.17 Measure the piston ring-to-groove clearance using a feeler gauge

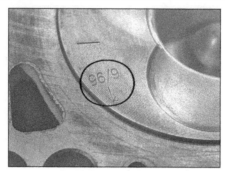

7.19a The piston crown is marked with an arrow which must point towards the timing belt end of the engine

the groove. Compare the measurements with those listed; if the clearances are outside of the tolerance band, then the piston must be renewed. Confirm this by checking the width of the piston ring with a micrometer.

18 Examine the small-end bearing and gudgeon pin for wear and damage. If excessive, the gudgeon pin will have to be renewed and a new bush fitted to the connecting rod. This work must be entrusted to an engine reconditioning specialist.

19 The orientation of the piston with respect to the connecting rod must be correct when the two are reassembled. The piston crown is marked with an arrow (which may be obscured by carbon deposits); this must point towards the timing belt end of the

engine when the piston is installed. On some engines, the connecting rod and its bearing cap both have recesses/lugs machined into them, close to their mating surfaces – these recesses/lugs must both face the same way as the arrow on the piston crown (ie, towards the timing belt end of the engine) when correctly installed **(see illustrations)**. Reassemble the two components to satisfy this requirement. Other engines are fitted with 'fractured' split connecting rods. On these engines, the bearing caps are split from the connecting rod during the manufacturing process. The resultant mating surfaces are unique, and consequently, will only fit properly to their original positions. Any attempt to fit them in an alternative position

with ruin both connecting rod and bearing cap.

20 Lubricate the gudgeon pin and small-end bush with clean engine oil. Slide the pin into the piston, engaging the connecting rod small-end. Fit two new circlips to the piston at either end of the gudgeon pin. Repeat this operation for the remaining pistons.

8 Crankshaft – removal and inspection

Note: *If no work is to be done on the pistons and connecting rods, then removal of the cylinder head and pistons will not be necessary. Instead, the pistons need only be pushed far enough up the bores so that the connecting rods are positioned clear of the crankpins. The use of an engine stand is strongly recommended.*

Removal

1 With reference to Chapter 2A or 2B as applicable, carry out the following:
a) *Remove the timing belt and crankshaft sprocket.*
b) *Remove the flywheel.*
c) *Remove the sump, oil pump and balancer shaft assembly.*
d) *Remove the crankshaft oil seals and housings.*

2 Remove the pistons and connecting rods or disconnect them from the crankshaft as described in Section 7 (see Note above).

3 With the cylinder block upside down on the bench, carry out a check of the crankshaft endfloat as follows. **Note:** *This can only be accomplished when the crankshaft is still installed in the cylinder block/crankcase, but is free to move.* Set up a DTI gauge so that the probe is in line with the crankshaft axis and is in contact with a fixed point on the end of the crankshaft. Push the crankshaft along its axis to the end of its travel, and then zero the gauge. Push the crankshaft fully the other way, and record the endfloat indicated on the dial **(see illustration)**. Compare the result with the figure given in the Specifications and establish whether new thrustwashers are required.

4 If a dial gauge is not available, feeler blades

7.19b Piston assembly

1 Piston	4 Connecting rod	7 Oil jet for piston cooling	9 Big-end bearing cap bolts
2 Gudgeon pin	5 Bearing shell	8 Oil jet retaining bolt	10 Piston rings
3 Circlips	6 Bearing shell		11 Bearing cap
A Connecting rod/bearing cap identification marks		B Connecting rod/bearing cap orientation marks	

8.3 Measure the crankshaft endfloat using a DTI gauge...

8.4 ...or feeler gauges

8.5 Manufacturer's identification markings on the main bearing caps (arrowed)

8.7 Lift the crankshaft from the crankcase

can be used. First push the crankshaft fully towards the flywheel end of the engine, then use a feeler blade to measure the gap between cylinder No 3 crankpin web and the main bearing thrustwasher **(see illustration)**. Compare the results with the Specifications.

5 Observe the manufacturer's identification marks on the main bearing caps. The number indicates the cap position in the crankcase, as counted from the timing belt end of the engine **(see illustration)**.

6 Loosen the main bearing cap bolts half a turn at a time, until they can be removed. Using a soft-faced mallet, strike the caps lightly to free them from the crankcase. Recover the lower main bearing shells, using tape to attach them to the cap for safe-keeping. Mark them to aid identification, but do not score or scratch them in any way. Remove the thrustwashers from each side of the No 3 main bearing cap where applicable.

7 Carefully lift the crankshaft out, taking care not to dislodge the upper main bearing shells **(see illustration)**.

8 Extract the upper main bearing shells from the crankcase, and tape them to their respective bearing caps. Remove the two thrustwasher bearings from either side of No 3 bearing saddle (where applicable).

9 With the shell bearings removed, observe the recesses machined into the bearing caps and crankcase – these provide location for the lugs which protrude from the shell bearings and so prevent them from being fitted incorrectly.

Inspection

10 Wash the crankshaft in a suitable solvent and allow it to dry. Flush the oil holes thoroughly, to ensure they are not blocked.

11 Inspect the main bearing and crankpin journals carefully. If uneven wear, cracking, scoring or pitting are evident then the crankshaft should be reground by an engineering workshop, and refitted to the engine with undersize bearings.

12 Have the crankshaft measured and inspected by an engine reconditioning specialist. If the crankshaft is worn and can be reground, they will be able to carry out the work and supply suitable undersize bearing shells.

9 Cylinder block/crankcase – cleaning and inspection

Cleaning

1 Remove all external components as applicable including lifting eyes, mounting brackets, the coolant pump, oil cooler and filter mounting housing and electrical switches/sensors from the block. For complete cleaning, the core plugs should ideally be removed. Drill a small hole in the plugs, then insert a self-tapping screw into the hole. Extract the plugs by pulling on the screw with a pair of grips, or by using a slide hammer.

2 Scrape all traces of gasket and sealant from the cylinder block/crankcase, taking care not to damage the sealing surfaces.

3 Remove all oil gallery plugs (where fitted). The plugs are usually very tight – they may have to be drilled out, and the holes re-tapped. Use new plugs when the engine is reassembled.

4 If the casting is extremely dirty, it should be steam-cleaned. After this, clean all oil holes and galleries one more time. Flush all internal passages with warm water until the water runs clear. Dry thoroughly, and apply a light film of oil to all mating surfaces and cylinder bores, to prevent rusting. If you have access to compressed air, use it to speed up the drying process, and to blow out all the oil holes and galleries.

9.6 Use a correct-sized tap to clean the cylinder block threads

Warning: Wear eye protection when using compressed air.

5 If the castings are not very dirty, you can do an adequate cleaning job with hot, soapy water and a stiff brush. Take plenty of time, and do a thorough job. Regardless of the cleaning method used, be sure to clean all oil holes and galleries very thoroughly, and to dry all components well. Protect the cylinder bores as described above, to prevent rusting.

6 All threaded holes must be clean, to ensure accurate torque readings during reassembly. To clean the threads, run the correct-size tap into each of the holes to remove rust, corrosion, thread sealant or sludge, and to restore damaged threads **(see illustration)**. If possible, use compressed air to clear the holes of debris produced by this operation. *Caution: Take extra care to exclude all liquid from blind tapped holes, as the casting may be cracked by hydraulic action if a bolt is threaded into a hole containing liquid.*

7 Apply suitable sealant to the new oil gallery plugs, and insert them into the holes in the block. Tighten them securely. Similarly, apply sealant to the core plugs and tap them into the cylinder block using a close-fitting tube or socket.

8 If the engine is not going to be reassembled immediately, cover it with a large plastic bag to keep it clean; protect all mating surfaces and the cylinder bores as described above, to prevent rusting.

Inspection

9 Visually check the casting for cracks and corrosion. Look for stripped threads in the threaded holes. If there has been any history of internal water leakage, it may be worthwhile having an engine overhaul specialist check the cylinder block/crankcase with professional equipment. If defects are found, have them renewed or if possible, repaired.

10 Check the cylinder bores for scuffing or scoring. Any evidence of this kind of damage should be cross-checked with an inspection of the pistons (see Section 7 of this Chapter). If the damage is in its early stages, it may be possible to repair the block by reboring it. Seek the advice of an engineering workshop.

11 Have the cylinder bores measured and inspected by an engine reconditioning specialist. If the bores are worn/damaged, they will be able to carry out any remedial work (reboring) and supply suitable oversize pistons, etc.

12 Apply a light coating of engine oil to the mating surfaces and cylinder bores to prevent rust forming.

13 Refit all the components removed in paragraph 1.

10 Main and big-end bearings – inspection and selection

Inspection

1 Even though the main and big-end bearings should be renewed during the engine overhaul, the old bearings should be retained for close examination, as they may reveal valuable information about the condition of the engine **(see illustration)**.

2 Bearing failure can occur due to lack of lubrication, the presence of dirt or other foreign particles, overloading the engine, or corrosion. Regardless of the cause of bearing failure, the cause must be corrected before the engine is reassembled, to prevent it from happening again.

3 When examining the bearing shells, remove them from the cylinder block/crankcase, the main bearing caps, the connecting rods and the connecting rod big-end bearing caps. Lay them out on a clean surface in the same general position as their location in the engine. This will enable you to match any bearing problems with the corresponding crankshaft journal. Do not touch any shell's internal bearing surface with your fingers while checking it, or the delicate surface may be scratched.

10.1 Typical bearing failures

4 Dirt and other foreign matter gets into the engine in a variety of ways. It may be left in the engine during assembly, or it may pass through filters or the crankcase ventilation system. It may get into the oil, and from there into the bearings. Metal chips from machining operations and normal engine wear are often present. Abrasives are sometimes left in engine components after reconditioning, especially when parts are not thoroughly cleaned using the proper cleaning methods. Whatever the source, these foreign objects often end up embedded in the soft bearing material, and are easily recognised. Large particles will not embed in the bearing, but will score or gouge the bearing and journal. The best prevention for this cause of bearing failure is to clean all parts thoroughly, and keep everything spotlessly-clean during engine assembly. Frequent and regular engine oil and filter changes are also recommended.

5 Lack of lubrication (or lubrication breakdown) has a number of interrelated causes. Excessive heat (which thins the oil), overloading (which squeezes the oil from the bearing face) and oil leakage (from excessive bearing clearances, worn oil pump or high engine speeds) all contribute to lubrication breakdown. Blocked oil passages, which usually are the result of misaligned oil holes in a bearing shell, will also oil-starve a bearing, and destroy it. When lack of lubrication is the cause of bearing failure, the bearing material is wiped or extruded from the steel backing of the bearing. Temperatures may increase to the point where the steel backing turns blue from overheating.

6 Driving habits can have a definite effect on bearing life. Full-throttle, low-speed operation (labouring the engine) puts very high loads on bearings, tending to squeeze out the oil film. These loads cause the bearings to flex, which produces fine cracks in the bearing face (fatigue failure). Eventually, the bearing material will loosen in pieces, and tear away from the steel backing.

7 Short-distance driving leads to corrosion of bearings, because insufficient engine heat is produced to drive off the condensed water and corrosive gases. These products collect in the engine oil, forming acid and sludge. As the oil is carried to the engine bearings, the acid attacks and corrodes the bearing material.

8 Incorrect bearing installation during engine assembly will lead to bearing failure as well. Tight-fitting bearings leave insufficient bearing running clearance, and will result in oil starvation. Dirt or foreign particles trapped behind a bearing shell result in high spots on the bearing, which lead to failure.

9 Do not touch any shell's internal bearing surface with your fingers during reassembly as there is a risk of scratching the delicate surface, or of depositing particles of dirt on it.

10 As mentioned at the beginning of this Section, the bearing shells should be renewed as a matter of course during engine overhaul. To do otherwise is false economy.

Bearing selection

11 Main and big-end bearings for the engines described in this Chapter are available in standard sizes and a range of undersizes to suit reground crankshafts. Refer to an engine reconditioning specialist for details.

11 Engine overhaul – reassembly sequence

1 Before reassembly begins, ensure that all new parts have been obtained, and that all necessary tools are available. Read through the entire procedure to familiarise yourself with the work involved, and to ensure that all items necessary for reassembly of the engine are at hand. In addition to all normal tools and materials, thread-locking compound will be needed. A suitable tube of liquid sealant will also be required for the joint faces that are without gaskets. It is recommended that the manufacturer's own products are used, which are specially formulated for this purpose; the relevant product names are quoted in the text of each Section where they are required.

2 In order to save time and avoid problems, engine reassembly should ideally be carried out in the following order:

a) *Crankshaft (see Section 12).*
b) *Piston/connecting rod assemblies (see Section 13 and Section 14).*
c) *Oil pump and (where fitted) balancer shaft assembly (see Chapter 2A Section 15 or Chapter 2B Section 13).*
d) *Sump (see Chapter 2A Section 14 or Chapter 2B Section 12).*
e) *Flywheel (see Chapter 2A Section 16 or Chapter 2B Section 14).*
f) *Cylinder head (see Chapter 2A Section 13 or Chapter 2B Section 11).*
g) *Timing belt tensioner, sprockets and timing belt (see Chapter 2A Section 7 and 2A Section 8 or Chapter 2B Section 7 and 2B Section 8).*
h) *Inlet and exhaust manifolds (see Chapter 4A Section 6 and Chapter 4B Section 4).*
i) *Engine external components and ancillaries (see list in Section 5 of this Chapter).*

3 At this stage, all engine components should be absolutely clean and dry, with all faults repaired. The components should be laid out (or in individual containers) on a completely clean work surface.

12 Crankshaft – refitting

1 Where removed, the oil jets must be refitted at this stage and their mounting bolts tightened to the specified torque.

2 If new shells are being fitted, ensure that all traces of the protective grease are cleaned off using paraffin.

12.4 Upper main bearing shells correctly fitted

A Recess in the bearing saddle
B Lug on the bearing shell
C Oil hole

3 Clean the backs of the bearing shells, and the bearing locations in both the cylinder block/crankcase and the main bearing caps.

4 With the cylinder block positioned on a clean work surface, with the crankcase opening uppermost, press the bearing shells into their locations, ensuring that the tab on each shell engages in the notch in the cylinder block or bearing cap, and that the oil holes in the cylinder block and bearing shell are aligned **(see illustration)**. Note that the shells with the oil groove are fitted to the cylinder block, whilst the ones without the groove are fitted to the bearing caps. Take care not to touch any shell's bearing surface with your fingers.

5 Wipe off the rear surfaces of the new lower

12.5 Fit the new lower half main bearing shells into the main bearing caps

half main bearing shells and fit them to the main bearing caps, ensuring the locating lugs engage correctly **(see illustration)**.

6 At this point, it is assumed that the crankshaft, cylinder block/crankcase and bearings have been cleaned, inspected and reconditioned or renewed.

7 Give the newly-fitted main bearing shells and the crankshaft journals a final clean with a cloth. Check that the oil holes in the crankshaft are free from dirt, as any left here will become embedded in the new bearings when the engine is first started.

8 Liberally coat the bearing shells in the crankcase with clean engine oil of the appropriate grade **(see illustration)**. Install the new thrustwashers each side of the No 3 bearing position in the cylinder block. Use a small quantity of grease to hold them in place. Ensure that they are seated correctly in

12.8 Lubricate the upper main bearing shells...

the machined recesses, with the oil grooves facing outwards.

9 Lower the crankshaft into position so that No 1 cylinder crankpin is at BDC, ready for fitting No 1 piston.

10 Lubricate the lower bearing shells in the main bearing caps with clean engine oil, then fit the thrustwashers to each side of No 3 bearing cap. Use a small quantity of grease to hold them in place. Ensure that they are seated correctly in the machined recesses, with the oil grooves facing outwards **(see illustrations)**.

11 Fit the main bearing caps in the correct order and orientation – No 1 bearing cap must be at the timing belt end of the engine and the bearing shell locating recesses in the bearing saddles and caps must be adjacent to each other **(see illustrations)**. Insert the new bearing cap bolts and hand-tighten them only.

12.10a ...and lower main bearing shells with clean engine oil...

12.10b ...then fit the thrustwashers each side of the bearing cap...

12.10c ...and/or bearing saddle (see text)

12.11a Fit the No 3 main bearing cap

12.11b Fit the No 1 main bearing cap

12.11c No 1 main bearing cap

12.12a Tighten the main bearing cap bolts to the specified torque...

12.12b ...and angle

12 Working from the centre bearing cap outwards, tighten the new retaining bolts to their specified torques and angles in the stages given **(see illustrations)**.
13 Check that the crankshaft rotates freely by turning it manually.
14 Carry out a check of the crankshaft endfloat as described at the beginning of Section 8. If the thrust surfaces of the crankshaft have been checked and new thrustwashers have been fitted, then the endfloat should be within specification.
15 Refit the pistons and connecting rods or reconnect them to the crankshaft as described in Section 14.
16 With reference to Chapter 2A or 2B as applicable, carry out the following:
a) Refit the crankshaft oil seal housings, together with new oil seals.
b) Refit the balancer shaft assembly (where fitted), oil pump, baffle plate and sump.
c) Refit the flywheel.
d) Refit the crankshaft sprocket and timing belt.

13 Pistons and piston rings – assembly

1 At this point it is assumed that the pistons have been correctly assembled to their respective connecting rods and that the piston ring-to-groove clearances have been checked. If not, refer to the end of Section 7.

2 Before the rings can be fitted to the pistons, the end gaps must be checked with the rings fitted into the cylinder bores.
3 Lay out the piston assemblies and the new ring sets on a clean work surface so that the components are kept together in their groups during and after end gap checking. Place the crankcase on the work surface on its side, allowing access to the top and bottom of the bores.
4 Take the No 1 piston top ring and insert it into the top of the bore. Using the No 1 piston, push the ring close to the bottom of the bore, at the lowest point of the piston travel. Ensure that it is perfectly square in the bore.
5 Use a set of feeler blades to measure the gap between the ends of the piston ring. The correct blade will just pass through the gap with a minimal amount of resistance **(see illustration)**. Compare this measurement with that listed in Specifications. Check that you have the correct ring before deciding that a gap is incorrect. Repeat the operation for the remaining rings.
6 If new rings are being fitted, it is unlikely that the end gaps will be too small. If a measurement is found to be undersize, it must be corrected or there is the risk that the ends of the ring may contact each other during operation, possibly resulting in engine damage. This is achieved by gradually filing down the ends of the ring, using a file clamped in a vice. Fit the ring over the file such that both its ends contact opposite faces of the file. Move the ring along the file, removing small amounts of material at a time.

Take great care as the rings are brittle and form sharp edges if they fracture. Remember to keep the rings and piston assemblies in the correct order.
7 When all the piston ring end gaps have been verified, they can be fitted to the pistons. Work from the lowest ring groove (oil control ring) upwards. Note that the oil control ring may be two side rails separated by a expander ring, or a one-piece oil control ring with a internal expander spring. Note also that the two compression rings are different in cross-section, and so must be fitted in the correct groove and the right way up, using a piston ring fitting tool. Both of the compression rings may have marks stamped on one side to indicate the top facing surface. Ensure that these marks face up when the rings are fitted **(see illustration)**.
8 Distribute the end gaps around the piston, spaced at 120° intervals to the each other.
Note: If the piston ring manufacturer supplies specific fitting instructions with the rings, follow these exclusively.

14 Piston/connecting rod assemblies – refitting

Note: At this point, it is assumed that the crankshaft has been fitted to the engine, as described in Section 12. A piston ring compressor tool will be required for this operation.
1 Clean the backs of the bearing shells, and the bearing locations in both the connecting rods and the big-end bearing caps.
2 Press the bearing shells into their locations in the connecting rods and caps. The shells are not positively located by lugs and recesses – simply ensure the shells are fitted squarely and centrally into place **(see illustration)**. On all engines, the upper bearing shell is more wear-resistant than the lower, and on a new shell is identified by a black line on the bearing surface in the area of the bearing joint. Take care not to touch any shell's bearing surface with your fingers.
3 Lubricate the cylinder bores, the pistons, piston rings and upper bearing shells with clean engine oil **(see illustrations)**. Lay out

13.5 Check the piston ring end gap using feeler gauges

13.7 Piston ring top marking

14.2 Ensure the shells are fitted squarely into place

each piston/connecting rod assembly in order on a work surface. Where the bearing caps are secured with nuts, pad the threaded ends of the bolts with insulating tape to prevent them scratching the crankpins and bores when the pistons are refitted.

4 Start with piston/connecting rod assembly No 1. Make sure that the piston rings are still spaced as described in Section 13, then clamp them in position with a piston ring compressor.

5 Insert the piston/connecting rod assembly into the top of cylinder No 1. Lower the big-end in first, guiding it to protect the cylinder bores. Where oil jets are located at the bottoms of the bores, take particular care not to break them off when guiding the connecting rods onto the crankpins.

6 Ensure that the orientation of the piston in its cylinder is correct – the piston crown, connecting rods and big-end bearing caps have markings, which must point towards the timing belt end of the engine when the piston is installed in the bore – refer to Section 7 for details.

7 The piston crowns are specially shaped to improve the engine's combustion characteristics. Because of this, on SOHC engines, pistons 1 and 2 are different to pistons 3 and 4. When correctly fitted, the larger inlet valve chambers on pistons 1 and 2 must face the flywheel end of the engine, and the larger inlet valve chambers on the remaining pistons must face the timing belt end of the engine. New pistons have number markings on their crowns to indicate their type – 1/2 denotes piston 1 or 2, 3/4 indicates piston 3 or 4 **(see illustration)**.

8 Using a block of wood or hammer handle against the piston crown, tap the assembly into the cylinder until the piston crown is flush with the top of the cylinder **(see illustration)**.

9 Ensure that the bearing shell is still correctly installed. Liberally lubricate the crankpin and both bearing shells with clean engine oil. Taking care not to mark the cylinder bores, tap the piston/connecting rod assembly down the bore and onto the crankpin. Fit the big-end bearing cap,lubricate the threads and under the heads of its new retaining bolts and install them, finger-tight at first. Note that the orientation of the bearing cap with respect to the connecting rod must be correct when the two components are reassembled. These engines are fitted, with 'fractured' split connecting rods. The bearing caps are split from the connecting rod during the manufacturing process. The resultant mating surfaces are unique, and consequently will only fit properly to their original positions. Any attempt to fit them in an alternative position will ruin both connecting rod and bearing cap.

10 Tighten the retaining bolts to the specified Stage 1 torque **(see illustration)**.

11 Angle-tighten the retaining bolts to the specified Stage 2 angle **(see illustration)**.

14.3a Lubricate the pistons...

14.3b ...and the big-end upper bearing shells

12 Refit the remaining three piston/connecting rod assemblies in the same way.

13 Rotate the crankshaft by hand. Check that it turns freely; some stiffness is to be expected if new parts have been fitted, but there should be no binding or tight spots.

14 If new pistons are fitted or if a new short engine is installed, the projection of the piston crowns above the cylinder head at TDC must be measured, to determine the type of head gasket that should be fitted. Follow the procedure description given in Chapter 2A or 2B as applicable.

15 Note that if the original pistons have been refitted, then a new head gasket of the same type as the original item must be fitted.

16 Refer to Part A or B of this Chapter (as applicable) and refit the oil pump, balancer shaft assembly (where fitted), sump, baffle plate, flywheel and cylinder head.

15 Engine –
initial start-up after overhaul and reassembly

1 Refit the remainder of the engine components in the order listed in Section 11 of this Chapter. Refit the engine to the vehicle as described in Section 4 of this Chapter. Double-check the engine oil and coolant levels and make a final check that everything has been reconnected. Make sure that there are no tools or rags left in the engine compartment.

2 Prime the fuel system with reference to Chapter 4A Section 16

3 Start the engine, but be aware that as fuel system components have been disturbed, the cranking time may be a little longer than usual.

14.7 Piston orientation and coding

14.8 Use a hammer handle to tap the piston into its bore

14.10 Tighten the big-end bearing cap bolts to the Stage 1 setting...

14.11 ...and then angle-tighten them to the Stage 2 setting

4 During cranking and initial start up ensure that the oil pressure warning lamp remains off, should it illuminate switch off immediately and check the oil level and oil filter security, if these are in order then it will be necessary to satisfy yourself that the oil is being pumped around the engine at sufficient pressure, before progressing any further.

5 While the engine is idling, check for fuel, water and oil leaks. Don't be alarmed if there are some odd smells and the occasional plume of smoke as components heat up and burn off oil deposits.

6 Assuming all is well, keep the engine idling until hot water is felt circulating through the top hose.

7 After a few minutes, recheck the oil and coolant levels, and top-up as necessary.

8 There is no need to retighten the cylinder head bolts once the engine has been run following reassembly.

9 If new pistons, rings or crankshaft bearings have been fitted, the engine must be treated as new, and run-in for the first 600 miles. Do not operate the engine at full-throttle, or allow it to labour at low engine speeds in any gear. It is recommended that the engine oil and filter are changed at the end of this period.

Chapter 3
Cooling, heating and ventilation systems

Contents

Degrees of difficulty

Easy, suitable for novice with little experience	Fairly easy, suitable for beginner with some experience	Fairly difficult, suitable for competent DIY mechanic	Difficult, suitable for experienced DIY mechanic	Very difficult, suitable for expert DIY or professional

Specifications

Engine codes*

PD unit injector engines:

1.9 litre (1896 cc), 8-valve, SOHC	BJB, BKC, BLS and BXE

2.0 litre (1968 cc):

8-valve, SOHC	BMM
16-valve, DOHC	BKD and BMN

Common rail injection engines:

2.0 litre (1968 cc), 16-valve, DOHC	CBBB, CBDB and CEGA (1st Generation)
	CLCA, CLCB, CFHC and CFHF (2nd Generation)

*See 'Vehicle identification' at the end of this manual for the location of engine code markings.

General

Maximum system pressure	1.4 to 1.6 bar

Thermostat

Operating temperature:

Opening begins.	87°C (approx)
Fully open	102°C (approx)

Air conditioning

Refrigerant capacity.	525 ± 25 g

Torque wrench settings

	Nm	lbf ft
Air conditioning compressor mountings	25	18
Air conditioning refrigerant pipes to compressor.	23	17
Coolant pipe to cylinder block bolt (engine code CEGA).	10	7
Coolant pump.	15	11
Receiver/dryer screws (Showa and Fujikoki)	5	4
Thermostat housing-to-cylinder block bolts	15	11

1 General information and precautions

1 The cooling system is of the pressurised type, comprising a coolant pump, an aluminium radiator, cooling fan(s), a thermostat, heater matrix, and all associated hoses and switches. The coolant pump is driven by the camshaft timing belt. All models are fitted with an electrically-operated fan. Common rail engines are also fitted with an electrically-driven coolant circulation pump. The system functions as follows.

2 When the engine is cold, the coolant in the engine is pumped around the cylinder block and head passages, and through an engine oil cooler. After cooling the cylinder bores, combustion surfaces and valve seats, the coolant passes through the heater, and is returned via the cylinder block to the coolant pump. The thermostat is initially closed, preventing the cold coolant from the radiator entering the engine.

3 When the coolant in the engine reaches a predetermined temperature, the thermostat opens. The cold coolant from the radiator is then allowed to enter the engine through the bottom hose and the hot coolant from the engine flows through the top hose to the radiator. As the coolant circulates through the radiator, it is cooled by the inrush of air when the car is in forward motion. The airflow is supplemented by the action of the cooling fan(s) when necessary. As the coolant reduces in temperature, it passes to the bottom of the radiator and the cycle is repeated.

4 On all models, the cooling fan(s) are electrically-powered, and are controlled by the engine management ECM, which receives data from the engine coolant temperature sensor and radiator outlet temperature sensor (where fitted). At a predetermined coolant temperature, the sensor actuates the fan. The switch then cuts the power supply to the fan when the coolant temperature has reduced sufficiently.

5 On models with an automatic transmission unit, a transmission fluid cooler is built into the radiator. The transmission unit is linked to the radiator by two pipes and the fluid

2.3 Prise out the clip a little, and pull the radiator hose from the union

is circulated around the cooler to keep its temperature stable under arduous operating conditions.

⚠ *Warning: Do not attempt to remove the expansion tank filler cap, or to disturb any part of the cooling system, while the engine is hot, as there is a high risk of scalding. If the expansion tank filler cap must be removed before the engine and radiator have fully cooled (even though this is not recommended), the pressure in the cooling system must first be relieved. Cover the cap with a thick layer of cloth to avoid scalding, and slowly unscrew the filler cap until a hissing sound is heard. When the hissing has stopped, indicating that the pressure has reduced, slowly unscrew the filler cap until it can be removed; if more hissing sounds are heard, wait until they have stopped before unscrewing the cap completely. At all times, keep well away from the filler cap opening, and protect your hands.*

• *Do not allow antifreeze to come into contact with your skin, or with the painted surfaces of the vehicle. Rinse off spills immediately, with plenty of water. Never leave antifreeze lying around in an open container, or in a puddle in the driveway or on the garage floor. Children and pets are attracted by its sweet smell, but antifreeze can be fatal if ingested.*

• *If the engine is hot, the electric cooling fan may start rotating even if the engine is not running. Be careful to keep your hands, hair, and any loose clothing well clear when working in the engine compartment.*

• *Refer to Section 10 for precautions to be observed when working on models equipped with air conditioning.*

2 Cooling system hoses – disconnection and renewal

Note: *Refer to the warnings given in Section 1 of this Chapter before proceeding. Hoses should only be disconnected once the engine has cooled sufficiently to avoid scalding.*

1 If the checks described in Chapter 1 Section 10 reveal a faulty hose, it must be renewed as follows.

2 First drain the cooling system (see Chapter 1 Section 37). If the coolant is not due for renewal, it may be re-used, providing it is collected in a clean container.

3 In order to disconnect the moulded connectors of the radiator inlet and outlet hoses, and the heater hoses on some models, apply pressure to hold the hose on to the relevant union, pull out the spring clip and pull the hose from the union **(see illustration)**. Note that the radiator inlet and outlet unions are fragile; do not use excessive force when attempting to remove the hoses. If a hose proves to be difficult to remove, try the

application of a penetrating spray (such as WD-40) into the connection union and then gently push and pull the union to encourage it to release. (Note that the connection O-ring seals should always be renewed, especially if they have been in contact with a penetrating spray).

4 To disconnect a hose clamped to a stub, release the retaining clips, then move them along the hose, clear of the relevant inlet/outlet. Carefully work the hose free. The hoses can be removed with relative ease when new – on an older car, they may have stuck.

5 If a hose proves to be difficult to remove, try to release it by rotating its ends before attempting to free it. Gently prise the end of the hose with a blunt instrument (such as a flat-bladed screwdriver), but do not apply too much force, and take care not to damage the pipe stubs or hoses. Note in particular that the radiator inlet stub is fragile; do not use excessive force when attempting to remove the hose. If all else fails, cut the hose with a sharp knife, then slit it so that it can be peeled off in two pieces. Although this may prove expensive if the hose is otherwise undamaged, it is preferable to buying a new radiator. Check first, however, that a new hose is readily available.

6 When fitting a hose, first slide the clips onto the hose, then work the hose into position. On some hose connections alignment marks are provided on the hose and union; if marks are present, ensure they are correctly aligned.

7 Ensure the hose is correctly routed, then slide each clip back along the hose until it passes over the flared end of the relevant inlet/outlet, before tightening the clip securely. Prior to refitting a radiator inlet or outlet hose, renew the connection O-ring regardless of condition. The connections are a push-fit over the radiator unions, always ensuring that the securing spring clip is correctly engaged in the groove of the radiator union and is fully pushed in.

8 Refill the cooling system with reference to the relevant part of Chapter 1 Section 37.

9 Check thoroughly for leaks as soon as possible after disturbing any part of the cooling system.

3 Radiator – removal, inspection and refitting

Removal

1 Remove the cooling fan and shroud assembly as described in Section 5.

2 Drain the cooling system as described in Chapter 1 Section 37.

3 Disconnect the radiator top and bottom coolant hoses (see Section 2), noting the correct fitted locations **(see illustration 2.3)**. **Note:** *On some models, quick-release couplings are fitted to the hoses.*

3.4a Undo the radiator mounting screws on the left-hand side (upper screw arrowed)...

3.4b ...and the right-hand side (upper screw arrowed)...

3.4c ...then lift the radiator from place

4 Undo the radiator mounting screws, pull the radiator rearwards and remove it from the vehicle **(see illustrations)**.

Inspection

5 If the radiator has been removed due to suspected blockage, reverse-flush it as described in Chapter 1 Section 37. Clean dirt and debris from the radiator fins, using an airline (in which case, wear eye protection) or a soft brush. Be careful, as the fins are sharp, and easily damaged.
6 If necessary, a radiator specialist can perform a flow test on the radiator, to establish whether an internal blockage exists.
7 A leaking radiator must be referred to a specialist for permanent repair. Do not attempt to weld or solder a leaking radiator, as damage to the plastic components may result.
8 If the radiator is to be sent for repair or renewed, remove all hoses and switches (where fitted).

Refitting

9 Refitting is a reversal of removal, bearing in mind the following points.
a) Ensure that the radiator is correctly positioned before refitting and tightening the mounting screws.
b) Make sure all coolant hoses are correctly reconnected and securely retained by their clips.
c) Refill the cooling system with new antifreeze as described in Chapter 1 Section 37

4.7a Thermostat housing bolts (arrowed)

4 Thermostat – removal, testing and refitting

Removal

1 The thermostat is located behind the alternator at the front right-hand side of the engine cylinder block. There are two types of thermostat fitted to diesel models:
a) Single hose to the thermostat cover – the thermostat can be renewed separately.
b) Four connections to the thermostat housing – the thermostat is part of the housing and can only be renewed as a complete assembly.
2 Drain the cooling system as described in Chapter 1 Section 37. If the coolant is not due for renewal, it may be re-used if it is collected in a clean container.

PD engines

3 Remove the plastic cover on the top of the engine by pulling it upwards from its mountings.
4 Remove the alternator as described in Chapter 5 Section 5.
5 Release the securing clip and disconnect the coolant hose from the thermostat housing.
6 Disconnect the temperature sensor wiring plug from the sensor in the thermostat housing (where fitted).
7 Unscrew the two securing bolts, and remove the thermostat housing complete with the thermostat. Note the locations of any

4.7b Renew the thermostat cover O-ring seal

brackets secured by the bolts. Recover the O-ring if it is loose **(see illustrations)**.
8 To remove the thermostat from the cover, twist the thermostat 90° clockwise, and pull it from the housing **(see illustration)**.

Common rail engines with a single outlet housing

9 Remove the cover from the top of the engine.
10 Remove the radiator cooling fans with reference to Section 5
11 Remove the right charge air hose from it's connections to the intercooler and front charge air pipe.
12 Remove the two bolts securing the front charge air pipe to the engine, release the coolant hose clipped to it, disconnect the charge pressure sender wiring plug and slacken the upper clamp. Remove the front charge air pipe.
13 Remove the inlet manifold flap housing (see Chapter 4A Section 4).
14 Release the clamp and remove the coolant hose from the thermostat housing.
15 Unscrew the two securing bolts, and remove the thermostat housing complete with the thermostat. Recover the O-ring if it is loose.
16 To remove the thermostat from the housing, twist the thermostat 90° clockwise, and pull it from the housing.

Common rail engines (1st generation, engine code CEGA) with four connection housing

17 Remove the cover from the top of the engine.

4.8 Twist the thermostat 90° clockwise and withdraw it from the housing

4.28 Charge air pipe lower mounting bolt.

18 Remove the alternator as described in Chapter 5 Section 5.

19 Remove the right charge air hose from it's connections to the intercooler and front charge air pipe.

20 Remove the two bolts securing the front charge air pipe to the engine, release the coolant hose clipped to it, disconnect the charge pressure sender wiring plug and slacken the upper clamp. Remove the front charge air pipe **(see illustration)**.

21 Remove the inlet manifold flap housing (see Chapter 4A Section 4).

22 Slacken and remove the bolt securing the front coolant pipe across the cylinder block, behind the oil filter housing.

23 Release the clamps and remove the three coolant hoses from their connections to the thermostat housing.

24 Remove the two bolts securing the thermostat housing to the cylinder block, pull the housing away from the block and the towards the right of the vehicle to release the housing from the front coolant pipe. Remove the housing from the vehicle.

Note: *The thermostat is integral with the four connection housing and can only be renewed as a complete unit.*

Common rail engines (2nd generation, engine codes CLCA, CLCB, CFHC and CFHF) with four connection housing

25 Remove the cover from the top of the engine.

26 Remove the alternator as described in Chapter 5 Section 5

27 Remove the right charge air hose from it's connections to the intercooler and front charge air pipe.

28 Remove the two bolts securing the front charge air pipe to the engine, release the coolant hose clipped to it, disconnect the charge pressure sender wiring plug and slacken the upper clamp. Remove the front charge air pipe **(see illustration)**.

29 Remove the oil dipstick, unbolt the dipstick guide tube upper mounting, release the pressed in lower mounting clip and pull the dipstick guide tube upwards to release it from the cylinder block.

30 Remove the air filter housing (see Chapter 4A Section 3).

31 Remove the battery and battery tray (see Chapter 5 Section 3).

32 Remove the left charge air hose from it's connections to the intercooler and left charge air pipe.

33 Release any wiring or hoses secured to the left charge air pipe, remove the mounting bolts for the left charge air pipe at the front and left of the engine, release the clamp at the turbocharger outlet and remove the left charge air pipe.

34 Release the clamp and remove the lower coolant hose from the coolant housing on the left end of the cylinder head.

35 Unplug and remove the wiring connection for the camshaft position sensor from the coolant pipe across the front of the cylinder block.

36 Remove the coolant pipe mounting bolts located at the left of the engine above the transmission, pull the coolant pipe to the left of the vehicle to release it from it's connection to the thermostat housing. Note that the pipe is still connected to the engine by coolant hoses but should have sufficient movement to enable it to release from the thermostat housing.

37 Release the clamps and remove the three coolant hoses from their connections to the thermostat housing.

38 Remove the two bolts securing the thermostat housing, pull the housing away from the cylinder block and recover the sealing ring. **Note:** *The thermostat is integral with the 4 connection housing and can only be renewed as a complete unit.*

Testing

Note: *If there is any question about the operation of the thermostat, it's best to renew it – they are not usually expensive items. Testing involves heating in, or over, an open pan of boiling water, which carries with it the risk of scalding. A thermostat which has seen more than five years' service may well be past its best already.*

39 A rough test of the thermostat may be made by suspending it with a piece of string in a container full of water, but not touching the container. Heat the water to bring it to the boil – the thermostat must open by the time the water boils. If not, renew it.

40 If a thermometer is available, the precise opening temperature of the thermostat may be determined, and compared with the figure given in the Specifications. The opening temperature is also marked on the thermostat. It will not be possible to achieve the fully open temperature given in the specifications outside of the pressurised enviroment found in a sealed cooling system.

41 A thermostat which fails to close as the water cools must also be renewed.

Refitting

42 Refitting is a reversal of removal, with reference to any sections referred to during removal and bearing in mind the following points.

Single outlet thermostat housing

a) *Refit the thermostat using a new O-ring.*

b) *Insert the thermostat into the cover and twist 90° anti-clockwise.*

c) *The thermostat should be fitted with the brace almost vertical.*

d) *Ensure that any brackets are in place on the thermostat cover bolts as noted before removal.*

e) *Use a new seal when refitting the inlet manifold flap housing.(common rail engine)*

f) *Refill the cooling system with the correct type and quantity of coolant as described in Chapter 1 Section 37*

Four connection housing

a) *Refit the thermostat housing using a new O-ring seal.*

b) *Use a new O-ring at the coolant pipe to thermostat housing connection.*

c) *Use a new seal when refitting the inlet manifold flap housing.*

d) *Refill the cooling system with the correct type and quantity of coolant as described in Chapter 1 Section 37*

---

5 Cooling fan(s) – testing, removal and refitting

Testing

1 Depending on the model, there may be one or two electric cooling fans fitted. The cooling fans are supplied with current through the ignition switch, cooling fan control unit (located on the motor), temperature sensor(s), the relays and fuses/fusible link (see Chapter 12 Section 3). The engine management ECU activates the fan(s) according to the engine coolant temperature sensor(s). Testing of the cooling fan circuit is as follows:

2 If a fan does not appear to work, first check the fuses and fusible links. If they are good, run the engine until normal operating temperature is reached, then allow it to idle. If the fan does not cut-in within a few minutes, the cause may be the temperature sender (where applicable), which can be checked by a Skoda dealer (or suitably equipped garage) using specialist diagnostic equipment.

3 The motors can be checked, by disconnecting the motor wiring connector and connecting a 12-volt supply directly to the motor terminals. If the motor is faulty, it must be renewed, as no spares are available.

4 If the fan still fails to operate, check the cooling fan circuit wiring (Chapter 12 Section 2). Check each wire for continuity and ensure that all connections are clean and free of corrosion.

5 On models with a cooling fan control unit, if no fault can be found, then it is likely that the cooling fan control unit is faulty. Testing of the unit should be entrusted to a Skoda dealer or specialist; if the unit is faulty it must be renewed.

5.11 Disconnect the fan motor wiring plug

5.12a The fan shroud is secured by 2 screws on the right-hand side (upper screw arrowed)…

5.12b …and 2 screws on the left-hand side (upper screw arrowed)

Removal

Note: *Although it may not be necessary on some models, it is recommended to position the lock carrier in the service position for removal of the radiator fans and shroud due to the limited access and risk of damage to the radiator.*

6 Jack up and support the front of the vehicle (see Chapter 13 Section 5).

7 Remove the engine undershield.

8 Disconnect and remove the air filter intake pipe/duct from the lock carrier and air filter housing with reference to Chapter 4A Section 3

9 Disconnect and remove the left charge air hose from between the intercooler and charge air pipe.

10 Place the lock carrier assembly in the 'Service position' as described in Chapter 11 Section 10.

11 Unplug the fan motor wiring plug, located at the bottom left of the fan shroud. Move the wiring to one side **(see illustration)**.

12 Slacken and remove the fan shroud retaining screws (2 each side) and remove the fan shroud assembly from the rear of the radiator **(see illustrations). Note:** *The fan motor wiring plug and lower shroud retaining bolts are more easily accessed from beneath the vehicle.*

13 Unclip the motor wiring from the rear of the shroud then undo the fasteners and pull the motor assembly away from the shroud **(see illustration)**. If the motor is faulty, the complete unit may have to be renewed – consult your Skoda dealer or parts specialist.

5.12c Lift the fan and shroud assembly upwards from the engine compartment

Refitting

14 Fit the motor assembly to the shroud and securely tighten its retaining nuts. Ensure the motor wiring is correctly routed and clipped securely in position.

15 Refit the shroud assembly to the radiator and securely tighten its retaining screws.

16 Reconnect the wiring plug.

17 The remainder of refitting is the reversal of removal.

<table>
<tr><td>6</td><td>Cooling system sensors – testing, removal and refitting</td></tr>
</table>

Testing

1 All models have two coolant temperature sensors fitted. One sensor is fitted into the

5.13 Undo the fasteners (arrowed) and separate the fan motor(s) from the shroud

coolant housing on the left-hand end of the cylinder head **(see illustrations 6.1a and 6.1b)**, the other coolant sensor is fitted into a coolant hose with different locations as follows:

a) *On 1.9 litre PD engines BXE, BKC and BJB, the sensor is located in the left-hand lower radiator hose, near to the connection to the radiator* **(see illustration 6.1c)**.

b) *On 1.9 litre PD engine BLS and all 2.0 litre PD engines the sensor is located in the thermostat housing, located to the rear of the alternator.*

c) *On all common rail engines the sensor is located in a coolant pipe on the right-hand side of the engine, adjacent to the fuel filter* **(see illustration 6.1d)**.

2 The sensor is a thermistor. A thermistor is

6.1c Radiator outlet coolant temperature sensor (arrowed) is at the left-hand side of the radiator – PD unit injector engines (BXE, BKC and BJB)

6.1a Coolant temperature sensor (arrowed) – PD unit injector engines

6.1b Coolant temperature sensor (arrowed) – common rail injection engines

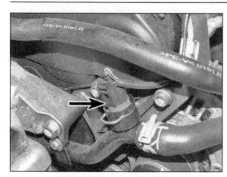

6.1d The radiator outlet coolant temperature sensor (arrowed) is at the right-hand end of the cylinder head – common rail injection engines

an electronic component whose electrical resistance changes at a predetermined rate as the temperature changes. The engine management electronic control module (ECM) supplies the sensor with a set voltage and then, by measuring the current flowing in the sensor circuit, determines the engine's temperature. This information is then used, in conjunction with other inputs, to control the injector timing, the temperature gauge/warning light, the idle speed, etc. It is also used to determine the glow plug preheating and post-heating times.

3 If the sensor circuit should fail to provide adequate information, the ECM's back-up facility will override the sensor signal. In this event, the ECM assumes a predetermined setting which will allow the engine management system to run, albeit at reduced efficiency. When this occurs, the warning light on the instrument panel will come on, and a fault code will be stored by the system's self-diagnosis facility – the advice of a Skoda dealer or specialist should be sought. The sensor itself can only be tested using special diagnostic equipment. Do not attempt to test the circuit using any other equipment, as there is a high risk of damaging the ECM.

Removal

Note: *If the intention is to remove the sensor*

7.4a Coolant pump – PD unit injector engines...

without draining the cooling system, ensure that the cooling system has been depressurised by unscrewing the coolant expansion tank cap with reference to Chapter 1 Section 37. Tighten the cap once any pressure has been released.

Coolant housing sensor

4 Pull the plastic cover on the top of the engine upwards from its mountings.

5 To access the temperature sensor fitted at the left-hand end of the cylinder head, remove the air cleaner assembly as described in Chapter 4A Section 3.

6 Slacken the retaining clip, undo the retaining bolts and move the charge air ducting away from the coolant housing.

7 Either partially drain the cooling system to just below the level of the sensor (as described in Chapter 1 Section 37), or have a suitable plug which can be used to plug the sensor aperture whilst it is removed. If a plug is used, take great care not to damage the sensor unit aperture, and do not use anything which would allow foreign matter to enter the cooling system. If a new sensor is to be fitted, by having the sensor and a new sealing ring ready, it is possible to quickly change the sensor with a minimal amount of coolant loss.

8 Disconnect the sensor wiring plug.

9 Press the sensor unit in, and slide out the retaining clip. Withdraw the sensor from the housing and recover the sealing ring (see illustration 6.1a or 6.1b).

Coolant hose sensor

1.9 litre PD engine codes BXE, BKC and BJB

10 Either partially drain the cooling system to just below the level of the sensor (as described in Chapter 1 Section 37), or have a suitable plug which can be used to plug the sensor aperture whilst it is removed. If a plug is used, take great care not to damage the sensor unit aperture, and do not use anything which would allow foreign matter to enter the cooling system. If a new sensor is to be fitted, by having the sensor and a new sealing ring ready, it is possible to quickly change the sensor with a minimal amount of coolant loss.

11 Disconnect the sensor wiring plug.

12 Press the sensor unit in, and slide out the retaining clip. Withdraw the sensor from the hose and recover the sealing ring.

7.4b ...and common rail injection engines

1.9 litre PD engine code BLS and all 2.0 litre PD engines

13 Drain the cooling system as described in Chapter 1 Section 37.

14 Remove the alternator as described in Chapter 5 Section 5.

15 Disconnect the sensor wiring plug.

16 Press the sensor unit in, and slide out the retaining clip. Withdraw the sensor from the housing and recover the sealing ring.

Common rail engines

17 Either partially drain the cooling system to just below the level of the sensor (as described in Chapter 1), or have a suitable plug which can be used to plug the sensor aperture whilst it is removed. If a plug is used, take great care not to damage the sensor unit aperture, and do not use anything which would allow foreign matter to enter the cooling system. If a new sensor is to be fitted, by having the sensor and a new sealing ring ready, it is possible to quickly change the sensor with a minimal amount of coolant loss.

18 Undo the bolt and two nuts and move the fuel filter housing to one side for access to the sensor (leave fuel pipes connected).

19 Disconnect the sensor wiring plug.

20 Press the sensor unit in, and slide out the retaining clip. Withdraw the sensor from the pipe and recover the sealing ring.

Refitting

21 Refitting is the reversal of removal. Bearing in mind the following points:

a) Fit a new sealing ring, then push the sensor fully into the aperture and slide in the retaining clip.

b) Reconnect the wiring plug, and refill the cooling system as described in Chapter 1 Section 37, or top-up as described in 'Weekly checks'.

---

7 Coolant pump – removal and refitting

Primary coolant pump

Note: *Best practise is to always replace the coolant pump when the timing belt is replaced. If replacing the coolant pump because it is faulty (leaking) always replace the timing belt and tensioners.*

Removal

1 Drain the cooling system as described in Chapter 1 Section 37.

2 Remove the auxiliary drivebelt as described in Chapter 1 Section 11.

3 With reference to Chapter 2A or 2B, remove the timing belt.

4 Unscrew and remove the coolant pump securing bolts. Carefully withdraw the pump from the cylinder block and recover the sealing O-ring (see illustrations).

Refitting

5 Ensure that the pump and housing mating

surfaces are clean and free from all traces of corrosion.

6 Obtain a new sealing O-ring and moisten it with undiluted antifreeze of the specified type (see *Lubricants and fluids 0 Section 6*). Position the sealing ring on the pump **(see illustration)**.

7 Fit the coolant pump to the cylinder block

8 Insert the mounting bolts and tighten them evenly and progressively to the specified torque.

9 Refit the timing belt as described in Chapter 2A or 2B.

10 On completion refill the cooling system as described in Chapter 1 Section 37.

Electric circulation pump

Note: *This pump is only fitted to common rail engines.*

Removal

11 Raise the front of the vehicle and support is securely on axle stands (see *Jacking and vehicle support*).

12 Undo the fasteners and remove the engine undershield.

13 Remove the right-hand charge air hose from the intercooler and front charge air pipe

14 Remove the mounting bolts for the front charge air hose, slacken the upper clamp and move the front charge air pipe to access the bolt securing the circulation pump bracket.

15 Drain the cooling system (see Chapter 1 Section 37) or fit hose clamps to the coolant hoses connected to the pump, release the clips and disconnect the hoses from the pump **(see illustration)**.

16 Disconnect the pump wiring plug.

17 Undo the retaining bolt and remove the pump **(see illustration)**.

Refitting

18 Refitting is a reversal of removal. Top-up or refill the coolant as described in *Weekly checks* and Chapter 1 Section 37, as appropriate.

<table><tr><td>**8**</td><td>**Heating and ventilation system –** general information</td></tr></table>

1 The heating/ventilation system consists of a fully-adjustable blower motor (housed behind the facia), face level vents in the centre and at each end of the facia, and air ducts to the front and rear footwells.

2 The heater control unit is located in the facia, and the controls operate flap valves to deflect and mix the air flowing through the various parts of the heating/ventilation system. The flap valves are contained in the air distribution housing, which acts as a central distribution unit, passing air to the various ducts and vents.

3 Cold air enters the system through the grille at the rear of the engine compartment. If required, the airflow is boosted by the blower, and then flows through the various ducts, according to the settings of the controls. Stale air is expelled through ducts at the rear of

7.6 Position the sealing ring on the pump

the vehicle. If warm air is required, the cold air is passed over the heater matrix, which is heated by the engine coolant.

4 The outside air supply to the vehicle can be closed off which is useful to prevent unpleasant odours entering from outside the vehicle. This is achieved either by setting the blower motor switch to position 0 or by operating the recirculation switch (depending on model). This facility should only be used briefly, as the recirculated air inside the vehicle will soon become stale.

5 The heating and air conditioning systems fitted to the Skoda Octavia are equipped with a sophisticated self-diagnosis facility. Should a fault occur, before attempting a repair procedure, have the facility interrogated using Skoda's diagnosis equipment (VAS 5051) or a suitable alternative. This may reveal any stored fault codes, and pin-point the problem area. Consult a Skoda dealer or suitably-equipped specialist. Note that the control unit communicates with the rest of the vehicle's electrical system by means of a databus network. Traditional 'back-probing' of connectors should not be attempted without first identifying the databus connections.

<table><tr><td>**9**</td><td>**Heater/ventilation components –** removal and refitting</td></tr></table>

General information

1 The information in this Section is applicable to heating/ventilation element of the vehicle.

9.4 Carefully prise the control panel trim from place

7.15 Disconnect the hoses from the circulation pump (arrowed)

7.17 Circulation pump bracket retaining bolt (arrowed – shown with the charge air pipe removed for clarity)

The air conditioning elements are described in Section 11.

Heater/ventilation/ air conditioning control panel

2 On models with manual heating/air conditioning controls, set the heater control knob to 'cold', the blower motor to '0' and the vent direction to 'footwell'.

3 Disconnect the battery negative lead (see Chapter 5 Section 3).

4 Use a blunt, flat-bladed tool to prise away the control panel surround trim **(see illustration)**.

5 Undo the retaining screws and pull the control panel from place **(see illustration)**.

6 Note their fitted positions, then prise up the locking catches, squeeze together the retaining tabs and disconnect the wiring plugs from the rear of the panel **(see illustration)**.

9.5 Heater control panel retaining screws (arrowed)

9.6 Prise up the wiring plug locking catches, and disconnect the plug from the heater panel

9.11a Undo the screw (where fitted) and release the catch (arrowed)...

Unclip the operating cable from the rear of the distribution knob.

7 Refitting is a reversal of removal. When refitting the cable to the distribution knob on the control panel, removing the side cover of the centre console gives access to the rear of the control panel making refitting easier. **Note:** *If a replacement fully-automatic Climatronic control panel has been fitted, it will be necessary to carry out the basic setting procedure. This procedure necessitates the use of Skoda diagnostic equipment VAS5051/1. Consequently, this task should be entrusted to a Skoda dealer, or suitably-equipped specialist.*

Blower motor

8 Remove the passenger's glovebox as described in Chapter 11 Section 27.

9.15 Heater blower motor resistor wiring plug

9.9 Closure panel fixings (arrowed)

9.11b ...then rotate the motor clockwise and remove it (shown with the heater housing removed for clarity)

9 Undo and remove the footwell closure panel beneath the blower motor and the footwell vent on the passenger side **(see illustration)**.
10 Disconnect the wiring plug from the blower motor.
11 Undo the retaining screw (where fitted), release the catch, rotate the blower motor anti-clockwise and lower it from the housing **(see illustrations)**. **Note:** *If no screw is fitted to secure the blower motor housing, provision is made at the location shown to enable the use of a screw if the catch should become defective.*
12 Refitting is a reversal of removal.

Blower motor resistor

13 Remove the passenger's glovebox as described in Chapter 11 Section 27.
14 Undo and remove the footwell closure

9.18 Prise out the clips and disconnect the heater hoses

panel beneath the blower motor **(see illustration 9.9)**.
15 Disconnect the resistor wiring plug, depress the clip and pull the resistor from the housing **(see illustration)**.
16 Refitting is a reversal of removal.

Heater matrix

Note: *Skoda advise that this operation can be carried out with the heater unit in situ. However, it may be easier to undertake this with the heater unit removed from the vehicle.*
17 If air conditioning is fitted, switch on the ignition, set the temperature to the highest setting, then switch off ignition.
18 Using hose clamps, clamp the heater matrix inlet and return hoses located on the bulkhead at the rear of the engine compartment. Note that removing the air inlet duct at the rear of the engine improves access. Place a container beneath the hoses, then prise out the clips and disconnect them **(see illustration)**. Note the location of the hoses for correct refitting.
19 With the hoses disconnected, remove the coolant from the matrix by blowing air into the upper tube, preferably using a compressed air line.
Caution: Always use eye protection when using compressed air.
20 Using a 6 mm socket, loosen (but do not remove) the bolt located between the matrix upper and lower tubes **(see illustration)**. This will make removal of the matrix easier.
21 On the centre console, remove the left-hand side cover and footwell vent.
22 Remove the glovebox as described in Chapter 11 Section 27.
23 Disconnect the wiring plug, remove the screw and remove the control unit for the left side temperature flap.
24 Undo the bolts and remove the cover from the heater matrix **(see illustration)**.
25 Place cloth rags or similar on the floor beneath the heater matrix, then release the pipe clamps and pull the coolant pipes from the matrix **(see illustration)**. Discard the pipes-to-matrix seals – new ones must be fitted.
26 Slide the heater matrix from the heater unit.
27 Refitting is a reversal of removal, noting the following.

9.20 Slacken the bolt (arrowed) between the matrix tubes

9.24 Heater matrix cover bolts (arrowed)

9.25 Undo the pipe clamps

9.27 Moisten the new seals with coolant (arrowed)

a) Make sure the seal is fitted correctly around the perimeter of the matrix.

b) When reconnecting the coolant pipes, moisten the seals with coolant and fit them to the matrix, not the pipes **(see illustration)**. After reconnecting the pipes, the clamps must turn easily before tightening them securely.

c) Check that the rubber grommet around the pipes in the bulkhead is correctly located in its hole.

d) Check the coolant level before and after running the engine with reference to Weekly checks and Chapter 1 Section 37.

Heater/distribution unit

28 Have the air conditioning system discharged by a suitably-equipped specialist.
29 Using hose clamps, clamp the heater matrix inlet and return hoses located on the bulkhead at the rear of the engine compartment. Place a container beneath the hoses, then prise out the clips and disconnect them. Note the location of the hoses for correct refitting.

30 With the hoses disconnected, remove the coolant from the matrix by blowing air into the upper tube, preferably using a compressed air line.

31 Undo the bolts and disconnect the refrigerant pipes from the engine compartment bulkhead**(see illustration)**. Plug the openings to prevent contamination.

32 Remove the facia as described in Chapter 11 Section 26.

33 Remove the steering column as described in Chapter 10 Section 20.

34 Remove the side covers from the centre console as described in Chapter 11 Section 25.

35 Undo the retaining screws and remove the footwell vents on the driver and passenger side **(see illustration)**.

36 Unclip any wiring and remove the metal crossbeam support bracket located each side of the distribution unit. These are held in place by 2 bolts at the bottom on each side, 1 bolt at the top on the left hand side, and 2 bolts at the top on the right hand side. Remove the screw at either side attaching the support brackets to a metal bracket located beneath the distribution unit. Remove the support brackets and their connecting bracket **(see illustrations)**.

37 Detach the drain tube from the base of the distribution unit at the back **(see illustration)**.

38 Note their fitted positions and disconnect the wiring plugs from the fresh air/recirculating air flap motor, and from the temperature sensors.

9.31 Undo the Torx bolts (arrowed) securing the refrigerant pipes at the bulkhead

9.35 Left-hand footwell vent securing screw (arrowed)

9.36a Right-hand side support bracket lower bolts (arrowed)

9.36b Left-hand side support bracket upper bolt (arrowed)

9.36c Right-hand side support bracket upper bolts (arrowed)

9.36d Bracket located below the heater unit (shown with heater removed for clarity)

9.37 Disconnect the drain tube (arrowed)

9.39 Mounting screws for the convenience unit bracket (arrowed)

9.40 Undo the 2 screws (arrowed) and detach the fusebox from the crossbeam

39 Undo the screw holding the convenience unit bracket to the crossbeam, and move the unit to one side **(see illustration)**.

40 Undo the 2 retaining screws and detach the fusebox from the crossbeam, and move to one side **(see illustration)**.

41 Carefully unclip the air vents on top of the distribution unit, and undo the clips holding the demister vents to the top of the crossbeam **(see illustration)**.

42 Release any clips holding the wiring loom to the rear of the crossbeam and unbolt the crossbeam. The crossbeam is attached by 1 nut at the left-hand end, 2 nuts at the right-hand end, 2 bolts at the rear of the beam above the passenger airbag bracket, 2 bolts at the rear of the beam on the passenger side, 2 bolts above the steering column mounting, 2 bolts behind the beam at the right-hand end that retain the relay panel, 1 bolt behind

the fusebox, and 1 transverse bolt at the rear of the steering column bracket. Remove the two bolts each side of the distribution unit, mounting it to brackets on the crossbeam.

43 Detach the crossbeam from the heater distribution unit and the mounting studs at each end and remove the crossbeam from the vehicle, checking that all cabling has been released as it is removed **(see illustrations)**.

44 Undo the retaining screw attaching the wiring loom to the rear of the blower motor. Note that this fixing is out of sight and best reached from the rear of the passenger footwell.

45 Move the distribution unit upwards to release it from the vents at the centre console, where it attaches to the vents running to the rear.

46 With the help of an assistant, remove the unit from the vehicle, keeping it upright to avoid spilling the residual coolant.

47 Refitting is the reverse of removal, noting the following points:
a) Ensure the ducts and the wiring/cables are correctly routed before securing the housing in position.
b) Ensure the relay panel is in its correct position before the crossbeam is refitted.
c) When refitting the crossbeam, ensure the locating pins at each end sit in the centre of their holes.

Fresh air/recirculating/ temperature/flap positioning motors

Note: Depending on whether the unit is manually or automatically controlled there may be three or five flap servomotors fitted. On models with manual control there are two motors on the left side of the heater housing and one by the blower motor housing, on

9.41 Undo the clips holding the middle air vent to the crossbeam

9.43a Undo the bolts (arrowed) on the front face of the crossmember

9.43b Undo the bolt (arrowed) at the left-hand of the crossbeam...

9.43c ...and the 2 bolts (arrowed) at the right-hand of the crossbeam

9.43d Undo the bolts (arrowed) that attach the crossbeam to the heater unit

9.43e Undo the bolts (arrowed) that attach the crossbeam to the heater unit on the left-hand side

automatically controlled units there are two motors each side of the housing and one by the blower motor. Note that if any servo motor is replaced its basic settings will require programming using Skoda diagnostic equipment or a suitable alternative.

Fresh/recirculating air flap motor

48 Situated above the blower motor housing, remove the glovebox assembly as described in Chapter 11 Section 27 to access this motor.
49 Disconnect the wiring plug from the motor.
a) *On early models release the motor from its mountings and remove it, take note of the air flap position and ensure it does not move while the motor is removed.*
b) *On later models (May 2007 onward) undo the motor retaining bolts, turn the motor approximately 15° clockwise to release it from the guide and remove it.*
50 Refitting is the reversal of removal.

Temperature flap control motor (left)

51 Located on the lower left side of the heater housing to access this motor remove the glovebox and centre console side panel as described in Chapter 11 Sections 25 and 27.
52 Remove the lower footwell vent.
53 Disconnect the motor wiring plug, remove the mounting screw and release the motor from the housing by turning it slightly, as the motor is removed disengage it from the connecting link.
54 Refitting is the reversal of removal.

Temperature flap control motor (right)

55 Where fitted this motor is located on the lower right side of the heater housing, to access this motor remove the right lower facia panel with reference to Chapter 11 Section 26.
56 Remove the lower footwell vent.
57 Disconnect the motor wiring plug, remove the mounting screws and release the motor from the housing, as the motor is removed turn it slightly to disengage it from the connecting link.
58 Refitting is the reversal of removal.

Central flap motor

59 Situated on the upper left side of the heater housing to access this motor it will be necessary to remove the facia as described in Chapter 11 Section 26.
60 Disconnect the wiring plug, remove the mounting screws and detach the motor from the housing.
61 Refitting is the reversal of removal.

Defroster flap motor (where fitted)

62 Situated on the upper right side of the heater housing to access this motor it will be necessary to remove the facia as described in Chapter 11 Section 26.
63 Remove the lower footwell vent.
64 Undo the bolts and remove the bracket over the motor.
65 Disconnect the wiring plug, remove the

9.68 Footwell vent sensor (arrowed)

mounting screws and detach the motor from the housing, disengage the motor from the linkage as it is removed.
66 Refitting is the reversal of removal.

Air vent temperature sensors

Footwell vent (right)

67 Remove the centre console side panel and lower dash panel on the driver's side with reference to Chapter 11 Sections 25 and 26. Remove the footwell vent.
68 Disconnect the sensor wiring plug, then rotate the sensor 90° and remove it from the air duct **(see illustration)**.
69 Refitting is a reversal of removal.

Footwell vent (left)

70 Remove the glovebox and centre console side panel with reference to Chapter 11 Sections 25 and 26, then release and remove the footwell vent.
71 Disconnect the sensor wiring plug, then rotate the sensor 90° and remove it from the air duct.

Evaporator vent

72 Remove the lower dash panel on the driver's side as described in Chapter 11, Section 26.
73 Rotate the sensor 90° and remove it from the air duct. Disconnect the wiring plug as the sensor is withdrawn **(see illustration)**.
74 Refitting is a reversal of removal.

Middle vent

75 These are only accessible with the facia removed.
76 Rotate the sensor 90° and remove it from the air duct. Disconnect the wiring plug as the sensor is withdrawn **(see illustration)**.
77 Refitting is a reversal of removal.

Air quality sensor

78 Remove the wiper arms as described in Chapter 12 Section 13.
79 Pull up the rubber sealing strip, the starting in the middle, pull the plenum chamber cover upwards from the base of the windscreen. Unclip the washer jet pipe from the cover as it's withdrawn. Undo the screw at each end and remove the baffle plate below the plenum cover at the rear of the engine.
80 Remove the cover over the air intake, and

9.73 Evaporator vent sensor (arrowed)

rotate the sensor 90°. Disconnect the wiring plug as the sensor is withdrawn.
81 Refitting is a reversal of removal.

10 Air conditioning system – general information and precautions

1 Air conditioning is fitted as standard equipment to all models. It combines a conventional air heating system with an air cooling and dehumidifying system. This allows greater control over the temperature and humidity of the air inside the car, giving increased comfort and rapid window demisting.
2 The cooling side of the system works in the same way as a domestic refrigerator. Refrigerant gas, contained in a sealed network of alloy pipes, is drawn into a belt-driven compressor, and is forced through a condenser mounted on the front of the radiator. On entering the condenser, the refrigerant changes state from gas to liquid and releases heat, which is absorbed by the air flowing into the front of the engine compartment through the condenser. The liquid refrigerant passes through an expansion valve to an evaporator, where it changes from liquid under high pressure to gas under low pressure. This change in state is accompanied by a drop in temperature, which cools the evaporator. Air passing through the evaporator is cooled before flowing into the air distribution unit. The refrigerant then returns to the compressor, and the cycle begins again.

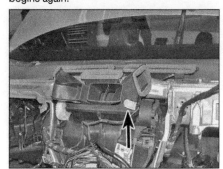

9.76 Middle air vent sensor (arrowed)

10.6 Refrigerant circuit service ports (arrowed)

3 The cooled air passes to the air distribution unit/heater housing, where it is blended with hot air blown through the heater matrix to achieve the desired temperature in the passenger compartment. When the air conditioning system is operating in Automatic mode, a series of air valves controlled by servo motors automatically regulate the cabin temperature by blending hot and cold air.

4 The heating side of the system operates as described in Section 8.

5 The operation of the air conditioning system is managed by an electronic control module, which controls the electric cooling fan, the compressor, and the facia-mounted warning light. The heating and air conditioning systems fitted to the Skoda Octavia are equipped with a sophisticated self-diagnosis facility. Should a fault occur, before attempting a repair procedure, have the facility interrogated using Skoda's diagnosis equipment (VAS 5051).

This may reveal any stored fault codes, and pin-point the problem area. Consult a Skoda dealer or suitably-equipped specialist. Note that the control unit communicates with the rest of the vehicle's electrical system by means of a databus network. Traditional 'back-probing' of connectors should not be attempted without first identifying the databus connections.

6 When working on the air conditioning system, it is necessary to observe special precautions. If for any reason the refrigerant lines must be disconnected, you must entrust this task to a Skoda dealer or an air conditioning specialist. Similarly, the system can only be evacuated and recharged by a dealer or air conditioning specialist. The refrigerant circuit service ports are located in the right-hand front corner of the engine compartment (see illustration).

⚠ *Warning: The air conditioning system contains a pressurised liquid refrigerant. If the system is discharged in an uncontrolled manner without the aid of specialist equipment, the refrigerant will boil as soon as it is exposed to the atmosphere, causing severe frostbite if it comes into contact with unprotected skin. In addition, certain refrigerants, in the presence of a naked flame (including a lit cigarette), will oxidise to form a highly poisonous gas. It is therefore extremely dangerous to disconnect any part of the air conditioning system without specialised knowledge and equipment.*

7 Uncontrolled discharging of the refrigerant can also be damaging to the environment, as certain refrigerants contain CFCs.

8 As no clutch is fitted to the air conditioning compressor (the compressor operates continuously), do not operate the engine if at all possible if the system is known to be short of refrigerant, as this will damage the compressor.

11 Air conditioning system components – removal and refitting

⚠ *Warning: Do not attempt to discharge the refrigerant circuit yourself (refer to the precautions given in Section 10). Have the air conditioning system discharged by a suitably-equipped specialist. On completion, have the engineer fit new O-rings to the line connections and evacuate and recharge the system.*

Compressor

1 Have the air conditioning system discharged by a suitably-equipped specialist.

2 Place the lock carrier in the 'Service position' (see Chapter 11 Section 10).

3 Remove the auxiliary drivebelt as described in Chapter 1 Section 11.

4 Unscrew the retaining bolts and disconnect the refrigerant lines from the compressor (see illustration). Remove the O-ring seals and renew them if necessary. Plug the open pipes and ports to prevent the ingress of moisture.

5 Disconnect the wiring plug, then unscrew the retaining bolts from the compressor, then remove the compressor from its mounting bracket (see illustration). **Note:** *The engine must not be started if the refrigerant lines are disconnected from the compressor. A lack of lubrication to the compressor could lead to overheating and damage to the unit.*

6 Refitting is a reversal of the removal procedure;fit new O ring seals to the refrigerant pipe connections and ensure that all fixings are tightened to the specified torque. On completion, have a refrigerant engineer connections evacuate and recharge the refrigerant circuit.

Evaporator

7 Remove the heater/distribution unit as described in Section 9.

8 Completely remove the bolt securing the matrix pipe to the heater housing, then remove the rubber grommet and foam seal (see illustrations).

9 Slacken the clamps and pull the two coolant pipes from the heater matrix (see illustration 9.25). Be prepared for coolant spillage.

10 Remove the fresh air/recirculating air flap motor as described in Section 9.

11 Undo the retaining bolts, remove the cover then slide the heater matrix from the housing (see illustration).

12 Disconnect the wiring plugs from the temperature sensors on the right-hand side of the housing.

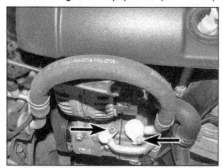

11.4 Undo the bolts (arrowed) and remove the refrigerant lines from the compressor

11.5 Compressor mounting bolts (arrowed)

11.8a Remove the matrix pipe retaining bolt (arrowed)...

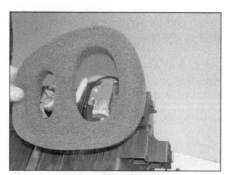

11.8b ...and the foam seal

11.11 After removing the cover, slide the matrix from the housing

11.13 Separating the matrix from the distributor housing

11.15 Undo the bolts (arrowed) and remove the cover

13 Undo the 4 retaining bolts, release the 2 catches, and separate the matrix housing from the distributor housing **(see illustration)**.
14 Undo the retaining bolt (where fitted), slide the cover across and remove the pollen filter.
15 Undo the bolts and remove the plastic cover from the front side of the housing **(see illustration)**.
16 Remove the 13 retaining bolts around the circumference of the evaporator/blower motor housing, release the catches, and separate the halves of the housing **(see illustration)**.
17 Lift the evaporator from position**(see illustration)**.
18 If required, remove the rubber seal, undo the retaining bolts and detach the expansion valve from the evaporator pipes. Recover the seals between the pipes and valve.
19 Refitting is the reverse of removal, noting the following points.
a) *Check the condition of the evaporator seal and renew it if necessary.*
b) *Reconnect the coolant pipes to the heater matrix using new seals and clamps.*
c) *Top-up the cooling system as described in Chapter 1 Section 37.*
d) *On completion, have the refrigerant engineer fit new O-rings to the line connections and then evacuate and recharge the refrigerant circuit.*

Sunlight photo-sensor

20 Carefully prise up the rear edge of the facia panel around the sensor a maximum of 15 mm. If the panel is lifted more than this, there is a risk of damage. Use a piece of cardboard on the facia to prevent damage.
21 Insert a long, flat-bladed screwdriver beneath the panel, position a small block of wood as a pad, then push the screwdriver handle downwards, release the clip and prise the sensor upwards from position. Disconnect the sensor wiring plug as it is withdrawn, and tie the connector back to prevent it from disappearing down inside the facia.
22 Refitting is a reversal of removal.

Receiver/drier

Note: *Skoda use more than one type of receiver/drier depending on model. Refer to a Skoda dealer or specialist if you are unsure which type is fitted.*

11.16 Remove the various bolts securing the halves of the housing, release the catches, then separate the halves

23 Damage can occur to an air conditioning system if it contains excess moisture. The material of the receiver drier absorbs and stores any moisture found in the in the system, but is only capable of storing a certain amount of moisture. If the system has been open to the atmosphere for any length of time then the receiver/drier should be replaced.

Showa and Fujikoki units

24 Have the air conditioning refrigerant discharged by a suitably-equipped specialist.
25 Remove the condenser as described in paragraphs 36 to 41.
26 Undo the screw holding the mounting at the top of the receiver/drier and remove the mounting. Undo the 2 screws at the bottom of the condenser. The receiver/drier unit can then be withdrawn from the bottom of the condenser. **(see illustration)**.

11.26 Bottom screws (arrowed) on Showa and Fujikoki receiver/drier unit

11.17 Lift the evaporator from place

27 Connect a new receiver/drier unit to the condenser using new seals and tighten the screws to the specified torque. The remainder of refitting is the reversal of removal.
28 Have the refrigerant recharged by a suitably-equipped specialist.

Modine unit

29 Have the air conditioning refrigerant discharged by a suitably-equipped specialist.
30 Remove the condenser as described in paragraphs 36 to 41.
31 Unscrew the protective cap from the condenser unit **(see illustration)**.
32 Push the cap on top downwards and remove the circlip. Pull out the cap, and remove the drier element using a thin pair of pointed pliers or a long pick-up tool.
33 Below the desiccant element is a mesh

11.31 Protective cap location

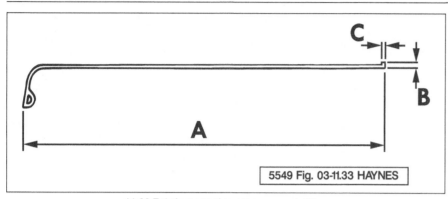

5549 Fig. 03-11.33 HAYNES

11.33 Fabricate tool to remove mesh filter

a = 390 mm   b = 7 mm max   c = 6 mm

filter, which can also be replaced, to remove it fabricate a hooked tool from a piece of 2mm diameter wire **(see illustration)** and carefully hook the mesh filter and remove it from the condenser.

34 Refitting is a reversal of removal, ensuring any seals are renewed and correctly located. Have the refrigerant recharged by a suitably-equipped specialist.

Denso unit

35 The receiver/drier is integral with the condenser in this unit and cannot be separated.

Condenser

36 Have the air conditioning refrigerant discharged by a suitably-equipped specialist.
37 Remove the radiator (see Section 3).
38 Remove the intercooler as described in Chapter 4A Section 13.
39 Undo the bolts and detach the refrigerant pipes from the condenser. Renew the O-ring seals on the connections where necessary **(see illustration)**. Plug/seal the openings to prevent contamination.
40 Lift the condenser from place **(see illustration)**.

41 Refitting is a reversal of removal. Have the refrigerant recharged by a suitably-equipped specialist.

Ambient temperature sensor

42 Raise the front of the vehicle and support it securely on axle stands (see *Jacking and vehicle support*).
43 Undo the fasteners and remove the engine undershield. Alternatively, removing the air grille from the left hand side of the bumper may allow access to the sensor.
44 The sensor is fitted behind the front bumper towards the left of the vehicle. Unclip the sensor and disconnect the wiring plug **(see illustration)**.
45 Refitting is a reversal of removal.

Expansion valve

46 Have the air conditioning refrigerant discharged by a suitably-equipped specialist.
47 Undo the bolts and disconnect the refrigerant pipes from the engine compartment bulkhead. Plug the openings to prevent contamination. Renew the O-ring seals if necessary.
48 Undo the 2 bolts and remove the expansion valve. Recover the seals between the expansion valve and refrigerant pipes.
49 Refitting is a reversal of removal, remembering to renew the valve-to-pipe seals where necessary.

11.39 The refrigerant pipes are secured by Torx bolts (arrowed)

11.40 Lift the condenser from place

11.44 Ambient temperature sensor (arrowed)

Chapter 4 Part A
Fuel system

Contents

Degrees of difficulty

Easy, suitable for novice with little experience	Fairly easy, suitable for beginner with some experience	Fairly difficult, suitable for competent DIY mechanic	Difficult, suitable for experienced DIY mechanic	Very difficult, suitable for expert DIY or professional

Specifications

Engine codes*

PD unit injector engines:
   1.9 litre (1896 cc), 8-valve, SOHC . . . .   BJB, BKC, BLS and BXE
   2.0 litre (1968 cc):
      8-valve, SOHC . . . .   BMM
      16-valve, DOHC . . . .   BKD and BMN
Common rail injection engines:
   2.0 litre (1968 cc), 16-valve, DOHC . . . .   CBBB, CBDB and CEGA (1st Generation)
                                            CLCA, CLCB, CFHC and CFHF (2nd Generation)

*See 'Vehicle identification' at the end of this manual for the location of engine code markings.

General

Fuel injection system . . . .   Electronic, direct injection
Firing order   1-3-4-2
Maximum engine speed. . . . .   N/A (ECM controlled)
Engine fast idle speed . . . .   N/A (ECM controlled)

Tandem pump (PD unit injector engines only)

Fuel pressure at 4000 rpm:
   SOHC engines . . . .   7.5 bar minimum
   DOHC engines . . . .   10.5 bar minimum

Turbocharger

Type . . . .   Garrett or KKK

Torque wrench settings

	Nm	lbf ft
Camshaft position sensor	10	7
EGR pipe flange to exhaust manifold nuts	25	18
EGR pipe flange bolts:		
Engine codes CLCA, CLCB, CFHC and CFHF	10	7
All other engine codes	22	16
EGR valve mounting bolt	10	7
Engine speed/TDC sender	5	4
Exhaust gas temperature sensor		
(where fitted to turbocharger/exhaust manifold)	45	33
Exhaust manifold nuts*	25	18
Fuel pressure regulating valve (common rail)	80	59
Fuel pressure sensor (common rail)	100	74
Fuel rail mounting bolts (common rail)	22	16
High-pressure fuel pipe unions:		
Engine code CEGA:		
Stage 1	15	11
Stage 2	Angle-tighten a further 60°	
Engine codes CLCA, CLCB, CFHC and CFHF	28	21
High-pressure fuel pump bolts:		
Stage 1	20	15
Stage 2	Angle-tighten lower bolts a further 180°	
	Angle-tighten upper bolt a further 45°	
Injector clamp/mounting:		
PD unit injector engines: *		
1.9 litre:		
Stage 1	12	9
Stage 2	Angle-tighten a further 270°	
2.0 litre:		
Stage 1	3	2
Stage 2	Angle-tighten a further 90°	
Stage 3	Angle-tighten a further 180°	
Common rail injector engines with engine code CEGA:		
Clamp nut	10	7
Cover bolt	5	4
Common rail injector engines with engine codes CLCA, CLCB, CFHC and CFHF:		
Stage 1	8	6
Stage 2	Angle-tighten a further 270°	
Inlet manifold flap motor housing	10	7
Inlet manifold to cylinder head: *		
PD unit injector engines	22	16
Common rail injection engines	8	6
Pump injector rocker shaft bolts: *		
Stage 1	20	15
Stage 2	Angle-tighten a further 90°	
Tandem pump bolts:		
SOHC engines:		
Upper	20	15
Lower	8	6
DOHC engines	20	15
Throttle valve module	10	7
Turbocharger oil feed pipe connection to cylinder block		
(engine codes CLCA, CLCB, CFHC and CFHF)	30	22
Turbocharger oil feed pipe union (at turbo)	22	16
Turbocharger support bracket (incorporating turbo oil return):		
To engine block: *		
Engine codes CLCA, CLCB, CFHC and CFHF	40	30
Engine codes BLS, BMM, BMN and CEGA	60	44
To turbocharger:		
Engine codes BLS,BMM,BMN and CEGA	25	18
Engine codes CLCA, CLCB, CFHC and CFHF	20	15
Turbocharger oil return pipe to adaptor at cylinder block:		
Engine codes BJB, BKC, BXE and BKD	30	22
Turbocharger oil return pipe adaptor to cylinder block:		
Engine codes BJB, BKC, BXE and BKD	40	30
Turbocharger oil return pipe to turbo:		
Engine codes BJB, BKC, BXE and BKD	17	12
Engine codes BLS, BMM, BMN and CEGA	15	11
Engine codes CLCA, CLCB, CFHC and CFHF	20	15

* Do not re-use

1 General information and precautions

1 All engines covered by this Manual are fitted with a direct-injection fuelling system, incorporating a fuel tank, an engine-bay mounted fuel filter with an integral water separator, fuel supply and return lines and four fuel injectors. Models with the PD unit injector engines also have a fuel cooler mounted beneath the right-hand side of the car, on the underbody. All engines are fitted with a turbocharger.

2 Two different types of fuel injection system are fitted to the Octavia model. The first is first is known as the PD (Pumpe Duse) or unit injector system, where fuel is delivered by a camshaft-driven 'tandem pump' at low pressure to the injectors (known as unit injectors). A 'roller rocker' assembly, mounted above the camshaft bearing caps, uses an extra set of camshaft lobes to compress the top of each injector once per firing cycle. This arrangement creates high injection pressures. The precise timing of the pre-injection and main injection is controlled by the engine management ECM and a solenoid on each injector.

3 The second type is the familiar common rail system, where fuel is supplied from a timing belt-driven high-pressure pump to a common fuel rail (or reservoir). The four injectors are fitted into the cylinder head and are connected to the fuel rail by rigid metal pipes. The precise timing of the pre, main, and post-injections are controlled by the engine management ECM and electrically-operated Piezo crystal or electro-magnetically controlled injectors.

4 The direct-injection fuelling system is controlled electronically by a diesel engine management system, comprising an Electronic Control Module (ECM) and its associated sensors, actuators and wiring. In addition, the ECM manages the operation of the Exhaust Gas Recirculation (EGR) emission control system (Chapter 4B Section 3), the turbocharger boost pressure control system and the glow plug control system (Chapter 5 Section 11).

5 A flap valve/throttle valve module fitted to the inlet manifold is closed by the ECM for 3 seconds as the engine is switched off, to minimise the air intake as the engine shuts down. This minimises the vibration felt as the pistons come up against the volume of highly compressed air present in the combustion chambers.

6 It should be noted that fault diagnosis of the diesel engine management system is only possible with dedicated electronic test equipment. Problems with the system's operation should therefore be referred to a Skoda dealer or suitably-equipped specialist for assessment. Once the fault has been identified, the removal/refitting sequences detailed in the following Sections will then allow the appropriate component(s) to be renewed as required.

7 The EOBD diagnostic connector is located under the driver's side of the facia.

Precautions

8 Many of the operations described in this Chapter involve the disconnection of fuel lines, which may cause an amount of fuel spillage. Before commencing work, refer to the warnings below and the information in *Safety first!* at the beginning of this manual.

⚠ *Warning: When working on any part of the fuel system, avoid direct contact skin contact with diesel fuel – wear protective clothing and gloves when handling fuel system components. Ensure that the work area is well-ventilated to prevent the build-up of diesel fuel vapour.*

⚠ *Warning: Fuel injectors operate at extremely high pressures and the jet of fuel produced at the nozzle is capable of piercing skin, with potentially fatal results. When working with pressurised injectors, take care to avoid exposing any part of the body to the fuel spray. It is recommended that a diesel fuel systems specialist should carry out any pressure testing of the fuel system components.*

⚠ *Warning: Under no circumstances should diesel fuel be allowed to come into contact with coolant hoses – wipe off accidental spillage immediately. Hoses that have been contaminated with fuel for an extended period should be renewed.*

⚠ *Warning: Diesel fuel systems are particularly sensitive to contamination from dirt, air and water. Pay particular attention to cleanliness when working on any part of the fuel system, to prevent the ingress of dirt. Thoroughly clean the area around fuel unions before disconnecting them. Only use lint-free cloths and clean fuel for component cleansing.*

⚠ *Warning: Store dismantled components in sealed containers to prevent contamination and the formation of condensation.*

2 Fuel pipes and fittings – general information and disconnection

1 Disconnect the cable from the negative battery terminal (Chapter 5 Section 3) before proceeding.

2 The fuel supply pipe connects the fuel pump in the fuel tank to the fuel rail on the engine.

3 Whenever you're working under the vehicle, be sure to inspect all fuel and evaporative emission pipes for leaks, kinks, dents and other damage. Always replace a damaged fuel pipe immediately.

4 If you find signs of dirt in the pipes during disassembly, disconnect all pipes and blow them out with compressed air. Inspect the fuel strainer on the fuel pump pick-up unit for damage and deterioration.

Steel tubing

5 It is critical that the fuel pipes be replaced with pipes of equivalent type and specification.

6 Some steel fuel pipes have threaded fittings. When loosening these fittings, hold the stationary fitting with a spanner while turning the union nut.

Plastic tubing

⚠ *Warning: When removing or installing plastic fuel tubing, be careful not to bend or twist it too much, which can damage it. Also, plastic fuel tubing is NOT heat resistant, so keep it away from excessive heat.*

7 When replacing fuel system plastic tubing, use only original equipment replacement plastic tubing.

Flexible hoses

8 When replacing fuel system flexible hoses, use original equipment replacements, or hose to the same specification.

9 Don't route fuel hoses (or metal pipes) within 100 mm of the exhaust system or within 280 mm of the catalytic converter. Make sure that no rubber hoses are installed directly against the vehicle, particularly in places where there is any

2.10a Two-tab type fitting; depress both tabs with your fingers, then pull the fuel pipe and the fitting apart

2.10b On this type of fitting, depress the two buttons on opposite sides of the fitting, then pull it off the fuel pipe

2.10c Threaded fuel pipe fitting; hold the stationary portion of the pipe or component (A) while loosening the union nut (B) with a flare-nut spanner

2.10d Plastic collar-type fitting; rotate the outer part of the fitting

2.10e Metal collar quick-connect fitting; pull the end of the retainer off the fuel pipe and disengage the other end from the female side of the fitting...

2.10f ... insert a fuel pipe separator tool into the female side of the fitting, push it into the fitting and pull the fuel pipe off the pipe

2.10g Some fittings are secured by lock tabs. Release the lock tab (A) and rotate it to the fully-opened position, squeeze the two smaller lock tabs (B)...

2.10h ... then push the retainer out and pull the fuel pipe off the pipe

2.10i Spring-lock coupling; remove the safety cover, install a coupling release tool and close the tool around the coupling...

2.10j ... push the tool into the fitting, then pull the two pipes apart

2.10k Hairpin clip type fitting: push the legs of the retainer clip together, then push the clip down all the way until it stops and pull the fuel pipe off the pipe

3.1 Disconnect the airflow meter wiring plug (arrowed) and the vacuum hose

vibration. If allowed to touch some vibrating part of the vehicle, a hose can easily become chafed and it might start leaking. A good rule of thumb is to maintain a minimum of 8.0 mm clearance around a hose (or metal pipe) to prevent contact with the vehicle underbody.

Disconnecting fuel pipe fittings

10   Typical fuel pipe fittings **(see illustrations 2.10a to 2.10b)**

3   Air cleaner assembly – removal and refitting

Removal

1   Disconnect the wiring from the air mass meter. Also disconnect the vacuum hose from the air filter housing **(see illustration)**.

3.2 Disconnect the air intake hose

3.3 Unclip the cover from the intake ducting

3.5 Air cleaner assembly retaining bolt (arrowed)

2 Loosen the clip and disconnect the turbocharger air intake hose at the connection to the air mass meter **(see illustration)**.

3 Release the air filter intake pipe, where the intake pipe is attached to plastic ducting on the lock carrier unclip the plastic cover from the air intake ducting **(see illustration)**, then release the two securing clips (one at each side) and remove the ducting from the lock carrier. Note on some models there may be retaining screws securing the inner part of the lower ducting to the lock carrier.

4 Press in the tabs and release the air filter intake pipe from the housing.

5 Undo the retaining bolt located at the base of the air cleaner assembly at the back, and pull the assembly upwards releasing the locating pins from their grommets. Manoeuvre the filter housing from the engine compartment, taking note of the routing of the attached drain tubing **(see illustration)**.

Refitting

6 Refitting is the reverse of removal, making sure that the assembly mounting pegs and grommets are correctly engaged and the drain tube is correctly routed.

**4 Engine management system
– component removal
and refitting**

Throttle pedal/position sensor

Removal

1 Prise out the plastic cap, and undo the retaining bolt at the top of the pedal assembly **(see illustration)**.

2 Insert Skoda tool into the slots at the base of the assembly to release the clips and lift it from place (note that the slots may be obscured by carpet). In the absence of the special tool, insert a small screwdriver into the slots, and release the clips. Push the right-hand clip rearwards to release it, and the left-hand clip to the right **(see illustration)**.

3 Disconnect the sensor wiring plug.

4 No further dismantling of the assembly is recommended – no component parts are available. If the assembly if faulty, a new one must be fitted.

Refitting

5 Position the assembly, ensuring that the two pins on the floor and the centring pin on the bulkhead locate correctly.

6 The remainder of refitting is a reversal of removal. Note that renewal of the throttle pedal module on vehicles fitted with an automatic gearbox requires resetting of the engine ECM. This is carried out using Skoda diagnostic equipment VAS5051, and should be undertaken by a Skoda dealer or suitably-equipped specialist.

Coolant temperature sensor

7 Refer to Chapter 3 Section 6.

Fuel temperature sensor

Removal

8 The fuel temperature sensor is located in the fuel line at the front of the cylinder head

4.1 Prise out the cap and undo the bolt (arrowed) at the top of the pedal

4.11a Fuel temp sensor (arrowed) – PD unit injector engines

(PD unit injector engines) or on the top of the high-pressure fuel pump (common rail injection engines).

9 Pull the plastic cover on the top of the engine upwards from the rubber mountings.

10 Disconnect the wiring from the sensor.

11 On PD unit injector engines, release the clips and pull the sensor from the hoses. On common rail injection engines, release the clamps and disconnect the hoses from the sensor assembly **(see illustrations)**.

Refitting

12 Refit the fuel temperature sensor by reversing the removal procedure.

Intake air temperature/ charge pressure sensor

Removal

13 The intake air temperature/charge air pressure sensor is located in the charge air

4.2 Insert the Skoda tool/screwdrivers into the slots (arrowed)

4.11b Release the clamps (arrowed) and remove the fuel temperature sensor assembly – common rail injection engines

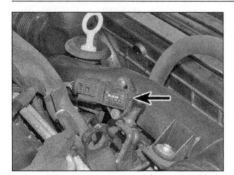

4.15a Charge pressure sensor (arrowed) – 1.9 litre PD unit injector engines (BJB, BKC and BXE)

4.15b Charge pressure sensor (arrowed) – 2.0 litre PD unit injector engines

4.15c Charge pressure sensor (arrowed) – common rail injection engines

trunking between the intercooler and the inlet manifold. On engine codes BLS and BMM the sensor is located in the outlet at the top right of the intercooler, on engine codes BJB, BKC and BXE the sensor is in the charge air pipe at the top front of the engine **(see illustration 4.15a)**, on other models the sensor is situated in the charge air pipe at the base or front of the engine **(see illustrations 4.15b and 4.15c)**.

14 To access the lower sensors it will be necessary to raise the vehicle and support it on axle stands with reference to *Jacking and vehicle support*, and remove the engine undertray.

15 On common rail engines, disconnect the charge air hoses at each end, undo the mounting bolts and remove the charge air pipe, releasing the sensor wiring plug as it is withdrawn **(see illustrations)**.

16 On all models release the wiring plug (where still connected), undo the bolts and remove the sensor from the charge air pipe.

Refitting

17 Refitting is a reversal of removal.

Engine speed sensor

Removal

18 The engine speed sensor is mounted on the front left-hand side of the cylinder block, adjacent to the mating surface of the block and transmission bellhousing. Raise the front of the vehicle, and support is securely on axle stands (see *Jacking and vehicle support*).

19 Undo the fasteners and remove the engine undershield.

4.20 Oil cooler/filter housing bolts (arrowed)

20 Remove the oil filter housing with reference to Chapter 2A Section 19 or Chapter 2B Section 17 **(see illustration)**.

21 Disconnect wiring plug from engine speed sensor, remove the retaining bolt and withdraw the sensor from the cylinder block **(see illustration)**.

Refitting

22 Refit the sensor by reversing the removal procedure. Re-fill the coolant and top-up the engine oil as described in Chapter 1 Section 37 and *Weekly checks*.

Airflow meter

Removal

23 On all models the air flow meter is located in the outlet from the air cleaner assembly on the left-hand side of the engine compartment.

24 Disconnect the airflow meter wiring plug **(see illustration 2.1)**

25 Loosen the clip and disconnect the air intake hose between the airflow meter and the turbocharger.

26 Undo the two screws and pull the air flow meter from its connection to the air cleaner housing. Handle the airflow meter carefully, as it is a delicate component.

Refitting

27 Refitting is a reversal of removal. Renew the O-ring seal if it appears damaged.

Inlet manifold flap motor/ housing (PD engines)

Removal

Note: *On model engine code BJB the inlet manifold flap is vacuum operated and shares a housing with the EGR valve, whereas all other PD engine codes have a separate electrically-operated flap motor.*

28 As diesel engines have a very high compression ratio, when the engine is turned off, the pistons still compress a large quantity of air for a few revolutions and cause the engine unit to shudder. The inlet manifold shut-off flap is located in a housing bolted to the inlet manifold. When the ignition switch is turned to the 'off' position, the engine management ECM-controlled flap is closed, which shuts off the air supply to the cylinders.

This allows the pistons to compress very little air, and the engine runs softly to a halt. The flap opens again approximately 3 seconds after switching off the ignition switch.

29 Remove the plastic cover from the top of the engine.

30 Release any charge air intake pipe/hose fixings and attachments and disconnect the charge air intake pipe/hose from the inlet manifold flap housing. Remove the charge air intake pipe or position it to enable access to the bolts securing the flap motor housing.

31 Disconnect the wiring plug or vacuum hose (as applicable) from the inlet manifold flap motor. Where required, undo the bolts and disconnect the EGR pipe from the housing.

32 Undo the bolts, and remove the flap motor from the inlet manifold. Discard the O-ring seal, a new one must be fitted.

Refitting

33 Refitting is a reversal of removal. Tighten the inlet manifold flap motor housing bolts to the specified torque.

Throttle valve housing/module (common rail engines)

Removal

34 Remove the cover from the top off the engine.

35 Slacken the clips and disconnect the charge air hose from the right-hand side of the intercooler and plastic charge air pipe. Undo the fixings securing the charge air

4.21 Engine speed sensor bolt (arrowed) – shown with flywheel removed for clarity

4.35 Charge air hose connected to throttle valve housing

4.37 Undo the dipstick tube retaining bolt

4.38 Undo the three retaining bolts

pipe to the engine, disconnect the intake air temperature/charge air pressure sender wiring plug, release the attached coolant hose and slacken the clamp at the charge air hose connection to the throttle valve housing (see illustration). Remove the charge air pipe/hose from the front of the engine.

36 Disconnect the wiring plug from the throttle valve housing.

37 Undo the retaining bolt and disconnect the dipstick guide tube upper mounting from the throttle housing (see illustration).

38 Unscrew and remove the retaining bolts (see illustration), then lift the throttle valve housing/module away from the inlet manifold or EGR valve (engine code CEGA). Recover the O-ring seal a new one will be required for refitting.

Refitting

39 Refitting is the reversal of removal, noting the following:

a) Use a new O-ring seal between the throttle housing and inlet manifold. (EGR valve housing on engine code CEGA).

b) Tighten the throttle housing bolts evenly to the specified torque.

c) Ensure that all hoses and electrical connectors are refitted securely.

Clutch position sensor

Removal

40 Remove the plastic cover from the top of the engine by pulling it up from the mountings.

41 Undo the nuts and remove the heat shield over the particulate filter, and the heat shield over the clutch master cylinder at the engine compartment bulkhead (where fitted).

42 Apply a hose clamp to the fluid supply hose to the clutch master cylinder.

43 Prise out the retaining clip a little, then pull the pressure hose from the master cylinder at the engine compartment bulkhead (see illustrations).

44 Unclip the position sensor and slide it from the master cylinder. Disconnect the wiring plug as the sensor is withdrawn.

Refitting

45 Refitting is a reversal of removal. If necessary, bleed the clutch hydraulic system as described in Chapter 6 Section 2.

Electronic control module (ECM)

Removal

Caution: The ECM is programmed and identified specifically for the vehicle it is fitted to, and the identity coding must be transferred to any new module. This process requires the use of dedicated Skoda diagnostic equipment VAS 5051/2. For this reason, it is recommended that ECM renewal is carried out by a Skoda dealer or suitably-equipped specialist, however removal and refitting of the original ECM is possible by the home mechanic. Note also that if the ECM is renewed, the identification of the new ECM must be transferred to the immobiliser control module by a Skoda dealer or specialist.

Caution: Always wait at least 30 seconds after switching off the ignition before disconnecting the wiring from the ECM.

4.43a Press the clip (arrowed) across...

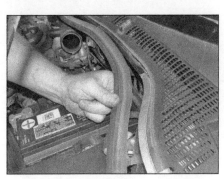

4.48a Pull up the rubber sealing strip

When the wiring is disconnected, all the learned values may be erased, although any Specifications of the fault memory are retained. After reconnecting the wiring, the vehicle must be driven for several miles so that the ECM can learn its basic settings. If the engine still runs erratically, the basic settings may be reinstated by a Skoda dealer or specialist using a special test instrument.

Note: Removing the wiper motor improves access when carrying out this task.

46 The electronic control module is located on the bulkhead at the rear of the engine compartment. Disconnect the battery negative (earth) lead (see Chapter 5 Section 3).

47 Remove the wiper arms as described in Chapter 12 Section 13.

48 Pull up the rubber sealing strip, the starting in the middle, pull the plenum chamber cover upwards from the base of the windscreen (see illustrations). Unclip the washer jet pipe from

4.43b ... and slide the clutch position sensor downwards

4.48b Starting at one end, pull the plenum chamber cover from the base of the windscreen

the cover as it's withdrawn. Undo the screw at each end and remove the front section of the plenum chamber below the plenum cover at the rear of the engine.

49 Disconnect the wiring plug from the windscreen heater control unit (where fitted).

50 Being careful not to damage any part of the wiring loom, use a small saw to cut slots in the 2 shear bolts **(see illustration)** and undo.

51 With the screws removed, move the cover plate to the left to access the locking tab. Using a screwdriver, lift the locking tab and slide the cover plate to the left, manoeuvre it past the ECM wiring, and remove **(see illustrations)**.

52 The ECM can now be slid to the left, the wiring plug disconnected, and the unit removed**(see illustration)**.

Refitting

53 Refitting is a reversal of removal, using new shear bolts to refit the cover plate. Reconnect the battery as described in Chapter 5 Section 3.

Camshaft position sensor

Removal
(1.9 litre PD unit injector engines)

54 With reference to Chapter 2A Section 6, remove the timing belt upper cover.

55 Undo the retaining bolt, and remove the sensor from the cylinder head. Trace the sensor wiring back to the connector on the engine bulkhead and unplug.

56 Prise out the grommet in the timing belt

4.51a Slide the cover plate to one side and lift the locking tab

4.52 Slide the ECM from place

4.50 Use a small saw to cut slots in the shear bolts. Take care not to damage the wiring loom

rear cover and manoeuvre the sensor out through the hole.

Refitting

57 Refitting is a reversal of removal, noting that the sensor has a locating peg which must be fitted into the hole in the cylinder head**(see illustration)**. Tighten the sensor retaining bolt to the specified torque.

Removal
(2.0 litre PD unit injector engines)

58 Remove the timing belt from the camshaft pulleys and idler roller as described in Chapter 2A Section 7.Trace the wiring to the connecting plug, then undo the retaining bolt and remove the sensor.

Refitting

59 Refitting is a reversal of removal, noting that the sensor has a locating peg which must

4.51b Remove the cover plate

4.57 The camshaft position sensor has a locating peg which must locate into the hole in the cylinder head

be fitted into the hole in the cylinder head **(see illustration 4.57)**. Tighten the sensor retaining bolt to the specified torque.

Removal (Common rail engines)

60 Remove the timing belt as described in Chapter 2B Section 7.

61 Disconnect the camshaft position sensor wiring plug and release it from the retaining bracket.

62 Use a screwdriver to remove the repair aperture webs from the timing belt inner cover.

63 Unscrew the retaining bolt and manoeuvre the camshaft position sensor and wiring plug through the repair aperture in the timing belt cover **(see illustration)**.

Refitting

64 Refitting is a reversal of removal, noting that the repair aperture must be re-covered. Tighten the sensor retaining bolt to the specified torque.

---

5 Injectors –
general information, removal and refitting

> ⚠️ *Warning: Exercise extreme caution when working on the fuel injectors. Never expose the hands or any part of the body to injector spray, as the high working pressure can cause the fuel to penetrate the skin, with possibly fatal results. You are strongly advised to have any work which involves testing the injectors under pressure carried out by a dealer or fuel injection specialist. Refer to the precautions given in Section 1 of this Chapter before proceeding.*

General information

1 Injectors deteriorate with prolonged use, and it is reasonable to expect them to need reconditioning or renewal once high mileages have been reached. Accurate testing, overhaul and calibration of the injectors must be left to a specialist.

Removal

Note: *Take care not to allow dirt into the injectors or fuel pipes during this procedure. Do not drop the injectors or allow the needles at their tips to become damaged. The injectors*

4.63 Camshaft position sensor bolt

are precision-made to fine limits, and must not be handled roughly. Keep the injectors identified for position to ensure correct refitting.

1.9 litre PD unit injector engines

2 With reference to Chapter 2A Sections 4 and 6, remove the upper timing belt cover and camshaft cover.

3 Using a spanner or socket, turn the crankshaft pulley until the rocker arm for the injector which is to be removed, is at its highest, ie, the injector plunger spring is under the least amount of tension.

4 Slacken the locknut of the adjustment bolt on the end of the rocker arm above the injector, and undo the adjustment bolt until the rocker arm lies against the plunger pin of the injector **(see illustration)**.

5 Starting at the outside and working in, gradually and evenly slacken and remove the rocker shaft retaining bolts. Lift off the rocker shaft. Check the contact face of each adjustment bolt, and renew any that show signs of wear.

6 Undo the clamping block securing bolt and remove the block from the side of the injector **(see illustration)**.

7 Using a small screwdriver, carefully prise the wiring connector from the injector.

8 Skoda technicians use a slide hammer (tool T10055) to pull the injector from the cylinder head. This is a slide hammer which engages in the side of the injector. If this tool is not available, it is possible to fabricate an equivalent using a short section of angle-iron, a length of threaded rod, a cylindrical weight, and two locknuts. Weld/braze the rod to the angle-iron, slide the weight over the rod, and lock the two nuts together at the end of the rod to provide the stop for the weight **(see illustration)**. Seat the slide hammer/tool in the slot on the side on the injector, and pull the injector out using a few gently taps. Recover circlip, the heat shield and O-rings and discard. New ones must be used for refitting **(see illustration)**.

9 If required, the injector wiring loom/rail can be removed from the cylinder head by undoing the two retaining nuts/bolts at the left-hand end of the head. To prevent the wiring connectors

5.4 Undo the adjustment bolt until the rocker arm lies against the plunger pin of the injector

5.6 Remove the clamping block securing bolt (arrowed)

5.8a Unit injector removal tool

a = 5 mm
b = 15 mm
c = 25 mm
d Weld/braze the rod to the angle iron
e Threaded rod
f Cylindrical weight
g Locknuts

fouling the cylinder head casting as the assembly is withdrawn, insert the connectors into the storage slots in the plastic wiring rail. Carefully push the assembly to the rear, and out of the casting **(see illustrations)**.

2.0 litre PD unit injector engines

10 With reference to Chapter 2A Sections 4 and 6, remove the upper timing belt cover and camshaft cover.

11 Slacken the locknut of the adjustment bolt on the end of the rocker arm above the respective injector, and undo the adjustment bolt until the rocker arm lies against the plunger pin of the injector.

12 Starting at the outside and working in, gradually and evenly slacken and remove the rocker shaft retaining bolts. Lift off the rocker shaft. Check the contact face of each adjustment bolt, and renew any that show signs of wear.

13 Using a pair of pliers, carefully pull the wiring connector from the injector.

14 The unit injectors have two mounting bolts each. Unscrew and remove the two bolts.

15 Skoda technicians use a slide hammer (tool T10133) to pull the injector from the cylinder head. This is a slide hammer which engages in the injector bolt holes. If this tool is not available, it is possible to fabricate an

5.8b Seat the slide hammer/tool in the slot on the side of the injector, and pull the injector out

5.9a Undo the two nuts at the left-hand end of the head and slide the injector loom/rail out

5.9b The injector connectors will slide into the loom/rail to prevent them from being damaged as the assembly is withdrawn/inserted into the cylinder head

5.17 Lever up the clip (arrowed) and disconnect the injector wiring plugs

5.18a Hold down the outer tabs, and prise up the centre piece (arrowed)...

5.18b... then pull the return hose connector upwards from the injector

5.19 Undo the unions and remove the high-pressure pipes between the common rail and the injectors

5.20a Undo the injector clamp cover bolts (arrowed)...

5.20b... then lift and rotate it 90°

equivalent using a short section of angle-iron, a length of threaded rod, a cylindrical weight, and two locknuts. Weld/braze the rod to the angle-iron, slide the weight over the rod, and lock the two nuts together at the end of the rod to provide the stop for the weight **(see illustration 5.8a)**. Pull the injector out of the cylinder head. Recover the heat shield and O-rings and discard. New ones must be used for refitting.

Common rail engines

16 Pull the plastic cover over the engine upwards from its mountings. Where fitted, remove the foam insulation over the injectors.
17 Disconnect the injector wiring plugs **(see illustration)**.
18 Ensure the area around the injectors and the pipes/return hoses is clean and free from debris. The use of a vacuum cleaner

is recommended. Push the return hose connector downwards at its tabs, then pull up the centre piece and disconnect them from the injectors **(see illustrations)**. Plug the openings to prevent contamination.
19 Undo the unions remove the high-pressure pipes between the common fuel rail and the injectors **(see illustration)**. Where provision is given counterhold the injector union to avoid damaging the injector as the pipe union is slackened. Plug the openings to prevent contamination.

Engine code CEGA

20 Undo the bolts securing the injector clamp cover, the slightly lift the cover and rotate it 90° for access to the injector retaining nuts **(see illustrations)**.
21 Unscrew the injector retaining nuts.
22 Skoda technicians use a slide hammer

(tool T10055) to pull the injector from the cylinder head. This is a slide hammer with an adapter which bolts onto the top of the. If this tool is not available, it is possible to fabricate an equivalent using slide hammer with the union from an old injector pipe brazed/welded onto the end. Screw the tool onto the top of the injector, and pull the injector out using a few gently taps. Recover the clamping piece, copper seal and O-rings and discard. New ones must be used for refitting **(see illustrations)**. **Note:** *The injectors should only be refitted to their original positions. Mark the injectors to avoid confusion if refitting the original injectors.*

Engine codes CLCA, CLCB, CFHC and CFHF

23 Undo the bolt securing the injector clamp between the two injectors, note that one

5.22a We affixed an old injector pipe union onto the end of the slide hammer...

5.22b ... screwed it onto the top of the injector...

5.22c ... and pulled it from the cylinder head

5.23 Remove the injector clamp retaining bolt

5.25 Remove two injectors with retaining clamp

5.27 Great care must be used to ensure that the injector O-rings are fitted without being twisted

clamp secures two injectors in place **(see illustration)**.

24 Skoda technicians use a slide hammer (tool T10055) and adapter (T10415) to release the injectors from the cylinder head. If this tool is not available it may be possible to to fabricate an equivalent tool using a slide hammer, fastened to the injector using an old pipe union nut. (ensuring that any tool pulls the injector straight up out of the cylinder head).

25 Either the left or right pair of injectors will have to be released and removed together as one retaining clamp is slotted into two injectors **(see illustration)**.

26 Recover the copper seals and O-rings and discard. New ones must be used for refitting. **Note:** *The injectors and retaining clamps should only be refitted to their original positions. Mark the injectors to avoid confusion if refitting the original injectors*

Refitting

1.9 litre PD unit injector engines

27 Prior to refitting the injectors, the three O-rings, heat insulation washer and clip must be renewed. Due to the high injection pressures, it is essential that the O-rings are fitted without being twisted. Skoda recommend the use of three special assembly sleeves to install the O-rings squarely (tool T10056), although suitably-equivalent tools are available from automotive tool manufacturers. It may be prudent to entrust O-ring renewal to a Skoda dealer or suitably-equipped injection specialist, rather than risk subsequent leaks **(see illustration)**.

28 After renewing the O-rings, fit the heat shield and secure it in place with the circlip **(see illustration)**.

29 Smear clean engine oil onto the O-rings, and push the injector evenly down into the cylinder head onto its stop.

30 Fit the clamping block alongside the injector, but only hand-tighten the new retaining bolt at this stage.

31 It is essential that the injectors are fitted at right-angles to the clamping block. In order to achieve this, measure the distance from the end of the cylinder head to the rounded section of the injector **(see illustrations)**. The dimensions (a) are as follows:

Cylinder 1 = 333.0 ± 0.8 mm
Cylinder 2 = 245.0 ± 0.8 mm
Cylinder 3 = 153.6 ± 0.8 mm
Cylinder 4 = 65.6 ± 0.8 mm

5.28 Unit injector

1	Bolt	3	Cylinder head	5	Rocker arm	8	Unit injector	11	O-ring
2	Clamping block	4	Bolt	6	Nut	9	O-ring	12	Heat shield
				7	Adjuster	10	O-ring	13	Circlip

5.31a Measure the distance (a) from the end of the cylinder head to the rounded section of the injector

5.31b Use a set square against the rounded edge of the injector...

5.31c ... and measure the distance to the end of the cylinder head

5.34 Attach a DTI (Dial Test Indicator) gauge to the cylinder head upper surface, and position the DTI probe against the top of the adjustment bolt

32 Once the injector(s) are aligned correctly, tighten the clamping bolt to the specified Stage 1 torque setting, and the Stage 2 angle tightening setting. **Note:** *If an injector has been renewed, it is essential that the adjustment bolt, locknut of the corresponding rocker and ball-pin are renewed at the same time. The ball-pins simply pull out of the injector spring cap. There is an O-ring in each spring cap to stop the ball-pins from falling out.*

33 Smear some grease (No G000 100) onto the contact face of each rocker arm adjustment bolt, and refit the rocker shaft assembly to the camshaft bearing caps, tightening the retaining bolts as follows. Starting from the inside out, hand-tighten the bolts. Again, from the inside out, tighten the bolts to the Stage 1 torque setting. Finally, from the inside out, tighten the bolts to the Stage 2 angle tightening setting.

34 The following procedure is only necessary if an injector has been removed. Attach a DTI (Dial Test Indicator) gauge to the cylinder head upper surface, and position the DTI probe against the top of the adjustment bolt **(see illustration)**. Turn the crankshaft until the rocker arm roller is on the highest point of its corresponding camshaft lobe, and the adjustment bolt is at its lowest. Once this position has been established, remove the DTI gauge, screw the adjustment bolt in until firm resistance is felt, and the injector spring cannot be compressed further. Turn the adjustment bolt anti-clockwise 180°, and tighten the locknut securely. Repeat this procedure for any other injectors that have been removed.

35 Reconnect the wiring plug to the injector.
36 Refit the camshaft cover and upper timing belt cover, as described in Chapter 2A Sections 4 and 6.
37 Start the engine and check that it runs correctly.

2.0 litre PD unit injector engines

38 Prior to refitting the injectors, the O-ring and heat insulation washer must be renewed. Due to the high injection pressures, it is essential that the O-ring is fitted without being twisted. Skoda recommend the use of a special assembly sleeve to install the O-ring squarely. It may be prudent to entrust O-ring renewal to a Skoda dealer or suitably-equipped injection specialist, rather than risk subsequent leaks. In addition, Skoda recommend that the adjustment bolts and the ball-pins (located on the tops of the injectors) are renewed.

39 Smear clean engine oil onto the O-ring, and push the injector together with the heat shield evenly down into the cylinder head onto its stop. It is absolutely important that the injector is inserted fully at this stage, as subsequent tightening of the mounting bolts may otherwise cause damage. Skoda technicians use a special lever to press the injectors fully into the head.

40 Insert the mounting bolts and tighten in the three stages given in the Specifications.

41 Smear some grease (No G000 100) onto the contact face of each rocker arm adjustment bolt, and refit the rocker shaft assembly, tightening the retaining bolts as follows. Starting from the inside out,

hand-tighten the bolts. Again, from the inside out, tighten the bolts to the Stage 1 torque setting. Finally, from the inside out, tighten the bolts to the Stage 2 angle tightening setting.

42 The following procedure is only necessary if an injector has been removed. Attach a DTI (Dial Test Indicator) gauge to the cylinder head upper surface, and position the DTI probe against the top of the adjustment bolt **(see illustration 5.34)**. Turn the crankshaft until the rocker arm roller is on the highest point of its corresponding camshaft lobe, and the adjustment bolt is at its lowest. Once this position has been established, remove the DTI gauge, bolt the adjustment bolt in until firm resistance is felt, and the injector spring cannot be compressed further. Turn the adjustment bolt anti-clockwise 180°, and tighten the locknut securely. Repeat this procedure for any other injectors that have been refitted.

43 Reconnect the wiring plug to the injector.
44 Refit the camshaft cover and upper timing belt cover, as described in Chapter 2A Sections 4 and 6.
45 Start the engine and check that it runs correctly.

Common rail engines

46 Ensure the area around the injector locations in the cylinder head are clean and free from debris. Use a vacuum cleaner if available. Clean any carbon deposits from the injector and sealing surfaces with a cloth soaked in clean engine oil or rust-releasing spray.

Engine code CEGA

47 If new cover plates are to be fitted, slide them on now **(see illustration)**.
48 To remove the copper seal, spray rust-releasing spray around the injector nozzle, then clamp the seal in a vice, and use a twisting motion to pull the injector from the seal. Push the new copper seal into place **(see illustration)**.
49 Apply a little clean engine oil to the return pipe connection on the injector, and fit the new O-ring **(see illustration)**.
50 To renew the main injector O-ring seal, Skoda specify the use of tool No T10377.

5.47 Slide the new cover plate onto the injector

5.48 Push the new copper seal (arrowed) into place

This tool allows the O-ring to slide over the end of the injector without twisting. With care, the seals can be fitted without the tool **(see illustration)**.

51 Slide the new clamping piece onto injector as shown **(see illustration)**.

52 Apply a smear of clean engine oil to the main O-ring seal, and insert the injector into place in the cylinder head. Note that if the original injectors are being refitted, they must go into their original positions. Tighten the injector clamping piece retaining nuts to the specified torque.

53 Rotate the cover back to position and tighten the retaining bolt to the specified torque.

54 Refit the high-pressure fuel pipes and tighten the unions to the specified torque. Note that the pipes may be re-used providing the tapered seats are undamaged, and the pipes are not deformed, constricted or corroded. If a new injector is being fitted then a new pipe should be used.

55 Refit the return pipe connectors to the top of the injectors, ensure they are pushed fully on and the locking catch is pressed down.

Engine codes CLCA, CLCB, CFHC and CFHF

56 If required, renew the injector seals in the top of the camshaft cover. Using a screwdriver, prise the seal out from the cover; the new seal can then be pressed firmly into the cover. There are different size seals depending on engine code, make sure the correct seals are supplied. Also make sure the spring on the inside lip of the seal does not drop into the camshaft cover.

57 To remove the copper seal, spray rust-releasing spray around the injector nozzle, then clamp the seal in a vice, and use a twisting motion to pull the injector from the seal. Push the new copper seal into place. Do not touch the very end of the injector as you could damage or block the injector nozzle.

58 To renew the main injector O-ring seal, Skoda specify the use of tool No T10377. This tool allows the O-ring to slide over the end of the injector without twisting. With care, the seals can be fitted without the tool **(see illustration)**.

59 Apply a smear of clean engine oil to the main O-ring, fit two injectors into the retaining clamp and locate in their original position in the cylinder head. Install a new bolt into the retaining clamp and tighten hand tight at this stage.

60 Refit the high pressure fuel pipes in their original locations and tighten the unions hand tight at this stage, twist the injectors slightly, if required, to ensure the pipes are installed stress free. Note that the high pressure pipes can be re-used providing the tapered seats are undamaged and the pipes are not deformed, constricted or corroded. If a new injector is being fitted then a new pipe should be used.

5.49 Fit the new return pipe O-ring (arrowed) to the top of the injector

5.51 Slide the new clamping piece (arrowed) onto the injector

61 Tighten the injector retaining clamp bolt to the specified torque.

62 Tighten the fuel pipe unions at the fuel rail and injectors to the specified torque, counterhold the injector with an open-ended spanner to prevent damage as the union is tightened.

63 Apply a little engine oil to the return pipe O-rings and fit them to the return pipe connectors, push the connectors into the injectors and ensure they are fully home and then press down the locking catch.

All common rail engines

64 The remainder of refitting is a reversal of removal, noting the following:

a) *If one or more injectors have been renewed, the injector delivery and injector voltage calibration values must be entered into the ECM using Skoda diagnostic equipment (VAS 5051). Entrust this task to a Skoda dealer or suitably-equipped specialist.*

b) *After completion of the work, the fuel system must be bled as described in Section 16.*

6 Inlet manifold – removal and refitting

PD engines

Removal

1 All PD engines have a conventional inlet

5.50 Fit a new main O-ring (arrowed) without twisting it

5.58 Fit a new main O-ring seal without twisting it

manifold. 1.9 litre engines have a simple manifold fitted with an EGR control and throttle valve/shut down valve mounted at one end. 2.0 litre engines (BKD and BMN) have an inlet manifold with a centrally mounted EGR control and throttle valve/ shut down valve **(see illustrations overleaf)**. Note the illustrations show typical manifolds – there are variations, but all are similar.

2 Remove the engine cover by pulling it up.

3 Remove the flap motor and EGR valve with reference to Section 4 of this Chapter, and to Chapter 4B Section 3.

4 On engine code BMN, disconnect and unbolt the swirl control vacuum unit from the end of the manifold.

5 Access to manifolds at the rear of the engine can be improved, where required, if the front section of the plenum chamber is removed as described in the Electronic control module procedure in Section 4.

6 Where applicable, remove the heat shield from the manifold, then unscrew the mounting bolts and remove the inlet manifold from the cylinder head. Note the locations of any brackets retained by the mounting bolts. Recover the gasket and discard, as a new one must be used on refitting.

Refitting

7 Ensuring that all mating surfaces are clean, carry out refitting in the reverse of removal, using new manifold, EGR pipe and manifold flap assembly gaskets/O-rings. Tighten the mounting bolts to the specified torque.

6367 Fig. 04a-05.01 HAYNES

6.1a Inlet manifold – 2.0 litre PD engines BKD and BMN

1 Inlet manifold
2 Gasket
3 EGR pipe

4 Shut down flap control motor (anti shudder control)
5 EGR valve

6 Gasket
7 O-ring seal

H46298

6.1b Inlet manifold – 1.9 litre PD engine

1 Inlet manifold
2 O-ring seal
3 Combined EGR and flap housing (engine code BJB). The EGR and flap housings are seperate on other versions.
4 Screw
5 Gasket
6 EGR pipe
7 Screw
8 Bracket
9 Vacuum actuator for shut down flap (electrically controlled on BXE, BKC and BLS)
10 Vacuum hose to solenoid

Common rail engines

Removal

8 Raise the vehicle and support on axle stands (see *Jacking and vehicle support*). Remove the engine undertray.

9 Pull the plastic cover on the top of the engine upwards from its mountings and remove the foam insulation (where fitted). Ensure the area around the fuel rail and pipes is clean and free from debris. If available, use a vacuum cleaner.

10 Undo the clamp and release the charge air pipe and connecting hose from the throttle valve housing (it may be necessary to remove the lower right charge air hose and unbolt the charge air pipe from the front of the engine).

11 Using thin, long-nosed pliers, carefully pull the wiring plugs from the top of the glow plugs **(see illustration)**.

12 On engine code CEGA, with reference to Section 5, disconnect the fuel return pipes from the injectors, fuel rail, and high-pressure pump, undo the retaining nut and remove the fuel return pipe **(see illustration)**.

13 On models with a plastic manifold remove the fuel rail with reference to Section 7, on aluminium manifold versions only remove the high pressure pipe from between the fuel rail and high pressure pump.

14 Disconnect the wiring from the throttle and EGR housings.

15 Remove the EGR pipe from the manifold by releasing the clamp, or from the EGR housing by removing the bolts (according to model).

16 Remove the dipstick guide tube upper bolt from the throttle housing.

17 Undo the unions and disconnect the high-pressure fuel pipe between the pump and fuel rail.

18 Disconnect the wiring plug from the manifold change-over motor (where fitted)

19 Unbolt the bracket and move the EGR cooler by-pass solenoid valve to the side.

20 Disconnect the wiring plug from the EGR valve and throttle valve control unit.

21 Undo the retaining bolts, starting from the outside and working inwards in a diagonal sequence, then manoeuvre the manifold from position.

6.11 Pull the wiring plugs (arrowed) from the glow plugs

Refitting

22 Refitting is a reversal of removal, using new manifold bolts, seals, EGR pipe and manifold flap assembly gaskets. Remember to renew any self-locking nuts and bleed the fuel system with reference to Section 16.

7 Common fuel rail – removal and refitting

Note: *Observe the precautions in Section 1 before working on any component in the fuel system.*

Removal

1 Pull the plastic cover on the top of the engine upwards from its mountings and remove the foam insulation (where fitted). Ensure the area around the fuel rail and pipes is clean and free from debris. If available, use a vacuum cleaner.

2 Disconnect the wiring plugs from the fuel pressure regulating valve, and the fuel pressure sensor at each end of the fuel rail.

3 Undo the retaining bolts, disconnect the coolant return hose from the expansion tank, and move the coolant pipe/hose to one side (only engine code CEGA).

4 Release the vacuum hose from its connection to the camshaft cover (engine codes CLCA, CLCB, CFHC and CFHF).

5 Unplug the wiring from the glow plugs.

6 Disconnect the fuel return hoses from the high-pressure pump and common fuel rail,

6.12 Fuel return pipe nut (arrowed)

then undo the retaining nuts and remove the fuel return pipe from the inlet manifold **(see illustration 6.12)**. Plug the openings to prevent contamination (engine code CEGA).

7 Disconnect the fuel return hose from the common fuel rail. Plug the openings to prevent contamination (engine codes CLCA, CLCB, CFHC and CFHF).

8 Unclip the wiring loom guide from the common fuel rail and move the wiring guide to one side.

9 If they are to be re-used, note their fitted positions, then undo the unions and remove the high-pressure pipes from the common fuel rail to the injectors. Plug the openings to prevent contamination.

10 Note their fitted positions and release the retaining clip(s) on the high pressure pipe between the common fuel rail and the high pressure pump, undo the unions and remove the pipe **(see illustration)**. Plug the openings to prevent contamination. **Note:** *When slackening or tightening fuel pipe unions, if the injector, fuel pump or fuel rail has provision for counter-holding with an open ended spanner then this should always be used to prevent possible damage to the component.*

11 Undo the multispline retaining bolts and remove the common rail **(see illustration)**. If required, note their fitted positions, then unscrew the fuel pressure sensor and pressure regulating valve from the common rail **(see illustrations)**. Plug the openings to prevent contamination. **Note:** *Skoda insist that once removed, the pressure regulating valve cannot be re-used.*

7.10 Remove the high-pressure pipe between the pump and common rail (arrowed)

7.11a Undo the bolts (arrowed) securing the common rail

7.11b Unscrew the pressure sensor...

Refitting

12 Where applicable, refit the fuel pressure sensor and the new regulating valve to the common rail, and tighten them to the specified torque. Note that the threads of the sensors must be clean and free from oil and grease.

13 The remainder of refitting is a reversal of removal, noting the following points:
a) Refit the high-pressure fuel pipes and tighten the unions to the specified torque. Note that the high-pressure fuel pipes may be re-used providing the tapered seats are undamaged, and the pipes are not deformed, constricted or corroded.
b) After completion of the work, the fuel system must be bled as described in Section 16.

8 Fuel gauge sender unit – removal and refitting

Note: *Observe the precautions in Section 1 before working on any component in the fuel system.*

⚠️ **Warning: Avoid direct skin contact with fuel – wear protective clothing and gloves when handling fuel system components. Ensure that the work area is well-ventilated to prevent the build-up of fuel vapour.**

Removal

1 The fuel gauge sender unit is mounted in the top of the fuel tank. The access cover

7.11c... and pressure regulator

is beneath the rear seat cushion. The unit protrudes into the fuel tank, and its removal involves exposing the Specifications of the tank to the atmosphere.

2 Ensure that the vehicle is parked on a level surface, then disconnect the battery negative (earth) lead (see Chapter 5 Section 3).

3 Refer to Chapter 11 Section 29, and remove the rear seat cushion. Fold back the carpet from the right-hand side of the vehicle floor.

4 Lift the carpet, and prise the access hatch away from the floorpan **(see illustration)**, then unplug the wiring connector from the pump/sender unit.

5 Place rags beneath the fuel hoses to catch spilt fuel. Depress the retaining tabs and disconnect the fuel supply and return hoses **(see illustration)**. Mark/identify each hose for position – the blue hose is fuel return, and the black hose is fuel supply.

6 Unscrew the metal ring securing the pump/

sender unit in the tank. Skoda technicians use a special tool (T30101) to unscrew the ring, however a home-made equivalent will suffice **(see illustration)**. Observe any arrows indicating the position of the ring for refitting.

7 Remove the fuel pump/sender unit from the tank **(see illustration)**. Take great care not to bend or damage the sender unit float and arm as they are removed from the tank. **Note:** *There may be fuel sitting within the unit, so beware of spillage when removing.*

8 Inspect the float on the sender unit swinging arm for punctures and fuel ingress, and renew it if it appears damaged. The sender and float unclips from the main assembly.

Refitting

9 Refitting is a reversal of removal, noting the following points:
a) Renew the fuel tank aperture seal if necessary, and refit it dry **(see illustration)**.
b) Do not bend the float arm during refitting.
c) Ensure all hoses are securely reconnected to their original positions.
d) The flange will only fit in one position – extended lug at the rear **(see illustration)**.
e) Reconnect the battery as described in Chapter 5 Section 3.

9 Fuel tank – removal and refitting

Note: *Observe the precautions in Section 1 before working on any component in the fuel system.*

8.4 Prise the access hatch from the floor

8.5 Depress the retaining tabs (arrowed) and disconnect the fuel hoses

8.6 Undoing the metal securing ring with a home-made tool

8.7 Manoeuvre the fuel pump/sender unit from the tank

8.9a Fit the new seal dry

8.9b The flange will only fit with the extended lug (arrowed) at the rear

Removal

1 As no drain plug is provided, it is preferable to carry out this operation with the tank almost empty.
2 Open the fuel filler flap, and unscrew the fuel filler cap – leave the cap loosely in place.
3 Disconnect the battery negative lead and position it away from the terminal as described in Chapter 5 Section 3. Using a hand pump or siphon, remove any remaining fuel from the bottom of the tank.
4 Gain access to the top of the fuel tank sender unit as described in Section 8. Unplug the wiring connector and disconnect the fuel pipes from the sender unit.
5 Loosen the rear wheel bolts, then jack up the rear of the car and support it securely on axle stands (see *Jacking and vehicle support*). Remove the rear roadwheels.
6 Remove the right-hand rear wheel arch liner as described in Chapter 11 Section 11.
7 Unscrew the filler pipe from the body, and unclip the wiring harness from the pipe**(see illustration)**.
8 Unbolt and remove the exhaust tunnel bridge, loosen the front clamping sleeve and push it to the rear.
9 Undo the mountings for the rear exhaust silencer then slightly lower the exhaust pipe. Support the lowered pipe by tying it to a suitable part of the body or suspension.
10 Depress the release buttons and disconnect the fuel supply and return pipes located at the front of the tank **(see illustration)**.
11 Position a trolley jack under the centre of the tank. Insert a block of wood between the jack head and the tank to prevent damage to the tank surface. Raise the jack until it just takes the weight of the tank.
12 Unscrew the mounting bolts and detach the tank straps**(see illustrations)**.
13 Lower the jack and tank away from the underside of the vehicle. Guide the filler neck between the rear axle and body.
14 If the tank is contaminated with sediment or water, remove the fuel pump/sender unit (see Section 8) and swill the tank out with clean fuel. The tank is injection-moulded from a synthetic material, and if damaged, it should be renewed. However, in certain cases it may be possible to have small leaks or minor damage repaired. Seek the advice of a suitable specialist before attempting to repair the fuel tank.

Refitting

15 Refitting is the reverse of the removal procedure, noting the following points:
a) When lifting the tank back into position, make sure the mounting rubbers are correctly positioned, and take care to ensure none of the hoses get trapped between the tank and vehicle body.
b) Ensure that all pipes and hoses are correctly routed, are not kinked, and are securely held in position with their retaining clips.
c) Be especially careful not to mix up the fuel feed and return pipes when refitting.

9.7 Fuel filler pipe retaining bolts (arrowed)

9.12a Fuel tank left-hand strap retaining bolt (arrowed)

d) Tighten all fasteners to their specified torque where given.
e) On completion, refill the tank with fuel, and exhaustively check for signs of leakage prior to taking the vehicle out on the road.

10 Tandem fuel pump – removal and refitting

Note: *The tandem fuel pump is only fitted on PD unit injection engines and is located on the left-hand end of the cylinder head. It is effectively a vacuum pump (for the braking system) and a fuel lift pump (for the fuel injection system).*

Removal

1 Remove the air cleaner housing (Section 3.
2 Pull the plastic cover on the top of the engine upwards to release the mountings.

10.4 Fuel supply hose (A) and return (B) – PD unit injection engine shown

9.10 Depress the release buttons (arrowed) and pull the connections apart

9.12b Fuel tank right-hand strap retaining bolt

3 Release the retaining clip (where fitted) and disconnect the brake servo pipe from the tandem pump.
4 Disconnect the fuel supply hose (marked white) from the tandem pump **(see illustration)**. Be prepared for fuel spillage.
5 Unscrew the four retaining bolts and move the tandem pump away from the cylinder head. As the pump is lifted up, disconnect the fuel return hose (marked blue). Be prepared for fuel spillage. There are no serviceable parts within the tandem pump. If the pump is faulty, it must be renewed.

Refitting

6 Reconnect the fuel return hose to the pump and refit the pump to the cylinder head, using new rubber seals, and ensuring that the pump pinion engages correctly with the drive slot in the camshaft **(see illustration)**.

10.6 Ensure the pump pinion engages correctly with the drive slot in the camshaft

11.19 Turbocharger oil supply pipe union (arrowed)

7 Refit the pump retaining bolts, and tighten them to the specified torque.

8 Re-attach the fuel supply hose and brake servo hose to the pump.

9 The remainder of refitting is a reversal of removal. Upon completion, attach a hand-held vacuum pump to the return outlet from the pump, and operate the pump until a steady stream of fuel appears from the outlet. Start the engine and check for leaks.

11 Turbocharger – general information, removal and refitting

General information

1 A turbocharger which is integral with the inlet manifold is fitted to all the engines covered in this manual.

2 The turbocharger increases engine efficiency by raising the pressure in the inlet manifold above atmospheric pressure, this results in the air being forced into the cylinders rather than simply sucked in.

3 Energy for the operation of the turbocharger comes from the exhaust gas. The gas flows through a specially shaped housing (the turbine housing) and in so doing, spins the turbine wheel. The turbine wheel is attached to a shaft, at the end of which is another vaned wheel, known as the compressor wheel. The compressor wheel spins in its own housing, and compresses the inducted air on the way to the inlet manifold.

4 Between the turbocharger and the inlet manifold, the compressed air passes through an intercooler. The purpose of the intercooler is to remove from the inducted air some of the heat gained in being compressed. Because cooler air is denser, removal of this heat further increases engine efficiency.

5 According to model, boost pressure (the pressure in the inlet manifold) is regulated by either an integral wastegate valve (which diverts the exhaust gas away from the turbine) or by using variable vanes in the turbine housing (arranged around the turbine, their angle can be adjusted to control the effect of the exhaust gas on the turbine). Control of the wastegate or variable vanes is achieved using

11.20 Unscrew the exhaust gas temperature sensor

a vacuum operated lever. An electrical sensor relays the position of the operating lever to the electronic control module (ECM) on some models.

6 The turbo shaft is pressure-lubricated by an oil feed pipe connected to the engine oil filter housing or the engine oil gallery. The shaft 'floats' on a cushion of oil. Oil is returned to the sump through a return pipe that connects to the rear of the cylinder block. On some models the tubular turbocharger support bracket also functions as an oil return pipe with a hollow connection bolt at the base of the cylinder block through which oil returns to the sump.

Precautions

7 The turbocharger operates at extremely high speeds and temperatures. Certain precautions must be observed to avoid premature failure of the turbo, or injury to the operator.

8 Do not operate the turbo with any parts exposed – foreign objects falling onto the rotating vanes could cause excessive damage and (if ejected) personal injury.

9 Cover the turbocharger air inlet ducts to prevent debris entering, and clean using lint-free cloths only.

10 Do not race the engine immediately after start-up, especially if it is cold. Give the oil a few seconds to circulate.

11 Observe the recommended intervals for oil and filter changing, and use a reputable oil of the specified quality. Neglect of oil changing, or use of inferior oil, can cause carbon

11.21 Remove the EGR pipe between the exhaust manifold and cooler (engine CEGA shown)

formation on the turbo shaft and subsequent failure. Thoroughly clean the area around all oil pipe unions before disconnecting them, to prevent the ingress of dirt. Store dismantled components in a sealed container to prevent contamination.

Removal

Caution: Thoroughly clean the area around all oil pipe unions before disconnecting them, to prevent the ingress of dirt. Store dismantled components in a sealed container to prevent contamination. Cover the turbocharger air intake ducts to prevent debris entering, and clean using lint-free cloths only.

12 Apply the handbrake, then jack up the front of the vehicle and support it on axle stands (see *Jacking and vehicle support*). Remove the engine compartment undertray and engine top cover.

13 Remove the air cleaner housing as described in Section 3.

14 Remove the plenum chamber cover with reference to Chapter 12 Section 13, then release the screws at each end and remove the front section of the plenum chamber.

15 Disconnect the wiring plug from the oil level sensor.

16 Remove the right-hand driveshaft as described in Chapter 8 Section 2 and the driveshaft heat shield (where fitted).

17 Remove the particulate filter/catalytic converter as described in Chapter 4B Section 5.

18 Undo the nuts/bolts and remove the heat shields form the turbocharger (as applicable).

19 Disconnect the oil supply pipe from the turbocharger. Check that the oil supply pipe can be positioned to allow removal of the turbocharger, on some models it will be necessary to disconnect the oil supply pipe at both ends, release the support brackets and remove the pipe. On models with a pipe union nut **(see illustration)**, counter-hold the union adaptor to ensure it does not unscrew as the pipe nut is released.

20 Where fitted, release the wiring and unscrew the exhaust gas temperature sensor from the exhaust manifold/turbocharger **(see illustration)**.

21 Undo the nuts/clamps and remove the EGR pipe between the exhaust manifold and EGR cooler **(see illustration)**, on engine codes CLCA, CLCB, CFHC and CFHF remove the second EGR pipe between the cooler and cylinder head.

22 On Common Rail and particulate filter equipped PD engines, undo the bolts/ nuts and remove the support bracket from the underside of the turbocharger **(see illustration)**. Note that this bracket doubles as an oil return pipe, with the return pipe from the underside of the turbocharger fitting inside the support bracket at its upper end. If necessary, twist and pull the bracket from the pipe and unbolt the oil return pipe from the turbocharger **(see illustrations)**.

23 On catalytic converter PD engines, disconnect the oil return pipe at the union with the cylinder block, counter-holding the union adaptor to ensure that it does not unscrew as the pipe nut is released.

24 On catalytic converter PD engines, undo the nuts/bolts and remove the turbocharger support bracket.

25 Release the fasteners and detach the charge air pipes/hoses and air intake pipes/hoses from the turbocharger, releasing from the crankcase breather pipe if necessary.

26 Remove the two retaining bolts and withdraw the charge air pulsation damper from the turbocharger outlet (where fitted).

27 Note their fitted positions, then disconnect the vacuum hose/wiring plug from the turbocharger boost control unit.

28 Check around the turbocharger/exhaust manifold and unclip any wiring or hoses still connected, noting their fitted position and the routing of all cables.

29 Undo the bolts/nuts securing the exhaust manifold to the cylinder head, then tilt the bottom of the engine forwards a little, and lower the manifold and turbocharger assembly from place **(see illustration)**.

30 The turbocharger is integral with the exhaust manifold. If defective, the complete assembly will require specialist overhaul or replacement.

Refitting

31 Refit the turbocharger by following the removal procedure in reverse, noting the following points:

a) Renew all gaskets, seals and O-rings.

b) Ensure all sealing and gasket mating surfaces are clean before assembly.

c) Fit a new banjo bolt to the oil return pipe connection at the base of the cylinder block.

d) Renew all self-locking nuts.

e) Before reconnecting the oil supply pipe, fill the turbocharger with fresh oil using an oil can.

f) Apply high-temperature grease to the turbocharger/exhaust pipe mounting studs.

g) Tighten all nuts and bolts to the specified torque where given.

h) When the engine is started after refitting, allow it to idle for approximately one minute to give the oil time to circulate around the turbine shaft bearings.

---

12 Turbocharger charge control system components –
description, removal and refitting

Description

1 The turbocharger charge (boost) pressure control mechanism is operated by a vacuum controlled lever. The vacuum is supplied by the vacuum pump mounted on the left-hand end of the cylinder head. The vacuum supply is controlled by an electrically operated solenoid

11.22a Undo the bolts (arrowed) and remove the turbocharger support bracket

11.22c Return pipe bolts (arrowed). Note the O-ring seals where the pipe slides into the support bracket (arrowed)

valve activated by the engine management ECM. This charge pressure control solenoid valve is mounted on the bulkhead at the rear of the engine compartment **(see illustration)**. The valve has three hoses connecting it to the air cleaner, turbocharger and vacuum pump, it is important that these hoses are connected correctly to the solenoid valve. **Note:** *On engine codes BJB, BKC, BXE and BKD the charge pressure control solenoid valve is incorporated into the vacuum valve block, refer to EGR control valve in Chapter 4B Section 3 for more information.*

Charge pressure control solenoid valve

2 The charge pressure control solenoid valve is mounted at the rear of the engine compartment on the bulkhead.

3 Release the catch and disconnect the

12.1 Charge pressure control solenoid valve

11.22b Remove the banjo bolt with copper washer and O-ring (arrowed)

11.29 Exhaust manifold/turbocharger nuts (arrowed)

wiring plug from the solenoid valve **(see illustration)**.

4 Undo the retaining nuts and pull the solenoid valve away from the bulkhead, unclipping the vacuum hoses from any retaining clips.

5 Remove the vacuum hoses from their connections to the solenoid valve, noting their positions to aid correct refitting.

6 Refitting is the reversal of removal.

---

13 Intercooler –
removal and refitting

1 The intercooler is effectively an 'air radiator' used to cool the pressurised inlet air before it enters the engine.

2 When the turbocharger compresses the inlet

12.3 Disconnect the wiring plug

13.8a Remove the left-hand charge air hose from the bottom of the intercooler...

13.8b... and the right-hand charge air hose

air, one side-effect is that the air is heated, causing the air to expand. If the inlet air can be cooled, a greater effective volume of air will be inducted, and the engine will produce more power.

3 The compressed air from the turbocharger, which would normally be fed straight into the inlet manifold, is instead ducted around the engine to the intercooler. The intercooler is mounted at the front of the car, in the airflow. The heated air entering the unit is pushed through a network of tubes which are cooled by the airflow through their connected fins, much as with the radiator. When it leaves the intercooler, the cooled air is then ducted into the throttle housing.

4 There is a charge air pressure/temperature sensor fitted to the inlet ducting from the intercooler to the inlet manifold. See Section 4 for removal and refitting procedures.

Removal

5 Apply the handbrake, then jack up the front of the vehicle and support it on axle stands (see *Jacking and vehicle support*). Remove the engine compartment undershield.

6 Remove the radiator as described in Chapter 3 Section 3.

7 Remove the front bumper as described in Chapter 11 Section 9.

8 Detach the charge air hoses from each side of the intercooler **(see illustrations)**.

9 Disconnect the wiring plug from the charge air pressure/temperature sender unit on models where the unit is in the intercooler outlet.

10 From the front of the vehicle undo the four condenser mounting screws and then remove the screws from the intercooler mountings each side.

11 Taking care not to damage the air

conditioning refrigerant pipes, lift the intercooler and condenser from the lock carrier and tilt them backwards to gain access to the screw on the right-hand lower side securing the refrigerant pipe bracket to the intercooler. Remove the screw and withdraw the intercooler downwards.

 Warning: Refer to the precautions given in Chapter 3 Section 10, before working on the air conditioning system.

12 Secure the condenser to the front crossmember or support it to prevent any damage to the fins or refrigerant pipes.

Refitting

13 Refitting is the reversal of removal, noting the following points:

a) *Check the grommets are correctly located in the lock carrier lower section.*

b) *Make sure the lugs at the base of the intercooler are located in the grommets.*

c) *Ensure that all intercooler hoses are free from oil and grease before assembly.*

d) *Refer to Chapter 3 Section 3, when refitting the radiator.*

14 High-pressure fuel pump (common rail engines only)

Removal

1 Remove the timing belt and pump sprocket as described in Chapter 2B Section 7.

2 Release the wiring plug for the fuel temperature sensor and disconnect the fuel supply hose from the pump **(see illustration)**. Plug all openings to prevent contamination.

3 Disconnect the wiring plug from the control valve on the pump.

4 Undo the bolts securing the pump-to-common rail high-pressure pipe support brackets **(see illustration)**.

5 Unclip and release the glow plug wiring from the wiring guide, pulling only under the ridge at the top of the connectors, disconnect the glow plug wiring connectors **(see illustration 6.11)**.

Caution: Take care not to damage the connectors or wiring, as the glow plug wiring loom/connectors are only available as a complete assembly.

6 Undo the bolts securing the coolant pipe to the inlet manifold, and position the pipe to one side.

7 Disconnect the fuel return pipes from the pump and the common fuel rail **(see illustration)**.

8 Undo the unions and disconnect the high-pressure fuel pipe between the pump and common fuel rail.

9 Counterhold the pump hub using Skoda tool No T10051, and undo the pump hub nut. In the absence of this special tool, counterhold the hub using a suitable C-spanner **(see illustration)**.

14.2 Release the clip (arrowed) and disconnect the fuel supply hose

14.4 High-pressure pipe support bracket bolts (arrowed)

14.7 Fuel pump return hose (arrowed)

14.9 Counter-hold the pump hub with a C-spanner, and undo the nut

14.10a Use a two-legged puller and 8 mm bolts to pull the hub from the pump shaft

14.10b Note the locating peg (arrowed) in the pump shaft

10 Using a suitable two-legged puller and two 8 mm bolts, remove the hub from the pump shaft **(see illustrations)**.
11 Undo the 3 retaining bolts and remove the pump.

Refitting

12 Refitting is a reversal of removal, noting the following points:
a) Ensure all fuel pipes/hose connections are clean and free from debris.
b) The high-pressure fuel pipe from the pump to the common rail maybe re-used providing it's not been damaged.
c) Tighten all fasteners to their specified torque where given.
d) Fill the pump with clean fuel through the fuel supply pipe aperture prior to starting **(see illustration)**.
e) Bleed the fuel system as described in Section 16.

15 Supplementary fuel pump (common rail engines only)

1 The supplementary fuel pump is not fitted to all models, where fitted, it is located on a bracket bolted to the top of the right-hand engine mounting **(see illustration)**.

Removal

2 Disconnect the wiring plug from the exhaust gas pressure sensor, then undo the retaining bolt and slide the mounting bracket to release it. Move the sensor and bracket to one side and place on a cloth or similar. Note the internals of the sensor are easily damaged and care should be taken when moving it.
3 Undo the retaining bolts on the bracket above the fuel pump, release the fuel hoses from the retaining clips on the bracket and remove the bracket.
4 Undo the retaining bolts and lift the supplementary fuel pump upwards to access the fuel pipe connections and wiring plug.

5 Disconnect the fuel pump wiring plug..
6 Place absorbent cloths or similar and be prepared for fuel spillage, then release the clamps and disconnect the fuel pipes from the supplementary fuel pump. Plug/cover the openings to prevent contamination.

Refiting

7 Refitting is a reversal of removal, noting the following points:
a) Ensure the hoses are not kinked.
b) Ensure all connections are clean and free from debris.
c) Bleed the system as described in Section 16.

16 Fuel system bleeding

PD unit injector engines

1 Attach a hand-held vacuum pump to the return outlet (coloured blue) from the tandem fuel pump, and operate the pump until a steady stream of fuel appears from the outlet. Start the engine and check for leaks. Refer also to Chapter 1 Section 30

Common rail engines

2 Prime the high-pressure fuel pump by filling

14.12 The triangles adjacent to the pump apertures indicate fuel flow (arrowed)

it with clean diesel through the fuel supply aperture**(see illustration 14.12)**, then operate the starter for short bursts (no more than 10 seconds at a time) until the engine starts. Operate the engine at a fast idle (approx 2000 rpm) for several minutes before allowing it to return to its normal idle speed.
3 If the engine fails to start, it must be filled/bled using Skoda or other suitable diagnostic equipment. Using this equipment operates the electric fuel pumps for 3 minutes, circulating fuel and purging the system of air.
4 Once the engine has been started, test drive the vehicle over a distance of at least 15 miles with at least one period of full acceleration. If there is any air left in the fuel system, the engine management ECM may switch to 'limp home' mode, and store a fault code. Have the fault code cleared and road test the vehicle again.

17 Fuel cooler – removal and refitting

Removal

1 Raise the right-hand side of the vehicle and support is securely on axle stands (see *Jacking and vehicle support*).

15.1 Supplementary fuel pump location

17.2 Undo the fasteners and remove the underbody panel

17.3 Depress the release buttons (arrowed) and pull the hoses from the cooler

17.4 Undo the retaining bolts and lower the cooler from place

2 Undo the 8 bolts and lower the underbody panelling around the fuel cooler **(see illustration)**.
3 Note their fitted positions, then depress the release buttons and disconnect the fuel feed and return hoses from the cooler **(see illustration)**. Plug the openings to prevent contamination.
4 Undo the retaining nuts and lower the cooler from place **(see illustration)**.

Refitting

5 Refitting is a reversal of removal. Check the system for leaks before refitting the panelling.

Chapter 4 Part B
Emission control and exhaust systems

Contents

Degrees of difficulty

Easy, suitable for novice with little experience	Fairly easy, suitable for beginner with some experience	Fairly difficult, suitable for competent DIY mechanic	Difficult, suitable for experienced DIY mechanic 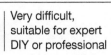	Very difficult, suitable for expert DIY or professional

Specifications

Engine codes*
PD unit injector engines:
 1.9 litre (1896 cc), 8-valve, SOHC . . . . BJB, BKC, BLS and BXE
 2.0 litre (1968 cc):
  8-valve, SOHC . . . . BMM
  16-valve, DOHC . . . . BKD and BMN
Common rail injection engines:
 2.0 litre (1968 cc), 16-valve, DOHC . . . . CBBB, CBDB and CEGA (1st Generation)
  CLCA, CLCB, CFHC and CFHF (2nd Generation)

*See 'Vehicle identification' at the end of this manual for the location of engine code markings.

Emissions equipment
Exhaust Gas Recirculation system. . . . . All engines
Catalytic converter . . . . All engines
Particulate filter. . . . . PD unit injector engine codes BLS, BMM and BMN.
 Common rail injection engines CFHC and CFHF

Torque wrench settings

	Nm	lbf ft
Catalytic converter support bracket.	40	30
EGR cooler mounting bolts	10	7
EGR cooler to flap housing	10	7
EGR pipe flange connection bolts (All Engines EXCEPT: CLCA, CLCB, CFHC and CFHF)	22	16
EGR pipe flange connection bolts (CLCA, CLCB, CFHC and CFHF)	10	7
EGR pipe flange connection to exhaust manifold nuts *	25	18
EGR pipe to inlet manifold clamp (CLCA, CLCB, CFHC and CFHF) *	5	4
EGR valve to inlet manifold	10	7
Exhaust gas temperature probe to exhaust manifold	45	33
Exhaust gas temperature sensor probe to particulate filter (All Engines EXCEPT: CLCA, CLCB, CFHC and CFHF)	45	33
Exhaust gas temperature sensor probe to particulate filter (CLCA, CLCB, CFHC and CFHF)	60	44
Exhaust system clamp		
Sleeve with individual clamps	25	18
Sleeve with single clamp	35	26
Exhaust mounting brackets to underbody.	23	17
Lambda (O2) sensor.	50	37
Particulate filter/catalytic converter clamp (to turbocharger) *	7	5
Particulate filter mounting bracket (on subframe)	25	18
Particulate filter pressure sensor line (at filter)	45	33
Particulate filter support brackets (to engine)	25	18
Underfloor crossmember (tunnel brace).	23	17

* Use new fixings

3.11 EGR pipe-to-valve bolts (arrowed)

1 General Information

Emission control systems

1 All models have a crankcase emission control system, and in addition are fitted with a catalytic converter, and an Exhaust Gas Recirculation (EGR) system to reduce exhaust emissions. Some models are also fitted with a particulate filter in the exhaust system to further reduce harmful emissions from the exhaust (see Specifications).

Crankcase emission control

2 To reduce the emission of unburned hydrocarbons from the crankcase into the atmosphere, the engine is sealed and the blow-by gases and oil vapour are drawn from inside the crankcase, through a wire mesh oil separator, into the inlet tract to be burned by the engine during normal combustion.
3 Under all conditions the gases are forced out of the crankcase by the (relatively) higher crankcase pressure. All engines have a pressure-regulating valve on the camshaft cover to control the flow of gases from the crankcase.

Exhaust emission control

4 An oxidation catalyst is fitted in the exhaust system of all models. This has the effect of removing a large proportion of the gaseous hydrocarbons, carbon monoxide and particulates present in the exhaust gas. Some models covered in this manual have a particulate filter, which is fitted behind the catalytic converter in order to filter out soot particles produced by the combustion process.
5 An Exhaust Gas Recirculation (EGR) system is also fitted to all models. This reduces the level of nitrogen oxides produced during combustion by introducing a proportion of the exhaust gas back into the inlet manifold under certain engine operating conditions. The system is controlled electronically by the engine management ECM.

Exhaust systems

6 On all models, the exhaust system comprises the exhaust manifold/turbocharger, front pipe and integral catalytic converter/ particulate filter, a short connecting pipe, intermediate pipe and silencer, and tailpipe and silencer. The system is supported by rubber bushes and/or rubber mounting rings.
7 Initially, the exhaust intermediate and rear sections are manufactured as one unit, however they are available separately as service items.

2 Crankcase emission system – general information

1 The crankcase emission control system consists of hoses connecting the crankcase to the air cleaner or inlet manifold. A pressure regulating valve is fitted to all engines.
2 The system requires no attention other than to check at regular intervals that the hoses, valve and oil separator are free of blockages and in good condition.

3 Exhaust Gas Recirculation (EGR) system – information and component removal

Information

1 Fitted to all the engines in this manual the EGR system comprises of an EGR valve (which controls the flow of exhaust gas from the exhaust to inlet manifold), an EGR cooler (through which the gases can be channelled for cooling), a cooler by-pass flap (to allow the gases to avoid being cooled when not necessary and metal pipes to connect the components between the exhaust and inlet manifolds.
2 The EGR valve operation is controlled by the engine management control unit (ECM) via a vacuum control solenoid and diaphragm actuator or integral electric motor and position sensor according to model.
3 The EGR cooler by-pass flap is controlled by the engine management control unit (ECM) via a vacuum control solenoid and diaphragm actuator.

EGR valve

Engine codes BJB, BXE, BKC, BLS and BMM

Note: *On all these versions of the PD engine the EGR valve is attached to the inlet manifold at the rear of the engine. Engine code BJB has a combined housing for the intake shut-off flap and EGR valve, both are vacuum operated. Engine codes BXE and BKC have a vacuum operated EGR valve with a separate housing from the intake manifold flap housing. On engine codes BLS and BMM the EGR valve is electrically controlled and can be removed without its housing on the intake manifold if required. The principle of removal (and refitting) is the same for all these versions, bearing in mind the points just made.*

Removal

4 Remove the plastic cover from the top of the engine.
5 Release any hoses/wiring fastened to the charge air pipe at the right side of the engine.
6 Release the fasteners, then disconnect and remove the charge air pipe from the inlet manifold flap housing.
7 On engine codes BLS and BMM disconnect the wiring plug, remove the securing bolts and remove the EGR valve from its housing.
8 On other models undo and remove the bolts securing the EGR pipe flange to the EGR valve, disconnect the vacuum hoses (or wiring plugs) from the EGR valve actuator and the intake flap actuator, noting their orientation.
9 Undo the bolts and detach the inlet manifold flap housing and EGR valve housing from the inlet manifold. Discard the O-ring seals and EGR pipe gasket as new ones must be fitted.

Refitting

10 Refitting is the reversal of removal.
Note: *On engine codes BMM and BLS if the EGR valve is replaced it will be necessary to carry out the following initialisation procedure:*
a) *Switch ignition on then off. Wait for one minute.*
b) *Start engine and allow to idle for more than one minute.*
c) *Check vehicle diagnostic trouble codes, if any codes are present clear them from the memory and repeat the procedure.*

Engine codes BKD, BMN and CEGA

Note: *On these versions of the PD and common rail engines the EGR valve housing is attached to the inlet manifold at the front of the engine. The procedure required for removal is essentially the same for all versions.*

Removal

11 Undo the bolts securing the pipe to the EGR valve **(see illustration)**.
12 Disconnect the EGR valve vacuum hose or wiring plug as applicable.
13 Remove the inlet manifold flap motor housing/throttle valve housing as described in Chapter 4A Section 4
14 Undo the bolts and detach the valve from the inlet manifold. Discard the O-ring seal, a new one must be fitted.

Refitting

15 Refitting is a reversal of removal, using a new EGR pipe gasket and O-ring seals. Tighten the retaining bolts to the specified torque.

Engine codes CLCA, CLCB, CFHC and CFHF

16 On these second generation, common rail versions the EGR valve is incorporated into the EGR cooler, for removal and refitting refer to paragraphs 49 – 61 of this section. At the time of writing, it was not possible to separate the EGR valve from the cooler.

3.17a Typical EGR cooler as fitted to catalytic converter equipped PD engines (with removable by-pass flap housing).

1 EGR cooler
2 Inlet manifold
3 By-pass (change-over) flap housing
4 Connection pipes
5 Gaskets

EGR cooler

17 A cooler is fitted in the exhaust gas recirculation system of all the engines covered by this manual (except engine code BJB). Located at the rear of the cylinder block and connected into the engine cooling system, under certain operating conditions the recirculated exhaust gases can be directed via the cooler to reduce their temperature, various designs of cooler are used (see illustrations), however the operating principles remain the same.

Engine codes BXE and BKC

Removal

18 Remove the upper engine cover.
19 Remove the inlet manifold flap motor housing with reference to Chapter 4A Section 4.
20 Remove the air filter housing and turbocharger air intake pipe with reference to Chapter 4A Section 3.
21 To save draining the complete system, clamp the EGR cooler and by-pass housing coolant hoses or drain the cooling system as

3.17b EGR cooler with integral by-pass flap (engine codes BMN and CEGA)

1 EGR cooler	3 Vacuum unit	5 Gaskets
2 Connecting pipes	4 Vacuum hose	6 Heat shield

3.17c EGR cooler with integral EGR valve and by-pass flap (engine codes CLCA, CLCB, CFHC and CFHF)

1 EGR cooler, valve and by-pass unit	2 Recirculation pipes	4 Gasket
	3 Vacuum line	5 Clamp

3.53a Disconnect left-hand coolant hose from cooler

3.53b Release right-hand cooler hose retaining clips and remove hose

described in Chapter 1 Section 37, release the hose clamps and being prepared for some coolant spillage, remove the hoses from the cooler and by-pass housing.

22 Disconnect the vacuum hose from the by-pass flap actuator.

23 Disconnect the main vacuum pipe at its connection to the vacuum pump, then unbolt and remove the engine lifting eye at the right hand rear of the cylinder head.

24 Unbolt the EGR pipes at their flange connections to the EGR cooler by-pass flap housing.

25 Remove the EGR cooler mounting bolts and remove the cooler and by-pass assembly.

Refitting

26 Refitting is the reversal of removal, bearing in mind the following points:
a) Replace EGR pipe connection flange gaskets.
b) Fit new O-ring seal at inlet manifold flap motor housing.
c) Tighten all mountings to the specified torque.
d) Check/refill the cooling system with reference to 'Weekly checks' and Chapter 1 Section 37.

Engine code BKD

Removal

27 Remove the upper engine cover.

28 Remove the wiper arms as described in Chapter 12 Section 13.

29 Pull up the rubber sealing strip, the starting in the middle, pull the plenum chamber cover upwards from the base of the windscreen. Unclip the washer jet pipe from the cover as it's withdrawn. Undo the screw at each end and remove the front section of the plenum chamber below the plenum cover at the rear of the engine.

30 Remove the air filter housing and turbocharger air intake pipe with reference to Chapter 4A Section 3.

31 To save draining the complete system clamp the EGR cooler and by-pass housing coolant hoses or drain the cooling system as described in Chapter 1 Section 37, release the hose clamps and being prepared for some coolant spillage, remove the hoses from the cooler and by-pass housing

32 Unbolt the upper EGR pipe at the flange connection to the EGR cooler by-pass flap housing.

33 Remove the nuts securing the lower EGR pipe flange connection to the exhaust manifold.

34 Disconnect the vacuum hose from the EGR cooler by-pass actuator.

35 Undo the bolts securing the EGR cooler to its mounting bracket and remove the cooler.

Refitting

36 Refitting is the reversal of removal, bearing in mind the following points:
a) Replace EGR pipe connection flange gaskets.
b) Use new nuts at EGR pipe connection to exhaust manifold.
c) Tighten all mountings to the specified torque.
d) Check/refill the cooling system with reference to 'Weekly checks' and Chapter 1 Section 37.

Engine codes BLS, BMM, BMN and CEGA

Removal

37 Remove the upper engine cover.

38 Remove the air filter housing and turbocharger air intake pipe with reference to Chapter 4A Section 3.

39 Remove the battery and battery tray as described in Chapter 5 Section 3.

40 Refer to Section 6 and remove the diesel particulate filter.

41 Unbolt and remove the EGR pipe between the EGR cooler and the exhaust manifold.

3.54 Remove exhaust manifold to cooler EGR pipe

42 Drain the cooling system with reference to Chapter 1 Section 37, or if suitable clamps are available clamp the coolant hoses to save draining the complete system, then disconnect them from the EGR cooler, being prepared for some coolant spillage.

43 Undo the upper bolts and lower banjo bolt and remove the turbocharger oil return pipe/support bracket from the rear of the engine.

44 Remove the particulate filter support bracket (if not already removed).

45 Remove the heat shielding (where fitted) and disconnect the vacuum hose from the by-pass flap actuator.

46 Disconnect remaining EGR pipe at its flange connection.

47 Remove the bolts securing the cooler at the rear of the cylinder block and withdraw the cooler.

Refitting

48 Refitting is the reversal of removal, bearing in mind the following points:
a) Replace EGR pipe connection flange gaskets.
b) Use new nuts at EGR pipe connection to exhaust manifold.
c) Renew gaskets,seals banjo bolt and washers on turbocharger oil return/support bracket.
d) Tighten all mountings to the specified torque.
e) Check/refill the cooling system with reference to 'Weekly checks' and Chapter 1 Section 37.

Engine codes CLCA, CLCB, CFHC and CFHF

Removal

49 Remove the upper engine cover.

50 Remove the air filter housing and turbocharger air intake pipe with reference to Chapter 4A Section 3.

51 Remove the battery and battery tray as described in Chapter 5 Section 3.

52 Remove the exhaust front pipe/catalytic converter/particulate filter as described in Section 6.

53 Drain the cooling system with reference to Chapter 1 Section 37, or if suitable clamps are available clamp the coolant hoses to save draining the complete system, then release the retaining clips and disconnect the hoses from the EGR cooler, being prepared for some coolant spillage (see illustrations).

54 Undo the two retaining bolts from the cooler, the two retaining nuts from the exhaust manifold, and remove the EGR metal connecting pipe (see illustration).

55 Undo the two retaining bolts from the cooler, the two retaining bolts from the cylinder head and remove the EGR metal connecting pipe (see illustrations).

56 Disconnect the turbocharger oil feed pipe at the union at the top of the turbocharger, counter-hold the adaptor as the union is released to prevent it from unscrewing from the turbocharger body. Remove the banjo bolt

3.55a Undo the EGR pipe to cooler bolts and....

3.55b .... the EGR pipe bolts to the cylinder head

3.57 Oil feed and return banjo bolts

3.59 Disconnect the wiring plug connector from the EGR valve

3.61 Fit new gasket to EGR pipe

3.62 Control valve

from the oil feed pipes connection to the base of the cylinder block.

57 Undo the upper bolts and lower banjo bolt from the turbocharger oil return pipe/support bracket. Remove the oil feed pipe and oil return pipe/support bracket from the vehicle **(see illustration)**.

58 Disconnect the vacuum hose from the by-pass flap actuator.

59 Disconnect the wiring plug connector from the EGR valve **(see illustration)**.

60 Undo the four retaining bolts and remove the EGR valve/cooler unit from the rear of the engine.

Refitting

61 Refitting is the reversal of removal, bearing in mind the following points:
a) Replace EGR pipe connection flange gaskets **(see illustration)**.
b) Renew gaskets,seals banjo bolt and sealing washers on turbocharger oil return pipe/support bracket. Renew sealing washers on oil supply banjo bolt.
c) Use new nuts at EGR pipe connection to exhaust manifold.
d) Tighten all mountings to the specified torque.
e) Check/refill the cooling system with reference to 'Weekly checks' and Chapter 1 Section 37.
f) If the EGR valve/cooler unit has been replaced it will require adaptation to the engine management system using Skoda diagnostic equipment or a suitable alternative.

EGR vacuum control valve

62 On engine codes BJB, BKC, BXE and BKD the EGR valve is vacuum operated, control of the vacuum supply is from a control valve block **(see illustration)**, mounted on the bulkhead to the left of the engine. This unit utilises solenoid valves to enable the ECM to control the vacuum actuated components in the engine bay.

Removal

63 Note their fitted locations, and disconnect the vacuum hoses from the control valve **(see illustration)**.

64 Disconnect the wiring plug from the control valve.

65 Undo the two retaining bolts and remove the control valve.

Refitting

66 Refitting is a reversal of removal.

EGR cooler 'by-pass' (change-over) solenoid valve

67 All models fitted with an EGR cooler have a vacuum operated cooler by-pass flap, an ECM operated solenoid valve controls

3.63 Vacuum hose connections to control valve block

1 Vacant
2 Vacuum supply
3 EGR valve
4 Bypass (change over) flap of EGR cooler (intake manifold flap on engine code BJB
5 Air filter
6 Vacuum reservoir
7 Turbocharger vacuum control

3.67 EGR cooler solenoid valve (common rail engines)

the vacuum supply to the by-pass flap. On common rail engines the solenoid valve is mounted above the oil filter housing **(see illustration)** and on PD engines it is mounted at the rear of the engine, except on engine codes BJB, BKC, BXE and BKD, where it is integrated into the vacuum control valve block (for removal/refitting of the valve block refer to the ' EGR vacuum control valve' in this section). Do not confuse the EGR solenoid with the turbo charge pressure control solenoid which is mounted on the bulkhead.

Removal

68 Disconnect the wiring plug from the solenoid valve.
69 Release the valve from its mounting, then identify the vacuum hoses for refitting and disconnect them from the valve.

Refitting

70 Refitting is the reversal of removal.

5.8a Exhaust/turbo securing clamp (catalytic converter)

5.9 Undo upper mounting bolt

Ensure that the hoses and wiring plug are reconnected securely and correctly.

4 Exhaust manifold – removal and refitting

1 The exhaust manifold is integral with the turbocharger and cannot be renewed separately. Refer to Chapter 4A Section 11 for the turbocharger removal and refitting procedure details.

5 Catalytic converter/ particulate filter – removal and refitting

⚠️ *Warning: Allow ample time for the exhaust system to cool before starting work. In particular, note that the catalytic converter runs at very high temperatures. If there is any chance that the system may still be hot, wear suitable gloves.*

⚠️ *Warning: DO NOT use fuel or engine oil additives – these may contain substances harmful to the catalytic converter/particulate filter.*

⚠️ *Warning: DO NOT continue to use the car if the engine burns (engine) oil to the extent of leaving a visible trail of blue smoke.*

⚠️ *Warning: Remember that the catalytic converter is FRAGILE – do not strike it with tools during servicing work, and take care handling*

5.8b Exhaust/turbo securing clamp (particulate filter)

5.12 Brace the flexible pipe with a flat metal bar and clips.

it when removing it from the car for any reason.

Note: *This section describes removal of the exhaust front flexible pipe complete with the catalytic converter or combined particulate filter and catalytic converter (depending on the model). On Common rail (CR) engines equipped with a particulate filter, it will be necessary to remove the front subframe assembly to enable removal of the particulate filter/catalytic converter unit. On catalytic converter equipped CR engines and PD engines with particulate filter and/or catalytic converter, removal (whilst awkward) is possible with the subframe in position.*

Removal

1 Disconnect the battery negative lead and position it away from the terminal (or insulate the terminal) to prevent accidental reconnection – see disconnection and reconnection in Chapter 5 Section 3.
2 Remove the engine top cover.
3 On engine codes BJB, BKC, BXE, BLS and BMM remove the EGR valve as described in Section 3.
4 Trace the wiring of the oxygen (lambda) sensor to its connector at the bulkhead, disconnect the wiring plug, release the wiring, then unscrew and remove the sensor.
5 On particulate filter equipped vehicles trace the wiring from the exhaust gas temperature sensors to their connectors at the bulkhead, disconnect the wiring plug and release the wiring from any retainers.
6 Release the wiring plug from the particulate filter differential pressure sensor slacken the bolt and remove the sensor unit's mounting bracket from the supplementary fuel pump mounting. Disconnect the sensor from the pressure line flexible hoses and remove the sensor.
7 Apply the handbrake, then jack up the front of the vehicle and support it on axle stands (see *Jacking and vehicle support*). Undo the fasteners and remove the engine compartment undershield.
8 Slacken the retaining bolt to release the clamp between the turbocharger and the particulate filter/catalytic converter **(see illustrations)**.
9 Working at the right-hand rear corner of the cylinder head, slacken and remove the particulate filter/catalytic converter upper mounting bolt **(see illustration)**.
10 On common rail engines with a particulate filter, remove the front subframe with reference to Chapter 10 Section 21 (note that it is not necessary to unbolt the steering gear from the subframe). On all other variants remove the rear engine mounting (torque arm) as described in Chapter 2A Section 18 or Chapter 2B Section 16.
11 Remove the right-hand driveshaft and driveshaft heat shield (where fitted) as described in Chapter 8 Section 2.
12 To prevent damage to the front pipe flexible section, brace that part of the pipe with a suitable length of bar and some clips **(see illustration)**.

5.13 Slide the exhaust clamp along the exhaust

5.17a Undo the support bracket upper bolt (arrowed)...

5.17b ... and the lower bolt (arrowed) at the gearbox casing

Caution: Handle the flexible, braided section of the front pipe carefully and do not bend it excessively, if it is bent more than 10° it can be damaged.

13 To disengage the exhaust front pipe from the rest of the system, slacken the exhaust sleeve clamp nuts and slide the sleeve rearwards **(see illustration)**.

14 Unbolt and remove the flooring/transmission tunnel front cross brace.

15 On particulate filter equipped engines remove the exhaust gas temperature sensors from the filter.

16 Where the subframe is still in position, unbolt the exhaust mounting bracket from the subframe, release the rubber mounts from the exhaust and remove the bracket. Disconnect the wiring plug from the oil level sensor at the base of the sump and push the sump forward (taking care not to damage the radiator fans or any front of engine components) to give as much room as possible for removal of the particulate filter/catalytic converter. Secure the engine in this position using a ratchet strap, wooden block or other suitable means.

17 On catalytic converter equipped engines undo the upper and lower bolts and remove the converter support bracket **(see illustrations)**.

18 On particulate filter equipped engines, undo the nuts securing the lower mounting bracket to the filter and the cylinder block, then remove the bracket **(see illustrations)**.

19 Carefully manoeuvre the catalytic converter/particulate filter downwards from place. Where the subframe is still in place it will be necessary to rotate the particulate filter assembly as it is removed. Make sure that all wiring has been released and take care not to damage any wiring or sensors. Also take care not to bend the flexible section of the exhaust more than 10°.

Refitting

20 Refit the catalytic converter/particulate filter assembly by following the removal procedure in reverse, noting the following points:
a) *Renew all gaskets.*
b) *Replace any specified fasteners.*
c) *Tighten all fasteners to their specified torque where given.*

d) *Use a suitable high temperature anti-seize grease on the threads of the O2 sensor before installing.*
e) *Fully tighten catalytic converter/particulate filter to turbocharger clamp only after the catalytic converter/particulate filter mounting brackets are fitted and tightened.*

Note: *If a new particulate filter has been fitted access to Skoda or other suitable diagnostic equipment will be required to carry out adaptation of the new particulate filter to the engine management system, this will reset the stored ash deposit mass to zero and ensure correct monitoring and regeneration of the new filter.*

6 Exhaust system – component renewal

⚠️ *Warning: Allow ample time for the exhaust system to cool before starting work. In particular, note that the catalytic converter runs at very high temperatures. If there is any chance that the system may still be hot, wear suitable gloves.*

Note: *If the original exhaust system is fitted the intermediate and rear sections may be in one piece, it will be necessary to locate the indentation markings and cut through the pipe at 90°, in line with the centre indentation, to remove/replace either the intermediate or rear sections. A sliding sleeve and clamps will be required for refitting.*

1 Each exhaust section can be removed

5.18a Undo the upper securing nuts...

individually, however because the system is located above the rear axle, the system cannot be removed complete.

2 To remove part of the system, first jack up the front or rear of the car and support it on axle stands (see *Jacking and vehicle support*). Alternatively, position the car over an inspection pit or on car ramps.

Front pipe (catalytic converter/ particulate filter) removal

Caution: Handle the flexible, braided section of the front pipe carefully, and do not bend it excessively, if it is bent more than 10° it could get damaged.

3 The front flexible pipe section is part of the catalytic converter/particulate filter, remove the front pipe assembly as described in Section 5.

Intermediate pipe and silencer removal

4 Working under the car, support the front pipe on an axle stand or trolley jack.

5 If the original intermediate/tail pipe is fitted, it will be necessary to cut through the middle pipe in order to separate it from the tailpipe and silencer. The pipe should have an indentation to indicate where the cut must be made before the rear silencer. Using a hacksaw, cut through the pipe at right-angles.

6 If the service pipe has been fitted, unscrew the clamp bolts and separate the intermediate pipe from the tailpipe.

7 Note the fitted position of the clamp attaching the intermediate pipe to the catalytic converter or short pipe (the bolts should be on

5.18b ... and lower securing nuts

the left-hand side of the clamp, and the lower ends of the bolts should not be below the bottom of the pipe), then unscrew the clamp bolts and separate the catalytic converter.

8 Disconnect the rubber mounting and withdraw the intermediate pipe and silencer from under the car.

Tailpipe and silencer removal

9 If the original intermediate/tail pipe is fitted, it will be necessary to cut through the middle pipe in order to separate it from the tailpipe and silencer. The pipe has an indentation to indicate where the cut must be made. Using a hacksaw, cut through the pipe at right-angles.

10 If the service pipe has been fitted, unscrew the clamp bolts and separate the tailpipe from the intermediate pipe. Note that the fitted position of the clamp should be with the bolts facing the rear of the car, and the bolt ends should not be below the bottom of the pipe.

11 Disconnect the rubber mountings and withdraw the tailpipe and silencer from under the car.

Refitting

12 Each section is refitted by a reversal of the removal sequence, noting the following points.

a) *Ensure that all traces of corrosion have been removed from the flanges or pipe ends and renew all necessary gaskets.*

b) *Inspect the rubber mountings for signs of damage or deterioration and renew as necessary.*

c) *Prior to tightening the exhaust system mounting, ensure that all rubber mountings are correctly located and that there is adequate clearance between the exhaust system and vehicle underbody.*

d) *Renew all self-locking nuts.*

e) *Apply high-temperature anti-seize grease to any mounting studs.*

Chapter 5
Starting and charging systems

Contents

Degrees of difficulty

Easy, suitable for novice with little experience	Fairly easy, suitable for beginner with some experience	Fairly difficult, suitable for competent DIY mechanic	Difficult, suitable for experienced DIY mechanic	Very difficult, suitable for expert DIY or professional

Specifications

General

System type	12 volt, negative earth

Manufacturer's engine codes: *
   PD unit injector engines:

1.9 litre (1896 cc), 8-valve, SOHC	BJB, BKC, BLS and BXE

      2.0 litre (1968 cc):

8-valve, SOHC	BMM
16-valve, DOHC	BKD and BMN

   Common rail injection engines:

2.0 litre (1968 cc), 16-valve, DOHC	CBBB, CBDB and CEGA (1st Generation)
	CLCA, CLCB, CFHC and CFHF (2nd Generation)

*See 'Vehicle identification' at the end of this manual for the location of engine code markings.

Starter motor

Type	Pre-engaged

Battery

Rating	44 to 80 Ah (depending on model and market)

Alternator

Type	Bosch or Valeo
Rating	90 or 120 amp
Minimum brush length	5.0 mm

Torque wrench settings

	Nm	lbf ft
Alternator connections (B+)	20	15
Alternator freewheel pulley nut	80	59
Alternator mounting bolt	23	17
Battery clamp bolt	22	16
Battery terminal clamp	6	4
Glow plug:		
PD unit injector engines (engine code BKD)	10	7
PD unit injector engines (all except engine code BKD):		
Ceramic	12	9
Metal	15	11
Common rail injection engines:		
Engine code CEGA	17	12
Engine codes CLCA, CLCB, CFHC and CFHF	18	13
Starter motor mounting bolts:		
M10	40	30
M12	80	59
Starter motor negative (earth) cable connection *	20	15
Starter motor positive (+) cable connection to solenoid:		
Starter solenoid with steel connection threads *	20	15
Starter solenoid with copper connection threads *	16	12

Use new fixings

1 General information and precautions

1 The engine electrical system consists mainly of the charging, starting, and preheating systems. Because of their engine-related functions, these are covered separately from the body electrical devices such as the lights, instruments, etc, which are covered in Chapter 12.

2 The electrical system is of the 12 volt negative earth type.

3 The battery, which may be of the low maintenance or maintenance-free (sealed for life) type, is charged by the alternator, which is belt-driven from the crankshaft pulley.

4 Most models are fitted with a freewheeling alternator belt pulley, designed with a one-way clutch mechanism in the hub this type of pulley transmits drive from the belt to the alternator as engine speed increases, when engine speed decreases, the pulley disconnects the drive allowing the alternator to overrun. On some versions the hub incorporates a spring/damper system to help cushion the drive. These types of pulley have the advantages of reducing vibration and noise in the belt drive when compared to a fixed pulley and this relieves the belt and alternator of some of the stresses which constant changes in speed produce.

5 The starter motor is of the pre-engaged type, with an integral solenoid. On starting, the solenoid moves the drive pinion into engagement with the flywheel ring gear before the starter motor is energised. Once the engine has started, a one-way clutch prevents the motor armature being driven by the engine until the pinion disengages from the flywheel.

6 Two primary earth straps are fitted; one from the battery negative terminal to the body, and one from the engine to the body (see Chapter 12 Section 2).

7 To assist cold starting, a preheating system is fitted which comprises four glow plugs, a glow plug control unit (incorporated in the ECM), a facia-mounted warning lamp and the associated electrical wiring.

8 The glow plugs are miniature electric heating elements, encapsulated in a metal or ceramic case with a probe at one end and electrical connection at the other. Each combustion chamber has a glow plug threaded into it, which is positioned directly in line with the incoming spray of fuel. When the glow plug is energised, the air in the combustion chamber is heated, allowing optimum combustion temperature to be achieved more quickly.

9 The duration of the preheating period is governed by the ECM, which monitors the temperature of the engine via the coolant temperature sensor and alters the preheating time to suit the conditions. Preheating only takes place at coolant temperatures below 9ºC.

10 A facia-mounted warning light informs the driver that preheating is taking place. The light extinguishes when sufficient preheating has taken place to allow the engine to be started, but power will still be supplied to the glow plugs for a further period until the engine is started. If no attempt is made to start the engine, the power supply to the glow plugs is switched off to prevent battery drain and glow plug burn-out. After the engine is started, there is a period of post-heating which takes place irrespective of whether it is preceded by preheating or not. This period lasts for a maximum of 4 minutes after the engine has been started, at engine speeds of under 2500 rpm. The heating is switched off after this period, or if the engine speed exceeds 2500 rpm. Post-heating reduces combustion noise and improves idling quality, and additionally reduces hydrocarbon emissions.

11 The warning light comes on when the ignition is initially switched on with a cold engine, and indicates that the glow plugs are being energised. If the light does not come on in these conditions, there is a defect in the glow plug system which should be investigated. When the engine is warm, the light may not come on, and the engine can be started straight away, and any post-heating will take place automatically.

12 Further details of the various systems are given in the relevant Sections of this Chapter. While some repair procedures are given, the usual course of action is to renew the component concerned.

⚠ *Warning: It is necessary to take extra care when working on the electrical system to avoid damage to semi-conductor devices (diodes and transistors), and to avoid the risk of personal injury. In addition to the precautions given in 'Safety first!', observe the following when working on the system:*

⚠ *Warning: Always remove rings, watches, etc, before working on the electrical system. Even with the battery disconnected, capacitive discharge could occur if a component's live terminal is earthed through a metal object. This could cause a shock or nasty burn.*

⚠ *Warning: Do not reverse the battery connections. Components such as the alternator, electronic control modules, or any other components having semi-conductor circuitry could be irreparably damaged.*

⚠ *Warning: Never disconnect the battery terminals, the alternator, any electrical wiring or any test instruments when the engine is running.*

⚠ *Warning: Do not allow the engine to turn the alternator when the alternator is not connected.*

 Warning: Never test for alternator output by 'flashing' the output lead to earth.

Warning: Always ensure that the battery negative lead is disconnected when working on the electrical system.

Warning: If the engine is being started using jump leads and a slave battery, connect the batteries negative-to-negative and positive-to-positive (see Jump starting at the beginning of the manual). This also applies when connecting a battery charger.

Warning: Before using electric-arc welding equipment on the car, disconnect the battery, alternator and components such as electronic control modules to protect them from the risk of damage.

Caution: The audio unit fitted as standard equipment has a built-in security code to deter thieves. If the power source to the unit is cut, the anti-theft system will activate. Even if the power source is immediately reconnected, the audio unit will not function until the correct security code has been entered. Therefore, if you do not know the correct security code for the radio, do not disconnect the battery negative terminal or remove the radio from the vehicle.

2 Battery –
testing and charging

Testing

1 All original equipment batteries are sealed for life maintenance-free batteries. These may be one of three types:
a) *Standard lead acid. Sealed for life with a visual charge indicator fitted.*
b) *Absorbent Glass Mat (AGM) Lead acid battery with the electrolyte absorbed in a glass matrix. No visual indicator fitted.*
c) *Enhanced Flooded Battery (EFB). Visual indicator fitted. Used on some stop-start models.*
2 Topping-up and testing of the electrolyte in each cell is not possible. The condition of the battery can therefore only be tested using a battery condition indicator or a voltmeter.
3 All models (except those with AGM batteries) are fitted with a maintenance-free battery with a built-in charge condition indicator. The indicator is located in the top of the battery casing, and indicates the condition of the battery from its colour. If the indicator shows green, then the battery is in a good state of charge. If the indicator turns darker, eventually to black, then the battery requires charging, as described later in this Section. If the indicator shows clear/yellow, then the electrolyte level in the battery is too low to allow further use, and the battery should be renewed. **Do not** attempt to charge, load or jump-start a battery when the indicator shows clear/yellow. **Note:** *From 2009 Skoda introduced batteries that only have a two colour visual indicator. If the indicator*

2.4 Checking the battery voltage

shows black there is sufficient electrolyte in the cell, if the indicator shows light yellow the electrolyte level is low and the battery must be replaced. Note that the indicator is only a guide to the electrolyte level on one cell and is not a guide to the state of charge.
4 If testing the battery using a voltmeter, connect the voltmeter across the battery and note the voltage **(see illustration)**. The test is only accurate if the battery has not been subjected to any kind of charge for the previous six hours. If this is not the case, switch on the headlights for 30 seconds, then wait four to five minutes before testing the battery after switching off the headlights. All other electrical circuits must be switched off, so check that the doors and tailgate are fully shut when making the test.
5 If the voltage reading is less than 12.2 volts, then the battery is discharged, whilst a reading of 12.2 to 12.4 volts indicates a partially discharged condition. The battery should be recharged as described later in this Section.
6 The preferable method of testing the battery is to use a digital battery analyser. Most garages (and battery supply specialists) will have one. These machines are capable of assessing the condition and performance of the battery without removing it from the vehicle or disconnecting the battery terminals. Note also that many modern battery chargers will also have some battery test abilities **(see illustration)**.

Charging

Note: *The following is intended as a guide only. Always refer to the manufacturer's recommendations (often printed on a label attached to the battery) before charging a battery.*
7 If the battery is to be recharged, we recommend that you use an 'intelligent' charger. Where an AGM or EFB battery is fitted it is essential that the charger is specifically capable of charging these types of battery. Whilst some chargers are capable of safely charging the battery with the battery connected to the vehicle, if you are unsure, always disconnect the battery. If the battery is disconnected (e.g. if it is to be removed and recharged on the bench), note that certain 'learned' values will be lost from the

2.6 Modern battery chargers can often test battery capacity

engine management ECU memory, requiring the car to be driven over a short distance after refitting the battery. Also, when the battery is reconnected, the warning lights for the ESP and electro-mechanical steering will light up and stay on. They will extinguish if you drive briefly in a straight line at a speed of 9 to 13 mph.

3 Battery –
disconnection, reconnection, removal and refitting

Disconnecting the battery

Note: *If the vehicle has a security-coded audio/ navigation unit, check that you have a copy of the code number before disconnecting the battery cable; refer to the caution in Section 1.*

Warning: There are two methods of battery disconnection: If working on the airbag system then the battery must be disconnected and reconnected with the ignition ON. When working on all other systems the battery must be disconnected and connected with the ignition OFF.

1 Lower the drivers window and remove the key from the ignition. Note the warning above!
2 The battery is located on the left-hand side of the engine compartment. Release the catch and remove the battery cover (where fitted).
3 Loosen the clamp nut and disconnect the battery negative (-) lead from the terminal **(see illustration)**.

3.3 Slacken the clamp nut and disconnect the battery negative (-) lead

3.12 Slacken the clamp nut and disconnect the battery positive (+) lead

3.15 Undo the battery clamp bolt (arrowed)

3.17 Undo the bolts (arrowed) and remove the battery tray

4 Move the negative (earth) lead away from the terminal. Cover the lead (or battery terminal) with a suitable insulator (a plastic bag over the lead clamp or a short length of plastic tube over the terminal post is ideal) or simply secure it to the side with a cable tie, to prevent accidental reconnection.

 Warning: If the battery has been disconnected with the ignition ON, prior to work on the airbag system, wait at least five minutes for any residual electrical energy to dissipate before commencing work on the system.

Reconnecting the battery

5 Reconnect the negative (-) lead. Push it down until it is flush with the battery terminal post and then tighten the nut to the specified torque.
6 Refit the battery cover and close the bonnet. **Note:** *If the battery has been disconnected prior to work on the airbag system, ensure that no-one is in the passenger cabin, and the ignition is switched ON before reconnecting the battery.*
7 Reach through the open drivers window and turn on the ignition. Wait a minute or so to allow the on board computer systems to boot up and for the battery voltage to stabilise.
8 Start the vehicle (from outside where possible) and then open and close all the power windows. Adjust the clock time and re-activate the audio unit by inserting the security code (where applicable).
9 Restore the electric window automatic opening/closing function by following the procedure in Chapter 11 Section 20 for each window.
10 After reconnecting the battery and starting the vehicle the ESP (Electronic Stability Programme) the TCS (Traction Control System) and the power steering warning light will remain on until the vehicle is driven in a straight line at a speed of 10 mph or more.

Removal

11 Disconnect the battery negative (-) lead as described above.
12 Loosen the clamp nut and disconnect the battery positive (+) lead from the terminal **(see illustration)**.

13 Where fitted, disconnect the vent pipe from the battery. Note on some models the vent incorporates a flashback arrester.
14 Lift the front section of the battery surround/box from place, or lift the fabric-type box from around the battery.
15 Undo the clamp bolt **(see illustration)**.
16 Lift out the battery and withdraw it from the engine compartment.
17 If required, remove the air cleaner assembly as described in Chapter 4A Section 3, then undo the 3 bolts and remove the battery tray **(see illustration)**.

Refitting

18 Clean the battery mounting, then refit the battery in position and refit the clamp. Tighten the bolt to the specified torque.
19 Refit the battery box/surround.
20 Where fitted, refit the vent pipe.
21 Reconnect the positive battery (+) lead and tighten to the specified torque.
22 Reconnect the negative (-) lead as described above. **Note:** *The battery positive (+) lead must always be connected before the negative (-) lead.*

4 Alternator/charging system – testing in vehicle

Note: *Refer to Section 1 of this Chapter before starting work.*
1 If the charge warning light fails to illuminate when the ignition is switched on, first check the alternator wiring connections for security. If the light still fails to illuminate, check the continuity of the warning light feed wire from the alternator to the dash warning lamp. If all is satisfactory, the alternator is at fault and should be renewed or taken to an auto-electrician for testing and repair.
2 Similarly, if the charge warning light comes on with the ignition, but is then slow to go out when the engine is started, this may indicate an impending alternator problem. Check all the items listed in the preceding paragraph, and refer to an auto-electrical specialist if no obvious faults are found.
3 If the charge warning light illuminates when the engine is running, stop the engine and

check that the drivebelt is correctly tensioned (see Chapter 1 Section 11), check the freewheel alternator pulley (where fitted) and that the alternator connections are secure. If all is so far satisfactory, check the alternator brushes and slip-rings as described in Section 6. If the fault persists, the alternator should be renewed, or taken to an auto-electrician for testing and repair.
4 If the alternator output is suspect even though the warning light functions correctly, the regulated voltage may be checked as follows.
5 Connect a voltmeter across the battery terminals, and start the engine.
6 Increase the engine speed until the voltmeter reading remains steady; the reading should be approximately 12 to 13 volts, and no more than 14 volts.
7 Switch on as many electrical accessories as possible (eg, the headlights, heated rear window and heater blower), and check that the alternator maintains the regulated voltage at around 13 to 14 volts.
8 If the regulated voltage is not as stated, this may be due to worn brushes, weak brush springs, a faulty voltage regulator, a faulty diode, a severed phase winding or worn or damaged slip-rings. Have the alternator checked and tested by an auto-electrician.

5 Alternator – removal and refitting

Removal

1 The alternator is fitted to the right-hand front of the engine. First, disconnect the battery negative lead and position it away from the terminal – refer to Section 3. Remove the plastic cover from the top of the engine.

8 valve PD unit injector engines

2 Disconnect the hoses at each end, release the fixings and attachments, then remove the charge air pipe from above the alternator
3 Undo the bolts/nut and lift the fuel filter from place **(see illustration)**. There's no need to disconnect the fuel hoses – place the filter to one side.

5.3 Undo the bolts/nut (arrowed) and move the fuel filter to one side

5.5a Undo the bolt (arrowed) and detach the vacuum reservoir from the bracket...

5.5b ...then undo the bolt (arrowed) and remove the bracket

4 Remove the auxiliary drivebelt as described in Chapter 1 Section 11.

16 valve PD unit injector engines

5 On engine code BKD, disconnect the vacuum pipes, undo the retaining bolt and detach the vacuum reservoir, then undo the bolts and remove the bracket from the front of the engine(see illustrations). Unscrew the oil level dipstick guide tube bracket at the same time.

6 On engine code BMN, release the vacuum solenoid valve from the bracket above the alternator, then undo the bolts and remove the bracket from the front of the engine.

7 Remove the auxiliary drivebelt as described in Chapter 1 Section 11.

8 Undo the bolts/nut and lift the fuel filter from place (see illustration 5.3). There's no need to disconnect the fuel hoses.

Common rail injection engines

9 Place the lock carrier in the 'Service position' as described in Chapter 11 Section 10.

10 Remove the auxiliary drivebelt as described in Chapter 1 Section 11.

11 Disconnect the hoses at each end, release the fixings and attachments, then remove the charge air pipe from the front of the engine.

12 Disconnect the wiring plug, undo the bolts and move the air conditioning compressor to one side. Suspend the compressor from a suitable position using wire, etc. There is no need to disconnect the refrigerant pipes.

13 Undo the nut securing the wiring loom retainer to the rear of the alternator.

5.15 Disconnect the wiring (arrowed) from the rear of the alternator

14 Undo the bolts/nut and lift the fuel filter to one side (see illustration 5.3). There is no need to disconnect the fuel hoses.

All engines

15 Note their fitted positions, then disconnect the wiring from the rear of the alternator (see illustration). Where necessary, release the wiring loom from any clips on the rear of the alternator.

16 Support the alternator, then unscrew and remove the mounting bolts (see illustration).

Refitting

17 Refitting is a reversal of removal. Refer to Chapter 1 Section 11 for details of refitting the drivebelt. Tighten the alternator mounting bolts, and the alternator wiring connections to the specified torque.

5.16 Alternator mounting bolts (arrowed)

6 Alternator – brush holder/voltage regulator module renewal

Removal

1 Remove the alternator, as described in Section 5.

2 Place the alternator on a clean work surface, with the pulley facing down.

Bosch

3 Undo the bolt and the two retaining nuts, and lift away the outer plastic cover (see illustration).

4 Unscrew the three securing bolts, and remove the voltage regulator (see illustrations).

6.3 On the Bosch type, remove the outer cover...

6.4a ...undo the bolts (arrowed)...

6.4b ...and remove the brush holder/ regulator

6.5 On the Valeo type, remove the outer plastic cover...

6.6a ...undo the bolts and nut (arrowed)...

6.6b ...and remove the voltage regulator

Valeo

5 Prise off the spring clips, and remove the outer plastic cover **(see illustration)**.
6 Undo the two bolts and single nut, and remove the voltage regulator **(see illustrations)**.
7 Slide off the brush cover by depressing the lugs on each side.

Inspection

8 Measure the free length of the brush contacts **(see illustration)**. Check the measurement with the Specifications; renew the module if the brushes are worn below the minimum limit.
9 Clean and inspect the surfaces of the slip-rings at the end of the alternator shaft **(see illustration)**. If they are excessively worn, or damaged, the alternator must be renewed.

Refitting

Bosch

10 Refit the voltage regulator using a reversal of the removal procedure, tightening the bolts securely. On completion, refer to Section 5 and refit the alternator.

Valeo

11 Depress the carbon brushes into the housing, then refit the voltage regulator and tighten the bolts and nut securely. Slide on the brush cover until it is heard to engage. On completion, refer to Section 5 and refit the alternator.

7 **Alternator freewheel pulley**
– checking, removing
and refitting

Checking

Caution: Keep loose clothing and long hair well out of the way of moving mechanical parts.
1 With the engine running, observe the area of the auxiliary belt drive for unusual vibration, noise or excessive belt tensioner movement, any of these can indicate a possible fault with the belt pulley. A problem with the pulley can also be the cause of a charging fault.
2 Observe the direction of rotation of the alternator, then switch off the engine. Disconnect the battery (see Section 3), and

6.8 Measure the brush length

remove the auxiliary belt as described in Chapter 1 Section 11.
3 Insert a screwdriver, or similar tool, carefully through the casing at the drive end of the alternator to engage with the fan on the rotor, preventing the rotor from turning.
4 Attempt to turn the pulley by hand in its normal direction of rotation, with the rotor held stationary the pulley should not turn in this direction.
5 With the rotor still held, turn the pulley against the normal direction of rotation, the pulley should turn freely and smoothly with no roughness or play.
6 Remove the tool used for locking the rotor.
7 Refit the auxiliary belt (Chapter 1 Section 11) and reconnect the battery with reference to Section 3.

Removal and refitting

Note: *Special tools will be required to remove*

7.10 Tools to engage with splines in pulley and alternator shaft

6.9 Clean and inspect the surfaces of the slip-rings

and refit the freewheel alternator pulley, at the time of writing these are widely available from many tool outlets.
8 Remove the alternator as described in Section 5. **Note:** *It may be possible on some models to change the pulley without removal of the alternator, this will depend on the model and what tools are available.*
9 Prise out the cap from the end of the alternator pulley.
10 Select the correct tools to engage with the internal splines of the pulley and the end of the alternator shaft **(see illustration)**.
11 Fit the hollow adaptor into the splines of the pulley and pass the other splined tool through into the end of the alternator shaft. Hold the shaft with a suitable spanner on the tool, whilst unscrewing the pulley using a spanner on the hollow adaptor **(see illustration)**.
12 The threads on the alternator shaft may

7.11 Unscrew the pulley using a spanner on the hollow adaptor be left or right handed, this will depend on the direction of driven rotation of the alternator. An alternator pulley that drives the alternator in a clockwise direction will need turning in an anti-clockwise direction to release it from the alternator shaft and vice-versa **(see illustration)**. Note: *Ensure that any replacement pulley is a compatible match to the original.*

13 Refitting is the reversal of removal, making sure that the pulley is tightened to the specified torque and a new end cap is fitted.

8 Starting system – testing

Note: *Refer to Section 1 of this Chapter before starting work.*

1 If the starter motor fails to operate when the ignition key is turned to the appropriate position, the following possible causes may be to blame:
a) *The battery is faulty.*
b) *The electrical connections between the switch, solenoid, battery and starter motor are somewhere failing to pass the necessary current from the battery through the starter to earth.*
c) *The solenoid is faulty.*
d) *The starter motor is mechanically or electrically defective.*

2 To check the battery, switch on the headlights. If they dim after a few seconds, this indicates that the battery is discharged – recharge (see Section 2) or renew the battery. If the headlights glow brightly, operate the ignition switch and observe the lights. If they dim, then this indicates that current is reaching the starter motor, therefore the fault must lie in the starter motor. If the lights continue to glow brightly (and no clicking sound can be heard from the starter motor solenoid), this indicates that there is a fault in the circuit or solenoid – see following paragraphs. If the starter motor turns slowly when operated, but the battery is in good condition, then this indicates that either the starter motor is faulty, or there is considerable resistance somewhere in the circuit.

3 If a fault in the circuit is suspected, disconnect the battery leads (including the earth connection to the body), the starter/ solenoid wiring and the engine/transmission earth strap. Thoroughly clean the connections, and reconnect the leads and wiring, then use a voltmeter or test light to check that full battery voltage is available at the battery positive lead connection to the solenoid, and that the earth is sound.

4 If the battery and all connections are in good condition, check the circuit by disconnecting the wire from the solenoid blade terminal. Connect a voltmeter or test light between the wire end and a good earth (such as the battery negative terminal), and check that the wire is live when the ignition switch is turned to the start position. If it is, then the circuit is sound – if not the circuit wiring can be checked as described in Chapter 12 Section 2.

5 The solenoid contacts can be checked by connecting a voltmeter or test light between the battery positive feed connection on the starter side of the solenoid, and earth. When the ignition switch is turned to the start position, there should be a reading or lighted bulb, as applicable. If there is no reading or lighted bulb, the solenoid is faulty and should be renewed.

6 If the circuit and solenoid are proved sound, the fault must lie in the starter motor. It may be possible to have the starter motor overhauled by a specialist, but check on the availability and cost of spares before proceeding, as it may prove more economical to obtain a new or exchange motor.

9 Starter motor – removal and refitting

Removal

1 Disconnect the battery negative lead as described in Section 3.
2 Remove the air cleaner housing as described in Chapter 4A Section 3.
3 Slide off the protective cap, then note their fitted positions and disconnect the wiring from the starter **(see illustration)**.
4 Undo the nut and detach the earth strap from the starter mounting bolt **(see illustration)**.
5 Raise the front of the vehicle and support it securely on axle stands (see *Jacking and*

7.12 Remove the pulley from the alternator shaft

vehicle support). Undo the fasteners and remove the engine undershield.
6 Undo the retaining bolts and remove the starter. Note the wiring loom support bracket shares a starter mounting bolt**(see illustration)**.

Refitting

7 Refit the starter motor by following the removal procedure in reverse. Tighten the mounting bolts to the specified torque.

10 Starter motor – testing and overhaul

1 If the starter motor is thought to be defective, it should be removed from the vehicle and taken to an auto-electrician for assessment. In the majority of cases, new starter motor brushes can be fitted at a reasonable cost. However, check the cost of repairs first as it may prove more economical to purchase a new or exchange motor.

11 Glow plugs – testing, removal and refitting

Testing

1 If the system malfunctions, testing is ultimately by substitution of known good units, but some preliminary checks may be made as described in the following paragraphs.

9.3 Disconnect the wiring plug and power lead from the starter motor

9.4 Disconnect the earth lead from the upper starter motor mounting bolt

9.6 Detach the wiring loom support bracket from the lower starter motor mounting bolt (arrowed)

11.19 Pull the connector (arrowed) from the top of the glow plug

11.24 Disconnect the wiring plugs from the injectors (arrowed)

2 Before testing the system, check that the battery voltage is at least 11.5 volts using a voltmeter. Switch off the ignition.

3 Where necessary for access, remove the engine top cover.

4 Disconnect the wiring plug from the coolant temperature sender at the rear of the engine. Disconnecting the sender in this way simulates a cold engine, which is a requirement for the glow plug system to activate.

5 Disconnect the wiring connector from the most convenient glow plug, and connect a suitable voltmeter between the wiring connector and a good earth.

6 Have an assistant switch on the ignition. Battery voltage should be displayed for approximately 20 seconds – note that the voltage will drop to zero when the pre- and post-heating periods end.

7 If no supply voltage can be detected at the glow plug, then either the glow plug relay (where applicable) or the supply wiring must be faulty. Also check that the glow plug fuse has not blown – if it has, this may indicate a serious wiring fault; consult a Skoda dealer or specialist for advice.

8 To locate a faulty glow plug, first disconnect the battery negative cable and position it away from the terminal (see Section 3).

9 Disconnect the wiring plug from the glow plug terminal. Measure the electrical resistance between the glow plug terminal and the engine earth. Ceramic glow plugs should have a resistance of no more than 1 ohm, and as a guide on metal glow plugs, more than a few ohms indicates that the plug

is defective. Ceramic glow plugs are identified by a white or silver seal around the top of the plug. Metal plugs have a red seal around the top of the plug.

10 If a suitable ammeter is available, connect it between the glow plug and its wiring connector, and measure the steady-state current consumption (ignore the initial current surge, which will be about 50% higher). As a guide, high current consumption (or no current draw at all) indicates a faulty glow plug.

11 As a final check, remove the glow plugs and inspect their stems for signs of damage. A badly burned or charred stem may be an indication of a faulty fuel injector.

Removal – PD unit injector engines

Note: *The glow plugs tend to be easier to remove from a warm engine. Snapping a glow plug whilst removing it will likely lead to the need to remove the cylinder head.*

Ceramic glow plugs

12 Ceramic glow plugs are identified by a white or silver seal at the top of the plug. Due to the materials used in their construction, special rules must be followed regarding their handling:

a) *Do not remove the plugs from the packaging until you are ready to fit them.*

b) *Ceramic plugs are very delicate. Protect them from knocks. Skoda claim that plugs which have been dropped (even from 2.0 cm) must not be fitted.*

c) *Damaged glow plugs may cause engine*

damage. Remove any fragments of damaged ceramic heater tips from the combustion chamber.

d) *The software within the ECM is specific to ceramic plugs. Therefore, these type of plugs are not interchangeable with metal plugs.*

13 Remove the plastic cover on the top of the engine.

14 On the 2.0 litre engines (BKD, BMN), remove the camshaft cover as described in Chapter 2A Section 4.

15 Carefully pull the connector(s) from the top of the glow plug(s).

16 Using a universal joint, extension and a deep socket, unscrew and remove the glow plug(s) from the cylinder head. Note that the plug must be kept 'straight' when being removed – if the ceramic heater tip touches the cylinder head, etc, it can easily be damaged.

Metal glow plugs

17 Remove the plastic cover on the top of the engine.

18 On the 2.0 litre engines (BKD, BMN), remove the camshaft cover as described in Chapter 2A Section 4.

19 Carefully pull the connector(s) from the top of the glow plug(s) **(see illustration)**.

20 Using a universal joint, extension and a deep socket, unscrew and remove the glow plug(s) from the cylinder head.

Removal – common rail injection engines

Note: *The glow plugs tend to be easier to remove from a warm engine. Snapping a glow plug whilst removing it will likely lead to the need to remove the cylinder head.*

21 Pull the plastic cover on the top of the engine upwards from its mountings.

22 Remove the noise insulation from above the injectors (where fitted).

23 Disconnect the wiring plug from the fuel rail pressure sensor.

24 Disconnect the wiring plugs from the injectors **(see illustration)** and exhaust gas pressure sensor (only engine code CEGA).

25 Undo the retaining screws and detach the coolant pipe from the inlet manifold. Move the pipe to the front of the manifold.

26 Release the wiring from the wiring guide, then carefully pull the connectors from the top of the glow plugs. Be sure to only pull on the underside of the ridge at the top of the connectors **(see illustrations)**.

27 Undo the screws retaining the fuel return pipe to the inlet manifold, then release the clamp and disconnect the fuel return pipes hose connection from the fuel rail. Be prepared for fuel spillage.

28 Push down the tabs, pull up the centre piece and disconnect the fuel return connectors from the top of the injectors (only engine code CEGA). Plug the openings to prevent contamination **(see illustrations)**.

11.26a Using long nose pliers...

11.26b ...pull the connectors from the top of the glow plugs

29 Move the fuel return pipe assembly to the front of the manifold.

30 Lay the glow plug wiring harness to one side.

31 Clean the area around the glow plugs; use a vacuum cleaner if possible. Spray brake cleaner (or similar) around the glow plug opening, letting it penetrate briefly, before blowing out with compressed air.

Caution: Always wear safety goggles to protect your eyes when using compressed air.

32 Using a universal joint, extension and a deep socket, unscrew and remove the glow plug(s) from the cylinder head. Note that the plug must be kept 'straight' when being removed – if the ceramic heater tip touches the cylinder head, etc, it can easily be damaged.

Refitting

Ceramic glow plugs

33 Ensure the threads in the cylinder head and on the glow plugs are clean and dry, and free of oil or grease. Clean any combustion deposits from the area around the glow plug apertures in the cylinder head.

34 Fit the glow plugs finger-tight only, taking great care not to allow the ceramic heater tips to contact any part of the cylinder head, etc.

11.28a Hold down the tabs (arrowed)...

35 Tighten the plugs to the specified torque.

36 Using a hand-held multimeter, check the resistance of the plugs. If the resistance of any of the plugs exceeds 1 ohm, remove it and check the ceramic heater tip is not damaged. If any of the tips are damaged, the ceramic fragments must be removed from the combustion chamber before the engine is started, otherwise extensive engine damage may result.

37 Reconnect the glow plug wiring plugs.

38 Skoda insist that the engine management ECM self-diagnosis system must be interrogated for any stored faults relating to

11.28b ...and pull up the centre piece of the fuel return connectors (arrowed)

the glow plugs before the engine is started. If any glow plug related faults are stored, do not start the engine. Remove the plugs and inspect them for damage.

39 The remainder of refitting is a reversal of removal.

Metal glow plugs

40 Ensure the threads in the cylinder head and glow plugs are clean, then refit the plugs to the cylinder head.

41 Tighten the plugs to the specified torque.

42 Reconnect the glow plug wiring plugs.

43 The remainder of refitting is a reversal of removal.

Notes

Chapter 6
Clutch

Contents

Degrees of difficulty

Easy, suitable for novice with little experience	Fairly easy, suitable for beginner with some experience	Fairly difficult, suitable for competent DIY mechanic	Difficult, suitable for experienced DIY mechanic 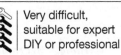	Very difficult, suitable for expert DIY or professional

Specifications

General

Type:

Luk clutch..   Single dry friction disc, diaphragm spring with spring-loaded hub, self-adjusting pressure plate (SAC)

Sachs clutch..   Single dry friction disc, diaphragm spring with spring-loaded hub

Operation ....   Hydraulic with slave and master cylinders

Torque wrench settings

	Nm	lbf ft
Clutch pedal bracket mounting nuts*	20	15
Clutch pedal pivot nut*	25	18
Clutch slave cylinder mounting bolt:		
5-speed gearbox	20	15
6-speed gearbox: *		
Metal slave cylinder	12	9
Non-metallic slave cylinder	15	11
Hydraulic pipe unions	15	11
Pressure plate-to-flywheel bolt:		
M6	13	10
M7	20	15

Use new fasteners

1 General Information

1 The clutch is of single dry plate type, incorporating a diaphragm spring pressure plate, and is hydraulically-operated.

2 The clutch cover (pressure plate) is bolted to the rear face of the flywheel, and the friction disc is located between the pressure plate and the flywheel friction surface. The disc hub is splined to the transmission input shaft and is free to slide along the splines. Friction lining material is riveted to each side of the disc and the disc hub incorporates cushioning springs to absorb transmission shocks and ensure a smooth take-up of drive. The flywheel is manufactured in two parts instead of the conventional single unit; the friction surface has a limited buffered movement in relation to the main flywheel mass bolted to the rear of the crankshaft. This has the effect of absorbing the initial clutch engagement shock and makes for a smoother gearchange.

3 When the clutch pedal is depressed, the slave cylinder pushrod moves the release lever forwards (on 5-speed gearboxes) or the concentric slave cylinder acts directly upon the release bearing (6-speed gearboxes), and the release bearing is forced onto the diaphragm spring fingers. As the centre of the spring is pushed in, the outer part of the spring moves out and releases the pressure plate from the friction disc. Drive then ceases to be transmitted to the transmission.

4 When the clutch pedal is released, the diaphragm spring forces the pressure plate into contact with the linings on the friction disc, and at the same time pushes the disc slightly forward along the input shaft splines into engagement with the flywheel.

The friction disc is now firmly sandwiched between the pressure plate and flywheel. This causes drive to be taken up.

5 An over-centre spring is fitted to the clutch pedal to equalise the operating effort over the full pedal stroke.

6 As the linings wear on the friction disc, the pressure plate rest position moves closer to the flywheel resulting in the 'rest' position of the diaphragm spring fingers being raised. Some vehicles may have a self-adjusting clutch (SAC) fitted. On these units, as the friction disc wears, an adjustment ring of varied thickness within the pressure plate assembly rotates slightly to compensate. This should ensure a more consistent feel to the clutch pedal. The hydraulic system requires no adjustment since the quantity of hydraulic fluid in the circuit automatically compensates for wear every time the clutch pedal is operated.

2.10a Clutch slave cylinder bleed screw (arrowed) – 5-speed transmission...

2.10b ... and 6-speed transmission (arrowed)

2 Hydraulic system – bleeding

⚠️ *Warning: Hydraulic fluid is poisonous; thoroughly wash off spills from bare skin without delay. Seek immediate medical advice if any fluid is swallowed or gets into the eyes. Certain types of hydraulic fluid are inflammable and may ignite when brought into contact with hot components. Hydraulic fluid is also an effective paint stripper. If spillage occurs onto painted bodywork or fittings, it should be washed off immediately, using copious quantities of cold water. It is also hygroscopic (it absorbs moisture from the air) therefore old fluid should never be re-used.*

1 The correct operation of any hydraulic system is only possible after removing all air from the components and circuit; this is achieved by bleeding the system.
2 During the bleeding procedure, add only clean, unused hydraulic fluid of the recommended type; never re-use fluid that has already been bled from the system. Ensure that sufficient fluid is available before starting work.
3 If there is any possibility of incorrect fluid being already in the system, the hydraulic circuit must be flushed completely with uncontaminated, correct fluid.
4 If hydraulic fluid has been lost from the system, or air has entered because of a leak, ensure that the fault is cured before continuing further.
5 The bleed screw is located on the slave cylinder located on the left-hand upper side of the transmission. As access to the bleed screw is limited it will be necessary to remove the air cleaner assembly as described in Chapter 4A Section 3.
6 Check that all pipes and hoses are secure, unions tight and the bleed screw is closed. Clean any dirt from around the bleed screw.
7 Unscrew the master cylinder fluid reservoir cap (the clutch shares the same fluid reservoir as the braking system), and top the master cylinder reservoir up to the upper (MAX) level line. Refit the cap loosely, and remember to maintain the fluid level at least above the lower

(MIN) level line throughout the procedure, or there is a risk of further air entering the system.
8 There are a number of one-man, do-it-yourself bleeding kits currently available from motor accessory shops. It is recommended that one of these kits is used whenever possible, as they greatly simplify the bleeding operation, and reduce the risk of expelled air and fluid being drawn back into the system. If such a kit is not available, the basic (two-man) method must be used, which is described in detail below.
9 If a kit is to be used, prepare the vehicle as described previously, and follow the kit manufacturer's instructions, as the procedure may vary slightly according to the type being used; generally, they are as outlined below in the relevant sub-section.

Bleeding

Basic (two-man) method

10 Collect a clean glass jar, a suitable length of plastic or rubber tubing which is a tight fit over the bleed screw **(see illustrations)**, and a ring spanner to fit the screw. The help of an assistant will also be required.
11 Remove the dust cap from the bleed screw. Fit the spanner and tube to the screw, place the other end of the tube in the jar, and pour in sufficient fluid to cover the end of the tube.
12 Ensure that the fluid level is maintained at least above the lower level line in the reservoir throughout the procedure.
13 Have the assistant fully depress the clutch pedal several times to build-up pressure, then maintain it on the final downstroke.
14 While pedal pressure is maintained, unscrew the bleed screw (approximately one turn) and allow the compressed fluid and air to flow into the jar. The assistant should maintain pedal pressure and should not release it until instructed to do so. When the flow stops, tighten the bleed screw again, have the assistant release the pedal slowly, and recheck the reservoir fluid level.
15 Repeat the steps given in paragraphs 13 and 14 until the fluid emerging from the bleed screw is free from air bubbles. If the master cylinder has been drained and refilled allow approximately five seconds between cycles for the master cylinder passages to refill.
16 When no more air bubbles appear, tighten

the bleed screw securely, remove the tube and spanner, and refit the dust cap. Do not overtighten the bleed screw.

Using a one-way valve kit

17 As their name implies, these kits consist of a length of tubing with a one-way valve fitted, to prevent expelled air and fluid being drawn back into the system; some kits include a translucent container, which can be positioned so that the air bubbles can be more easily seen flowing from the end of the tube.
18 The kit is connected to the bleed screw, which is then opened. The user returns to the driver's seat, depresses the clutch pedal with a smooth, steady stroke, and slowly releases it; this is repeated until the expelled fluid is clear of air bubbles.
19 Note that these kits simplify work so much that it is easy to forget the fluid reservoir level; ensure that this is maintained at least above the lower level line at all times.

Using a pressure-bleeding kit

20 These kits are usually operated by the reservoir of pressurised air contained in the spare tyre. However, note that it will probably be necessary to reduce the pressure to a lower level than normal; refer to the instructions supplied with the kit.
21 By connecting a pressurised, fluid-filled container to the fluid reservoir, bleeding can be carried out simply by opening the bleed screw and allowing the fluid to flow out until no more air bubbles can be seen in the expelled fluid.
22 This method has the advantage that the large reservoir of fluid provides an additional safeguard against air being drawn into the system during bleeding.

All methods

23 When bleeding is complete, and correct pedal feel is restored, tighten the bleed screw securely and wash off any spilt fluid. Refit the dust cap to the bleed screw.
24 Check the hydraulic fluid level in the master cylinder reservoir, and top-up if necessary (see *Weekly checks*).
25 Discard any hydraulic fluid that has been bled from the system; it will not be fit for re-use.
26 Check the operation of the clutch pedal. If the clutch is still not operating correctly, air must still be present in the system, and further bleeding is required. Failure to bleed satisfactorily after a reasonable repetition of the bleeding procedure may be due to worn master cylinder/release cylinder seals.

3 Clutch pedal – removal and refitting

Removal

1 To improve access, the driver's seat should be pushed back as far as possible and the steering wheel moved to its highest position.

2 Remove the lower part of the facia panel on the driver's side (see Chapter 11, Section 26).

3 Unbolt the crash strut mounted in front of the clutch pedal and remove the mounting damper where fitted.

4 Undo the pivot bolt attaching the pedal to the bracket, and pulling the pedal forwards slightly remove the over-centre helper spring from its mounting **(see illustration)**.

5 Using a suitable pair of pliers compress the clips at the top of the pedal that hold it to the master cylinder pushrod. The pedal can now be removed **(see illustration)**.

Refitting

6 Refitting is a reversal of removal. Renew any self-locking nuts.

4 Master cylinder – removal, overhaul and refitting

Note: *Refer to the warning at the beginning of Section 2 regarding the hazards of working with hydraulic fluid.*

Removal

1 Follow steps 1 to 3 as described in Section 3.

2 Disconnect the fluid supply pipe for the clutch master cylinder at the brake master cylinder fluid reservoir **(see illustration)**.

3 Prise out the clip and pull the fluid pressure pipe from the clutch master cylinder. Plug the openings to prevent contamination **(see illustration)**.

4 Disconnect the wiring plug from the clutch position sensor on the cylinder.

5 Undo the 3 bolts and remove the pedal assembly, complete with master cylinder.

6 Compress the clips each side and separate the clutch master cylinder pushrod from the pedal **(see illustration 3.5)**.

7 Insert a 40 mm spacer (eg, a socket) between the clutch pedal and the stop.

8 Release the clip, and pull the master cylinder from the bracket.

Overhaul

9 Check with your local Skoda dealer or parts specialist regarding the availability of repair kits.

Refitting

10 Refitting is a reversal of removal, but tighten all nuts and bolts to the specified torques where given. When repositioning the pedal bracket onto the bulkhead, have an assistant guide the clutch master cylinder through the location hole from the engine compartment side. When reconnecting the fluid pressure line, the clip must engage audibly. Bleed the clutch hydraulic system as described in Section 2.

3.4 Clutch pedal pivot bolt (arrowed)

5 Slave cylinder – removal, overhaul and refitting

Note: *Refer to the warning at the beginning of Section 2 regarding the hazards of working with hydraulic fluid.*

Removal

5-speed gearbox

1 The slave cylinder is located on top of the transmission on the left-hand side.

2 Remove the air filter housing as described in Chapter 4A Section 3 and if required remove the battery and battery tray as described in Chapter 5 Section 3.

3 Remove the retaining clips and disconnect the gear selector cables from the pins on the levers **(see illustration)**.

4.2 Disconnect the fluid supply pipe from the brake master cylinder (arrowed)

5.3 Slide off the retaining clips (arrowed)

3.5 Depress the clip (arrowed) on each side of the pedal

4 Undo the 3 bolts and move the gearchange cable support bracket (complete with cables) to one side, to ease access to the slave cylinder **(see illustration)**.

5 Remove the slave cylinder pressure pipe support bracket from the transmission casing.

6 Clamp the rubber section of the hydraulic hose leading from the master cylinder to the slave cylinder using a brake hose clamp to prevent loss of hydraulic fluid.

7 Using a screwdriver, prise out the spring clip and disconnect the hydraulic line from the slave cylinder. Tape over or plug the end of the line and the slave cylinder aperture.

8 Unscrew the mounting bolts and withdraw the slave cylinder **(see illustration)**.

Caution: Do not depress the clutch pedal with the slave cylinder removed.

4.3 Prise out the clip (arrowed) a little and disconnect the pressure pipe

5.4 Undo the bolts (arrowed) securing the gearchange cable bracket

5.8 Undo the slave cylinder retaining bolts (arrowed)

5.10 Prise up the clip (arrowed) and pull the bleed screw connection assembly from place

5.11 Slave cylinder/release bearing retaining bolts (arrowed)

6-speed gearbox

9 Remove the transmission as described in Chapter 7A Section 3.
10 Prise out the retaining clip and pull the bleed screw connection assembly from the slave cylinder (see illustration).
11 Undo the 3 retaining bolts and remove the slave cylinder along with the release bearing (see illustration). Note that the cylinder is integral with the release bearing. Renew the retaining bolts.

Overhaul

12 Check with your local Skoda dealer or spare parts specialist regarding the availability of overhaul kits.

Refitting

13 Refitting is a reversal of removal, noting the following points:
a) Tighten all fasteners to their specified torque where given.
b) Adjust the gearchange cables as described in Chapter 7A Section 2 (where applicable).
c) Bleed the clutch hydraulic system as described in Section 2.

---

6 Clutch friction disc and pressure plate – removal, inspection and refitting

⚠ *Warning: Dust created by clutch wear and deposited on the clutch components may contain asbestos,*

6.3a Undo the pressure plate retaining bolts (arrowed)

which is a health hazard. DO NOT blow it out with compressed air or inhale any of it. DO NOT use petrol or petroleum-based solvents to clean off the dust. Brake system cleaner or methylated spirit should be used to flush the dust into a suitable receptacle. After the clutch components are wiped clean with clean rags, dispose of the contaminated rags and cleaner in a sealed container.

Removal

1 Access to the clutch is obtained by removing the transmission as described in Chapter 7A Section 3.
2 Mark the clutch pressure plate and flywheel in relation to each other.
3 Hold the flywheel stationary, then unscrew the clutch pressure plate bolts ¼ of a turn at a time (see illustration). With the bolts unscrewed two or three turns, check that the pressure plate is not binding on the dowel pins. If necessary, use a screwdriver to release the pressure plate. On models with the Sachs clutch, the stop-pin must slacken as the bolts are removed. If it doesn't, press the pin towards the flywheel (see illustration).
4 Remove all the bolts, then lift the clutch pressure plate and friction disc from the flywheel.

Inspection

Note: *Due to the amount of work necessary to remove and refit clutch components, it is usually considered good practice to renew the clutch friction disc, pressure plate assembly and release bearing as a matched set, even if only*

6.3b Ensure the stop-pin is free to move

one of these is actually worn enough to require renewal. It is also worth considering the renewal of the clutch components on a preventive basis if the engine and/or transmission have been removed for some other reason.

5 Clean the pressure plate friction surface, clutch friction disc and flywheel. Do not inhale the dust, as it may contain asbestos which is dangerous to health.
6 Examine the fingers of the diaphragm spring for wear or scoring. If the depth of wear exceeds half the thickness of the fingers, a new pressure plate assembly must be fitted.
7 Examine the pressure plate for scoring, cracking, distortion and discoloration. Light scoring is acceptable, but if excessive, a new pressure plate assembly must be fitted. If the distortion of the friction surface exceeds 1.0 mm, renew it.
8 Examine the friction disc linings for wear and cracking, and for contamination with oil or grease. The linings are worn excessively if they are worn down to, or near, the rivets. Check the disc hub and splines for wear by temporarily fitting it on the transmission input shaft. Renew the friction disc as necessary.
9 Examine the flywheel friction surface for scoring, cracking and discoloration (caused by overheating). If excessive, it may be possible to have the flywheel machined by an engineering works, otherwise it should be renewed.
10 Ensure that all parts are clean, and free of oil or grease, before reassembling. Apply just a small amount of lithium-based grease (Skoda No G000100) to the splines of the friction disc hub. Do not use copper-based grease. Note that new pressure plates and clutch covers may be coated with protective grease. It is only permissible to clean the grease away from the friction disc lining contact area. Removal of the grease from other areas will shorten the service life of the clutch.

Refitting

11 Commence reassembly by locating the friction disc on the flywheel, with the raised side of the hub facing outwards (normally marked 'Getriebeseite' or 'Gearbox side'). If possible, the centralising tool (see paragraph 19) should be used to hold the disc on the flywheel at this stage (see illustration).

Self-adjusting clutch (SAC)

12 On models with a self-adjusting clutch (SAC), where a new friction disc is fitted, but the pressure plate is to be re-used, it is necessary to reset the pressure plate adjusting ring prior to assembly as follows.

13 Insert three 8 mm bolts into the pressure plate mounting holes at intervals of 120°. The bolts should be inserted from the flywheel side, and retained by nuts **(see illustration)**.

14 Place the pressure plate face down on the bed of an hydraulic press so that only the heads of the bolts make contact with the press bed, then place a circular spacer over the ends of the diaphragm springs fingers.

15 Use 2 screwdrivers to attempt to rotate the adjuster ring anti-clockwise. Apply just enough pressure with the hydraulic press until it's just possible to move the adjuster ring **(see illustration)**.

16 Once the adjuster ring edges are between the notches, relieve the pressure. The ring is now reset. **Note:** *New pressure plates are supplied in this reset position.*

All models

17 Locate the clutch pressure plate on the disc, and fit it onto the location dowels **(see illustration)**. If refitting the original pressure plate, make sure that the previously-made marks are aligned.

18 Insert the bolts finger-tight to hold the pressure plate in position.

19 The friction disc must now be centralised, to ensure correct alignment of the transmission input shaft with the disc centre. To do this, a proprietary tool may be used, or alternatively, use a wooden mandrel made to fit inside the friction disc and the hole in the centre of the crankshaft. Insert the tool through the friction disc into the crankshaft, and make sure that it is central.

20 Tighten the pressure plate bolts progressively and in diagonal sequence, until the specified torque setting is achieved, then remove the centralising tool **(see illustration)**.

21 Check the release bearing in the transmission bellhousing for smooth operation, and if necessary renew it with reference to Section 7.

22 Refit the transmission with reference to Chapter 7A Section 3.

---

7 Release bearing and lever
– removal, inspection and refitting

Note: *The following only applies to models with a 5-speed transmission. On the 6-speed transmission, the release bearing is integral with the slave cylinder and both parts are renewed as a single unit as described in Section 5.*

Removal

1 Remove the transmission as described in Chapter 7A Section 3.

6.11 The friction disc should be marked 'Getriebeseite' or 'Gearbox side'

6.13 Insert three 8 mm bolts from the flywheel side, and secure with nuts

6.15 The edges of the adjuster ring (B) must be between the notches (A)

2 Use a screwdriver to prise the release lever from the ball-stud inside the transmission bellhousing. If this proves difficult, push the spring clip from the pivot end of the release lever by pushing it through the hole. This will release the pivot end of the lever from the ball-stud. Now withdraw the lever together with the release bearing from the guide sleeve **(see illustrations)**.

3 Use a screwdriver to depress the plastic

6.17 Fit the pressure plate over the locating dowel pins (arrowed)

6.20 With the pressure plate bolts tightened, remove the centralising tool

7.2a Push the spring clip to release the lever from the ball-stud

7.2b Release lever and bearing removed from the transmission

7.3a Depress the retaining tabs...

7.3b ... and remove the release bearing from the lever

7.5 Lubricate the ball-stud with a little grease

7.6a Locate the spring over the end of the release lever...

7.6b ... and press the spring into the hole...

7.6c ... then press the release lever onto the ball-stud until the spring clip holds it in position

tabs and separate the bearing from the lever **(see illustrations)**.

Inspection

4 Spin the release bearing by hand, and check it for smooth running. Any tendency to seize or run rough will necessitate renewal of the bearing. If it is to be re-used, wipe it clean with a dry cloth; on no account should the bearing be washed in a liquid solvent, otherwise the internal grease will be removed.

Refitting

5 Commence refitting by lubricating the ball-stud and plastic pivot with a little lithium-based grease (No G000100)**(see illustration)**. Smear a little grease on the release bearing surface which contacts the diaphragm spring fingers and the release lever, and also on the guide sleeve. Wipe off any excess grease.
6 Fit the spring onto the release lever, and make sure the plastic pivot is in place on the

ball-stud. Refit the lever together with the bearing and press the release lever onto the ball-stud until the spring holds it in position **(see illustrations)**.

8 Clutch pedal position sensor
– removal and refitting

1 Refer to Chapter 4A Section 4.

Chapter 7 Part A
Manual transmission

Contents

Degrees of difficulty

Easy, suitable for novice with little experience	Fairly easy, suitable for beginner with some experience	Fairly difficult, suitable for competent DIY mechanic	Difficult, suitable for experienced DIY mechanic 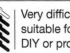	Very difficult, suitable for expert DIY or professional

Specifications

General

Type	Transversely-mounted, front-wheel-drive layout with integral transaxle differential/final drive, 5 or 6 forward speeds and 1 reverse

Application:
1.9 litre models	5-speed transmission (0A4)
2.0 litre models	6-speed transmission (02Q)

Oil capacities

5-speed (OA4) transmission*	1.8 litres
6-speed (O2Q) transmission*	2.15 litres

Capacities are the refill amounts for a previously filled transmission.

Torque wrench settings

	Nm	lbf ft
Gearchange bracket	20	15
Reversing light switch	20	15
Selector lever	23	17
Transmission to engine:		
M12 bolts	80	59
M10 bolts	40	30
Drain plug (5-speed, OA4)**	30	22
Pivot pin securing bolt (5-speed, OA4)	25	19
Drain, fill/level plug (6-speed, O2Q)**		
Multi-point socket head	45	33
Hexagon socket head	30	22
Locking cap screw (filler) (6-speed, O2Q)*		
Metal	45	33
Plastic	30	22

* not to be re-used
** drain/level plug sealing washers (where fitted) should be renewed when plug is removed.

1 General Information

1 The manual transmission is bolted directly to the left-hand end of the engine. This layout has the advantage of providing the shortest possible drive path to the front wheels, as well as locating the transmission in the airflow through engine bay, optimising cooling. The unit is cased in aluminium alloy.

2 Drive from the crankshaft is transmitted through the clutch to the gearbox input shaft, which is splined to accept the clutch friction disc.

3 All forward gears are fitted with synchromesh. The floor-mounted gear lever is connected to the gearbox by shift cables. Levers on the transmission actuate internal selector forks which are connected to the synchromesh sleeves. The sleeves are locked to the gearbox shafts but can slide axially by means of splined hubs, and they press baulk rings into contact with the respective gear/ pinion. The coned surfaces between the baulk rings and the pinion/gear act as a friction clutch that progressively matches the speed of the synchromesh sleeve (and hence the gearbox shaft) with that of the gear/pinion. This allows gearchanges to be carried out smoothly.

4 Drive is transmitted to the differential crownwheel, which rotates the differential case and planetary gears, thus driving the sun gears and driveshafts. The rotation of the differential planetary gears on their shaft allows the inner roadwheel to rotate at a slower speed than the outer roadwheel during cornering.

2.2 Pull the collar down and lock in position

2.3 Push down the selector shaft, then push the locking pin (arrowed) inwards whilst turning it clockwise

2.4 Lock the gear lever in position using a drill bit (arrowed)

2 Gearchange linkage – adjustment

1 Remove the air cleaner housing as described in Chapter 4A Section 3.
2 With the gearchange set in the neutral position, push the two locking collars (one on each cable) forwards to compress the springs, turn them clockwise (looking from the driver's seat) to lock into position **(see illustration)**.
3 Press down on the selector shaft on the top of the transmission, and push the locking pin into the transmission while turning it clockwise until it engages and the selector shaft cannot move **(see illustration)**.
4 Working inside the vehicle, unclip the gear lever gaiter from the centre console. Still in the neutral position, insert the locking pin (or drill bit) through the hole in the base of the gear lever and into the hole in the housing **(see illustration)**.
5 Working back in the engine bay, turn the two locking collars on the cables anti-clockwise so that the springs will release them back into position and lock the cables.
6 With the cable adjustment set, the locking pin can now be turned anti-clockwise to its original position.
7 Inside the vehicle, remove the locking pin from the gear lever, then check the operation of the selector mechanism. When the gear lever is at rest in neutral, it should be central, ready to select 3rd or 4th. The gear lever gaiter can now be refitted to the centre console.

8 Refit the air cleaner housing as described in Chapter 4A Section 3.

3 Manual transmission – removal and refitting

Removal

1 Select a solid, level surface to park the vehicle upon. Give yourself enough space to move around it easily. Apply the handbrake and chock the rear wheels.
2 Raise the front of the vehicle and support it securely on axle stands (see *Jacking and vehicle support*). Where fitted, remove the engine/transmission undershield. Position a suitable container beneath the transmission, then unscrew the drain plug and drain the transmission oil.
3 Remove the air cleaner assembly as described in Chapter 4A Section 3.
4 Remove the battery and battery tray with reference to Chapter 5 Section 3.
5 Prise off the clips and disconnect the gear selector cables from the gear selector levers. Note that on some models, the left-hand cable is not retained by a clip, and must be prised from place. Extract the clip and remove the relay lever, then unscrew the nut and remove the selector lever from the top of the transmission. Unscrew and remove the gearchange cables bracket **(see illustration and illustrations 5.3 and 5.4 in Chapter 6)**.

6 On 5-speed transmissions, undo the gearbox support bracket, then unscrew the clutch slave cylinder from the transmission and place to one side.
7 On 6-speed transmissions, seal the slave cylinder flexible hose using a hose clamp, then prise out the clip and pull the fluid pipe from the bleeder connection on the slave cylinder **(see illustration)**.
8 Unscrew the earth cable from the transmission or vehicle body **(see illustration)**.
9 Disconnect the wiring from the reversing light switch, and the neutral position sensor (vehicles with Stop-Start system only).
10 Unscrew and remove the upper bolts securing the transmission to the engine.
11 With reference to Chapter 5 Section 9, remove the starter motor.
12 Remove the lower left-hand wheel arch liner.
13 Unscrew the driveshaft protective cover.
14 Remove both driveshafts as described in Chapter 8 Section 2.
15 With reference to Chapter 4B Section 6, loosen the clamp and slide the connecting tube between the front and rear sections of the exhaust pipe. This will allow the engine to be moved forwards and backwards during the transmission removal and alignment procedures.
16 Remove the subframe as described Chapter 10 Section 21. Note there is no need to detach the steering gear or anti-roll bar from the subframe.
17 Where applicable, unscrew the cover

3.5 Prise up the edge (arrowed) and slide the retaining clip to one side

3.7 Prise up the clip a little and pull the hose from the bleeder connection

3.8 Earth cable (arrowed)

plate from the transmission bellhousing **(see illustration)**.

18 Using a suitable hoist, support the weight of the engine.

19 Unscrew the bolts securing the transmission mounting to the bracket on the transmission, then unscrew the mounting bracket from the transmission**(see illustration)**.

20 Lower the engine/transmission assembly slightly and, using a trolley jack, support the transmission. Position the jack so that it can be withdrawn from the left-hand side of the car.

21 Unscrew and remove the remaining lower transmission-to-engine mounting bolts, including the bolt located on the left-hand rear of the engine.

22 Carefully pull the transmission directly away from the engine, taking care not to allow its weight to rest on the clutch friction disc hub. A second person is helpful to pull the engine as far forwards as possible.

⚠️ *Warning: Support the transmission to ensure that it remains steady on the jack head. Keep the transmission level until the input shaft is fully withdrawn from the clutch friction disc.*

23 When the transmission is clear of the locating dowels and clutch components, lower the transmission to the ground and withdraw from under the car.

Refitting

24 Refitting the transmission is essentially a reversal of the removal procedure, but note the following points:

a) *Apply a smear of high melting-point grease (Skoda No G000100) to the clutch friction disc hub splines; take care to avoid contaminating the friction surfaces.*

b) *In order to align the transmission with the flywheel, gently pull the engine forward as the transmission is manoeuvred into place.*

c) *Tighten the transmission-to-engine bolts to the specified torque.*

d) *Refer to the relevant part of Chapter 2 and tighten the engine mounting bolts to the correct torque.*

e) *Refer to Chapter 8 Specifications and tighten the driveshaft bolts to the specified torque.*

f) *On completion, refer to Section 2 and check the gearchange linkage/cable adjustment.*

g) *Refill the transmission with the correct grade and quantity of oil. Refer to 'Lubricants and fluids', Chapter 1 Section 16 and Section 6 of this chapter.*

4 Manual transmission overhaul – general information

1 The overhaul of a manual transmission is a complex (and often expensive) task for the DIY

3.17 Undo the bolt (arrowed) and remove the cover plate

home mechanic to undertake, which requires access to specialist equipment. It involves dismantling and reassembly of many small components, measuring clearances precisely and if necessary adjusting them by selecting shims and spacers. Internal transmission components are also often difficult to obtain and in many instances, extremely expensive. Because of this, if the transmission develops a fault or becomes noisy, the best course of action is to have the unit overhauled by a specialist repairer or to obtain an exchange reconditioned unit.

2 Nevertheless, it is not impossible for the more experienced mechanic to overhaul the transmission if the special tools are available and the job is carried out in a deliberate step-by-step manner, to ensure nothing is overlooked.

3 The tools necessary for an overhaul include internal and external circlip pliers, bearing pullers, a slide hammer, a set of pin punches, a dial test indicator and possibly a hydraulic press. In addition, a large, sturdy workbench and a vice will be required.

4 During dismantling of the transmission, make careful notes of how each component is fitted to make reassembly easier and accurate.

5 Before dismantling the transmission, it will help if you have some idea of where the problem lies. Certain problems can be closely related to specific areas in the transmission, which can make component examination and renewal easier. Refer to the Fault finding Section in this manual for more information.

5.7a Reversing light switch (arrowed) – 5-speed transmission...

3.19 Mounting-to-bracket bolts (arrowed)

5 Reversing light switch – testing, removal and refitting

Testing

1 Ensure that the ignition switch is turned to the OFF position.

2 Remove the engine underpanel for easier access and unplug the wiring harness from the reversing light switch at the connector. The switch is located on the front, top of the casing.

3 Connect the probes of a continuity tester, or multimeter set to the resistance measurement function, across the terminals of the reversing light switch.

4 The switch contacts are normally open, so with any gear other than reverse selected, the tester/meter should indicate an open circuit or infinite resistance. When reverse gear is selected, the switch contacts should close, causing the tester/meter to indicate continuity or zero resistance.

5 If the switch does not operate correctly, it should be renewed.

Removal

6 Ensure that the ignition switch is turned to the OFF position.

7 Unplug the wiring harness from the reversing light switch at the connector **(see illustrations)**.

8 Unscrew the switch from the transmission casing, and recover the sealing ring.

5.7b ... and 6-speed transmission (arrowed)

6.7 Oil drain plug (A) and pivot pin (B)

Refitting

9 Refitting is a reversal of removal.

6 Transmission oil –
draining and refilling

With the vehicle on flat ground, find a level location on the vehicle with a spirit level (e.g. the luggage area floor), use the spirit level in the same location to ensure the vehicle is level when raised on axle stands or ramps.

5-speed (OA4) transmissions

1 On these transmissions, it is impossible to check the level of the oil through the 'filler' plug, due to the engine/transmission installation angle; the level of the fluid is above the lower edge of the filler hole. The only method of ensuring the correct fluid level is to completely drain and refill the transmission – as described below.

2 The vehicle must be on level ground to check/fill the transmission. This can be accomplished by using wheel ramps to raise the front of the vehicle and then raising the rear of the vehicle using a jack and axle stands (see *Jacking and vehicle support*).

3 Undo the fasteners and remove the engine undershield.

4 Remove the air filter housing as described in Chapter 4A Section 3

5 Place a container under the transmission casing.

6 Unscrew the drain plug from the base of the transmission housing and allow the oil to drain.

7 In order to fully drain the transmission, a pivot pin must be removed from the underside of the transmission casing. To prevent the position of the selector forks being altered, from above, press the selector shaft down, then press in and turn the angled locking rod upwards to lock the shaft in position **(see illustration 2.3)**. On the underside of the gearbox, remove the retaining bolt and pull out the pivot pin nearest the left front roadwheel to allow the oil to drain **(see illustration)**.

8 When the oil has finished draining, clean the surrounding area, refit the drain plug and tighten it to the specified torque

9 Renew the O-ring on the pivot pin, prior to refitting, install the retaining bolt and tighten to the specified torque.

10 Rotate the selector-shaft locking rod to its original position.

11 Unscrew the reversing light switch from the top of the transmission casing.

12 Using a 600 mm length of 10 mm (external) diameter hose, and funnel, add the specified quantity of new oil to the transmission.

13 Refit the reversing light switch, and tighten it to the specified torque.

14 Refit the air filter housing and undershield before lowering the vehicle to the ground.

6-speed (O2Q) transmissions

Note: *Two variants of this transmission can be found in these vehicles, one has a level/filler plug on the front face of the transmission through which oil can be added and the level checked, the other has no filler/level plug, this transmission requires draining and refilling with the correct quantity to establish the correct oil level.*

With oil level/filler plug

15 Apply the handbrake, then jack up the front and rear of the vehicle and support it on axle stands (see *Jacking and vehicle support*). To ensure an accurate check, make sure that the vehicle is level. Undo the fasteners and remove the engine/transmission undershield.

16 Remove the filler/level plug from the transmission

17 Position a drain tray or suitable container beneath the transmission, then unscrew the drain plug and drain the transmission oil.

18 When the oil has finished draining, clean the surrounding area, refit the drain plug and tighten it to the specified torque. Note that two versions of the oil drain plug are fitted and they have different torque settings.

19 Fill the transmission with oil until it is at the lower edge of the filler hole. Allow time for the oil to drain down into the transmission and then re-check the level.

20 Refit the filler/level plug and tighten to the

6.26 Gearshift locking cap screw location

specified torque (again there are two versions of filler/level plug with different torque settings.

21 Refit the undershield and lower the vehicle to the ground.

Without oil level/filler plug

22 Apply the handbrake, then jack up the front and rear of the vehicle and support it on axle stands (see *Jacking and vehicle support*). To ensure an accurate check, make sure that the vehicle is level. Undo the fasteners and remove the engine/transmission undershield.

23 Position a drain tray or suitable container beneath the transmission, then unscrew the drain plug and drain the transmission oil.

24 When the oil has finished draining, clean the surrounding area, refit the drain plug and tighten it to the specified torque. Note that two versions of the oil drain plug are fitted and they have different torque settings.

25 Remove the air filter housing as described in Chapter 4A Section 3

26 Ensure that the gear linkage mechanism is in the neutral position and remove the gearshift locking cap screw, located on the transmission housing adjacent to the linkage mechanism **(see illustration)**.

27 Using a 600 mm length of 16mm (external) diameter hose, and a funnel, add the specified quantity of new oil to the transmission through the hole that the locking cap screw was removed from.

28 Fit a new locking cap screw and tighten to the specified torque. Note thatthe torque setting for this component depends on whether it is made from metal or plastic.

29 Refit the air filter housing and undershield before lowering the vehicle to the ground.

Chapter 7 Part B
Automatic transmission

Contents

Degrees of difficulty

Easy, suitable for novice with little experience	Fairly easy, suitable for beginner with some experience	Fairly difficult, suitable for competent DIY mechanic	Difficult, suitable for experienced DIY mechanic	Very difficult, suitable for expert DIY or professional

Specifications

General

Description	DSG (Direct Shift Gearbox) semi-automatic 6-speed transmission with dual multi-plate clutch and differential
Transmission type number	02E

Transmission capacity:
Initial fill at factory	7.2 litres
Change quantity	5.2 litres (approximately)

Torque wrench settings

	Nm	lbf ft
Transmission fluid drain plug	45	33
Transmission fluid level elbow tube	3	2.2
Transmission filter housing	20	15
Transmission mounting -to-bracket bolts: *		
Stage 1	60	44
Stage 2	Angle-tighten a further 90°	
Transmission mounting bracket-to-transmission bolts: *		
Stage 1	40	30
Stage 2	Angle-tighten a further 90°	
Transmission-to-engine bolts:		
M10 bolts	40	30
M12 bolts	80	59

Do not re-use

1 General Information

1 The Skoda type 02E semi-automatic DSG (Direct Shift Gearbox) has six forward speeds (and one reverse). In contrast to traditional automatic transmissions where a fluid flywheel (torque converter) transmits the power from the engine to the gearbox, the DSG has two multi-plate clutches. The twin-clutch transmission is essentially two separate gearboxes with a pair of clutches between them. One gearbox provides odd-numbered speeds (first, third and fifth gear), the other provides even-numbered speeds (second, fourth and sixth). Initially, the 'odd' gearbox is in first gear and the 'even' gearbox is in second gear. The clutch engages the odd gearbox and the car proceeds in first gear. To change to second gear, the transmission uses the clutches to switch from the odd gearbox to the even gearbox. The odd gearbox immediately pre-selects third gear. At the next change the transmission swaps gearboxes again, engaging third gear, and the even gearbox pre-selects fourth gear. The transmission ECM (Electronic Control Module) calculates the next likely gearchange based on vehicle speed and driver behaviour and has the 'idle' gearbox pre-select that gear. The main advantages of the DSG is near-instant gearchanges, with seamless, highly efficient drive, resulting in less exhaust emissions and fuel consumption.

2 A fault diagnosis system is integrated into the control unit, but analysis can only be undertaken with specialised equipment. It is important that any transmission fault be identified and rectified at the earliest possible opportunity. A Skoda dealer or suitably-equipped specialist can 'interrogate' the ECM fault memory for stored fault codes, enabling him to pin-point the fault quickly. Once the fault has been corrected and any fault codes have been cleared, normal transmission operation is restored.

3 Because of the need for special test equipment, the complexity of some of the parts, and the need for scrupulous cleanliness when these transmissions, the work which the owner can do is limited. Most major repairs and overhaul operations should be left to a Skoda dealer or specialist, who will be equipped with the necessary equipment for fault diagnosis and repair. The information in this Chapter is therefore limited to a description of the removal and refitting of the transmission as a complete unit, the removal, refitting and adjustment of the selector cable and changing of the transmission fluid.

4 In the event of a transmission problem occurring, consult a Skoda dealer or transmission specialist before removing the transmission from the vehicle, since the majority of fault diagnosis is carried out with the transmission in situ.

2.7 Selector cable clip and outer cable circlip (arrowed)

2.8 Clamp the transmission cooler hoses (arrowed)

2.9 Transmission wiring plug and earth cable (arrowed)

2 Transmission –
removal and refitting

Removal

1 The automatic transmission is removed downwards from the engine compartment. First, select a solid, level surface to park the vehicle upon. Give yourself enough space to move around it easily. Select P, apply the handbrake, and chock the rear wheels.
2 Loosen the front wheel bolts, and the driveshaft hub bolts, then raise the front of the vehicle and rest it securely on axle stands (see *Jacking and vehicle support*). Remove the front wheels. Allow a suitable working clearance underneath for the eventual withdrawal of the transmission. Undo the fasteners and remove the engine/transmission undershield.
3 Remove the air cleaner housing as described in Chapter 4A Section 3.
4 Remove the turbocharger intake hose.
5 Remove the battery and battery tray as described in Chapter 5 Section 3.
6 Remove the starter motor as described in Chapter 5 Section 9.
7 Remove the retaining clip, lever off the end of the selector cable from the selector shaft lever, then prise up the circlip and remove the outer cable from the support bracket. Position the cable to one side. Note that both the retaining clip and circlip must be renewed**(see illustration)**.
8 Clamp off the automatic transmission fluid cooler hoses with brake hose type clamps. Release the retaining clips and detach the hoses from the cooler (located on the top of the transmission)**(see illustration)**.
9 Rotate the collar anti-clockwise and disconnect the transmission wiring plug **(see illustration)**. Undo the nuts and detach the wiring loom retainer from the gearbox cover.
10 Remove the upper engine-to-transmission mounting bolts.
11 Release the clips and remove the air hose between the intercooler and the charge air pipe.
12 Remove the radiator cooling fan assembly as described in Chapter 3 Section 5.

13 Disconnect the wiring plug from the engine oil level/temperature sensor on the sump.
14 Undo the bolts securing the exhaust pipe front mounting bracket to the subframe.
15 Undo the bolts and slide rearwards the tubular exhaust pipe connecting piece between the front and rear sections of the exhaust system.
16 Remove both driveshafts as described in Chapter 8 Section 2.
17 Undo the bolts and remove the engine rear mounting (torque arm). Position a block of wood between the sump and the subframe to prevent the engine from swinging rearwards.
18 Support the engine with a hoist or support bar located on the front wing inner channels. Depending on the engine, temporarily remove components as necessary to attach the hoist.
19 Position a trolley jack underneath the transmission, and raise it to just take the weight of the unit.
20 Undo and remove the bolts securing the left-hand gearbox mounting to the mounting spacer, and the bolts securing the spacer to the transmission casing. By controlling both the engine hoist/support bar and the trolley jack, lower the transmission approximately 60 mm. Remove the transmission mounting spacer.
21 Remove the transmission-to-engine bolt located in the starter motor aperture.
22 Undo the retaining bolt and remove the small cover plate located above the right-hand driveshaft flange.
23 Lower the engine/transmission until there is sufficient clearance between the upper edge of the transmission and the left-hand chassis member.
24 Unscrew and remove the lower bolts securing the transmission to the engine, noting the bolt locations, as they are of different sizes and lengths.
25 Check that all the fixings and attachments are clear of the transmission. Enlist the aid of an assistant to help in guiding and supporting the transmission during its removal.
26 The transmission is located on engine alignment dowels, and if stuck on them, it may be necessary to carefully tap and prise the transmission free of the dowels to allow separation. Once the transmission is disconnected from the location dowels, swivel the unit out and lower it out of the vehicle.

 Warning: Support the transmission to ensure that it remains steady on the jack head.

Refitting

27 Refitting is a reversal of the removal procedure, but note the following points:
a) *Apply a little high-temperature grease (Skoda No G052133A2) to the needle bearing in the crankshaft.*
b) *When reconnecting the transmission to the engine, ensure that the location dowels are in position, and that the transmission is correctly aligned with them before pushing it fully into engagement with the engine.*
c) *Tighten all retaining bolts to their specified torque wrench settings.*
d) *Be sure to guide the selector cable into the support bracket as the transmission is refitted – renew the retaining clips.*
e) *Adjust the selector cable, as described in Section 4.*
f) *On completion, check the transmission fluid level (see Section 6) and coolant level (see 'Weekly checks')*
g) *If a new transmission unit has been fitted, it may be necessary to have the transmission ECM 'matched' to the engine management ECM electronically, to ensure correct operation – seek the advice of your Skoda dealer or suitably-equipped specialist.*

3 Transmission overhaul –
general information

1 In the event of a fault occurring, it will be necessary to establish whether the fault is electrical, mechanical or hydraulic in nature, before repair work can be contemplated. Diagnosis requires detailed knowledge of the transmission's operation and construction, as well as access to specialised test equipment, and so is deemed to be beyond the scope of this manual. It is therefore essential that problems with the automatic transmission are referred to a Skoda dealer or specialist for assessment.
2 Note that a faulty transmission should not be removed before the vehicle has been assessed by a dealer or specialist, as fault diagnosis is carried out with the transmission in situ.

4 Selector cable – removal, refitting and adjustment

Removal

1 Move the selector lever to the S position, and remove the battery and battery tray as described in Chapter 5 Section 3.

2 Slacken the adjustment bolt on the cable end fitting at the transmission end **(see illustration)**.

3 Prise out the clips securing the cable to the lever on the transmission, and the outer cable to the support bracket. Discard the clips – new ones must be fitted.

4 Pull the cable from the lever and support bracket on the transmission.

5 Raise the front of the vehicle and support it securely on axle stands (see *Jacking and vehicle support*).

6 Separate the exhaust downpipe from the intermediate pipe with reference to Chapter 4B Section 6.

7 Remove the centre tunnel heat shield from the underside of the vehicle to gain access to the selector lever housing.

8 Undo the securing nuts and remove the cover from the selector lever housing.

9 Remove the clip securing the outer cable to the selector lever housing.

10 Push the retaining tab forwards, then using a screwdriver from beneath, push out the pin from the selector cable end fitting. Remove the cable.

Refitting

11 Refit the selector cable by reversing the removal procedure, noting the following points:

a) *Do not grease the cable end fittings. This is stated by Skoda.*

b) *Ensure that the cable is correctly routed, as noted on removal, and that it is securely held by its retaining clips.*

c) *Take care not to bend or kink the cable.*

d) *Carry out the cable adjustment procedure described below before reconnecting the cable at the transmission end.*

e) *When refitting the outer cable to the selector lever housing and the support bracket, use new clips.*

Adjustment

12 Inside the car, move the selector lever to the P position.

13 At the transmission, slacken the cable adjusting bolt at the ball socket. Check that both the selector lever inside the car and the lever on the transmission are in their P positions by gently rocking them backwards and forwards to settle the cable. Do not move either lever out of the P position.

14 Tighten the cable locking bolt.

15 Verify the operation of the selector lever by shifting through all gear positions and checking that every gear can be selected smoothly and without delay.

5 Emergency release of selector lever

1 If the vehicle's battery is disconnected or discharged, it is possible to release the selector lever from its locked position. First, ensure the handbrake is fully applied.

2 Carefully prise up the selector lever gaiter surround trim from the console and move it to the left-hand side **(see illustration)**.

3 Press the yellow plastic wedge inwards. It should now be possible to move the selector lever to the desired position.

6 Transmission fluid

Note: *To obtain an accurate fluid level it will be necessary to ensure that the fluid is at a temperature of between 35°C and 45°C. Skoda use dedicated equipment connected via the on-board diagnostics socket to access the transmission temperature. at the time of writing various aftermarket tools are available that will access this information via the diagnostics socket. Skoda also use tools VAS6262 or VAS6262A to fill the transmission with fluid, these basically consist of a plastic tube with adaptors at each end for connection to the transmission and the transmission fluid bottle. Once again after-market versions are widely available.*

4.2 Slacken the cable adjustment bolt (arrowed)

Transmission fluid and filter change

1 Start the engine and run at idle speed until the transmission fluid is between 35°C and 45°C (this will aid draining later)

2 Engage Park on the gear selector lever and switch off the engine.

3 Remove the complete air filter housing as described in Chapter 4A Section 3

4 Remove the battery and battery tray as described in Chapter 5 Section 3

5 Clean the area around the transmission filter housing, then using a 24 mm socket, slacken the upper filter housing **(see illustration)** and after allowing the fluid time to drain into the transmission, fully unscrew and remove the upper housing **(see illustration)**.

6 Pull up on the filter to release it from the centre stub, inclining the filter to let the fluid drain back into the transmission **(see illustration)**. When

5.2 Prise up the selector lever gaiter surround trim

6.5a Slacken upper filter housing

6.5b Remove upper housing

6.6 Allow filter to drain

6.7a Replace seal...

6.7b ... and lubricate with clean transmission fluid

6.8a Lubricate seal at base of filter

6.8b Tighten upper housing to specified torque

6.12 Slacken and remove drain plug

6.13 Remove the overflow tube

it has drained, remove the filter from the vehicle.

7 Using clean lint free cloth clean the upper and lower filter housings, replace the O-ring seal on the upper housing and lubricate it with a smear of clean transmission fluid **(see illustrations)**.

8 Lubricate the seal at the base of the new filter with clean transmission fluid **(see illustration)** and insert the filter into the lower housing, install the upper housing (initially by hand) and tighten to the specified torque **(see illustration)**.

9 Refit the battery tray, battery and air filter housing.

10 Raise the front and rear of the vehicle and support it on axle stands (see *Jacking and vehicle support*), ensuring the vehicle is kept level. Undo the retaining screws and remove the undershield to gain access to the base of the transmission unit.

11 Unbolt and remove the protective panel on the underside of the transmission (where fitted).

Caution: Wear gloves and eye protection and be aware that the transmission fluid could be hot!

12 Position a drain tray under the vehicle and using a 14 mm hex key slacken and remove the drain plug, approximately 0.5 litres of fluid should run out **(see illustration)**.

13 Using an 8 mm hex key inside the drain plug aperture unscrew and remove the overflow tube, this will allow the remaining transmission fluid to drain (approximately 5 litres) **(see illustration)**.

14 When the transmission has finished draining, refit the overflow tube and tighten to the specified torque **(see illustration)**.

15 Connect the filling tool (VAS 6262 or equivalent) to the transmission by attaching

at the drain plug location and threading the pipework up between the transmission casing and the radiator, so that the bottle connection is higher than the transmission **(see illustration)**.

16 After shaking the contents of a transmission fluid bottle, attach it to the filler tube and invert the bottle, make a small hole at the base of the bottle to allow air to enter and then providing it is kept higher than the transmission the fluid will flow into it. Use this method to add 5.5 litres of fluid to the transmission **(see illustration)**.

17 Connect equipment for transmission fluid temperature monitoring to the vehicle diagnostic socket.

Caution: Take care while working on the vehicle with the engine running, keep clear of moving components and be aware that the exhaust and other parts will get very hot.

6.14 Refit the overflow tube

6.15 Connect filling tool to the transmission

6.16 Add fluid to the transmission

18 Ensure that the filling tool is positioned away from any moving parts, start the engine and with the brake pedal depressed move the selector lever through each position, pausing for at least 3 seconds with each move. This will distribute the fluid around the transmission. Return the lever to the **P** position but do not turn off the engine.

19 Disconnect the filling tool adaptor from the transmission, have the drain tray in position as excess fluid will drain from the overflow tube. As the fluid temperature in the transmission rises the fluid will expand and will flow out of the overflow tube, monitor the fluid temperature **(see illustration)** and when it is between 35°C and 45°C and as soon as the fluid flow from the overflow tube is a steady drip then the level is correct. Fit the drain plug with a new sealing washer and tighten to the specified torque **(see illustration)**.

Caution: Make sure that the fluid level check is completed before the fluid temperature passes 45°C

Note: Slight amounts of fluid from the overflow tube in pulses at approximately 30 second intervals are to be disregarded when looking for the steady drips of fluid indicating the correct level. This is a characteristic of the oil circulation in the transmission.

20 Switch off the engine, remove the filler tool, wipe clean the underside of the transmission and refit the protective panel (where fitted).

21 Refit the undershield and lower the vehicle to the ground.

Transmission fluid check

Note: No recommended interval for checking the fluid is given, if it is suspected that the fluid level is low the following procedure will enable checking and topping up. Between scheduled fluid changes the level should not drop, as an incorrect fluid level can impair the operation of the transmission, the cause of any significant drop in the transmission fluid level should be investigated and the problem rectified.

22 Raise the front and rear of the vehicle and

6.19a Check transmission fluid temperature

support it on axle stands (see *Jacking and vehicle support*), ensuring the vehicle is kept level. Undo the retaining screws and remove the undershield to gain access to the base of the transmission unit.

23 Unbolt and remove the protective panel on the underside of the transmission (where fitted).

24 Connect equipment for transmission fluid temperature monitoring.

25 Start the engine and run it at idle speed until the transmission fluid temperature reaches 35°C. Note that the level is checked with the engine running.

26 Position a drain tray under the transmission and remove the drain plug, some fluid will be in the overflow tube and will run out.

27 If fluid continually drips from the overflow tube with the fluid temperature within the range of 35°C to 45°C, the level is correct and the drain plug can be refitted with a new sealing washer and tightened to the specified torque **(see illustration)**.

28 If no fluid drips from the overflow tube, even when the fluid temperature has reached 45°C, it will be necessary to add fluid. Allow the transmission to cool and connect the filling tool (VAS 6262 or equivalent) to the transmission by attaching at the drain plug location and threading the pipework

6.19b Fit the drain plug with new sealing washer

up between the transmission casing and the radiator, so that the bottle connection is higher than the transmission **(see illustration)**.

29 Shake the contents and connect a bottle of transmission fluid to the filler tool, invert and squeeze the bottle to transfer fluid to the transmission. As there is no method of establishing the required quantity when topping up we would suggest adding 0.5 litres at a time.

30 Start the engine and allow it to run at idle, monitor the transmission fluid temperature and when it reaches 35°C remove the filling tool adaptor from the transmission, excess oil will drain from the transmission.

31 Continue to monitor the fluid temperature and when it is between 35°C and 45°C and as soon as the fluid flow from the overflow tube is a steady drip then the level is correct. Fit the drain plug with a new sealing washer and tighten to the specified torque **(see illustration)**. If no fluid drips from the overflow tube then the fluid level is still low, repeat the procedure from paragraph 28 above.

32 Switch off the engine, remove the filler tool, wipe clean the underside of the transmission and refit the protective panel (where fitted).

33 Refit the undershield and lower the vehicle to the ground.

6.27 Fluid drip from overflow tube

6.28 Filling tool connected to transmission

6.31 Fit the drain plug

Notes

Chapter 8
Driveshafts

Contents

Degrees of difficulty

Easy, suitable for novice with little experience	Fairly easy, suitable for beginner with some experience	Fairly difficult, suitable for competent DIY mechanic	Difficult, suitable for experienced DIY mechanic	Very difficult, suitable for expert DIY or professional

Specifications

General

Driveshaft type	Steel shafts with outer constant velocity joints and inner tripod or constant velocity joints (according to type)

Type code differences:

VL 90	CV joints each end, inner joint diameter 90 mm bolted to transmission drive flanges on each side
VL 100	CV joints each end, inner joint diameter 100 mm bolted to transmission drive flanges on each side
VL 107	CV joints each end, inner joint diameter 107 mm bolted to drive flange on transmission
AAR 2600i	CV outer joint, tripod inner joint located in housing splined to sun gear
AAR 3300i	CV outer joint, tripod inner joint housing bolted to transmission drive flange or splined to sun gear

Lubrication

Overhaul and repair	Use only special grease supplied in sachets with gaiter/overhaul kits; joints are otherwise pre-packed with grease and sealed

Joint grease quantity:
Outer joint:

Joint diameter 81 mm	80 g
Joint diameter 90 mm	100 g
Joint diameter 94 – 98 mm	120 g
Joint diameter 100 mm	140 g

inner joint:

VL90	80 g
VL100	110 g
VL107	140 g
AAR 2600i and AAR3300i	130 g

Torque wrench settings

	Nm	lbf ft
Driveshaft-to-transmission flange bolts: *		
Stage 1	10	7
Stage 2:		
M8	40	30
M10	70	52
Hub bolt: *		
Hexagon (6-sided) and bi-hexagonal bolt (black) without ribbing on the face:		
Stage 1	200	148
Stage 2	Angle-tighten a further 180°	
Bi-hexagonal bolt (silver) without ribbing on the face:		
Stage 1	200	148
Stage 2	Angle-tighten a further 90°	
Bi-hexagonal (12-sided) bolt with ribbing on the face:		
Stage 1	70	52
Stage 2	Angle-tighten a further 90°	
Lower arm-to-balljoint nuts: *		
Cast steel lower arm	60	44
Sheet steel or aluminium lower arm	100	74
Wheel bolts	120	89

* Use new bolt/nuts

1 General Information

1 Drive is transmitted from the differential to the front wheels by means of two steel driveshafts of either solid or hollow construction (depending on model). Both driveshafts are splined at their outer ends, to accept the wheel hubs, and are secured to the hub by a large bolt. The inner end of each driveshaft is either bolted to a transmission drive flange or splined directly into the differential sun gear.

2 Ball-bearing type constant velocity (CV) joints are fitted to the outer ends of each driveshaft, to ensure the smooth and efficient transmission of drive at all the angles possible as the roadwheels move up-and-down with the suspension, and as they turn from side-to-side under steering.

3 Gaiters are fitted over both CV joints with steel clips. The gaiters contain the grease which lubricates the joints, and also protect the joints from the entry of dirt and debris.

2 Driveshafts – removal and refitting

Removal

1 Remove the wheel trim/hub cap (as applicable) then apply the handbrake, and partially unscrew, by a maximum of 90°, the relevant hub bolt with the vehicle resting on its wheels – note that the bolt is very tight, and a suitable extension bar will probably be required to aid unscrewing. Also unscrew the roadwheel securing bolts. **Note:** *Do not loosen the bolt more than 90° with the vehicle standing on the ground, as the wheel bearings may be damaged.*

2 Apply the handbrake, then jack up the front

2.4 Undo the driveshaft/hub bolt

of the vehicle and support it on axle stands (see *Jacking and vehicle support*). Remove the appropriate front roadwheel.

3 Remove the fasteners, and remove the undershield from beneath the engine/transmission unit to gain access to the driveshafts. Where fitted, also unscrew the heat shield above the right-hand inner joint to improve access.

4 Unscrew and remove the hub bolt **(see illustration)**. Discard the bolt and obtain a new one.

5 Unscrew the three nuts securing the front suspension lower arm balljoint to the lower arm. Discard the nuts as new ones must be used on refitting.

6 Lever the lower arm downwards to release it from the balljoint studs, then pull the hub carrier outwards, and at the same time withdraw the driveshaft outer constant velocity joint from the hub. If the joint splines are a tight fit in the hub, tap the joint out of the hub using a soft-faced mallet and drift. If this fails to free the driveshaft from the hub, the joint will have to be pressed out using a suitable tool bolted to the hub.

7 Proceed as follows according to type.

Caution: Support the driveshaft by suspending it with wire or string – do not allow it to hang under its own weight, or the joint may be damaged.

Inner joint with drive flange

8 Using a multisplined tool, unscrew and remove the bolts securing the inner driveshaft joint to the transmission flange and, where applicable, recover the retaining plates from underneath the bolts **(see illustration)**. Discard the bolts – new ones must be fitted.

Inner joint splined to sun gear

9 Position a container beneath the transmission to catch spilt oil, then pull out the driveshaft. The internal driveshaft circlip may be tight in the transmission side gear, in which case careful use of a lever against the transmission casing will be required. Lever against a block of wood to prevent damage to the casing, and take care not to damage the oil seal as the driveshaft is being removed. **Note:** *Pull only on the inner joint housing, not the driveshaft itself, otherwise the gaiter/joint may be damaged.*

All types

10 Manoeuvre the driveshaft out from underneath the vehicle and (where fitted) recover the gasket from the end of the inner constant velocity joint. Discard the gasket a new one will be needed for refitting.

Caution: Do not allow the vehicle to rest on its wheels with one or both driveshaft(s) removed, as damage to the wheel bearings may result.

11 If moving the vehicle is unavoidable, temporarily insert the outer end of the driveshaft(s) in the hub(s), and tighten the driveshaft retaining bolt(s); in this case, the inner end(s) of the driveshaft(s) must be supported, for example by suspending with rope or wire from the vehicle underbody.

Refitting

12 Where applicable, check the condition of the circlip on the inner end of the driveshaft, and if necessary, renew it.

13 As applicable, clean the splines on each end of the driveshaft and in the hub and apply a little oil, and where applicable wipe clean

2.8 Driveshaft inner joint and flange bolts (arrowed)

2.14 Locate a new gasket on the inner joint

the oil seal in the transmission casing. Check the oil seal and if necessary renew it. Smear a little oil on the lips of the oil seal before fitting the driveshaft.

Inner joint with drive flange

14 Ensure that the transmission flange and inner joint mating surfaces are clean and dry. Where necessary, fit a new gasket to the joint by peeling off its backing foil and sticking it in position **(see illustration)**.

15 Manoeuvre the driveshaft into position, and align the inner joint holes with those on the transmission flange. Fit the new retaining bolts and where necessary, the plates. Tighten the retaining bolts in a diagonal pattern to the specified torque.

Inner joint splined to sun gear

16 Locate the inner end of the driveshaft into the transmission – turn the driveshaft as necessary to engage the splines. Press in the

driveshaft until the internal circlip engages the groove. Check that the circlip is engaged by attempting to pull out the driveshaft with only moderate force.

All types

17 With the lower arm levered downwards, engage the outer joint with the hub. Fit the new hub bolt and use it to draw the joint fully into position.

18 Align the balljoint studs with the holes in the lower arm, then release the arm and fit the three new nuts. Tighten the nuts to the specified torque.

19 With the wheel clear of the ground, tighten the driveshaft bolt to the Stage 1 torque (see Specifications).

20 Refit the roadwheel and lower the vehicle to the ground, then angle-tighten the driveshaft bolt through the Stage 2 angle (see Specifications).

21 Once the driveshaft bolt is correctly

tightened, tighten the wheel bolts to the specified torque and refit the wheel trim/hub cap.

3 Driveshaft rubber gaiters – renewal

1 Remove the driveshaft from the car, as described in Section 2. Continue as described under the relevant sub-heading. Driveshafts with a tripod type inner joint can be identified by the shape of the inner CV joint; the driveshaft retaining bolt holes are in extensions from the joint, giving it a six-pointed star-shaped exterior, in contrast to the smooth, circular shape of the ball-and-cage joint **(see illustrations)**. Note that for illustrative purposes the layout for types VL90 and VL100 are effectively the same.

3.1a VL 100 driveshaft details

1 Dished spring	4 Circlip	8 Clamp	12 Dished spring	16 Right-hand driveshaft
2 Inner constant velocity joint	5 Bolts	9 Gaiter	13 Clamp	17 Bolt
	6 Retaining plate	10 Circlip	14 Gaiter	18 Outer constant velocity joint
3 Seal	7 Left-hand driveshaft	11 Thrustwasher	15 Clamp	

3.1b VL 107 driveshaft details

1 Bolt
2 Cover
3 Circlip
4 Gasket
5 Inner constant velocity joint
6 Cap
7 Retaining plate
8 Clamp
9 Gaiter
10 Clamp
11 Driveshaft
12 Clamp
13 Gaiter
14 Clamp
15 Dished spring
16 Spacer ring
17 Circlip
18 Bolt
19 Outer constant velocity joint

3.1c AAR 2600i driveshaft details

1 Tripod roller
2 Circlip
3 Inner joint body
4 Circlip
5 Clamp
6 Gaiter
7 Clamp
8 Circlip
9 Spacer ring
10 Dished spring
11 Clamp
12 Gaiter
13 Clamp
14 Right-hand driveshaft
15 Left-hand driveshaft
16 Bolt
17 Outer constant velocity joint

3.1d AAR 3300i driveshaft details

1 Inner joint body – manual transmission
2 Bolt
3 Circlip
4 Inner joint body – automatic transmission
5 Circlip
6 Tripod roller
7 Clamp
8 Gaiter
9 Clamp
10 Driveshaft
11 Clamp
12 Gaiter
13 Clamp
14 Dished spring
15 Spacer ring
16 Circlip
17 Bolt
18 Outer constant velocity joint

Outer CV joint gaiter

2 Secure the driveshaft in a vice equipped with soft jaws, and release the two outer joint gaiter retaining clips **(see illustration)**. If necessary, the retaining clips can be cut to release them.

3 Slide the rubber gaiter down the shaft to expose the constant velocity joint, and scoop out excess grease **(see illustration)**.

4 Using a soft-faced mallet, tap the joint off the end of the driveshaft **(see illustration)**.

5 Remove the circlip from the driveshaft groove, and slide off the thrustwasher/spacer ring and dished washer, noting which way around it is fitted**(see illustration)**.

6 Slide the rubber gaiter off the driveshaft and discard it**(see illustration)**.

7 Thoroughly clean the constant velocity joint(s) using paraffin, or a suitable solvent, and dry thoroughly. Carry out a visual inspection as follows.

8 Move the inner splined driving member from side-to-side to expose each ball in turn at the top of its track. Examine the balls for cracks, flat spots or signs of surface pitting.

9 Inspect the ball tracks on the inner and outer members. If the tracks have widened,

the balls will no longer be a tight fit. At the same time, check the ball cage windows for wear or cracking between the windows.

10 If on inspection any of the constant velocity joint components are found to be worn or damaged, it will be necessary to

3.2 Release the outer joint gaiter clips...

3.3 ... and slide the gaiter away from the joint

3.4 Use a mallet to drive the outer joint from the driveshaft

3.5 Remove the circlip, thrustwasher and dished washer

3.6 Remove the outer gaiter

3.11 Temporarily tape over the splines to protect the new gaiter

3.14a Pack half of the grease in the joint...

3.14b ... and the remaining half in the gaiter

3.15a Fit a new circlip...

3.15b ... then refit the outer joint

3.16 Seat the gaiter on the outer joint and driveshaft, then lift its inner lip to equalise the air pressure

renew the complete joint assembly. If the joint is in satisfactory condition, obtain a new gaiter and retaining clips, a constant velocity joint circlip and the correct type of grease. Grease is usually supplied with the joint repair kit – if not, use a good-quality molybdenum disulphide grease.

11 Tape over the splines on the end of the driveshaft to protect the new gaiter as it is slid into place**(see illustration)**.

12 Slide the new gaiter onto the end of the driveshaft, then remove the protective tape from the driveshaft splines.

13 Slide on the dished washer, making sure its convex side is innermost, followed by the thrustwasher.

14 Pack the joint with half the quantity of grease. Work the grease well into the bearing tracks whilst twisting the joint, and fill the rubber gaiter with the remaining half **(see illustrations)**.

15 Fit a new circlip to the driveshaft, then tap the joint onto the driveshaft until the circlip engages in its groove **(see illustrations)**. Make sure that the joint is securely retained by the circlip.

16 Ease the gaiter over the joint, and ensure that the gaiter lips are correctly located on both the driveshaft and constant velocity joint. Lift the outer sealing lip of the gaiter to equalise air pressure within the gaiter **(see illustration)**.

17 Fit the large metal retaining clip to the gaiter. Pull the clip as tight as possible, and locate the hooks on the clip in their slots. Remove any slack in the gaiter retaining clip by carefully compressing the raised section of the clip. In the absence of the special tool, a pair of side-cutters may be used, taking care not to cut the clip **(see illustrations)**. Secure the small retaining clip using the same procedure.

18 Check the constant velocity joint moves freely in all directions, then refit the driveshaft to the vehicle, as described in Section 2.

Tripod inner CV joint gaiter

19 Release the two outer joint gaiter retaining clips. If necessary, the retaining clips can be cut to release them. Slide the rubber gaiter down the shaft, away from the joint outer member.

20 Carefully secure the joint outer member in a vice equipped with soft jaws.

21 Scoop out excess grease from the joint, then on models with a splined inner joint, remove the circlip from the groove in the end of the joint splined member.

22 Using a suitable marker pen or a scriber, make alignment marks between the end of the driveshaft, the tripod roller assembly, and the outer member.

23 Support the driveshaft and the joint, and withdraw the outer member from the vice. As the assembly is removed from the vice, make sure that the rollers do not fall off the tripod.

24 Slowly slide the joint outer member down the driveshaft, away from the joint, making sure that the rollers stay on the tripod.

25 Mark the rollers and the arms of the tripod, so that the rollers can be refitted in their original positions, then lift off the rollers and place them to one side on a dry, clean surface.

26 Remove the circlip from the end of the driveshaft.

27 Press or drive the driveshaft from the tripod, taking great care not to damage the surfaces of the roller locating arms.

3.17a Fit the large metal retaining clip...

3.17b ... and use a suitable tool to tighten it

3.30 Check the tripod rollers and outer member for signs of wear

3.32a Tape over the driveshaft splines to protect the new gaiter...

3.32b ... then lever the gaiter carefully over the ridge on the driveshaft

28 Slide the outer member and the rubber gaiter from the end of the driveshaft.

29 Thoroughly clean the joint components using paraffin, or a suitable solvent, and dry thoroughly. Carry out a visual inspection as follows.

30 Inspect the tripod rollers and the joint outer member for signs of wear, pitting or scuffing on their mating surfaces. Check that the joint rollers rotate smoothly, with no traces of roughness **(see illustration)**.

31 If the rollers or outer member shown signs of wear or damage, it will be necessary to renew the complete driveshaft, since the joint is not available separately. If the joint is in satisfactory condition, obtain a repair kit, consisting of a new gaiter, retaining clips, circlip, and the correct type and quantity of grease.

32 Tape over the splines on the end of the driveshaft, to protect the new gaiter as it is slid into place, then slide the new gaiter and securing clips, and the joint outer member over the end of the driveshaft **(see illustrations)**. Remove the protective tape from the driveshaft splines.

33 Press or drive the tripod onto the end of the driveshaft until it contacts the stop, ensuring that the marks made on the end of the driveshaft and the tripod before dismantling are aligned. Note that the chamfered edge of the internal splines on the tripod should face towards the driveshaft.

34 Fit the new circlip to retain the tripod on the end of the driveshaft.

35 Refit the rollers to the tripod, ensuring that they are refitted in their original locations, as noted before removal.

3.37 Work the grease into the joint outer member

36 Work half of the grease supplied with the repair kit into the inner end of the joint outer member, then slide the outer member over the tripod, ensuring that the marks made during dismantling are aligned, and clamp the outer member in the vice.

37 Work the rest of the grease supplied with the repair kit into the rear of the joint outer member **(see illustration)**.

38 Slide the rubber gaiter up the driveshaft onto the joint outer member, and secure with the large clip, as described in paragraph 17.

39 Lift the gaiter outer end to equalise the air pressure in the gaiter, then secure the outer gaiter securing clip in position using the same method used previously **(see illustration)**.

40 Check that the grease in the joint outer member is evenly distributed around the tripod rollers.

41 Check the driveshaft joint moves freely in all directions, then refit the driveshaft to

3.39 Lift the gaiter outer end to equalise the air pressure

the vehicle, as described in Section 2. To prevent the tripod joint from being pushed back down the driveshaft during refitting, temporarily stick adhesive tape over the open end of the joint outer member **(see illustration)**. Remove the tape just before reconnecting the inner end of the driveshaft to the transmission.

Ball-and-cage type inner CV joint

42 Secure the driveshaft in a vice equipped with soft jaws, then release the gaiter clamp(s), securing the gaiter to the driveshaft **(see illustration)**.

43 Using a hammer and a small drift, carefully drive the gaiter metal ring from the joint outer member **(see illustration)**.

44 Slide the gaiter down the driveshaft to expose the constant velocity joint, and scoop out excess grease.

3.41 Tape over the end of the driveshaft joint

3.42 Release the gaiter small securing clip...

3.43 ... and drive the metal ring from the joint outer member

3.46 Remove the circlip...

3.47a ... followed by the joint...

3.47b ... dished washer...

3.48 ... and gaiter

3.49a Tilt the splined hub and cage to remove the ball-bearings...

3.49b ... then separate the hub from the cage

45 Where fitted, prise the metal cover from the end of the driveshaft.
46 Remove the circlip from the end of the driveshaft using circlip pliers **(see illustration)**.
47 Press or drive the driveshaft from the

3.49c Inner CV joint gaiter repair kit

joint, taking great care not to damage the joint. Recover the dished washer (where fitted) between the constant velocity joint and the shaft **(see illustrations)**.
48 Slide the gaiter from the end of the driveshaft **(see illustration)**.

3.53a Pack the inner joint with half of the grease...

49 Proceed as described previously in paragraphs 7 to 12 **(see illustrations)**.
50 Slide the dished washer (where fitted) onto the driveshaft, making sure its convex side is innermost.
51 Fit the joint to the end of the driveshaft, noting that the chamfered edge of the internal splines on the joint should face towards the driveshaft. Drive or press the joint into position until it contacts the shoulder on the driveshaft.
52 Fit a new circlip to retain the joint on the end of the driveshaft.
53 Pack the joint with the half the recommended quantity of grease (see Specifications), then pack the gaiter with the remaining half **(see illustrations)**.
54 Slide the gaiter up the driveshaft, and press or drive the gaiter metal ring onto the joint outer member. To ensure the bolt holes are correctly positioned, temporarily fit one of the flange bolts **(see illustrations)**.

3.53b ... then pack the gaiter with the remaining grease

3.54a Temporarily fit one of the flange bolts to ensure the bolt holes are correctly aligned...

3.54b ... then drive the metal ring onto the joint outer member

55 Slide the outboard end of the gaiter into position on the driveshaft, then secure the gaiter securing clamps in position as described in paragraph 17**(see illustration)**.

56 Position the new gasket in place on the inner joint body, then (where applicable) press on the new metal cover.

57 Check the driveshaft joint moves freely in all directions, then refit the driveshaft to the vehicle, as described in Section 2.

4 Driveshaft overhaul – general information

1 If any of the checks described in Chapter 1 Sections 18 or 19 reveal wear in any driveshaft joint, first remove the roadwheel trim or centre cap (as applicable) and check that the hub bolt is tight. If the bolt is loose, obtain a new one, and tighten it to the specified torque (see Section 2). If the bolt is tight, refit the centre cap/trim, and repeat the check on the other hub bolt.

2 Road test the vehicle, and listen for a metallic clicking from the front of the vehicle as the vehicle is driven slowly in a circle on full-lock. If a clicking noise is heard, this indicates wear in the outer constant velocity joint; this means that the joint must be renewed.

3 If vibration consistent with roadspeed is felt through the car when accelerating, there is a possibility of wear in the inner constant velocity joints.

4 To check the joints for wear, remove the driveshafts, then dismantle them as described in Section 3. If any wear or free play is found, the affected joint must be renewed. Refer to a Skoda dealer for information on the availability of driveshaft components.

3.55 Installation position of inner joint gaiter

A Vent chamber in gaiter
B Vent hole

Chapter 9
Braking system

Contents

Degrees of difficulty

| Easy, suitable for novice with little experience | Fairly easy, suitable for beginner with some experience | Fairly difficult, suitable for competent DIY mechanic | Difficult, suitable for experienced DIY mechanic | Very difficult, suitable for expert DIY or professional |

Specifications

Front brakes

1.9 litre PD engines

Type:
1.9 litre engine with manual transmission . . . . Ventilated disc, with single-piston sliding FSIII calipers
All other models . . . . As above, but with FN3 calipers
Disc diameter:
FSIII caliper. . . . . 280 mm
FN3 caliper . . . . 288 mm
Disc thickness:

	New	Minimum
FSIII	22 mm	19 mm
FN3	25 mm	22 mm

Maximum disc run-out. . . . . 0.05 mm
Brake pad wear limit (friction material only – not including backing plate) . 2 mm

2.0 litre PD engine

Type . . . . Ventilated disc, with single-piston sliding FN3 calipers
Disc diameter:
Engine codes BKD and BMM. . . . . 288 mm
Engine code BMN . . . . 312 mm
Disc thickness:
New . . . . 25 mm
Minimum. . . . . 22 mm
Maximum disc run-out. . . . . 0.05 mm
Brake pad wear limit (friction material only – not including backing plate) . 2 mm

2.0 litre common rail engine

Type . . . . Ventilated disc, with single-piston sliding FN3 or FSIII calipers
Disc diameter:
81 kw engines (code CLCA and CFHF) with FSIII caliper . . . . 280 mm
103 kw engine (code CLCB and CFHC) with FN3 caliper . . . . 288 mm
125 kw engine (code CEGA) with FN3 caliper . . . . 312 mm
Disc thickness:

	New	Minimum
FSIII caliper.	22 mm	19 mm
FN3 caliper	25 mm	22 mm

Maximum disc run-out. . . . . 0.05 mm
Brake pad wear limit (friction material only – not including backing plate) . 2 mm

Rear brakes

1.9 litre PD engine

Type:
Auto transmission (up to 04/2006)	Disc, with single-piston sliding CII 41 caliper
All 1.9 PD engine (except above)	Disc, with single-piston sliding CI 38 caliper

Disc diameter:
CII 41 caliper.	260 mm
CI 38 caliper	255 mm (253 mm on vehicles from 04/2009)

Disc thickness:
	New	Minimum
CII 41 caliper.	12 mm	10 mm
CI 38 caliper	10 mm	8 mm

Maximum disc run-out . . . . 0.05 mm
Brake pad wear limit (friction material only – not including backing plate) . 2 mm

2.0 litre PD engine

Type . . . . Disc, with single-piston sliding CII 41 or Bosch caliper

Disc diameter:
CII 41 caliper:	
Engine codes BKD and BMM.	260 mm (256 mm from 04/2009)
Engine code BMN.	286 mm
Bosch caliper	272 mm

Disc thickness:
	256, 260 and 286 mm diameter	272 mm diameter
New	12.0 mm	10.0 mm
Minimum thickness.	10.0 mm	8.0 mm

Maximum disc run-out . . . . 0.05 mm
Brake pad wear limit (friction material only – not including backing plate) . 2 mm

2.0 litre common rail engine

Type . . . . Disc, with single-piston sliding CI 38, CII 41 or Bosch caliper

Disc diameter:
CII 41 caliper	286 mm (282 mm from 04/2009 on)
CI 38 caliper	253 mm
Bosch caliper	272 mm

Disc thickness:
	New	Minimum
CI 38 and Bosch calipers.	10 mm	8 mm
CI 41 caliper	12 mm	10 mm

Maximum disc run-out . . . . 0.05 mm
Brake pad wear limit (friction material only – not including backing plate) . 2 mm

Torque wrench settings

	Nm	lbf ft
ABS hydraulic unit mounting bolts.	8	6
Brake disc retaining screw	4	3
Brake pedal pivot bolt nut*	25	18
Caliper bleed screw	10	7
Front brake caliper:		
Guide pins	30	22
Mounting bracket bolts (FN3 caliper)*	190	140
Wiring/brake hose bracket bolt	15	11
Handbrake lever mounting plate to floorpan nuts	20	15
Hydraulic pipe union:		
To ABS hydraulic unit	14	10
To front caliper	35	26
To rear caliper:		
CII 41 and CI 38	14	10
Bosch (banjo bolt)	35	26
To master cylinder	14	10
Master cylinder retaining nuts*	50	37
Rear brake caliper:		
Guide pin bolts*	35	26
Mounting bracket bolts: *		
Stage 1	90	66
Stage 2	Angle-tighten a further 90°	
Roadwheel bolts.	120	89
Vacuum pump bolts (common rail injection engines).	10	7
Vacuum servo-to-bulkhead/pedal bracket through-bolts*	25	18
Wheel speed sensor bolt	8	6

* Use new fasteners

1 General Information

1 All models have disc brakes fitted at the front and rear wheels as standard. ABS (Anti-lock Braking System) is also fitted as standard on all models (refer to Section 20 for further information on ABS operation).

2 The front and rear disc brakes are actuated by single-piston sliding type calipers, which ensure that equal pressure is applied to each disc pad. An independent mechanical handbrake mechanism is incorporated into the rear brakes.

3 Because the diesel engines have no throttle valve, there is insufficient vacuum in the inlet manifold to operate the braking system servo effectively at all times. To overcome this problem, a vacuum pump is fitted to these models, to provide sufficient vacuum to operate the servo unit. The vacuum pump is mounted on the rear of the cylinder head and driven by the camshaft.

4 ESP (Electronic Stability Program) is fitted to all models. The ESP incorporates the ABS, EBS (Electronic Brake Assist) system and TCS (Traction Control System). It stabilises the vehicle when oversteering or understeering by applying the brake, or applying increased power to the relevant roadwheel, to increase the driver's control of the vehicle. In order for the ESP system to function, it utilises sensors which provide data concerning the speed of the vehicle around a vertical axis, the lateral movement of the vehicle, the brake pressure and the angle of the front wheels.

Note: *When servicing any part of the system, work carefully and methodically; also observe scrupulous cleanliness when overhauling any part of the hydraulic system. Always renew components (in axle sets, where applicable) if in doubt about their condition, and use only genuine Skoda parts, or at least those of known good quality. Note the warnings given in 'Safety first!' and at relevant points in this Chapter concerning the dangers of asbestos dust and hydraulic fluid.*

2 Hydraulic system – bleeding

⚠ *Warning: Hydraulic fluid is poisonous; wash off immediately and thoroughly in the case of skin contact, and seek immediate medical advice if any fluid is swallowed or gets into the eyes. Certain types of hydraulic fluid are inflammable, and may ignite when allowed into contact with hot components; when servicing any hydraulic system, it is safest to assume that the fluid is inflammable, and to take precautions against the risk of fire as though it is petrol that is being handled.*

Hydraulic fluid is also an effective paint stripper, and will attack plastics; if any is spilt, it should be washed off immediately, using copious quantities of fresh water. Finally, it is hygroscopic (it absorbs moisture from the air) – old fluid may be contaminated and unfit for further use. When topping-up or renewing the fluid, always use the recommended type, and ensure that it comes from a freshly-opened sealed container.

Note: *If the hydraulic circuit upstream of (before) the ABS modulator/hydraulic unit has been disturbed, the system may need to be bled using Skoda diagnostic equipment. Entrust this task to a Skoda dealer or suitably-equipped specialist.*

General

1 The correct operation of any hydraulic system is only possible after removing all air from the components and circuit; this is achieved by bleeding the system.

2 During the bleeding procedure, add only clean, unused hydraulic fluid of the recommended type; never re-use fluid that has already been bled from the system. Ensure that a sufficient quantity of new fluid is available before starting work.

3 If there is any possibility of incorrect fluid being already in the system, the brake components and circuit must be flushed completely with uncontaminated, correct fluid, and new seals should be fitted to the various components.

4 If hydraulic fluid has been lost from the system, or air has entered because of a leak, ensure that the fault is cured before proceeding further.

5 Park the vehicle on level ground, securely chock the wheel then release the handbrake.

6 Check that all pipes and hoses are secure, unions tight and bleed screws closed. Clean any dirt from around the bleed screws.

7 Unscrew the master cylinder reservoir cap, and top the master cylinder reservoir up to the MAX level line; refit the cap loosely, and remember to maintain the fluid level at least above the MIN level line throughout the procedure, or there is a risk of further air entering the system.

8 There are a number of one-man, do-it-yourself brake bleeding kits currently available from motor accessory shops. It is recommended that one of these kits is used whenever possible, as they greatly simplify the bleeding operation, and also reduce the risk of expelled air and fluid being drawn back into the system. If such a kit is not available, the basic (two-man) method must be used, which is described in detail below.

9 If a kit is to be used, prepare the vehicle as described previously, and follow the kit manufacturer's instructions, as the procedure may vary slightly according to the type being used; generally, they are as outlined below in the relevant sub-section.

10 Whichever method is used, the same sequence must be followed (see paragraphs 11 and 12) to ensure the removal of all air from the system.

Bleeding

Sequence

11 If the system has been only partially disconnected, and suitable precautions were taken to minimise fluid loss, it should be necessary only to bleed that part of the system (ie, the primary or secondary circuit).

12 If the complete system is to be bled, then it should be done working in the following sequence:

a) *Left-hand front brake.*

b) *Right-hand front brake.*

c) *Left-hand rear brake.*

d) *Right-hand rear brake.*

Basic (two-man) method

13 Collect a clean glass jar, a suitable length of plastic or rubber tubing which is a tight fit over the bleed screw, and a ring spanner to fit the screw. The help of an assistant will also be required.

14 Remove the dust cap from the first bolt in the sequence. Fit the spanner and tube to the bolt, place the other end of the tube in the jar, and pour in sufficient fluid to cover the end of the tube.

15 Ensure that the master cylinder reservoir fluid level is maintained at least above the MIN level line throughout the procedure.

16 Have the assistant fully depress the brake pedal several times to build-up pressure, then maintain it on the final downstroke.

17 While pedal pressure is maintained, unscrew the bleed screw (approximately one turn) and allow the compressed fluid and air to flow into the jar.

18 The assistant should maintain pedal pressure, following it down to the floor if necessary, and should not release it until instructed to do so. When the flow stops, tighten the bleed screw again, have the assistant release the pedal slowly, and recheck the reservoir fluid level.

19 Repeat the steps given in paragraphs 16 to 18 inclusive until the fluid emerging from the bleed screw is free from air bubbles. If the master cylinder has been drained and refilled, and air is being bled from the first screw in the sequence, allow approximately five seconds between cycles for the master cylinder passages to refill.

20 When no more air bubbles appear, tighten the bleed screw securely, remove the tube and spanner, and refit the dust cap. Do not overtighten the bleed screw.

21 Repeat the procedure on the remaining screws in the sequence, until all air is removed from the system and the brake pedal feels firm again. On completion, lower the vehicle to the ground (where necessary).

2.23 Attach the bleeding kit to the bleed screw on the caliper

Using a one-way valve kit

22 As their name implies, these kits consist of a length of tubing with a one-way valve fitted, to prevent expelled air and fluid being drawn back into the system; some kits include a translucent container, which can be positioned so that the air bubbles can be more easily seen flowing from the end of the tube.

23 The kit is connected to the bleed screw, which is then opened **(see illustration)**. The user returns to the driver's seat, depresses the brake pedal with a smooth, steady stroke, and slowly releases it; this is repeated until the expelled fluid is clear of air bubbles.

24 Note that these kits simplify work so much that it is easy to forget to watch the master cylinder reservoir fluid level; ensure that this is maintained at least above the MIN level line at all times, otherwise air will be reintroduced into the system.

Using a pressure-bleeding kit

25 These kits are usually operated by the reservoir of pressurised air contained in the spare tyre. However, note that it will probably be necessary to reduce the pressure to a lower level than normal; refer to the instructions supplied with the kit.

26 By connecting a pressurised, fluid-filled container to the master cylinder reservoir, bleeding can be carried out simply by opening each screw in turn (in the specified sequence), and allowing the fluid to flow out until no more air bubbles can be seen in the expelled fluid.

27 This method has the advantage that the large reservoir of fluid provides an additional safeguard against air being drawn into the system during bleeding.

28 Pressure-bleeding is particularly effective when bleeding difficult systems, or when bleeding the complete system at the time of routine fluid renewal.

All methods

29 When bleeding is complete, and firm pedal feel is restored, wash off any spilt fluid, tighten the bleed screws securely, and refit their dust caps.

30 Check the hydraulic fluid level in the master cylinder reservoir, and top-up if necessary (see *Weekly checks*).

31 Discard any hydraulic fluid that has been bled from the system; it will not be fit for re-use.

32 Check the feel of the brake pedal. If it feels at all spongy, air must still be present in the system, and further bleeding is required. Failure to bleed satisfactorily after a reasonable repetition of the bleeding procedure may be due to worn master cylinder seals.

33 Because the clutch hydraulic system shares the same fluid reservoir, we recommend that the clutch is bled at the same time (see Chapter 6 Section 2).

3 Hydraulic pipes and hoses – renewal

Note: Before starting work, refer to the note at the beginning of Section 2 concerning the dangers of hydraulic fluid.

1 If any pipe or hose is to be renewed, minimise fluid loss by first removing the master cylinder reservoir cap, then tightening it down onto a piece of polythene to obtain an airtight seal. Alternatively, flexible hoses can be sealed, if required, using a proprietary brake hose clamp; metal brake pipe unions can be plugged (if care is taken not to allow dirt into the system) or capped immediately they are disconnected. Place a wad of rag under any union that is to be disconnected, to catch any spilt fluid.

2 If a flexible hose is to be disconnected, unscrew the brake pipe union nut and remove the spring clip which secures the hose to its mounting bracket.

3 To unscrew the union nuts, it is preferable to obtain a brake pipe spanner of the correct size; these are available from most large motor accessory shops. Failing this, a close-fitting open-ended spanner will be required, though if the nuts are tight or corroded, their flats may be rounded-off if the spanner slips. In such a case, a self-locking wrench is often the only way to unscrew a stubborn union, but it follows that the pipe and the damaged nuts must be renewed on reassembly. Always clean a union and surrounding area before disconnecting it. If disconnecting a component with more than one union, make a careful note of the connections before disturbing any of them.

4 If a brake pipe is to be renewed, it can be obtained, cut to length with the union nuts and end flares in place, from Skoda dealers. All that is then necessary is to bend it to shape, following the line of the original, before fitting it to the car. Alternatively, most motor accessory shops can make up brake pipes from kits, but this requires very careful measurement of the original, to ensure that the new one is of the correct length. The safest answer is usually to take the original to the shop as a pattern.

5 On refitting, do not overtighten the union

nuts. It is not necessary to exercise brute force to obtain a sound joint.

6 Ensure that the pipes and hoses are correctly routed, with no kinks, and that they are secured in the clips or brackets provided. After fitting, remove the polythene from the reservoir, and bleed the hydraulic system as described in Section 2. Wash off any spilt fluid, and check carefully for fluid leaks.

4 Front brake pads – renewal

⚠ *Warning: Renew both sets of front brake pads at the same time – never renew the pads on only one wheel, as uneven braking may result. Note that the dust created by wear of the pads may contain asbestos, which is a health hazard. Never blow it out with compressed air, and don't inhale any of it. An approved filtering mask should be worn when working on the brakes. DO NOT use petrol or petroleum-based solvents to clean brake parts; use brake cleaner or methylated spirit only.*

Note: One of two types of front caliper may be fitted. The main difference between the FS III caliper that is shown and the FN3 caliper, is that the FN3 caliper has an external retaining spring, instead of the spring fitted to the back of the outer pad (this requires the pad to be fitted into the caliper carrier during assembly, not the caliper). Removal and refitting of the brake pads is essentially the same for both types of caliper.

1 Apply the handbrake, then loosen the front roadwheel bolts. Jack up the front of the vehicle and support it on axle stands (*Jacking and vehicle support*). Remove both front roadwheels.

2 Follow the accompanying photos for the pad renewal procedure **(illustrations 4.2a to 4.2l)** Be sure to stay in order and read the caption under each illustration, and note the following points:

a) *The inner pad (with a spring) may be marked with an arrow. The arrow must point in the direction of brake disc rotation.*

b) *New pads may have an adhesive foil on the backplates. Remove this foil prior to installation.*

c) *Thoroughly clean the caliper guide pin surfaces, and apply a little brake assembly grease (polycarbamide).*

d) *Thoroughly clean caliper and caliper bracket at brake pad contact points.*

e) *For removal disconnect pad wear wiring connectors (where fitted). During refitting ensure pads with wear sensors are fitted in the correct position and wiring plugs are connected.*

f) *When pushing the caliper piston back to accommodate new pads, keep a close eye on the fluid level in the reservoir.*

Caution: Pushing back the piston causes

a reverse-flow of brake fluid, which has been known to 'flip' the master cylinder rubber seals, resulting in a total loss of braking. Best practice to avoid this is to clamp the caliper flexible hose and open the bleed screw – as the piston is pushed back, the fluid can be directed into a suitable container using a hose attached to the bleed screw. Close the screw just before the piston is pushed fully back, to ensure no air enters the system.

3 Depress the brake pedal repeatedly, until the pads are pressed into firm contact with the brake disc, and normal (non-assisted) pedal pressure is restored.

4 Repeat the above procedure on the remaining front brake caliper.

5 Refit the roadwheels, then lower the vehicle to the ground and tighten the roadwheel bolts to the specified torque.

6 Check the hydraulic fluid level as described in *Weekly checks*.

Caution: New pads will not give full braking efficiency until they have bedded-in. Be prepared for this, and avoid hard braking as far as possible for the first hundred miles or so after pad renewal.

4.2a Remove the guide pin rubber caps...

4.2b Use an Allen socket to unscrew the guide pins

4.2c If there's a wear/rust lip around the disc, use a screwdriver to force the inner pad away from the disc a little

4.2d Slide the caliper from the brake disc

4.2e Remove the outer brake pad from the caliper...

4.2f ...and pull the inner pad from the caliper piston

4.2g Measure the thickness of the pad's friction material – the minimum is 2 mm

4.2h If new pads are to be fitted, push the piston back into the caliper body using a pad retraction tool. Keep an eye on the fluid level in the master cylinder reservoir

4.2i Clip the inner pad into the caliper piston...

4.2 j ...and fit the outer brake pad into the caliper

4.2k Slide the caliper back over the brake disc...

4.2l ...and screw in the guide pins, tightening to the specified torque. Refit the rubber caps

5 Rear brake pads – renewal

Warning: Renew both sets of rear brake pads at the same time – never renew the pads on only one wheel, as uneven braking may result. Note that the dust created by wear of the pads may contain asbestos, which is a health hazard. Never blow it out with compressed air, and don't inhale any of it. An approved filtering mask should be worn when working on the brakes. DO NOT use petrol or petroleum-based solvents to clean brake parts; use brake cleaner or methylated spirit only.

1 There are three types of rear brake caliper fitted. Removal and refitting of the brake pads is essentially the same, regardless of the type of caliper fitted.

2 Chock the front wheels, then jack up the rear of the vehicle and support it on axle stands (see *Jacking and vehicle support*). Remove the rear wheels.

3 With the handbrake released, follow the accompanying photos for the pad renewal procedure **(see illustrations 5.3a to 5.3k)**. Be sure to stay in order and read the caption under each illustration, and note the following points:

a) If re-installing the original pads, ensure they are fitted to their original positions.

b) For removal disconnect pad wear wiring connectors (where fitted). During refitting ensure pads with wear sensors are fitted in the correct position and wiring plugs are connected.

c) Check that the guide pins slide freely, clean and lubricate as required.

d) Thoroughly clean caliper and caliper bracket at brake pad contact points.

e) The piston will have to be rotated clockwise into the caliper using a suitable tool **(see illustration 5.3f)**.

f) Use new caliper guide pin bolts and fitting shims (where fitted) – included in the Skoda repair kit.

g) If new pads are to be fitted, extract some of the brake fluid from the reservoir prior to retracting the caliper piston – keep an eye on the fluid level in the reservoir whilst retracting the piston.

Caution: Pushing back the piston causes a reverse-flow of brake fluid, which has been known to 'flip' the master cylinder rubber seals, resulting in a total loss of braking. Best practice to avoid this is to clamp the caliper flexible hose and open the bleed screw – as the piston is wound back, the fluid can be directed into a suitable container using a hose attached to the bleed screw. Close the screw just before the piston is wound fully back, to ensure no air enters the system.

4 Depress the brake pedal repeatedly, until the pads are pressed into firm contact with the brake disc, and normal (non-assisted) pedal pressure is restored.

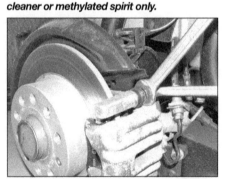

5.3a Using an open-ended spanner to counterhold the guide pin, undo the upper and lower guide pin bolts (arrowed)

5.3b Remove the guide pin bolts...

5.3c ...and slide the caliper from the bracket

5.3d Remove the outer brake pad from the caliper...

5.3e ...and the inner pad

5.3f Use a retraction tool to wind the piston back into the caliper body. Keep an eye on the fluid level in the master cylinder reservoir

5.3g Slide the new inner pad into place....

5.3h ...followed by the outer pad

5.3i Slide the caliper over the pads and into place on the bracket

5 Repeat the above procedure on the remaining brake caliper.
6 If necessary, adjust the handbrake as described in Section 15.
7 Refit the roadwheels, then lower the vehicle to the ground and tighten the roadwheel bolts to the specified torque.
8 Check the hydraulic fluid level as described in *Weekly checks*.
Caution: New pads will not give full braking efficiency until they have bedded-in. Be prepared for this, and avoid hard braking as far as possible for the first hundred miles or so after pad renewal.

5.3j Fit the new guide pin bolts...

5.3k ...and tighten them to the specified torque

6 Front brake disc – inspection, removal and refitting

Note: *Before starting work, refer to the note at the beginning of Section 4 concerning the dangers of asbestos dust.*

Inspection

Note: *If either disc requires renewal, BOTH should be renewed at the same time, to ensure even and consistent braking. New brake pads should also be fitted.*

1 Apply the handbrake, then jack up the front of the car and support it on axle stands (see *Jacking and vehicle support*). Remove the appropriate front roadwheel.
2 Slowly rotate the brake disc so that the full area of both sides can be checked; remove the brake pads if better access is required to the inboard surface. Light scoring is normal in the area swept by the brake pads, but if heavy scoring or cracks are found, the disc must be renewed.
3 It is normal to find a lip of rust and brake dust around the disc's perimeter; this can be scraped off if required. If, however, a lip has formed due to excessive wear of the brake pad swept area, then the disc's thickness must be measured using a micrometer. Take measurements at several places around the disc, at the inside and outside of the pad swept area; if the disc has worn at any point to the specified minimum thickness or less, the disc must be renewed **(see illustration)**.
4 If the disc is thought to be warped, it can be checked for run-out.

5 Either use a dial gauge mounted on any convenient fixed point, while the disc is slowly rotated, or use feeler blades to measure (at several points all around the disc) the clearance between the disc and a fixed point, such as the caliper mounting bracket **(see illustration)**. If the measurements obtained are at the specified maximum or beyond, the disc is excessively warped, and must be renewed, however, it is worth checking first that the hub bearing is in good condition (see Chapter 1 Section 19).
6 Check the disc for cracks, especially around the wheel bolt holes, and any other wear or damage, and renew if necessary.

Removal

7 Where applicable, disconnect the wiring connector from the brake pad wear sensor connector and unclip the connector from the bracket.

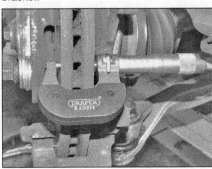

6.3 Use a micrometer to measure the thickness of the disc

8 On vehicles fitted with the FS III caliper, remove the guide pin caps, slacken and remove the guide pins and slide the caliper from the disc. Tie the caliper to the front coil spring, using a piece of wire or string, to avoid placing any strain on the hydraulic brake hose and retrieve the brake pads.
9 On vehicles fitted with the FN3 caliper, unscrew and remove the two bolts securing the brake caliper mounting bracket to the hub carrier. Slide the whole caliper assembly off the hub and away from the disc and tie the assembly to the front coil spring, using a piece of wire or string, to avoid placing any strain on the hydraulic brake hose. The caliper mounting bracket can be unscrewed and separated from the caliper if required.
10 Remove the screw holding the disc to the hub, and remove the disc. If it is tight, lightly tap its rear face with a hide or plastic mallet to free it from the hub.

6.5 Use a DTI gauge to measure the disc run-out

Refitting

11 Refitting is the reverse of the removal procedure, noting the following points:

a) *Ensure that the mating surfaces of the disc and hub are clean and flat.*

b) *If a new disc has been fitted, use a suitable solvent to wipe any preservative coating from the disc, before refitting the caliper. Note that new brake pads should always be fitted when the disc is renewed.*

c) *On FN3 caliper equipped vehicles, slide the caliper into position, making sure the pads pass either side of the disc, fit new caliper mounting bracket bolts and tighten them to the specified torque setting.*

d) *On FS III caliper equipped vehicles refer to Section 4, for details of brake pad and caliper fitting.*

e) *Refit the roadwheel then lower the vehicle to the ground and tighten the wheel bolts to the specified torque. Apply the footbrake several times to force the pads back into contact with the disc before driving the vehicle.*

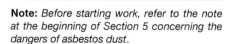

7 Rear brake disc – inspection, removal and refitting

Note: *Before starting work, refer to the note at the beginning of Section 5 concerning the dangers of asbestos dust.*

Inspection

Note: *If either disc requires renewal, BOTH should be renewed at the same time, to ensure even and consistent braking. New brake pads should be fitted also.*

1 Firmly chock the front wheels, engage 1st gear (or P), then jack up the rear of the car and support it on axle stands (see *Jacking and vehicle support*). Remove the appropriate rear roadwheel.

2 Inspect the disc as described in Section 6.

Removal

3 Unscrew the two bolts securing the brake caliper mounting bracket in position, then slide the whole caliper, bracket and pads off the disc. The bolts should be discarded and new ones fitted. If preferred, the caliper and pads can be removed separately before unscrewing the mounting bracket. Using a piece of wire or string, tie the caliper to the exhaust hanger/vehicle body, to avoid placing any strain on the hydraulic brake hose.

4 Remove the screw holding the disc to the hub, and remove the disc. If it is tight, lightly tap its rear face with a hide or plastic mallet to free it from the hub.

Refitting

5 Refitting is the reverse of the removal procedure, noting the following points:

a) *Ensure that the mating surfaces of the disc and hub are clean and flat.*

b) *If a new disc has been fitted, use a suitable*

solvent to wipe any preservative coating from the disc, before refitting the caliper. Note that new brake pads should always be fitted when the disc is renewed.

c) *Prior to installation, renew the caliper bracket mounting bolts. Slide the caliper into position, making sure the pads pass either side of the disc, and tighten the caliper bracket bolts to the specified torque setting.*

d) *Refit the roadwheel then lower the vehicle to the ground and tighten the wheel bolts to the specified torque. Apply the footbrake several times to force the pads back into contact with the disc before driving the vehicle.*

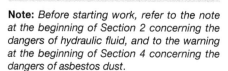

8 Front brake caliper – removal, overhaul and refitting

Note: *Before starting work, refer to the note at the beginning of Section 2 concerning the dangers of hydraulic fluid, and to the warning at the beginning of Section 4 concerning the dangers of asbestos dust.*

Removal

1 Apply the handbrake, then jack up the front of the vehicle and support it on axle stands (see *Jacking and vehicle support*). Remove the front roadwheels.

2 Minimise fluid loss by first removing the master cylinder reservoir cap, and then tightening it down onto a piece of polythene, to obtain an airtight seal. Alternatively, use a brake hose clamp to clamp the flexible hose.

3 Where applicable, disconnect the wiring connector from the brake pad wear sensor connector. Unclip the connector from the bracket.

4 Clean the area around the caliper brake hose union then slacken the union. Release the brake hose from the mounting bracket at the base of the suspension strut.

5 Remove the end caps from the guide bushes then unscrew and remove the caliper guide pins.

6 Lift the caliper out of position and unscrew it from the flexible brake hose union. Plug/cap the hose end and caliper openings to minimise fluid loss and prevent the entry of dirt into the hydraulic system. Remove the brake pads (where fitted to the caliper).

Overhaul

Note: *Check with a Skoda dealer or parts specialist regarding the availability of caliper overhaul kits.*

7 With the caliper on the bench, wipe away all traces of dust and dirt, but avoid inhaling the dust, as it is injurious to health.

8 Withdraw the partially-ejected piston from the caliper body, and remove the dust seal. If the caliper piston is reluctant to move, apply low air pressure (eg, from a foot pump) to the fluid inlet, but note that the piston may be ejected with some force.

9 Using a soft flat-bladed instrument, such as a plastic spatula, extract the piston hydraulic seal, taking great care not to damage the caliper bore.

10 Thoroughly clean all components, using only methylated spirit, isopropyl alcohol or clean brake fluid as a cleaning medium. Never use mineral-based solvents such as petrol or paraffin, as they will attack the hydraulic system's rubber components. Dry the components immediately, using compressed air or a clean, lint-free cloth. Use compressed air to blow clear the fluid passages.

11 Check all components, and renew any that are worn or damaged. Check particularly the cylinder bore and piston; these should be renewed if they are scratched, worn or corroded in any way (note that this means the renewal of the complete body assembly). Similarly check the condition of the guide pins and the bushes in the caliper body; both pins should be undamaged and (when cleaned) a reasonably tight sliding fit in the bushes. If there is any doubt about the condition of any component, renew it.

12 If the caliper is fit for further use, obtain the appropriate repair kit. All rubber seals should be renewed as a matter of course; these should never be re-used.

13 On commencement of re-assembly, ensure that all components are clean and dry.

14 Soak the seals in the special fluid provided in the overhaul kit for at least 45 minutes – check with the instructions provided in the kit. Smear some of the special fluid on the cylinder bore surface.

15 Fit the new piston (fluid) seal, using only your fingers (no tools) to manipulate it into the cylinder bore groove.

16 Fit the new dust seal to the rear of the piston and seat the outer lip of the seal in the caliper body groove. Carefully ease the piston squarely into the cylinder bore using a twisting motion. Press the piston fully into position and seat the inner lip of the dust seal in the piston groove.

17 If the guide bushes are being renewed, push the old bushes out from the body and press the new ones into position, making sure they are correctly seated.

18 Prior to refitting, fill the caliper with fresh hydraulic fluid by unscrewing the bleed screw and pumping the fluid through the caliper until bubble-free fluid is expelled from the union hole.

Refitting

19 Screw the caliper fully onto the flexible hose union.

20 Refit the brake pads with reference to Section 4, then manoeuvre the caliper into position over the brake disc.

21 Fit the caliper guide pins, tightening them to the specified torque setting, and refit the end caps to the guide bushes.

22 Tighten the brake hose union to the specified torque and secure the hose to the bracket at the base of the suspension strut.

Caution: The brake hose must not be twisted or strained, if a replacement caliper is fitted it may be necessary to slacken the brake hose at the connection to the vehicle body, to enable re-alignment of the hose. Tighten unions to the specified torque once the hose is correctly positioned.

23 Ensure the wiring is correctly routed, then clip the pad wear sensor wiring connector onto its bracket. Securely reconnect the wiring connector.

24 Remove the brake hose clamp or polythene (where fitted) and bleed the hydraulic system as described in Section 2. Note that, providing the precautions described were taken to minimise brake fluid loss, it should only be necessary to bleed the relevant front brake.

25 Refit the roadwheel, then lower the vehicle to the ground and tighten the roadwheel bolts to the specified torque.

9 Rear brake caliper – removal, overhaul and refitting

Note: *Before starting work, refer to the note at the beginning of Section 2 concerning the dangers of hydraulic fluid, and to the warning at the beginning of Section 5 concerning the dangers of asbestos dust.*

Note: *New guide pin bolts must be used on refitting.*

Removal

1 Chock the front wheels, release the handbrake, then jack up the rear of the vehicle and support it on axle stands (see *Jacking and vehicle support*). Remove the relevant rear wheel.

2 Detach the handbrake cable from the lever on the caliper, remove the spring clip and pull the outer cable from the bracket.

3 Minimise fluid loss by first removing the master cylinder reservoir cap, and then tightening it down onto a piece of polythene, to obtain an airtight seal. Alternatively, use a brake hose clamp to clamp the flexible hose **(see illustration)**.

4 Clean the area around the caliper brake pipe and undo the pipe unions, then remove the clip and release the brake hose from the bracket. (On Bosch calipers remove the banjo bolt from the brake hose to caliper union).

5 Unscrew and remove the caliper fixings, using a slim open-ended spanner to prevent the guide pins from rotating. Discard the fixings – new ones must be used on refitting **(see illustration)**.

6 Lift the brake caliper away from its mounting bracket. Plug/cover the pipe end and caliper port to minimise fluid loss and prevent the entry of dirt into the hydraulic system. Wash off any spilt fluid immediately with cold water. Remove the inner and outer brake pads.

Overhaul

7 Check with a Skoda dealer or parts specialist regarding the availability of caliper overhaul kits. The procedure is much the same as given in Section 8 for the front caliper, although note that the piston will need to be 'unscrewed' from the caliper body and rotated back in. **Note:** *It is not possible to overhaul the brake caliper handbrake mechanism. If the mechanism is faulty, or fluid is leaking from the handbrake lever seal the caliper assembly must be renewed.*

8 With the caliper on the bench, wipe away all traces of dust and dirt, but avoid inhaling the dust, as it is injurious to health.

9 Using a small screwdriver, carefully prise out the dust seal from the caliper, taking care not to damage the piston.

10 Remove the piston from the caliper bore by rotating it in an anti-clockwise direction. This can be achieved using a suitable pair of circlip pliers engaged in the caliper piston slots. Once the piston turns freely but does not come out any further, the piston can be withdrawn by hand.

11 Using a small screwdriver, extract the piston hydraulic seal(s), taking care not to damage the caliper bore.

12 Withdraw the guide pins from the caliper, and remove the guide sleeve gaiters.

13 Thoroughly clean all components, using only methylated spirit, isopropyl alcohol or clean hydraulic fluid as a cleaning medium. Never use mineral-based solvents such as petrol or paraffin, as they will attack the hydraulic system rubber components. Dry the components immediately, using compressed air or a clean, lint-free cloth. Use compressed air to blow clear the fluid passages.

14 Check all components, and renew any that are worn or damaged. Check particularly the cylinder bore and piston; these should be renewed (note that this means the renewal of the complete caliper body assembly) if they are scratched, worn or corroded in any way. Similarly check the condition of the spacers/guide pins and their bushes/bores (as applicable); both spacers/pins should be undamaged and (when cleaned) a reasonably tight sliding fit in their bores. If there is any doubt about the condition of any component, renew it.

15 If the assembly is fit for further uses obtain the appropriate repair kit; the components are available from Skoda dealers in various combinations.

16 Renew all rubber seals, dust covers and caps disturbed on dismantling as a matter of course; these should never be re-used.

17 On reassembly, ensure that all components are clean and dry.

18 Smear a thin coat of brake fitting paste on the piston, seal and caliper bore. This should be included in the overhaul/repair kit. Fit the new piston (fluid) seal, using only the fingers (no tools) to manipulate into the cylinder bore groove.

19 Fit the new dust seal to the piston groove, then refit the piston assembly. Turn the piston in a clockwise direction, using the method

9.3 Use a brake hose clamp to clamp the flexible hose

employed on dismantling, until it is fully retracted into the caliper bore.

20 Press the dust seal into position in the caliper housing.

21 Apply the grease supplied in the repair kit, or a brake grease or anti-seize compound, to the guide pins. Fit the new gaiters to the guide pins and fit the pins to the caliper ensuring that the gaiters are correctly located in the grooves on both the pins and caliper.

22 Prior to refitting, fill the caliper with fresh hydraulic fluid by slackening the bleed screw and pumping the fluid through the caliper until bubble-free fluid is expelled from the union hole.

Refitting

23 Refit the brake pads to the caliper mounting bracket with reference to Section 5.

24 Manoeuvre the caliper into position over the pads then fit the new guide pin bolts, tightening them to the specified torque setting.

25 Connect the brake pipe unions to the caliper and flexible brake hose, fit the brake hose securing clip and tighten the pipe unions to the specified torque. (On Bosch calipers fit the banjo bolt to the brake hose union and tighten to the specified torque).

26 Remove the brake hose clamp or polythene (where used) and securely tighten the brake pipe union, and secure the pipe bracket to the caliper.

27 Reattach the handbrake cable through the bracket and onto the lever on the caliper.

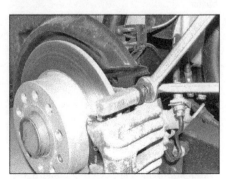

9.5 Using an open-ended spanner to counterhold the guide pin, undo the upper and lower guide pin bolts (arrowed)

10.8 Disconnect the clutch master cylinder supply hose (arrowed) from the brake fluid reservoir

10.10 Master cylinder retaining nuts (arrowed)

10.11 Fluid reservoir retaining bolt (arrowed in mirror)

28 Bleed the hydraulic system as described in Section 2. Note that, providing the precautions described were taken to minimise brake fluid loss, it should only be necessary to bleed the relevant rear brake.

29 Refit the roadwheel, then lower the vehicle to the ground and tighten the roadwheel bolts to the specified torque.

10 Master cylinder –
removal, overhaul and refitting

Note: *If the hydraulic circuit upstream of (before) the ABS modulator/hydraulic unit has been disturbed, the system may need to be bled using Skoda diagnostic equipment.*

Removal

1 Disconnect the battery negative lead as described in Chapter 5 Section 3.
2 Remove the engine top cover.
3 On non DPF (diesel particulate filter) PD engine models remove the air inlet trunking and top timing belt cover with reference to Chapter 2A Section 6.
4 On DPF (diesel particulate filter) equipped models, remove the DPF as described in Chapter 4B Section 5.
5 Disconnect brake fluid level sensor wiring plug, unscrew the reservoir cap, and siphon the hydraulic fluid from the reservoir. **Note:** *Do not siphon the fluid by mouth as it is poisonous; use a syringe or an old poultry baster.*
6 On common rail engine models release

11.2a Improvised special tool constructed from a modified exhaust clamp, used to release the brake pedal from the servo pushrod

the fuel supply and return pipes from their retainers in the area of the master cylinder and remove the coolant reservoir fixings to enable the reservoir to be moved aside.
7 Disconnect the wiring plug from the brake light switch located on the master cylinder body (where fitted).
8 On manual transmission models, clamp the clutch master cylinder supply hose and disconnect from the brake fluid reservoir **(see illustration)**.
9 Wipe clean the area around the brake pipe unions on the side of the master cylinder, and place absorbent rags beneath the pipe unions to catch any leaking fluid. Make a note of the correct fitted positions of the unions, then unscrew the union nuts and carefully withdraw the pipes. Plug or tape over the pipe ends and master cylinder orifices to minimise the loss of brake fluid, and to prevent the entry of dirt into the system. Wash off any spilt fluid immediately with cold water.
10 Unscrew and remove the two nuts and washers securing the master cylinder to the vacuum servo unit, remove the heat shield (where fitted), then withdraw the unit from the engine compartment **(see illustration)**. Remove the O-ring from the rear of the master cylinder, and discard it. Discard the nuts, new ones must be fitted.

Overhaul

11 Check with a Skoda dealer or parts specialist regarding the availability of repair kits. Items which can be renewed are the mounting seals for the fluid reservoir; if these show signs of deterioration remove the

11.2b Use the tool to release the brake pedal from the servo pushrod

retaining bolt **(see illustration)** and pull the reservoir from the seals, prise out the seals with a screwdriver, lubricate new seals with clean brake fluid, and press them into the master cylinder ports, push the reservoir into position and fit the retaining bolt.

Refitting

12 Remove all traces of dirt from the master cylinder and servo unit mating surfaces, and fit a new O-ring to the groove on the master cylinder body.
13 Fit the master cylinder to the servo unit, ensuring that the servo unit pushrod enters the master cylinder bore centrally. Refit the heat shield (where applicable), and the new master cylinder mounting nuts and washers, and tighten them to the specified torque.
14 Wipe clean the brake pipe unions, then refit them to the master cylinder ports and tighten them securely.
15 On manual transmission models, reconnect the clutch master cylinder supply hose to the reservoir.
16 Refill the master cylinder reservoir with new fluid, and bleed the complete hydraulic system as described in Section 2.
17 Reconnect the wiring to the brake level sender unit and brake light switch (where fitted).
18 The remainder of refitting is the reversal of removal.

11 Brake pedal –
removal and refitting

Removal

1 Remove the trim panel beneath the facia on the driver's side as described in Chapter 11, Section 26.
2 The end of the servo pushrod is shaped as a ball, and engages with a retaining clip in the back of the lever/pedal. To release the clip a special Skoda tool is available, but a suitable alternative can be improvised as shown. Note that the plastic lugs are very stiff, and it will not be possible to release them by hand. Using the tool, release the securing lugs and pull the pedal from the servo pushrod **(see illustrations)**.

3 Hold the nut and unscrew the brake pedal pivot bolt **(see illustration)**. Note that the steering column may need to be lowered slightly to ease access to the pivot bolt. Withdraw the bolt and remove the pedal.

4 Examine all components for signs of wear or damage, renewing them as necessary.

Refitting

5 Apply a smear of multipurpose grease to the pedal pivot bore and the pushrod ball.

6 The remainder of the refitting procedure is a reversal of the removal procedure, noting the following points:

a) *A new nut must be fitted to the brake pedal pivot bolt before tightening it to the specified torque.*

b) *Tighten all fixings to the correct torque, where specified.*

---

12 Vacuum servo unit – testing, removal and refitting

Testing

1 To test the operation of the servo unit, depress the footbrake several times to exhaust the vacuum, then start the engine whilst keeping the pedal firmly depressed. As the engine starts, there should be a noticeable give in the brake pedal as the vacuum builds-up. Allow the engine to run for at least two minutes, then switch it off. If the brake pedal is now depressed it should feel normal, but further applications should result in the pedal feeling firmer, with the pedal stroke decreasing with each application.

2 If the servo does not operate as described, first inspect the servo unit check valve as described in Section 13. Also check the vacuum pump as described in Section 22.

3 If the servo unit still fails to operate satisfactorily, the fault may lie within the unit itself. Repairs to the unit are not possible – if faulty, the servo unit must be renewed.

Removal

4 Remove the driver's side footwell cover. Unclip the diagnostic plug as the cover is withdrawn.

5 Working underneath the facia, locate the servo unit pushrod. The end of the servo pushrod is shaped as a ball, and engages with a retaining clip in the back of the lever/pedal. To release the clip a special Skoda tool is available, but a suitable alternative can be improvised as shown. Note that the plastic lugs are very stiff, and it will not be possible to release them by hand. Using the tool, release the securing lugs and pull the pedal from the servo pushrod **(see illustrations 11.2a and 11.2b)**.

6 Unplug the connector from the brake light switch and remove the switch as described in Section 19 (where fitted to the pedal bracket).

7 Remove the wiper arms as described in Chapter 12 Section 13.

8 Pull up the rubber sealing strip, the starting in the middle, pull the plenum chamber cover upwards from the base of the windscreen. Unclip the washer jet pipe from the cover as it's withdrawn. Undo the screw at each end and remove the front section of the plenum chamber below the plenum cover at the rear of the engine.

9 Disconnect the sensor wiring plug (where fitted) and carefully ease the vacuum hose connection out from the servo unit, taking care not to damage the grommet.

10 Remove the master cylinder as described in Section 10.

11 On PD engine models with the inlet manifold at the rear of the engine, remove the manifold as described in Chapter 4A Section 6.

12 To gain enough room to remove the brake servo the engine must be moved forward, if not already removed, jack and support the vehicle (see *Jacking and vehicle support*) and remove the rear engine mounting link from the transmission and subframe.

13 Install an engine crane to support the engine and remove the right- hand engine mounting.

14 In the engine compartment remove the two bolts securing the brake servo unit (located through the centre of the master cylinder mounting studs) and release the servo unit. Lower the engine slightly and pull it forward, taking care that no remaining attachments are placed under any strain, manoeuvre the servo unit out of the vehicle.

15 Recover any gaskets/seals from the rear of the master cylinder and servo unit and discard them as new ones must be fitted.

Overhaul

16 Check with a Skoda dealer or parts specialist regarding the availability of overhaul kits.

Refitting

17 Ensure the servo unit and bulkhead mating surfaces are clean, fit the gasket to the rear of the servo unit (where applicable) and then manoeuvre the unit into position.

18 From inside the vehicle, make sure the pushrod is correctly engaged with the rear of the pedal then press the pushrod firmly into position until the balljoint can be felt to engage. Lift the brake pedal by hand to check that the pushrod is securely reconnected.

19 Fit new servo mounting bolts and tighten them to the specified torque.

20 The remainder of refitting is a reversal of removal, bearing in mind the following points:

a) *Replace the seal between the master cylinder and servo unit and secure the master cylinder with new nuts tightened to the specified torque.*

b) *When connecting the vacuum hose connection to the servo, take care not to displace the sealing grommet.*

11.3 Brake pedal pivot bolt (arrowed)

c) *Replace any fixings where indicated in the relevant specification sections and observe the correct tightening values.*

d) *Refit and reset the brake light switch as described in Section 19.*

e) *Bleed the brake system with reference to Section 2.*

---

13 Vacuum servo unit check valve – removal, testing and refitting

Removal

1 Carefully ease the vacuum hose connections from the check valve located at the rear of the vacuum pump at the left-hand end of the cylinder head **(see illustration)**.

2 Slacken the retaining clip then disconnect the vacuum hose from the vacuum pump and remove it from the vehicle.

Testing

3 Examine the vacuum hose for signs of damage, and renew if necessary. The valve may be tested by blowing through it in both directions. Air should flow through the valve in one direction only – when blown through from the servo unit end of the valve. Renew the valve if this is not the case.

Refitting

4 Refitting is a reversal of removal. On completion, start the engine and check the check valve-to-servo unit connection for signs of air leaks.

13.1 Vacuum check valve (arrowed)

15.3 Remove the storage tray to access the adjustment nut (arrowed)

14 Vacuum servo unit pressure sensor – removal and refitting

Removal

1 Pull the plastic cover on the top of the engine upwards to release it from its mountings.
2 Disconnect the wiring plug from the sensor.
3 Pull the vacuum hose, complete with pressure sensor (where fitted), from the servo.
4 Using a pair of pliers, release the two clips and pull the sensor from place.

Refitting

5 Refitting is a reversal of removal.

15 Handbrake – adjustment

1 To check the handbrake adjustment, first apply the footbrake firmly several times to establish correct pad-to-disc clearance, then apply and release the handbrake 3 times.
2 Applying normal moderate pressure, pull the handbrake to the fully-applied position, counting the number of clicks from the handbrake ratchet mechanism. If adjustment is correct, there should be approximately 4 to 7 clicks before the handbrake is fully applied. If this is not the case, adjust as follows.
3 Remove the storage tray from the rear of the centre console to gain access to the adjustment nut (see illustration).

17.1 Handbrake cable equaliser plate (arrowed)

16.4 Handbrake lever retaining nuts (arrowed)

4 Chock the front wheels, then jack up the rear of the vehicle and support it on axle stands.(Jacking and vehicle support).
5 With the handbrake fully released, slacken the adjustment nut until both rear caliper handbrake levers are back against their stops.
6 Tighten the adjustment nut until both handbrake levers just move off the caliper stops. The gap between each lever and its stop must be between 1.0 and 1.5 mm.
7 Apply the handbrake 3 times, then release it and check that both wheels rotate freely. Check the adjustment by counting the clicks (see paragraph 2) and re-adjust if required.
8 Refit the rear storage tray.

16 Handbrake lever – removal and refitting

Removal

1 Remove the centre console as described in Chapter 11 Section 25.
2 Disconnect the plug from the handbrake warning light switch.
3 Slacken the handbrake cable adjuster nut sufficiently to allow the cables to be removed from the equaliser plate.
4 Undo the retaining nuts and remove the lever and bracket assembly from the floor (see illustration).

Refitting

5 Refitting is a reversal of the removal procedure. Adjust the handbrake as described

18.3 Warning light switch (arrowed)

in Section 15, and check the operation of the warning light switch before refitting the centre console.

17 Handbrake cables – removal and refitting

Removal

1 Remove the centre console as described in Chapter 11 Section 25. The handbrake cables consist of two sections which are linked to the lever by an equaliser plate. Each cable can be removed individually (see illustration).
2 Chock the front wheels, then jack up the rear of the vehicle and support it on axle stands.
3 Slacken the handbrake cable adjuster nut sufficiently to allow the cables to be disengaged from the equaliser plate.
4 Working back along the length of the cable, note its correct routing, and free it from all relevant guides and retaining clips.
5 Pulling the caliper lever forward slightly, disengage the inner cable from the lever, then remove the outer cable retaining bracket from the suspension trailing arm. Detach the cable from the bracket and withdraw the cable from underneath the vehicle.

Refitting

6 Refitting is a reversal of the removal procedure. Adjust the handbrake as described in Section 15 before refitting the centre console.

18 Handbrake 'on' warning light switch – removal and refitting

Removal

1 Disconnect the battery negative lead as described in Chapter 5 Section 3.
2 Remove the centre console as described in Chapter 11 Section 25.
3 Disconnect the wiring plug from the switch, squeeze the securing lugs, and withdraw the switch from the handbrake assembly (see illustration).

Refitting

4 Refitting is a reversal of the removal procedure.

19 Brake light switch – removal and refitting

Models up to 10/05

Removal

1 The brake light switch is located on the pedal bracket beneath the facia. Disconnect the battery negative lead before commencing work (Chapter 5 Section 3).

2 Remove the lower facia panel in the driver's footwell and the air duct above the pedal assembly.

3 Reach up behind the facia and disconnect the wiring connector from the switch.

4 Twist the switch 45 degrees to the left and remove it from the bracket.

Refitting

5 Before installation, fully extend the switch plunger. Guide the switch through the opening in the bracket, push it against the brake pedal (which must be in the 'released' position, ie, brakes off) and twist it 45 degrees to the right.

6 Refit the wiring connector and check the operation of the brake lights before refitting the air duct and lower facia panel.

Models from 10/05

Removal

7 The brake light switch is located on the master cylinder.

8 Pull the plastic cover on the top of the engine upwards to release it from its mountings.

9 Disconnect the wiring connector from the switch body located on the underside of the master cylinder.

10 Undo the retaining bolt, then lower the switch from place. Note the locating lug at the top of the switch **(see illustrations)**.

Refitting

11 Refitting is a reversal of removal.

20 Anti-lock braking system (ABS) – general information

1 ABS is fitted as standard to all models in the range. The system comprises a hydraulic unit, an electronic control unit (ECM) and four roadwheel sensors. The hydraulic unit contains the eight hydraulic solenoid valves (two for each brake – one inlet and one outlet) and the electrically-driven return pump. The purpose of the system is to prevent the roadwheels locking during heavy braking. This is achieved by automatic release of the brake on the relevant wheel, followed by re-application of the brake. In the case of the rear wheels, both rear brakes are released and applied at the same time.

2 The solenoid valves are controlled by the ECM, which itself receives signals from the four wheel sensors (front sensors are fitted to the hubs and the rear sensors are fitted to the rear axle), which monitor the speed of rotation of each wheel. By comparing these signals, the ECM can determine the speed at which the vehicle is travelling. It can then use this speed to determine when a wheel is decelerating at an abnormal rate, compared to the speed of the vehicle, and therefore predicts when a wheel is about to lock. During normal operation, the system functions in the same way as a non-ABS braking system.

3 If the ECM senses that a wheel is about

19.10a Brake light switch retaining bolt (arrowed)

to lock, it closes the relevant outlet solenoid valves in the hydraulic unit, which then isolates the relevant brake on the wheel which is about to lock from the master cylinder, effectively sealing-in the hydraulic pressure.

4 If the speed of rotation of the wheel continues to decrease at an abnormal rate, the ECM opens the inlet solenoid valves on the relevant brake and operates the electrically-driven return pump which pumps the hydraulic fluid back into the master cylinder, releasing the brake. Once the speed of rotation of the wheel returns to an acceptable rate, the pump stops; the solenoid valves switch again, allowing the hydraulic master cylinder pressure to return to the caliper, which then re-applies the brake. This cycle can be carried out many times a second.

5 The action of the solenoid valves and return pump creates pulses in the hydraulic circuit. When the ABS system is functioning, these pulses can be felt through the brake pedal.

6 The operation of the ABS system is entirely dependent on electrical signals. To prevent the system responding to any inaccurate signals, a built-in safety circuit monitors all signals received by the ECM. If an inaccurate signal or low battery voltage is detected, the ABS system is automatically shut down, and the warning light on the instrument panel is illuminated to inform the driver that the ABS system is not operational. Normal braking should still be available, however.

7 On all models, the ABS system also includes Electronic Differential Lock (EDL) and Traction Control (TCS) functions. If under acceleration the ECM senses that a wheel is spinning, it uses the hydraulic unit to gradually apply the brake on that wheel until traction is regained. Once the wheel regains traction, the brake is released.

8 The ESP (Electronic Stability Program) function is a further expansion of the ABS system which takes into consideration the angle of the steering wheel, using a steering angle sender and a combined lateral acceleration, yaw rate, and longitudinal acceleration sensor.

9 The ABS/ESP/TCS ECM and hydraulic unit are combined into one unit, and must not be separated.

10 If a fault does develop in the system, the

19.10b Note the lug (arrowed) at the top of the switch

vehicle must be taken to a Skoda dealer or suitably-equipped specialist for fault diagnosis and repair.

21 Anti-lock braking system (ABS) components – removal and refitting

Hydraulic unit

1 Removal and refitting of the hydraulic unit is best entrusted to a Skoda dealer as fault diagnosis and coding of the control unit must be performed on completion using specialist equipment.

Front wheel sensor

Removal

2 Apply the handbrake, then jack up the front of the vehicle and support securely on axle stands (see *Jacking and vehicle support*). To improve access, remove the roadwheel.

3 Disconnect the sensor wiring plug.

4 Undo the retaining bolt, then carefully pull the sensor out from the wheel bearing housing and remove it from the vehicle **(see illustration)**.

Refitting

5 Ensure that the mating faces of the sensor and hub carrier are clean and dry then lubricate the wheel sensor surfaces with a small quantity of copper-based grease.

6 Ensure the sensor wiring is correctly positioned then push the sensor firmly into position until it is fully home in the hub carrier,

21.4 Front ABS wheel sensor retaining bolt (arrowed)

21.11 Rear ABS wheel sensor retaining bolt (arrowed)

22.3 Pull the vacuum hose from the pump

22.5 Vacuum pump retaining bolts (arrowed)

and tighten the retaining bolt to the specified torque.

7 Ensure the sensor is securely retained then work along the sensor wiring, making sure it is correctly routed, securing it in position with all the relevant clips and ties. Reconnect the wiring connector.

8 Refit the wheel then lower the vehicle and tighten the wheel bolts to the specified torque.

Rear wheel sensor

Removal

9 Chock the front wheels, then jack up the rear of the vehicle and support it on axle stands (see *Jacking and vehicle support*). To improve access, remove the appropriate roadwheel.

10 Working underneath the vehicle, disconnect the wiring plug from the sensor.

11 Note the fitted position of the speed sensor, then undo the retaining bolt and carefully prise the sensor from the wheel bearing housing **(see illustration)**.

Refitting

12 Ensure that the mating faces of the sensor and axle are clean and dry, then lubricate the wheel sensor surfaces with a little copper-based grease.

13 Ensure the sensor wiring is correctly positioned then push the sensor firmly into position until it is fully home in the hub carrier, and tighten the retaining bolt to the specified torque.

14 Reconnect the sensor wiring plug.

15 Refit the roadwheel then lower the vehicle to the ground and tighten the wheel bolts to the specified torque.

22 Vacuum pump – removal and refitting

PD unit injector engines

1 Refer to Chapter 4A, Section 10.

Common rail injection engines

Removal

2 Remove the air cleaner housing as described in Chapter 4A Section 3.

3 Disconnect the vacuum hose from the top of the pump **(see illustration)**.

4 Undo the charge air pipe retaining bolts, then push the pipe down a little to access the rearmost pump retaining bolt.

5 Undo the 4 bolts and remove the pump **(see illustration)**. Recover the seal.

Refitting

6 Renew the pump seal, then fit the pump, ensuring it seats properly in the camshaft.

7 Tighten the pump retaining bolts to the specified torque.

8 The remainder of refitting is a reversal of removal.

23 ESP system components – removal and refitting

1 The ESP system comprises of the ABS, TCS and EDL system. The ESP, TCS and EDL systems rely on the ABS system

components for measuring and reducing wheel speed. In addition to the wheel sensors and brake pressure sensors, the ESP receives information concerning the steering wheel angle, lateral acceleration, vehicle rotational speed (yaw rate), and longitudinal acceleration. Testing of the various system components should be entrusted to a Skoda dealer or specialist.

Lateral acceleration/yaw rate/ longitudinal acceleration sensor

2 Depending on model, this sensor is integrated into the ABS unit or mounted beneath the right-hand front seat. As specialist equipment is required to reset the sensor after refitting or renewal, it is advised that this work is entrusted to a Skoda dealer or specialist.

Brake pressure sensor

3 The brake pressure sensor is fitted to the ABS hydraulic control unit. Skoda state that the sensor should not be detached from the control unit.

Steering angle sensor

4 The steering angle sensor is incorporated into the airbag contact unit between the steering wheel and column switch, or on later models incorporated as part of the steering gear and cannot be renewed separately. Note that if the sensor has been renewed, specialist equipment is required to perform a 'zero comparison'. Removal and refitting should therefore be entrusted to a Skoda dealer or specialist.

Chapter 10
Suspension and steering

Contents

Degrees of difficulty

Easy, suitable for novice with little experience	Fairly easy, suitable for beginner with some experience	Fairly difficult, suitable for competent DIY mechanic	Difficult, suitable for experienced DIY mechanic	Very difficult, suitable for expert DIY or professional

Specifications

Front suspension

Type .... Independent, with MacPherson struts incorporating coil springs, telescopic shock absorbers and anti-roll bar

Rear suspension

Type .... Trailing arm with Multilink transverse arms, separate gas-filled telescopic shock absorbers, coil springs and anti-roll bar

Steering

Type .... Rack-and-pinion. Electro-mechanical power assistance standard

Wheel alignment and steering angles*

Front wheel

Camber angle:
- Standard and self-levelling suspension .... -30' ± 30'
- Sports suspension .... -41' ± 30'
- Heavy duty suspension .... -8' ± 30'
- Maximum difference between sides .... 30'

Castor angle:
- Standard and self-levelling suspension .... 7° 34' ± 30'
- Sports suspension .... 7° 47' ± 30'
- Heavy duty suspension .... 7° 14' ± 30'
- Maximum difference between sides .... 30'

Toe setting .... 10' ± 10'

Toe-out on turns (20° left or right):
- Standard and self-levelling suspension .... 1° 38' ± 20'
- Sports suspension .... 1° 40' ± 20'
- Heavy duty suspension .... 1° 20' ± 20'

Ride height:
- Standard and self-levelling suspension (2UA) .... 391 ± 10 mm
- Sports suspension (2UC) .... 376 ± 10 mm
- Heavy duty suspension (2UB) .... 416 ± 10 mm

Refer to a Skoda dealer for the latest recommendations.

Rear wheel

Camber angle:
Vehicles up to 02/05 . . . .   -1°45' ± 30'
Vehicles from 02/05 . . . .   -1°20' ± 30'
Maximum difference between sides . . . .   30'
Toe setting . . . .   +10' ± 10'
Ride height:
Standard suspension (up to 12/05) . . . .   398 ± 10 mm
Standard suspension (from 01/06) . . . .   394 ± 10 mm
Sports suspension (up to 12/05) . . . .   386 ± 10 mm
Sports suspension (from 01/06) . . . .   380 ± 10 mm
Heavy duty suspension . . . .   419 ± 10 mm

* Refer to a Skoda dealer for the latest recommendations.

Torque wrench settings

	Nm	lbf ft
Front suspension		
Anti-roll bar link nut*	65	48
Anti-roll bar to subframe: *		
Stage 1	20	15
Stage 2	Angle-tighten a further 90°	
Balljoint to lower arm: *		
Cast steel arm	60	44
Sheet steel arm.	100	74
Balljoint to wheel bearing housing: *	60	44
Hub bolt*	See Chapter 8	
Hub to wheel bearing housing: *		
Stage 1	70	52
Stage 2	Angle-tighten a further 90°	
Lower arm (steel subframe):		
Mountings to subframe: *		
Stage 1	70	52
Stage 2	Angle-tighten a further 180°	
Lower arm (aluminium subframe):		
Front mounting to subframe (console): *		
Stage 1	70	52
Stage 2	Angle-tighten a further 180°	
Rear mounting bracket to underbody: *		
Stage 1	70	52
Stage 2	Angle-tighten a further 135°	
Rear mounting bracket to subframe (console): *		
Stage 1	50	37
Stage 2	Angle-tighten a further 90°	
Rear engine mounting:		
To subframe: *		
Stage 1	100	74
Stage 2	Angle-tighten a further 90°	
To transmission: *		
Class 8.8 bolts:		
Stage 1	40	30
Stage 2	Angle-tighten a further 90°	
Class 10.9 bolts:		
Stage 1	50	37
Stage 2	Angle-tighten a further 90°	
Splash plate to wheel bearing housing	12	9
Subframe-to-underbody bolts (aluminium subframe): *		
Stage 1	70	52
Stage 2	Angle-tighten a further 135°	
Subframe-to-underbody bolts (steel subframe): *		
Stage 1	90	66
Stage 2	Angle-tighten a further 180°	
Suspension strut:		
Bottom clamp: *		
Stage 1	70	52
Stage 2	Angle-tighten a further 90°	
Upper mounting: *		
Stage 1	15	11
Stage 2	Angle-tighten a further 90°	
Upper piston rod*	60	44
Vehicle level sender to subframe and lower arm	9	7

Torque wrench settings (continued)

	Nm	lbf ft
Rear suspension		
ABS speed sensor	8	6
Anti-roll bar link *	45	33
Anti-roll bar to subframe: *		
Stage 1	20	15
Stage 2	Angle-tighten a further 90°	
Hub to wheel bearing housing: *		
Stage 1	200	147
Stage 2	Angle-tighten a further 90°	
Lower suspension arm to wheel bearing housing: *		
Stage 1	70	52
Stage 2	Angle-tighten a further 180°	
Shock absorber:		
To body: *		
Stage 1	50	37
Stage 2	Angle-tighten a further 45°	
To wheel bearing housing: *	180	133
Splash plate to wheel bearing housing	12	9
Subframe to body: *		
Stage 1	70	52
Stage 2	Angle-tighten a further 180°	
Track control rod:		
To subframe: *		
Stage 1	70	52
Stage 2	Angle-tighten a further 180°	
To wheel bearing housing: *		
Stage 1	130	96
Stage 2	Angle-tighten a further 180°	
Trailing arm:		
Mounting bracket to underbody: *		
Stage 1	50	37
Stage 2	Angle-tighten a further 45°	
To mounting bracket: *		
Stage 1	90	66
Stage 2	Angle-tighten a further 90°	
To wheel bearing housing: *		
Stage 1	70	52
Stage 2	Angle-tighten a further 90°	
Upper suspension arm:		
To subframe*	95	70
To wheel bearing housing: *		
Stage 1	130	96
Stage 2	Angle-tighten a further 180°	
Vehicle level sender	5	4
Steering		
Steering column:		
Mounting bracket to body	20	15
Frequency link to body	25	18
To frequency link	20	15
To mounting bracket*	20	15
Universal joint to steering gear*	30	22
Steering gear:		
Heat shield (not fitted to all models)*	6	4
To subframe: *		
Stage 1	50	37
Stage 2	Angle-tighten a further 90°	
Steering wheel to column: *		
4 spoke wheel	30	22
3 spoke wheel	50	37
Track rod end:		
To track rod	55	41
To wheel bearing housing: *		
Stage 1	20	15
Stage 2	Angle-tighten a further 90°	
Track rod to steering gear	100	74
Roadwheels		
Roadwheel bolts	120	89

* Do not re-use

1 General Information

1 The independent front suspension is of the MacPherson strut type, incorporating coil springs and integral telescopic shock absorbers. The struts are located by transverse lower suspension arms, which use rubber inner mounting bushes, and incorporate a balljoint at the outer ends. The front wheel bearing housings, which carry the wheel bearings, brake calipers and the hub/disc assemblies, are attached to the MacPherson struts by clamp bolts, and connected to the lower arms through the balljoints. A front anti-roll bar is fitted to all models. The anti-roll bar is rubber-mounted, and is connected to both lower suspension struts by short links.

2 The rear suspension consists of a trailing arm, rubber-mounted at its front end to the underbody, a wheel bearing housing, lower transverse suspension arm and coil spring, track control rod, upper suspension arm, and separate shock absorber. A rear anti-roll bar is fitted to all models. The anti-roll bar is rubber-mounted on the rear subframe, and is connected to the wheel bearing housings on each side by a short connecting link.

3 The safety steering column incorporates an intermediate shaft at its lower end. The intermediate shaft is connected to both the steering column and steering gear by universal joints, although the shaft is supplied as part of the column assembly and cannot be separated. Both the inner steering column and intermediate shaft have splined sections which collapse during a major frontal impact. The outer column is also telescopic with two sections, to facilitate reach adjustment.

4 The steering gear is mounted onto the front subframe, and is connected by two track rods, with balljoints at their inner and outer ends, to the steering arms projecting rearwards from the wheel bearing housings. The track rod ends are threaded to the track rods in order to allow adjustment of the front wheel toe setting. The steering gear has electro-mechanical assistance, and incorporates an integral control unit. It is only functional when the engine is running. There are no hydraulic components, and steering assistance is automatically matched to the vehicle speed, steering wheel torque and steering wheel angle.

5 All models are fitted with an Anti-lock Brake System (ABS), and can also be fitted with a Traction Control System (TCS), an Electronic Differential Lock (EDL) system and an Electronic Stability Program (ESP). The ABS may also be referred to as including EBD (Electronic Brake Distribution) which means it adjusts the front and rear braking forces according to the weight being carried. The TCS may also be referred to as ASR (Anti Slip Regulation).

6 The TCS system prevents the front wheels from losing traction during acceleration by reducing the engine output. The system is switched on automatically when the engine is started, and it utilises the ABS system sensors to monitor the rotational speeds of the front wheels.

7 The ESP system extends the ABS, TCS and EDL functions to reduce wheel spin in difficult driving conditions. It does this by using highly-sensitive sensors which monitor the speed of the vehicle, lateral movement of the vehicle, the brake pressure, and the steering angle of the front wheels. If, for example, the vehicle is tending to oversteer, the brake will be applied to the front outer wheel to correct the situation. If the vehicle is tending to understeer, the brake will be applied to the rear inside wheel. The steering angle of the front wheels is monitored by an angle sensor on the top of the steering column.

8 The TCS/ESP systems should always be switched on, except when driving with snow chains, driving in snow or driving on loose surfaces, when some wheel spin may be advantageous. The ESP switch is located in the centre of the facia.

9 Some models are also fitted with an Electronic Differential Lock (EDL) which reduces unequal traction from the front wheels. If one front wheel spins 100 rpm or more faster than the other, the faster wheel is slowed down by applying the brake to that wheel. The system is not the same as the traditional differential lock, where the actual differential gears are locked. Because the system applies a front brake, in the event of a brake disc overheating the system will shut down until the disc has cooled. No warning light is displayed if the system shuts down. As is the case with the TCS system, the EDL system uses the ABS sensors to monitor front wheel speeds.

2 Front wheel bearing housing – removal and refitting

Note: *Renewal of the hub bearings does not require removal of the wheel bearing housing (see Section 3). This Section describes removal of the wheel bearing housing leaving*

2.4 Brake pipe/ABS sensor bracket retaining bolt (arrowed)

the suspension strut in situ, however, if necessary it can be removed together with the suspension strut, then separated on the bench. All self-locking nuts and bolts disturbed on removal must be renewed as a matter of course.

Removal

1 Remove the wheel trim/hub cap (as applicable) and loosen the driveshaft retaining bolt (hub bolt) by 90° with the vehicle resting on its wheels. Also loosen the wheel bolts. **Note:** *Do not loosen the hub bolt more than 90° at this stage, or the wheel bearing may be damaged.*

2 Apply the handbrake, then jack up the front of the vehicle and support it on axle stands (see *Jacking and vehicle support*). Remove the front roadwheel.

3 Unscrew and remove the driveshaft retaining bolt.

4 Unbolt the bracket for the brake pipe/ABS sensor wiring from the bearing housing **(see illustration)**.

5 Remove the brake disc as described in Chapter 9 Section 6. This procedure includes removing the brake caliper, however do not disconnect the hydraulic brake hose from the caliper. Using a piece of wire or string, tie the caliper to the front suspension coil spring, to avoid placing any strain on the hydraulic brake hose.

6 Unscrew the splash plate from the wheel bearing housing. Undo the bolt securing the brake pipe and wiring to the housing.

7 Loosen the nut securing the steering track rod balljoint to the wheel bearing housing. To do this, fit a ring spanner to the nut, then hold the balljoint pin stationary using an Allen key. With the nut removed, it may be possible to release the balljoint from the wheel bearing housing by turning the balljoint pin with an Allen key. If not, leave the nut on by a few turns to protect the threads, then use a universal balljoint separator to release the balljoint. Remove the nut completely once the taper has been released.

8 Unscrew the front suspension lower balljoint-to-lower arm retaining nuts **(see illustration 4.6a)**, then lever the lower arm down to release the balljoint studs from the arm. Now use a soft-faced mallet to tap the driveshaft from the hub splines while pulling out the bottom end of the wheel bearing housing. If the driveshaft is tight on the splines, it may be necessary to use a puller bolted to the hub to remove it. Tie the driveshaft to one side.

9 Note which way round it is fitted, then unscrew the nut and remove the clamp bolt securing the wheel bearing housing to the bottom of the strut.

10 The wheel bearing housing must now be released from the strut. To do this, Skoda technicians insert a special tool into the split wheel bearing housing, and turn it through 90° to open up the clamp. A similar tool can be made out of an old screwdriver, or alternatively

a suitable cold chisel can be driven into the split as a wedge. Slightly press the top of the wheel bearing housing inwards, then push it downwards from the bottom of the strut (see illustrations).

Refitting

11 Ensure that the driveshaft outer joint and hub splines are clean and dry, then lubricate the splines with fresh engine oil. Also lubricate the threads and contact surface of the hub bolt with oil.

12 Lift the wheel bearing assembly into position, and engage the hub with the splines on the outer end of the driveshaft. Fit the new hub bolt, tightening it by hand only at this stage.

13 Engage the wheel bearing housing with the bottom of the suspension strut, making sure that the hole in the side plate aligns with the holes in the split housing. Remove the tool used to open the split.

14 Insert the strut-to-wheel bearing housing clamp bolt from the rear, and fit the new retaining nut. Tighten the nut to the specified torque.

15 Refit the lower arm balljoint to the lower arm, and tighten the new nuts to the specified torque.

16 Refit the track rod balljoint to the wheel bearing housing, then fit a new retaining nut and tighten it to the specified torque. If necessary, hold the balljoint pin with an Allen key while tightening the nut.

17 Refit the splash plate and tighten the bolts.

18 Refit the brake disc and caliper with reference to Chapter 9 Section 6.

19 Refit the ABS wheel sensor as described in Chapter 9 Section 21.

20 Ensure that the outer joint is drawn fully into the hub, then refit the roadwheel.

21 Have an assistant depress the brake pedal, then tighten the driveshaft retaining bolt in the stages given in the Specifications. It is recommended that an angle gauge is used to ensure the correct tightening angle. **Note:** *The car must not be standing on its wheels when tightening the bolt, or the wheel bearing may be damaged.*

22 Lower the vehicle to the ground, tighten the roadwheel bolts, and refit the wheel trim/hub cap.

23 Have the front wheel alignment checked by a Skoda dealer or specialist at the earliest opportunity.

3 Front hub bearings – renewal

Note: *The bearing is a sealed, pre-adjusted and pre-lubricated, double-row roller type, and requires no maintenance. It is bolted to the wheel bearing housing.*

1 Remove the wheel trim/hub cap (as applicable) and loosen the driveshaft retaining bolt (hub bolt) and the wheel bolts, with the

2.10a Use a cold chisel to carefully open up the split in the wheel bearing housing and release the strut

vehicle resting on its wheels. **Note:** *Do not loosen the hub bolt more than 90° at this stage, or the wheel bearing may be damaged.*

2 Apply the handbrake, then jack up the front of the vehicle and support it on axle stands (see *Jacking and vehicle support*). Remove the front roadwheel.

3 Unscrew and remove the driveshaft retaining bolt.

4 Remove the ABS wheel sensor as described in Chapter 9 Section 21.

5 Remove the brake disc as described in Chapter 9 Section 6. This procedure includes removing the brake caliper, however do not disconnect the hydraulic brake hose from the caliper. Using a piece of wire or string, tie the caliper to the front suspension coil spring, to avoid placing any strain on the hydraulic brake hose.

6 Press the driveshaft outer stub towards the transmission as far as possible, then unscrew and remove the wheel bearing retaining bolts from the rear of the housing (see illustration).

7 Remove the hub/wheel bearing complete with hub from the outside of the housing while sliding it from the driveshaft splines.

8 Ensure all hub/wheel bearing and housing mating surfaces are clean and free of corrosion.

9 Fit the new wheel bearing to the housing and engage the hub splines with the driveshaft outer stub. Fit the new bolts and tighten them to the specified torque.

10 Refit the brake disc and caliper with reference to Chapter 9 Section 6.

3.6 Front wheel bearing retaining bolts (arrowed)

2.10b Withdraw the wheel bearing housing from the bottom of the suspension strut

11 Refit the ABS wheel sensor as described in Chapter 9 Section 21.

12 Pull the driveshaft outer stub fully into the hub and fit a new hub bolt, hand-tight at this stage.

13 Ensure that the outer joint is drawn fully into the hub, then refit the roadwheel.

14 Tighten the new driveshaft retaining bolt in the stages given in the Specifications. It is recommended that an angle gauge is used to ensure the correct tightening angle.

Note: *The car must not be standing on its wheels when tightening the bolt, or the wheel bearing will be damaged.*

15 Lower the vehicle to the ground, tighten the roadwheel bolts, and refit the wheel trim/hub cap.

4 Front strut – removal, overhaul and refitting

Note: *This section describes removal of the suspension strut leaving the wheel bearing housing in situ, however, if necessary it can be removed together with the wheel bearing housing, then separated on the bench. All self-locking nuts and bolts disturbed on removal must be renewed as a matter of course.*

Removal

1 Remove the wheel trim/hub cap (as applicable) and loosen the driveshaft retaining bolt (hub bolt) and the wheel bolts, with the vehicle resting on its wheels. **Note:** *Do not loosen the hub bolt more than 90° at this stage, or the wheel bearing may be damaged.*

2 Apply the handbrake, then jack up the front of the vehicle and support it on axle stands (see *Jacking and vehicle support*). Remove the appropriate roadwheel.

3 Unscrew the nut and disconnect the anti-roll bar link from the strut (see illustration 7.3b).

4 Unhook the cable for the ABS sensor from the suspension strut.

5 Unscrew and remove the driveshaft retaining bolt (see illustration). Refit 2 of the roadwheel bolts, then have an assistant

4.5 Undo the driveshaft bolt

4.6a Undo the balljoint-to-lower arm nuts

4.6b Pull the driveshaft from the hub splines

apply the brakes to prevent the disc/hub from rotating whist slackening the bolt.

6 Unscrew the front suspension lower balljoint-to-lower arm retaining nuts, then lever the lower arm down to release the balljoint studs. Now use a soft-faced mallet to tap the driveshaft from the hub splines while pulling out the bottom end of the wheel bearing housing (see illustrations). If the driveshaft is tight on the splines, it may be necessary to use a puller bolted to the hub to remove it. Tie the driveshaft to one side, then refit the lower balljoint to the lower arm and secure with the nuts, hand-tightened.

7 Note which way round it is fitted, then unscrew the nut and remove the clamp bolt securing the wheel bearing housing to the bottom of the strut (see illustration).

8 The wheel bearing housing must now be released from the strut. To do this, Skoda technicians insert a special tool into the split

wheel bearing housing, and turn it through 90° to open up the clamp. A similar tool such as an Allen key can be used, or alternatively a suitable cold chisel can be driven into the split as a wedge. Slightly press the top of the wheel bearing housing inwards, then push it downwards from the bottom of the strut (see illustrations 2.10a and 2.10b). Support the wheel bearing housing to one side without straining the hydraulic brake hose.

9 Remove the plenum cover as described in Chapter 4A, Section 4.

10 To ensure correct refitting, mark the strut upper mounting in relation to the body. If the reason for removing the strut is overhaul, loosen the upper mounting centre nut one turn, while holding the piston rod with an Allen key.

11 Support the strut, then unscrew the upper mounting bolts and lower the strut from under the wheel arch (see illustration).

Overhaul

⚠ *Warning: Before attempting to dismantle the suspension strut, a suitable tool to hold the coil spring in compression must be obtained. Adjustable coil spring compressors are readily available, and are recommended for this operation. Any attempt to dismantle the strut without such a tool is likely to result in damage or personal injury.*

12 With the strut removed from the car, clean away all external dirt. If necessary, mount it upright in a vice during the dismantling procedure.

13 Fit the spring compressor, and compress the coil spring until all tension is relieved from the upper spring seat (see illustration).

14 Unscrew and remove the upper centre retaining nut, whilst retaining the strut piston with a suitable Allen key, then remove the mounting/ thrust bearing, and coil spring (see illustrations).

4.7 Undo the nut (arrowed) and pull the strut lower clamp bolt from place

4.11 Undo the strut upper mounting bolts (arrowed)

4.13 Compressor tool (double clamp type) fitted to the front suspension coil spring

4.14a Hold the piston with an Allen key and undo the centre nut

4.14b Remove the upper mounting/thrust bearing...

4.14c ...and coil spring

15 Remove the gaiter, bump stop and protective sleeve **(see illustrations)**.
16 With the strut assembly now completely dismantled, examine all the components for wear, damage or deformation, and check the bearing for smoothness of operation. Renew any of the components as necessary.
17 Examine the strut for signs of fluid leakage. Check the strut piston for signs of pitting along its entire length, and check the strut body for signs of damage. While holding it in an upright position, test the operation of the strut by moving the piston through a full stroke, and then through short strokes of 50 to 100 mm. In both cases, the resistance felt should be smooth and continuous. If the resistance is jerky, or uneven, or if there is any visible sign of wear or damage to the strut, renewal is necessary.
18 If any doubt exists about the condition of the coil spring, carefully remove the spring compressors, and check the spring for distortion and signs of cracking. Renew the spring if it is damaged or distorted, or if there is any doubt as to its condition.
19 Inspect all other components for signs of damage or deterioration, and renew as necessary.
20 Fit the protective sleeve to the strut, then assemble the bump stop to the upper mounting, and refit the gaiter to the mounting. The larger diameter of the bump stop must be against the upper mounting, and the lower edge of the gaiter must be pulled down around the protective sleeve.
21 Fit the coil spring (together with the compressor tool) onto the strut, making sure its lower (larger diameter) end is correctly located against the spring seat stop.
22 Refit the thrust bearing and upper mounting, then screw on a new retaining nut. Tighten the nut to the specified torque while holding the piston rod with an Allen key.

Refitting

23 Manoeuvre the strut into position under the wheel arch, and locate in the suspension strut turret in the previously-noted position. If a new strut is being fitted, locate it so that one of the two arrows marked on the upper mounting points forwards, and the bolt holes are aligned **(see illustration)**. Insert the new bolts and tighten to the specified torque.
24 Refit the plenum cover.
25 Engage the wheel bearing housing with the bottom of the suspension strut, making sure that the hole in the side plate aligns with the holes in the split housing. Raise the housing, while pressing it inwards to assist entry. Use a trolley jack if necessary. When fully entered, remove the tool used to open the split.
26 Insert the new strut-to-wheel bearing housing clamp bolt from the rear, and fit the new retaining nut. Tighten the nut to the specified torque.
27 Unscrew the nuts from the lower balljoint and lever down the lower arm to release it from the wheel bearing housing. Insert the

4.15a Remove the gaiter...

4.15b ...bump stop...

4.15c ...and protective sleeve

4.23 One of the two arrows must point forwards

outer end of the driveshaft through the hub and engage it with the splines. Fit the new hub bolt, tightening it by hand only at this stage.
28 Refit the lower arm balljoint to the lower arm, and tighten the new nuts to the specified torque. Where applicable, refit the headlight range control sensor arm to the lower arm and tighten the nut.
29 Refit the ABS wheel sensor as described in Chapter 9 Section 21.
30 Ensure that the outer joint is drawn fully into the hub, then refit the roadwheel.
31 Have an assistant depress the brake pedal, then tighten the driveshaft retaining bolt in the stages given in the Specifications. It is recommended that an angle gauge is used to ensure the correct tightening angle. **Note:** *The car must not be standing on its wheels when tightening the bolt, or the wheel bearing may be damaged.*
32 Lower the vehicle to the ground, tighten the roadwheel bolts, and refit the wheel trim/hub cap. We recommend the front wheel alignment is checked at the earliest opportunity.

5 Front lower arm –
removal, overhaul and refitting

Note: *The lower arm (also referred to as the track control arm) is available in either cast steel or sheet steel – when renewing the arm, make sure the correct type is fitted according to model. Different design arms are fitted depending on whether a steel or aluminium*

subframe assembly is fitted to the vehicle. For aluminium subframe equipped vehicles Skoda subframe locating pins (T10096) or similar are required for the work in this Section, to ensure correct front wheel alignment. All self-locking nuts and bolts disturbed on removal must be renewed as a matter of course.
Note: *Following the removal and refitting of the front lower arm(s) have the front wheel alignment checked and if necessary adjusted by a Skoda dealer or suitably equipped garage.*
Note: *Removal of the left front lower arm on automatic gearbox models will require the subframe to be lowered slightly (refer to Section 21).*

Aluminium subframe equipped vehicles

Removal

1 Apply the handbrake, then jack up the front of the vehicle and support it on axle stands (see *Jacking and vehicle support*). Remove the appropriate front roadwheel and the engine compartment undershield.
2 If removing the left-hand side lower arm, the coupling rod for the vehicle level sensor (where fitted) will need to be removed.
3 Unscrew the front suspension lower balljoint-to-lower arm retaining nuts, then lever down the lower arm to release the arm from the balljoint studs.
4 At this stage, Skoda technicians use locating pins T10096 in place of the rear outer subframe mounting bolts to ensure correct front wheel alignment. If these pins are not

5.5 Rear outer mounting bolt (arrowed)

available, only remove and refit one lower arm at a time, and mark the position of the subframe accurately with dabs of paint.

5 Unscrew and remove the rear outer mounting bolt and, where available, substitute it with a locating pin tightened to 20 Nm (15 lbf ft) **(see illustration)**.

6 Unscrew and remove the front mounting bolt, then support the lower arm and unscrew the two rear inner mounting bolts. Remove the lower arm from beneath the car.

Overhaul

7 Thoroughly clean the lower arm, then check carefully for cracks or any other signs of wear or damage, paying particular attention to the rubber/metal mounting bushes. If either bush requires renewal, take the lower arm to a Skoda dealer or suitably-equipped garage. Where access to a hydraulic press and suitable spacers are available these may be used to remove the rubber bushes and install new ones. Alternatively, consider whether it is more cost effective to fit a new lower arm supplied complete with bushes.When fitting new bushes, note the following:

a) *When fitting a new front mounting bush, it must be initially tilted with one lip in the bore. As the bush is inserted, it will straighten up. Make sure the bush is centred in its bore.*

b) *Dip rubber bushes in a mild solution of washing-up liquid and water to aid installation.*

c) *The rear mounting bush is integral with the mounting bracket, make note of the brackets fitted position before removal from the arm, ensure that the new bracket is correctly aligned and that the hexagonal section of the arm is pushed fully into the bush of the rear mounting bracket.*

Refitting

8 Locate the lower arm on the subframe and insert the new front mounting bolt loosely.

9 Insert the two new inner rear mounting bolts loosely, then position the outer bolt hole in the exact position noted during removal. If a Skoda location pin was used on removal, the bracket will be correctly positioned on the pin. Tighten the two inner bolts to the specified torque, then remove the pin and fit the new outer bolt, and tighten to the specified torque.

10 Lever down the lower arm and locate the

balljoint studs in their holes. Fit the new nuts and tighten to the specified torque.

11 Raise the arm using a suitable jack until the suspension is at the correct specified ride height, measured from the centre of the hub bolt, vertically, to the edge of the wheel arch.

Caution: Exercise extreme care as the vehicle may be lifted off of the axle stand during this procedure. An alternative approach is to refit the wheel and tighten the arm bolts with the vehicle on the ground (or wheel ramps).

Note: *The type of running gear (and other vehicle information) can be found on a label attached to the luggage area floor panel.*

12 Tighten the front mounting bolt to the specified torque with the suspension at the specified ride height.

13 If working on the left-hand side lower arm, refit the coupling rod for the vehicle level sensor (where fitted).

14 Refit the roadwheel and undershield, and lower the car to the ground.

Steel subframe equipped vehicles

Removal

15 Apply the handbrake, then jack up the front of the vehicle and support it on axle stands (see *Jacking and vehicle support*). Remove the appropriate front roadwheel and the engine compartment undershield.

16 If removing the left-hand side lower arm, the coupling rod for the vehicle level sensor (where fitted) will need to be removed.

17 Unscrew the front suspension lower balljoint-to-lower arm retaining nuts, then lever down the lower arm to release the arm from the balljoint studs.

18 Slacken and remove the front mounting bolt.

19 Counter-hold the nut, then slacken and remove the lower arm rear mounting bolt.

20 Pull the lower arm from the subframe.

Overhaul

21 Thoroughly clean the lower arm, then check carefully for cracks or any other signs of wear or damage, paying particular attention to the rubber/metal mounting bushes. If either bush requires renewal, take the lower arm to a Skoda dealer or suitably-equipped garage. Where access to a hydraulic press and suitable spacers are available these may be used to remove the rubber bushes and install new ones. Alternatively, consider whether it is more cost effective to fit a new lower arm supplied complete with bushes.When fitting new bushes, note the following:

a) *When fitting a new front mounting bush, it must be initially tilted with one lip in the bore. As the bush is inserted, it will straighten up. Make sure the bush is centred in its bore.*

b) *Dip the rubber bushes in a mild solution of washing-up liquid and water to aid installation.*

c) *Identify the alignment markings on the lower arm and rear bush before removing*

the bush, position the marking on a new bush so that it is aligned between the two markings on the arm, this will ensure that the bush is fitted in the correct position.

Refitting

22 Fit the lower arm to the subframe and align to enable a new rear mounting nut and bolt to be fitted. Do not tighten at this stage.

23 Manipulate the lower arm so that the front mounting is correctly aligned with the subframe and install a new mounting bolt, but do not tighten.

24 Lever down the lower arm and locate the balljoint studs in their holes. Fit the new nuts and tighten to the specified torque.

25 Tighten the rear lower arm mounting bolt to the specified torque, counter-hold the nut with a spanner and ensure is does not turn as the bolt is tightened. Raise the arm using a suitable jack until the suspension is at the correct specified ride height, measured from the centre of the hub bolt, vertically, to the edge of the wheel arch.

Caution: Exercise extreme care as the vehicle may be lifted off of the axle stand during this procedure. An alternative approach is to refit the wheel and tighten the arm bolts with the vehicle on the ground (or wheel ramps).

Note: *The type of running gear (and other vehicle information) can be found on a label attached to the luggage area floor panel.*

26 Tighten the front lower arm mounting bolt to the specified torque with the suspension at the specified ride height.

27 If working on the left-hand side lower arm, refit the coupling rod for the vehicle level sensor (where fitted).

28 Refit the roadwheel and undershield, and lower the car to the ground.

---

6 Front lower arm balljoint – removal, inspection and refitting

Note: *All self-locking nuts and bolts disturbed on removal must be renewed as a matter of course.*

Removal

1 Remove the wheel trim/hub cap (as applicable) and loosen the driveshaft retaining bolt (hub bolt) and the wheel bolts, with the vehicle resting on its wheels. **Note:** *Do not loosen the hub bolt more than 90° at this stage, or the wheel bearing may be damaged.*

2 Apply the handbrake, then jack up the front of the vehicle and support it on axle stands (see *Jacking and vehicle support*). Remove the appropriate roadwheel.

3 Unscrew and remove the driveshaft retaining bolt.

4 Unscrew the front suspension lower balljoint-to-lower arm retaining nuts, then lever the lower arm down to release the balljoint studs **(see illustration 4.6a)**. Now use a soft-faced mallet to tap the driveshaft

from the hub splines while pulling out the bottom end of the wheel bearing housing. If the driveshaft is tight on the splines, it may be necessary to use a puller bolted to the hub to remove it. It is not necessary to remove the driveshaft completely from the hub. Retain the wheel bearing housing away from the lower arm by inserting a block of wood between the strut and the inner body panel.

5 Unscrew and remove the balljoint retaining nut, then release the balljoint from the wheel bearing housing using a universal balljoint separator. Withdraw the balljoint (see illustration).

Inspection

6 With the balljoint removed, check that it moves freely, without any sign of roughness. Check also that the balljoint rubber gaiter shows no sign of deterioration, and is free from cracks and splits. Renew as necessary.

Refitting

7 Fit the balljoint to the wheel bearing housing and fit the new retaining nut. Tighten the nut to the specified torque setting, noting that the balljoint shank can be retained with an Allen key if necessary to prevent it from rotating.

8 Remove the wooden block and move the strut inwards, then refit the balljoint to the lower arm using new nuts, and tighten them to the specified torque.

9 Refit the driveshaft retaining bolt and tighten it sufficiently to draw the driveshaft fully into the hub, then refit the roadwheel.

10 Have an assistant depress the brake pedal, then tighten the driveshaft retaining bolt in the stages given in the Specifications. It is recommended that an angle gauge is used to ensure the correct tightening angle. Note that the car must not be standing on its wheels when tightening the bolt, or the wheel bearing may be damaged.

11 Lower the vehicle to the ground, tighten the roadwheel bolts, and refit the wheel trim/hub cap.

7 Front anti-roll bar – removal and refitting

Note: *As the subframe must be lowered during this procedure, Skoda subframe locating pins (T10096) or similar are required to ensure correct front wheel alignment. All self-locking nuts and bolts disturbed on removal must be renewed as a matter of course.*

Removal

1 Remove the front subframe as described in Section 21, covering removal of the steering gear assembly.

2 Manoeuvre the steering gear rearward, to enable removal of the anti-roll bar from the subframe.

3 Carefully examine the anti-roll bar components for signs of wear, damage or

deterioration, paying particular attention to the rubber mounting bushes. Renew worn components as necessary.

Refitting

4 Refitting is a reversal of removal but tighten all nuts and bolts to the specified torque where given. When refitting the subframe, align it with the marks made on removal, or use the special Skoda location pins before tightening the mounting bolts. To assist entry of the steering gear gaiter through the bulkhead, apply a soapy solution to it. Have the front wheel alignment checked at the earliest opportunity. It may also be necessary to carry out resetting of the steering angle sensor, which requires specialist equipment. This should be entrusted to a Skoda dealer or suitably equipped specialist.

8 Front anti-roll bar connecting link – removal and refitting

1 All self-locking nuts and bolts disturbed on removal must be renewed as a matter of course.

Removal

2 Apply the handbrake, then jack up the front of the vehicle and support it on axle stands (see *Jacking and vehicle support*). Remove the relevant front roadwheel.

3 Unscrew and remove the nuts securing the link to the strut and anti-roll bar (see illustrations).

4 Inspect the link rubbers for signs of damage or deterioration. If evident, renew the link complete.

Refitting

5 Refitting is a reversal of removal, but tighten the nuts to the specified torque.

9 Rear wheel bearing housing – removal and refitting

Removal

1 Chock the front wheels, then jack up the

6.5 Undo the nut and use a balljoint splitter to separate the balljoint from the bearing housing

rear of the vehicle and support it on axle stands (see *Jacking and vehicle support*).

2 Remove the rear coil spring as described in Section 14.

3 Remove the rear hub as described in Section 10.

4 Unscrew the splash plate from the rear wheel bearing housing.

5 Disconnect the wiring, then unscrew the mounting bolt and remove the ABS sensor from the rear wheel bearing housing.

6 Unscrew the bolt securing the rear shock absorber to the rear wheel bearing housing.

7 Unscrew the bolts securing the top suspension arm and bottom suspension arm to the rear wheel bearing housing.

8 Unscrew the bolt securing the rear track control rod to the rear wheel bearing housing.

9 Support the rear wheel bearing housing, then unscrew the mounting bolts from the trailing arm. Also, undo the nut and disconnect the anti-roll bar link from the trailing arm.

10 Withdraw the rear wheel bearing housing from the car.

Refitting

11 Fit the wheel bearing housing to the trailing arm and hand-tighten the bolts.

12 Attach the rear wheel bearing housing to the rear track control rod, and the top and bottom suspension arms, and hand-tighten the bolts.

13 Attach the anti-roll bar link rod to the housing/trailing arm and hand-tighten the nut.

14 Refit the splash plate and tighten the bolts to the specified torque.

8.3a Anti-roll bar link lower mount

8.3b Anti-roll bar link upper mount

9.18 Measure from the centre of the wheel arch to the centre of the hub

15 Refit the shock absorber lower mounting bolt and hand-tighten.

16 Refit the coil spring.

17 Refit the rear hub with reference to Section 10.

18 Position the centre of the rear hub at the correct ride-height distance (see Specifications) measured from the centre of the wheel arch, according to model **(see illustration)**. Use the trolley jack to adjust the position.

Caution: Exercise extreme care as the vehicle may be lifted off of the axle stand during this procedure. An alternative approach is to refit all the components and tighten the suspension bolts with the vehicle on the ground (or wheel ramps).

19 Tighten the following bolts to their specified torque, in the order given:
a) *Track control rod.*
b) *Upper suspension arm.*
c) *Lower suspension arm.*
d) *Shock absorber lower mounting bolt.*
e) *Trailing arm to wheel bearing housing*
f) *Anti-roll bar link nut*

20 Remove the trolley jack used to set the suspension at the specified ride height.

21 Refit the ABS sensor and tighten the mounting bolt. Reconnect the wiring.

22 Refit the roadwheel, then lower the vehicle to the ground, tighten the roadwheel bolts, and refit the wheel trim/hub cap. Have the rear wheel alignment checked and if necessary adjusted by a Skoda dealer or specialist.

10.3 Prise the dust cap from the hub

10 Rear hub/wheel bearings – checking and renewal

Note: *The rear wheel bearings cannot be renewed independently of the rear hub, because the outer races are formed in the hub itself. If excessive wear is evident, the rear hub must be renewed complete. The rear hub nut must always be renewed after removal.*

Removal

1 Chock the front roadwheels, then jack up the rear of the vehicle and support on axle stands (see *Jacking and vehicle support*). Release the handbrake and remove the relevant rear roadwheel.

2 Remove the brake disc and caliper as described in Chapter 9 Section 7.

3 Remove the dust cap from the centre of the hub using a screwdriver or cold chisel **(see illustration)**.

4 Unscrew and remove the hub bolt, using a multispline key. Note that it is tightened to a high torque and a socket extension bar may be required to loosen it. The bolt must be renewed whenever removed.

5 Using a suitable puller, pull the hub and bearings from the stub axle.

6 Examine the hub and bearings for wear, pitting and damage. If any damage is evident, renew the hub complete.

Refitting

7 Wipe clean the stub axle, then check that

the bearing races are adequately lubricated with suitable grease.

8 Locate the hub as far as possible on the stub axle.

9 Screw on the new bolt and tighten it to the specified torque.

10 Check the dust cap for damage and renew it if necessary. Use a hammer to carefully tap the cap into the hub. **Note:** *A badly fitting dust cap will allow moisture to enter the bearing, reducing its service life.*

11 Refit the brake disc and caliper as described in Chapter 9 Section 7.

12 Refit the roadwheel and lower the vehicle to the ground.

11 Rear track control rod – removal and refitting

Removal

1 Chock the front roadwheels, then jack up the rear of the vehicle and support on axle stands (see *Jacking and vehicle support*). Remove the relevant rear roadwheel.

2 Remove the coil spring as described in Section 14.

3 Remove the rear anti-roll bar as described in Section 16. This is to allow removal of the control rod inner bolt.

4 Note the fitted position of the rear track control rod, with the 'closed' side facing forwards. Also, note which way round the mounting bolts are fitted.

5 Unscrew the inner bolt retaining nut, then use a large adjustable spanner to counteract the 'twist' loading on the control rod to allow the inner bolt to be removed **(see illustrations)**.

6 Unscrew and remove the outer mounting bolt and nut, and withdraw the track control rod from under the vehicle. Note the location of the special 'star' washer beneath the head of the bolt securing the outer end of the rod to the wheel bearing housing **(see illustration)**.

Refitting

7 Refitting is a reversal of removal, but delay fully-tightening the mounting bolts until the rear suspension is set to the correct ride-height as described in Section 9. Check that a clearance

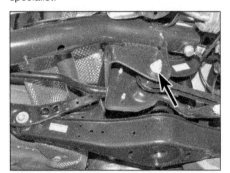

11.5a Undo the track control rod inner bolt and nut...

11.5b ...then 'twist' the control rod and remove the bolt

11.6 Undo the track control rod outer mounting bolt

exists between the special 'star' washer and the track control rod. Have the rear wheel alignment checked and if necessary adjusted by a Skoda dealer or specialist.

12 Rear suspension arms – removal and refitting

Upper arm

Removal

1 Chock the front roadwheels, then jack up the rear of the vehicle and support on axle stands (see *Jacking and vehicle support*). Remove the roadwheel.
2 Remove the rear coil spring as described in Section 14.
3 Release the ABS speed sensor wiring from the upper arm, then unscrew the bolt securing the arm to the wheel bearing housing **(see illustration)**.
4 At the inner end of the upper arm, mark the position of the eccentric bolt and subframe in relation to each other. This alignment determines the camber setting of the rear wheels **(see illustration)**.
5 Note which way round the eccentric bolt is fitted, then unscrew and remove it, and withdraw the upper arm.

Refitting

6 Refitting is a reversal of removal, but delay fully-tightening the mounting bolts until the rear suspension is set to the correct ride-height as described in Section 9. Make sure the eccentric bolt is correctly aligned as previously-noted, and also position the 'star' washer to provide a clearance between one of its points and the splash plate. Have the rear wheel alignment checked and if necessary adjusted by a Skoda dealer or specialist.

Lower arm

Removal

7 Chock the front roadwheels, then jack up the rear of the vehicle and support on axle stands (see *Jacking and vehicle support*). Remove the roadwheel.
8 Remove the rear coil spring as described in Section 14.
9 Unscrew the bolt securing the lower suspension arm to the wheel bearing housing **(see illustration)**.
10 On models with headlight range control, unscrew the nut and disconnect the sensor arm from the link.
11 At the inner end of the upper link, mark the position of the eccentric bolt and subframe in relation to each other **(see illustration)**. This alignment determines the camber setting of the rear wheels.
12 Refer to Chapter 4B Section 6 and lower the rear section of the exhaust system for improved access. Support the exhaust on an axle stand.
13 Unscrew and remove the inner bolt and

12.3 Rear upper arm outer bolt

12.9 Lower suspension arm mounting bolt (arrowed) at the wheel bearing housing

withdraw the lower suspension arm from under the car.

Refitting

14 Refitting is a reversal of removal, but delay fully-tightening the mounting bolts until the rear suspension is set to the correct ride-height as described in Section 9. Make sure the eccentric bolt is correctly aligned as previously-noted, and also position the 'star' washer to provide a clearance between one of its points and the splash plate. Have the rear wheel alignment checked and if necessary adjusted by a Skoda dealer or specialist.

13 Rear trailing arm and bracket – removal, overhaul and refitting

Removal

1 Chock the front roadwheels, then jack up the rear of the vehicle and support on axle stands (see *Jacking and vehicle support*). Remove the roadwheel.
2 Remove the rear coil spring as described in Section 14.
3 Undo the fixing holding the handbrake cable to the trailing arm.
4 Unscrew the nut and detach the anti-roll bar link.
5 Unscrew the bolts securing the trailing arm to the rear wheel bearing housing.
6 Mark the position of the trailing arm front mounting bracket in relation to the underbody **(see illustration)**.

12.4 Mark the position of the eccentric washer (arrowed) – upper arm

12.11 Lower suspension arm inner mounting bolts (arrowed) at subframe

7 Support the front mounting bracket on a trolley jack, then unscrew the bolts, lower the assembly and withdraw the rear trailing arm and bracket from under the vehicle.

Overhaul

8 Thoroughly clean the trailing arm and bracket, then unscrew the front pivot bolt and separate the arm from the bracket. Check carefully for cracks or any other signs of wear or damage, paying particular attention to the rubber mounting bush.
9 If the bush requires renewal, take the arm to a Skoda dealer or suitably-equipped garage. Alternatively, a hydraulic press and suitable spacers may be used to press the bush out of the arm, and to install the new one. Dip the bush in a mild solution of washing-up liquid and water. When fitting the new bush to the front of the trailing arm, it is important to position

13.6 Mark the position of the trailing arm front bracket in relation to the underbody

13.9a Make a vertical line on the arm as shown...

A = 114.0 mm

it correctly. Make a vertical line on the arm as shown in the accompanying illustration, then press in the new bush so that the line is between the two projections shown **(see illustrations)**.

10 With the new bush in position, locate the front of the arm in the bracket, and insert the bolt. Position the arm in relation to the bracket as shown **(see illustration)** then tighten the bolt/nut to the specified torque. There may be two types of bush.

Refitting

11 Fit the trailing arm to the wheel bearing housing and insert the bolts loosely.
12 Fit the anti-roll bar link and bolt on the nut loosely.
13 Raise the front mounting bracket and locate it on the underbody in its previously-

noted position. Insert the new bolts and tighten to the specified torque.
14 Lower the jack then refit the rear coil spring with reference to Section 14.
15 Position the centre of the rear hub at the correct ride-height distance (see Section 9) measured from the centre of the wheel arch, according to model. Use a trolley jack to adjust the position.
Caution: Exercise extreme care as the vehicle may be lifted off of the axle stand during this procedure. An alternative approach is to refit all the components and tighten the suspension bolts with the vehicle on the ground (or wheel ramps).
16 Tighten the arm-to-housing bolts to the specified torque.
17 Tighten the anti-roll bar link nut.

18 Lower the jack used to set the ride height.
19 Refit the handbrake cable to the trailing arm.
20 Refit the roadwheel and lower the vehicle to the ground. Have the rear wheel alignment checked and if necessary adjusted by a Skoda dealer or specialist.

14 Rear coil spring – removal and refitting

Warning: Adjustable coil spring compressors are readily available, and are recommended for this operation. Any attempt to remove the coil spring without such a tool is likely to result in damage or personal injury.

Removal

1 Chock the front roadwheels, then jack up the rear of the vehicle and support on axle stands (see *Jacking and vehicle support*). Remove the relevant rear roadwheel.
2 Fit the tool to the coil spring and compress it until it can be removed from the transverse arm and underbody **(see illustration)**. With the coil spring on the bench, carefully release the tension of the tool and remove it.
3 With the coil spring removed, recover the upper and lower spring seats and check them for damage. Obtain new ones if necessary,

13.9b ...then press in the new bush so that the line is between the two projections (1)

13.10 Bracket position on the rear trailing arm

14.2 Compress the coil spring with a special tool

14.4a The lug on the underside of the spring seat (arrowed)...

14.4b ...must locate in the hole (arrowed)

but note that they are different: the lower one having a location pin which enters a hole in the lower suspension arm. Also clean the spring locations on the underbody and trailing arm thoroughly.

Refitting

4 Refitting is a reversal of removal, but make sure that the lower spring seat engages the hole in the lower suspension arm, the lower end of the coil spring abuts the stop on the seat, and the upper seat is correctly engaged with the lug on the underbody**(see illustrations)**.

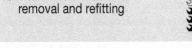

15 Rear shock absorber – removal and refitting

Note: *All self-locking nuts and bolts disturbed on removal must be renewed as a matter of course.*

Removal

1 Before removing the shock absorber, an idea of how effective it is can be gained by depressing the rear corner of the car. If the shock absorber is in good condition, the body should rise then settle in its normal position. If the body oscillates more than this, the shock absorber is probably defective. **Note:** *To ensure even rear suspension, both rear shock absorbers should be renewed at the same time.*

2 Chock the front roadwheels, then jack up the rear of the vehicle and support on axle stands (see *Jacking and vehicle support*). Remove the relevant rear roadwheel.

3 Remove the wheel arch liner.

4 Position a trolley jack and block of wood beneath the coil spring position on the trailing arm, and raise the arm so that the shock absorber is slightly compressed. Note on some models, it may be necessary to remove the stone protection guard first. If preferred, the rear coil spring may be removed completely at this stage as described in Section 14.

5 Unscrew the lower mounting bolt, then unscrew the upper mounting bolts and withdraw the shock absorber **(see illustrations)**.

Refitting

6 Locate the shock absorber in the rear wheel arch, then insert the upper mounting bolts and tighten to the specified torque.

7 Extend the shock absorber if necessary, and insert the lower mounting bolt loosely. Note the washer between the shock absorber and wheel bearing housing.

8 Raise the trailing arm until the rear suspension is set to the correct ride-height given as described in Section 9, then fully- tighten the shock absorber lower mounting bolt.

9 Refit the rear coil spring with reference to Section 14.

14.4c The upper end of the coil spring must locate around the lug (arrowed) on the underbody

10 Refit the wheel arch liner.
11 Refit the roadwheel and lower the vehicle to the ground.

16 Rear anti-roll bar – removal and refitting

Removal

1 Chock the front roadwheels, then jack up the rear of the vehicle and support on axle stands (see *Jacking and vehicle support*). Remove both rear roadwheels.

2 Working on each side in turn, unscrew the nut and detach the side links from the anti-roll bar. Discard the nuts – new ones must be fitted. Use a multispline bit to counterhold the nut **(see illustration 17.2)**.

15.5a Rear shock absorber lower mounting bolt...

16.4 Undo the anti-roll bar clamp bolts (lower one arrowed)

3 Mark the anti-roll bar to indicate which way round it is fitted, and the position of the rubber mounting bushes; this will aid refitting.
4 Unscrew the multispline bolts securing the anti-roll bar clamps to the rear subframe, and recover the clamps**(see illustration)**.
5 If required, prise off the clamps and remove the split bushes from the bar **(see illustration)**.

Refitting

6 Refitting is a reversal of removal but tighten all nuts and bolts to the specified torque only when the weight of the vehicle is back on the wheels.

17 Rear anti-roll bar connecting link – removal and refitting

Removal

1 Chock the front roadwheels, then jack up the rear of the vehicle and support on axle stands (see *Jacking and vehicle support*). Remove the relevant rear roadwheel.
2 Unscrew the nuts securing the link to the anti-roll bar and trailing arm, and withdraw it from under the vehicle. Discard the nuts – new ones must be fitted. Use a multispline bit to counterhold the nuts **(see illustration)**.
3 Inspect the link rubbers/balljoints for signs of damage or deterioration. If evident, renew the link complete.

15.5b ...and upper mounting bolts (arrowed)

16.5 Prise off the clamps and remove the split rubber bushes

17.2 Anti-roll bar connecting link bolts (arrowed)

Refitting

4 Refitting is a reversal of removal, but tighten the nuts to the specified torque only when the weight of the vehicle is back on the wheels.

18 Vehicle level sender –
removal and refitting

1 The front sender for the headlight range control system is located on the left-hand side of the front subframe, and incorporates an arm and link attached to the left-hand front lower suspension arm. The rear sender is bolted to the rear subframe, and an arm and link is attached to a bracket on the lower suspension arm. The system is controlled by an ECM located behind a cover on the passenger's side of the instrument panel.

Removal

2 To remove the front sender, apply the handbrake then jack up the front of the vehicle and support it on axle stands (see *Jacking and vehicle support*). Remove the front roadwheel, then note the position of the sender on the lower arm. Unscrew the nut and disconnect the link and bracket from the lower arm. Disconnect the wiring then unscrew the bolt and remove the sender from the front subframe.

3 To remove the rear sender, chock the front roadwheels then jack up the rear of the vehicle and support on axle stands (see *Jacking and vehicle support*). Disconnect the wiring from

20.5a Undo the lower shroud retaining screw...

19.3 Unscrew the steering wheel bolt using a multispline bit. Note any markings for refitting (arrowed)

the sender. Unscrew the bolts securing the link and bracket to the lower suspension arm, then unscrew the bolts and remove the sender from the rear subframe.

Refitting

4 Refitting is a reversal of removal, but tighten the mounting bolts to the specified torque. If a sender has been renewed, the basic setting of the system needs to be performed using dedicated diagnostic equipment. Entrust this task to a Skoda dealer or suitably-equipped specialist.

19 Steering wheel –
removal and refitting

Removal

1 Remove the driver's airbag as described in Chapter 12 Section 24.

2 Adjust the steering column to its highest position, then extend it into the passenger compartment as far as possible, and lock it in this position.

3 Using a multispline bit, unscrew and remove the retaining bolt, while holding the steering wheel stationary **(see illustration)**. Discard the bolt – a new one must be fitted.

4 Check if the steering wheel is marked in relation to the column. If not, use a dab of paint to mark them, then ease the steering wheel from the column splines by firmly rocking it side-to-side.

20.5b ...and unclip the upper shroud

Refitting

5 Locate the steering wheel on the column splines making sure that the previously-made marks are correctly aligned.

6 Fit the new retaining bolt and tighten to the specified torque while holding the steering wheel stationary.

7 Refit the driver's airbag with reference to Chapter 12 Section 24.

20 Steering column –
removal, inspection and refitting

Removal

1 Move the front wheels to the straight-ahead position.

2 Adjust the steering column to its lowest position and extend it into the passenger compartment as far as possible, then lock it in this position.

3 Remove the steering wheel as described in Section 19.

4 Undo the 2 screws and remove the steering column adjustment handle.

5 Undo the screw beneath the lower cover, then unclip and remove the upper shroud from the steering column **(see illustrations)**.

6 Undo the two upper screws either side of the steering column and remove the lower shroud from the steering column **(see illustration)**. As the shroud is being removed, release it from the height and reach adjustment handle.

7 Undo the retaining bolts and remove the trim panel above the driver's pedals. Unclip the diagnostic connector from the panel as it's withdrawn.

8 Remove the combination switch assembly from the top of the steering column as described in Chapter 12 Section 6.If it is not imperative to remove the assembly, it can be left it in position on the steering column, provided the wiring plugs are disconnected.

9 Unscrew the nut and disconnect the earth cable, then disconnect the wiring plugs from the steering column ECM and from the immobiliser reading coil.

10 Remove the crash strut above the clutch pedal, and brake pedal (where fitted).

20.6 Undo the screws (arrowed) and remove the lower shroud

11 To ease access, remove the lower air vent (located above the pedals) by undoing the screw at the right-hand end.

12 Remove the cable guide from below the steering column. To do this, carefully prise up the lugs from the retaining clips.

13 Undo the retaining screws and remove the trim beneath the foot pedals for access to the steering column universal joint. Unscrew the pinch-bolt and pull the universal joint from the steering gear pinion **(see illustration)**. Note that the pinion shaft has a cut-out to enable fitting of the pinch-bolt, and the splined pinion shaft incorporates a flat making it impossible to assemble the joint to the shaft in the wrong position. Discard the pinch-bolt; a new one should be used on refitting.

14 Note that the inner and outer columns, and the intermediate shaft, are telescopic, to facilitate the reach adjustment. It is important to keep the splined sections of the inner steering column engaged with each other while the steering column is removed. If they become detached due to the outer column sections being separated, especially on a vehicle which has completed a high mileage, it is possible that rattling noises may occur.

15 Unscrew and remove two diagonally-opposite mounting bolts, then support the steering column and unscrew the two remaining bolts **(see illustration)**. Withdraw the steering column from inside the car. Discard the bolts as new ones must be used on refitting. Note that the mounting bracket on the bulkhead has location pins which align the steering column.

Caution: Do not carry the steering column by suspending it from the universal joint or intermediate shaft, as this will damage the universal joint and steering column bushes. Also, do not bend the joints by more than 90°.

Inspection

16 The steering column is designed to collapse in the event of a front-end crash, to prevent the steering wheel injuring the driver. Before refitting the steering column, examine the column and mountings for signs of damage and deformation.

17 Check the inner column sections for signs of free play in the column bushes. If any damage or wear is found on the steering column bushes, the column must be renewed as an assembly.

18 The intermediate shaft is permanently attached to the inner column and cannot be renewed separately. Inspect the universal joints for excessive wear. If evident, the complete steering column must be renewed.

Refitting

19 Refit the steering column to the bulkhead bracket, insert the new mounting bolts, and tighten to the specified torque.

20 Reconnect the earth cable and tighten the bolt. Refit the wiring harness.

21 Attach the universal joint on the steering

20.13 Universal joint pinch-bolt (arrowed)

gear pinion splines, insert the new pinch-bolt, and tighten to the specified torque.

22 The remainder of refitting is a reversal of removal. Note that the steering angle sensor basic settings may need to be set using dedicated diagnostic equipment. Entrust this task to a Skoda dealer or suitably-equipped specialist.

21 Steering gear assembly – removal, overhaul and refitting

Note: Two different steering gear assemblies may be fitted. Vehicles up to model year 2008 are fitted with a '2nd Generation' assembly, and vehicles from model year 2009 are fitted with a '3rd Generation' assembly. If the 2nd Generation steering gear is to be renewed, only 3rd Generation assemblies are available, and the electrical wiring harness from the engine electrical box to the steering gear will also have to be renewed.

Note: As the subframe must be removed during this procedure, Skoda subframe locating pins (T10096 for aluminium subframe, T10096/T10452 for steel subframe) or similar are required to ensure correct front wheel alignment. All self-locking nuts and bolts disturbed on removal must be renewed as a matter of course.

Note: Varying lengths of bolt secure the subframe, note the length and location of each bolt as it is removed.

Removal

1 Disconnect the battery negative lead and remove the battery tray as described in Chapter 5 Section 3.

2 Disconnect the steering gear loom wiring from the engine compartment fusebox, earth connection and wiring plug. Release the loom retaining clip, then release the loom from the from the plastic cable guide.

3 Apply the handbrake, then jack up the front of the vehicle and support it on axle stands positioned on the underbody, leaving the subframe free (see *Jacking and vehicle support*). Position the steering straight-ahead, then remove both front roadwheels. Also remove the engine compartment undershield.

20.15 Steering column mounting bolts (arrowed)

4 Inside the vehicle, undo the screws and remove the plastic cover for access to the universal joint connecting the steering inner column to the steering gear pinion. Unscrew and remove the pinch-bolt, and pull the universal joint from the pinion splines. Take note that the steering gear pinion incorporates a cut-out for the pinch-bolt, and therefore the joint can only be correctly fitted in one position. Discard the pinch-bolt, a new one should be used on refitting.

5 Working on each side in turn, unscrew the nuts from the track rod ends, then use a balljoint separator tool to release the ends from the steering arms on the front wheel bearing housings.

6 Working on each side in turn, unscrew the nuts securing the anti-roll bar links to the struts. Use an Allen key to counterhold the link balljoint shanks.

7 Working on each side in turn, unscrew the front suspension lower balljoint-to-lower arm retaining nuts, then lever the lower arms down to release the balljoint studs. Discard the nuts – new ones must be fitted.

8 Disconnect the plug from the front left vehicle level sender (where fitted).

9 Unscrew and remove the engine/transmission rear mounting bolts from the transmission and disconnect the wiring from the oil level sensor.

10 Unscrew the exhaust system mounting from the subframe **(see illustration)**.

11 Undo the bolts and detach the heat shield from the steering gear (where fitted). Unclip any wiring loom from the heat shield.

21.10 Exhaust mounting bolts (arrowed)

21.12 Steering gear and anti-roll bar bolts (arrowed)

12 Undo the bolts securing the steering gear and anti-roll bar to the subframe **(see illustration)**.

13 Support the subframe with a trolley jack and block of wood. If not using the special Skoda locating pins, to facilitate refitting, accurately mark the position of the subframe to ensure correct alignment.

14 Unscrew the mounting bolts in turn and where available install the Skoda locating pins to a torque of 20 Nm (15 lb ft). Remove the remaining mounting bolts, slightly lower the subframe and check that all electrical wiring is released.

Note: *For aluminium subframe models, the fitting pins (T10096) should be fitted in the positions occupied by the front and outer rear subframe mounting bolts, for Steel subframe models the fitting pins (T10096/T10452) should be fitted in the positions occupied by the front and inner rear subframe mounting bolts.*

15 Remove the heat shield from over the steering gear.

16 Lower the subframe together with the steering gear to the floor.

17 Remove the cable guide and disconnect the wiring plugs from the steering gear. Release the wiring from all clips.

Caution: Do not touch the wiring terminals on the electronic control module, as a static electricity discharge may damage the internal components.

18 Manoeuvre the steering gear from place, and carefully place it on the floor taking care not to damage the electronic control module.

22.2 Steering gear gaiter clips (arrowed)

Overhaul

19 Examine the steering gear assembly for signs of wear or damage, and check that the rack moves freely throughout the full length of its travel, with no signs of roughness or excessive free play between the steering gear pinion and rack.

20 It is not possible to overhaul the steering gear assembly housing components, and if it is faulty, the assembly must be renewed. The only components which can be renewed individually are the steering gear gaiters, the track rod end balljoints and the track rods, as described later in this Chapter.

Refitting

21 Locate the steering gear on the subframe, and reconnect the wiring loom. Ensure the loom is clipped into place in its original locations.

22 Insert and tighten the new bolts for the gear and anti-roll bar.

23 Refit the heat shield, then raise the subframe onto the underbody and align it with the Skoda location pins or marks made on removal, to assist entry of the steering gear gaiter through the bulkhead, apply a soapy solution to it. Install and tighten the new mounting bolts in the reverse order of removal, removing the locating pins where fitted and tightening each bolt to the specified stage one torque, with all the subframe mounting bolts installed carry out the specified second stage tightening of each bolt. Lower and remove the support used to lift the subframe.

24 Refit the exhaust mounting, then refit the engine/transmission rear mounting bolts to the transmission and tighten to the specified torque.

25 Locate the front suspension lower balljoints in the lower arms, screw on the new nuts and tighten to the specified torque.

26 Refit the track rod ends with new nuts, and tighten to the specified torque.

27 Inside the car, attach the universal joint on the steering gear pinion splines, insert the new pinch-bolt, and tighten to the specified torque.

28 The remainder of refitting is a reversal of removal. Have the front wheel alignment checked at the earliest opportunity. If a new steering gear has been fitted, the steering angle sensor basic settings must be set using dedicated diagnostic equipment, and it must also be adapted to the vehicle by a Skoda dealer or specialist.

22 Steering gear rubber gaiters and track rods – renewal

Steering gear rubber gaiters

1 Remove the track rod end balljoint as described in Section 23. Also, unscrew the locking nut after noting its position.

2 Wipe clean the rubber gaiter to prevent entry of dirt or moisture. Note the fitted position of the gaiter on the track rod, then release the retaining clips and slide the gaiter off the steering gear housing and track rod **(see illustration)**.

3 Carefully slide the new gaiter onto the track rod, and locate it on the steering gear housing. Position the gaiter as noted on removal, making sure that it is not twisted, then lift the outer sealing lip of the gaiter to equalise air pressure within the gaiter.

4 Secure the gaiter in position with new retaining clips. Where crimped-type clips are used, pull the clip as tight as possible, and locate the hooks in their slots. Remove any slack in the clip by carefully compressing the raised section. In the absence of the special crimping tool, a pair of side-cutters may be used, taking care not to cut the clip.

5 Screw on the locking nut, then refit the track rod end balljoint as described in Section 23.

Track rods

6 Remove the relevant steering gear rubber gaiter as described earlier. If there is insufficient working room with the steering gear mounted in the car, remove it as described in Section 22 and hold it in a vice while renewing the track rod.

7 Hold the steering rack stationary with one spanner on the flats provided, then loosen the balljoint nut with another spanner. Fully unscrew the nut and remove the track rod from the rack.

8 Locate the new track rod on the end of the steering rack and bolt on the nut. Hold the rack stationary with one spanner and tighten the balljoint nut to the specified torque. A crow's foot adapter may be required since the track rod prevents access with a socket, and care must be taken to apply the correct torque in this situation.

9 Refit the steering gear or rubber gaiter with reference to the earlier paragraphs or Section 22. On completion check and, if necessary, adjust the front wheel alignment as described in Section 24.

23 Track rod end – removal and refitting

Removal

1 Apply the handbrake, then jack up the front of the vehicle and support it on axle stands (see *Jacking and vehicle support*). Remove the relevant roadwheel.

2 If the track rod end is to be re-used, mark its position in relation to the track rod to facilitate refitting.

3 Unscrew the track rod end locknut by a quarter of a turn. Do not move the locknut from this position, as it will serve as a handy reference mark on refitting.

4 Loosen and remove the nut securing the track rod end balljoint to the wheel bearing

23.4 Use a balljoint splitter to separate the track rod end balljoint from the bearing housing

housing, and release the balljoint tapered shank using a universal balljoint separator. Note that the balljoint shank has a hexagon hole – hold the shank with an Allen key while loosening the nut **(see illustration)**.

5 Counting the exact number of turns necessary to do so, unscrew the track rod end from the track rod.

6 Carefully clean the balljoint and the threads. Renew the balljoint if its movement is sloppy or too stiff, if excessively worn, or if damaged in any way; carefully check the stud taper and threads. If the balljoint gaiter is damaged, the complete balljoint assembly must be renewed; it is not possible to obtain the gaiter separately.

Refitting

7 Screw the track rod end onto the track rod by the number of turns noted on removal. This should bring the track rod end to within a quarter of a turn of the locknut, with the alignment marks that were made on removal (if applicable) lined up. Tighten the locknut.

8 Refit the balljoint shank to the steering arm on the wheel bearing housing, then fit a new retaining nut and tighten it to the specified torque. Hold the shank with an Allen key if necessary.

9 Refit the roadwheel, then lower the car to the ground and tighten the roadwheel bolts to the specified torque.

10 Check and, if necessary, adjust the front wheel toe setting as described in Section 24.

24 Wheel alignment and steering angles – general information

Definitions

1 A car's steering and suspension geometry is defined in three basic settings – all angles are expressed in degrees; the steering axis is

defined as an imaginary line drawn through the axis of the suspension strut, extended where necessary to contact the ground **(see illustration)**.

Camber

2 Camber is the angle between each roadwheel and a vertical line drawn through its centre and tyre contact patch, when viewed from the front or rear of the car. Positive camber is when the roadwheels are tilted outwards from the vertical at the top; negative camber is when they are tilted inwards.

3 Camber angle is only adjustable by loosening the front suspension subframe mounting bolts and moving it slightly to one side. This also alters the castor angle. The camber angle can be checked using a camber checking gauge.

Castor

4 Castor is the angle between the steering axis and a vertical line drawn through each roadwheel's centre and tyre contact patch, when viewed from the side of the car. Positive castor is when the steering axis is tilted so that it contacts the ground ahead of the vertical; negative castor is when it contacts the ground behind the vertical. Slight castor angle adjustment is possible by loosening the front suspension subframe bolts and moving it slightly to one side. This also alters the camber angle.

5 Castor is not easily adjustable, and is given for reference only; while it can be checked using a castor checking gauge, if the figure obtained is significantly different from that specified, the car must be taken for careful checking by a professional, as the fault can only be caused by wear or damage to the body or suspension components.

Toe

6 Toe is the difference, viewed from above, between lines drawn through the roadwheel centres and the car's centre-line. Toe-in is when the roadwheels point inwards, towards each other at the front, while toe-out is when they splay outwards from each other at the front.

7 The front wheel toe setting is adjusted by screwing the track rod(s) in/out of the outer balljoint(s) to alter the effective length of the track rod assembly.

8 Rear wheel toe setting is not adjustable, and is given for reference only. While it can be checked, if the figure obtained is significantly different from that specified, the car must be taken for careful checking by a professional, as the fault can only be caused by wear or damage to the body or suspension components.

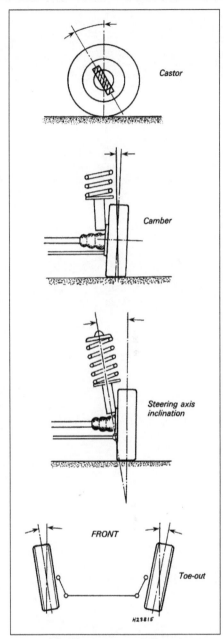

24.1 Front wheel geometry

Checking and adjustment

9 Due to the special measuring equipment necessary to check the wheel alignment, and the skill required to use it properly, the checking and adjustment of these settings is best left to a Skoda dealer or similar expert. Note that most tyre-fitting centres now possess sophisticated checking equipment.

Notes

Chapter 11
Bodywork and fittings

Contents

Degrees of difficulty

Easy, suitable for novice with little experience 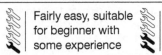	Fairly easy, suitable for beginner with some experience 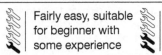	Fairly difficult, suitable for competent DIY mechanic	Difficult, suitable for experienced DIY mechanic	Very difficult, suitable for expert DIY or professional

Specifications

Torque wrench settings	Nm	lbf ft
Bonnet hinge bolts	20	15
Bonnet lock bolts	20	15
Door hinge pin nuts	30	22
Door lock bolts	20	15
Door mirror bolt	20	15
Front bumper bracket-to-bodywork bolts:		
Top corner and lower inner bolts	9	7
All other bolts	30	22
Seat mounting bolts	40	30
Seat belt lower anchor bolts	45	33
Seat belt upper anchor bolts (front)	35	26
Seat belt stalk mounting bolt (front)	22	16
Seat belt stalk mounting bolt (rear)	45	33
Seat belt inertia reel bolt (front)	35	26
Seat belt inertia reel bolt (left and right outer rear)	45	33
Seat belt inertia reel nut (centre rear)	35	26
Tailgate lock bolts.	20	15
Tailgate mounting bolts/nuts	20	15

* Do not re-use

1 General description

1 Two body types are covered by this manual – the five-door Hatchback and the five-door Estate. The body is of all-steel construction, and incorporates calculated impact crumple zones at the front and rear, with a central safety cell passenger compartment.

2 During manufacture, the underbody is treated with underseal and, as a further anti-rust aid, some of the more exposed body panels are galvanised. The bumpers and wheel arch liners are plastic mouldings, for durability and strength.

2 Maintenance – bodywork and underframe

1 The general condition of a vehicle's bodywork is the one thing that significantly affects its value. Maintenance is easy, but needs to be regular. Neglect, particularly after minor damage, can lead quickly to further deterioration and costly repair bills. It is important also to keep watch on those parts of the vehicle not immediately visible, for instance the underside, inside all the wheel arches, and the lower part of the engine compartment.

2 The basic maintenance routine for the bodywork is washing – preferably with a lot of water, from a hose. This will remove all the loose solids which may have stuck to the vehicle. It is important to flush these off in such a way as to prevent grit from scratching the finish. The wheel arches and underframe need washing in the same way, to remove any accumulated mud which will retain moisture and tend to encourage rust. Paradoxically enough, the best time to clean the underframe and wheel arches is in wet weather, when the mud is thoroughly wet and soft. In very wet weather, the underframe is usually cleaned of large accumulations automatically, and this is a good time for inspection.

3 Periodically, except on vehicles with a wax-based underbody protective coating, it is a good idea to have the whole of the underframe of the vehicle steam-cleaned, so that a thorough inspection can be carried out to see what minor repairs and renovations are necessary. Steam cleaning is available at many garages, and is necessary for the removal of the accumulation of oily grime, which sometimes is allowed to become thick in certain areas. If steam-cleaning facilities are not available, there are some excellent grease solvents available which can be brush-applied; the dirt can then be simply hosed off. Note that these methods should not be used on vehicles with wax-based underbody protective coating, or the coating will be removed. Such vehicles should be inspected annually, preferably just before Winter, when the underbody should be washed down, and any damage to the wax coating repaired. Ideally, a completely fresh coat should be applied.

4 After washing paintwork, wipe off with a chamois leather to give an unspotted clear finish. A coat of clear protective wax polish will give added protection against chemical pollutants in the air. If the paintwork sheen has dulled or oxidised, use a cleaner/polisher combination to restore the brilliance of the shine. This requires a little effort, but such dulling is usually caused because regular washing has been neglected. Care needs to be taken with metallic paintwork, as special non-abrasive cleaner/polisher is required to avoid damage to the finish. Always check that the door and ventilator opening drain holes and pipes are completely clear, so that water can be drained out. Brightwork should be treated in the same way as paintwork. Windscreens and windows can be kept clear of the smeary film which often appears, by proprietary glass cleaner. Never use any form of wax or other body or chromium polish on glass.

3 Maintenance – upholstery and carpets

1 Mats and carpets should be brushed or vacuum-cleaned regularly, to keep them free of grit. If they are badly stained, remove them from the vehicle for scrubbing or sponging, and make quite sure they are dry before refitting. Seats and interior trim panels can be kept clean by wiping with a damp cloth. If they do become stained (which can be more apparent on light-coloured upholstery), use a little liquid detergent and a soft nail brush to scour the grime out of the grain of the material. Do not forget to keep the headlining clean in the same way as the upholstery. When using liquid cleaners inside the vehicle, do not over-wet the surfaces being cleaned. Excessive damp could get into the seams and padded interior, causing stains, offensive odours or even rot. In addition, if the vehicle is fitted with a seat-heating system, seat cloth should not be wet-cleaned. You should instead use special cleaning agents such as dry foam to prevent damage to system components. If the inside of the vehicle gets wet accidentally, it is worthwhile taking some trouble to dry it out properly, particularly where carpets are involved. Do not leave oil or electric heaters inside the vehicle for this purpose.

4 Minor body damage – repair

Minor scratches

1 If the scratch is very superficial, and does not penetrate to the metal of the bodywork, repair is very simple. Lightly rub the area of the scratch with a paintwork renovator or a very fine cutting paste to remove loose paint from the scratch, and to clear the surrounding bodywork of wax polish. Rinse the area with clean water.

2 Apply touch-up paint to the scratch using a fine paint brush; continue to apply fine layers of paint until the surface of the paint in the scratch is level with the surrounding paintwork. Allow the new paint at least two weeks to harden, then blend it into the surrounding paintwork by rubbing the scratch area with a paintwork renovator or a very fine cutting paste. Finally, apply wax polish.

3 Where the scratch has penetrated right through to the metal of the bodywork, causing the metal to rust, a different repair technique is required. Remove any loose rust from the bottom of the scratch with a penknife, then apply rust-inhibiting paint to prevent the formation of rust in the future. Using a rubber or nylon applicator, fill the scratch with bodystopper paste. If required, this paste can be mixed with cellulose thinners to provide a very thin paste which is ideal for filling narrow scratches. Before the stopper-paste in the scratch hardens, wrap a piece of smooth cotton rag around the top of a finger. Dip the finger in cellulose thinners, and quickly sweep it across the surface of the stopper-paste in the scratch; this will ensure that the surface of the stopper-paste is slightly hollowed. The scratch can now be painted over as described earlier in this Section.

Dents

4 When deep denting of the vehicle's bodywork has taken place, the first task is to pull the dent out, until the affected bodywork almost attains its original shape. There is little point in trying to restore the original shape completely, as the metal in the damaged area will have stretched on impact, and cannot be reshaped fully to its original contour. It is better to bring the level of the dent up to a point which is about 3 mm below the level of the surrounding bodywork. In cases where the dent is very shallow anyway, it is not worth trying to pull it out at all. If the underside of the dent is accessible, it can be hammered out gently from behind, using a mallet with a wooden or plastic head. Whilst doing this, hold a suitable block of wood firmly against the outside of the panel, to absorb the impact from the hammer blows and thus prevent a large area of the bodywork from being 'belled-out'.

5 Should the dent be in a section of the bodywork which has a double skin, or some other factor making it inaccessible from behind, a different technique is called for. Drill several small holes through the metal inside the area – particularly in the deeper section. Then bolt long self-tapping screws into the holes, just sufficiently for them to gain a good purchase in the metal. Now the dent can be pulled out by pulling on the protruding heads of the bolts with a pair of pliers. Alternatively, suction tools that perform this function without requiring bodywork to be drilled are available from specialist suppliers.

6 The next stage of the repair is the removal of the paint from the damaged area, and from an inch or so of the surrounding 'sound' bodywork. This is accomplished most easily by using a wire brush or abrasive pad on a power drill, although it can be done just as effectively by hand, using sheets of abrasive paper. To complete the preparation for filling, score the surface of the bare metal with a screwdriver or the tang of a file. This will provide a good 'key' for the filler paste.

7 To complete the repair, see the Section on filling and respraying.

Rust holes or gashes

8 Remove all paint from the affected area, and from an inch or so of the surrounding 'sound' bodywork, using an abrasive pad or a wire brush on a power drill. If these are not available, a few sheets of abrasive paper will do the job most effectively. With the paint removed, you will be able to judge the severity of the corrosion, and therefore decide whether to renew the whole panel (if this is possible) or to repair the affected area. New body panels are not as expensive as most people think, and it is often quicker and more satisfactory to fit a new panel than to attempt to repair large areas of corrosion.

9 Remove all fittings from the affected area, except those which will act as a guide to the original shape of the damaged bodywork (eg, headlight shells, etc). Then, using tin snips or a hacksaw blade, remove all loose metal and any other metal badly affected by corrosion. Hammer the edges of the hole inwards, to create a slight depression for the filler paste.

10 Wire-brush the affected area to remove the powdery rust from the surface of the remaining metal. Paint the affected area with rust-inhibiting paint; if the back of the rusted area is accessible, treat this also.

11 Before filling can take place, it will be necessary to block the hole in some way. This can be achieved with aluminium or plastic mesh, or aluminium tape.

12 Aluminium or plastic mesh, or glass-fibre matting, is probably the best material to use for a large hole. Cut a piece to the approximate size and shape of the hole to be filled, then position it in the hole so that its edges are below the level of the surrounding bodywork. It can be retained in position by several blobs of filler paste around its periphery.

13 Aluminium tape should be used for small or very narrow holes. Pull a piece off the roll, trim it to the approximate size and shape required, then pull off the backing paper (if used) and stick the tape over the hole; it can be overlapped if the thickness of one piece is insufficient. Burnish down the edges of the tape with the handle of a screwdriver or similar, to ensure that the tape is securely attached to the metal underneath.

Filling and respraying

14 Before using this Section, see the Sections on dent, deep scratch, rust holes and gash repairs.

15 Many types of bodyfiller are available,

but generally speaking, those proprietary kits which contain a tin of filler paste and a tube of resin hardener are best for this type of repair which can be used directly from the tube. A wide, flexible plastic or nylon applicator will be found invaluable for imparting a smooth and well-contoured finish to the surface of the filler.

16 Mix up a little filler on a clean piece of card or board – measure the hardener carefully (follow the maker's instructions on the pack), otherwise the filler will set too rapidly or too slowly. Using the applicator, apply the filler paste to the prepared area; draw the applicator across the surface of the filler to achieve the correct contour and to level the surface. When a contour that approximates to the correct one is achieved, stop working the paste – if you carry on too long, the paste will become sticky and begin to 'pick-up' on the applicator. Continue to add thin layers of filler paste at 20-minute intervals, until the level of the filler is just proud of the surrounding bodywork.

17 Once the filler has hardened, the excess can be removed using a metal plane or file. From then on, progressively-finer grades of abrasive paper should be used, starting with a 40-grade production paper, and finishing with a 400-grade wet-and-dry paper. Always wrap the abrasive paper around a flat rubber, cork, or wooden block – otherwise the surface of the filler will not be completely flat. During the smoothing of the filler surface, the wet-and-dry paper should be periodically rinsed in water. This will ensure that a very smooth finish is imparted to the filler at the final stage.

18 At this stage, the 'dent' should be surrounded by a ring of bare metal, which in turn should be encircled by the finely 'feathered' edge of the good paintwork. Rinse the repair area with clean water or a proprietary panel wiping fluid, until all the dust produced by the rubbing-down operation has gone.

19 Spray the whole area with a light coat of primer – this will show up any imperfections in the surface of the filler. Repair these imperfections with fresh filler paste or bodystopper, and again smooth the surface with abrasive paper. If bodystopper is used, it can be mixed with cellulose thinners, to form a thin paste which is ideal for filling small holes. Repeat this spray-and-repair procedure until you are satisfied that the surface of the filler, and the feathered edge of the paintwork, are perfect. Clean the repair area with clean water, and allow to dry fully.

20 The repair area is now ready for final spraying. Paint spraying must be carried out in a warm, dry, windless and dust-free atmosphere. This condition can be created artificially if you have access to a large indoor working area, but if you are forced to work in the open, you will have to pick your day very carefully. If you are working indoors, dousing the floor in the work area with water will help

to settle the dust which would otherwise be in the atmosphere. If the repair area is confined to one body panel, mask off the surrounding panels; this will help to minimise the effects of a slight mismatch in paint colours. Bodywork fittings (e.g. chrome strips, door handles etc) will also need to be masked off. Use genuine masking tape, and several thickness of newspaper, for the masking operations.

21 Before starting to spray, agitate the aerosol can thoroughly, then spray a test area (an old tin, or similar) until the technique is mastered. Cover the repair area with a thick coat of primer; the thickness should be built up using several thin layers of paint, rather than one thick one. Using 400 grade wet-and-dry paper, rub down the surface of the primer until it is smooth. While doing this, the work area should be thoroughly doused with water, and the wet-and-dry paper periodically rinsed in water. Allow to dry before spraying on more paint.

22 Spray on the top coat, again building up the thickness by using several thin layers of paint. Start spraying at one edge of the repair area, and then, using a side-to-side motion, work until the whole repair area and about 2 inches of the surrounding original paintwork is covered. Remove all masking material 10 to 15 minutes after spraying on the final coat of paint.

23 Allow the new paint at least two weeks to harden, then, using a paintwork renovator or a very fine cutting paste, blend the edges of the paint into the existing paintwork. Finally, apply wax polish.

Plastic components

24 With the use of more and more plastic body components by the vehicle manufacturers (e.g. bumpers, spoilers, and in some cases major body panels), rectification of more serious damage to such items has become a matter of either entrusting repair work to a specialist in this field, or renewing complete components. Repair of such damage by the DIY owner is not feasible, owing to the cost of the equipment and materials required for effecting such repairs. The basic technique involves making a groove along the line of the crack in the plastic, using a rotary burr in a power drill. The damaged part is then welded back together, using a hot air gun to heat up and fuse a plastic filler rod into the groove. Any excess plastic is then removed, and the area rubbed down to a smooth finish. It is important that a filler rod of the correct plastic is used, as body components can be made of a variety of different types (e.g. polycarbonate, ABS, polypropylene).

25 Damage of a less serious nature (abrasions, minor cracks etc) can be repaired by the DIY owner using a two-part epoxy filler repair material which can be used directly from the tube. Once mixed in equal proportions, this is used in similar fashion to the bodywork filler used on metal panels. The filler is usually cured in twenty to thirty minutes, ready for sanding and painting.

26 If the owner is renewing a complete component himself, or if he has repaired it with epoxy filler, he will be left with the problem of finding a suitable paint for finishing which is compatible with the type of plastic used. At one time, the use of a universal paint was not possible, owing to the complex range of plastics met with in body component applications. Standard paints, generally speaking, will not bond to plastic or rubber satisfactorily, but professional matched paints, to match any plastic or rubber finish, can be obtained from some dealers. However, it is now possible to obtain a plastic body parts finishing kit which consists of a pre-primer treatment, a primer and coloured top coat. Full instructions are normally supplied with a kit, but basically the method of use is to first apply the pre-primer to the component concerned, and allow it to dry for up to 30 minutes. Then the primer is applied, and left to dry for about an hour before finally applying the special-coloured top coat. The result is a correctly coloured component, where the paint will flex with the plastic or rubber, a property that standard paint does not normally possess.

5 Major body damage – repair

1 Where serious damage has occurred, or large areas need renewal due to neglect, it means that complete new panels will need welding-in, and this is best left to professionals. If the damage is due to impact,

8.1a Remove the intake hood screw (arrowed)

8.2 Open the coupling and disconnect the bonnet release cable (arrowed)

7.3 Bonnet-to-hinge bolts (arrowed)

it will also be necessary to check completely the alignment of the bodyshell, and this can only be carried out accurately by a Skoda dealer or specialist bodyshop using special jigs. If the body is left misaligned, it is primarily dangerous, as the car will not handle properly, and secondly, uneven stresses will be imposed on the steering, suspension and possibly transmission, causing abnormal wear, or complete failure, particularly to such items as the tyres.

6 Door rattles – tracing and rectification

1 Check first that the door is not loose at the hinges, and that the latch is holding the door firmly in position. Check also that the door lines up with the aperture in the body.

8.1b Remove the plastic panel at the rear of the lock mechanism

8.3 Undo the bolts (arrowed) and withdraw the lock mechanism

If the door is out of alignment, adjust it with reference to Section 21.
2 If the latch is holding the door in the correct position, but the latch still rattles, the lock mechanism is worn and should be renewed.
3 Other rattles from the door could be caused by wear in the window operating mechanism, interior lock mechanism, loose glass channels or loose wiring.

7 Bonnet – removal, refitting and adjustment

Removal

1 Fully open the bonnet, then place some cardboard or rags beneath the corners by the hinges to protect the bodywork.
2 Prop the bonnet open using two stout lengths of wood, one positioned at each corner. Alternatively, enlist the help of an assistant to support the bonnet.
3 Mark the location of the hinges with a pencil, then slacken the four hinge-to-bonnet retaining bolts (two each side) **(see illustration)**.
4 Support the bonnet as the securing bolts are unscrewed, then withdraw the bonnet from the car.

Refitting and adjustment

5 Refitting is a reversal of removal. Ensure that the hinges are adjusted to their original positions. Close the bonnet very carefully initially; misalignment may cause the edges of the bonnet to damage the bodywork. If necessary, adjust the hinges to their original positions and check that the bonnet is level with the surrounding bodywork. If necessary, adjust the height of the bonnet front edge by screwing the rubber buffers in or out.
6 Check that the bonnet lock operates in a satisfactory manner. In particular, check that the safety catch holds the bonnet after the bonnet release cable has been pulled.

8 Bonnet lock and release cable – removal and refitting

Bonnet lock

Removal

1 Remove the plastic panel at the rear of the lock mechanism (above the radiator). Unscrew the intake hood, then undo the 2 screws in the middle and the screw at each end **(see illustrations)**.
2 Unclip the coupling mounted on the lock carrier, open the coupling and disconnect the bonnet release cable **(see illustration)**.
3 Slacken the nuts and withdraw the 2 securing bolts and move the lock mechanism away from the slam panel **(see illustration)**. Disconnect the wiring plug and bonnet release cable as the assembly is withdrawn.

Refitting

4 Reconnect the lock wiring plug and bonnet release cable.

5 Position the lock mechanism on the slam panel, and tighten the retaining bolts to the specified torque.

6 Reconnect the cable as described in this Section, then refit plastic panel at the rear of the lock mechanism. Check the action of the release cable/lock before closing the bonnet.

Cable

Removal

7 Pull the release handle to open the bonnet, then use a small, flat-bladed screwdriver to release the retaining clip, and remove the handle **(see illustrations)**.

8 Disconnect the cable from the handle.

9 Unclip the coupling mounted on the lock carrier, open the coupling and disconnect the bonnet release cable **(see illustration 8.2)**.

10 Free the release cable from all its retaining clips in the engine compartment and wheel arch.

11 Attach a suitable length of strong cord to the end of the release cable at the release handle end, then carefully draw the cable through into the engine compartment.

12 Undo the cord from the cable, and leave the cord ends exposed in the engine compartment and footwell.

Refitting

13 Refit in the reverse order of removal. Tie the inner end of the cable to the exposed cord in the engine compartment, carefully pull the cable through to the release handle, then untie the cord.

14 When positioning the cable in the engine compartment and wheel arch, ensure that it is re-routed correctly to avoid kinks, sharp bends and chafing. Check for satisfactory operation of the cable and the lock before closing the bonnet. Ensure that the bonnet locks properly when closed, and also that the safety catch operates correctly when the bonnet release cable is actuated.

8.7a Use a screwdriver to release the retaining clip

9 Bumpers and radiator grille
– removal and refitting

Front bumper

1 Slacken the front roadwheel bolts, jack up the front of the vehicle and support it securely on axle stands (see *Jacking and vehicle support*). Remove the front roadwheels.

2 Undo the 3 screws each side securing the front lower section of the wheel arch liner to the bumper **(see illustration)**.

3 Remove the headlights as described in Chapter 12 Section 10.

4 Remove the grilles at each end of the bumper **(see illustration)** and undo the screw exposed in the aperture.

9.2 Undo the screws between the bumper and the wheel arch liner

8.7b Pull the clip out to release the handle

5 On models from 11/08, it may also be necessary to remove the fog/daytime driving lights mounted within the bumper.

6 Undo the 3 Torx bolts at the top edge of the bumper **(see illustration)**.

7 Prise up the centre pin and lever out the 2 expansion rivets at the top on each side. On models from 11/08 these rivets were replaced by screws **(see illustration)**.

8 Undo the 2 screws underneath securing the front section of the wheel arch liner each side **(see illustration)**.

9 Undo the 3 expansion rivets underneath securing the lower rear edge of the bumper in the centre **(see illustration)**.

10 Pull back the wheel arch liners, then undo 1 screw each side securing the lower section of the bumper **(see illustration)**.

11 With the help of an assistant, pull out

9.4 Remove the bumper grilles and undo the screw in the recess

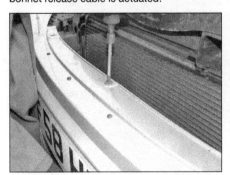

9.6 Undo the 3 bolts on the top of the bumper

9.7 Lever out the expansion rivets at each side of the bumper

9.8 Undo the 2 screws (arrowed) securing the front of the bumper to the wheel arch liner...

9.9 ... and lever out the 3 expansion rivets underneath

9.10 Pull back the wheel arch liner and undo the screw (arrowed)

9.15a Undo the 2 bolts on the left-hand side...

9.15b ... and the 2 bolts on the right-hand side

9.16a Release the clips and remove the cover strips at each end of the bumper

9.16b Remove the 2 screws behind the cover strips

the rear edges, then pull the front bumper forwards, and withdraw it from the car.

12 Disconnect any wiring plugs as the bumper is withdrawn. On models with headlight washers, depress the release clip and disconnect the washer hose as the bumper is withdrawn.

13 Refitting is a reversal of removal. On completion, check for satisfactory operation of the accessory components as applicable.

Rear bumper

Hatchback models

14 Remove the body-mounted tail lights as described in Chapter 12 Section 10 and the tailgate/luggage compartment cover.

15 Remove the side trim panels in the luggage compartment and undo the bolts behind **(see illustrations)**. Those on the

left-hand side also locate the frame for the CD changer where fitted.

16 Remove the cover strips located above and at each end of the bumper by carefully releasing the 4 clips at the top and pushing the strip down to release the lower clips. Remove the two screws **(see illustrations)**.

17 These covers are not fitted to models after 10/08. Instead remove the 2 expanding rivets mounted on the top of the bumper at either end.

18 Undo the 4 screws in the wheel arch area each side and the 1 screw securing the mudflap to the wheel arch liner **(see illustration)**.

19 From under the bumper, undo the 4 screws in the centre, and the 2 screws on the right-hand side **(see illustrations)**.

20 With the help of an assistant, pull the

bumper rearwards and withdraw it from the rear of the car. Disconnect any wiring plugs as the bumper is withdrawn.

21 Where parking aid sensors are fitted, disconnect the wiring plug from the control unit mounted on the left-hand rear wheel arch (exposed when the side trim panel is removed) and withdraw the wiring through the grommet in the rear body panel as the bumper is removed.

22 Refit in the reverse order of removal. Loosely fit all retaining bolts and bolts before fully-tightening them.

Estate models

23 Remove the trim panels from the bottom of the D-pillar as described in Section 30. Remove the body-mounted tail lights as described in Chapter 12 Section 10.

24 Remove the side trim panels in the

9.18 Undo the screws (arrowed) securing the bumper to the wheel arch liner

9.19a Undo the screws (arrowed) in the centre of the bumper...

9.19b ... and the 2 screws (arrowed) on the right-hand side

luggage compartment and undo the bolts behind **(see illustration)**.

25 Undo the 4 screws each side in the wheel arch area and the 1 screw securing the mudflap to the wheel arch liner.

26 Remove the 2 expansion rivets located at the top of the bumper at either end.

27 From under the bumper, undo the 4 securing bolts in the centre, and the 2 bolts securing the panel on the right-hand side.

28 With the help of an assistant, pull the bumper rearwards and remove it from the vehicle (see paragraph 21 above if parking aid sensors are fitted).

29 Refit in the reverse order of removal. Loosely fit all retaining bolts and screws before fully-tightening them.

Radiator grille

30 Open the bonnet then undo the screw at the top edge of the grille **(see illustration)**.

31 Using a pair of pliers, carefully release the clips around the inside of the grille **(see illustration)**.

32 Use a suitable wedge to release the clips at the lower edge **(see illustration)**.

33 Refitting is a reversal of removal.

10 Lock carrier – removal and refitting

General information

1 The lock carrier is the name given to the section of bodywork that is mounted across the front of the engine compartment. A number of major components, including the bonnet lock mechanism, front bumper, radiator, automatic transmission fluid cooler and front light clusters are mounted on the lock carrier. The construction of the Skoda Octavia bodywork is such that the lock carrier and its associated components can be removed without being extensively dismantled. In addition, the lock carrier can be moved forward several centimetres to a 'Service position' without having to disconnect the various hoses, pipes and wiring harnesses that serve the components mounted on it. In this position, access to components at the front of the engine compartment is greatly improved.

Removal

2 Refer to Section 9 and remove the front bumper. Undo the 3 screws and remove the bumper guide sections at each side **(see illustration)**. Remove the engine undershield.

3 Release the pipe from the intake hood **(see illustrations)**.

4 Disconnect the temperature sensor plug.

5 Disconnect the bonnet cable coupling mounted on the lock carrier and disconnect the plug from the switch for the flap lock **(see illustration)**.

6 Undo the bolt at the top of the lock carrier

9.24 Undo the bolts behind the side trim panels (right-hand side shown)

9.31 Release the clips around the inside of the grille

10.2 Undo the screws (outer two arrowed) and remove the bumper guide sections

10.3b ... and release the pipe

9.30 Undo the screw (arrowed)

9.32 Carefully release the clips at the lower edge

on each side, the bolt behind each bumper guide section, and the 4 bolts on the front at each side. Loosen the radiator and the condenser from the lock carrier and secure to a suitable part of the engine compartment using cable-ties or wire.

7 Withdraw the lock carrier from the front of the vehicle.

10.3a Unclip the top of the intake hood...

10.5 Disconnect the bonnet cable coupling

10.12a Undo the bolt at the top of the lock carrier at each side

10.12b Undo the 4 bolts (arrowed) on the front of the lock carrier on each side

10.13 Insert the fabricated tool (arrowed) and pull the lock carrier forwards

Refitting

8 Refit in the reverse order of removal. Check the operation of the front lights, and the bonnet lock and safety catch, on completion.

Setting the Service position

Note: *To carry out this procedure, Skoda use a tool to hold the lock carrier in position. Alternatively it will be necessary to fabricate two service tools, using two 10 mm diameter 300 mm lengths of threaded rod and a selection of hex nuts.*

9 Refer to Section 9 and remove the front bumper and unbolt the bumper guide sections at each side. Remove the engine undershield.
10 Disconnect the bonnet cable coupling mounting on the lock carrier and release the pipe from the intake hood.
11 Protect the corner of each front wing using adhesive tape.
12 Undo the bolt at the top of the lock carrier

on each side, the bolt behind each bumper guide section, and the 4 bolts on the front at each side **(see illustrations)**.
13 With the help of an assistant, carefully draw the lock carrier forwards approximately 10 cm **(see illustration)**.
14 The lock carrier can be refitted by following the removal procedure in reverse. Ensure that all fixings are tightened to the correct torque wrench setting, where specified. On completion, have the headlights checked for correct beam alignment.

11 Wheel arch liners – removal and refitting

Removal

1 Loosen the relevant wheel bolts, then raise

the front or rear of the car and support on axle stands (see *Jacking and vehicle support*). Remove the roadwheel.
2 The liner is secured by various fasteners. It may be helpful to remove any accumulated dirt to make locating these easier.
3 Undo and remove the liner securing screws.
4 Lower the liner out of position, and manoeuvre it out from under the wing.

Refitting

5 Refitting is a reversal of removal. Renew any fasteners which were broken on removal.

12 Tailgate – removal and refitting

Removal

1 Remove the lower trim panel from the tailgate. Undo the screw at the tailgate handle and using a suitable wedge carefully prise the sides and top of the panel from the clips in the tailgate and remove the trim **(see illustration)**. This operation is similar for the estate model.
2 Remove the luggage compartment cover.
3 Remove the upper trim panel from the tailgate. Remove the screws at the lower part of the trim panel, unscrew the supports for the luggage compartment cover, and using a suitable wedge carefully prise the sides and top of the panel from the clips in the tailgate and remove **(see illustrations)**.
4 Unplug the wiring connector and pull the cable from the tailgate.

12.1 Unclip the lower trim panel from the tailgate

12.3a Unscrew the supports for the luggage cover

12.3b Undo the screw each side securing the upper trim panel...

12.3c ... release the clips, and remove the panel

12.7 Tailgate hinge retaining bolts (arrowed)

5 Remove the gas support struts as described in Section 14.
6 Mark the relationship between the tailgate and the hinges by drawing around the outside of each hinge with a marker pen.
7 Enlist the aid of an assistant to support the tailgate, then unscrew and remove the hinge-to-tailgate retaining bolts **(see illustration)**, and lift the tailgate clear.

Refitting

8 Refit in the reverse order of removal. Check the lid for correct alignment, and if necessary loosen off the hinge bolts to adjust, then retighten them; there should be an even gap between the outside edge of the tailgate and the surrounding bodywork.

13 Tailgate lock – removal and refitting

1 Remove the lower trim from inside the tailgate, see Section 12.

Lock unit

Removal

2 Disconnect the lock wiring plug.
3 Mark the fitted position of the lock with a marker pen, then unscrew the retaining nuts and withdraw the lock unit from the tailgate.

Refitting

4 Refit in the reverse order of removal.

Lock motor – Estate models

Removal

5 Undo the 2 Torx screws and withdraw the lock from the rear sill panel. Undo the 2 screws, release the wiring plug, and separate the motor from the lock unit **(see illustration)**.

Refitting

6 Refit in the reverse order of removal.

Emergency tailgate lock release

7 Fold the rear seats forward, and from inside the luggage compartment unclip the lock cover. Unlock by pressing the emergency release lever downwards.

14 Tailgate support strut(s) – removal and refitting

Removal

1 On all models, disconnect the strut(s) at the upper and lower balljoints by lifting (not removing) the locking elements, and pulling the strut from the ball-stud **(see illustration)**.
2 If a strut is defective in operation, it must be renewed. Do not attempt to dismantle and repair the strut. Note that the struts are filled with pressurised gas, so should not be punctured or disposed of by incineration.

13.5 Tailgate lock retaining screws (arrowed)

Refitting

3 Refit in the reverse order of removal. Ensure that the strut is securely engaged with the balljoints.

15 Door trim panel – removal and refitting

Note: *Switch off ignition and all electrical items before commencing work.*

Front door

Driver's door

1 Using a blunt, flat-bladed tool, carefully prise up the handle recess from the door trim. Alternatively, pull sharply upwards on the interior handle to release the retaining clips.

15.1 Prise or pull up the interior door handle to remove

15.3 Prise off the handle cover

14.1 Use a screwdriver to lift the locking element on the strut

Where applicable, disconnect any wiring plugs as the trim is removed **(see illustration)**.
2 Undo the 3 Torx bolts exposed in the handle recess aperture **(see illustration)**.

Passenger's door

3 Using a blunt, flat-bladed tool, carefully prise out the pull-handle cover **(see illustration)**.
4 Undo the 2 bolts in the handle recess **(see illustration)**.

Both doors

5 Unclip the cover over the treble speaker, disconnect the wiring plug and remove the screw exposed in the recess **(see illustrations)**.
6 Undo the 2 Torx bolts at the base of the door trim in the centre **(see illustration)**.
7 Pull the trim away from the door frame at

15.2 Undo the 3 bolts (arrowed) exposed in the aperture

15.4 Undo the 2 bolts (arrowed)

15.5a Unclip the speaker cover...

15.5b ... disconnect the wiring plug...

15.5c ... and undo the screw in the recess

15.6 Undo the 2 bolts at the base of the door panel

15.7 Carefully pull the trim panel from the door, releasing the clips

15.8 Unhook the cable from the door handle

the lower, front and rear edges, releasing the retaining clips, then lift the trim panel up squarely **(see illustration)**. Be prepared for some of the clips to break as the trim is removed.

8 Unhook the operating cable from the rear of the interior handle as it becomes accessible **(see illustration)**.

9 Note their fitted positions, and disconnect the various wiring plugs as the panel is withdrawn.

10 Refit in the reverse order of removal, noting the following points:
a) *Ensure that the wiring and connections are secure and correctly routed, clear of the window regulator and latch/lock components.*
b) *Renew any damage retaining clips.*

Rear door

11 On models with manual windows, pull the spring collar rearwards and slide the window handle from the shaft **(see illustrations)**. Note the fitted position of the handle for refitting.

12 Using a blunt, flat-bladed tool, carefully prise out the pull handle cover **(see illustration 15.3)**.

13 Undo the 2 bolts in the handle recess **(see illustration 15.4)**.

14 Unclip the cover over the treble speaker, disconnect the wiring plug and remove the screw exposed in the recess.

15 Pull the trim away from the door frame at the lower, front and rear edges, releasing the retaining clips, then lift the trim panel up squarely. Be prepared for some of the clips to break as the trim is removed.

16 Unhook the operating cable from the rear of the interior handle as it becomes accessible **(see illustration 15.8)**.

17 Note their fitted positions, and disconnect the various wiring plugs as the panel is withdrawn.

18 Check the door trim for any missing or broken clips, and renew where necessary.

19 Refit in the reverse order of removal, noting the following points:
a) *Ensure that the wiring and connections are secure and correctly routed, clear of the window regulator and latch/lock components.*
b) *The window winder handle (where fitted) should be positioned at approximately ± 5° from the horizontal pointing forwards with the window closed.*

16 Door lock – removal and refitting

Removal

1 Refer to Section 18 and remove the door carrier assembly.

2 Disconnect the lock wiring plug.

3 Undo the 2 Torx bolts on the door edge and withdraw the lock **(see illustrations)**.

4 If required, the interior handle cable can be detached by unclipping from the operating lever on the lock assembly **(see illustration)**.

Refitting

5 Refitting is a reversal of the removal

15.11a Pull the spring collar rearwards...

15.11b ... and remove the handle

16.3a Undo the 2 Torx bolts on the door's edge

16.3b Withdraw the lock mechanism

16.4 Unhook the cable from the lock mechanism (lock removed for clarity)

procedure. Check that the door striker enters the lock centrally when the door is closed, and if necessary adjust the position of the striker.

17 Door handles and lock cylinder – removal and refitting

Exterior handles

Removal

1 Remove the lock cylinder/housing as described in this Section.
2 Undo the clip and swivel the handle from the door **(see illustrations)**.

Refitting

3 Refitting is a reverse of removal. Note the door handle should remain in the 'open' position. Any attempt to close the handle will result in damage to the lock bracket.
4 Refit the lock cylinder/housing as described in this Section.

Lock cylinder/housing

Note: *There is a risk that the retaining screws could fall into the door if they are completely removed. Retrieval would require the removal of the carrier assembly.*
Note: *The door handle should remain in the 'open' position. Any attempt to close the handle will result in damage to the lock bracket.*

Removal

5 Remove the caps from the door edge. Loosen the lower screw but do not undo completely. Pull out the exterior handle and loosen the upper retaining screw approximately 3.5 turns. Insert the key into the lock, turn clockwise 90 degrees and pull the lock from the door. If the lock does not withdraw immediately, continue to loosen the bottom retaining screw (though not removing completely) until the lock can be removed **(see illustrations)**.

Refitting

6 Insert the lock cylinder/housing into the aperture, and gradually tighten the retaining screws.

Interior handles

7 Refer to Section 15.

17.2a Use a screwdriver to release the clip...

18 Door carrier assembly – removal and refitting

Removal

1 Remove the door inner trim panel as described in Section 15.
2 Remove the lock cylinder and door handle as described in Section 17.
3 Lever out the plastic caps (1 at each end of the carrier), and align the window so the spreader pin and spreader plug are visible **(see illustrations)**. The window needs to be approximately two thirds of the way up – the electric window switch plug can be reconnected in order to move the window.
4 Screw a 5 mm bolt, 70 mm long, into the

17.2b ... and swivel the handle from the door

17.5a Remove the caps (arrowed) from the door edge

17.5b Loosen the lower screw

17.5c Using the ignition key, withdraw the lock from the door

18.3a Lever out the plastic caps

18.3b Align the window so the spreader pin and plug are visible

18.4 Remove the spreader pin with a 5 mm bolt

18.5 Remove the spreader plug with an 8 mm bolt

18.7a Pull the rubber gaiter from the A-pillar...

18.7b ... and disconnect the wiring plug

window spreader pin and pull it from the spreader plug **(see illustration)**. Discard the pin – a new one must be fitted.

5 Screw an 8 mm bolt, 80 mm long, into the spreader plug and pull the plug from the window clamp/regulator **(see illustration)**. Discard the plug – a new one must be fitted.

6 Lift the window glass by hand and secure to the door using sticky tape.

7 Pull the rubber gaiter from the A-pillar and disconnect the wiring plugs **(see illustrations)**.

8 Using a 10 mm drill, carefully drill out the rivets around the edge of the carrier assembly **(see illustration)**.

9 Pulling the carrier assembly forward slightly, disconnect the wiring plugs for the door lock mechanism and door mirror (speaker on rear doors). The cable that connects the door lock to the interior handle can be pulled through

the hole in the carrier as the carrier panel is withdrawn.

Refitting

10 Refitting is a reversal of removal.

19 Door window glass and regulator – removal and refitting

Window glass

Removal

1 Remove the door trim as described in Section 15 and remove the weather strip at the base of the glass **(see illustration)**.

2 Lever out the plastic caps, and align the window so the spreader pin/plug is visible **(see illustrations 18.3a and 18.3b)**.

3 Screw a 5 mm bolt, 70 mm long, into the window spreader pin and pull it from the plug **(see illustration 18.4)**. Discard the pin – a new one must be fitted.

4 Screw an 8 mm bolt, 80 mm long, into the spreader plug and pull the plug from the window clamp/regulator**(see illustration 18.5)**. Discard the plug – a new one must be fitted.

5 Pull the rear of the window glass upwards and manoeuvre it from the door. To facilitate removal, you may need to remove both the internal and external weather seals from the base of the window. If so, these can be carefully prised out.

Refitting

6 Fit the new spreader plug into the window fitting, then push the new spreader pin into place until it's flush with the plug **(see illustrations)**.

18.8 Using a 10 mm drill, drill out the rivets around the edge of the door carrier

19.1 Remove the weather strip at the base of the glass

19.6a Press in the spreader pin...

19.6b ... until it's flush with the spreader plug

7 Lower the window into place, then gently push the window down to engage it with the regulator.

8 The remainder of refitting is a reversal of removal. On models with electric rear windows, initialise the window positions as described in Chapter 5, Section 3.

Regulator

9 The regulator is integral with the carrier assembly. Follow instructions for removing the carrier assembly as described in Section 18. The regulator can then be removed.

20 Door window lift motors –
removal and refitting

Removal

1 Remove the door inner trim panel as described in Section 15.

2 Disconnect the wiring plugs from the motor.

3 Remove the 3 fixing screws **(see illustration)** and remove the motor from the carrier assembly.

Refitting

4 Refitting is a reversal of removal.

5 After refitting, the lifting mechanism will need to be reset as follows. Switch the ignition on and off. Switch the ignition on again and raise the window until it reaches the stop at the top of its travel. Continue to press the window switch for approximately a further 3 seconds.

21.2a Remove the screw from the door check strap (arrowed)...

21 Doors –
removal and refitting

Note: *The doors are heavy – the help of an assistant is essential.*

Removal

Front doors

1 Pull the wiring loom rubber gaiter from the door pillar and disconnect the wiring plug **(see illustrations 18.7a and 18.7b)**.

2 Remove the nuts from the upper and lower hinges and remove the screw from the door check strap **(see illustrations)**.

3 Lift the door upwards from place.

Rear doors

4 The procedure is identical to that described for front doors.

Refitting

5 Refitting is a reversal of the removal procedure. On completion, shut the door and check it for closure and alignment. Check the depth at which the striker enters the lock. If adjustment is required, slacken the securing bolts and reposition the striker plate.

22 Windscreen, rear window glass and rear side window glass – general information

1 The windscreen, rear window glass and rear side window glass are directly bonded to the metalwork. Their removal and refitting requires the use of special tools not readily available to the home mechanic. This work should therefore be left to a Skoda dealer, or a specialist glass renewal company.

23 Sunroof –
general

1 A sliding/tilting sunroof is fitted to some models. When fitted correctly, the roof

21.2b ... the nut from the upper hinge...

20.3 Remove the 3 screws (arrowed) and remove the motor

panel in the fully closed position should be level with, or no more than 1.0 mm lower than, the roof panel at the leading edge. The rear edge must be level with, or no more than 1.0 mm higher than, the roof panel at the rear.

2 Removal and refitting, and adjustments to the roof panel, are best entrusted to a Skoda dealer or specialist, as specialised tools are required.

3 The sunroof panel motor can be removed and refitted as described in Chapter 12 Section 17. If the motor malfunctions when the roof panel is in the open position, it can be wound shut manually; refer to Chapter 12 Section 17 or the Owners Handbook supplied with the vehicle.

Drain tubes

4 It is advisable to check the sunroof water drain tubes on a periodic basis. If they become blocked, they may be cleared by probing them with a length of suitable cable (an old speedometer drive cable is ideal).

5 The front drain tubes terminate just below the A-pillars, between the pillar and the door – cleaning is carried out from the sunroof end.

6 The rear drain tubes terminate in the water channel for the tailgate (accessible when the tailgate is open). Cleaning is carried out from the bottom end of the tube.

21.2c ... and from the lower hinge

24.2a Release the clips at the rear of the mirror housing

24.2b Lift the housing from the mirror assembly

24.3 Remove the 2 screws (left-hand one arrowed) at the base of the assembly

24 Door mirror components – removal and refitting

Mirror housing

Models up to 10/08

1 Remove the mirror as described in this Section.
2 Remove the mirror housing by carefully releasing the clips and removing the mirror housing upwards **(see illustrations)**.
3 Remove the 2 screws at the bottom of the housing **(see illustration)**.
4 Remove the lower part with the indicator repeater light and disconnect the plug connection **(see illustration)**.
5 Refitting is a reversal of removal

Models from 11/08

6 Remove the mirror as described in this Section.
7 Remove the 2 screws and unclip the housing using a screwdriver **(see illustration)**. Remove the mirror housing upwards.
8 To remove the lower section with the indicator lens, remove the 2 screws and release the 2 clips at the front and the one at the rear, and disconnect the wiring plug **(see illustrations)**.
9 Refitting is a reversal of removal.

Mirror

⚠ **Warning: Wear gloves and eye protection when carrying out this operation, particularly if the mirror glass is broken.**

10 Press in the bottom of the mirror, then insert a flat-bladed blunt tool behind the mirror, and carefully prise the upper part of the mirror from the retaining clips**(see illustration)**.
11 Disconnect the heater element wiring plugs (where fitted) as the mirror is withdrawn.
12 To refit, reconnect the wiring plugs, and press firmly at the centre of the mirror glass to engage the retaining clip. On completion, check the operation of the mirror adjustment mechanism using the adjustment knob/buttons.

Complete assembly

13 Remove the door inner trim panel as described in Section 15.
14 Release the mirror wiring loom from any retaining clips, and disconnect the wiring plug.
15 Carefully prise the triangular trim from the top, front of the door **(see illustration)**.

24.4 Remove the indicator section, unplugging the wiring as it is withdrawn

24.7 Remove the 2 upper screws and unclip the mirror housing

24.8a Remove the 2 screws within the assembly...

24.8b ... and unclip the indicator lens

24.8c Undo the wiring plug as the lens is withdrawn

24.10 Use a flat-bladed tool to prise the mirror glass from the retaining clips

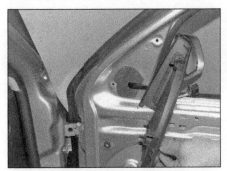

24.15 Prise the triangular trim from the door

24.16 Undo the retaining bolts

25.2 Prise up the gear lever gaiter

16 Undo the retaining bolts and withdraw the mirror from the door. Guide the wiring loom through as the mirror is withdrawn **(see illustration)**.

17 Refitting the mirror is a reversal of the removal procedure. Check the operation of the mirror adjustment on completion.

25 Centre console – removal and refitting

Removal

1 Before commencing work, ensure the ignition and all electrical items are switched off.

Manual transmission models

2 Using a blunt, flat-bladed tool prise up the gear lever gaiter from the surround trim **(see illustration)**. Pull the gaiter up around the gear lever knob.

3 Where fitted lift the gear lever insulation panel from around the lever. Note the arrow on the insulation panel indicating direction of travel.

Automatic transmission models

4 Using a blunt, flat-bladed tool, prise up the selector lever surround trim, and position it to one side.

All models

5 Pull the gear/selector lever surround panel from the console **(see illustration)**. Disconnect any wiring plugs as the panel is withdrawn.

6 Undo the 2 retaining bolts and pull the ashtray/storage tray from place **(see illustrations)**. Disconnect any wiring plugs as the tray is withdrawn.

7 Remove the side panels. Undo the retaining screw at the front of each panel in the footwell, remove the ashtray ahead of the gear lever and undo the screws revealed in the aperture, slide the panel forwards to release the clips at the base of the facia, and release the Velcro attachment located on each side ahead of the gear lever **(see illustration)**.

8 Remove the 2 screws at the front of the centre console (1 each side), where it meets the base of the facia panel **(see illustration)**.

9 Remove the rear ashtray and disconnect the wiring plug for the ashtray illumination or the rear seat heating control (where fitted).

10 Carefully prise out the rear air vent/ storage compartment (as fitted), and remove the 2 screws that are exposed in the aperture **(see illustration)**.

25.5 Pull up the gear/selector lever surround panel

25.6a Undo the 2 bolts exposed by removing the gear/selector lever surround panel

25.6b Pull the ashtray from place

25.7 Remove the centre console side panels

25.8 Undo the screw on each side where the console meets the base of the facia

25.10 Remove the rear storage compartment and undo the screws (arrowed)

25.11a Unclip the trim piece beneath the handbrake lever

25.11b Manoeuvre the console from place, pulling it over the gear lever surround

26.6 Undo the 2 screws and remove the column adjustment lever handle

11 Apply the handbrake and unclip the trim piece beneath **(see illustration)**. Manoeuvre the console from place, carefully pulling it over the gear lever surround, and disconnecting any wiring plugs as the console is withdrawn **(see illustration)**.

Refitting

12 Refitting is a reversal of the removal procedure.

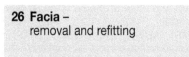

26 Facia –
removal and refitting

Note: *Removing the A-pillar trim panels can make removing and refitting the fascia easier.*

Removal

1 Disconnect the battery negative lead (refer to Chapter 5 Section 3).
2 Remove the centre console as described in Section 25.
3 Remove the sunlight photo sensor as described in Chapter 3, Section 11 (where applicable).
4 Remove the steering wheel as described in Chapter 10 Section 19.
5 Remove the steering column switch unit as described in Chapter 12 Section 6.
6 Remove the 2 fixing screws and remove the steering wheel height adjustment lever, followed by the steering column lower trim panel **(see illustration)**.
7 Carefully prise out the trim panel on the top of the facia containing the centre air vents

and storage compartment, disconnecting the plug for the hazard light switch as the trim is withdrawn **(see illustration)**.
8 Using a blunt, flat-bladed tool, carefully prise out the trim pieces to the right and left of the steering wheel (the right-hand trim surrounds the main light switch), and the side covers at both ends of the facia panel **(see illustrations)**.
9 Remove the main light switch as described in Chapter 12 Section 7.
10 Remove the panel above the pedals. This is secured by 2 screws at the top of the panel located behind the trim pieces either side of the steering column, 2 screws at the bottom, and 1 screw behind the fuse cover at the end of the facia. Unclip and detach the diagnostic socket as the panel is withdrawn **(see illustrations)**.

26.7 Carefully lever out the panel containing the upper air vents

26.8a Prise out the trim piece to the right of the steering wheel (surrounding the main light switch)...

26.8b ... and the trim piece to the left of the steering wheel

26.10a Undo the screws (arrowed) either side of the steering column

26.10b Undo the lower screw on the left-hand side...

26.10c ... on the right-hand side...

26.10d ... and the screw behind the fuse panel cover

26.14 Undo the screws (arrowed) for the passenger airbag support (right-hand screw arrowed)

26.16a Undo the screw in the radio aperture

11 Remove the infotainment unit as described in Chapter 12 Section 20.

12 Remove the heater control panel as described in Chapter 3 Section 9, and remove the switches below as described in Chapter 12 Section 7.

13 Remove the glovebox as described in Section 27.

14 With the glovebox removed, undo the 2 fixing screws for the front passenger airbag support **(see illustration)** and disconnect the wiring plug for the airbag.

15 Undo the 2 retaining bolts and remove the instrument cluster as described in Chapter 12 Section 12. Note that as the cluster is withdrawn, the wiring plug is automatically disconnected.

16 The facia is now secured by 1 bolt behind the radio, 2 bolts behind the right-hand end panel, 3 bolts behind the left-hand end panel, and 2 bolts in the centre (1 each side of the centre console, towards the top). Undo the bolts and with the help of an assistant, pull the facia panel rearwards to release the retaining clips **(see illustrations)**. Manoeuvre the facia from the cabin.

Refitting

17 Refitting is a reversal of the removal process. Ensure that the heater control cables and all wiring harnesses are correctly routed and clipped in position.

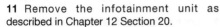

27 Glovebox –
removal and refitting

Removal

1 Using a blunt, flat-bladed tool, carefully prise out the trim panel at the end of the facia panel.

2 The glovebox is secured by 2 bolts at its lower edge, 3 at its upper edge, and 1 behind the trim panel at the end of the facia.

3 Pull the glovebox rearwards slightly and disconnect the wiring plugs for the glovebox light and the key switch for the passenger airbag (where fitted). Also disconnect the hose for the glovebox cooling system **(see illustrations)**.

4 Withdraw the glovebox from the facia panel.

26.16b Undo the 2 screws (arrowed) behind the fuse panel cover

Refitting

5 Refit in the reverse order of removal. It can be difficult to refit the wiring plug for the passenger airbag with the switch in position. If so, undo the 2 screws on the top of the glovebox that hold the switch in position, lower the switch and feed the wiring plug through the hole and reconnect. Screw the switch back in position before continuing to refit the glovebox.

28 Interior mirror –
removal and refitting

⚠️ **Warning: Use extreme care whilst attempting this procedure; the windscreen is easily cracked.**

27.3a Disconnect the wiring plugs for the glovebox light and passenger airbag switch

26.16c Undo the screw each side (right-hand side arrowed)

Basic mirror with rigid base

Removal

1 Twist the mirror 90° clockwise, and remove it from the mounting plate.

Refitting

2 To refit, position the support arm at 90° to the vertical, then carefully turn it anti-clockwise to the point where the lock spring is felt to engage.

Mirror with rain sensor

Removal

3 Carefully prise apart the 2 halves of the trim around the mirror mounting base **(see illustration)**.

4 Slide the mirror down the windscreen from the mounting. Disconnect the wiring plugs

27.3b Disconnect the glovebox cooling hose

28.3 Prise apart the two halves of the trim

28.4 Slide the mirror down from the mounting

as the mirror assembly is withdrawn **(see illustration)**.

Refitting

5 Refitting is a reversal of removal.

Mirror mounting plate

6 Renewal of the mirror mounting plate should be entrusted to a Skoda dealer or specialist, due to the use of dangerous chemicals used in the bonding process.

29 Seats –
removal and refitting

Front seat

Warning: Where front seats are equipped with side airbags, it is essential you are electrostatically

29.5 Undo the seat rail bolts (front bolt arrowed)

29.15a Undo the rear seat clamp retaining bolt...

discharged prior to disconnecting the airbag wiring plug by briefly touching a door lock or vehicle body.

Removal

1 Disconnect the battery negative cable with reference to Chapter 5 Section 3.
2 Move the seat forwards to the extent of its travel.
3 Undo the bolt at the rear of each seat rail securing the seat to the vehicle body.
4 Move the seat fully rearwards.
5 Undo the bolt at the front of the each seat rail **(see illustration)**.
6 Lift up the cover in the floor then unplug the airbag wiring plug (see warning above), and where fitted, disconnect the wiring plugs for the seat heating and motor systems. Remove the seat from the vehicle. **Note:** *Due to the risk of injury or component failure, no further dismantling of the seats is recommended.*

29.12 Remove the rear seat side upholstery

29.15b ... and disengage the backrests from their locating pins

Refitting

7 Refit the seat in the reverse order of removal. Note that after refitting the seat(s), the airbag warning light on the dash may signal a fault. Take the vehicle to a Skoda dealer or suitably-equipped specialist to have the self-diagnosis system interrogated and the fault code erased.

Rear seat bench

8 On all models, grasp the front lower edge of the seat and pull it forwards.
9 Once released at the rear, tip the seat base towards the front of the vehicle and release the wire clips located at the front edge. Disconnect any wiring plugs as the seat is removed.
10 Refit the seat bench in the reverse order of removal.

Side upholstery

11 Remove the seat bench as described above.
12 Press the side upholstery inwards towards the centre of the car and slide down to remove **(see illustration)**.
13 To refit, press inwards and slide upwards until secure.

Rear seat backrest

14 Fold the seat benches forwards and fold down the backrests.
15 Undo the retaining bolt, lift out the clamp and remove the backrests, disengaging the backrests from the locating pins at each side at the base of the side pad **(see illustrations)**. Disconnect any wiring plugs as the backrest is withdrawn.
16 Refit the seat backrest in the reverse order of removal.

30 Interior trim –
removal and refitting

Interior trim panels

1 The interior trim panels are secured using either bolts or various types of trim fasteners, usually studs or clips.
2 Check that there are no other panels overlapping the one to be removed; usually there is a sequence that has to be followed, and this will only become obvious on close inspection.
3 Remove all obvious fasteners, such as bolts. If the panel will not come free, it is held by hidden clips or fasteners. These are usually situated around the edge of the panel and can be prised up to release them; note, however that they can break quite easily so new ones should be available. The best way of releasing such clips without the correct type of tool is to use a large flat-bladed screwdriver. Note in many cases that the adjacent sealing strip must be prised back to release a panel.
4 When removing a panel, never use excessive

30.12 Undo the various fixing screws (end screws arrowed) and remove the side support

30.16a Unscrew the luggage retaining hooks...

30.16b ... and the remaining screws

force or the panel may be damaged; always check carefully that all fasteners or other relevant components have been removed or released before attempting to withdraw a panel.

5 Refitting is the reverse of the removal procedure; secure the fasteners by pressing them firmly into place and ensure that all disturbed components are correctly secured to prevent rattles.

Carpets

6 The passenger compartment floor carpet is in one piece and is secured at its edges by bolts or clips, usually the same fasteners used to secure the various adjoining trim panels.

7 Carpet removal and refitting is reasonably straightforward but very time-consuming because all adjoining trim panels must be removed first, as must components such as the seats, the centre console and seat belt lower anchorages.

Headlining

8 The headlining is clipped to the roof and can be withdrawn only once all fittings such as the grab handles, sunvisors, sunroof (if fitted), windscreen and rear quarter windows and related trim panels have been removed and the door, tailgate and sunroof aperture sealing strips (as applicable) have been prised clear.

9 Note that headlining removal requires considerable skill and experience if it is to be carried out without damage and is therefore best entrusted to an expert.

Luggage compartment cover side supports

Hatchback models

10 Remove the luggage compartment cover.

11 Remove the luggage compartment side trim panel as described later in this section, and the rear seat side pads as described in Section 29.

12 Remove the 3 fixing screws, undo the bolt below the side support that locates the seat belt guide, and remove **(see illustration)**.

13 Refitting is a reverse of removal, repositioning the seat belt guide as the side support is fitted back into position and ensuring that the top of the support clips into the base of the C-pillar trim.

30.18 Where fitted, prise out the label at the top of the A-pillar trim, and undo the bolt revealed

Estate models

14 Remove the luggage compartment cover and the rear seat side pads.

15 Remove the D-pillar lower trim panel as described below.

16 Remove the screw for the luggage hook and the 3 remaining fixing screws **(see illustrations)**.

17 Refitting is a reversal of removal, ensuring that the luggage hook is in place before the support is refitted.

A-pillar trim

Caution: Skoda recommend disconnecting the battery negative terminal (Chapter 5 Section 3) before commencing any work where an airbag is present.

Upper section

18 On models fitted with a head airbag, prise

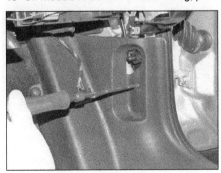

30.22a Undo the screw exposed by the removal of the bonnet release lever

30.19 Carefully release the clips and withdraw the trim panel from the A-pillar

out the airbag label then undo the bolt in the label aperture **(see illustration)**.

19 Pull the A-pillar trim from place, releasing the push-on clips, then pull it to the rear to release it from the facia panel. Manoeuvre the trim from the cabin **(see illustration)**.

20 Refitting is a reversal of removal, ensuring the lug at the front edge of the trim engages correctly.

Lower section

21 Remove the B-pillar upper and lower trim panels as described below.

22 On the driver's side, remove the bonnet release lever, then remove the screw that is exposed in the aperture **(see illustrations)**. Undo the fixing ahead of the throttle pedal.

23 On both sides, pull the pillar trim inwards to release the any clips.

24 Disengage the trim from the door

30.22b Undo the fixing ahead of the throttle pedal

30.26 Starting at the top, pull the pillar trim inwards to release the retaining clips

30.31 Pull the trim panel upwards to release the retaining clips

30.40 Carefully slide the trim panel from the headlining

weatherstrip, and pull the trim rearwards unclipping it from the sill.

25 Refitting is a reversal of removal.

B-pillar trim

Upper section

26 Loosen the trim panel from the door weatherstrip and pull the top of the pillar trim inwards to release the 2 clips. Feed the seat belt through the slot in the pillar trim (see illustration).

27 Remove the retaining bolt and loosen the seat belt anchorage.

28 On models fitted with a head airbag, lever out the airbag label and remove the screw in the label aperture. Loosen the trim from the door weatherseal and remove.

29 Refitting is a reversal of removal, ensuring the seat belt height adjuster mechanism aligns correctly with the inside of the trim. The

height adjuster needs to be at the top position for refitting.

Lower section

30 Remove the upper section of the B-pillar trim as previously described.

31 Pull the sill trim panel upwards to release the retaining clips where it overlaps the pillar trim (see illustration).

32 Pull the trim panel from the door weatherstrips, then pull the panel inwards to release the retaining clips. Disconnect any wiring plugs as the panel is withdrawn.

33 Refitting is a reversal of removal.

C-pillar trim – Hatchback models

34 On models with a head airbag, lever out the airbag label and remove the screw in the label aperture.

35 Remove the supports for the luggage cover as described previously in this Section.

36 Remove the trim strip from the rear of the headlining.

37 Remove the screw from the front edge of the trim and pull the trim inwards to release it from the retaining clips.

38 Refitting is a reversal of removal.

C-pillar trim – Estate models

Upper section

39 Remove the support for the luggage cover as described previously in this Section.

40 Carefully slide the trim panel from the headlining (see illustration).

41 On models fitted with a head bag, lever out the airbag label, remove the screw in the label aperture, and remove the trim panel.

42 Refitting is a reversal of removal.

Lower section

43 Remove the lower B-pillar trim panel as described previously in this Section.

44 Remove the rear seat bench and side upholstery as described in Section 29, and fold the seat forwards.

45 Remove the fixing screws and remove trim panel.

46 Refitting is a reversal of removal.

D-pillar trim panel

47 Unclip the trim strip from the rear of the headlining (see illustration).

48 Remove the luggage compartment cover supports as described previously in this Section.

49 Starting at the top, unclip the trim panel from the D-pillar and remove (see illustration).

Luggage compartment side trim

Hatchback models

50 Remove the rear sill trim as described in the section below, and the side upholstery.

51 Unscrew the luggage retaining hooks. Where a luggage net is fitted to this panel, its rearmost fixing attaches the trim panel to the body and will need to be carefully released before withdrawing the side trim (see illustrations).

52 Where a CD changer is fitted, there are 4 clips around the mounting frame that need to be released.

53 Pull the side trim from beneath the luggage

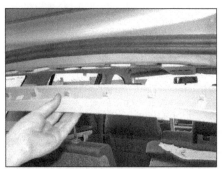

30.47 Unclip the trim strip from the rear of the headlining

30.49 Starting at the top, unclip the trim panel from the D-pillar

30.51a Remove the 2 screws (arrowed) and remove the luggage hook

30.51b Unscrew any remaining hooks

30.51c If a luggage net is fitted, pull back the trim panel and unclip the mounting from the bodywork

30.57 Undo the screws at the rear of the trim panel

30.64 Undo the 3 plastic nuts and unclip the centre trim panel

compartment side supports and disconnect any wiring plugs as the trim is withdrawn.
54 Refitting is a reversal of removal.

Estate models

55 Remove the luggage compartment cover supports as described previously in this Section.
56 Remove the sill trim end panels as described below.
57 Remove the 3 screws at the top of the panel, and the 2 screws at the rear **(see illustration)**.
58 Disconnect any wiring plugs as the trim is withdrawn.
59 Refitting is a reversal of removal.

Luggage compartment rear sill trim

Hatchback models

60 Lift the luggage compartment floor covering.
61 Slacken the 2 fixing screws at the base of the panel, unclip from the boot edge and remove.
62 Refitting is a reversal of removal. Ensure the trim sits below weatherstrips when in place.

Estate models

63 The sill trim is in 3 sections, the outer ones acting as the base of the D-pillar.
64 Remove the centre section first by lifting the floor covering, undoing the 3 plastic nuts, and unclipping the panel from the boot edge **(see illustration)**.
65 To remove the end sections, prise the cap from the luggage hook and undo the screw. Undo the remaining screw and unclip the panel **(see illustrations)**.
66 Refitting is a reversal of removal.

31 Seat belt tensioning mechanism – general information

1 All models are fitted with seat belt pretensioners that are integrated into the airbag control system. The system is designed to instantaneously take up any slack in the seat belt in the case of a direct or oblique frontal impact, therefore reducing

the possibility of injury to the occupants. Each front seat inertia reel is fitted with its own tensioner, which is triggered by a frontal impact above a predetermined force. Lesser impacts and impacts to the rear of the vehicle will not trigger the system.
2 When the system is triggered, the explosive gas in the tensioner mechanism retracts and locks the seat belt. This prevents the seat belt moving and keeps the occupant firmly in position in the seat. Once the tensioner has been triggered, the seat belt will be permanently locked and the assembly must be renewed, together with the impact sensors.
3 Always disconnect the battery negative lead (see Chapter 5 Section 3) before working on the pretensioners.
4 Note the following warnings before contemplating any work on the front seat belts.

 Warning: Do not expose the tensioner mechanism to temperatures in excess of 100°C.
 Warning: Do not use electric or impact screwdrivers to remove or install the tensioners.
 Warning: If the tensioner mechanism is dropped, it must be renewed, even it has suffered no apparent damage.
Warning: Do not allow any solvents to come into contact with the tensioner mechanism.
Warning: Do not attempt to open the tensioner mechanism as it contains explosive gas.

30.65a Remove the plastic caps and undo the screw that retains the luggage hook

Warning: Tensioners must be discharged before they are disposed of, but this task should be entrusted to a Skoda dealer.

32 Seat belts – general, removal and refitting

Note: *Refer to the warnings in Section 31 before working on the front seat belts.*

General

1 Periodically check the belts for fraying or other damage. If evident, renew the belt.
2 If the belts become dirty, wipe them with a damp cloth, using a little liquid detergent only.
3 Check the tightness of the anchor bolts, and if they are ever disconnected, make quite sure that the original sequence of fitting of washers, bushes, and anchor plate is retained.
4 Access to the front belt height adjuster and inertia reel units can be made by removing the trim from the B-pillar on the side concerned.
5 The rear seat belt anchorages can be checked by removing the rear seat bench. Access to the rear seat inertia reel units is made by removing the rear seat backrest, luggage compartment cover and luggage area side trim.
6 The torque wrench settings for the seat belt anchor bolts and other attachments are given in the Specifications at the start of this Chapter.
7 Never modify the seat belts, or alter the attachments to the body, in any way.

30.65b Undo any remaining screws and unclip the trim panel

32.10 Undo the seat belt inertia reel bolt (arrowed)

32.11 Seat belt upper anchorage bolt

32.12 Seat belt guide bolts (arrowed)

Front seat belt

8 Disconnect the battery negative lead as described in Chapter 5 Section 3.

9 Remove the upper and lower B-pillar trims as described in Section 30.

10 Undo the inertia reel mounting bolt and manoeuvre the reel from the pillar. Disconnect the pretensioners wiring plug by opening the locking element, depressing the clip and disconnecting the plug **(see illustration)**.

11 Undo the bolt at the upper seat belt anchorage point **(see illustration)**.

12 Undo the 2 bolts and remove the seat belt guide from the B-pillar **(see illustration)**.

13 To remove the seat belt stalk, remove the relevant front seat as described in Section 29, then undo the bolt on the underside of the seat, and remove the stalk. Disconnect the wiring as the stalk is withdrawn **(see illustration)**.

14 Refitting is a reversal of removal, ensuring all fasteners are tightened to their specified torque where given.

Rear side seat belt

Hatchback models

15 Remove the luggage compartment cover, and side supports as described in Section 30.

16 On models with pretensioners, disconnect the wiring plug, and undo the bolt securing the pretensioner to the vehicle body. Undo the lower seat belt anchorage point/relay bracket bolt.

17 Undo the retaining bolt and remove the inertia reel, along with the seat belt **(see illustration)**.

18 To remove the seat belt stalk, remove the rear seat backrest as described in Section 29. Undo the plastic rivets holding the carpet and pull the carpet to one side. Undo the bolt and remove the stalk **(see illustration)**.

19 Refitting is a reversal of removal, ensuring all fasteners are tightened to their specified torque where given.

Estate models

20 Remove the rear seats as described in Section 29, and the luggage compartment side panel trims as described in Section 30. On models with pretensioners, disconnect the wiring plug, and undo the bolt securing the pretensioner to the vehicle body.

21 Undo the lower seat belt anchorage point/relay bracket bolt and remove the belt.

22 Undo the 2 bolts and remove the seat belt guide (where fitted).

23 Undo the retaining bolt, and remove the inertia reel along with the seat belt.

24 To remove the seat belt stalk, remove the rear seat bench as described in Section 29, undo the bolt and remove the stalk.

25 Refitting is a reversal of removal, ensuring all fasteners are tightened to their specified torque where given.

Rear centre seat belt

26 Remove the rear seat bench as described in Section 29.

27 The centre rear seat belt reel is attached to the rear seat backrest. Remove the backrest as described in Section 29 (the larger of the two sections if the backrest is split). Depress the release buttons on the guide collars, and remove the headrests from the backrest.

28 Pull back the carpet and undo the bolt securing the bottom of the centre seat belt to the floor (this also releases the seat belt stalk) **(see illustration)**.

29 Use a screwdriver to release the plastic

32.13 Seat belt stalk bolt (arrowed)

32.17 Rear seat belt inertia reel bolt (arrowed)

32.18 Rear seat belt stalk retaining bolt (arrowed)

32.28 Rear seat centre seat belt anchorage

32.29 Prise the seat belt guide from the rear seat back

32.30 Unclip the seat cover beading

32.31 Seat belt inertia reel bolt

33.2 Prise open the cap and undo the sunvisor hinge screw

seat belt guide on top of the backrest **(see illustration)**.

30 Unclip the seat cover beading from the bottom and outside edges of the backrest frame. Take care not to mark the seat covering **(see illustration)**.

31 Carefully fold back the covering and padding, then undo the retaining nut and remove the inertia reel **(see illustration)**.

32 Refitting is a reversal of removal, ensuring all fasteners are tightened to their specified torque where given.

33 Sunvisors –
removal and refitting

Removal

1 Swing the sunvisor out of its retaining clip.

Prise off the plastic cover to expose the clip retaining screws. Undo the screws and remove the retaining clip.

2 To remove the sunvisor/hinge, prise out the plastic cap and undo the retaining screw **(see illustration)**.

Refitting

3 Refitting is a reversal of removal.

34 Grab handles –
removal and refitting

Removal

1 Hold down the grab handle, and prise out the plastic caps. Undo the retaining screws and remove the handles **(see illustration)**.

34.1 Prise open the caps and undo the grab handle screws

Refitting

2 Refitting is a reversal of removal.

Notes

Chapter 12
Body electrical systems

Contents

Degrees of difficulty

 Easy, suitable for novice with little experience | 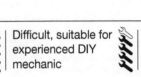 Fairly easy, suitable for beginner with some experience | Fairly difficult, suitable for competent DIY mechanic | Difficult, suitable for experienced DIY mechanic | Very difficult, suitable for expert DIY or professional

Specifications

General

System type . . . . 12 volt, negative earth

Bulbs — **Power rating (watts)**

Brake lights (body-mounted and high-level)	21/LEDs
Direction indicators	PY21
Direction indicator side repeaters	LEDs
Door entry lights	5
Foglight: Front	35 H8
Rear	21
Footwell lights	5
Glovebox light	5
Headlights (halogen): Dipped	55 H7
Main	55 H1
Interior lights: Bulb without base	5
'Soffitte' type bulb	10
Luggage compartment light	5
Number plate light	5
Reading lights	5
Reversing light	21
Sidelights	3

Torque wrench settings

	Nm	lbf ft
Airbag control unit nuts	10	7
Passenger airbag unit nuts/bolts	7	5
Rear window wiper arm nut	12	9
Windscreen wiper arm nuts	17	13
Windscreen wiper linkage bolts	10	7

1 General information and precautions

⚠️ *Warning: Before carrying out any work on the electrical system, read through the precautions given in 'Safety first!' at the beginning of this manual, and in Chapter 5.*

1 The electrical system is of 12 volt negative earth type. Power for the lights and all electrical accessories is supplied by a lead-acid type battery which is charged by the alternator.

2 This Chapter covers repair and service procedures for the various electrical components not associated with the engine. Information on the battery, alternator and starter motor can be found in Chapter 5.

3 It should be noted that prior to working on any component in the electrical system, the battery negative terminal should first be disconnected to prevent the possibility of electrical short-circuits and/or fires.

2 Electrical fault finding – general information

Note: *Refer to the precautions given in 'Safety first!' and in Chapter 5 before starting work. The following tests relate to testing of the main electrical circuits, and should not be used to test delicate electronic circuits (such as anti-lock braking systems), particularly where an electronic control module is used.*

Caution: The Skoda Octavia electrical system is extremely complex. Many of the ECMs are connected via a Databus system, where they are able to share information from the various sensors, and communicate with each other. For instance, as the automatic gearbox approaches a gear ratio shift point, it signals the engine management ECM via the Databus. As the gearchange is made by the transmission ECM, the engine management ECM retards the ignition timing, momentarily reducing engine output, to ensure a smoother transition from one gear ratio to the next. Due to the design of the Databus system, it is not advisable to backprobe the ECMs with a multimeter in the traditional manner. Instead, the electrical systems are equipped with a sophisticated self-diagnosis system, which can interrogate the various ECMs to reveal stored fault codes, and help pin-point faults. In order to access the self-diagnosis system, specialist test equipment (fault code reader/scanner) is required.

General

1 Typically, the electrical circuit consists of an electrical component, any switches, relays, motors, fuses, fusible links or circuit breakers related to that component, and the wiring and connectors which link the component to both the battery and the chassis. To help to pin-point a problem in an electrical circuit, wiring diagrams are included at the end of this Chapter.

2 Have a good look at the appropriate wiring diagram, before attempting to diagnose an electrical fault, to obtain a complete understanding of the components included in the particular circuit concerned. The possible sources of a fault can be narrowed down by noting if other components related to the circuit are operating properly. If several components or circuits fail at one time, the problem is likely to be related to a shared fuse or earth connection.

3 An electrical problem will usually stem from simple cause, such as loose or corroded connections, a faulty earth connection, a blown fuse, or a faulty relay (refer to Section 3 for details of testing relays). Visually inspect the condition of all fuses, wires and connections in a problem circuit before testing the components. Use the wiring diagrams to determine which terminal connections will need to be checked in order to pin-point the trouble-spot.

4 The basic tools required for electrical fault finding include a circuit tester or voltmeter (a 12 volt bulb with a set of test leads can also be used for certain tests); a self-powered test light (sometimes known as a continuity tester); an ohmmeter (to measure resistance); a battery and set of test leads; and a jumper wire, preferably with a circuit breaker or fuse incorporated, which can be used to bypass suspect wires or electrical components. Before attempting to locate a problem with test instruments, use the wiring diagram to determine where to make the connections.

5 Sometimes, an intermittent wiring fault (usually caused by a poor or dirty connection, or damaged wiring insulation) can be pin-pointed by performing a wiggle test on the wiring. This involves wiggling the wiring by hand to see if the fault occurs as the wiring is moved. It should be possible to narrow down the source of the fault to a particular section of wiring. This method of testing can be used in conjunction with any of the tests described in the following sub-Sections.

6 Apart from problems due to poor connections, two basic types of fault can occur in an electrical circuit: open-circuit, or short-circuit.

7 Largely, open-circuit faults are caused by a break somewhere in the circuit, which prevents current from flowing. An open-circuit fault will prevent a component from working, but will not cause the relevant circuit fuse to blow.

8 Low resistance or short-circuit faults are caused by a 'short'; a failure point which allows the current flowing in the circuit to 'escape' along an alternative route, somewhere in the circuit. This typically occurs when a positive supply wire touches either an earth wire, or an earthed component such as the bodyshell. Such faults are normally caused by a breakdown in wiring insulation, A short circuit fault will normally cause the relevant circuit fuse to blow.

9 Fuses are designed to protect a circuit from being overloaded. A blown fuse indicates that there may be problem in that particular circuit and it is important to identify and rectify the problem before renewing the fuse. Always renew a blown fuse with one of the correct current rating; fitting a fuse of a different rating may cause an overloaded circuit to overheat and even catch fire.

Finding an open-circuit

10 One of the most straightforward ways of finding an open-circuit fault is by using a circuit test meter or voltmeter. Connect one lead of the meter to either the negative battery terminal or a known good earth. Connect the other lead to a connector in the circuit being tested, preferably nearest to the battery or fuse. Switch on the circuit, bearing in mind that some circuits are live only when the ignition switch is moved to a particular position. If voltage is present (indicated either by the tester bulb lighting or a voltmeter reading, as applicable), this means that the section of the circuit between the relevant connector and the battery is problem-free. Continue to check the remainder of the circuit in the same fashion. When a point is reached at which no voltage is present, the problem must lie between that point and the previous test point with voltage. Most problems can be traced to a broken, corroded or loose connection.

Warning: Under no circumstances may live measuring instruments such as ohmmeters, voltmeters or a bulb and test leads be used to test any of the airbag circuitry. Any testing of these components must be left to a Skoda dealer or specialist, as there is a danger of activating the system if the correct procedures are not followed.

Finding a short-circuit

11 Loading the circuit during testing will produce false results and may damage your test equipment, so all electrical loads must be disconnected from the circuit before it can be checked for short circuits. Loads are the components which draw current from a circuit, such as bulbs, motors, heating elements, etc.

12 Keep both the ignition and the circuit under test switched off, then remove the relevant fuse from the circuit, and connect a circuit test meter or voltmeter to the fuse connections.

13 Switch on the circuit, bearing in mind that some circuits are live only when the ignition switch is moved to a particular position. If voltage is present (indicated either by the tester bulb lighting or a voltmeter reading, as applicable), this means that there is a short-circuit. If no voltage is present, but the fuse still blows with the load(s) connected, this indicates an internal fault in the load(s).

2.14a The main earth strap connection is on the left-hand side chassis member in the engine compartment under the air cleaner (arrowed)

2.14b Other locations include behind the left-hand footwell panel (arrowed)...

2.14c ... and on the rear wheel arch (arrowed)...

Finding an earth fault

14 The battery negative terminal is connected to 'earth': the metal of the engine/transmission and the car body – and most systems are wired so that they only receive a positive feed, the current returning through the metal of the car body. This means that the component mounting and the body form part of that circuit. Loose or corroded mountings can therefore cause a range of electrical faults, ranging from total failure of a circuit, to a puzzling partial fault. In particular, lights may shine dimly (especially when another circuit sharing the same earth point is in operation), motors (eg, wiper motors or the radiator auxiliary cooling fan motor) may run slowly, and the operation of one circuit may have an apparently unrelated effect on another. Note that on many vehicles, earth straps are used between certain components, such as the engine/transmission and the body, usually where there is no metal-to-metal contact between components due to flexible rubber mountings, etc **(see illustrations)**.

15 To check whether a component is properly earthed, disconnect the battery and connect one lead of an ohmmeter to a known good earth point. Connect the other lead to the wire or earth connection being tested. The resistance reading should be zero; if not, check the connection as follows.

16 If an earth connection is thought to be faulty, dismantle the connection and clean back to bare metal both the bodyshell and the wire terminal, or the component earth connection

mating surface. Be careful to remove all traces of dirt and corrosion, then use a knife to trim away any paint, so that a clean metal-to-metal joint is made. On reassembly, tighten the joint fasteners securely; if a wire terminal is being refitted, use serrated washers between the terminal and the bodyshell to ensure a clean and secure connection. When the connection is remade, prevent the onset of corrosion in the future by applying a coat of petroleum jelly or silicone-based grease or by spraying on (at regular intervals) a proprietary ignition sealer or a water dispersant lubricant.

3 Fuses and relays – general information

Main fuses

1 The fuses are located on a single panel at the right-hand end of the facia on RHD models, at the left-hand end on LHD models, and in the engine compartment adjacent to the battery.

2 Access to the fuses is gained by pulling open the cover panel on the facia, or unclipping the fusebox cover in the engine compartment **(see illustrations)**.

3 Each fuse is numbered; the fuses ratings and circuits they protect are listed on the rear face of the cover panel. A list of fuses is given with the wiring diagrams.

4 To remove a fuse, first switch off the circuit concerned (or the ignition), then pull the fuse out of its terminals. The wire within the fuse

should be visible; if the fuse is blown the wire will have a break in it, which will be visible through the plastic casing.

5 Always renew a fuse with one of an identical rating; never use a fuse with a different rating from the original or substitute anything else. Never renew a fuse more than once without tracing the source of the trouble. The fuse rating is stamped on top of the fuse; note that the fuses are also colour-coded for easy recognition.

6 If a new fuse blows immediately, find the cause before renewing it again; a short to earth as a result of faulty insulation is most likely. Where a fuse protects more than one circuit, try to isolate the defect by switching on each circuit in turn (if possible) until the fuse blows again. Always carry a supply of spare fuses of each relevant rating on the vehicle, a spare of each rating should be clipped into the base of the fusebox.

Relays

7 The main relays are located behind a panel on the driver's side of the facia. The facia relays are mounted on a common base, which is accessed by removing the driver's side lower facia panel as described in Chapter 11, Section 26 **(see illustration)**.

8 The relays are of sealed construction, and cannot be repaired if faulty. The relays are of the plug-in type, and may be removed by pulling directly from their terminals. In some cases, it will be necessary to prise the two plastic clips outwards before removing the relay.

3.2a Fuses are located behind a panel at the end of the facia on the driver's side...

3.2b ... and beneath a cover in the engine compartment

3.7 The main relay panel is located behind the driver's side lower facia panel

4.5a Most electrical connectors have a single release tab that you depress to release the connector

4.5b Some electrical connectors have a retaining tab which must be pried up to free the connector

4.5c Some connectors have two release tabs that you must squeeze to release the connector

9 If a circuit or system controlled by a relay develops a fault and the relay is suspect, operate the system; if the relay is functioning, it should be possible to hear it click as it is energised. If this is the case, the fault lies with the components or wiring of the system. If the relay is not being energised, then either the relay is not receiving a main supply or a switching voltage, or the relay itself is faulty. Testing is by the substitution of a known good unit, but be careful; while some relays are identical in appearance and in operation, others look similar but perform different functions.

10 To renew a relay, first ensure that the ignition switch is off. The relay can then be pulled out from the socket (or the clips released as appropriate) and the new relay pressed in.

4 Electrical connectors

1 Most electrical connections on these vehicles are made with multiwire plastic connectors. The mating halves of many connectors are secured with locking clips molded into the plastic connector shells. The mating halves of some large connectors, such as some of those under the instrument panel, are held together by a bolt through the center of the connector.

2 To separate a connector with locking clips, use a small screwdriver to pry the clips apart carefully, then separate the connector halves. Pull only on the shell, never pull on the wiring

harness, as you may damage the individual wires and terminals inside the connectors. Look at the connector closely before trying to separate the halves. Often the locking clips are engaged in a way that is not immediately clear. Additionally, many connectors have more than one set of clips.

3 Each pair of connector terminals has a male half and a female half. When you look at the end view of a connector in a diagram, be sure to understand whether the view shows the harness side or the component side of the connector. Connector halves are mirror images of each other, and a terminal shown on the right side end-view of one half will be on the left side end-view of the other half.

4 It is often necessary to take circuit voltage measurements with a connector connected. Whenever possible, carefully insert a small straight pin (not your meter probe) into the rear of the connector shell to contact the terminal inside, then clip your meter lead to the pin. This kind of connection is called "backprobing." When inserting a test probe into a terminal, be careful not to distort the terminal opening. Doing so can lead to a poor connection and corrosion at that terminal later. Using the small straight pin instead of a meter probe results in less chance of deforming the terminal connector. "T" pins are a good choice as temporary meter connections. They allow for a larger surface area to attach the meter leads too.

5 Typical electrical connectors:

4.5d Some connectors use wire retainers that you squeeze to release the connector

4.5e Critical connectors often employ a sliding lock (1) that you must pull out before you can depress the release tab (2)

4.5f Here's another sliding-lock style connector, with the lock (1) and the release tab (2) on the side of the connector

4.5g On some connectors the lock (1) must be pulled out to the side and removed before you can lift the release tab (2)

4.5h Some critical connectors, like the multi-pin connectors at the Electronic Control Module employ pivoting locks that must be flipped open

5 Ignition switch/ steering column lock – removal and refitting

Ignition switch

Removal

1 Remove the top and bottom steering column trim panels as described in Chapter 10, Section 20.
2 Remove the cover for the switch (if present) by inserting a small screwdriver in the opening at the top and levering the cover upwards. Disconnect the wiring plug from the switch.
3 Release the switch by inserting two small screwdrivers in the openings at the top and bottom of the switch and releasing the pegs.
4 Pull the switch out of the steering lock.

Refitting

5 Refitting is a reversal of removal.

Steering column lock

Removal

6 Disconnect the battery negative terminal.
7 Remove the steering wheel as described in Chapter 10 Section 19.
8 Undo the screws and remove the column height and reach adjustment handle.
9 Remove the upper and lower covers from the steering column as described in Chapter 10, Section 20.
10 Remove the plastic cover from the steering lock shear bolts on top of the steering column and release the cable-tie securing the wiring loom.
11 Mark the position of the combination switch on the column, then unscrew the clamp bolt and withdraw the switch.
12 On automatic transmission models, move the selector lever to position P, then turn the ignition key to the 'On' position. Release the wire clip by pressing it either up or down (according to type), then pull out the steering lock locking cable.
13 Carefully pull the wiring plug from the ignition switch and disconnect the wiring from the ignition key immobiliser coil.
14 The lock is secured to the outer column by shear-head bolts, and the heads are broken off in the tightening procedure. To remove the old bolts, either drill them out, or use a sharp cold chisel to cut off their heads or turn them anti-clockwise. Withdraw the lock from the steering column.
15 The lock cylinder can be removed from the steering lock housing as described below.

Refitting

16 If removed, refit the lock cylinder with the ignition key in the 'On' position, then remove the wire. Make sure that the immobiliser coil connection is located correctly in the guide when inserting the lock cylinder.
17 Locate the lock on the outer column and insert the new shear-head bolts. Tighten the bolts until their heads break off.

18 Reconnect the wiring plug to the ignition switch and ignition key immobiliser coil.
19 On automatic transmission models, with the selector lever in position P and the ignition key in the 'On' position, slide the locking cable into the lock housing until the wire clip engages. Check that it is possible to move the selector lever out of the P position. If not, refer to Chapter 7B and adjust the cable. Check also that it is only possible to remove the ignition key with the selector in the P position. With the ignition key in the 'Off' position, it must not be possible to move the selector lever out of the P position.
20 Locate the combination switch on the column, align it with the previously-made mark, and tighten the clamp bolt.
21 The remainder of refitting is a reversal of the removal.

Ignition switch lock cylinder

Removal

22 Disconnect the battery negative terminal with reference to Chapter 5 Section 3.
23 Remove the steering wheel as described in Chapter 10 Section 19.
24 Undo the screws and column height and reach adjustment handle.
25 Remove the upper and lower covers from the steering column as described in Chapter 10, Section 20.
26 Disconnect the wiring from the sensor coil, insert the ignition key and turn it to the ignition 'On' position.
27 Insert a 1.5 mm diameter wire of drill into the hole in the lock cylinder located next to the key, then withdraw the key, lock cylinder and sensor from the housing **(see illustration)**.

Refitting

28 Refitting is a reversal of removal.

6 Steering column switch assembly – removal and refitting

Electronic steering control unit

Note: *On models from 06/10, this unit is integrated with the airbag contact unit. See below.*

6.3 Undo the screw (arrowed) on the front of the control unit

5.27 Insert a piece of wire or a drill bit into the hole in the lock cylinder, insert the ignition key and withdraw the lock cylinder

1 Disconnect the battery negative terminal (see Chapter 5 Section 3), and remove the steering wheel as described in Chapter 10 Section 19.
2 Remove the upper and lower steering column trims as described in Chapter 10, Section 20.
3 Release the screw at the front of the control unit, and insert a 2.5 mm drill in the opening. Swivel the drill to the right to release the clip on the top of the control unit. Use a suitable screwdriver to release the clip at the rear of the unit above the connectors **(see illustration)**.
4 Pull the control unit down without tilting it, and carefully disconnect the wiring plug.
5 Refitting is a reversal of removal.
6 The unit must be coded after installation using dedicated diagnostic equipment. Entrust this task to a Skoda dealer or suitably-equipped specialist.

Airbag contact unit

Models up to 05/10

7 Remove the electronic steering column control unit as previously described in this Section.
8 Carefully release the clips at the rear and pull the contact assembly from the column **(see illustration)**. **Note:** *Do not allow the contact unit to rotate as it's withdrawn. If the unit is rotated accidentally it must be reset to the middle position during refitting, as follows. Put the front wheels in the straight-ahead*

6.8 Releasing the clips at the rear will allow the contact unit to be withdrawn from the steering column

6.11a Undo the 2 screws (arrowed)...

6.11b ... and slide the unit from the steering column

6.14 Release the clips and remove the steering angle sender

position. Slowly turn the unit to the right until it stops, then turn it to the left until it stops, counting the number of turns. Slowly turn the unit to the right again by half the number of counted turns.

9 Refitting is a reversal of removal.

Models from 06/10

10 On models from 06/10, this unit is integrated with the electronic steering control unit.

11 For removal, lock the contact unit in the centre position with adhesive tape. Remove the screws on each side at the top of the unit and the screw at the bottom. Disconnect the wiring plugs and slide from the steering column **(see illustrations)**.

12 On refitting, ensure that the indicator stalk is in the 0 position to prevent the reset segment from being broken. The unit must be

coded after installation by a Skoda dealer or suitably-equipped specialist.

Steering angle sender

13 Remove the airbag contact unit as previously described in this Section.

14 Release the clips and pull the sender from the column switch unit **(see illustration)**.

15 Refitting is a reversal of removal. The sender must be reset after installation using dedicated diagnostic equipment. Entrust this task to a Skoda dealer or suitably-equipped specialist.

Column switch unit

Models up to 05/10

16 Remove the electronic steering control unit, airbag contact unit, and steering angle sender as previously described in this section.

17 Remove the left and right column stalks by using a 1 mm feeler gauge to release the retaining lugs **(see illustrations)**. The indicator stalk has a further clip on the left side, while the wiper stalk has a clip just behind the stalk.

18 Drill out the fixing bolts for the steering lock and lock cylinder, and slide the switch mounting and steering lock from the column. No further dismantling of the switch unit is recommended. If faulty, the complete unit must be renewed.

19 Refitting is a reversal of removal.

Models from 06/10

20 Remove the airbag contact unit as described previously.

21 Using a small screwdriver, release the bottom fixing peg through the hole at the bottom of the switch unit, then release the catch pegs at the rear of the switch unit at both sides **(see illustrations)**. Slide the unit from the steering column. No further dismantling of the switch unit is recommended. If faulty, the complete unit must be renewed.

22 Refitting is a reversal of removal.

7	Switches – removal and refitting	

Facia-mounted light switch

1 With the light switch in position O, press the switch centre inwards and turn it slightly to the right. Hold this position and pull the switch from the facia **(see illustration)**.

6.17a Use a screwdriver and a feeler gauge to release the clips, and remove the left-hand column stalk...

6.17b... and the right-hand column stalk

6.21a Use a screwdriver inserted in the hole (arrowed) to release the fixing peg at the bottom of the unit

6.21b Release the catches at the rear on each side and slide the unit from the steering column

7.1 Removing the main light switch

7.9 Unclip the cover for the treble speaker

7.10 Undo the wiring connector and unclip the switch from the cover

7.16 With the centre console removed, the release clips for the central locking switch can be accessed

7.19a Prise down the rear of the cover using a blunt, flat-bladed tool

7.19b Undo the 2 screws visible in the aperture and remove the switch/sensor unit

7.21 Carefully prise the interior monitoring deactivation switch from the B-pillar trim

2 As the switch is withdrawn from the facia, disconnect the wiring plug.

3 To refit, reconnect the wiring plug.

4 Hold the switch and press the rotary part inwards and slightly to the right.

5 Insert the switch into the dash, turn the rotary part to position O and release. Check the switch for correct operation.

Glovebox light switch

6 Remove the glovebox (see Chapter 11 Section 27).

7 Prise out the actuating arm pin, rotate the switch body/arm clockwise and detach it from the glovebox.

8 Refitting is a reversal of removal.

Door mirror adjuster

9 Unclip the cover for the treble speaker (see illustration).

10 Detach the wiring connector, release the fixings and remove the switch downwards from the panel (see illustration).

11 Refit in the reverse order of removal.

Sunroof control

12 Remove the interior light assembly as described in Section 9.

13 Disconnect the sunroof switch wiring plug, then release the 3 retaining clips and remove the switch.

14 Refit in the reverse order of removal.

Central locking switch

15 Remove the centre console as described in Chapter 11 Section 25.

16 Release the retaining clips, then press the switch from the console (see illustration).

17 Refitting is a reversal of removal.

Interior monitoring switch/ vehicle inclination sensor

18 The switch and sensor are located behind a cover at the front of the headlining to the rear of the interior light.

19 Use a blunt, flat-bladed tool to prise down the rear of the cover (end furthest from screen) and remove. The switch/sensor is held in place by 2 screws (see illustrations).

20 Refitting is a reversal of removal.

21 These functions can be deactivated using a switch located on the driver's side B-pillar. To remove the switch, carefully prise it from the B-pillar trim. Disconnect the wiring plug as the switch is withdrawn. Refitting is a reverse of removal (see illustration).

7.23 Prise or pull up the switch panel on the driver's door

Courtesy light switches

22 The courtesy light are controlled by microswitches incorporated into the door locks. The switches are not available separately. If defective, the door lock assembly must be renewed (see Chapter 11 Section 16).

Window switches

Driver's door switch panel

23 Using a blunt, flat-bladed tool, carefully prise up the switch panel from the door trim (see illustration). Alternatively, firmly hold the door handle section and pull sharply upwards to release the retaining clips.

24 Unclip and disconnect the wiring plug from the underside of the panel.

25 Release any retaining clips and remove the switch assembly from the panel (see illustration).

7.25 Release any retaining clips, undo the wiring plug, and remove the switch panel from the handle

7.27 Unclip the cover for the treble speaker

7.28 Disconnect the wiring plugs, release the 2 clips, and remove the window switch from the speaker cover

7.35 It may be possible to attach a sticky pad or piece of tape to the hazard light switch and pull it from place. Otherwise, prise it out carefully with a suitable tool

26 Refitting is a reversal of removal.

Front passenger and rear door switches

27 Unclip the cover for the treble speaker **(see illustration)**.
28 Disconnect the wiring plug from the switch, and release the 2 clips on each side to remove the switch **(see illustration)**.
29 Refitting is a reversal of removal.

Brake light switch

30 Refer to Chapter 9 Section 19.

Steering column switch

31 Refer to Section 6.

Headlight control

32 Remove the driver's side lower facia panel as described in Chapter 11, Section 26, and disconnect any wiring plugs.
33 Working from the rear, push in the securing tabs and pull the switch from the facia panel.
34 Refit in the reverse order of removal.

Hazard warning switch

35 It may be possible to remove the switch by applying a sticky pad or piece of tape to the face of the switch and pulling it from place. If not, use a blunt, flat-bladed tool to carefully prise the trim containing the centre air vents and storage compartment from the top of the facia. Push the switch out from the rear and disconnect the wiring plug **(see illustration)**.
36 Refitting is a reversal of removal.

Centre console switches

37 The switches in the centre console control a number of functions, including the ESP, parking aid, and warning light for passenger airbag deactivation. The process for removal and refitting is the same for each switch.
38 Using a blunt, flat-bladed tool, carefully prise away the panel that surrounds the radio, heating controls and switches. Take great care not to damage the surrounding area.
39 Lever out the relevant switch and disconnect the wiring plugs.
40 Refitting is the reversal of removal.

Seat heating switches

41 The front seat heating switches are integral with the heating/air conditioning control panel, and cannot be renewed separately. Removal of the panel is described in Chapter 3.
42 To remove the rear seat switches, open the rear ashtray.
43 Carefully unclip the panel containing the switches from the centre console and disconnect the wiring plug.
44 Unclip the relevant switch from the panel.
45 Refitting is a reversal of removal.

8 Exterior light bulbs – renewal

Note: *Whenever a bulb is renewed, note the following points*:

a) *Remember that if the light has just been in use, the bulb may be extremely hot.*
b) *Do not touch the bulb glass with the fingers, as the small deposits can cause the bulb to cloud over.*
c) *Always check the bulb contacts and holder, ensuring that there is clean metal-to-metal contact. Clean off any corrosion or dirt before fitting a new bulb.*
d) *Wherever bayonet-type bulbs are fitted, ensure that the live contacts bear firmly against the bulb contact.*
e) *Always ensure that the new bulb is of the correct rating and that it is completely clean before fitting it.*

Halogen headlights

Note: *This section does not cover bulb renewal on models fitted with gas discharge headlights; refer to Section 11.*
Note: *Removing the headlight can make bulb renewal easier but beam adjustment may be required after refitting.*

Vehicles up to model year 2008

1 To renew the dipped and main beam bulbs, remove the relevant cover from the rear of the headlight (larger square cover for dipped beam, circular cover for main beam), unplug the wiring connector, release the wire spring clamp and pull the bulb from the holder **(see illustrations)**.
2 If the bulb is to be refitted, do not touch the glass with the fingers. If the glass is accidentally touched, clean it with methylated spirit.
3 Refitting is a reversal of removal.

Vehicles from model year 2009

4 To remove the dipped beam bulb, remove the larger of the two rubber caps, turn the lifting eye anti-clockwise and remove the fitting and bulb from the headlight. To remove the main beam bulb, remove the smaller of the two rubber caps, unplug the wiring connector, release the wire spring clamp and remove the bulb **(see illustrations)**.
5 If the bulb is to be refitted, do not touch the glass with the fingers. If the glass is accidentally touched, clean it with methylated spirit.

8.1a Removing the larger cover on the rear of the headlamp gives access to the dipped beam bulb

8.1b Removing the smaller cover gives access to the main beam bulb

8.4a Remove the larger of the 2 rubber caps and remove the dipped beam bulb

8.4b Remove the smaller of the rubber caps to access the main beam bulb

8.8 Remove the larger cover from the headlight and use a pair of thin pliers to pull the parking light bulb from place

6 Refitting is a reversal of removal

Parking light

Vehicles up to model year 2008

7 Remove the larger plastic cover from the rear of the headlight.
8 Pull the bulbholder from the headlight **(see illustration)**.
9 Pull the wedge-type bulb directly from the bulbholder.
10 Fit the new bulb using a reversal of the removal procedure.

Vehicles from model year 2009

11 Remove the larger of the two rubber caps.
12 Using a pair of pliers, pull the bulbholder from the headlight and remove the bulb from the holder **(see illustration)**.
13 Fit the new bulb using a reversal of the removal procedure.

Front foglight

14 Remove the foglight (see Section 10).
15 Rotate the bulb and holder assembly anti-clockwise and remove it. Note that the bulb is integral with the holder.
16 Refitting is a reversal of removal.

Direction indicator

17 Rotate the bulbholder anti-clockwise and pull it from place.
18 Depress and twist the bulb to remove it from the bulbholder **(see illustrations)**.
19 Fit the new bulb using a reversal of the removal procedure.

Direction indicator side repeater

20 Additional indicator repeaters are mounted in the side mirror housings.

Vehicles up to model year 2008

21 Remove the mirror housing as described in Chapter 11 Section 24, and unplug the wiring connector.
22 Remove the screws at each end to release the indicator lens from the mirror housing. At the time of writing it appears that the bulb is integral with the lens and cannot be renewed separately, so a new lens may be required. Consult a Skoda dealer.

Vehicles from model year 2009

23 Remove the mirror glass and the upper and lower mirror covers as described in Chapter 11 Section 24.

24 The indicator LEDs are fitted as part of the lower cover.

Rear lights

25 Open the tailgate and open the access flap in the trim panel **(see illustration)**.
26 Disconnect the wiring plug connector, release the locking clips and remove the bulbholder **(see illustration)**.
27 Press and twist the relevant bulb anti-clockwise, and withdraw it from the bulbholder.
28 Fit the new bulb using a reversal of the removal procedure.

Number plate light

29 Undo the 2 screws, remove the number plate light and remove the bulb from its holder **(see illustration)**.

8.12 Remove the larger rubber cap and use a pair of pliers to pull the bulb from place

8.18a Turn the indicator bulbholder anti-clockwise and pull it from place

8.18b Depress and twist the bulb for removal

8.25 Undo the plastic screw and open the access flap

8.26 Release the locking clips and withdraw the bulbholder

8.29 Under the 2 screws (arrowed) to remove the number plate light lens

30 Fit the new bulb using a reversal of the removal procedure.

High-level brake light

31 Light Emitting Diodes (LEDs) are soldered to a printed circuit board to provide illumination for the high-level brake light. It is not possible to renew them. Where an LED is not functioning, the complete brake light unit must be renewed as described in Section 10.

9   Interior light bulbs –
      renewal

Note: *Whenever a bulb is renewed, note the following points:*
a) Remember that if the light has just been in use, the bulb may be extremely hot.
b) Always check the bulb contacts and holder, ensuring that there is clean metal-to-metal contact between the bulb and its live and earth. Clean off any corrosion or dirt before fitting a new bulb.
c) Wherever bayonet-type bulbs are fitted, ensure that the live contact(s) bear firmly against the bulb contact.
d) Always ensure that the new bulb is of the correct rating and that it is completely clean before fitting it.

Front and rear interior lights

1 Carefully lever down the light cover/lens of the interior light unit.

10.1a Undo the plastic nut (arrowed) at the top of the headlamp unit...

9.2 Carefully prising off the lens gives access to the interior light bulb, which can then be pulled from its holder

2 Remove the bulb from its holder **(see illustration)**.
3 Fit the new bulb using a reversal of the removal procedure.

Glovebox light

4 Insert a flat-bladed screwdriver behind the end of the lens, and prise free the light lens/unit. Remove the bulb from its holder.
5 Fit the new bulb using a reversal of the removal procedure.

Instrument panel bulbs

6 On all models covered by this Manual, it is not possible to renew the instrument panel bulbs individually as they are of LED design and soldered to a printed circuit board. Where an LED is not functioning, the complete instrument panel must be renewed.

Luggage compartment light

7 Insert a flat-bladed screwdriver behind the end of the lens, and prise free the light lens/unit. Disconnect the wiring plug and remove the bulb from its holder.
8 Fit the new bulb using a reversal of the removal procedure.

Switch illumination

9 Switch illumination bulbs are usually built into the switch itself, and cannot be renewed separately. Refer to Section 7 and remove the switch – bulb renewal should then be self-evident, if it is possible; otherwise, renew the switch.

10.1b ...and pull out the lever (arrowed)

Heater/air conditioning control panel illumination

10 The control panel is illuminated by non-renewable LEDs. If defective, the control panel may need to be renewed.

Door courtesy light

11 Using a screwdriver, carefully prise the light lens from place and pull the bulb from its holder.
12 Fit the new bulb using a reversal of the removal procedure.

Footwell light

13 Insert a flat-bladed screwdriver behind the end of the lens, and prise free the light lens/unit.
14 Unclip the heat shield, and pull the capless bulb from its holder.
15 Fit the new bulb using a reversal of the removal procedure.

10 Exterior light units –
     removal, refitting
     and beam adjustment

Headlight unit

Caution: On models equipped with gas discharge headlights, disconnect the battery negative lead, as described in Chapter 5 Section 3, prior to working on the headlights.

1 Undo the plastic nut at the top of the headlight and loosen the headlight by pulling on the lever **(see illustrations)**.
2 Disconnect the wiring plugs and carefully push the headlight forward to remove.
3 Refitting is a reversal of the removal procedure. On completion check for satisfactory operation, and have the headlight beam adjustment checked as soon as possible.

Front foglight

4 Remove the cover fitted next to the foglight.
5 On vehicles up to model year 2008, undo the 2 screws and pull the foglight forwards. Disconnect the wiring plug as the unit is withdrawn. On vehicles from model year 2009, the foglight is held in place by a catch accessed through the aperture when the cover is removed. When the catch is released, the foglight can be swivelled out of position.
6 Refitting is a reversal of removal, but have the foglight beam setting checked at the earliest opportunity.

Direction indicator

7 On all models, direction indicators are an integral part of the headlight unit and cannot be renewed separately.

Direction indicator side repeater

8 On all models, side repeaters are fitted within the exterior mirrors and are accessed by disassembling the mirror housings as described in Chapter 11 Section 24.

Rear lights

9 Open the access flap in the luggage compartment trim panel.
10 Disconnect the wiring plug from the rear of the light unit.
11 Undo the 4 retaining nuts and remove the light unit from the rear **(see illustration)**.
12 Refitting is a reversal of removal. Before tightening the retaining nuts, ensure the light unit is correctly aligned with the surrounding body panels with an even gap all round.

Number plate light

13 Undo the 2 screws and remove the light. Disconnect the wiring plug as the unit is withdrawn **(see illustration 7.29)**.
14 Refitting is a reversal of removal.

High-level brake light

Hatchback models

15 Remove the tailgate upper trim panel as described in Chapter 11, Section 12.
16 Undo the 2 retaining screws and release the 2 locking tabs, taking care not to damage the unit **(see illustration)**. Disconnect the wiring plug and remove the unit.
17 Refitting is a reversal of removal.

Estate models

18 Remove the tailgate upper trim panel as described in Chapter 11, Section 12.
19 Undo the 3 plastic retaining nuts **(see illustration)**.
20 Pull the light unit forward slightly and disconnect the wiring plug and rear screen washer hose **(see illustration)**. Remove the unit from the tailgate.
21 Refitting is a reversal of removal.

Headlight beam adjustment

22 Accurate adjustment of the headlight beam is only possible using optical beam setting equipment, and this work should therefore be carried out by a Skoda dealer or suitably-equipped workshop.

11 Gas discharge headlight system – general information

1 Gas discharge headlights were available as an optional extra on all models covered in this Manual. The headlights are fitted with bulbs that produce light by means of an electric arc, rather than by heating a metal filament as in conventional halogen bulbs. The arc is generated by a control circuit which operates at voltages of above 28 000 volts. The intensity of the emitted light means that the headlight beam has to be controlled dynamically to avoid dazzling other road users. An electronic control module monitors the vehicle's pitch and overall ride height by sensors mounted on the front and rear suspension, and adjusts the beam range accordingly, using the range control motors built into the headlight units. Additionally, gas discharge headlights fitted

10.11 To remove the rear light unit, undo the 4 nuts (arrowed)

10.19 On Estate models, undo the 3 plastic nuts (arrowed)

to the 2009 model year Octavia range are equipped with 'cornering' lights. On models with dynamic cornering lights, these are swivelled in relation to the steering wheel position, by means of electric motors integral with the headlights.
2 Refer to a Skoda dealer or suitably-equipped workshop for the renewal of bulbs or other components.

⚠ *Warning: Be aware that if you do decide to work on the system yourself, the discharge bulb starter circuitry operates at extremely high voltages. To avoid the risk of electric shock, ensure that the battery negative cable is disconnected before working on the headlight units (see Chapter 5 Section 3), then additionally switch the dipped beam on and off to discharge any residual voltage.*

12.4a With the steering column shrouds removed, undo the 2 screws (arrowed) at the base of the instrument panel

10.16 Undo the 2 screws (arrowed) and release the retaining clips. Take care not to damage the light unit

10.20 Disconnect the wiring plug and washer hose, and remove the light unit from the tailgate

12 Instrument panel – removal and refitting

Note: *If the instrument panel is being substituted with a new or exchange unit, a Skoda dealer or specialist is required to initialise/adapt the various instrument panel functions.*
1 Fully extend the steering column, and move it to its lowest position.
2 Remove the light switch as described in Section 6, and the two trim panels either side of the steering wheel.
3 Remove the upper steering column trim panel along with the cover between the steering column and facia panel.
4 Undo the 2 bolts securing the instrument panel at its lower edge **(see illustrations)**

12.4b Pull the top of the instrument panel rearwards to release the retaining clips. Take care as the panel is easily damaged

12.5 Undo the wiring plug at the rear and withdraw the instrument panel from the facia

and prise the top edge of the panel from its retaining clips. Note that the top clips can be difficult to release so care is needed to avoid damage to the instrument panel.

5 Pulling the instrument panel rearwards should

release the wiring connection. If not, carefully pull the panel and undo the wiring plug. The panel can now be removed **(see illustration)**.

6 Refitting is a reversal of removal, but see the note at the beginning of this Section.

13 Windscreen wiper components – removal and refitting

Wiper blades

1 Refer to *Weekly checks*.

Wiper arms

Removal

2 Switch on the ignition and turn it off again, then within 10 seconds briefly press the wiper control switch downwards and release it. This will cause the wipers to move to the 'Service' position.

13.3a With the wipers in the 'Service' position, remove the plastic cover and undo the spindle nut

13.3b If required, use a small two-legged puller to remove the arm

3 Before removing an arm, mark its parked position on the glass with a strip of adhesive tape. Prise off the cover and unscrew the spindle nut, if necessary using a small two-legged puller to remove the arm **(see illustrations)**.

4 To remove the tailgate wiper, raise the cover and carefully pull out the washer jet nozzle. Undo the spindle nut and ease the arm from the spindle by rocking it slowly from side-to-side. If necessary, use a small two-legged puller to remove the arm.

Refitting

5 Refitting the front wipers is a reversal of removal, but before tightening the spindle nuts, position the wiper blades as marked before removal. On Hatchback models, the distance between the wiper blade and the bottom edge of the rear screen should be 36 mm, and on Estate models 22 mm.

Wiper motor

Note: *See Section 15 for tailgate wiper motor.*

Removal

6 Remove the wiper arms as described above.
7 Remove the cover over the plenum chamber. Pull up the rubber sealing strip, then starting in the middle, pull the plenum chamber cover upwards from the base of the windscreen **(see illustration)**. Unclip the washer jet pipe from the cover as it's withdrawn.
8 Disconnect the motor wiring plug **(see illustration)**.
9 Undo the retaining bolts, then manoeuvre the assembly from place **(see illustrations)**.
10 Using a screwdriver, carefully prise the linkage arm from the balljoint stud.

13.7 Pull plenum chamber cover from the base of the windscreen

13.8 Disconnect the wiper motor wiring plug

13.9a Undo the 2 retaining bolts...

13.9b ... and manoeuvre the wiper motor from place

13.11 Undoing the nut (arrowed) releases the crank arm from the motor

13.12 Undo the 3 bolts (arrowed) to remove the motor from the linkage

11 Undo the nut and detach the crank arm from the wiper motor **(see illustration)**.
12 To separate the motor from the linkage, undo the three retaining bolts and remove the motor **(see illustration)**.

Refitting

13 When refitting, note the locating pin on the rear of the motor which engages with a grommet at the rear of the space for the motor. With the motor/linkage back in place, refit the crank arm so the distance between the stop on the retaining plate and the motor crank arm is 3 mm, and tighten the retaining nut securely. The remainder of refitting is a reversal of removal.

14 Washer system – general

1 All models are fitted with a windscreen washer system and also a tailgate washer; some models are fitted with headlight washers.
2 The fluid reservoir for the windscreen/headlight washer is located behind the right-hand side of the front bumper. The windscreen washer fluid pump is attached to the side of the reservoir body, and the level sensor is attached to the underside of the reservoir behind the headlight **(see illustration)**. Where headlight washers are fitted, a lift cylinder/accumulator is located in the supply tube, behind the front bumper. Access to the reservoir is achieved by removing the right-hand headlight and placing the lock carrier in the 'Service position' (Chapter 11 Section 10). In order to access the pump, only the bumper need be removed (Chapter 11 Section 9).
3 The tailgate washer is fed by the same reservoir and pump, operating in the reverse direction.
4 Access to the headlight washer lift cylinders is by removal of the front bumper (Chapter 11 Section 9). No dismantling of the lift cylinders is recommended. If defective, the complete assembly must be renewed.
5 The reservoir fluid level must be regularly topped-up with windscreen washer fluid containing an antifreeze agent, but not cooling system antifreeze – see *Weekly checks*.

14.2 The washer reservoir is located behind the front bumper on the right-hand side

6 The supply hoses are attached by rubber couplings to their various connections, and if required, can be detached by simply pulling them free from the appropriate connector **(see illustration)**.
7 The windscreen washer jets can be adjusted by using a small screwdriver and moving the nozzle up or down until the correct spray pattern is reached.
8 To remove the rear washer jet, pull open the plastic cover over the wiper spindle, and pull the jet from place. On Estate models, the washer jet is integral with the high-level brake light.
9 The headlight washer jets are best adjusted using the Skoda tool, and should therefore be entrusted to a Skoda garage to set.

15 Tailgate wiper motor – removal and refitting

1 Make sure the tailgate wiper is switched off and in its rest position, then remove the tailgate trim panel as described in Chapter 11, Section 12.
2 Remove the wiper arm and blade as described in Section 13.
3 Detach the wiring connector from the wiper motor, then disconnect the washer jet hose.
4 Undo the 3 wiper motor mounting nuts and remove the wiper motor from the tailgate **(see illustration)**. Check the condition of the spindle rubber grommet in the tailgate, and if necessary, renew it.

14.6 Washer hoses can simply be pulled from any connectors

5 Refit in the reverse order of removal. Refit the wiper arm and blade so that the arm is parked correctly.

16 Horns – removal and refitting

1 The horn is located at the front end of the vehicle behind the left-hand side of the bumper (or both sides for dual horns).
2 Remove the wheel arch liner as described in Chapter 11 Section 11.
3 Disconnect the horn wiring plug, undo the mounting nut and remove the horn from the vehicle **(see illustrations)**.
4 Refit in the reverse order of removal. Check for satisfactory operation on completion.

17 Sunroof motor – removal and refitting

Closing sunroof manually

1 If the motor malfunctions when the roof panel is in the open position, it can be wound shut manually. To do this, use a flat, blunt-edged tool to remove the cover adjacent to the interior light.
2 Insert a suitably-sized Allen key into the fitting on the motor and turn until the roof is closed.

15.4 Undo the 3 nuts (arrowed) to remove the rear wiper motor from the tailgate

16.3a For dual horns, undo the nut (arrowed) to remove the right-hand horn...

16.3b ... and the nut (arrowed) to remove the left-hand horn

19.3 The parking aid control unit is mounted on the left-hand wheel arch

19.7a Disconnect the parking sensor wiring plug

19.7b Release the retaining clips and pull the sensor from the bumper

Motor

3 Ensure the sunroof is fully closed, then turn off the ignition. Use a flat, blunt-edged tool to remove the cover adjacent to the interior light.
4 Undo the 3 retaining bolts and lower the motor from place. Disconnect the wiring plug as the motor is withdrawn. Discard the bolts – new ones must be fitted.
5 Refitting is a reversal of removal noting the process below.

Drive position adjustment

6 With the motor removed but the wiring plug connected, select 'tilt sunroof' with the control switch.
7 Now select 'close sunroof' using the control switch.
8 Now select 'open sunroof' using the control switch.
9 Again, select 'close sunroof' using the control switch.
10 In the motor drive aperture, the coloured marking must be aligned with the pre-set lug. The motor is now in the correct position for refitment.

18 Central locking system – general information

1 All models are equipped with a central door locking system, which automatically locks all doors and the tailgate in unison with the manual locking of the driver's front door. The system is operated electronically with motors/

19.12 The buzzer for the rear parking sensors is located behind the lower B-pillar trim panel on the left-hand side

switches incorporated into the door lock assemblies and is controlled by an electronic control unit.
2 The control unit is equipped with a self-diagnosis capability. Should the system develop a fault, have the control unit interrogated by a Skoda dealer or suitably-equipped specialist. Once the fault has been established, refer to the relevant Section of Chapter 11 to renew a door lock or tailgate lock as applicable.

19 Parking aid components – general, removal and refitting

General information

1 The parking aid system is available on all models. Four ultrasound sensors located in the bumpers measure the distance to the closest object behind or in front the car, and inform the driver using acoustic signals from a buzzer located behind the left-hand B-pillar trim or behind the instrument panel. The nearer the object, the more frequent the acoustic signals.
2 The system includes a control unit and self-diagnosis program, and therefore, in the event of a fault, the vehicle should be taken to a Skoda dealer or suitably-equipped specialist.

Control unit

3 The control unit is located behind the left-hand trim in the rear luggage compartment **(see illustration)**. Remove the luggage compartment side panel trim as described in Chapter 11, Section 30.
4 Disconnect the control unit wiring plugs, undo the fasteners and remove the control unit.
5 Refitting is a reversal of removal. If a new control unit is fitted, re-coding is required using Skoda diagnostic equipment. This work should be entrusted to a Skoda dealer or suitably-equipped specialist.

Range/distance sensor

Front sensors

6 Remove the front bumper as described in Chapter 11 Section 9.

7 Disconnect the sensor wiring plug, release the retaining clips, and pull the sensor from position **(see illustrations)**.
8 Refitting is a reversal of removal. Press the sensor firmly into position until the retaining clips engage.

Rear sensors

9 Remove the rear bumper as described in Chapter 11 Section 9.
10 Disconnect the sensor wiring plug, release the retaining clips, and pull the sensor from position **(see illustrations 18.7a and 18.7b)**.
11 Refitting is a reversal of removal. Press the sensor firmly into position until the retaining clips engage.

Warning buzzer

Rear buzzer

12 The rear warning buzzer is located behind the lower trim panel of the left-hand B-pillar **(see illustration)**. Remove the lower B-pillar trim as described in Chapter 11, Section 30. Remove the button rivets, lift the buzzer from position, and disconnect the wiring plug.
13 Refitting is a reversal of removal.

Front buzzer

14 Remove the instrument panel as described in Section 12.
15 Disconnect the wiring plug, lever out the plastic expansion rivets, and remove the buzzer.
16 Refitting is a reversal of removal.

20 Infotainment unit and autochanger – removal and refitting

Note: *This Section applies only to standard-fit audio equipment. The radio/CD unit may have a security code which requires inputting on refitting. Ensure that you have this before disconnecting any wiring plugs.*

Removal

Radio/CD unit

1 Carefully prise the infotainment unit/heater control surround trim from place using a blunt, flat-bladed tool.

2 Remove the covers at each corner of the unit and undo the 4 retaining bolts **(see illustration)**.

3 Withdraw the infotainment unit from the mounting case, then disconnect the wiring plugs as the unit is withdrawn **(see illustration)**.

4 Refitting is a reversal of removal.

Autochanger

5 The CD changer is located in the luggage compartment behind the left-hand side trim panel.

6 Remove the trim panel as described in Chapter 11, Section 30. Insert the special Skoda tools into the slots in the front face of the autochanger **(see illustration)**.

7 Pull the autochanger from position, then disconnect the wiring plugs.

8 Refitting is a reversal of removal.

Multimedia control unit

9 Amongst other functions, the Multimedia control unit (where fitted) provides an audio input (AUX-IN), a USB input, and an iPod connection interface.

10 To remove the control unit, remove the glovebox as described in Chapter 11 Section 27. Undo the 2 nuts and pull the control unit and bracket downwards.

11 Disconnect the wiring plugs as the unit is withdrawn.

12 Refitting is a reversal of removal. If the unit is renewed, recoding is required using Skoda diagnostic equipment. This work should be entrusted to a Skoda dealer or suitably-equipped specialist.

13 An external connection for other audio devices may also be fitted in the centre console. Removing the connection requires removal of the centre console as described in Chapter 11 Section 25.

21 Audio amplifier – removal and refitting

1 The audio amplifier (where fitted) is located under the passenger's seat, either slide the seat fully back, or to improve access, remove the seat as described in Chapter 11 Section 29.

2 Unclip the amplifier cover, and pull it forwards.

3 Undo the securing bolts and remove the amplifier. Disconnect the wiring plugs as the amplifier is withdrawn.

4 Refitting is a reversal of removal. Recoding of the audio system may be required and should be entrusted to a Skoda dealer or suitably-equipped specialist.

22 Speakers – removal and refitting

1 The audio system speakers are fitted in the front and rear door trim panels and there are separate mid-range and high frequency

20.2 Lever out the plastic cover at each corner of the radio and undo the bolts (arrowed)

speakers. Other speakers may be also be fitted depending on the specification of the audio system.

Door speakers

Low frequency speaker

2 To remove a door-mounted speaker, remove the appropriate door trim as described in Chapter 11 Section 15.

3 Drill out the rivets and remove the speaker. Disconnect the speaker wiring plugs as the speaker is withdrawn.

4 Refit in the reverse order of removal.

High frequency speaker

5 Remove the trim surrounding the door interior release handle as described in Chapter 11 Section 15.

6 Disconnect the wiring plug from the speaker and slide the speaker/trim from the handle.

7 Refit in the reverse order of removal.

23 Airbag system – general information and precautions

⚠ *Warning: Before carrying out any operations on the airbag system, disconnect the battery negative terminal (see Chapter 5 Section 3), then wait at least 5 minutes for any residual electric energy to dissipate before proceeding. When operations are complete, make sure no one is inside the vehicle when the battery is reconnected.*

⚠ *Warning: Note that the airbag(s) must not be subjected to temperatures in excess of 90°C. When the airbag is removed, ensure that it is stored with the pad uppermost to prevent possible inflation.*

⚠ *Warning: Do not allow any solvents or cleaning agents to contact the airbag assemblies. They must be cleaned using only a damp cloth.*

⚠ *Warning: The airbags and control unit are both sensitive to impact. If either is dropped or damaged they should be renewed.*

20.3 Pull out the wiring plug as the radio is withdrawn

⚠ *Warning: Disconnect the airbag control unit wiring plug prior to using arc-welding equipment on the vehicle.*

1 Both a driver's and passenger's airbag are fitted as standard equipment to models in the Skoda Octavia range. The driver's airbag is fitted to the centre of the steering wheel. The passenger's airbag is fitted to the upper surface of the facia, above the glovebox. The airbag system comprises the airbag units (complete with gas generators), an impact sensor, the control unit and a warning light in the instrument panel. Seat-mounted side airbags, overhead curtain airbags and rear side airbags are also fitted on certain models, and seat belt tensioners are incorporated in the front seat belt reels and rear seat belt anchors.

2 The airbag system is triggered in the event of a direct or offset frontal impact above a predetermined force. The airbag is inflated within milliseconds, and forms a safety cushion between the driver and the steering wheel or the passenger and the facia. This prevents contact between the upper body and the steering wheel, column and facia, and therefore greatly reduces the risk of injury. The airbag then deflates almost immediately through vents in the side of the airbag.

3 Every time the ignition is switched on, the airbag control unit performs a self-test. The self-test takes approximately 3 seconds, and during this time the airbag warning light on the

20.6 Insert the release tools in the slots in the front of the CD unit and pull it from place

24.2 Insert a small screwdriver into the 2 access holes in the rear of the steering wheel and turn clockwise to release the airbag clips

facia is illuminated. After the self-test has been completed, the warning light should go out. If the warning light fails to come on, remains illuminated after the initial 3-second period, or comes on at any time when the vehicle is being driven, there is a fault in the airbag system. The vehicle should then be taken to a Skoda dealer or specialist for examination at the earliest possible opportunity.

24 Airbag system components – removal and refitting

Note: *Refer to the warnings in Section 23 before carrying out the following operations.*

Driver's airbag

1 Release the steering column adjustment lever, and pull the wheel out and down as far as possible.
2 Locate the access holes in the reverse side of the steering wheel. Insert a flat-bladed screwdriver approximately 5 mm, and turn the screwdriver clockwise (anti-clockwise from the driver's seat) from to release the fastener **(see illustration)**. Turn the wheel 180° and release the second fastener on the opposite side.
3 Temporarily touch the striker plate of the front door to discharge any electrostatic electricity then carefully lift the airbag assembly away from the steering wheel, disconnecting the wiring connector(s) **(see illustration)**. Note that the airbag must not be

24.3 Release the wiring plug from the steering wheel as the airbag unit is withdrawn

knocked or dropped, and should be stored with its padded surface uppermost.
4 On refitting, reconnect the wiring connectors and locate the airbag unit in the steering wheel, making sure the wire does not become trapped, and the connectors audibly engage (click). Ensure no-one is in the vehicle when the battery is reconnected.

Passenger airbag

5 Remove the passenger's glovebox as described in Chapter 11 Section 27.
6 Release the locking catch, then disconnect the airbag wiring plug.
7 Temporarily touch the striker plate of the front door to discharge any electrostatic electricity then undo the 4 retaining bolts **(see illustrations)**, and manoeuvre the airbag from place.
8 Refitting is a reversal of removal. Apply a little thread-locking compound to the bolts. Ensure that the wiring connector is securely reconnected. Ensure that no-one is inside the vehicle when the battery is reconnected.

Airbag wiring contact unit

9 Removal and refitting the contact unit is described in Section 6.

Airbag control unit

10 Refer to Chapter 11 Section 25 and remove the side covers of the centre console on both sides.
11 Release the locking device and disconnect the wiring plug for the control unit.

12 Undo the 3 retaining nuts and remove the control unit **(see illustration)**.
13 Refitting is a reversal of removal. If a new control unit has been fitted, it must be coded using Skoda diagnostic equipment. Entrust this task to a Skoda dealer or suitably-equipped specialist.

Side airbags

14 The side airbags are incorporated into the side of the front and rear seats. Removal of the units requires the seat upholstery to be removed. This is a specialist task, which we recommend should be entrusted to a Skoda dealer or specialist.

Head airbags

15 The head airbags run from the rear of the passenger cabin to the front A-pillars on each side. Removal of the airbags requires the headlining to be lowered. This is a specialist task, and should be entrusted to a Skoda dealer or upholstery specialist.

Rear side airbags

16 The side airbags are incorporated into the side padding adjacent to the rear seat backrests. Removal of the units is a specialist task, which we recommend should be entrusted to a Skoda dealer or specialist.

25 Anti-theft alarm system – general information

1 An anti-theft alarm and immobiliser system is fitted as standard equipment. Should the system become faulty, the vehicle should be taken to a Skoda dealer or specialist for examination. They will have access to a special diagnostic tester which will quickly trace any fault present in the system.

26 Convenience system electronic control module – removal and refitting

Note: *The convenience system electronic control module (ECM) – and on later models the vehicle voltage control unit (VVCU) – is*

24.7a Undo the 4 retaining bolts (left-hand bolts arrowed)...

24.7b ... and lower the passenger airbag unit from place

24.12 Airbag control unit retaining nuts (arrowed)

26.2 Undo the 2 retaining screws (arrowed) to remove the ECM bracket

responsible for the operation of a number of functions including the central locking, sunroof and window lifter controls, and the anti-theft alarm.

Removal

Vehicles up to model year 2008

1 The ECM is located behind the glovebox on the passenger side of the facia panel.
2 Remove the glovebox as described in Chapter 11 Section 27. The ECM bracket is held in place by 2 screws, an upper screw to the left of the ECM and a lower screw behind the passenger side facia end panel. Undo the 2 retaining screws and remove the bracket, complete with the ECM **(see illustration)**.
3 Disconnect the wiring plug.
4 If required, slide across the locking catch and detach the ECM from the bracket.

Vehicles from model year 2009

5 The convenience functions were no longer controlled by the convenience system ECM but were integrated into the vehicle voltage control unit. See Section 28 for removal and refitting.

Refitting

6 Refitting is a reversal of removal. If a new ECM is being fitted, it will be necessary for the units to be initialised prior to use by means of dedicated test equipment. Consult your local Skoda dealer or suitably-equipped specialist.

27 Fuel filler flap locking motor – removal and refitting

1 Remove the right-hand side luggage compartment side trim panel, as described in Chapter 11, Section 30.
2 Disconnect the motor wiring plug.
3 Undo the 2 screws and pull the motor and actuating rod rearwards **(see illustration)**.
4 To refit, manoeuvre the motor into position, reconnect the wiring plug and tighten the retaining bolts securely.
5 Refit the luggage compartment side trim panel.

28 Vehicle voltage control unit – removal and refitting

1 The vehicle voltage control unit (VVCU) is

27.3 Undo the 2 screws (arrowed) and pull the motor rearwards

responsible for supplying power to various vehicle systems and accessory circuits and communicates with other control units via a databus network. The control unit is located behind the driver's side of the facia.
2 To remove the VVCU, remove the lower facia panel on the driver's side as described in Chapter 11, Section 26.
3 Push together the catches and push the relay carrier from the brackets on the VVCU.
4 Release the catches on each of the plug connections and remove from the VVCU.
5 Push out the locking tabs at each side of the VVCU and carefully pull it away from its mounting.
6 Refitting is a reversal of removal, noting that if a new unit is fitted, it may need to be adapted/initialised using Skoda diagnostic equipment. Entrust this task to a Skoda dealer or suitably-equipped specialist.

Skoda Octavia wiring diagrams

Diagram 1

At the time of writing, certain wiring diagram technical information was unavailable. As a result these diagrams are intended as a representative set covering most major electrical systems typically encountered on this model range.

WARNING: This vehicle is fitted with a supplemental restraint system (SRS) consisting of a combination of driver (and passenger) airbag(s), side impact protection airbags and seatbelt pre-tensioners. The use of electrical test equipment on any SRS wiring systems may cause the seatbelt pre-tensioners to abruptly retract and airbags to explosively deploy, resulting in potentially severe personal injury. Extreme care should be taken to correctly identify any circuits to be tested to avoid choosing any of the SRS wiring in error.
For further information see airbag system precautions in body electrical systems chapter.
Note: The SRS wiring harness can normally be identified by yellow and/or orange harness or harness connectors.

Key to symbols

Solenoid actuator

Earth point and location

Wire colour
(red with black tracer) — Ro/Sw

Dashed outline denotes part of a larger item, containing in this case an electronic or solid state device.
6a/3 refers to pin 3 of a single connector 6a.
30 refers to standard DIN terminal designation, in this instance for permanent battery supply.

Bulb

Switch

Fuse/Fusible link **F26**

Resistor

Variable resistor

Variable resistor

Heating element

Wire splice, soldered joint, or unspecified connector

Connecting wires

Diode

Light-emitting diode

Item number **12**

Motor/pump

Earth locations

E1   Near battery
E2   LH engine bay, lower longitudinal member
E3   Lower LH 'A' pillar
E4   Lower RH 'A' pillar
E5   On steering column
E6   LH luggage compartment
E7   LH luggage compartment
E8   RH engine bay, lower longitudinal member
E9   Lower RH 'A' pillar
E10 Below centre console
E11 Lower LH 'A' pillar
E12 Lower LH 'B' pillar
E13 Lower RH 'B' pillar
E14 LH engine bay, lower longitudinal member

Battery fusebox 4

FA1   150A   Alternator
         200A   Alternator
FA2   80A   Power steering
FA3   80A   Radiator cooling fan
FA4   -   Spare
FA5   100A   Auxiliary heater
FA6   80A   Supply to fuses
FA7   -   Spare

Key to circuits

Diagram 1   Information for wiring diagrams.
Diagram 2   Information for wiring diagrams.
Diagram 3   Starting, charging, horn, cigar lighter and accessory socket
Diagram 4   Side, tail number plate & headlights, stop, reversing & fog lights.
Diagram 5   Hazard warning & direction indicators, headlight levelling, heated rear window.
Diagram 6   Heater blower & wash/wipe.
Diagram 7   Audio system & interior lighting.
Diagram 8   Instrument cluster.
Diagram 9   Electric power steering & electric mirrors.
Diagram 10   Central locking.
Diagram 11   Electric windows.

Skoda Octavia wiring diagrams

Diagram 2

Engine fusebox 5

FB1	30A	ABS
FB2	30A	ABS
FB3	20A	Convenience system control unit
FB4	5A	On-board supply control unit
FB5	20A	Horn
FB6	20A	Engine management
FB7	5A	Engine management
FB8	10A	Engine management
FB9	10A	Engine management
FB10	10A	Engine management
FB11	30A	Engine management
FB12	15A	Engine management
FB13	15A	Automatic transmission
FB14	-	Spare
FB15	40A	Starter
FB16	15A	Steering column control unit
FB17	10A	Instrument cluster
FB18	30A	Amplifier
FB19	15A	Audio system, navigation
FB20	5A	Telephone
FB21	-	Spare
FB22	-	Spare
FB23	-	Spare
FB24	10A	Data bus diagnostic interface
FB25	-	Spare
FB26	10A	Engine management
FB27	10A	Engine management
FB28	20A	Automatic transmission
FB29	20A	Engine management
FB30	-	Spare

FB31	30A	Wiper motor
FB32	10A	Engine management
FB33	15A	Engine management
FB34	-	Spare
FB35	-	Spare
FB36	-	Spare
FB37	-	Spare
FB38	10A	Headlight levelling
FB39	5A	Oil level/temperature sender
FB40	20A	Interior voltage supply
FB41	-	Spare
FB42	10A	Engine management
FB43	20A	Vacuum pump for brakes
FB44	-	Spare
FB45	15A	Engine management
FB46	-	Spare
FB47	40A	On-board supply control unit
FB48	40A	On-board supply control unit
FB49	-	Spare
FB50	-	Spare
FB51	50A	Engine management
FB52	50A	On-board supply control unit, 'x' contact relay
FB53	50A	Interior voltage supply
FB54	50A	Engine cooling fan

Passenger fusebox 13

FC1	10A	Diagnostic connector supply
FC2	5A	TCS/ESP/ABS, tyre pressure monitor
FC3	10A	Power steering
FC4	5A	Heating and air conditioning
FC5	-	Spare
FC6	5A	Instrument cluster, data bus diagnostic interface, automatic transmission
FC7	5A	Headlight levelling
FC8	5A	Anti-dazzle interior mirror
FC9	5A	Four wheel drive control unit
FC10	5A	Telephone
FC11	5A	Trailer
FC12	10A	Front door control units (central locking)
FC13	10A	Light switch, diagnostic connector supply
FC14	5A	Stop light switch, automatic transmission
FC15	7.5A	On-board supply control unit, interior lighting
FC16	10A	Heating and air conditioning
FC17	10A	Rain and light sensor
FC18	5A	Parking aid
FC19	5A	Parking aid
FC20	-	Spare
FC21	-	Spare
FC22	40A	Heater blower control unit
FC23	30A	Front door control units (electric windows)
FC24	25A	Front accessory socket, cigar lighter
FC25	25A	Heated rear window
FC26	20A	Luggage compartment accessory socket
FC27	15A	Engine management

FC28	-	Spare
FC29	10A	Engine management
FC30	5A	Airbag
FC31	5A	Reversing light switch, automatic transmission
FC32	30A	Rear door control units
FC33	25A	Sunroof
FC34	-	Spare
FC35	5A	Alarm
FC36	20A	Headlight washer
FC37	30A	Heated front seats
FC38	-	Spare
FC39	-	Spare
FC40	40A	Heater blower
FC41	15A	Rear wiper
FC42	15A	On-board supply control unit
FC43	15A	Trailer
FC44	20A	Trailer
FC45	15A	Trailer
FC46	5A	Heated seats, heated washer jets
FC47	-	Spare
FC48	-	Spare
FC49	5A	Light switch

H47361

Colour codes

Ws	White	Or	Orange
Bl	Blue	Ro	Red
Gr	Grey	Rs	Pink
Ge	Yellow	Gn	Green
Br	Brown	Li	Purple
Sw	Black		

Key to items

1 Battery
2 Starter motor
3 Alternator
4 Battery fusebox
5 Engine fusebox
  R1 = terminal 15 supply relay
  R2 = terminal 50 supply relay
6 On-board power supply control unit
  a = horn relay
7 Steering column control unit

8 Ignition switch
9 High tone horn
10 Low tone horn (if fitted)
11 Steering wheel clock springs
12 Horn switch
13 Passenger fusebox
14 Cigar lighter
15 Luggage compartment accessory socket
16 Front ashtray light
17 Rear ashtray light

18 Ignition key lock solenoid

Diagram 3

H47362

Starting & charging

Horn

Cigar lighter & accessory socket

Colour codes

Ws	White	**Or**	Orange
Bl	Blue	**Ro**	Red
Gr	Grey	**Rs**	Pink
Ge	Yellow	**Gn**	Green
Br	Brown	**Li**	Purple
Sw	Black		

Key to items

1 Battery
4 Battery fusebox
5 Engine fusebox
 R1= terminal 15 supply relay
6 On-board power supply control unit
 b = 'x' contact relief relay
7 Steering column control unit
13 Passenger fusebox
20 Stop light switch
21 Reversing light switch
22 High level stop light

23 LH rear light unit
 a = stop light
 b = reversing light
 c = foglight
24 RH rear light unit (a to c as above)
25 Dir. indicator/headlight flash/dip switch
26 LH tail light
27 RH tail light
28 Number plate light
29 Light switch
 a = off/auto/side/headlight

b = control unit
c = switch illumination
d = front/rear foglight
30 LH headlight
 a = sidelight
 b = main beam
 c = dip beam
31 RH headlight (a to c as above)
32 Rain/light sensor
33 LH front foglight
34 RH front foglight

Diagram 4

H47363

Stop & reversing lights

Front/rear fog lights

Headlights, side, tail & number plate lights

Colour codes

Ws	White	**Or**	Orange
Bl	Blue	**Ro**	Red
Gr	Grey	**Rs**	Pink
Ge	Yellow	**Gn**	Green
Br	Brown	**Li**	Purple
Sw	Black		

Key to items

1 Battery
4 Battery fusebox
5 Engine fusebox
   R1= terminal 15 supply relay
6 On-board power supply control unit
   c = heated rear window relay
7 Steering column control unit
13 Passenger fusebox
23 LH rear light unit
   d = direction indicator
24 RH rear light unit (d as above)

25 Dir. indicator/headlight flash/dip switch
30 LH headlight
   d = direction indicator
   e = headlight levelling
31 RH headlight (d and e as above)
37 Hazard warning switch
38 Driver's door control unit
39 Passenger's door control unit
40 Driver's door mirror assembly
   a = indicator side repeater

41 Passenger's door mirror assembly
   a = indicator side repeater
42 Headlight levelling/lighting rheostat
43 Heated rear window
44 Heater control panel
   a = heated rear window switch
   b = heated rear window indicator

Diagram 5

H47364

Direction indicators & hazard warning lights

Headlight levelling

Heated rear window

Colour codes

Ws	White	**Or**	Orange
Bl	Blue	**Ro**	Red
Gr	Grey	**Rs**	Pink
Ge	Yellow	**Gn**	Green
Br	Brown	**Li**	Purple
Sw	Black		

Key to items

1 Battery
4 Battery fusebox
5 Engine fusebox
   R1= terminal 15 supply relay
6 On-board power supply control unit
   b = 'x' contact relay
   d = windscreen washer relay 1
   e = windscreen washer relay 2
7 Steering column control unit

13 Passenger fusebox
44 Heater control panel
   c = recirculation switch
   d = recirculation indicator
   e = switch illumination
   f = heater blower switch
47 Heater blower motor
48 Recirculation motor
49 Heater blower resistors

50 Wash/wipe switch
   a = intermittent delay
   b = front wiper
   c = rear wiper
51 Front wiper motor
52 Rear wiper motor
53 Washer pump

Diagram 6

H47365

Heater blower

Wash/wipe

Colour codes

Ws	White	**Or**	Orange
Bl	Blue	**Ro**	Red
Gr	Grey	**Rs**	Pink
Ge	Yellow	**Gn**	Green
Br	Brown	**Li**	Purple
Sw	Black		

Key to items

1 Battery
4 Battery fusebox
5 Engine fusebox
6 On-board supply control unit
  f = terminal 30 supply relay
13 Passenger fusebox
42 Headlight levelling/lighting rheostat
56 Audio unit
57 LH front bass speaker

58 LH rear bass speaker
59 RH front bass speaker
60 RH rear bass speaker
61 LH front tweeter
62 LH rear tweeter
63 RH front tweeter
64 RH rear tweeter
65 CD player
66 Antenna

67 Convenience control unit
68 Front interior light
69 Rear interior light
70 Glove box light
71 Luggage compartment light
72 LH luggage compartment light
73 Tailgate switch
  a = luggage compartment light switch

Diagram 7

H47366

Audio system

Interior lighting

Colour codes

Ws	White	Or	Orange
Bl	Blue	Ro	Red
Gr	Grey	Rs	Pink
Ge	Yellow	Gn	Green
Br	Brown	Li	Purple
Sw	Black		

Key to items

1 Battery
4 Battery fusebox
5 Engine fusebox
  R1= terminal 15 supply relay
6 On-board supply control unit
13 Passenger fusebox
75 Oil level/temperature sensor
76 Immobilizer reader coil
77 LH pad wear sensor
78 Low brake fluid switch
79 Oil pressure switch
80 Handbrake switch
81 Low coolant level sender
82 Low washer fluid sender
83 Ambient air temperature sensor
84 Fuel gauge sender/fuel pump
85 Instrument cluster
  a = buzzer
  b = immobilizer control unit

c = multifunction display
d = odometer
e = selector lever position indicator
f = speedometer
g = tachometer
h = coolant temperature gauge
i = fuel gauge
j = brake fluid/handbrake warning light
k = immobilizer warning light
l = coolant temp./level warning light
m = low washer fluid warning light
n = pad wear warning light
o = low oil level warning light
p = main beam warning light
q = dip beam warning light
r = LH indicator warning light
s = RH indicator warning light
t = rear foglight warning light
u = alternator warning light

v = ABS warning light
w = TCS/ESP warning light
x = airbag warning light
y = instrument cluster illumination
z = tailgate ajar warning light
a1 = door ajar warning light
b1 = bonnett ajar warning light
c1 = seatbelt warning light
d1 = bulb failure warning light
e1 = electronic fault warning light
f1 = glow plug warning light
g1 = exhaust emmission warning light
h1 = power steering warning light
i1 = tyre pressure warning light
j1 = selector lever warning light
k1 = oil pressure warning light
l1 = low fuel warning light

Diagram 8

H47367

Instrument cluster

Colour codes

Ws	White	Or	Orange
Bl	Blue	Ro	Red
Gr	Grey	Rs	Pink
Ge	Yellow	Gn	Green
Br	Brown	Li	Purple
Sw	Black		

Key to items

1 Battery
4 Battery fusebox
5 Engine fusebox
  R1= terminal 15 supply relay
6 On-board supply control unit
7 Steering column control unit
13 Passenger fusebox
38 Driver's door control unit
39 Passenger's door control unit

40 Driver's door mirror assembly
  b = entry light
  c = adjustment motor
  d = heating element
41 Passenger's door mirror assembly
  b = entry light
  c = adjustment motor
  d = heating element
88 Power steering control unit

89 Steering moment sensor
90 Steering angle sensor
91 Mirror control switch
  a = mirror heating switch
  b = LH/RH change-over switch
  c = mirror adjustment switch
  d = switch illumination

Diagram 9

H47368

Electric power steering

Electric mirrors

Colour codes

Ws	White	**Or**	Orange
Bl	Blue	**Ro**	Red
Gr	Grey	**Rs**	Pink
Ge	Yellow	**Gn**	Green
Br	Brown	**Li**	Purple
Sw	Black		

Key to items

1 Battery
4 Battery fusebox
5 Engine fusebox
6 On-board supply control unit
13 Passenger fusebox
38 Driver's door control unit
39 Passenger's door control unit
67 Convenience control unit
73 Tailgate switch
   b = central locking switch

95 Driver's door lock assembly
   a = door contact switch
   b = lock switch
   c = lock motor
   d = deadlock motor
96 Passenger's door lock assembly
   (a to d as above)
97 LH rear door lock assembly
   (a to d as above)

98 RH rear door lock assembly
   (a to d as above)
99 Rear lid handle release switch
100 Filler flap lock motor
101 Tailgate lock motor
102 Central locking warning light
103 Driver's door entry light
104 Passenger's door entry light

Diagram 10

H47369

Central locking

Colour codes

Ws	White	**Or**	Orange
Bl	Blue	**Ro**	Red
Gr	Grey	**Rs**	Pink
Ge	Yellow	**Gn**	Green
Br	Brown	**Li**	Purple
Sw	Black		

Key to items

1   Battery
4   Battery fusebox
5   Engine fusebox
13 Passenger fusebox
38 Driver's door control unit
    a = window motor
39 Passenger's door control unit
    a = window motor

106 LH rear door control unit
    a = window motor
107 RH rear door control unit
    a = window motor
108 Driver's window switch
    a = front LH window switch
    b = front RH window switch
    c = rear LH window switch

d = rear RH window switch
e = switch illumination
f = rear window isolator switch
109 Passenger's window switch
110 LH rear window switch
111 RH rear window switch

Diagram 11

H47370

Electric windows

Dimensions and weights

Note: *All figures are approximate, and may vary according to model. Refer to manufacturer's data for exact figures.*

Dimensions
Overall length	4572 mm
Overall width (including mirrors).	2018 mm
Overall height (unladen, including roof rails)	1462 mm

Weights
Kerb weight	1310 kg
Maximum towing weight:	
Trailer without brakes	650 kg
Trailer with brakes.	1400 to 1600 kg
Maximum roof rack load	75 kg

Conversion factors

Length (distance)

Inches (in)	x 25.4	= Millimetres (mm)	x 0.0394	= Inches (in)	
Feet (ft)	x 0.305	= Metres (m)	x 3.281	= Feet (ft)	
Miles	x 1.609	= Kilometres (km)	x 0.621	= Miles	

Volume (capacity)

Cubic inches (cu in; in³)	x 16.387	= Cubic centimetres (cc; cm³)	x 0.061	= Cubic inches (cu in; in³)	
Imperial pints (Imp pt)	x 0.568	= Litres (l)	x 1.76	= Imperial pints (Imp pt)	
Imperial quarts (Imp qt)	x 1.137	= Litres (l)	x 0.88	= Imperial quarts (Imp qt)	
Imperial quarts (Imp qt)	x 1.201	= US quarts (US qt)	x 0.833	= Imperial quarts (Imp qt)	
US quarts (US qt)	x 0.946	= Litres (l)	x 1.057	= US quarts (US qt)	
Imperial gallons (Imp gal)	x 4.546	= Litres (l)	x 0.22	= Imperial gallons (Imp gal)	
Imperial gallons (Imp gal)	x 1.201	= US gallons (US gal)	x 0.833	= Imperial gallons (Imp gal)	
US gallons (US gal)	x 3.785	= Litres (l)	x 0.264	= US gallons (US gal)	

Mass (weight)

Ounces (oz)	x 28.35	= Grams (g)	x 0.035	= Ounces (oz)	
Pounds (lb)	x 0.454	= Kilograms (kg)	x 2.205	= Pounds (lb)	

Force

Ounces-force (ozf; oz)	x 0.278	= Newtons (N)	x 3.6	= Ounces-force (ozf; oz)	
Pounds-force (lbf; lb)	x 4.448	= Newtons (N)	x 0.225	= Pounds-force (lbf; lb)	
Newtons (N)	x 0.1	= Kilograms-force (kgf; kg)	x 9.81	= Newtons (N)	

Pressure

Pounds-force per square inch (psi; lbf/in²; lb/in²)	x 0.070	= Kilograms-force per square centimetre (kgf/cm²; kg/cm²)	x 14.223	= Pounds-force per square inch (psi; lbf/in²; lb/in²)
Pounds-force per square inch (psi; lbf/in²; lb/in²)	x 0.068	= Atmospheres (atm)	x 14.696	= Pounds-force per square inch (psi; lbf/in²; lb/in²)
Pounds-force per square inch (psi; lbf/in²; lb/in²)	x 0.069	= Bars	x 14.5	= Pounds-force per square inch (psi; lbf/in²; lb/in²)
Pounds-force per square inch (psi; lbf/in²; lb/in²)	x 6.895	= Kilopascals (kPa)	x 0.145	= Pounds-force per square inch (psi; lbf/in²; lb/in²)
Kilopascals (kPa)	x 0.01	= Kilograms-force per square centimetre (kgf/cm²; kg/cm²)	x 98.1	= Kilopascals (kPa)
Millibar (mbar)	x 100	= Pascals (Pa)	x 0.01	= Millibar (mbar)
Millibar (mbar)	x 0.0145	= Pounds-force per square inch (psi; lbf/in²; lb/in²)	x 68.947	= Millibar (mbar)
Millibar (mbar)	x 0.75	= Millimetres of mercury (mmHg)	x 1.333	= Millibar (mbar)
Millibar (mbar)	x 0.401	= Inches of water (inH₂O)	x 2.491	= Millibar (mbar)
Millimetres of mercury (mmHg)	x 0.535	= Inches of water (inH₂O)	x 1.868	= Millimetres of mercury (mmHg)
Inches of water (inH₂O)	x 0.036	= Pounds-force per square inch (psi; lbf/in²; lb/in²)	x 27.68	= Inches of water (inH₂O)

Torque (moment of force)

Pounds-force inches (lbf in; lb in)	x 1.152	= Kilograms-force centimetre (kgf cm; kg cm)	x 0.868	= Pounds-force inches (lbf in; lb in)
Pounds-force inches (lbf in; lb in)	x 0.113	= Newton metres (Nm)	x 8.85	= Pounds-force inches (lbf in; lb in)
Pounds-force inches (lbf in; lb in)	x 0.083	= Pounds-force feet (lbf ft; lb ft)	x 12	= Pounds-force inches (lbf in; lb in)
Pounds-force feet (lbf ft; lb ft)	x 0.138	= Kilograms-force metres (kgf m; kg m)	x 7.233	= Pounds-force feet (lbf ft; lb ft)
Pounds-force feet (lbf ft; lb ft)	x 1.356	= Newton metres (Nm)	x 0.738	= Pounds-force feet (lbf ft; lb ft)
Newton metres (Nm)	x 0.102	= Kilograms-force metres (kgf m; kg m)	x 9.804	= Newton metres (Nm)

Power

Horsepower (hp)	x 745.7	= Watts (W)	x 0.0013	= Horsepower (hp)

Velocity (speed)

Miles per hour (miles/hr; mph)	x 1.609	= Kilometres per hour (km/hr; kph)	x 0.621	= Miles per hour (miles/hr; mph)

Fuel consumption*

Miles per gallon, Imperial (mpg)	x 0.354	= Kilometres per litre (km/l)	x 2.825	= Miles per gallon, Imperial (mpg)
Miles per gallon, US (mpg)	x 0.425	= Kilometres per litre (km/l)	x 2.352	= Miles per gallon, US (mpg)

Temperature

Degrees Fahrenheit = (°C x 1.8) + 32   Degrees Celsius (Degrees Centigrade; °C) = (°F - 32) x 0.56

It is common practice to convert from miles per gallon (mpg) to litres/100 kilometres (l/100km), where mpg x l/100 km = 282

Spare parts are available from many sources, including maker's appointed garages, accessory shops, and motor factors. To be sure of obtaining the correct parts, it will sometimes be necessary to quote the vehicle identification number. If possible, it can also be useful to take the old parts along for positive identification. Items such as starter motors and alternators may be available under a service exchange scheme – any parts returned should be clean.

Our advice regarding spare parts is as follows.

Officially appointed garages

This is the best source of parts which are peculiar to your car, and which are not otherwise generally available (eg, badges, interior trim, certain body panels, etc). It is also the only place at which you should buy parts if the car is still under warranty.

Accessory shops

These are very good places to buy materials and components needed for the maintenance of your car (oil, air and fuel filters, light bulbs, drivebelts, greases, brake pads, touch-up paint, etc). Components of this nature sold by a reputable shop are usually of the same standard as those used by the car manufacturer.

Besides components, these shops also sell tools and general accessories, usually have convenient opening hours, charge lower prices, and can often be found close to home. Some accessory shops have parts counters where components needed for almost any repair job can be purchased or ordered.

Motor factors

Good factors will stock all the more important components which wear out comparatively quickly, and can sometimes supply individual components needed for the overhaul of a larger assembly (eg, brake seals and hydraulic parts, bearing shells, pistons, valves). They may also handle work such as cylinder block reboring, crankshaft regrinding, etc.

Engine reconditioners

These specialise in engine overhaul and can also supply components. It is recommended that the establishment is a member of the Federation of Engine Re-Manufacturers, or a similar society.

Tyre and exhaust specialists

These outlets may be independent, or members of a local or national chain. They frequently offer competitive prices when compared with a main dealer or local garage, but it will pay to obtain several quotes before making a decision. When researching prices, also ask what extras may be added – for instance fitting a new valve, balancing the wheel and tyre disposal all both commonly charged on top of the price of a new tyre.

Other sources

Beware of parts or materials obtained from market stalls, car boot sales, on-line auctions or similar outlets. Such items are not invariably sub-standard, but there is little chance of compensation if they do prove unsatisfactory. In the case of safety-critical components such as brake pads, there is the risk not only of financial loss, but also of an accident causing injury or death.

Second-hand components or assemblies obtained from a car breaker can be a good buy in some circumstances, but this sort of purchase is best made by the experienced DIY mechanic.

Audio unit anti-theft system – precaution

The audio unit fitted as standard equipment by Skoda may be equipped with a built-in security code to deter thieves. If the power source to the unit is cut, the anti-theft system will activate. Even if the power source is immediately reconnected, the unit will not function until the correct security code has been entered. Therefore, if you do not know the correct security code for the unit, do not disconnect the battery negative lead, or remove the unit from the vehicle.

Whenever servicing, repair or overhaul work is carried out on the car or its components, observe the following procedures and instructions. This will assist in carrying out the operation efficiently and to a professional standard of workmanship.

Joint mating faces and gaskets

When separating components at their mating faces, never insert screwdrivers or similar implements into the joint between the faces in order to prise them apart. This can cause severe damage which results in oil leaks, coolant leaks, etc upon reassembly. Separation is usually achieved by tapping along the joint with a soft-faced hammer in order to break the seal. However, note that this method may not be suitable where dowels are used for component location.

Where a gasket is used between the mating faces of two components, a new one must be fitted on reassembly; fit it dry unless otherwise stated in the repair procedure. Make sure that the mating faces are clean and dry, with all traces of old gasket removed. When cleaning a joint face, use a tool which is unlikely to score or damage the face, and remove any burrs or nicks with an oilstone or fine file.

Make sure that tapped holes are cleaned with a pipe cleaner, and keep them free of jointing compound, if this is being used, unless specifically instructed otherwise.

Ensure that all orifices, channels or pipes are clear, and blow through them, preferably using compressed air.

Oil seals

Oil seals can be removed by levering them out with a wide flat-bladed screwdriver or similar implement. Alternatively, a number of self-tapping screws may be screwed into the seal, and these used as a purchase for pliers or some similar device in order to pull the seal free.

Whenever an oil seal is removed from its working location, either individually or as part of an assembly, it should be renewed.

The very fine sealing lip of the seal is easily damaged, and will not seal if the surface it contacts is not completely clean and free from scratches, nicks or grooves. If the original sealing surface of the component cannot be restored, and the manufacturer has not made provision for slight relocation of the seal relative to the sealing surface, the component should be renewed.

Protect the lips of the seal from any surface which may damage them in the course of fitting. Use tape or a conical sleeve where possible. Where indicated, lubricate the seal lips with oil before fitting and, on dual-lipped seals, fill the space between the lips with grease.

Unless otherwise stated, oil seals must be fitted with their sealing lips toward the lubricant to be sealed.

Use a tubular drift or block of wood of the appropriate size to install the seal and, if the seal housing is shouldered, drive the seal down to the shoulder. If the seal housing is unshouldered, the seal should be fitted with its face flush with the housing top face (unless otherwise instructed).

Screw threads and fastenings

Seized nuts, bolts and screws are quite a common occurrence where corrosion has set in, and the use of penetrating oil or releasing fluid will often overcome this problem if the offending item is soaked for a while before attempting to release it. The use of an impact driver may also provide a means of releasing such stubborn fastening devices, when used in conjunction with the appropriate screwdriver bit or socket. If none of these methods works, it may be necessary to resort to the careful application of heat, or the use of a hacksaw or nut splitter device. Before resorting to extreme methods, check that you are not dealing with a left-hand thread!

Studs are usually removed by locking two nuts together on the threaded part, and then using a spanner on the lower nut to unscrew the stud. Studs or bolts which have broken off below the surface of the component in which they are mounted can sometimes be removed using a stud extractor.

Always ensure that a blind tapped hole is completely free from oil, grease, water or other fluid before installing the bolt or stud. Failure to do this could cause the housing to crack due to the hydraulic action of the bolt or stud as it is screwed in.

For some screw fastenings, notably cylinder head bolts or nuts, torque wrench settings are no longer specified for the latter stages of tightening, "angle-tightening" being called up instead. Typically, a fairly low torque wrench setting will be applied to the bolts/nuts in the correct sequence, followed by one or more stages of tightening through specified angles.

When checking or retightening a nut or bolt to a specified torque setting, slacken the nut or bolt by a quarter of a turn, and then retighten to the specified setting. However, this should not be attempted where angular tightening has been used.

Locknuts, locktabs and washers

Any fastening which will rotate against a component or housing during tightening should always have a washer between it and the relevant component or housing.

Spring or split washers should always be renewed when they are used to lock a critical component such as a big-end bearing retaining bolt or nut. Locktabs which are folded over to retain a nut or bolt should always be renewed.

Self-locking nuts can be re-used in non-critical areas, providing resistance can be felt when the locking portion passes over the bolt or stud thread. However, it should be noted that self-locking stiffnuts tend to lose their effectiveness after long periods of use, and should then be renewed as a matter of course.

Split pins must always be replaced with new ones of the correct size for the hole.

When thread-locking compound is found on the threads of a fastener which is to be re-used, it should be cleaned off with a wire brush and solvent, and fresh compound applied on reassembly.

Special tools

Some repair procedures in this manual entail the use of special tools such as a press, two or three-legged pullers, spring compressors, etc. Wherever possible, suitable readily-available alternatives to the manufacturer's special tools are described, and are shown in use. In some instances, where no alternative is possible, it has been necessary to resort to the use of a manufacturer's tool, and this has been done for reasons of safety as well as the efficient completion of the repair operation. Unless you are highly-skilled and have a thorough understanding of the procedures described, never attempt to bypass the use of any special tool when the procedure described specifies its use. Not only is there a very great risk of personal injury, but expensive damage could be caused to the components involved.

Environmental considerations

When disposing of used engine oil, brake fluid, antifreeze, etc, give due consideration to any detrimental environmental effects. Do not, for instance, pour any of the above liquids down drains into the general sewage system, or onto the ground to soak away, as this is likely to pollute your local environment. Many local council refuse tips provide a facility for waste oil disposal, as do some garages. You can find your nearest disposal point by calling the Environment Agency on 03708 506 506 or by visiting www.oilbankline.org.uk.

Note: It is illegal and anti-social to dump oil down the drain. To find the location of your local oil recycling bank, call 03708 506 506 or visit www.oilbankline.org.uk.

The jack supplied with the vehicle locates in the jacking points on the underside of the sills – see *Wheel changing* at the front of this manual. Ensure that the jack head is correctly engaged before attempting to raise the vehicle.

The jack in the vehicle tool kit should only be used for changing the roadwheels; when carrying out any other kind of work, raise the vehicle using a hydraulic trolley jack, and always supplement the jack with axle stands positioned under the vehicle jacking points.

When using a trolley jack or axle stands, always position the jack head or axle stand head under, or adjacent to one of the relevant wheel changing jacking points under the sills **(see illustrations)**. Use a block of wood between the jack or axle stand and the sill.

Do not attempt to jack the vehicle under the front crossmember, the sump, or any of the suspension components.

Never work under, around, or near a raised vehicle, unless it is adequately supported in at least two places.

Front jacking point indicator arrow

Rear jacking point indicator arrow

Vehicle identification

Modifications are a continuing and unpublicised process in vehicle manufacture, quite apart from major model changes. Spare parts manuals and lists are compiled upon a numerical basis, the individual vehicle identification numbers being essential to correct identification of the component concerned.

When ordering spare parts, always give as much information as possible. Quote the car model, year of manufacture, body and engine numbers as appropriate.

The *vehicle identification plate* is situated at the base of the passenger's side B-pillar. The *vehicle identification number* is also attached to the front right suspension dome and repeated in the form of a plate visible through the windscreen on the passenger's side.

The *engine number* is stamped on the front, left-hand side of the cylinder block. The *engine code* can also be found on the vehicle data sticker in the luggage compartment on the left of the boot floor, and on a sticker on the timing belt cover.

Other identification numbers or codes are stamped on major items such as the gearbox, etc. These numbers are also printed on the *vehicle data sticker* located in the luggage compartment adjacent to the spare wheel.

Introduction

A selection of good tools is a fundamental requirement for anyone contemplating the maintenance and repair of a motor vehicle. For the owner who does not possess any, their purchase will prove a considerable expense, offsetting some of the savings made by doing-it-yourself. However, provided that the tools purchased meet the relevant national safety standards and are of good quality, they will last for many years and prove an extremely worthwhile investment.

To help the average owner to decide which tools are needed to carry out the various tasks detailed in this manual, we have compiled three lists of tools under the following headings: *Maintenance and minor repair, Repair and overhaul*, and *Special*. Newcomers to practical mechanics should start off with the *Maintenance and minor repair* tool kit, and confine themselves to the simpler jobs around the vehicle. Then, as confidence and experience grow, more difficult tasks can be undertaken, with extra tools being purchased as, and when, they are needed. In this way, a *Maintenance and minor repair* tool kit can be built up into a *Repair and overhaul* tool kit over a considerable period of time, without any major cash outlays. The experienced do-it-yourselfer will have a tool kit good enough for most repair and overhaul procedures, and will add tools from the *Special* category when it is felt that the expense is justified by the amount of use to which these tools will be put.

Maintenance and minor repair tool kit

The tools given in this list should be considered as a minimum requirement if routine maintenance, servicing and minor repair operations are to be undertaken. We recommend the purchase of combination spanners (ring one end, open-ended the other); although more expensive than open-ended ones, they do give the advantages of both types of spanner.

☐ *Combination spanners:*
  Metric - 8 to 19 mm inclusive
☐ *Adjustable spanner - 35 mm jaw (approx.)*
☐ *Spark plug spanner (with rubber insert) - petrol models*
☐ *Spark plug gap adjustment tool - petrol models*
☐ *Set of feeler gauges*
☐ *Brake bleed nipple spanner*
☐ *Screwdrivers:*
  Flat blade - 100 mm long x 6 mm dia
  Cross blade - 100 mm long x 6 mm dia
  Torx - various sizes (not all vehicles)
☐ *Combination pliers*
☐ *Hacksaw (junior)*
☐ *Tyre pump*
☐ *Tyre pressure gauge*
☐ *Oil can*
☐ *Oil filter removal tool (if applicable)*
☐ *Fine emery cloth*
☐ *Wire brush (small)*
☐ *Funnel (medium size)*
☐ *Sump drain plug key (not all vehicles)*

Repair and overhaul tool kit

These tools are virtually essential for anyone undertaking any major repairs to a motor vehicle, and are additional to those given in the *Maintenance and minor repair* list. Included in this list is a comprehensive set of sockets. Although these are expensive, they will be found invaluable as they are so versatile - particularly if various drives are included in the set. We recommend the half-inch square-drive type, as this can be used with most proprietary torque wrenches.

The tools in this list will sometimes need to be supplemented by tools from the *Special* list:

☐ *Sockets to cover range in previous list (including Torx sockets)*
☐ *Reversible ratchet drive (for use with sockets)*
☐ *Extension piece, 250 mm (for use with sockets)*
☐ *Universal joint (for use with sockets)*
☐ *Flexible handle or sliding T "breaker bar" (for use with sockets)*
☐ *Torque wrench (for use with sockets)*
☐ *Self-locking grips*
☐ *Ball pein hammer*
☐ *Soft-faced mallet (plastic or rubber)*
☐ *Screwdrivers:*
  Flat blade - long & sturdy, short (chubby), and narrow (electrician's) types
  Cross blade – long & sturdy, and short (chubby) types
☐ *Pliers:*
  Long-nosed
  Side cutters (electrician's)
  Circlip (internal and external)
☐ *Cold chisel - 25 mm*
☐ *Scriber*
☐ *Scraper*
☐ *Centre-punch*
☐ *Pin punch*
☐ *Hacksaw*
☐ *Brake hose clamp*
☐ *Brake/clutch bleeding kit*
☐ *Selection of twist drills*
☐ *Steel rule/straight-edge*
☐ *Allen keys (inc. splined/Torx type)*
☐ *Selection of files*
☐ *Wire brush*
☐ *Axle stands*
☐ *Jack (strong trolley or hydraulic type)*
☐ *Light with extension lead*
☐ *Universal electrical multi-meter*

Sockets and reversible ratchet drive

Brake bleeding kit

Torx key, socket and bit

Hose clamp

Angular-tightening gauge

Special tools

The tools in this list are those which are not used regularly, are expensive to buy, or which need to be used in accordance with their manufacturers' instructions. Unless relatively difficult mechanical jobs are undertaken frequently, it will not be economic to buy many of these tools. Where this is the case, you could consider clubbing together with friends (or joining a motorists' club) to make a joint purchase, or borrowing the tools against a deposit from a local garage or tool hire specialist.

The following list contains only those tools and instruments freely available to the public, and not those special tools produced by the vehicle manufacturer specifically for its dealer network. You will find occasional references to these manufacturers' special tools in the text of this manual. Generally, an alternative method of doing the job without the vehicle manufacturers' special tool is given. However, sometimes there is no alternative to using them. Where this is the case and the relevant tool cannot be bought or borrowed, you will have to entrust the work to a dealer.

☐ Angular-tightening gauge
☐ Valve spring compressor
☐ Valve grinding tool
☐ Piston ring compressor
☐ Piston ring removal/installation tool
☐ Cylinder bore hone
☐ Balljoint separator
☐ Coil spring compressors (where applicable)
☐ Two/three-legged hub and bearing puller
☐ Impact screwdriver
☐ Micrometer and/or vernier calipers
☐ Dial gauge
☐ Tachometer
☐ Fault code reader
☐ Cylinder compression gauge
☐ Hand-operated vacuum pump and gauge
☐ Clutch plate alignment set
☐ Brake shoe steady spring cup removal tool
☐ Bush and bearing removal/installation set
☐ Stud extractors
☐ Tap and die set
☐ Lifting tackle

Buying tools

Reputable motor accessory shops and superstores often offer excellent quality tools at discount prices, so it pays to shop around.

Remember, you don't have to buy the most expensive items on the shelf, but it is always advisable to steer clear of the very cheap tools. Beware of 'bargains' offered on market stalls, on-line or at car boot sales. There are plenty of good tools around at reasonable prices, but always aim to purchase items which meet the relevant national safety standards. If in doubt, ask the proprietor or manager of the shop for advice before making a purchase.

Care and maintenance of tools

Having purchased a reasonable tool kit, it is necessary to keep the tools in a clean and serviceable condition. After use, always wipe off any dirt, grease and metal particles using a clean, dry cloth, before putting the tools away. Never leave them lying around after they have been used. A simple tool rack on the garage or workshop wall for items such as screwdrivers and pliers is a good idea. Store all normal spanners and sockets in a metal box. Any measuring instruments, gauges, meters, etc, must be carefully stored where they cannot be damaged or become rusty.

Take a little care when tools are used. Hammer heads inevitably become marked, and screwdrivers lose the keen edge on their blades from time to time. A little timely attention with emery cloth or a file will soon restore items like this to a good finish.

Working facilities

Not to be forgotten when discussing tools is the workshop itself. If anything more than routine maintenance is to be carried out, a suitable working area becomes essential.

It is appreciated that many an owner-mechanic is forced by circumstances to remove an engine or similar item without the benefit of a garage or workshop. Having done this, any repairs should always be done under the cover of a roof.

Wherever possible, any dismantling should be done on a clean, flat workbench or table at a suitable working height.

Any workbench needs a vice; one with a jaw opening of 100 mm is suitable for most jobs. As mentioned previously, some clean dry storage space is also required for tools, as well as for any lubricants, cleaning fluids, touch-up paints etc, which become necessary.

Another item which may be required, and which has a much more general usage, is an electric drill with a chuck capacity of at least 8 mm. This, together with a good range of twist drills, is virtually essential for fitting accessories.

Last, but not least, always keep a supply of old newspapers and clean, lint-free rags available, and try to keep any working area as clean as possible.

Micrometers

Dial test indicator ("dial gauge")

Oil filter removal tool (strap wrench type)

Compression tester

Bearing puller

This is a guide to getting your vehicle through the MOT test. Obviously it will not be possible to examine the vehicle to the same standard as the professional MOT tester. However, working through the following checks will enable you to identify any problem areas before submitting the vehicle for the test.

It has only been possible to summarise the test requirements here, based on the regulations in force at the time of printing. Test standards are becoming increasingly stringent, although there are some exemptions for older vehicles.

An assistant will be needed to help carry out some of these checks.

The checks have been sub-divided into four categories, as follows:

1 Checks carried out **FROM THE VEHICLE INTERIOR**

2 Checks carried out **WITH THE VEHICLE ON THE GROUND**

3 Checks carried out **WITH THE VEHICLE RAISED AND THE WHEELS FREE TO TURN**

4 Checks carried out on **YOUR VEHICLE'S EXHAUST EMISSION SYSTEM**

1 Checks carried out **FROM THE VEHICLE INTERIOR**

Handbrake (parking brake)

☐ Test the operation of the handbrake. Excessive travel (too many clicks) indicates incorrect brake or cable adjustment.
☐ Check that the handbrake cannot be released by tapping the lever sideways. Check the security of the lever mountings.

☐ If the parking brake is foot-operated, check that the pedal is secure and without excessive travel, and that the release mechanism operates correctly.
☐ Where applicable, test the operation of the electronic handbrake. The brake should engage and disengage without excessive delay. If the warning light does not extinguish, or a warning message is displayed when the brake is disengaged, this could indicate a fault which will need further investigation.

Footbrake

☐ Depress the brake pedal and check that it does not creep down to the floor, indicating a master cylinder fault. Release the pedal, wait a few seconds, then depress it again. If the pedal travels nearly to the floor before firm resistance is felt, brake adjustment or repair is necessary. If the pedal feels spongy, there is air in the hydraulic system which must be removed by bleeding.

☐ Check that the brake pedal is secure and in good condition. Check also for signs of fluid leaks on the pedal, floor or carpets, which would indicate failed seals in the brake master cylinder.
☐ Check the servo unit (when applicable) by operating the brake pedal several times, then keeping the pedal depressed and starting the engine. As the engine starts, the pedal will move down. If not, the vacuum hose or the servo itself may be faulty.

Steering wheel and column

☐ Examine the steering wheel for fractures or looseness of the hub, spokes or rim.
☐ Move the steering wheel from side to side and then up and down. Check that the steering wheel is not loose on the column, indicating wear or a loose retaining nut. Continue moving the steering wheel as before, but also turn it slightly from left to right.
☐ Check that the steering wheel is not loose on the column, and that there is no abnormal movement of the steering wheel, indicating wear in the column support bearings or couplings.

☐ Check that the ignition lock (where fitted) engages and disengages correctly.
☐ Steering column adjustment mechanisms (where fitted) must be able to lock the column securely in place with no play evident.

Windscreen, mirrors and sunvisor

☐ The windscreen must be free of cracks or other significant damage within the 'swept area' of the windscreen. This is the area swept by the windscreen wipers. A second test area, known as 'Zone A', is the part of the swept area 290 mm wide, centred on the steering wheel centre line. Any damage in Zone A that cannot be contained in a 10 mm diameter circle, or any damage in the remainder of the swept area that cannot be contained in a 40 mm diameter circle, may cause the vehicle to fail the test.

☐ Any items that may obscure the drivers view, such as stickers, sat-navs, anything hanging from the interior mirror, should be removed prior to the test.
☐ Vehicles registered after 1st August 1978 must have a drivers side mirror, and either an interior mirror, or a passenger's side mirror. Cameras (or indirect vision devices) may replace the mirrors, but they must function correctly.
☐ The driver's sunvisor must be capable of being stored in the "up" position.

Seat belts, seats and supplementary restraint systems (SRS)

Note: *The following checks are applicable to all seat belts, front and rear.*

☐ Examine the webbing of all the belts (including rear belts if fitted) for cuts, serious fraying or deterioration. Fasten and unfasten each belt to check the buckles. If applicable, check the retracting mechanism. Check the security of all seat belt mountings accessible from inside the vehicle, ensuring any height adjustable mountings lock securely in place.

☐ Where the seat belt is attached to a seat, the frame and mountings of the seat form part of the belt mountings, and are to be inspected as such.

☐ Any airbag, or SRS warning light must extinguish a few seconds after the ignition is switched on. Failure to do so indicates a fault which must be investigated.

☐ Seat belts with pre-tensioners, once activated, have a "flag" or similar showing on the seat belt stalk. This, in itself, is a reason for test failure.

☐ Check that the original airbag(s) is/are present, and not obviously defective.

☐ The seats themselves must be securely attached and the backrests must lock in the upright position. The driver's seat must also be able to slide forwards/rearwards, and lock in several positions.

Doors

☐ Both front doors must be able to be opened and closed from outside and inside, and must latch securely when closed.

☐ The rear doors must open from the outside.

☐ Examine all door hinges, catches and striker plates for missing, deteriorated, or insecure parts that could effect the opening and closing of the doors.

Speedometer

☐ The vehicle speedometer must be present, and appear operative. The figures on the speedometer must be legible, and illuminated when the lights are switched on.

2 Checks carried out WITH THE VEHICLE ON THE GROUND

Vehicle identification

☐ Number plates must be in good condition, secure and legible, with letters and numbers correctly spaced – spacing at (A) should be 33 mm and at (B) 11 mm. At the front, digits must be black on a white background and at the rear

black on a yellow background. Other background designs (such as honeycomb) are not permitted.

☐ The VIN plate and/or homologation plate must be permanently displayed and legible.

Electrical equipment

☐ Switch on the ignition and check the operation of the horn.

☐ Check the windscreen washers and wipers, examining the wiper blades; renew damaged or perished blades. The wiper blades must clear a large enough area of the windscreen to provide an 'adequate' view of the road, and be able to be parked in a position where they will not affect the drivers' view.

☐ On vehicles first used from 1st September 2009, the headlight washers (where fitted) must operate correctly.

☐ Check the operation of the stop-lights. This includes any lights that appear to be connected – Eg. high-level lights.

☐ Check the operation of the sidelights and number plate lights. The lenses and reflectors must be secure, clean and undamaged.

☐ Check the operation and alignment of the headlights. The headlight reflectors must not be tarnished and the lenses must be undamaged. Where plastic lenses are fitted, check they haven't deteriorated to the extent where they affect the light ouput or beam image. It's often possible to restore the plastic lens using a suitable polish or aftermarket treatment.

☐ Where HID or LED headlights are fitted, check the operation of the cleaning and self-levelling functions.

☐ The headlight main beam warning lamp must be functional.

☐ On vehicles first used from 1st March 2018, the daytime running lights (where fitted) must operate correctly.

☐ Switch on the ignition and check the operation of the direction indicators (including the instrument panel tell-tale) and the hazard warning lights. Operation of the sidelights and stop-lights must not affect the indicators – if it does, the cause is usually a bad earth at the rear light cluster. Indicators should flash at a rate of between 60 and 120 times per minute – faster or slower than this could indicate a fault with the flasher unit or a bad earth at one of the light units.

☐ The hazard warning lights must operate with the ignition on and off.

☐ Check the operation of the rear foglight(s), including the warning light on the instrument panel or in the switch. Note that the foglight

must be positioned in the centre or driver's side of the vehicle. If only the passenger's side illuminates, the test will fail.

☐ The warning lights must illuminate in accordance with the manufacturers' design (this includes any warning messages). For most vehicles, the ABS and other warning lights should illuminate when the ignition is switched on, and (if the system is operating properly) extinguish after a few seconds. Refer to the owner's handbook.

☐ On vehicles first used from 1st September 2009, the reversing lights must operate correctly when reverse gear is selected.

☐ Check the vehicle battery for security and leakage.

☐ Check the visible/accessible vehicle wiring is adequately supported, with no evidence of damage or deterioration that could result in a short-circuit.

Footbrake

☐ Examine the master cylinder, brake pipes and servo unit for leaks, loose mountings, corrosion or other damage. If ABS is fitted, this unit should also be examined for signs of leaks or corrosion.

☐ The fluid reservoir must be secure and the fluid level must be between the upper (**A**) and lower (**B**) markings.

☐ Check the fluid in the reservoir for signs of contamination.

☐ Inspect both front brake flexible hoses for cracks or deterioration of the rubber. Turn the steering from lock to lock, and ensure that the hoses do not contact the wheel, tyre, or any part of the steering or suspension mechanism. With the brake pedal firmly depressed, check the hoses for bulges or leaks under pressure.

Steering and suspension

☐ Have your assistant turn the steering wheel from side to side slightly, up to the point where the steering gear just begins to transmit this movement to the roadwheels. Check for excessive free play between the steering wheel and the steering gear, indicating wear or insecurity of the steering column joints, the column-to-steering gear coupling, or the steering gear itself. With a standard (380 mm diameter) steering wheel, there should be no more than 13 mm of free play for rack-and-pinion systems, and no more than 75 mm for non-rack-and-pinion designs.

☐ Have your assistant turn the steering

wheel more vigorously in each direction, so that the roadwheels just begin to turn. As this is done, examine all the steering joints, linkages, fittings and attachments. Renew any component that shows signs of wear or damage. On vehicles with hydraulic power steering, check the security and condition of the steering pump, drivebelt and hoses.

☐ Note that all movement checks on power steering systems are carried out with the engine running.

☐ Check that the vehicle is standing level, and at approximately the correct ride height.

Exhaust system

☐ Start the engine. With your assistant holding a rag over the tailpipe, check the entire system for leaks. Repair or renew leaking sections.

3 Checks carried out
WITH THE VEHICLE RAISED AND THE WHEELS FREE TO TURN

Jack up the front and rear of the vehicle, and securely support it on axle stands. Position the stands clear of the suspension assemblies. Ensure that the wheels are clear of the ground and that the steering can be turned from lock to lock.

Steering mechanism

☐ Have your assistant turn the steering from lock to lock. Check that the steering turns smoothly, and that no part of the steering mechanism, including a wheel or tyre, fouls any brake hose or pipe or any part of the body structure.

☐ Examine the steering rack rubber gaiters for damage or insecurity of the retaining clips. If power steering is fitted, check for signs of damage or leakage of the fluid hoses, pipes or connections. Also check for excessive stiffness or binding of the steering, a missing split pin or locking device, or severe corrosion of the body structure within 30 cm of any steering component attachment point.

☐ Check the track rod end ball joint dust covers. Any covers that are missing, seriously damaged, deteriorated or insecure, may fail inspection.

Front and rear suspension and wheel bearings

☐ Starting at the front right-hand side, grasp the roadwheel at the 3 o'clock and 9 o'clock positions and rock gently but firmly. Check for free play or insecurity at the wheel bearings, suspension balljoints, or suspension mountings, pivots and attachments.

☐ Now grasp the wheel at the 12 o'clock and 6 o'clock positions and repeat the previous inspection. Spin the wheel, and check for roughness or tightness of the front wheel bearing.

☐ If excess free play is suspected at a component pivot point, this can be confirmed by using a large screwdriver or similar tool and levering between the mounting and the component attachment. This will confirm whether the wear is in the pivot bush, its retaining bolt, or in the mounting itself (the bolt holes can often become elongated).

☐ Carry out all the above checks at the other front wheel, and then at both rear wheels.

Springs and shock absorbers

☐ Examine the suspension struts (when applicable) for serious fluid leakage, corrosion, or damage to the casing. Also check the security of the mounting points.

☐ If coil springs are fitted, check that the spring ends locate in their seats, and that the spring is not corroded, cracked or broken.

☐ If leaf springs are fitted, check that all leaves are intact, that the axle is securely attached to each spring, and that there is no deterioration of the spring eye mountings, bushes, and shackles.

☐ The same general checks apply to vehicles fitted with other suspension types, such as torsion bars, hydraulic displacer units, etc. Ensure that all mountings and attachments are secure, that there are no signs of excessive wear, corrosion or damage, and (on hydraulic types) that there are no fluid leaks or damaged pipes.

☐ Check any suspension and anti-roll bar link ball joint dust covers. Any covers that are missing, seriously damaged, deteriorated or insecure, may fail inspection.

☐ Examine each shock absorber for signs of leakage, corrosion of the casing, missing, detached or worn pivots and/or rubber bushes.

Driveshafts (fwd vehicles only)

☐ Rotate each front wheel in turn and inspect the inner and outer joint gaiters for splits or damage. Also check that each driveshaft is straight and undamaged.

Braking system

☐ If possible without dismantling, check brake pad wear and disc condition. Ensure that the friction lining material has not worn excessively, (A) and that the discs are not fractured, pitted, scored or badly worn (B). As a general rule, if the friction material is less than 1.5 mm thick, the inspection will fail.

☐ Examine all the rigid brake pipes underneath the vehicle, and the flexible hose(s) at the rear. Look for corrosion, chafing or insecurity of the pipes, and for signs of bulging under pressure, chafing, splits or deterioration of the flexible hoses.

☐ Look for signs of fluid leaks at the brake calipers or on the brake backplates. Repair or renew leaking components.

☐ Slowly spin each wheel, while your assistant depresses and releases the footbrake. Ensure that each brake is operating and does not bind when the pedal is released.

☐ Examine the handbrake mechanism, checking for frayed or broken cables, excessive corrosion, or wear or insecurity of the linkage. Check that the mechanism works on each relevant wheel, and releases fully, without binding.

☐ Check the ABS sensors' wiring for signs of damage, deterioration or insecurity.

☐ It is not possible to test brake efficiency without special equipment, but a road test can be carried out later to check that the vehicle pulls up in a straight line.

Fuel and exhaust systems

☐ Inspect the fuel tank (including the filler cap), fuel pipes, hoses and unions. All components must be secure and free from leaks. Locking fuel caps must lock securely and the key must be provided for the MOT test.

☐ Examine the exhaust system over its entire length, checking for any damaged, broken or missing mountings, security of the retaining clamps and rust or corrosion.

☐ If the vehicle was originally equipped with a catalytic converter or particulate filter, one must be fitted.

Wheels and tyres

☐ Examine the sidewalls and tread area of each tyre in turn. Check for cuts, tears, lumps, bulges, separation of the tread, and exposure of the ply or cord due to wear or damage. Check that the tyre bead is correctly seated on the wheel rim, that the valve is sound and properly seated, and that the wheel is not distorted or damaged.

☐ Check that the tyres are of the correct size for the vehicle, that they are of the same size and type on each axle, and that the pressures are correct. The vehicle will fail the test if the tyres are obviously under-inflated.

☐ Check the tyre tread depth. The legal minimum at the time of writing is 1.6 mm over the central three-quarters of the tread width. Abnormal tread wear may indicate incorrect front wheel alignment or wear in steering or suspension components.

☐ Check that all wheel bolts/nuts are present.

☐ If the spare wheel is fitted externally or in a separate carrier beneath the vehicle, check that mountings are secure and free of excessive corrosion.

Body corrosion

☐ Check the condition of the entire vehicle structure for signs of corrosion in load-bearing areas. (These include chassis box sections, side sills, cross-members, pillars, and all suspension, steering, braking system and seat belt mountings and anchorages.) Any corrosion which has seriously reduced the thickness of a load-bearing area (or is within 30 cm of safety-related components such as steering or suspension) is likely to cause the vehicle to fail. In this case professional repairs are likely to be needed.

☐ Damage or corrosion which causes sharp or otherwise dangerous edges to be exposed will also cause the vehicle to fail.

Towbars

☐ Check the condition of mounting points (both beneath the vehicle and within boot/hatchback areas) for signs of corrosion, ensuring that all fixings are secure and not worn or damaged. There must be no excessive play in detachable tow ball arms or quick-release mechanisms.

☐ Examine the security and condition of the towbar electrics socket. If the later 13-pin socket is fitted, the MOT tester will check its' wiring functions/connections are correct.

General leaks

☐ The vehicle will fail the test if there is a fluid leak of any kind that poses an environmental risk.

4 Checks carried out on **YOUR VEHICLE'S EXHAUST EMISSION SYSTEM**

Petrol models

☐ The engine should be warmed up, and running well (ignition system in good order, air filter element clean, etc).

☐ Before testing, run the engine at around 2500 rpm for 20 seconds. Let the engine drop to idle, and watch for smoke from the exhaust. If the idle speed is too high, or if dense blue or black smoke emerges for more than 5 seconds, the vehicle will fail. Typically, blue smoke signifies oil burning (engine wear); black smoke means unburnt fuel (dirty air cleaner element, or other fuel system fault).

☐ An exhaust gas analyser for measuring carbon monoxide (CO) and hydrocarbons (HC) is now needed. If one cannot be hired or borrowed, have a local garage perform the check.

CO emissions (mixture)

☐ The MOT tester has access to the CO limits for all vehicles from 1st August 1992. The CO level is measured at idle speed, and at 'fast idle' (2500 to 3000 rpm). The following limits are given as a general guide:
  At idle speed – Less than 0.3% CO
  At 'fast idle' – Less than 0.2% CO
  Lambda reading – 0.97 to 1.03

☐ If the CO level is too high, this may point to poor maintenance, a fuel injection system problem, faulty lambda (oxygen) sensor or catalytic converter. Try an injector cleaning treatment, and check the vehicle's ECU for fault codes.

HC emissions

☐ The MOT tester has access to HC limits for all vehicles. The HC level is measured at 'fast idle' (2500 to 3000 rpm). The following limits are given as a general guide:
  At 'fast idle' – Less than 200 ppm

☐ Excessive HC emissions are typically caused by oil being burnt (worn engine), or by a blocked crankcase ventilation system ('breather'). If the engine oil is old and thin, an oil change may help. If the engine is running badly, check the vehicle's ECU for fault codes.

Diesel models

☐ If the vehicle was fitted with a DPF (Diesel Particulate Filter) when it left the factory, it will fail the test if the MOT tester can see smoke of any colour emitting from the exhaust, or finds evidence that the filter has been tampered with.

☐ The only emission test for diesel engines is measuring exhaust smoke density, using a calibrated smoke meter.

☐ This test involves accelerating the engine to its maximum unloaded speed a minimum of once, and a maximum of 6 times. With the smoke meter connected, the engine is accelerated quickly to its maximum speed. If the smoke level is at or below the limit specified, the vehicle will pass. If the level is more than the specified limit then two further accelerations are carried out, and an average of the readings calculated. If the vehicle is still over the limit, a further three accelerations are carried out, with the average of the last three calculated after each check.

Note: *On engines with a timing belt, it is VITAL that the belt is in good condition before the test is carried out.*

Vehicles registered after 1st July 2008
  Smoke level must not exceed 1.5m-1 – Turbo-charged and non-Turbocharged engines

Vehicles registered before 1st July 2008
  Smoke level must not exceed 2.5m-1 – Non-turbo vehicles
  Smoke level must not exceed 3.0m-1 – Turbocharged vehicles:

☐ If excess smoke is produced, try fitting a new air cleaner element, or using an injector cleaning treatment. If the engine is running badly, where applicable, check the vehicle's ECU for fault codes. Also check the vehicle's EGR system, where applicable. At high mileages, the injectors may require professional attention.

Engine

☐ Engine fails to rotate when attempting to start
☐ Engine rotates, but will not start
☐ Engine difficult to start when cold
☐ Engine difficult to start when hot
☐ Starter motor noisy or excessively-rough in engagement
☐ Engine starts, but stops immediately
☐ Engine idles erratically
☐ Engine misfires at idle speed
☐ Engine misfires throughout the driving speed range
☐ Engine hesitates on acceleration
☐ Engine stalls
☐ Engine lacks power
☐ Engine backfires
☐ Oil pressure warning light illuminated with engine running
☐ Engine runs-on after switching off
☐ Engine noises

Cooling system

☐ Overheating
☐ Overcooling
☐ External coolant leakage
☐ Internal coolant leakage
☐ Corrosion

Fuel and exhaust systems

☐ Excessive fuel consumption
☐ Fuel leakage and/or fuel odour
☐ Excessive noise or fumes from exhaust system

Clutch

☐ Pedal travels to floor – no pressure or very little resistance
☐ Clutch fails to disengage (unable to select gears)
☐ Clutch slips (engine speed increases, with no increase in vehicle speed)
☐ Judder as clutch is engaged
☐ Noise when depressing or releasing clutch pedal

Manual transmission

☐ Noisy in neutral with engine running
☐ Noisy in one particular gear
☐ Difficulty engaging gears
☐ Jumps out of gear
☐ Vibration
☐ Lubricant leaks

Automatic transmission (DSG)

☐ Fluid leakage
☐ General gear selection problems
☐ Transmission will not downshift (kickdown) with accelerator pedal fully depressed
☐ Engine will not start in any gear, or starts in gears other than Park or Neutral
☐ Transmission slips, shifts roughly, is noisy, or has no drive in forward or reverse gears

Driveshafts

☐ Vibration when accelerating or decelerating
☐ Clicking or knocking noise on turns (at slow speed on full-lock)

Braking system

☐ Vehicle pulls to one side under braking
☐ Noise (grinding or high-pitched squeal) when brakes applied
☐ Excessive brake pedal travel
☐ Brake pedal feels spongy when depressed
☐ Excessive brake pedal effort required to stop vehicle
☐ Judder felt through brake pedal or steering wheel when braking
☐ Pedal pulsates when braking hard
☐ Brakes binding
☐ Rear wheels locking under normal braking

Steering and suspension

☐ Vehicle pulls to one side
☐ Wheel wobble and vibration
☐ Excessive pitching and/or rolling around corners, or during braking
☐ Wandering or general instability
☐ Excessively-stiff steering
☐ Excessive play in steering
☐ Lack of power assistance
☐ Tyre wear excessive

Electrical system

☐ Battery will not hold a charge for more than a few days
☐ Ignition/no-charge warning light remains illuminated with engine running
☐ Ignition/no-charge warning light fails to come on
☐ Lights inoperative
☐ Instrument readings inaccurate or erratic
☐ Horn inoperative, or unsatisfactory in operation
☐ Windscreen/tailgate wipers inoperative, or unsatisfactory in operation
☐ Windscreen washers inoperative, or unsatisfactory in operation
☐ Electric windows inoperative, or unsatisfactory in operation

Introduction

The vehicle owner who does his or her own maintenance according to the recommended service schedules should not have to use this section of the manual very often. Modern component reliability is such that, provided those items subject to wear or deterioration are inspected or renewed at the specified intervals, sudden failure is comparatively rare. Faults do not usually just happen as a result of sudden failure, but develop over a period of time. Major mechanical failures in particular are usually preceded by characteristic symptoms over hundreds or even thousands of miles. Those components which do occasionally fail without warning are often small and easily carried in the vehicle.

With any fault-finding, the first step is to decide where to begin investigations. Sometimes this is obvious, but on other occasions, a little detective work will be necessary. The owner who makes half a dozen haphazard adjustments or renewals may be successful in curing a fault (or its symptoms), but will be none the wiser if the fault recurs, and ultimately may have spent more time and money than was necessary. A calm and logical approach will be found to be more satisfactory in the long run. Always take into account any warning signs or abnormalities that may have been noticed in the period preceding the fault – power loss, high or low gauge readings, unusual smells, etc – and remember that failure

of components such as fuses or spark plugs may only be pointers to some underlying fault.

The pages which follow provide an easy-reference guide to the more common problems which may occur during the operation of the vehicle. These problems and their possible causes are grouped under headings denoting various components or systems, such as Engine, Cooling system, etc. The general Chapter which deals with the problem is also shown in brackets; refer to the relevant part of that Chapter for system-specific information. Whatever the fault, certain basic principles apply. These are as follows:

Verify the fault. This is simply a matter of being sure that you know what the symptoms are before starting work. This is particularly important if you are investigating a fault for someone else, who may not have described it very accurately.

Don't overlook the obvious. For example, if the vehicle won't start, is there fuel in the tank? (Don't take anyone else's word on this particular point, and don't trust the fuel gauge either!) If an electrical fault is indicated, look for loose or broken wires before digging out the test gear.

Cure the disease, not the symptom. Substituting a flat battery with a fully-charged one will get you off the hard shoulder, but if the underlying cause is not attended to, the new battery will go the same way. Similarly, changing oil-fouled spark plugs for a new set will get you moving again, but remember that the reason for the fouling (if it wasn't simply an incorrect grade of plug) will have to be established and corrected.

Don't take anything for granted. Particularly, don't forget that a new component may itself be defective (especially if its been rattling around in the boot for months), and don't leave components out of a fault diagnosis sequence just because they are new or recently-fitted. When you do finally diagnose a difficult fault, you'll probably realise that all the evidence was there from the start.

Diesel fault diagnosis

The majority of starting problems on small diesel engines are electrical in origin. The mechanic who is familiar with petrol engines but less so with diesel may be inclined to view the diesel's injectors and pump in the same light as the spark plugs and distributor, but this is generally a mistake.

When investigating complaints of difficult starting for someone else, make sure that the correct starting procedure is understood and

is being followed. Some drivers are unaware of the significance of the preheating warning light – many modern engines are sufficiently forgiving for this not to matter in mild weather, but with the onset of winter, problems begin. Glow plugs in particular are often neglected – just one faulty plug will make cold-weather starting very difficult.

As a rule of thumb, if the engine is difficult to start but runs well when it has finally got going, the problem is electrical (battery, starter motor or preheating system). If poor performance is combined with difficult starting, the problem is likely to be in the fuel system. The low-pressure (supply) side of the fuel system should be checked before suspecting the injectors and high-pressure pump. The most common fuel supply problem is air getting into the system, and any pipe from the fuel tank forwards must be scrutinised if air leakage is suspected.

Engine

Engine fails to rotate when attempting to start
- [ ] Battery terminal connections loose or corroded (see *Weekly checks*).
- [ ] Battery discharged or faulty (Chapter 5).
- [ ] Broken, loose or disconnected wiring in the starting circuit (Chapter 5).
- [ ] Defective starter solenoid or switch (Chapter 5).
- [ ] Defective starter motor (Chapter 5).
- [ ] Starter pinion or flywheel/driveplate ring gear teeth loose or broken (Chapter 2A and 2B).
- [ ] Engine earth strap broken or disconnected (Chapter 5 or 12).

Engine rotates, but will not start
- [ ] Fuel tank empty.
- [ ] Battery discharged (engine rotates slowly) (Chapter 5).
- [ ] Battery terminal connections loose or corroded (see *Weekly checks*).
- [ ] Preheating system faulty (Chapter 5).
- [ ] Air in fuel system (Chapter 4A).
- [ ] Major mechanical failure (eg, timing belt) (Chapter 2A or 2B).

Engine difficult to start when cold
- [ ] Battery discharged (Chapter 5).
- [ ] Battery terminal connections loose or corroded (see *Weekly checks*).
- [ ] Preheating system faulty (Chapter 5).
- [ ] Low cylinder compressions (Chapter 2A or 2B).

Engine difficult to start when hot
- [ ] Air filter element dirty or clogged (Chapter 1).
- [ ] Low cylinder compressions (Chapter 2A or 2B).

Starter motor noisy or excessively-rough in engagement
- [ ] Starter pinion or flywheel ring gear teeth loose or broken (Chapter 2A or 2B and 5).
- [ ] Starter motor mounting bolts loose or missing (Chapter 5).
- [ ] Starter motor internal components worn or damaged (Chapter 5).

Engine starts, but stops immediately
- [ ] Air in fuel system (Chapter 4A).

Engine idles erratically
- [ ] Air filter element clogged (Chapter 1).
- [ ] Uneven or low cylinder compressions (Chapter 2A or 2B).
- [ ] Camshaft lobes worn (Chapter 2A or 2B).
- [ ] Timing belt incorrectly fitted (Chapter 2A or 2B).
- [ ] Faulty injector(s) (Chapter 4A).

Engine misfires at idle speed
- [ ] Faulty injector – diesel models (Chapter 4A).
- [ ] Air in fuel system (Chapter 4A).
- [ ] Uneven or low cylinder compressions (Chapter 2A or 2B).
- [ ] Disconnected, leaking, or perished crankcase ventilation hoses (Chapter 4B).

Engine misfires throughout the driving speed range
- [ ] Fuel filter choked (Chapter 1).
- [ ] Fuel tank vent blocked, or fuel pipes restricted (Chapter 4A).
- [ ] Faulty injector(s) (Chapter 4A).
- [ ] Uneven or low cylinder compressions (Chapter 2A or 2B).

Engine hesitates on acceleration
- [ ] Faulty mass airflow sensor (Chapter 4A).
- [ ] Faulty injector(s) (Chapter 4A).

Engine stalls
- [ ] Fuel filter choked (Chapter 1).
- [ ] Fuel pump faulty, or delivery pressure low (Chapter 4A).
- [ ] Fuel tank vent blocked, or fuel pipes restricted (Chapter 4A).
- [ ] Air in fuel system (Chapter 4A).
- [ ] Faulty injector(s) (Chapter 4A).

Engine lacks power
- [ ] Timing belt incorrectly fitted or tensioned (Chapter 2A or 2B).
- [ ] Fuel filter choked (Chapter 1).
- [ ] Fuel pump faulty, or delivery pressure low (Chapter 4A).
- [ ] Uneven or low cylinder compressions (Chapter 2A or 2B).
- [ ] Faulty injector(s) (Chapter 4A).
- [ ] Brakes binding (Chapter 9).
- [ ] Clutch slipping (Chapter 6).
- [ ] Air filter element clogged (Chapter 1).

Engine (continued)

Engine backfires

☐ Timing belt incorrectly fitted or tensioned (Chapter 2A or 2B).

Oil pressure warning light illuminated with engine running

☐ Low oil level, or incorrect oil grade (*Weekly checks*).
☐ Faulty oil pressure switch (Chapter 2A or 2B).
☐ Worn engine bearings and/or oil pump (Chapter 2C).
☐ High engine operating temperature (Chapter 3).
☐ Oil pressure relief valve defective (Chapter 2A or 2B).
☐ Oil pick-up strainer clogged (Chapter 2A or 2B).

Engine runs-on after switching off

☐ Excessive carbon build-up in engine (Chapter 2A).
☐ High engine operating temperature (Chapter 3).

Engine noises

Pre-ignition (pinking) or knocking during acceleration or under load

☐ Excessive carbon build-up in engine (Chapter 2A).

Whistling or wheezing noises

☐ Leaking exhaust manifold gasket or pipe-to-manifold joint (Chapter 4B).
☐ Leaking vacuum hose (Chapters 4A and 9).
☐ Blowing cylinder head gasket (Chapter 2A or 2B).

Tapping or rattling noises

☐ Worn valve gear or camshaft (Chapter 2A or 2B).
☐ Ancillary component fault (coolant pump, alternator, etc) (Chapters 3, 5, etc).

Knocking or thumping noises

☐ Worn big-end bearings (regular heavy knocking, perhaps less under load) (Chapter 2C).
☐ Worn main bearings (rumbling and knocking, perhaps worsening under load) (Chapter 2C).
☐ Piston slap (most noticeable when cold) (Chapter 2C).
☐ Ancillary component fault (coolant pump, alternator, etc) (Chapters 3, 5, etc).

Cooling system

Overheating

☐ Insufficient coolant in system (*Weekly checks*).
☐ Thermostat faulty (Chapter 3).
☐ Radiator core blocked, or grille restricted (Chapter 1 and 3).
☐ Electric cooling fan or thermostatic switch faulty (Chapter 3).
☐ Inaccurate temperature gauge sender unit (Chapter 3).
☐ Airlock in cooling system (Chapter 1).
☐ Expansion tank pressure cap faulty (Chapter 3).

Overcooling

☐ Thermostat faulty (Chapter 3).
☐ Inaccurate temperature gauge sender unit (Chapter 3).

External coolant leakage

☐ Deteriorated or damaged hoses or hose clips (Chapter 3).

☐ Radiator core or heater matrix leaking (Chapter 3).
☐ Pressure cap faulty (Chapter 3).
☐ Coolant pump internal seal leaking (Chapter 3).
☐ Coolant pump-to-housing seal leaking (Chapter 3).
☐ Boiling due to overheating (Chapter 3).
☐ Core plug leaking (Chapter 2C).

Internal coolant leakage

☐ Leaking cylinder head gasket (Chapter 2A or 2B).
☐ Cracked cylinder head or cylinder block (Chapter 2C).

Corrosion

☐ Infrequent draining and flushing (Chapter 1).
☐ Incorrect coolant mixture or inappropriate coolant type (see *Weekly checks*).

Fuel and exhaust systems

Excessive fuel consumption

☐ Air filter element dirty or clogged (Chapter 1).
☐ Faulty injector(s) (Chapter 4A).
☐ Faulty brake calipers (Chapter 9).
☐ Tyres under-inflated (see *Weekly checks*).

Fuel leakage and/or fuel odour

☐ Damaged fuel tank, pipes or connections (Chapter 4A).

Excessive noise or fumes from exhaust system

☐ Leaking exhaust system or manifold joints (Chapter 4B).
☐ Leaking, corroded or damaged silencers or pipe (Chapter 1 and 4B).
☐ Broken mountings causing body or suspension contact (Chapter 1).

Clutch

Pedal travels to floor – no pressure or very little resistance

☐ Faulty master or slave cylinder (Chapter 6).
☐ Faulty hydraulic release system (Chapter 6).
☐ Broken clutch release bearing or arm (Chapter 6).
☐ Broken diaphragm spring in clutch pressure plate (Chapter 6).

Clutch fails to disengage (unable to select gears)

☐ Faulty master or slave cylinder (Chapter 6).
☐ Faulty hydraulic release system (Chapter 6).
☐ Clutch disc sticking on gearbox input shaft splines (Chapter 6).
☐ Clutch disc sticking to flywheel or pressure plate (Chapter 6).
☐ Faulty pressure plate assembly (Chapter 6).
☐ Clutch release mechanism worn or incorrectly assembled (Chapter 6).

Clutch slips (engine speed increases, with no increase in vehicle speed)

☐ Faulty hydraulic release system (Chapter 6).
☐ Clutch disc linings excessively worn (Chapter 6).
☐ Clutch disc linings contaminated with oil or grease (Chapter 6).
☐ Faulty pressure plate or weak diaphragm spring (Chapter 6).

Judder as clutch is engaged

☐ Clutch disc linings contaminated with oil or grease (Chapter 6).
☐ Clutch disc linings excessively worn (Chapter 6).
☐ Faulty or distorted pressure plate or diaphragm spring (Chapter 6).
☐ Worn or loose engine or gearbox mountings (Chapter 2A or 2B).
☐ Clutch disc hub or gearbox input shaft splines worn (Chapter 6).

Noise when depressing or releasing clutch pedal

☐ Worn clutch release bearing (Chapter 6).
☐ Worn or dry clutch pedal pivot (Chapter 6).
☐ Faulty pressure plate assembly (Chapter 6).
☐ Pressure plate diaphragm spring broken (Chapter 6).
☐ Broken clutch friction plate cushioning springs (Chapter 6).

Manual transmission

Noisy in neutral with engine running

☐ Input shaft bearings worn (noise apparent with clutch pedal released, but not when depressed) (Chapter 7A).*
☐ Clutch release bearing worn (noise apparent with clutch pedal depressed, possibly less when released) (Chapter 6).

Noisy in one particular gear

☐ Worn, damaged or chipped gear teeth (Chapter 7A).*

Difficulty engaging gears

☐ Clutch fault (Chapter 6).
☐ Worn or damaged gear linkage (Chapter 7A).
☐ Worn synchroniser units (Chapter 7A).*

Jumps out of gear

☐ Worn or damaged gear linkage (Chapter 7A).

☐ Worn synchroniser units (Chapter 7A).*
☐ Worn selector forks (Chapter 7A).*

Vibration

☐ Lack of oil (Chapter 1 and 7A).
☐ Worn bearings (Chapter 7A).*

Lubricant leaks

☐ Leaking oil seal (Chapter 7A).
☐ Leaking housing joint (Chapter 7A).*
☐ Leaking input shaft oil seal (Chapter 7A).

Although the corrective action necessary to remedy the symptoms described is beyond the scope of the home mechanic, the above information should be helpful in isolating the cause of the condition, so that the owner can communicate clearly with a professional mechanic.

Automatic transmission (DSG)

Note: *Due to the complexity of the automatic transmission, it is difficult for the home mechanic to properly diagnose and service this unit. For problems other than the following, the vehicle should be taken to a dealer service department or automatic transmission specialist. Do not be too hasty in removing the transmission if a fault is suspected, as most of the testing is carried out with the unit still fitted.*

Fluid leakage

☐ To determine the source of a leak, first remove all built-up dirt and grime from the transmission housing and surrounding areas using a degreasing agent, or by steam-cleaning. Drive the vehicle at low speed, so airflow will not blow the leak far from its source. Raise and support the vehicle, and determine where the leak is coming from.

General gear selection problems

☐ Chapter 7B deals with checking and adjusting the selector mechanism on automatic transmissions. The following are common problems which may be caused by a poorly-adjusted mechanism:
a) *Engine starting in gears other than Park or Neutral.*

b) *Indicator panel indicating a gear other than the one actually being used.*
c) *Vehicle moves when in Park or Neutral.*
d) *Poor gear shift quality or erratic gear changes.*

Engine will not start in any gear, or starts in gears other than Park or Neutral

☐ Incorrect selector mechanism adjustment (Chapter 7B).

Transmission slips, shifts roughly, is noisy, or has no drive in forward or reverse gears

☐ There are many probable causes for the above problems, but unless there is a very obvious reason (such as a loose or corroded wiring plug connection on or near the transmission), the car should be taken to a franchised dealer or specialist for the fault to be diagnosed. The transmission control unit incorporates a self-diagnosis facility, and any fault codes can quickly be read and interpreted by a dealer with the proper diagnostic equipment.

Driveshafts

Vibration when accelerating or decelerating

- ☐ Worn inner constant velocity joint (Chapter 8).
- ☐ Bent or distorted driveshaft (Chapter 8).

Clicking or knocking noise on turns (at slow speed on full-lock)

- ☐ Worn outer constant velocity joint (Chapter 8).
- ☐ Lack of constant velocity joint lubricant, possibly due to damaged gaiter (Chapter 8).

Braking system

Note: *Before assuming that a brake problem exists, make sure that the tyres are in good condition and correctly inflated, that the front wheel alignment is correct, and that the vehicle is not loaded with weight in an unequal manner. Apart from checking the condition of all pipe and hose connections, any faults occurring on the anti-lock braking system should be referred to a Skoda dealer for diagnosis.*

Vehicle pulls to one side under braking

- ☐ Worn, defective, damaged or contaminated front or rear brake pads on one side (Chapters 1 and 9).
- ☐ Seized or partially-seized front or rear brake caliper (Chapter 9).
- ☐ A mixture of brake pad lining materials fitted between sides (Chapter 9).
- ☐ Brake caliper mounting bolts loose (Chapter 9).
- ☐ Worn or damaged steering or suspension components (Chapters 1 and 10).

Noise (grinding or high-pitched squeal) when brakes applied

- ☐ Brake pad friction lining material worn down to metal backing (Chapters 1 and 9).
- ☐ Excessive corrosion of brake disc – may be apparent after the vehicle has been standing for some time (Chapter 9).
- ☐ Foreign object (stone chipping, etc) trapped between brake disc and shield (Chapter 9).

Excessive brake pedal travel

- ☐ Faulty master cylinder (Chapter 9).
- ☐ Air in hydraulic system (Chapter 9).
- ☐ Faulty vacuum servo unit (Chapter 9).
- ☐ Faulty vacuum pump (Chapter 4A or 9).

Brake pedal feels spongy when depressed

- ☐ Air in hydraulic system (Chapter 9).
- ☐ Deteriorated flexible rubber brake hoses (Chapters 1 and 9).
- ☐ Master cylinder mountings loose (Chapter 9).
- ☐ Faulty master cylinder (Chapter 9).

Excessive brake pedal effort required to stop vehicle

- ☐ Faulty vacuum servo unit (Chapter 9).
- ☐ Disconnected, damaged or insecure brake servo vacuum hose (Chapter 9).
- ☐ Faulty vacuum pump (Chapter 4A or 9).
- ☐ Primary or secondary hydraulic circuit failure (Chapter 9).
- ☐ Seized brake caliper (Chapter 9).
- ☐ Brake pads incorrectly fitted (Chapter 9).
- ☐ Incorrect grade of brake pads fitted (Chapter 9).
- ☐ Brake pads contaminated (Chapter 9).

Judder felt through brake pedal or steering wheel when braking

- ☐ Excessive run-out or distortion of brake disc(s) (Chapter 9).
- ☐ Brake pad linings worn (Chapters 1 and 9).
- ☐ Brake caliper mounting bolts loose (Chapter 9).
- ☐ Wear in suspension or steering components or mountings (Chapters 1 and 10).

Pedal pulsates when braking hard

- ☐ Normal feature of ABS – no fault

Brakes binding

- ☐ Seized brake caliper piston(s) (Chapter 9).
- ☐ Faulty master cylinder (Chapter 9).

Rear wheels locking under normal braking

- ☐ Rear brake pad linings contaminated (Chapters 1 and 9).
- ☐ Rear brake discs warped (Chapter 9).

Steering and suspension

Note: *Before diagnosing suspension or steering faults, be sure that the trouble is not due to incorrect tyre pressures, mixtures of tyre types, or binding brakes.*

Vehicle pulls to one side

☐ Defective tyre (see *Weekly checks*).
☐ Excessive wear in suspension or steering components (Chapters 1 and 10).
☐ Incorrect front wheel alignment (Chapter 10).
☐ Accident damage to steering or suspension components (Chapters 1 and 10).

Wheel wobble and vibration

☐ Front roadwheels out of balance (vibration felt mainly through the steering wheel) (Chapter 1 or 10).
☐ Rear roadwheels out of balance (vibration felt throughout the vehicle) (Chapter 1 or 10).
☐ Roadwheels damaged or distorted (Chapter 1 or 10).
☐ Faulty or damaged tyre (*Weekly checks*).
☐ Worn steering or suspension joints, bushes or components (Chapters 1 and 10).
☐ Wheel bolts loose (Chapter 1 and 10).

Excessive pitching and/or rolling around corners, or during braking

☐ Defective shock absorbers (Chapters 1 and 10).
☐ Broken or weak coil spring and/or suspension component (Chapters 1 and 10).
☐ Worn or damaged anti-roll bar or mountings (Chapter 10).

Wandering or general instability

☐ Incorrect front wheel alignment (Chapter 10).
☐ Worn steering or suspension joints, bushes or components (Chapters 1 and 10).
☐ Roadwheels out of balance (Chapter 10).
☐ Faulty or damaged tyre (*Weekly checks*).
☐ Wheel bolts loose (Chapter 10).
☐ Defective shock absorbers (Chapters 1 and 10).

Excessively-stiff steering

☐ Seized track rod end balljoint or suspension balljoint (Chapters 1 and 10).
☐ Incorrect front wheel alignment (Chapter 10).
☐ Steering gear damaged (Chapter 10).

Excessive play in steering

☐ Worn steering column universal joint(s) (Chapter 10).
☐ Worn steering track rod end balljoints (Chapters 1 and 10).
☐ Worn steering gear (Chapter 10).
☐ Worn steering or suspension joints, bushes or components (Chapters 1 and 10).

Lack of power assistance

☐ Faulty steering gear (Chapter 10).

Tyre wear excessive

Tyres worn on inside or outside edges

☐ Incorrect camber or castor angles (Chapter 10).
☐ Worn steering or suspension joints, bushes or components (Chapters 1 and 10).
☐ Excessively-hard cornering.
☐ Accident damage.

Tyre treads exhibit feathered edges

☐ Incorrect toe setting (Chapter 10).

Tyres worn in centre of tread

☐ Tyres over-inflated (*Weekly checks*).

Tyres worn on inside and outside edges

☐ Tyres under-inflated (*Weekly checks*).
☐ Worn shock absorbers (Chapter 10).

Tyres worn unevenly

☐ Tyres/wheels out of balance (*Weekly checks*).
☐ Excessive wheel or tyre run-out (Chapter 10).
☐ Worn shock absorbers (Chapters 1 and 10).
☐ Faulty tyre (*Weekly checks*).

Electrical system

Note: *For problems associated with the starting system, refer to the faults listed under Engine earlier in this Section.*

Battery will not hold a charge more than a few days

☐ Battery defective internally (Chapter 5).
☐ Battery electrolyte level low – where applicable (*Weekly checks*).
☐ Battery terminal connections loose or corroded (*Weekly checks*).
☐ Auxiliary drivebelt worn – or incorrectly adjusted, where applicable (Chapter 1).
☐ Alternator not charging at correct output (Chapter 5).
☐ Alternator or voltage regulator faulty (Chapter 5).
☐ Short-circuit causing continual battery drain (Chapters 5 and 12).

Ignition/no-charge warning light remains illuminated with engine running

☐ Auxiliary drivebelt broken, worn, or incorrectly adjusted (Chapter 1).
☐ Internal fault in alternator or voltage regulator (Chapter 5).
☐ Broken, disconnected, or loose wiring in charging circuit (Chapter 12).

Ignition/no-charge warning light fails to come on

☐ Broken, disconnected, or loose wiring in warning light circuit (Chapter 12).
☐ Alternator faulty (Chapter 5).

Electrical system (continued)

Lights inoperative

- [ ] Bulb blown (Chapter 12).
- [ ] Corrosion of bulb or bulbholder contacts (Chapter 12).
- [ ] Blown fuse (Chapter 12).
- [ ] Faulty relay (Chapter 12).
- [ ] Broken, loose, or disconnected wiring (Chapter 12).
- [ ] Faulty switch (Chapter 12).

Instrument readings inaccurate or erratic

Fuel or temperature gauges give no reading

- [ ] Faulty gauge sender unit (Chapter 3 or 4A).
- [ ] Wiring open-circuit (Chapter 12).
- [ ] Faulty gauge (Chapter 12).

Fuel or temperature gauges give continuous maximum reading

- [ ] Faulty gauge sender unit (Chapters 3 or 4A).
- [ ] Wiring short-circuit (Chapter 12).
- [ ] Faulty gauge (Chapter 12).

Horn inoperative, or unsatisfactory in operation

Horn operates all the time

- [ ] Horn contacts permanently bridged or horn push stuck down (Chapter 12).

Horn fails to operate

- [ ] Blown fuse (Chapter 12).
- [ ] Cable or cable connections loose, broken or disconnected (Chapter 12).
- [ ] Faulty horn (Chapter 12).

Horn emits intermittent or unsatisfactory sound

- [ ] Cable connections loose (Chapter 12).
- [ ] Horn mountings loose (Chapter 12).
- [ ] Faulty horn (Chapter 12).

Windscreen/tailgate wipers inoperative, or unsatisfactory in operation

Wipers fail to operate, or operate very slowly

- [ ] Wiper blades stuck to screen, or linkage seized or binding (*Weekly checks* or Chapter 12).
- [ ] Blown fuse (Chapter 12).
- [ ] Cable or cable connections loose, broken or disconnected (Chapter 12).
- [ ] Faulty relay (Chapter 12).
- [ ] Faulty wiper motor (Chapter 12).

Wiper blades sweep over too large or too small an area of the glass

- [ ] Wiper arms incorrectly positioned on spindles (Chapter 12).
- [ ] Excessive wear of wiper linkage (Chapter 12).
- [ ] Wiper motor or linkage mountings loose or insecure (Chapter 12).

Wiper blades fail to clean the glass effectively

- [ ] Wiper blade rubbers worn or perished (*Weekly checks*).
- [ ] Wiper arm tension springs broken, or arm pivots seized (Chapter 12).
- [ ] Insufficient windscreen washer additive to adequately remove road film (*Weekly checks*).

Windscreen washers inoperative, or unsatisfactory in operation

One or more washer jets inoperative

- [ ] Blocked washer jet (Chapter 12).
- [ ] Disconnected, kinked or restricted fluid hose (Chapter 12).
- [ ] Insufficient fluid in washer reservoir (*Weekly checks*).

Washer pump fails to operate

- [ ] Broken or disconnected wiring or connections (Chapter 12).
- [ ] Blown fuse (Chapter 12).
- [ ] Faulty washer switch (Chapter 12).
- [ ] Faulty washer pump (Chapter 12).

Electric windows inoperative, or unsatisfactory in operation

Window glass will only move in one direction

- [ ] Faulty switch (Chapter 12).

Window glass slow to move

- [ ] Regulator seized or damaged, or in need of lubrication (Chapter 11).
- [ ] Door internal components or trim fouling regulator (Chapter 11).
- [ ] Faulty motor (Chapter 11).

Window glass fails to move

- [ ] Blown fuse (Chapter 12).
- [ ] Faulty relay (Chapter 12).
- [ ] Broken or disconnected wiring or connections (Chapter 12).
- [ ] Faulty motor (Chapter 12).

Central locking system inoperative, or unsatisfactory in operation

Complete system failure

- [ ] Blown fuse (Chapter 12).
- [ ] Faulty relay (Chapter 12).
- [ ] Broken or disconnected wiring or connections (Chapter 12).

Latch locks but will not unlock, or unlocks but will not lock

- [ ] Faulty switch (Chapter 12).
- [ ] Broken or disconnected latch operating rods or levers (Chapter 11).
- [ ] Faulty relay (Chapter 12).

One lock fails to operate

- [ ] Broken or disconnected wiring or connections (Chapter 12).
- [ ] Faulty motor (Chapter 11).
- [ ] Broken, binding or disconnected lock operating rods or levers (Chapter 11).
- [ ] Fault in door lock (Chapter 11).

A

ABS (Anti-lock brake system) A system, usually electronically controlled, that senses incipient wheel lockup during braking and relieves hydraulic pressure at wheels that are about to skid.

Air bag An inflatable bag hidden in the steering wheel (driver's side) or the dash or glovebox (passenger side). In a head-on collision, the bags inflate, preventing the driver and front passenger from being thrown forward into the steering wheel or windscreen.

Air cleaner A metal or plastic housing, containing a filter element, which removes dust and dirt from the air being drawn into the engine.

Air filter element The actual filter in an air cleaner system, usually manufactured from pleated paper and requiring renewal at regular intervals.

Air filter

Allen key A hexagonal wrench which fits into a recessed hexagonal hole.

Alligator clip A long-nosed spring-loaded metal clip with meshing teeth. Used to make temporary electrical connections.

Alternator A component in the electrical system which converts mechanical energy from a drivebelt into electrical energy to charge the battery and to operate the starting system, ignition system and electrical accessories.

Ampere (amp) A unit of measurement for the flow of electric current. One amp is the amount of current produced by one volt acting through a resistance of one ohm.

Anaerobic sealer A substance used to prevent bolts and screws from loosening. Anaerobic means that it does not require oxygen for activation. The Loctite brand is widely used.

Antifreeze A substance (usually ethylene glycol) mixed with water, and added to a vehicle's cooling system, to prevent freezing of the coolant in winter. Antifreeze also contains chemicals to inhibit corrosion and the formation of rust and other deposits that would tend to clog the radiator and coolant passages and reduce cooling efficiency.

Anti-seize compound A coating that reduces the risk of seizing on fasteners that are subjected to high temperatures, such as exhaust manifold bolts and nuts.

Asbestos A natural fibrous mineral with great heat resistance, commonly used in the composition of brake friction materials.

Asbestos is a health hazard and the dust created by brake systems should never be inhaled or ingested.

Axle A shaft on which a wheel revolves, or which revolves with a wheel. Also, a solid beam that connects the two wheels at one end of the vehicle. An axle which also transmits power to the wheels is known as a live axle.

Axleshaft A single rotating shaft, on either side of the differential, which delivers power from the final drive assembly to the drive wheels. Also called a driveshaft or a halfshaft.

B

Ball bearing An anti-friction bearing consisting of a hardened inner and outer race with hardened steel balls between two races.

Bearing The curved surface on a shaft or in a bore, or the part assembled into either, that permits relative motion between them with minimum wear and friction.

Bearing

Big-end bearing The bearing in the end of the connecting rod that's attached to the crankshaft.

Bleed nipple A valve on a brake wheel cylinder, caliper or other hydraulic component that is opened to purge the hydraulic system of air. Also called a bleed screw.

Brake bleeding Procedure for removing air from lines of a hydraulic brake system.

Brake bleeding

Brake disc The component of a disc brake that rotates with the wheels.

Brake drum The component of a drum brake that rotates with the wheels.

Brake linings The friction material which contacts the brake disc or drum to retard the vehicle's speed. The linings are bonded or riveted to the brake pads or shoes.

Brake pads The replaceable friction pads that pinch the brake disc when the brakes are applied. Brake pads consist of a friction material bonded or riveted to a rigid backing plate.

Brake shoe The crescent-shaped carrier to which the brake linings are mounted and which forces the lining against the rotating drum during braking.

Braking systems For more information on braking systems, consult the *Haynes Automotive Brake Manual*.

Breaker bar A long socket wrench handle providing greater leverage.

Bulkhead The insulated partition between the engine and the passenger compartment.

C

Caliper The non-rotating part of a disc-brake assembly that straddles the disc and carries the brake pads. The caliper also contains the hydraulic components that cause the pads to pinch the disc when the brakes are applied. A caliper is also a measuring tool that can be set to measure inside or outside dimensions of an object.

Camshaft A rotating shaft on which a series of cam lobes operate the valve mechanisms. The camshaft may be driven by gears, by sprockets and chain or by sprockets and a belt.

Canister A container in an evaporative emission control system; contains activated charcoal granules to trap vapours from the fuel system.

Canister

Carburettor A device which mixes fuel with air in the proper proportions to provide a desired power output from a spark ignition internal combustion engine.

Castellated Resembling the parapets along the top of a castle wall. For example, a castellated balljoint stud nut.

Castor In wheel alignment, the backward or forward tilt of the steering axis. Castor is positive when the steering axis is inclined rearward at the top.

Catalytic converter A silencer-like device in the exhaust system which converts certain pollutants in the exhaust gases into less harmful substances.

Catalytic converter

Circlip A ring-shaped clip used to prevent endwise movement of cylindrical parts and shafts. An internal circlip is installed in a groove in a housing; an external circlip fits into a groove on the outside of a cylindrical piece such as a shaft.

Clearance The amount of space between two parts. For example, between a piston and a cylinder, between a bearing and a journal, etc.

Coil spring A spiral of elastic steel found in various sizes throughout a vehicle, for example as a springing medium in the suspension and in the valve train.

Compression Reduction in volume, and increase in pressure and temperature, of a gas, caused by squeezing it into a smaller space.

Compression ratio The relationship between cylinder volume when the piston is at top dead centre and cylinder volume when the piston is at bottom dead centre.

Constant velocity (CV) joint A type of universal joint that cancels out vibrations caused by driving power being transmitted through an angle.

Core plug A disc or cup-shaped metal device inserted in a hole in a casting through which core was removed when the casting was formed. Also known as a freeze plug or expansion plug.

Crankcase The lower part of the engine block in which the crankshaft rotates.

Crankshaft The main rotating member, or shaft, running the length of the crankcase, with offset "throws" to which the connecting rods are attached.

Crankshaft assembly

Crocodile clip See Alligator clip

D

Diagnostic code Code numbers obtained by accessing the diagnostic mode of an engine management computer. This code can be used to determine the area in the system where a malfunction may be located.

Disc brake A brake design incorporating a rotating disc onto which brake pads are squeezed. The resulting friction converts the energy of a moving vehicle into heat.

Double-overhead cam (DOHC) An engine that uses two overhead camshafts, usually one for the intake valves and one for the exhaust valves.

Drivebelt(s) The belt(s) used to drive accessories such as the alternator, water pump, power steering pump, air conditioning compressor, etc. off the crankshaft pulley.

Accessory drivebelts

Driveshaft Any shaft used to transmit motion. Commonly used when referring to the axleshafts on a front wheel drive vehicle.

Drum brake A type of brake using a drum-shaped metal cylinder attached to the inner surface of the wheel. When the brake pedal is pressed, curved brake shoes with friction linings press against the inside of the drum to slow or stop the vehicle.

E

EGR valve A valve used to introduce exhaust gases into the intake air stream.

Electronic control unit (ECU) A computer which controls (for instance) ignition and fuel injection systems, or an anti-lock braking system. For more information refer to the *Haynes Automotive Electrical and Electronic Systems Manual*.

Electronic Fuel Injection (EFI) A computer controlled fuel system that distributes fuel through an injector located in each intake port of the engine.

Emergency brake A braking system, independent of the main hydraulic system, that can be used to slow or stop the vehicle if the primary brakes fail, or to hold the vehicle stationary even though the brake pedal isn't depressed. It usually consists of a hand lever that actuates either front or rear brakes mechanically through a series of cables and linkages. Also known as a handbrake or parking brake.

Endfloat The amount of lengthwise movement between two parts. As applied to a crankshaft, the distance that the crankshaft can move forward and back in the cylinder block.

Engine management system (EMS) A computer controlled system which manages the fuel injection and the ignition systems in an integrated fashion.

Exhaust manifold A part with several passages through which exhaust gases leave the engine combustion chambers and enter the exhaust pipe.

F

Fan clutch A viscous (fluid) drive coupling device which permits variable engine fan speeds in relation to engine speeds.

Feeler blade A thin strip or blade of hardened steel, ground to an exact thickness, used to check or measure clearances between parts.

Feeler blade

Firing order The order in which the engine cylinders fire, or deliver their power strokes, beginning with the number one cylinder.

Flywheel A heavy spinning wheel in which energy is absorbed and stored by means of momentum. On cars, the flywheel is attached to the crankshaft to smooth out firing impulses.

Free play The amount of travel before any action takes place. The "looseness" in a linkage, or an assembly of parts, between the initial application of force and actual movement. For example, the distance the brake pedal moves before the pistons in the master cylinder are actuated.

Fuse An electrical device which protects a circuit against accidental overload. The typical fuse contains a soft piece of metal which is calibrated to melt at a predetermined current flow (expressed as amps) and break the circuit.

Fusible link A circuit protection device consisting of a conductor surrounded by heat-resistant insulation. The conductor is smaller than the wire it protects, so it acts as the weakest link in the circuit. Unlike a blown fuse, a failed fusible link must frequently be cut from the wire for replacement.

G

Gap The distance the spark must travel in jumping from the centre electrode to the side electrode in a spark plug. Also refers to the spacing between the points in a contact breaker assembly in a conventional points-type ignition, or to the distance between the reluctor or rotor and the pickup coil in an electronic ignition.

Adjusting spark plug gap

Gasket Any thin, soft material - usually cork, cardboard, asbestos or soft metal - installed between two metal surfaces to ensure a good seal. For instance, the cylinder head gasket seals the joint between the block and the cylinder head.

Gasket

Gauge An instrument panel display used to monitor engine conditions. A gauge with a movable pointer on a dial or a fixed scale is an analogue gauge. A gauge with a numerical readout is called a digital gauge.

H

Halfshaft A rotating shaft that transmits power from the final drive unit to a drive wheel, usually when referring to a live rear axle.

Harmonic balancer A device designed to reduce torsion or twisting vibration in the crankshaft. May be incorporated in the crankshaft pulley. Also known as a vibration damper.

Hone An abrasive tool for correcting small irregularities or differences in diameter in an engine cylinder, brake cylinder, etc.

Hydraulic tappet A tappet that utilises hydraulic pressure from the engine's lubrication system to maintain zero clearance (constant contact with both camshaft and valve stem). Automatically adjusts to variation in valve stem length. Hydraulic tappets also reduce valve noise.

I

Ignition timing The moment at which the spark plug fires, usually expressed in the number of crankshaft degrees before the piston reaches the top of its stroke.

Inlet manifold A tube or housing with passages through which flows the air-fuel mixture (carburettor vehicles and vehicles with throttle body injection) or air only (port fuel-injected vehicles) to the port openings in the cylinder head.

J

Jump start Starting the engine of a vehicle with a discharged or weak battery by attaching jump leads from the weak battery to a charged or helper battery.

L

Load Sensing Proportioning Valve (LSPV) A brake hydraulic system control valve that works like a proportioning valve, but also takes into consideration the amount of weight carried by the rear axle.

Locknut A nut used to lock an adjustment nut, or other threaded component, in place. For example, a locknut is employed to keep the adjusting nut on the rocker arm in position.

Lockwasher A form of washer designed to prevent an attaching nut from working loose.

M

MacPherson strut A type of front suspension system devised by Earle MacPherson at Ford of England. In its original form, a simple lateral link with the anti-roll bar creates the lower control arm. A long strut - an integral coil spring and shock absorber - is mounted between the body and the steering knuckle. Many modern so-called MacPherson strut systems use a conventional lower A-arm and don't rely on the anti-roll bar for location.

Multimeter An electrical test instrument with the capability to measure voltage, current and resistance.

N

NOx Oxides of Nitrogen. A common toxic pollutant emitted by petrol and diesel engines at higher temperatures.

O

Ohm The unit of electrical resistance. One volt applied to a resistance of one ohm will produce a current of one amp.

Ohmmeter An instrument for measuring electrical resistance.

O-ring A type of sealing ring made of a special rubber-like material; in use, the O-ring is compressed into a groove to provide the sealing action.

Overhead cam (ohc) engine An engine with the camshaft(s) located on top of the cylinder head(s).

Overhead valve (ohv) engine An engine with the valves located in the cylinder head, but with the camshaft located in the engine block.

Oxygen sensor A device installed in the engine exhaust manifold, which senses the oxygen content in the exhaust and converts this information into an electric current. Also called a Lambda sensor.

P

Phillips screw A type of screw head having a cross instead of a slot for a corresponding type of screwdriver.

Plastigage A thin strip of plastic thread, available in different sizes, used for measuring clearances. For example, a strip of Plastigage is laid across a bearing journal. The parts are assembled and dismantled; the width of the crushed strip indicates the clearance between journal and bearing.

Plastigage

Propeller shaft The long hollow tube with universal joints at both ends that carries power from the transmission to the differential on front-engined rear wheel drive vehicles.

Proportioning valve A hydraulic control valve which limits the amount of pressure to the rear brakes during panic stops to prevent wheel lock-up.

R

Rack-and-pinion steering A steering system with a pinion gear on the end of the steering shaft that mates with a rack (think of a geared wheel opened up and laid flat). When the steering wheel is turned, the pinion turns, moving the rack to the left or right. This movement is transmitted through the track rods to the steering arms at the wheels.

Radiator A liquid-to-air heat transfer device designed to reduce the temperature of the coolant in an internal combustion engine cooling system.

Refrigerant Any substance used as a heat transfer agent in an air-conditioning system. R-12 has been the principle refrigerant for many years; recently, however, manufacturers have begun using R-134a, a non-CFC substance that is considered less harmful to the ozone in the upper atmosphere.

Rocker arm A lever arm that rocks on a shaft or pivots on a stud. In an overhead valve engine, the rocker arm converts the upward movement of the pushrod into a downward movement to open a valve.

Rotor In a distributor, the rotating device inside the cap that connects the centre electrode and the outer terminals as it turns, distributing the high voltage from the coil secondary winding to the proper spark plug. Also, that part of an alternator which rotates inside the stator. Also, the rotating assembly of a turbocharger, including the compressor wheel, shaft and turbine wheel.

Runout The amount of wobble (in-and-out movement) of a gear or wheel as it's rotated. The amount a shaft rotates "out-of-true." The out-of-round condition of a rotating part.

S

Sealant A liquid or paste used to prevent leakage at a joint. Sometimes used in conjunction with a gasket.

Sealed beam lamp An older headlight design which integrates the reflector, lens and filaments into a hermetically-sealed one-piece unit. When a filament burns out or the lens cracks, the entire unit is simply replaced.

Serpentine drivebelt A single, long, wide accessory drivebelt that's used on some newer vehicles to drive all the accessories, instead of a series of smaller, shorter belts. Serpentine drivebelts are usually tensioned by an automatic tensioner.

Serpentine drivebelt

Shim Thin spacer, commonly used to adjust the clearance or relative positions between two parts. For example, shims inserted into or under bucket tappets control valve clearances. Clearance is adjusted by changing the thickness of the shim.

Slide hammer A special puller that screws into or hooks onto a component such as a shaft or bearing; a heavy sliding handle on the shaft bottoms against the end of the shaft to knock the component free.

Sprocket A tooth or projection on the periphery of a wheel, shaped to engage with a chain or drivebelt. Commonly used to refer to the sprocket wheel itself.

Starter inhibitor switch On vehicles with an automatic transmission, a switch that prevents starting if the vehicle is not in Neutral or Park.

Strut See MacPherson strut.

T

Tappet A cylindrical component which transmits motion from the cam to the valve stem, either directly or via a pushrod and rocker arm. Also called a cam follower.

Thermostat A heat-controlled valve that regulates the flow of coolant between the cylinder block and the radiator, so maintaining optimum engine operating temperature. A thermostat is also used in some air cleaners in which the temperature is regulated.

Thrust bearing The bearing in the clutch assembly that is moved in to the release levers by clutch pedal action to disengage the clutch. Also referred to as a release bearing.

Timing belt A toothed belt which drives the camshaft. Serious engine damage may result if it breaks in service.

Timing chain A chain which drives the camshaft.

Toe-in The amount the front wheels are closer together at the front than at the rear. On rear wheel drive vehicles, a slight amount of toe-in is usually specified to keep the front wheels running parallel on the road by offsetting other forces that tend to spread the wheels apart.

Toe-out The amount the front wheels are closer together at the rear than at the front. On front wheel drive vehicles, a slight amount of toe-out is usually specified.

Tools For full information on choosing and using tools, refer to the *Haynes Automotive Tools Manual*.

Tracer A stripe of a second colour applied to a wire insulator to distinguish that wire from another one with the same colour insulator.

Tune-up A process of accurate and careful adjustments and parts replacement to obtain the best possible engine performance.

Turbocharger A centrifugal device, driven by exhaust gases, that pressurises the intake air. Normally used to increase the power output from a given engine displacement, but can also be used primarily to reduce exhaust emissions (as on VW's "Umwelt" Diesel engine).

U

Universal joint or U-joint A double-pivoted connection for transmitting power from a driving to a driven shaft through an angle. A U-joint consists of two Y-shaped yokes and a cross-shaped member called the spider.

V

Valve A device through which the flow of liquid, gas, vacuum, or loose material in bulk may be started, stopped, or regulated by a movable part that opens, shuts, or partially obstructs one or more ports or passageways. A valve is also the movable part of such a device.

Valve clearance The clearance between the valve tip (the end of the valve stem) and the rocker arm or tappet. The valve clearance is measured when the valve is closed.

Vernier caliper A precision measuring instrument that measures inside and outside dimensions. Not quite as accurate as a micrometer, but more convenient.

Viscosity The thickness of a liquid or its resistance to flow.

Volt A unit for expressing electrical "pressure" in a circuit. One volt that will produce a current of one ampere through a resistance of one ohm.

W

Welding Various processes used to join metal items by heating the areas to be joined to a molten state and fusing them together. For more information refer to the *Haynes Automotive Welding Manual*.

Wiring diagram A drawing portraying the components and wires in a vehicle's electrical system, using standardised symbols. For more information refer to the *Haynes Automotive Electrical and Electronic Systems Manual*.

Note: *References throughout this index are in the form "Chapter number"* • *"Page number". So, for example, 2C•15 refers to page 15 of Chapter 2C.*

Note: *References throughout this index are in the form* "**Chapter number**" • "**Page number**". *So, for example, 2C•15 refers to page 15 of Chapter 2C.*

Note: *References throughout this index are in the form "**Chapter number**" • "**Page number**". So, for example, 2C•15 refers to page 15 of Chapter 2C.*

REF•26 Index

Note: References throughout this index are in the form "Chapter number" • "Page number". So, for example, 2C•15 refers to page 15 of Chapter 2C.

Oil filter – 1•7
Oil level/temperature sensor
  Common rail injection engine – 2B•26
  PD unit injector engine – 2A•20
Oil pressure warning light switch
  Common rail injection engine – 2B•25
  PD unit injector engine – 2A•19
Oil pump
  Belt driven (engine codes CFHC, CFHF, CLCA and CLCB – 2B•19
  Chain driven (engine code CEGA) – 2B•19
Oil pump (Common rail injection engine) – 2B•18
Oil pump and drive chain (PD unit injector engine) – 2A•16
Oil pump drive chain/sprockets (PD unit injector engine) – 2A•16

P

Parking aid components – 12•14
  Control unit – 12•14
  Range/distance sensor – 12•14
  Warning buzzer – 12•14
Particulate filter ash deposit mass check – 1•15
Plenum chamber check – 1•13
Pollen filter element renewal – 1•11

R

Radiator grille – 11•7
Radiator removal – 3•2
Radio/CD unit – 12•14
Regular Maintenance – 1•6
Remote control battery renewal – 1•17
Resetting the service interval display – 1•8
Reversing light switch – 7A•3
Road test and exhaust emissions check – 1•13
Routine maintenance
  Component location – 1•3
  Maintenance schedule – 1•2
  Maintenance servicing specifications – 1•2

S

Safety First – 0•5
Screen washer fluid level – 0•13
Seats
  Front seat – 11•18
  Front seat belt – 11•22
  Rear centre seat belt – 11•22
  Rear seat backrest – 11•18
  Rear seat bench – 11•18
  Rear side seat belt – 11•22
  Seat bench side upholstery – 11•18
  Seat belt tensioning mechanism general information – 11•21
  Seat belts – 11•21
  Seat heating switches – 12•8
  Seats removal – 11•18
Service interval display – 1•8
Speakers removal – 12•15
Starter motor
  Removal – 5•7
  Testing/overhaul – 5•7
Starting and charging systems – 5•1 *et seq*
Steering and suspension – 10•1 *et seq*
  Front wheel bearing housing – 10•4
  Front anti-roll bar – 10•9
  Front anti-roll bar connecting link – 10•9

Front hub bearings – 10•5
Front suspension lower arm balljoint – 10•8
Front suspension lower arm removal/overhaul – 10•7
Front suspension strut removal/overhaul – 10•5
Rear anti-roll bar – 10•13
Rear anti-roll bar connecting link – 10•13
Rear coil spring – 10•12
Rear hub/wheel bearings checking/renewal – 10•10
Rear shock absorber – 10•13
Rear suspension arms – 10•11
Rear track control rod – 10•10
Rear trailing arm and bracket removal/overhaul – 10•11
Rear wheel bearing housing – 10•9
Steering and suspension check – 1•12
Steering angle sender – 12•6
Steering column – 10•14
Steering column lock – 12•5
Steering column switch assembly – 12•5
Steering column switch unit – 12•6
Steering gear assembly removal/overhaul – 10•15
Steering gear rubber gaiters and track rods – 10•16
Steering wheel – 10•14
Vehicle level sender – 10•14
Sump
  Common rail injection engine – 2B•17
  PD unit injector engine – 2A•16
Sunroof
  Check and lubrication – 1•13
  Control switch – 12•7
  General information – 11•13
  Motor – 12•13
Sunvisors – 11•23
Switches – 12•6
  Facia-mounted light switch – 12•6
  Front passenger and rear door switches – 12•8
  Interior monitoring switch/vehicle inclination sensor – 12•7
  Window switches – 12•7

T

Tailgate
  Removal – 11•8
  Emergency lock release – 11•9
  Lock – 11•9
  Lock motor (Estate models) – 11•9
  Lock unit – 11•9
  Support strut – 11•9
  Wiper motor – 12•13
Thermostat removal – 3•3
Throttle pedal/position sensor – 4A•5
Timing belt
  Belt/tensioning roller renewal
    1st generation common rail injection engines – 1•15
    2nd generation common rail injection engines – 1•15
    PD unit injector engines up to 2006 – 1•15
    PD unit injector engines after 2007 – 1•15
Timing belt covers
  Common rail injection engine – 2B•6
  PD unit injector engine – 2A•7
Timing belt Idler pulleys
  Common rail injection engine – 2B•10
  PD unit injector engine – 2A•9
  Belt removal
    Common rail injection engine – 2B•8
    PD unit injector engine – 2A•7

Note: *References throughout this index are in the form* **"Chapter number"** • **"Page number"**. *So, for example, 2C•15 refers to page 15 of Chapter 2C.*

Preserving Our Motoring Heritage

<
The Model J Duesenberg
Derham Tourster.
Only eight of these
magnificent cars were
ever built – this is the
only example to be found
outside the United States
of America

Almost every car you've ever loved, loathed or desired is gathered under one roof at the Haynes Motor Museum. Over 300 immaculately presented cars and motorbikes represent every aspect of our motoring heritage, from elegant reminders of bygone days, such as the superb Model J Duesenberg to curiosities like the bug-eyed BMW Isetta. There are also many old friends and flames. Perhaps you remember the 1959 Ford Popular that you did your courting in? The magnificent 'Red Collection' is a spectacle of classic sports cars including AC, Alfa Romeo, Austin Healey, Ferrari, Lamborghini, Maserati, MG, Riley, Porsche and Triumph.

A Perfect Day Out

Each and every vehicle at the Haynes Motor Museum has played its part in the history and culture of Motoring. Today, they make a wonderful spectacle and a great day out for all the family. Bring the kids, bring Mum and Dad, but above all bring your camera to capture those golden memories for ever. You will also find an impressive array of motoring memorabilia, a comfortable 70 seat video cinema and one of the most extensive transport book shops in Britain. The Pit Stop Cafe serves everything from a cup of tea to wholesome, home-made meals or, if you prefer, you can enjoy the large picnic area nestled in the beautiful rural surroundings of Somerset.

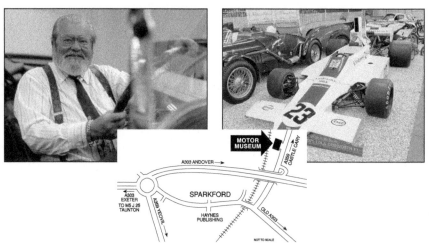

>
John Haynes O.B.E.,
Founder and
Chairman of the
museum at the wheel
of a Haynes Light 12.

<
Graham Hill's Lola
Cosworth Formula 1
car next to a 1934
Riley Sports.

The Museum is situated on the A359 Yeovil to Frome road at Sparkford, just off the A303 in Somerset. It is about 40 miles south of Bristol, and 25 minutes drive from the M5 intersection at Taunton.
Open 9.30am - 5.30pm (10.00am - 4.00pm Winter) 7 days a week, *except Christmas Day, Boxing Day and New Years Day*
Special rates available for schools, coach parties and outings Charitable Trust No. 292048